Handbook of
College and
University Teaching

The editors of this book join in respectfully thanking all of our colleagues and contributors, international and domestic, who care about the quality of teaching and learning worldwide. The global academic community is enriched by your efforts. Individually, we would like to share the following dedications:

James E. Groccia: To Chris, whose support and sacrifice have made my work on this book and indeed, my entire career, possible. To my Biggio Center colleagues, thanks for your cooperation and patience.

Mohammed A. T. Alsudairi: I dedicate this book to those who care about student learning all over the world.

William Buskist: To Connie, love of my life. Salida awaits!

Handbook of
College and University Teaching
A Global Perspective

Edited by
James E. Groccia
Auburn University

Mohammed A. T. Alsudairi
King Saud University

William Buskist
Auburn University

Los Angeles | London | New Delhi
Singapore | Washington DC

Los Angeles | London | New Delhi
Singapore | Washington DC

FOR INFORMATION:

SAGE Publications, Inc.
2455 Teller Road
Thousand Oaks, California 91320
E-mail: order@sagepub.com

SAGE Publications Ltd.
1 Oliver's Yard
55 City Road
London EC1Y 1SP
United Kingdom

SAGE Publications India Pvt. Ltd.
B 1/I 1 Mohan Cooperative Industrial Area
Mathura Road, New Delhi 110 044
India

SAGE Publications Asia-Pacific Pte. Ltd.
33 Pekin Street #02-01
Far East Square
Singapore 048763

Acquisitions Editor: Diane McDaniel
Editorial Assistant: Sarita Sarak
Production Editor: Astrid Virding
Copy Editor: Robin Gold
Typesetter: C&M Digitals (P) Ltd.
Proofreader: Dennis W. Webb
Indexer: Kathy Paparchontis
Cover Designer: Candice Harman
Marketing Manager: Liz Thornton
Permissions Editor: Karen Ehrmann

Copyright © 2012 by SAGE Publications, Inc.

Printed in the United States of America

Library of Congress Cataloging-in-Publication Data

Handbook of college and university teaching: a global perspective/editor James E. Groccia, Mohammed A. Al-Sudairy, William Buskist.

p. cm.

Includes bibliographical references and index.

ISBN 978-1-4129-8815-5 (cloth)

1. College teaching—Cross-cultural studies. 2. Learning—Cross-cultural studies. 3. Universities and colleges—Administration—Cross-cultural studies. I. Groccia, James E. II. Al-Sudairy, Mohammed A. III. Buskist, William.

LB2331.H3148 2012
378.1′25—dc23   2011033405

This book is printed on acid-free paper.

12 13 14 15 16 10 9 8 7 6 5 4 3 2 1

Contents _____

About the Editors _____

James E. Groccia is the Director of the Biggio Center for the Enhancement of Teaching and Learning and associate professor in the Department of Educational Foundations, Leadership, and Technology at Auburn University. He is a former president of the Professional and Organizational Development Network in Higher Education (POD Network), and was a 2011 Fulbright scholar at the University of Tartu, Estonia. Groccia has presented at dozens of national and international conferences, has conducted hundreds of workshops worldwide, has served as an advisor and consultant to institutions nationally and abroad, and has authored numerous articles and book chapters on teaching and learning issues. He is the author of *The College Success Book: A Whole-Student Approach to Academic Excellence* and coauthor with M. S. Hunter of *The First-Year Seminar: Designing, Implementing and Assessing Courses to Support Student Learning and Success: Vol. II. Instructor Training and Development.* Groccia is coeditor with Bill Buskist of *Evidence-Based Teaching*; coeditor with J. E. Miller of Volumes 29 and 30 of *To Improve the Academy, On Becoming a Productive University: Strategies for Reducing Costs and Increasing Quality in Higher Education; Enhancing Productivity: Administrative, Instructional, and Technological Strategies*; and coeditor with J. E. Miller and M. S. Miller on *Student-Assisted Teaching: A Guide to Faculty-Student Teamwork.*

Mohammed A. T. Alsudairi is assistant professor of management information systems (MIS) at King Saud University in Riyadh, Saudi Arabia. He is responsible for staff development and serves as Dean of Skills Development. He holds a PhD in business from Leicester University, United Kingdom, and received an MS in economics and an MBA in MIS from California State University, Pomona. His research interests are mainly in the areas of MIS, electronic business, electronic government, customer relations management, knowledge management, business process reengineering, and strategic uses of information systems. He has also founded the Saudi Teaching and Learning Society, authored the teaching manual of King Saud University, and presented various research papers in national and international conferences on teaching and learning, academic development, and knowledge acquisition and information technology.

William Buskist is the Distinguished Professor in the Teaching of Psychology at Auburn University and a Faculty Fellow at Auburn's Biggio Center for the Enhancement of Teaching and Learning. He has published widely on issues related to teaching and learning, both within his own discipline of psychology and more generally in higher education. His most recent publications include edited works with James Groccia (*Evidence-Based Teaching*) and with Victor Benassi (*Effective College and University Teaching: Strategies and Tactics for the New Professoriate*). Buskist has served as president for the Society for the Teaching of Psychology and is currently the editor-in-chief for the society's e-book program). He has won numerous teaching awards at both the local and national levels, as have many of his graduate student protégés. He is a Fellow of both the American Psychological Association and the Association for Psychological Science.

About the Contributors ___

Shakeer Abdullah is the director of Auburn University's Multicultural Center in Auburn, Alabama. He is a doctoral student in higher education administration, and his research interest is in multicultural competency, diversity in study abroad programs, and Muslim student identity development.

Solaiman M. AlHadlaq is associate professor of endodontics at King Saud University, College of Dentistry, Riyadh, Saudi Arabia. He is interested in promoting excellence in teaching, learning, and assessment in health education.

Saleh H. Alwasel is a physiologist in the College of Science at King Saud University, Riyadh, Saudi Arabia. He is a fellow in the Higher Education Academy, United Kingdom, and holds a postgraduate certificate in academic practice from King's College London, United Kingdom. He is interested in teaching enhancement in general, especially improving teaching microenvironments.

Virginia J. Anderson, a biologist and science educator at Towson University in Maryland, is a nationally known grading and assessment activist, author, workshop leader, and consultant. She chairs her department's assessment committee and the university's undergraduate assessment team, presents at Middle States Commission on Higher Education conferences frequently, and is currently serving as an evaluator on four National Science Foundation grants.

Carol M. Archer is professor of cross-cultural communication and English as a second language at the Language and Culture Center of the University of Houston, Texas. Her research and writing interests concern interpersonal, intercultural communication and its impact on teaching, learning, and developing human relationships.

Paul Blackmore is professor of higher education and director of the King's Learning Institute at King's College London. His research interests are in the conceptualization and exploration of professional expertise, particularly leadership roles in academic settings, and in strategic curriculum change.

Jeremy L. Brunson is an assistant professor of sociology and interpretation at Gallaudet University. His research interests are sociology of disability and sociology of work and the professions.

Andrew N. Christopher is professor of psychological science at Albion College in Albion, Michigan. He is editor of the Society for the Teaching of Psychology's journal, *Teaching of Psychology,* and has published numerous articles on topics in both economic and political psychology.

Margaret W. Cohen is associate provost for professional development and director of the Center for Teaching and Learning at the University of Missouri–St. Louis, where her faculty appointment is in the Division of Educational Psychology, Research, and Evaluation. Her commitment to mentoring and supporting the professional success of academic colleagues is reflected in her research and writing on faculty centers, collaborative learning, and the course syllabus.

Jacquelyn Cranney is an Australian Learning and Teaching Council National Teaching Fellow who has a special interest is undergraduate psychology education. She has served on a number of national committees concerned with the quality of education and training, and has contributed to reviews of the aims of undergraduate psychology education in the United States and in Britain.

Geoffrey Crisp is the dean of learning and teaching at RMIT University in Victoria, Australia. His research centers on faculty development, online assessment, and the use of the online environment for authentic learning and assessment.

Helen Dalton is a researcher and educator with a background in science and an interest in leadership in academic and curriculum development. She has been recognized for her contributions to student learning and has collaboratively undertaken a number of national studies into academic beliefs, curriculum, and leadership.

Shelda Debowski is Winthrop Professor for Higher Education Development and the director of Organisational and Staff Development Services at the University of Western Australia. Her research and professional interests relate to academic leadership, organizational and leadership development, and the provision of effective support to academics at all stages of their development.

Kevin Downing is a distinguished psychologist and education researcher currently working at City University of Hong Kong. He is the recipient of national and international awards for teaching excellence and is an acknowledged expert on metacognition.

Helen Fox heads the Social Theory and Practice Program at the University of Michigan. Her research and teaching interests include human rights, race and racism, international development, peace and justice education, and cultural issues in academic writing.

Dennis B. Galvan is professor and director of the undergraduate program in psychology at Gallaudet University, a liberal arts college for deaf and hard of hearing individuals in Washington, D.C. His research interests include the acquisition of American Sign Language by children and adults and excellence in college and university teaching.

Peter J. Giordano is professor and chair of the Psychological Science Department at Belmont University in Nashville, Tennessee. He has served as national president of Psi Chi and as the methods and techniques editor for the journal *Teaching of Psychology*. Recent scholarly interests include the infusion of Asian culture into psychology courses and the relevance of Asian philosophical traditions to the craft of teaching.

Regan A. R. Gurung is the Ben J. & Joyce Rosenberg Professor of Human Development & Psychology at the University of Wisconsin–Green Bay. His research interests include health across cultures, social objectification, and ways to improve teaching and student learning.

Mohammad M. Hassan is an associate professor in agricultural sciences and head of the Planning Department at the Deanship of Skills Development at King Saud University, Riyadh, Saudi Arabia. Besides his duties as an academic planner and developer in college teaching profession, he is a fellow of the Higher Education Academy, United Kingdom, and a distinguished external reviewer in academic accreditation. He is also an Excellence in College Teaching award winner at Cairo University in 2004 and 2006.

Angela Ho is the director of educational development at the Hong Kong Polytechnic University. Her research and professional interest include professional development of teachers in higher education; outcome-based approaches to teaching, learning, and assessment; and helping students learn to learn.

Emad A. Ismail is associate professor in agricultural sciences at Cairo University, Egypt; graduate of Post Graduate Certificate in Academic Practice (PGCAP) program at King's College London; a fellow of the Higher Education Academy, United Kingdom; and director of the research and publication unit at the Deanship of Skills Development, King Saud University, Riyadh, Saudi Arabia. His activities focus on research, awareness publications, and training for improving teaching skills of faculty members.

Kenneth Mølbjerg Jørgensen is associate professor in organizational learning at Aalborg University, Denmark. His research and teaching interests include organizational learning management education with a special focus on power, storytelling, ethics, and problem-based learning.

Camille B. Kandiko is a research associate in the King's Learning Institute at King's College London, United Kingdom. Her research focuses on international and comparative higher education, with areas of interest in curriculum and the student experience, interdisciplinarity, and PhD supervision.

Jared Keeley is assistant professor of psychology at Mississippi State University, Starkville, Mississippi. He is interested in furthering the scholarship of teaching and learning, particularly regarding how teachers are evaluated.

Kenneth D. Keith is professor of psychological sciences at the University of San Diego in San Diego, California. His writing and research encompass topics in cross-cultural psychology, the teaching of psychology, and education in the liberal arts.

Ian Kinchin is assistant director of the King's Learning Institute at King's College London, United Kingdom. His research interests focus on the development of university pedagogy through the perspective of knowledge structures as revealed by concept mapping.

Vesna Kovač is associate professor at the University of Rijeka in Croatia. Her research interests focus on higher education policy and management and on issues regarding academic staff development.

R. Eric Landrum is professor in the Department of Psychology at Boise State University. His research interests include various aspects of student success, broadly defined, such as pedagogy and scholarship of teaching and learning (SoTL), improving student writing, assessment of skills, and the multiple career paths for psychology baccalaureates.

Laurie Lomas has recently retired from King's College London, United Kingdom, where he is now visiting senior lecturer at the King's Learning Institute. His research interests and publications have been principally in international higher education management.

Stacey C. Nickson is the assistant director of the Biggio Center for the Enhancement of Teaching and Learning at Auburn University, Auburn, Alabama. Her research and writing interests include faculty development with an emphasis on intercultural communication and global initiatives to enhance access to the professoriate.

Einike Pilli is working as a faculty consultant at Tartu University (Lifelong Learning Centre) and as a trainer of faculty. Her main research topics include curriculum development and assessment, university didactics, informal lifelong learning, and accreditation of prior experiential learning.

Kristina Shin is a distinguished fashion design and education researcher currently working at the Polytechnic University of Hong Kong. She is founding editor-in-chief of the *International Journal of Fashion Design, Technology and Education*, and the recipient of an international award for teaching excellence.

Veena Singaram is a lecturer in the Department of Medical Education, at the Nelson R. Mandela School of Medicine, University of KwaZulu-Natal in Durban, South Africa. Her research and writing interests include problem-based learning, collaborative learning, academic coaching, and anatomical science education.

Ted Sommerville is associate professor in medical education at the Nelson R. Mandela School of Medicine, University of KwaZulu-Natal in Durban, South Africa. His research interests include curriculum, pedagogy, assessment, classics, anesthesia, and pain management.

Lorraine Stefani is professor and director of the Centre for Academic Development at the University of Auckland, New Zealand. Her current research interests are focused on the role of academic development in effecting sustainable organizational change and the leadership attributes required to deliver on this agenda

Anete M. Camille Strand is assistant professor in the Department of Communication at Aalborg University, Denmark. Her research and teaching interests include communication in organizations, material storytelling, and problem-based learning. She is particularly interested in experimenting with integrating new learning modalities such as body, space, and artifacts into the problem-based learning process.

Qi Sun is associate professor of adult education in the Department of Professional Studies at the University of Wyoming in Laramie, Wyoming. Her research and teaching focus on adult learning and transformative learning, lifelong learning and learning society, Eastern philosophical perspectives on education, and international and comparative (adult) education.

Po Li Tan is currently the visiting lecturer at the King's Learning Institute, King's College London, United Kingdom. Her interests include intercultural pedagogy in higher education, internationalization of global universities, intercultural sensitivity development, and coaching across cultures.

Anja Overgaard Thomassen is an assistant professor in the Department of Learning and Philosophy at Aalborg University, Denmark. Her research interests lie within the area of continuing education with special focus on problem-based learning (PBL). She is especially interested in how PBL can be a way of integrating education and work, thereby overcoming the gap between theory and practice.

Annie Trapp is director of the Higher Education Academy Psychology Network and a founding member of EUROPLAT, a European network to support psychology education. She has been involved in a wide range of teaching and learning initiatives relevant to psychology education and has special interests in bringing about organizational change within higher education and the use of technology to support teaching.

Marko Turk is a junior researcher and teaching assistant at the University of Rijeka in Croatia, and since 2008, a PhD student at the University of Zagreb. He is engaged in higher education issues, especially in the field of higher education teaching, governance, and academic profession.

Kätlin Vanari is head of the Department of Academic Affairs in the Estonian Academy of Security Sciences. Her research interests include learning to learn, learning and study skills, learning approaches, quality assurance in higher education institutions, and curriculum development, particularly outcome-based curricula.

Richard S. Velayo is professor of psychology at Pace University in New York City. His scholarly interests include the internationalization of the psychology curriculum, and pedagogical applications of multimedia and Internet-based technologies.

James E. Witte is associate professor at Auburn University in Auburn, Alabama, and teaches in the adult education program. His academic areas of interest include training program development and evaluation, individual learning styles, and how learning is assessed in both conventional and distance learning settings.

Maria Martinez Witte is associate professor at Auburn University in Auburn, Alabama, and teaches in the adult education program. Her academic areas of interest include analyzing effective content, context, and processes that enhance the teaching-learning environment, learning styles, and the assessment of learning.

Preface _____

When we think of college and university teaching, we generally think of it in terms of our own teaching—the knowledge, skills, attitudes, and values we share with our students; the pedagogy we use to share these things; and the strategies we use to measure whether our students have learned them. If we are fortunate enough to teach in a department that genuinely values teaching, then we may think of teaching as more of a collective effort and conceptualize our teaching by how it contributes to the overall mission of the department or institution. To be sure, though, relatively few of us think about teaching beyond the borders of our home institutions.

Nonetheless, the sphere that we call college and university teaching exists in myriad multidimensional forms throughout the world. Colleges and universities may be found in every nation, and they all have the same raisons d'être: to educate students with the knowledge, skills, attitudes, and values necessary to be productive members of their society, to be competitive in today's global job market, and to assist students to become lifelong learners. These goals are not mutually exclusive, although the former tends to be emphasized more than the latter in many, if not most, of the world's institutions of higher learning, especially in those college and universities that have adopted the student-as-consumer perspective of education.

Although most college and university teachers view teaching as a localized activity circumscribed by the needs of their institutions and communities, more and more students are traveling internationally to earn their college and university degrees. Having international students on campus—regardless of students' places of origin or the nation on whose campus they might now be studying—brings with it an infusion of multicultural perspectives, traditions, and values. Some teachers welcome the challenge of teaching these students, whereas other teachers are more reticent, unsure of how or what to teach or even how to interact with students who do not look like them or have the same native tongue.

But learning how to teach international students in our classrooms and helping them feel welcomed and supported in their host countries is not the only reason why we should broaden our perspectives on teaching and learning. Indeed, we can learn about the craft of teaching by seeking and understanding how teachers outside our own culture approach the challenge of educating the next generation of their students, many of whom will shape, for better or for worse, both the global economy and global politics.

As editors, we believe that, as the world "gets smaller," there is a growing and important need to pay attention to higher education at the cross-cultural, cross-national level. The globalization of higher education is a reality that has far-reaching consequences that call for increased awareness and modification of teaching and learning practices. The globalization of higher education has created universities where national boundaries are irrelevant; where the movement of students, teachers, ideas, and instructional methods crosses physical, cultural, and pedagogical barriers. According to Ben Wildavsky (2010), the consequences of globalization include

> the ever-more-intense recruitment of students and faculty; the swift spread of branch campuses; the well-financed efforts to create world-class universities, whether by upgrading existing institutions or by building brand-new ones; the innovative efforts by online universities and other for-profit players to fill unmet needs in higher education markets around the globe; and the closely watched rankings by which everyone keeps score. (pp. 4–5)

Beyond the economic and political impacts of this trend, why does globalization matter generally and to the individual university instructor? Nations around the globe have invested huge sums of financial and human capital to create higher education systems to capture their share of the educational market. As a result, competition for students and the faculty to teach them is increasing dramatically. The very notion of what it means to be an educated person is changing, in that such a product of our educational systems must be exposed to ideas, behaviors, cultures, and people that transcend physical space. Faculty members must also be exposed to the ideas and educational transformations occurring around the world so that they are better equipped to translate and transfer this knowledge to their students. Globalization of higher education represents a new kind of free trade, free trade in minds that should be embraced, not feared (Wildavsky, 2010). Globalization is not a zero-sum game where one country wins and another loses because the increase of knowledge benefits all.

Thus, we asked teachers from around the world to share with us, and with you, their perspectives on college and university teaching. Our authors rose brilliantly to the challenge. Some crafted chapters that address classroom teaching per se. Others contributed descriptions and perspectives of how national and global factors influence classroom teaching, learning, or curriculum development in their country. Still others offered theoretical perspectives on teaching accented by their culture. Finally, others shared their empirical research on issues of critical importance to teaching and learning at their universities. Thus, this volume presents international perspectives on critical issues affecting teaching and learning in a diverse range of higher education environments in the attempt to understand teaching and learning from multiple, although admittedly not all cultural perspectives.

Our volume is framed around James Groccia's seven-part model for understanding teaching and learning discussed in other publications (Groccia, 1997; Groccia, 2007; St. Clair & Groccia, 2009) and described in more detail in Chapter 1 in this volume. Using this model as the organizational structure of the book provides a guide for systemic thinking about what actions one should take, or suggest others take, when planning activities to improve teaching and learning, curriculum development, and assessment. The model indicates that college and university teaching consists of, and is influenced by, seven complex and interrelated variables: learning outcomes, teacher, learner, learning process, learning context, course content, and instructional processes. More specifically, these variables may be conceptualized as follows:

- *Learning outcomes:* The desired results of teaching, in short- and long-term learning outcomes, should be identified during the course design process, before teaching, and assessed on a regular basis throughout the instructional process. One can also include classroom assessment techniques as formative measures of learning outcomes.
- *Teacher:* Teachers differ, and their backgrounds, preparation, and individual characteristics influence why, when, and how they teach. Understanding who teachers are as individuals and professionals and what they bring to the learning situation can affect the quality of that experience.
- *Learner:* Learners differ in the same ways that teachers differ and their backgrounds, preparation, and individual characteristics influence why, when, and how they learn.
- *Learning process:* Knowledge of teaching and learning research and learning theory provides a foundation for good practice transfer of learning.
- *Learning context:* Learning context includes the emphasis an educational institution places on instruction, its mission and purposes, and the process of resource and reward allocation, which can influence what faculty and students do in and out of the classroom. Local, state, provincial, national, and international priorities shape what is taught, what our students learn and know, and how we teach.
- *Course content:* With the ever-increasing expansion of knowledge in many disciplines and the corresponding demands that it places on students, faculty need to ensure that what is taught in their courses is necessary, challenging, and well organized.
- *Instructional processes:* The most obvious variable in this model describes what faculty as teachers and students as learners actually do in the instructional environment: teaching strategies, teacher behaviors, and student learning responses.

We believe the contributors to this volume, many of whom are not native English speakers, did a marvelous job in so generously sharing their knowledge, experiences, and wisdom with us, and now you. We thank them for their willingness to contribute chapters to this volume, and doing so with good cheer. Indeed, as editors, we feel, on the one hand, that our world—our intellectual world—was enlarged substantially by our contributors' insights into college and university teaching. On the other hand, we feel our world—our social and cultural world—was shrunk substantially by the information shared as well as by the contributors' warm demeanor, graciousness, and goodwill.

Without the tireless efforts of several outstanding people at SAGE, this volume would not have come to fruition. We especially thank Senior Acquisitions Editor Christine Cardone for her unwavering support for this book despite several setbacks along the way. She is a marvelous friend and a magnificent editor. Sarita Sarak, Chris's talented and trusty editorial assistant, was faithfully by our sides all along the way. We thank her for taking care of the hundreds of the details that must be skillfully handled to bring this book into the light of day. We also offer our heartfelt thanks to Marketing Manager Liz Thornton for her excellent work in making sure that this volume made it safely into the hands of our readers. Our incredibly skilled copy editor, Robin Gold, did a wonderful job ensuring that every word in this volume is clear and understandable—and that was no easy task given that so many of our authors write and speak in a native tongue other than English.

Finally, our deepest appreciation is respectfully expressed to our wives and families for their patience and support through all phases of this project. The idea for this book is quite a simple one, but transforming that idea into words on a page, and hundreds of pages at that, meant that we spent many hours away from our families while we solicited and edited the draft manuscript and prepared the final manuscript. Special thanks to each of you.

James E. Groccia, Auburn, Alabama
Mohammed A. T. Alsudairi, Riyadh, Kingdom of Saudi Arabia
William Buskist, Auburn, Alabama

References

Groccia, J. E. (1997). A model for understanding teaching and learning. *Chalkboard* (Program for Excellence in Teaching, University of Missouri), *15*, 2–3.

Groccia, J. E. (2007). President's message—Planning faculty development activities: Using a holistic teaching and learning model. *POD Network News* (Professional and Organizational Development Network in Higher Education), 1, 3.

St. Clair, K. L., & Groccia, J. E. (2009). Change to social justice education: Higher education strategy. In K. Skubikowski, C. Wright, & R. Graf (Eds.), *Social justice education: Inviting faculty to transform their institutions* (pp. 70–84). Sterling, VA: Stylus.

Wildavsky, B. (2010). *The great brain race: How global universities are reshaping the world*. Princeton, NJ: Princeton University Press.

PART I

Introduction

CHAPTER 1

A Model for Understanding University Teaching and Learning

JAMES E. GROCCIA

> *"There is nothing more practical than a good theory."*
>
> Kurt Lewin (1952, p. 169)

The use of theories, metaphors, simulations, and models has been commonplace in higher education, especially in science-based disciplines, to comprehend the incomprehensible, to explain the unexplainable, or to view a picture of the unviewable. Complex issues can be made less complex and simple issues can be made complex through the use of an analog representation (model) that enables researchers or practitioners to develop intervention strategies or solve problems. It appears to me that one way to develop approaches to improve the teaching and learning in higher education is to develop and use a model that illustrates the multiple variables that fall under the term *college teaching*.

What Are Models?

In a general sense, a model is a simplified representation of a system that concentrates attention on specific aspects of the system (Ingham & Gilbert, 1991). A model allows aspects of the system (i.e., processes, structure, objects, events, ideas) that are complex or abstract to be rendered either visible or more easily understood (Gilbert, 1995; Gobert & Buckley, 2000). A model is an icon that embodies features from the original in a way that says, "*This* is how the original is" (Black, 1962, p. 221).

The *Oxford Advanced Learner's Dictionary* (Oxford University Press, 2011) provides two definitions of a *model* that are relevant to this discussion: a copy of something, usually smaller than the original object, and a simple description of a system used for explaining how something works or calculating what might happen. Paul Samuelson and William Nordhaus (1998) define a model as a formal framework for representing the basic features of a complex system by a few central relationships. Models can take the form of graphs, mathematical equations, and computer programs. David Begg, Stanley Fischer, and Rudiger Dornbusch (2000) indicate that a *model* or theory makes a series of simplifications from which it deduces how people will behave. It is a deliberate simplification of reality. Scientists and mathematicians use their models in problem-solving and problem-analyzing processes, and economists use models in economics to analyze and visualize economic problems (Kaewsuwan, 2002).

Characteristics of Good Models

Others have attempted to identify the characteristics of a "good" theory (Huberman & Miles, 1994; Popper, 1963; Swan, 1994; Ur, 2001), but I have been unable to find a list of the characteristics of a "good" model. Therefore, I will extrapolate from the characteristics of the former presented by Penny Ur (2001) to describe those of the latter:

- Plausibility: The model appears to be in accordance with experience and data. The model is truthful to what we know, as limited as that knowledge may be; it is true as far as we can assess from rational observation and experience.
- Simplicity: The model presents a representation or explanation that avoids complications and is as simple as possible. A good model is elegant in that it expresses its meaning with the least amount of words, figures, or ideas possible.
- Explicitness: The model is presented and stated in clear and understandable terms. It is easily communicated to others so that it can be used by others to extend knowledge and application.
- Comprehensiveness: A good model encompasses all of the data and variables necessary for understanding an application.
- Limited: The model includes what is necessary and clearly indicates where or to what it does and does not apply. The boundaries and demarcations of the model are clear.
- Usefulness: The model clearly explains what is going on so that it can generate, explain, or predict present and future action. A good model is useful and practical.

- Testable: The model presents ideas that can be tested, verified, or rejected.
- Aesthetic appeal: The model is visually, verbally, and graphically clear and elegant. A good model is not cluttered with unnecessary images or words and is visually attractive or stated in a compelling metaphor (Ellis, 1997).

Why Use a Model to Understand Teaching and Learning?

Models are communication tools to summarize, generalize, or transmit understanding to help make a complex process or concept more easily comprehended. Models inform practice. Models can lead to the building of theories, which in turn can lead to creation of hypotheses that lead to testing, intervention, and change. In the case of teaching and learning, a model can create a holistic conceptualization of teaching and learning to provide a framework for research and understanding to assist improvement efforts. A model illustrates the connections and interconnections between variables of interest. A model of teaching and learning helps the teacher and educational researcher understand the interplay between variables and their interdependence. Such awareness can provide multiple points of intervention as change in one element or variable in the model can stimulate change in others. This systemic approach can maximize efforts to improve teaching and learning and empower teachers in teaching improvement efforts.

A model also visually highlights the complexity of what is being modeled. A model of college teaching and learning says to teachers that there is more to teaching than what one does in front of students. Understanding the dynamic nature of the instructional process, and ways to improve it, requires knowledge about issues that take place before, during, and after the information-sharing process.

Understanding the complexity of teaching and learning can help avoid a "techquie" approach to teaching improvement. By this I mean the all too often attempt to improve teaching by the imitation or adoption of a teaching technique (e.g., "clickers," problem-based learning, cooperative learning, jigsaw teaching) without a full understanding of the pedagogical reasons for the use of such a technique, or of its impact on other variables in the teaching and learning process.

Precursor Models of Teaching and Learning

The Transmission Model of Teaching and Learning

Based on the prevalent form of instruction in the majority of higher education classrooms around the world, the lecture, one would assume that teaching and learning is a simple process. The teacher's (the expert) job is to transfer knowledge through talking to students (the novice) whose role is to receive knowledge through listening, watching, and maybe taking notes. The professor's job is to profess and the students' job is to receive, interpret, and internalize the "professtations"—the professor's words and actions. This top-down transition model of teaching "has prevailed throughout fundamental innovations including writing, books, computers, and the Internet." (Laurillard, n.d., p. 1). The transmission model can be called the default conceptualization of teaching and is illustrated in Figure 1.1.

This default model is fraught with difficulties, the most significant of which is its very simplicity. Such a conceptualization ignores the complexity of the teaching-learning process and the importance and interplay of many influential variables. Having a comprehensive model from which to view teaching and learning can guide individual faculty members in the design of teaching and learning actions and environments and guide educational developers in selecting and presenting the content for instructor training programs.

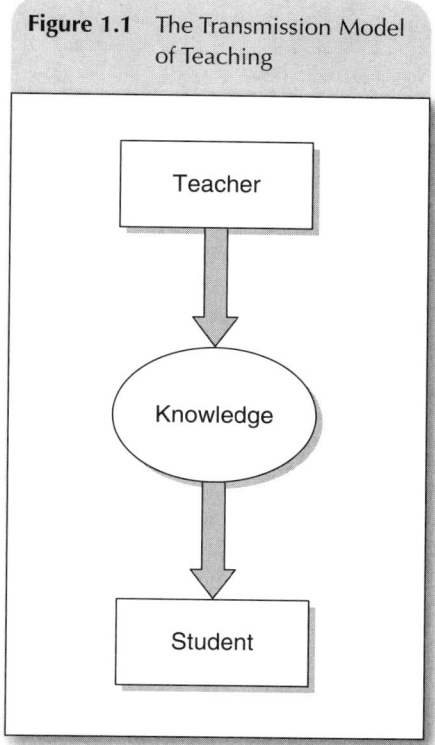

Figure 1.1 The Transmission Model of Teaching

Lowman's Two-Dimensional Conceptualization of Effective College Teaching

Joseph Lowman's (1995) model was developed as a result of his research analyzing the adjectives used to describe excellent teachers in letters submitted for the chancellor's teaching awards at the University of North Carolina. Lowman's factor analysis of student evaluations of teaching performance yielded two factors, teaching technique and rapport, as the most critical variables in effective teaching (see Table 1.1). Lowman identified a two-dimensional model of exemplary teaching that focused on intellectual excitement created by instructor clarity in the classroom, and interpersonal rapport and relationship building with students. This model can be characterized as teacher-centered and performance-based, and it does not focus on pre-instruction behaviors or the influence of the instructional setting. Classroom dynamics, such as student and teacher attitudes and class moral and some psychological issues of teachers and students are mentioned (i.e., sources of satisfaction and dissatisfaction, communication styles, interpersonal interaction between teachers and students, affective and classroom control measures) but Lowman's focus is primarily on the teaching skills of instructors.

Table 1.1   Lowman's Two-Dimensional Model of Effective College Teaching

Dimension 1: Intellectual Excitement
  • Clarity of presentations (what is presented)
  • Emotional impact on students (way material is presented)

Dimension 2: Interpersonal Rapport
  • Awareness of interpersonal nature of the classroom
  • Communication skills that enhance motivation and enjoyment of learning and that foster independent learning

Teaching-Learning Transactional Model of College Teaching

David Dees and colleagues (2007) developed their transactional model to provide a framework to guide college teacher reflection "before, in-the-moment, and after the event, that recognizes the complexity of the act of teaching, is sensitive to the aesthetic dimensions of both teaching and reflection, and provides a context to examine tacit decisions made during the act of teaching." (p. 130). The model is a qualitative description of the key elements of teaching to bring them out in the open to encourage reflection, discussion, and holistic inquiry. The transactional aspect of Dees et al.'s model (see Figure 1.2) illustrates the connected back and forth aspect of the various instructional elements.

Figure 1.2   Teaching-Learning Transactional Model of College Teaching (modified from Dees et al., 2007, p. 132)

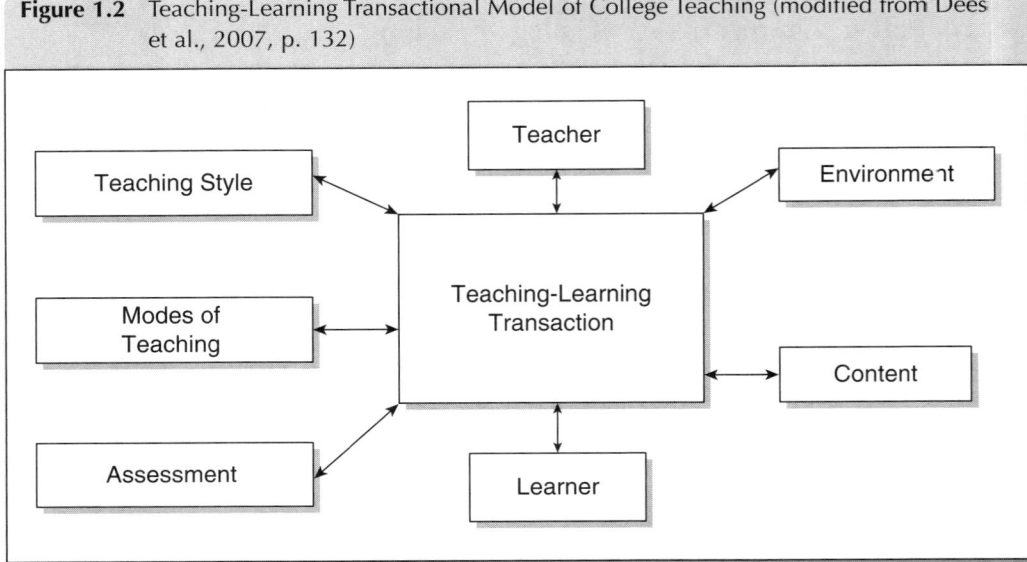

A Model for the Study of Classroom Teaching

Michael Dunkin and Bruce Biddle (1974), based on an earlier formulation by Harold Mitzel (1960), proposed a four-variable model to help educational researchers better understand the complex aspects of classroom instruction (see Figure 1.3). Developed primarily to assist researchers to organize findings of research on teaching, this model illustrated the complexity and interconnectedness of college teaching. Dunkin and Biddle's model contains four classes of variables for study: presage (teacher characteristics, experiences, training), context (properties of pupils, schools, community, classroom), process (teacher and student actions), and product (immediate and long-term effects). Each rectangle in the model represents a region of variables deserving of research, and the arrows presume a causative relationship between regions and are sources of hypotheses for future research. This model had "an enormous impact" (Shulman, 1986, p. 6) on the field of educational research by providing a theoretical framework and vocabulary for those studying teaching and learning.

Figure 1.3   A Model for the Study of Classroom Teaching (from Dunkin, *The Study of Teaching*, 1E. © 1974 Wadsworth, a part of Cengage Learning, Inc. Reproduced by permission. www.cengage.com/permissions)

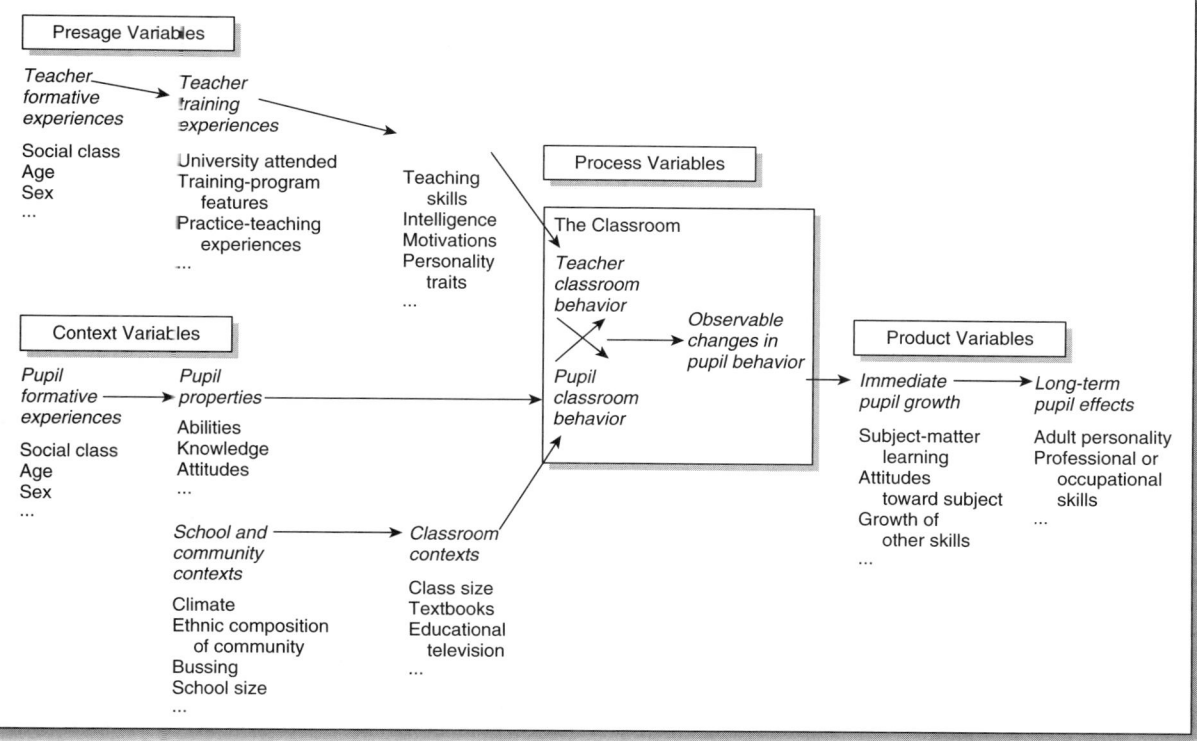

Groccia's Model for Understanding Teaching and Learning

I have developed a model for understanding university teaching and learning that share many of the components presented in the previous models. The model was initially described in a newsletter published at the University of Missouri (Groccia, 1997) as a way to organize and describe the activities of the campus teaching and learning center. The model also appeared in the *POD Network News* (Groccia, 2007) and in a book chapter on facilitating social justice education (St. Clair & Groccia, 2009) to provide a framework for faculty developers to conceptualize their activities.

This model consists of seven interrelated variables that influence teaching and learning: learning outcomes, instructional processes, course content, teacher and student characteristics, learning process, and learning context (Figure 1.4). These variables are not new to faculty in higher education. But, for many reasons, faculty members tend to focus on one or two of them and overlook the others. Each variable is represented by an oval, and the lines connecting the ovals represent their interconnectivity. Learning outcomes (product variables) are placed at the bottom of the model to illustrate that they are the foundation upon which all the other variables rest. In concert with the principles of backward course design, an understanding of university teaching and learning begins at the end—knowledge of teaching and learning goals and outcomes (i.e., determining what students are supposed to learn comes before the design of instructional or assessment methods). The large oval in the center of the model represents what the teacher and students do, the teaching and learning behaviors, techniques, and methods (process variables). The ovals at the top of the model can be considered indicator or preliminary variables, and represent factors that should be assessed and understood before teaching and determining appropriate learning outcomes. These are similar to L. Dee Fink's (2003) situational factors and Michael Dunkin and Bruce Biddle's (1974) presage and context variables. I believe that this model satisfies the conditions of a good model in that it is plausible, simple, explicit, comprehensive, limited, useful, and testable and has aesthetic appeal.

The first variable for instructors to consider in understanding teaching and learning is what they want students to get from the instructional experience, the *learning outcomes*. These are the short- and long-term learning goals and outcomes of the instructional experience. Assessment is a key function to determine whether identified learning outcomes have been met through the instructional processes that reflect the instructor, learner, learning process, learning context, and content variables of the model. Objective and subjective assessment techniques as well as summative and formative assessment methods to measure learning outcome attainment should be determined before instruction as well as throughout the teaching and learning experience. Included in this variable are also measures to assess teaching effectiveness.

Figure 1.4   Groccia's Model for Understanding Teaching and Learning (Groccia, 1997, used with permission of author)

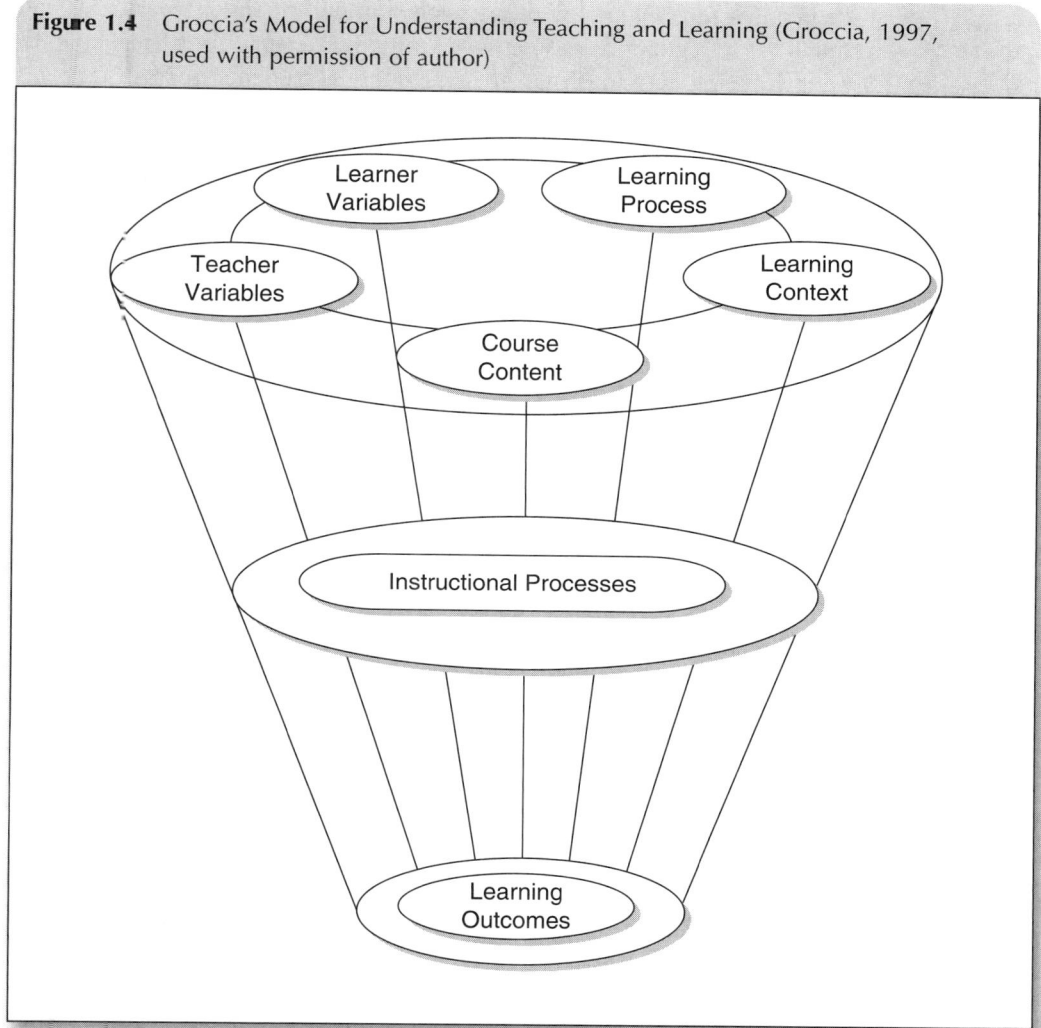

Moving to the top ring of ovals in this model, another variable to consider, *instructor variables*, emphasizes that instructors need to understand who they are and what they bring to the learning situation. Socioeconomic status, race, gender, age, and cultural background; academic preparation; and personal characteristics, such as thinking and learning styles, enthusiasm, rapport, and attitudes and values, all affect teaching and learning. The more instructors understand themselves, the better able they will be to capitalize on their strengths, minimize their weaknesses, and ultimately improve their teaching and students' learning.

A third set of variables relates to *the learner*. Like their instructors, learners' backgrounds, academic preparation, and individual characteristics influence learning. Armed with an understanding of the learners, through frequent and regular assessments, faculty members are better able to develop learning activities that are accessible to students in ways that are appropriate to their skills, interests, and needs.

Teaching and learning can be enhanced by knowledge of the *learning process*. Human learning has been thoroughly researched during the past 100 years (Ambrose, Bridges, DiPietro, Lovett, & Norman, 2010; Chickering & Gamson, 1987; Marchese, 1997). The wealth of information about human learning and how that knowledge can be applied to enhance teaching can provide a solid foundation for understanding the teaching and learning process. Additionally, knowledge of learning theory can provide suggestions for general and specific applications to enhance teaching and student learning. Table 1.2 provides a brief summary of four theories of learning, how

Table 1.2   Theories of Learning Applied to University Teaching

Theory	*General Applications to University Teaching*	*Specific Classroom Suggestions*
Behavioral Learning Theory	• Consequences of behavior determine future behavior • Learning occurs in response to rewards, absence of rewards, or punishment • Positive consequences shape learning better than negative consequences	• Attention and reward patterns will influence learning behaviors • Reward good behavior rather than punish bad • Match reward level with task difficulty • Provide frequent and clear feedback
Information Processing Theory of Learning	• Information is processed in stages in the brain • Amount of information that can be processed is limited • Learning is an interactive process	• Teach class as series of mini-units • Chunk information into connected parts • Teach new material first then practice and review
Cognitive Theory of Learning	• Learning occurs through struggle with mental imbalance • Learner actively constructs knowledge	• Use discovery, active learning techniques (cooperative learning, discussion, hands-on experiments) • Create opportunities for mental critical thinking and mental conflict (debates, case studies)
Humanistic Learning Theory	• Learning involves affective as well as cognitive growth • Students have natural need for knowledge • Cognitive growth only after lower order needs met (i.e., safety, belonging, esteem)	• Move from teacher-centered to student-centered learning • Reduce threat in classroom • Build on successful learning experiences • Scaffold task difficulty pairing challenge with support • Provide opportunities for students to take responsibility for own learning (e.g., choosing assignments and assessments)

they can be applied to university teaching, and a few specific suggestions for what a faculty member can do in the classroom.

Understanding the impact of the situation in which learning takes place, the *learning context* in this model, can provide valuable knowledge to instructors. Learning does not occur in a vacuum; physical surroundings influence instructor as well as learner behaviors. Besides the obvious classroom variables such as seating plan, room size and design, and access to instructional technologies, the learning context can include general elements of the educational institution that can affect seminar administration, instructor selection processes, values and goals of the instructional program, course evaluation methods, and learner selection policies. Context also addresses the cultural and global diversity within which teaching and learning takes place. Cultural realities affect teaching and learning in ways that are crucial to understanding and enhancing their effectiveness.

A critical element in the design and delivery of effective instruction is the selection or creation of appropriate course content. The accuracy, difficulty level, organization, and meaning of *course content*, what is taught and learned, must be appropriate to the desired learning outcomes, the learners being taught, and the expertise of instructors.

The variable that draws instructor, learner, learning process, learning context, and content together is *instructional processes*, or pedagogy. How the content is taught, the choice of one teaching method over another, should be made after consideration of desired learning outcomes, a careful review of the evidence on the effectiveness of different teaching approaches, the prior knowledge and present needs of learners, the expertise of instructors, and the limits or advantages presented by the classroom context.

Conclusion

Models are useful devices to represent and organize information or processes that can then be used to improve or enhance the information or processes. Models have been used in the physical, natural, engineering, and computer sciences to help render complex phenomena understandable and nonobservable variables visible. Disciplines within social sciences such as economics or management have developed models to help understand, explain, and predict human behavior. Models can also be extremely useful to help understand and improve university teaching and learning. The use of a model such as those described in this chapter can enable university instructors to develop teaching and learning environments that capitalize on and integrate a holistic understanding of the multiple variables that encompass the learning process. In this way, faculty members can become maximally effective in facilitating the kind of knowledge needed for today students within today's global realities.

References

Ambrose, S. A., Bridges, M. W., DiPietro, M., Lovett, M. C., & Norman, M. K. (2010). *How learning works: Seven research-based principles for smart teaching*. San Francisco, CA: Jossey-Bass.

Begg, D., Fischer, S., & Dornbusch, R. (2000). *Economics* (6th ed.), New York, NY: McGraw-Hill.

Black, M. (1962). *Models and metaphors: Studies in language and philosophy*. Ithaca, NY: Cornell University Press.

Chickering, A. W., & Gamson, Z. F. (1987). *Seven principles for good practice in undergraduate education*. Washington, DC: American Association for Higher Education Bulletin.

Dees, D. M., Ingram, A., Kovalik, C., Allen-Huffman, M., McClelland, A., & Justice, L. (2007). A transactional model of college teaching. *International Journal of Teaching and Learning in Higher Education, 19*(2), 130–139.

Dunkin, M., & Biddle, B. (1974). *The study of teaching*. New York, NY: Holt, Rinehart & Winston.

Ellis, R. (1997). *SLA research and language teaching*. Oxford, UK: Oxford University Press.

Fink, L. D. (2003). *Creating significant learning experiences: An integrated approach to designing college courses*. San Francisco, CA: Jossey-Bass.

Gilbert, J. K. (1995). *The role of models and modeling in some narratives in science learning*. In J. D. Gobert & B. C. Buckley. (2000). Introduction to model-based teaching and learning in science education. *International Journal of Science Education, 22*(9), 891–894.

Gobert, J. D., & Buckley, B. C. (2000). Introduction to model-based teaching and learning in science education. *International Journal of Science Education, 22*(9), 891–894.

Groccia, J. E. (1997). A model for understanding teaching and learning. *Chalkboard* (Program for Excellence in Teaching, University of Missouri), *15*, 2–3.

Groccia, J. E. (2007). President's message—Planning faculty development activities: Using a holistic teaching and learning model. *POD Network News* (Professional and Organizational Development Network in Higher Education), 1, 3.

Huberman, M., & Miles, M. B. (1994). *Qualitative data analysis*. London, UK: Sage.

Ingham, A. M., & Gilbert, J. K. (1991). The use of analog models by students of chemistry at higher education level. *International Journal of Science Education, 13*, 193–202.

Kaewsuwan, S. (2002). Importance of models in economics. Retrieved June 8, 2011, from http://www.gaoshan.de/university/tp/Importance_of_Models_in_Economics.pdf

Laurillard, D. (n.d.). Rethinking university teaching in the digital age. London, UK: Open University. Retrieved June 6, 2011, from http://net.educause.edu/ir/library/pdf/ffp0205s.pdf

Lewin, K. (1952). *Field theory in social science: Selected theoretical papers by Kurt Lewin*. London, UK: Tavistock.

Lowman, J. (1995). *Mastering the techniques of teaching* (2nd ed.). San Francisco, CA: Jossey-Bass.

Marchese, T. J. (1997). The new conversations about learning: Insights from neuroscience and anthropology, cognitive science and work-place studies. In E. E. Chaffee,

P. T. Ewell, S. B. Gelman, G. Kuh, T. J. Marchese, M. A. Miller, & G. Wiggins (Eds.), *Assessing impact: Evidence and action* (pp. 79–95). Washington, DC: American Association for Higher Education.

Mitzel, H. E. (1960). Teacher effectiveness. In C. W. Harris (Ed.), *Encyclopedia of educational research* (3rd ed., pp. 1481–1486). New York, NY: Macmillan.

Oxford University Press. (2011). *Oxford advanced learner's dictionary.* Oxford, UK: Oxford University Press. Retrieved June 7, 2001, from http://www.oxford advancedlearnersdictionary.com/dictionary/model

Popper, K. (1963). *Conjectures and refutations: The growth of scientific knowledge.* London, UK: Routledge & Kegan Paul.

Samuelson, P. A., & Nordhaus, W. D. (1998). *Economics* (16th ed.). New York, NY: McGraw-Hill.

Shulman, L. S. (1986). Paradigms and research programs in the study of teaching: A contemporary perspective. In M. C. Wittrock (Ed.), *Handbook of research on teaching* (3rd ed., pp. 3–36). New York, NY: Macmillan.

St. Clair, K. L., & Groccia, J. E. (2009). Change to social justice education: Higher education strategy. In K. Skubikowski, C. Wright, & R. Graf (Eds.), *Social justice education: Inviting faculty to transform their institutions* (pp. 70–84). Sterling, VA: Stylus.

Swan, M. (1994). Design criteria for pedagogic language rules. In M. Bygate, A. Tonkyn, & E. Williams (Eds.), *Grammar and the language teacher* (pp. 45–55). Hemel Hempstead, UK: Prentice Hall International.

Ur, P. (2001). There is nothing so practical as a good theory. *The PAC Journal, 1,* 33–40. Retrieved June 6, 2011, from http://www.pac-teach.org/jrnl-v1/pacj1-D.pdf

PART II

Outcomes of Teaching and Learning

CHAPTER **2**

Effective Grading and Assessment

Global Insights to Enhance
Student Learning, Faculty Satisfaction,
and Institutional Success

Virginia J. Anderson

A s you finish delivering one of the best lectures you have ever given, you
know it was on target, and the students, seemingly mesmerized by your
scholarship and clarity, know it too. For moments, a thoughtful hush lingers
in the lecture hall; it ends as a student in the fifth row gets your attention.
Pensively, he asks, "Will this information be on the test?" Whether you are
teaching English 101 at Wilson Technical College in North Carolina (United
States) or Cardiac Surgery at the Medical College of the University of
Sharjah (United Arab Emirates), you will find that grading and assessment
are volatile, but integral parts of the teaching and learning process.

Global Perspectives

I have presented grading and assessment workshops for faculty at more than
200 institutions of higher education throughout the United States. I have conducted workshops on the same topics in Canada, Tonga, Portugal, Mexico,
Puerto Rico, Nigeria, and the United Arab Emirates and "stateside" sessions
for visiting faculty from Japan, Italy, Germany, China, Costa Rica, Lebanon,
and the Marshall Islands. Within and across these workshops, faculty

members differed in academic discipline, teaching experience, gender, age, religious beliefs, lifestyle choices, cultural expectations, and institutional constraints, but there was one thing the participants all had in common—they all wanted to be better teachers. This chapter offers practical grading and assessment suggestions that my colleagues and I have found can reduce grading angst, enhance student learning, promote faculty satisfaction, and build institutional success in any classroom context—on any continent.

Grading

The entry on grading in *The Encyclopedia of Educational Psychology* (Anderson, 2008) notes

> To an outsider, grading may appear as perfunctory as writing a few marginal comments on a C+ essay or scoring an objective test with an 85%, but to experienced educators, grading is clearly a dynamic and demanding classroom interaction. Historically, teachers have complained about grading, students have complained about grades, and institutions have tinkered with grade reporting methodologies (whole letter grades, plus and minus grades, pass and fail grades, etc.), but grading is still here! It is the most entrenched and enduring educational practice found in American community colleges, colleges, and universities (p. 450).

At the Appalachian College Association weeklong summer Teaching and Learning Workshop in 2008, a Russian physicist, who had just completed his first year of teaching in the United States, asked the program director, "Since I am already grading all my tests on the Scantron machine, do I really need to attend the morning session on grading?" The answer was yes. Grading is not just, for example, the process of marking or scoring papers, averaging four numerical test scores, or posting a B– on the official grade roster. As faculty members plan for each new term, they should reconsider their grading processes and policies as carefully as their academic content.

Barbara Walvoord and Virginia Anderson (2010) defined grading as a "complex context-dependent process that serves multiple roles" (p. 2). These roles include evaluation, or the process of providing a valid and fair judgment about the quality of each individual student's work, and communication, motivation, organization, and reflection by both students and faculty. In accomplishing these roles, teachers construct context, meaning, format, and learning outcomes for each unit of academic instruction. They select tests and assignments to be completed (e.g., multiple-choice tests, essay questions, term papers, projects, electronic portfolios, discussions, performances) so that students can demonstrate how well they achieved those outcomes within the given period. In the final step of the grading process, teachers evaluate students' work, either individually for a single grade or collectively for a course grade, and give the grade to the students, official agencies, or both.

Misconceptions About Grading

Data from numerous *National Study of Student Engagement* surveys and focus group interviews reveal that U.S. students have several misconceptions about grades and grading (Kuh, 2001). The most pervasive misconception is that students think that a grade is a reward for effort. Haven't you heard their "I studied 27 hours for your test!" or "I work harder in your course than in all my other courses!" types of testimonials before exams? Students are essentially saying, "I tried so hard; I deserve a good grade." Other students view grades as "a ticket to a better life." They launch a campaign before class, after class, by e-mail, or by office visits to get that ticket. Haven't you heard their pleas as final exams approach: "I will lose my scholarship if I don't pass," "I have to make an A to get into medical school," or "If I don't pass your course, I can't get certified to be a teacher." A growing misconception among U.S. students today is that grades are a commodity purchased with tuition money. Yet, halfway around the world, Australian students, reacting to the "commodification" of their tertiary education system (increased fees, larger classes, and greater pressure on faculty to secure external funding), are reacting in the same way by positing themselves as "customers" and faculty as "service providers" (White, 2007, p. 602). The two most recurrent themes in Naomi Rosh White's (2007) 79 student interviews (first-year students excluded) on perceptions of teaching and grading were, "If one pays, one is entitled to satisfaction with the service and outcome," and "If you don't get it, complain." Interviewers also reported, "Roughly two thirds of the students interviewed felt it was acceptable to challenge or query a grade" (White, 2007, p. 600).

Globally, faculty members tend to be rather homogeneous in their belief that a grade is awarded for achievement or mastery of specific skills in the given academic period, but they have misconceptions about grading, too. For example, in most workshops in the United States and many abroad, I have found teachers believe that "hard teachers" will get lower student evaluations because their courses are more difficult and that "easy teachers" will get higher student evaluations. Research studies on student evaluations of faculty, although extremely prolific in the past 15 years, have not routinely supported either of these two assumptions (Berk, 2005). Students do, however, consistently give high evaluations to teachers they perceive to be fair (Arreola, 2000). Other traits correlated with higher teacher evaluations include being well organized, accessible, friendly, and enthusiastic or passionate (Berk, 2005; White, 2007).

A Framework for Being Fair

Creating a fair learning environment entails five critical steps.

Step 1. Begin by thinking carefully about what you want students to know and do by the end of the course, not what you will cover in the course. Be action oriented, but avoid verbs such as "understand" and "appreciate" in your structuring student learning outcomes. Students are novices and they do not understand "photosynthesis" or appreciate the "impact of market fluctuation" in the same ways that content experts do. For example, consider the following set of student learning outcomes a professor might place on the syllabus for a nonmajors course:

When you successfully complete Soil Sciences 101, you will be able to

A. Recognize, discuss, and apply basic concepts and key vocabulary terms related to soil composition, deposition, and agricultural use.

B. Identify, critique, and/or employ the components of the scientific method such as formulating a hypothesis, designing an experiment, controlling variables, defining terms operationally, and interpreting data.

C. Read and interpret graphic information (quantitative and qualitative) related to soil composition, deposition, and agricultural use.

D. Communicate to others a knowledge of, and ethical concern for, the importance of soil.

E. Operate selected scientific tools, common to the laboratory, safely and effectively.

These learning outcomes can be categorized by their intent (Bloom, 1956). Cognitive outcomes require students to demonstrate thinking, "knowing," or mental processing skills (outcomes A, B, and C). Affective outcomes require students to act in ways reflective of holding particular attitudes, feelings, or values (outcome D). Psychomotor outcomes require students to demonstrate appropriate actions and/or skills (outcome E).

Step 2. Whether you are a new instructor or a full professor, this next step may surprise you. Select the assessments (e.g., tests, problem sets, portfolios, oral presentations, lab reports) that you will use to enable you and your students to see how well they are achieving the course goals. By making these decisions first, you will be better able to plan and organize classroom content, topic sequences, and active learning strategies that will enable students to be successful in achieving the learning objectives. For example, our hypothetical soils sciences professor might choose to give and grade the following assessments:

A. Two lecture tests and a final examination (each would consist of 30 multiple-choice questions and five critical thinking, short-answer questions about a soil science research graphic, and a brief essay question)

B. A lab practical

C. A two-page reflection paper presenting the student's analysis of and personal action plan for a soils issue in the state

Step 3. Next, organize your course content materials and plan appropriate in-class and out-of-class activities to engage students in achieving these course goals. Other chapters in this book speak powerfully to these aspects of teaching and learning.

Step 4. Select your grading policies and procedures. Decide (or your institution may have already decided for you) how to score your student assessments: raw scores (e.g., 18/30 correct), numeric percentages (e.g., 62%, 90%), whole letter grades (e.g., A, D), letter grades (e.g., B–, C+), or pass/fail marks (e.g., P, F), and how to evaluate those raw scores. In criterion-referenced grading, all students' grades are based on their individual performance on the tested student learning outcomes regardless of the performance of others taking the test. In norm-referenced grading, the same student's grade is based on its relative position within the grade range of others (often used in departmental grading or national testing and referred to as "grading on the curve").

Identify for students how you will combine the tests and other assessment tasks to formulate the final course grade. Will homework count? Will class participation count? Walvoord and Anderson (2010) described the "how and why" of several grading systems: weighted letter grades, accumulated points, contract grading, and an innovative multiple category system in which both graded and ungraded work factor into the final course grade. In this system, students who have a B average on tests and graded projects at the end of the term can only get an B if they have turned in 83% or more of their pass/fail assigned work in that term. Students who have a B test and project average, but have only turned in 75% of pass/fail work would earn a C.

Step 5. Communicate, in writing, with students about the teaching, learning, and grading processes you will be using. Remember to begin your course syllabus with a welcome statement (this statement conveys to your students that you are enthusiastic and friendly). List the student learning outcomes for the course. Identify what will be graded, how much it counts (its value) toward the final grade, and when each exam or assignment is due. Do not forget to include any nonnegotiable course demands that you and your department have adopted (i.e., plagiarism consequences, lab attendance requirements, online discussions, or late assignments penalties).

Faculty-student communication about grading is important to both student and institutional success. The Middle States Commission on Higher Education's (2003) *Student Learning Assessment Handbook: Options and Resources* urges faculty to

> State your goals or outcomes "up front" on the syllabus, review them frequently with students, and then carefully and fairly design tests, assignments, and a grading system that values the kinds of learning that you most want to take place in your classroom. (p.78)

How Can Students Think I'm Unfair? ————————

When students criticize faculty members for being "unfair" on end-of-course evaluations, on local or large-scale surveys, in talking with other students, or, increasingly, on electronic sites (i.e., RateMyProfessor.com), they are usually reacting to one of several teacher behaviors.

Not Selecting Valid Tests or Graded Assignments

I have asked more than 8,000 faculty workshop participants to "think-pair-share" about what they want students to be able to know and do at the end of one of their courses. Not one has ever said, "I just want my students to be able to answer multiple-choice questions correctly." Most teachers have wonderful student learning outcomes in mind—for example, to communicate effectively and sensitively in sign language, describe historical events objectively, or use calculus principles to solve everyday problems—and yet many of these faculty only use multiple-choice tests to assess their students' achievement. If you tell students that it is important to write a literate e-mail in a business course, establish eye contact with the audience in a speech class, or use a microscope proficiently in a microbiology course, and you don't include these skills as part of the course grade, students will sense or say you are "unfair."

Not Using Grading or Feedback at the Appropriate Time

All instructors should jot down what percentage of a student's grade will be known at four time intervals in the academic term. Students should always receive "low threat" grades or feedback such as corrected practice tests or themes with constructive feedback before the first big test or assignment. This strategy will help students know whether their efforts are on target. After midterm, but at least 2 weeks before the final examination, is an appropriate time to have group projects, posters, or presentations become due. Group activities can increase student motivation, offer a different grading modality, and enhance students' higher-order thinking skills through peer discussion and reflection. Group work handed in at the final examination can do none of these things because there is not enough time at this point in the academic term. Students, who are passing with a C or better average for more than two thirds of the term and do not get intermediate feedback on a major assignment (e.g., research paper, art portfolio, teaching unit) due in right before the final, are often shocked and angered that they might fail in the last week of the course, and they will say such teachers are unfair.

Not Considering Make-Ups Policies in Advance

When you are giving and grading class or online quizzes, or reading summaries to help students keep up with the work routinely throughout the term, consider allowing students to drop their lowest grade. All students, regardless of their course average, appreciate this policy. It is a strong motivational incentive for students, especially if they have gotten off to a bad start, to keep on task and keep up their attendance. By letting students drop one formative grade over the term, you save yourself the unpleasant task of being the "judge and jury" of student excuses, eliminate keeping track of make-up work, and reduce the probability that students will think you are unfair.

Major exams are a different story. If a nursing student misses the only test that covers the cardiovascular system, the instructor cannot simply say, "Oh, that's all right. You get to drop one test." A make-up exam or graded assignment is essential. Allowing students to take make-ups without extra inconvenience rigor often elicits strong criticism from good students, such as "I took the test with a 101 degree fever on Friday and that teacher let two students take the same test on Monday. That's not fair."

There are more effective strategies for allowing students to make up missed examinations. One is to give all of your make-up examinations on one assigned day late in the term; this strategy consolidates the use of your proctoring time and greatly reduces criticism from students who took the tests as scheduled in the course. Test-dodgers dislike this policy, and good students with valid excuses are grateful they did not get a zero. Another strategy is to give a comprehensive final exam with intact subset questions testing concepts (not just repeat items) from earlier tests. Score the "missed test set" separately and use that score as the missing test, and then average all test items for final exam score.

Develop your grading policies within the context of your specific course, academic discipline, and institutional culture. Be creative, innovative, and fair. However, if you are a new teacher anywhere or a seasoned faculty veteran "teaching abroad," please consult your immediate supervisor or attend a campuswide grading workshop to be sure you are aware of any preexisting departmental, institutional, or national grading policies.

Assessment

Academic assessment is the systematic gathering and analyzing of information (excluding course grades) to inform and improve student learning or programs of learning in light of goal-oriented expectations (Anderson, 2006). As early as 1986, the American Council on Education defined assessment as "any measure other than end-of-course grading by which the college evaluates its students or programs" (El-Khawas, 1986, p. 5). Course grades were excluded, not because national leaders thought that faculty grades were arbitrary or unreliable, but because grades, as single artifacts (e.g., a C+), do not provide enough information to inform and improve programs of student learning. The differences in assessment policies and procedures worldwide are beyond the scope of this chapter, so I will focus on qualities of assessment that seem to be shared globally.

- Good assessment in the classroom or in the institution is systematic. It isn't over when grades are turned in or when the external evaluators have left and won't be back for another 5 years. "Assessment is a "perpetual work in progress" (Suskie, 2009, p. 36).
- Good assessment measures what matters most. It is easy to assess if science student teachers can reach 75% mastery on a standardized concept inventory, but it is imperative to see if they can explain key terms to young students and engage them in safe laboratory experiences.
- Good assessment of student learning requires at least one source of direct evidence of student learning and is enhanced by indirect evidence of student learning: Direct evidence is work that the student has produced. It may include themes; sculptures; musical scores; oral, written, or media presentations scored with a rubric; achievement records on locally designed multiple-choice tests accompanied by test blueprints; think-aloud tapes as students compose written work or solve problems; "clicker" data distributions; field supervisor reports; and capstone experiences. Indirect evidence of student learning is any product that indicates that students are learning course content and are on their way to achieving student learning outcomes. Examples of indirect evidence include assignment grades without rubric scoring, student ratings of their own knowledge or skills, many types of surveys, affective behavioral checklists, and more.
- Good assessment uses multiple measures at multiple times and evaluates multiple types of student achievement: cognitive, affective, and when appropriate, psychomotor skills.
- Good assessment is useful and used. It asks and answers questions about student learning and institutional support of that learning that the academic community wants to know. It then uses that new information to enhance student learning, faculty satisfaction, and intuitional success.

A Brief History of Assessment in the United States

After the Higher Education Act of 1965, postsecondary (tertiary) institutions were required to be periodically accredited by an approved regional or special interest agency if they wanted to receive federal funding (e.g., student grants, student loans, faculty grants, building funds, etc.). For at least the next 20 years, agencies considered how colleges and universities were prepared "to deliver" a quality education. They evaluated such factors as how many faculty had PhDs, how many books the library housed, how many academic majors were offered within institutions, and how many peer-reviewed articles faculty had published.

By the mid-1980s, many individuals in corporate America and independent educational organizations such as the National Institute of Education became concerned that the quality of college graduates was declining (Fink, 2003). These groups urged accrediting agencies to stop evaluating U.S. colleges and universities by their "inputs" and to start evaluating them by their "outputs"—for example, the percentage of graduating business majors who could construct a literate e-mail, the percentage of nursing students passing state boards, or the percentage of students who were employed in their chosen career within 1 year of graduation.

Soon, newly appointed assessment officers within colleges and universities began scrambling to get faculty to write student learning outcomes (not content outlines), give norm-referenced tests, and submit multiple measures of direct evidence of student learning. Faced with new jargon, more work, and having been told that their grades were useless (remember "excluding course grades"), faculty began to perceive assessment as something foreign to the classroom, an educational fad that would probably go away if ignored or resisted.

Assessment did not go away, and it is very likely that it will remain a part of the U.S. educational scene for decades to come. Three publications spurred U.S. faculty interest in assessment. The first was Thomas Angelo and K. Patricia Cross's (1993) *Classroom Assessment Techniques: A Handbook for College Teachers* that offered an exciting glimpse of how engaging students in class with 5- to 7-minute written assessments could provide faculty with immediate, useful teaching feedback. The second publication was the American Association of Higher Education's (1996) *Principles of Good Practice for Assessing Student Learning*, which linked good assessment to mission statements, educational values, faculty buy-in, and classroom practices. The third was Walvoord and Anderson's (1998) *Effective Grading: A Tool for Learning and Assessment*, which showed faculty how to use rubrics to grade student work more rigorously and quantitatively and how to use data from their grading processes rather than grades per se to improve student learning.

By 2000, the "add standardized tests and stir" approach to assessment had passed its zenith in higher education. Greater attention was being given to course-embedded assessment; in the United States, classroom assignments accompanied by rubrics had been recognized as direct evidence of student learning, test blueprinting was being used to extract specific, goal-oriented student achievement data from multiple-choice tests, and student reflections were no longer considered interesting, but useless. Correspondingly, in the United Kingdom, John Heywood (2000) concluded, "While attendance at institutions of higher learning would seem to have positive effects on development in the cognitive and moral spheres, much more can be done at the course, teaching, and assessment levels to enhance that experience" (p. 195).

A Closer Look at Rubrics ———————————————

Rubrics are criterion-referenced grading scales that allow teachers to examine integrated or complex student work (e.g., essay questions, themes, online discussion threads, math proofs, literature reviews) for specific goal-oriented expectations such as demonstrating contextual critical thinking or meeting written format demands. If a teacher grades a student's essay or research report holistically (having only one evaluative grade, for example, a C+), it can only be considered indirect evidence of student learning because the grade alone does not indicate how to inform and improve student learning. Using a criterion-referenced rubric allows teachers to grade how well each student is succeeding, but more importantly how well the whole class is achieving goal-oriented expectations.

For several semesters, I asked my students to compare and contrast prokaryotic cells (simple, bacterial-like cells) and eukaryotic cells (more complex cells with nuclei found in higher life forms) in four ways in a one or two paragraph format on the first test. I graded each paper holistically. I bemoaned to myself, and sometimes to colleagues, how poorly the students did on this important question.

After attending a Maryland Writing Across the Curriculum workshop, I decided maybe a rubric would give me a clue as to what wasn't working. I selected three traits, Comparison, Contrast, and Topic sentence(s) and constructed a 4-point rubric for each. Here is the rubric for one trait. (For entire rubric, see Anderson, 2008.)

TOPIC SENTENCE(S)

4 points: Each topic sentence is effective

3 points: Topic sentence or sentence(s) are present, but misleading

2 points: Paragraph format evident, but lacks topic sentence(s)

1 point: Not in paragraph format (p. 452)

I attached a rubric grading slip to each of the 90+ papers, graded them, and circled each student's performance level for each trait. I got the whole class average score for each of the rubric items (4 being top performance): Compare, 2.1; Contrast, 3.6; and Topic sentences, 2.8. Seeing the quantitative data, I realized that my students were able to explain how the two types of cells were different, but they could not identify ways in which they were similar (both have cell membranes, cytoplasm, DNA, and RNA; require energy; and can replicate asexually). When I returned the tests, I asked my students to read and sign the rubric slips and write on the back one way they might improve answering this kind of question on the next test (an example of a student reflection activity) and collected them.

At the start of the next unit (genetics), I drew a big Venn diagram (two overlapping circles with a shared intersect) on the blackboard and labeled the circles DNA and RNA. The students and I filled in the diagram. About 2 weeks later on the genetics test, I asked students to compare and contrast mitosis and meiosis in four ways in a one- to two-paragraph format. The class average essay score was higher (17%) than the first test, and the greatest gains occurred in the "comparison" scores. In popular U.S. assessment jargon, I was "closing the loop," meaning that I was using the assessment data I had collected to inform and improve teaching and learning.

Test Blueprinting

Across continents, institutions, and disciplines, faculty members give multiple-choice exams. They spend hours searching test banks, composing good questions, duplicating objective tests into multiple forms (to avoid cheating), scoring, and reporting test grades to students. Test blueprinting is a technique by which you can transform routine teaching artifacts such as unit tests, midterms, or final exams, indirect evidence of student learning, into stockpiles of direct evidence of student learning. Test blueprinting involves following four steps:

- Select the student learning outcomes you want to examine within the test.
- Identify questions that are good indicators for each outcome.
- Score all multiple-choice tests as you usually do (by hand or electronic marking device that denotes wrong choices.). Calculate and record each student's test grade.
- Return the test and hand out a copy of Table 2.1. Ask students to calculate their percentage correct for each question set, enter it on the form, sign on the front, and explain on the back how they planned to study differently for the next test.

Table 2.1   Summary of the Question and Outcome Alignment and Class Average for Each Learning Outcome (aspects of these data and more ideas on test blueprinting can be found in Suskie, 2009)

Learning Outcomes	Test items linked to this learning goal	Please calculate and enter your percentage correct score for each outcome set	Class average on each learning outcome set

When accompanied by an explanation of the process and selection of indicator items, test blueprint data are excellent sources of direct evidence. Students need help and practice in improving their quantitative reasoning skills. Test blueprinting is an effective means of assisting students in developing these important skills.

Affective Behavioral Checklists

Checklists of behaviors that are indicative of goal-oriented attitudes and values in sustained or intensive learning experiences (e.g., academic major, study abroad program, student teaching experiences, or service learning activities) can be valuable sources of indirect evidence of student learning. Items on an affective behavioral checklist do not ask students how they feel about the experience (that is, reflection, which is also a valuable assessment tool; Suskie [2009] offers detailed suggestions for constructing, analyzing, and reporting on reflective data). Instead, affective behavioral checklists ask students to self-report their actions or in more controlled situations, to work with an interviewer, who records the data and periodically asks for explanations.

Biology faculty at Towson University (TU) developed a 33-item affective behavioral checklist to examine if graduating seniors had participated in activities that indicated they valued the importance of research in science, technology competency, multicultural perspectives, and lifelong learning. Less than 3 percent of more than 270 seniors (over three semesters) had ever "assisted a faculty member in collecting research data," "presented a student paper at a professional science or research meeting," or "participated in a summer research program," and less than 1% had "read two or more articles independently (not assigned) in scientific journals in the last 3 months."

For a biology department that stated it valued student research its mission statement, these results were dismal. Yet, these same statistics served as a data-driven impetus to engage biology faculty to write and receive three consecutive National Science Foundation (NSF) Research Experiences for Undergraduates (REU) grants over the next 6 years (grants data on file with NSF and Towson University [www.towson.edu/OURS]).

Conclusion

Grading and assessment are no longer issues that isolated academics might have discussed over coffee in an ivy-covered building. Indeed, on either side of the Atlantic Ocean or above or below the equator, dedicated faculty in higher education are not only discussing, but contributing to, a "culture of assessment," which is and always will be a work in progress.

References

American Association of Higher Education. (1996). *AAHE's principles of good practice for assessing student learning.* Washington, DC: American Association of Higher Education.

Anderson, V. J. (2006). Assessing diversity in information technology: Strategies that enhance student learning and generate assessment data. In G. Trajkovski (Ed.), *Issues in information technology education: Issues and controversies* (pp. 153–165). Hershey, PA: Information Science.

Anderson, V. J. (2008). Grading. In N. Salkind (Ed.), *The encyclopedia of educational psychology* (Vol. 1, pp. 450–453). Thousand Oaks, CA: Sage.

Angelo, T. A., & Cross, K. P. (1993). *Classroom assessment techniques: A handbook for college teachers* (2nd ed.). San Francisco, CA: Jossey-Bass.

Arreola, R. A. (2000). *Developing a comprehensive faculty evaluation system: A handbook for college faculty.* Bolton, MA: Anker.

Berk, R. (2005). Survey of 12 strategies to measure teacher effectiveness. *International Journal of Teaching and Learning in Higher Education, 17,* 48–62.

Bloom, B. S. (Ed.). (1956). *Taxonomy of educational objectives.* New York, NY: McKay.

El-Khawas, E. (1986). *Campus trends.* Panel Report, no.73. Washington, DC: American Council on Higher Education.

Fink, L. D. (2003). *Creating significant learning experiences.* San Francisco, CA: Jossey-Bass.

Heywood, J. (2000). *Assessment in higher education: Student learning, teaching, programmes and institutions.* London, UK: Jessica Kingsley.

Kuh, G. D. (2001). Assessing what really matters to student learning: Inside the National Survey of Student Engagement. *Change, 33*(3), 10–17, 66.

Middle States Commission of Higher Education. (2003). *Student learning assessment handbook: Options and resources.* Philadelphia, PA: MSCHE.

Suskie, L. (2009). *Assessing student learning: A common sense guide* (2nd ed.). San Francisco, CA: Jossey-Bass.

Walvoord, B. E., & Anderson, V. J. (1998). *Effective grading: A tool for learning and assessment.* San Francisco, CA: Jossey-Bass.

Walvoord, B. E., & Anderson, V. J. (2010). *Effective grading: A tool for learning and assessment in college* (2nd ed.). San Francisco, CA: Jossey-Bass.

White, N. R. (2007). The customer is always right? Student discourse about higher education in Australia. *Higher Education, 54,* 593–604.

CHAPTER 3

Using the Scholarship of Teaching and Learning to Improve Learning Outcomes

REGAN A. R. GURUNG AND R. ERIC LANDRUM

The best place to start a story is the beginning, but when it comes to teaching and learning, we may want to start at the end. What do we want our students to know by the end of our classes? These goals are our learning outcomes (LOs) and are critical to effective pedagogical practices. What are LOs? How do we improve them using the scholarship of teaching and learning (SoTL)? These are central questions addressed in this chapter.

What Is SoTL?

SoTL is the intentional, systematic reflection on teaching and learning that results in peer-reviewed products made public (Gurung & Schwartz, 2010; see Irons & Buskist, 2008; Pan, 2009; Smith, in press; and Smith, 2008, for more on definitions).

Although SoTL is a relatively new field, thinking about how to improve teaching and learning is a centuries old activity (Berliner, 2006). Teachers have been reflecting on educational practices, both for formative improvement purposes and summative judgment purposes, for many years. Within U.S. psychology, this self-reflection on a discipline-wide basis was formalized in 1947 with the creation of Division 2 of the American Psychological Association (Buskist & Smith, 2008)—this division is now called the Society for the Teaching of Psychology (STP). In the United Kingdom, the Higher Education Academy Psychology Network is one of the Higher Education Academy's 24 subject centers that supports teaching and learning at the discipline level and serves similar purposes to that of STP.

SoTL catapulted into the national higher education consciousness in 1990 with Ernest L. Boyer's (1990) *Scholarship Reconsidered*, which catalyzed extensive examination of research on teaching and learning. Boyer proposed adding the scholarship of teaching to the other more traditional recognized forms of scholarship such as scholarship of discovery. SoTL is now recognized by colleges, universities, and national and international organizations as a legitimate, and indeed, vibrant area of scholarly inquiry (O'Meara & Rice, 2005). More recently, academic institutions have taken on the mantel of SoTL leadership by starting up specialized journals such as the *International Journal for the Scholarship of Teaching and Learning (IJSOTL)*, a peer-reviewed electronic journal published twice a year by the Center for Excellence in Teaching at Georgia Southern University, first published in January 2007 (http://academics.georgiasouthern.edu/ijsotl/index.htm).

Much has been written about the history of SoTL (e.g., Bender, 2005; Buskist & Smith, 2008), the prevalence of SoTL (e.g., Gurung, Ansburg, Alexander, Lawrence, & Johnson, 2008), and the potential benefit to faculty who engage in SoTL efforts (e.g., Goodburn & Savory, 2009; Russell, 2010; Smith, 2008; Weimer, 2006). Faculty-centered evidence about the beneficial effects of SoTL continue to emerge, such as the presentation of successful case studies based on particular institutions (Goodburn & Savory, 2009; Russell, 2010) and institution-wide survey efforts (Dewar, Dailey-Hebert, & Moore, 2010).

SoTL Around the World

Although SoTL was first championed in the United States, its practice is now common worldwide. For example, in the United Kingdom, Dai Hounsell and Noel Entwistle and others spearheaded the British Enhancing Teaching and Learning Project (ETL, n.d.), which developed subject-specific conceptual frameworks to guide institutional and faculty teaching-learning environments (see http://www.etl.tla.ed.ac.uk/publications.html). Based in Edinburgh, this group developed a number of useful tools for pedagogical research and mapped out key variables that influence learning (see Entwistle, 2009 for a review). One particularly useful tool that illustrates how SoTL can be used to increase learning is the *Approaches and Study Skills Inventory for Students* (ASSIST; Tait & Entwistle, 1996), a scale that has been used to explore student learning. For example, in Australia, the ASSIST survey was implemented at the beginning and end of a chiropractic class to identify changes in learning. When technology was integrated into the curriculum with appropriate learning activities, students using virtual microscopes moved more toward a strategic approach to learning but expressed a preference for a deep approach to teaching (Jonas-Dwyer & Sudweeks, 2007).

There are many compelling examples of SoTL being conducted around the world and published in a variety of outlets. In a study conducted in Australia, Krisztina Valter and Gerlese Akerlind's (2010) learning objective was to get students to think and act like researchers. Students engaged in research-like activities during lectures and in groups. The article provides numerous examples of introducing students to research practices within a course setting. Although this case study is based in the natural sciences, the same approach to teaching research skills could easily translate into other disciplines and illustrates how SoTL can be used to better student learning. A study conducted in Sweden addressed another common issue faced by many faculty—how does a teacher balance theory and practice? In a robotics course, Krister Wolff and Mattias Wahde's (2010) students used a custom-built robot consisting of standard electronic and mechanical components (instead of a commercial one) and modified time spent on teaching the theoretical background and time spent on robot assembly and programming to find what they considered a perfect balance of the two.

Global SoTL has evolved to a point where even cross-national data are available. For example, Susan Iverson and Amanda Espenschied-Reilly (2010) used interviews to study conceptions of academic service learning in the United States and the Republic of Ireland to determine if and how culture and social context shaped practitioners' perceptions and practices regarding service-learning pedagogy. The researchers found that "Irish participants distanced their practice from the historical and cultural context of U.S. service-learning, demonstrating the process of localization" (p. 1). The notion of culture and context is also seen in a study of memorization from Saudi Arabia. Muhammad Alfi (2004) reviewed research on memorization and educational theory, study of the Holy Qur'an, and methodologies in Islamic schools and used the amassed information to design classroom applications to optimize memorization.

SoTL is not always called by this name. A form of SoTL called *action research* in North America is called *teacher research* in the United Kingdom (Maclean & Mohr, 1999). Action research is any systematic inquiry conducted to gather information about how schools operate, how their faculty teach, and how well their students learn (Mills, 2007). In the United States, action research has its roots in the progressive education movement and the work of John Dewey (1916/2009). In the United Kingdom, teacher research fostered curricular reform and increased professionalism in teaching, and in Australia, action research catalyzed collaborative curriculum planning (Mills, 2007). Originating in the United Kingdom with the work of Lawrence Stenhouse (1975) and the Humanities Curriculum Project (McKernan, 1991), teacher research is now conducted around the globe.

Publishing SoTL Research

As a testament to the (mostly unknown) longevity of pedagogical research, the earliest journal articles on teaching and learning were published back in 1924 with the *Journal of Chemical Education*, which is still published. Many pedagogical journals started as newsletters (e.g., *Teaching of Psychology*), and conversely, many pedagogical publications are not "published" on paper at all—they appear only in electronic formats (e.g., *International Journal for the Scholarship of Teaching and Learning*).

In a review of the history and diversity of pedagogical research, Maryellen Weimer (2006) noted that almost all the major disciplines have pedagogical journals. In perhaps one of the most comprehensive listing of publication outlets for pedagogical research, Weimer's work clearly shows that if one is interested in learning more about how to optimize teaching and learning, there are many places to look. Some examples of SoTL outlets include *Academic Commons, Canadian Journal for the Scholarship of Teaching and Learning, College Teaching, International Journal for the Scholarship of Teaching and Learning, International Journal of Teaching and Learning in Higher Education, Journal of College Science Teaching, Journal of Effective Teaching, Journal of Teaching and Learning, Journal on Excellence in College Teaching*, and *Teaching in Higher Education*. For a comprehensive list, see http://ilstu.libguides.com/sotl or http://www4 .uwm.edu/sotl/help_support/pub_outlets/.

Doing SoTL: Major Research Designs

The steps for conducting research on teaching and learning mirror most of the steps used to conduct research on any topic. First, the teacher identifies a question of interest, and then reviews what has been published on the topic. Second, the teacher ascertains what is left to be discovered or needs to be researched, and then decides how to conduct that research. One common approach to this sort of research is to measure relevant aspects of what the students are learning, make a change or introduce a new method or assignment, and then measure students' learning again to determine the extent to which the manipulation affected it (see Gurung & Schwartz, 2009, for exemplars of conducting SoTL research). Many resources now provide excellent case studies from a variety of disciplines on how to conduct classroom research, for example, Thomas A. Angelo and K. Patricia Cross (1993); Nancy L. Chick, Aeron Haynie, and Regan A. R. Gurung (2012); Robert M. Diamond (2008); L. Dee Fink (2003); Gurung, Chick, and Haynie (2009); Pat Hutchins (2000); Kathleen McKinney (2007); Thomas Pusateri (2009); Laurie Richlin (2006); Paul Savory, Amy Nelson Burnett, and Amy M. Goodburn (2007); Jeffrey Seybert (2002); Linda Suskie (2009); Barbara E. Walvoord (2004); and Maryellen Weimer (2006).

These resources highlight many ways of researching whether students' learning improves as a result of changes teachers make to their teaching. To illustrate this point, we provide a few prototypical designs.

Semester-to-Semester Comparisons

The simplest way to study changes in learning is to compare grade distributions over semesters (or quarters or terms depending on the length of classes or the country). Are the class averages the same? What does the grade distribution look like? If the class averages are different across semesters, it is often a good idea to check if those differences are statistically significant. After all, any changes in grades could result from student characteristics (study habits, effort, ability), the teacher's characteristics (teaching technique, grading style, course design), or a combination of both. Other factors may play a smaller role in affecting student learning, such as teaching in different rooms, teaching at different times of day, changes in prerequisites to the course, and so on. The more factors that teachers can measure or control while manipulating only a single specific factor, the more likely that those teachers will be able to clearly and accurately determine the impact of that factor on their students' learning. Be mindful, though, that the semester-to-semester approach to conducting SoTL has an important shortcoming—the students in any course change from semester to semester, and many student characteristics may change as well and account for differences in student learning. Other research designs, particularly those involving within-semester changes avoid this problem.

As an exemplar study spanning multiple semesters, Randolph Smith (2008) suggested examining Patricia Connor-Greene's (2002) study. Using a problem-based service learning approach, Connor-Greene had students enrolled in an abnormal psychology course create community resources about specific psychiatric disorders. This course-based project involved reviewing the literature about various disorders, and students made on-site visits to mental health treatment facilities and worked to create resource materials that would be useful to the community. In her first iteration, Connor-Greene asked five evaluative questions that became key to teaching of the course because they allowed systematic analysis of the effectiveness of different assignment variations that would occur over a four-semester span. In the semester that Connor-Greene launched the project, it constituted about 10 percent of students' course grades, and the project was evaluated in the five evaluative questions. Student responses on the course evaluation prompted changes for the next implementation of this project—for instance, students believed that the project should be worth more than 10 percent of the course grade, and that noncontributing students in some groups should not be rewarded to the same extent as other hardworking students were.

In the second iteration, Connor-Greene (2002) increased the project's point value, and she graded students as individuals and as members of groups, although she noted that some groups did not integrate and synthesize information to the extent she desired. In the third iteration, Connor-Greene used multiple grading checkpoints for each of the five key components of the course, but this amount of additional work for both students and Connor-Greene consumed a lot of time. In the fourth iteration, Connor-Greene implemented online websites through which students could easily coordinate file sharing, and she could gain access to student work at any time during the semester. During the four semesters, Connor-Greene observed significant improvements in student understanding of disorders, treatment options in the area, empathy for individuals with mental disorders, and students' ability to locate treatments. Thus, the systematic and persistent application of SoTL principles lead to enhanced learning experiences for students over time.

Within-Semester Comparisons

There are many ways to examine changes in student learning within a semester (or quarter or term). The repeated measures design (RMD) works well in course designs that have a several similar exams or assignments. The term *RMD* is used in research when the assessment is identical such as when department learning outcomes or course objectives are measured year after year in the same college student sample. In such designs, the key is to identify changes in responses to similar questions over time. The measure used repeatedly consists of the same number of questions asked in the same order, and differences in the responses will be taken to indicate changes in knowledge (e.g., understanding diversity; Kernahan & Davis, 2010).

However, using identical questions is not always practical or possible in most courses. To avoid this problem, many teachers modify the RMD to include a pretest and a posttest. For example, many large general education courses give the same test at the beginning and end of the semester (e.g., a test of knowledge of governmental policy in a political science course). To test whether learning is changing during the semester, the teacher can test if the class average is changing over time, test if learning has changed from the beginning of the semester (using a class average), or even compare a single student's score to his or her previous score to determine if the student is improving during the semester. If there is a significant difference in student learning between the two assessments, it could be the result of the instruction the teacher provided in between the pretest and the posttest. Of course, teachers cannot be sure that the change resulted only from instruction unless they have measured and controlled for many other possible factors such as how much and how the student studied. If, while holding other variables constant, a teacher finds a significant difference between the pretest and posttest measures, then he or she may be confident that the finding is a good indicator that instructional changes produced increases in learning.

As an example of SoTL work achieved within the course of a semester, R. Eric Landrum and Karen Dietz (2006) recruited volunteers from four sections of an upper-division research methods course to complete the class in a "no-points" condition. That is, student work received letter grades, and typical feedback on assignments (e.g., comments on how to improve writing, multiple-choice items answered incorrectly) remained the same as normal except that the teacher did not reveal the actual number of points to students. The authors' goal in this study was to determine if student learning would improve when the possibility of a points-centered approach was removed from the class. Thirty percent of the enrolled students volunteered for the "no points" condition. The teacher used multiple instruments to determine whether pretreatment differences existed between volunteers and nonvolunteers (tests measured learning orientation-grade orientation, achievement anxiety, and locus of control) and found no significant pretreatment differences. Likewise, Landrum and Dietz found no significant differences in the grades earned by students in the points condition versus the no-points condition (although students did earn slightly more points in the no points condition, a fact the researchers did not reveal to them until the end of the semester). In this study, students realized that they can perform adequately and without penalty without receiving grades in the form of a specific number of points. Students also realized by being volunteers for a study about teaching and learning that pedagogical research questions can be addressed ethically in a classroom, and that the instructor modeling research methods in a research methods course helps to communicate the inherent values of thinking like a social scientist. Teachers learn (through application and vicariously through published journal articles) that different treatment interventions in a classroom environment can lead to interesting insights.

SoTL around the world and across disciplines, whether in Europe, Asia, or New Zealand, economics, chemistry, philosophy, or English, consists of a variation of these basic research designs. The key is that teachers methodologically and purposely examine how their students are learning, especially as a result of any changes the teachers implement. To best conduct SoTL, one should have a clear picture of one's learning outcomes.

What Are Learning Outcomes?

Learning outcomes (LOs) are the "knowledge, skills, attitudes, and habits of mind that student take with them from a learning experience" (Suskie, 2009, p. 117). LOs provide the evidence, after the fact, that learning has occurred. Well-written LOs possess three characteristics (Mager, 1962;

Marzano, 2009): performance, conditions, and criteria. First, a LO should describe what the student should know or be able to do after the learning experience. Second, a LO may describe the conditions or context in which the demonstration of knowledge or skills is to occur. Third, teachers should established a criterion—an acceptable level or of performance—to help determine if the student has achieved the LO. Here is an example of a LO: The student should be able to create a completely error free resume that will be used for postgraduation job applications.

There are three different kinds or types of LOs: (1) knowledge and conceptual understanding, (2) thinking and other skills, and (3) attitudes, values, dispositions, and habits of mind (Suskie, 2009). These types of LOs sometimes go by different labels. For example, Robert J. Marzano (2009) used the labels declarative, procedural, and noncognitive for the three categories listed, respectively. Thus, for Marzano (2009), a declarative learning goal (knowledge) would have the sentence structure "Students will understand _____," and a procedural learning goal (skill) would have the sentence structure "Students will be able to _____."

Although planning LOs for students sounds intuitive, the development of meaningful and measurable learning goals is challenging. Instructional designers typically recommend that the course design process start with LOs, but in reality, many teachers design and implement using LOs as an afterthought—called the typical approach by Grant P. Wiggins and Jay McTighe (1998). So rather than the "afterthought" design, one alternative would be to design the course "backward."

How Do Teachers Use Learning Outcomes?

If LOs and assessment practices are not centrally embedded in a course from the start, faculty may view LO assessment as additional work and view assessment in general as a burden rather than an opportunity to gauge the level to which students achieved LOs. Years ago, experts in course design suggested a different sequence of course planning steps; a sequence that is counterintuitive to many faculty members, hence the label *backward design* (Fink, 2003; Wiggins & McTighe, 1998). In backward design, teachers use LOs to guide course design, including both pedagogical decisions and assessment practices. Teachers articulate LOs with clarity and precision (similar to operational definitions in the social sciences) to be useful in the next step of backward design, which determines the assessment method. After LOs are defined and assessment processes are in place, *then* the teacher designing the course considers the pedagogical approach: Learning outcomes drive assessment practices, which in turn drive pedagogical decision making. Teachers may then examine evidence regarding the effectiveness of LOs and draw conclusions about the extent to which students achieved them.

Consideration of backward design might push teachers out of their comfort zones. Developing LOs first and an assessment plan second might lead to the conclusion, for example, that lecturing is not the optimum pedagogical approach. However, the strength of the backward design approach lies in the development of precise and clearly articulated course-relevant LOs.

SoTL and Learning Outcomes

There are many challenges to adequate measurement of LOs (e.g., Moore & Gayle, 2010). LOs can become a useful litmus test for consideration of pedagogical practices and using SoTL (Olson, 2009). In thinking about using clickers or other classroom response systems in a course—the key question for the teacher becomes "does the use of clickers help students achieve a desired LO in this course?" Similarly, many instructors have students work in groups. Does group work increase learning? Again a SoTL approach could help document potential impact on learning. In a qualitative case study of informal peer groups in a law program in Norway, Arne Vines (2010) focused on how students perceived and experienced participation in peer groups. Vines used a qualitative case study approach (monitoring student diaries and focus groups) and found that although the impact of informal peer groups on students' LOs could not be measured, peer groups play a crucial role in the total learning environment and the learning potential of such groupings. Some learning outcomes can be more specific. For example, Ihab Obaidat and Ehab Malkawi (2009) tested the extent to which students in the United Arab Emirates understood basic concepts of motion in a physics class. The authors developed a short research-based multiple-choice test and administered the test to students in engineering and science classes. Based on their findings, Obaidat and Malkawi identified reasons for students' failure to grasp basic concepts in physics and generated ways to modify their instructional practices in an effort to improve student learning.

LOs may be an individual teacher decision or dictated by departmental goals. Suskie (2009) likened the SoTL approach to learning objectives similarly to action research described earlier. The four steps we outline in Figure 3.1 may be helpful in identifying and tracking the usefulness and centrality of learning outcomes when teachers use a systematic SoTL-based approach to their instruction.

Entire volumes are devoted to providing detailed instruction on how to conduct assessments (e.g., Dunn, McCarthy, Baker, & Halonen, 2011; Maki, 2011)—the scope of this chapter only allows a cursory review of potential methodological approaches as seen earlier. The National Institute for Learning Outcomes Assessment (www.learningoutcomesassessment.org) provides many useful resources for the use and assessment of LOs at the collegiate level in the United States. We recommend that the assessment of

Figure 3.1   Key Steps in Identifying and Tracking the Usefulness and Centrality of Learning Outcomes (adapted from Suskie, 2009)

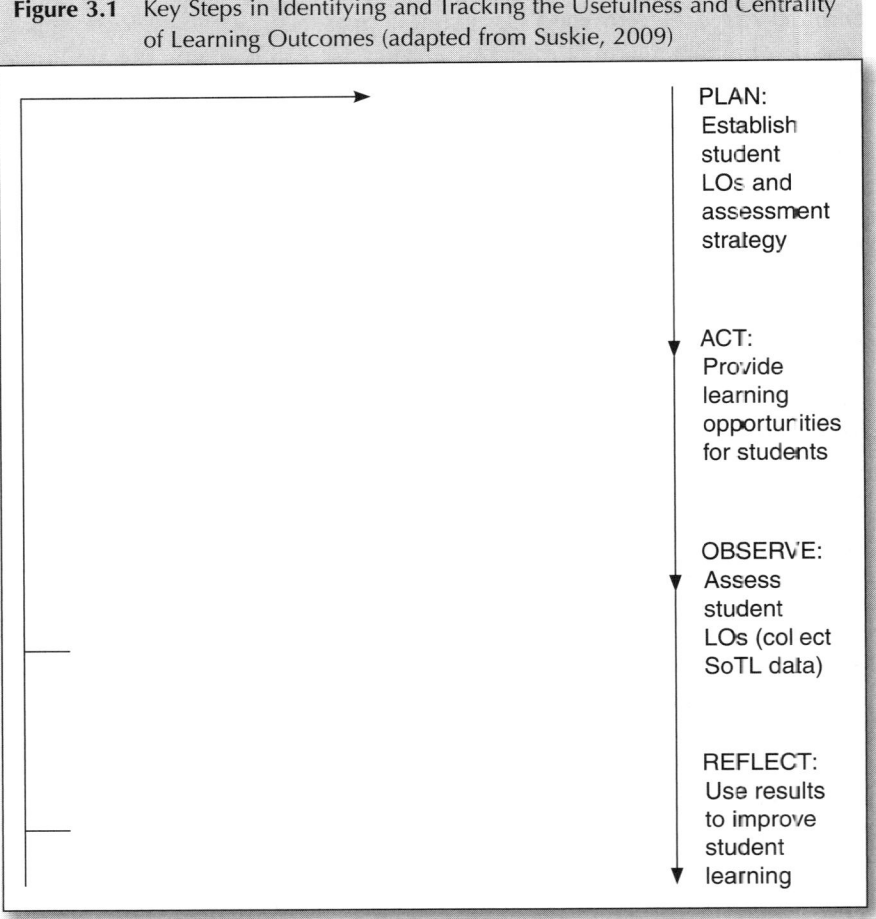

LOs use an evidence-based SoTL approach. As an organizational mechanism to frame discussions about assessment, considering the direct-indirect and objective-subjective dimensions can be valuable.

Direct-Indirect Dimension

Direct measures of student learning are what most teachers would call grading—the individual teacher's evaluation of student work such as exams, writing assignments, class projects, or other overt evidence (Weldy & Turnipseed, 2010). Indirect measures of student learning may be perceptual in nature—asking students about their opinions or attitudes about how much they learned, for example, through alumni surveys (Walvoord, 2004). To see the intended heuristic value of the direct-indirect continuum in reflecting about assessment practices, compare the items entered in the top half vs. the bottom half of Figure 3.2.

Figure 3.2   A 2 × 2 Matrix Integrating Evidence Source (Direct-Indirect) and Assessment Type (Subjective-Objective)

Direct Method: Behavior-Based Evidence From Students

Objective Assessments—Tend to Be More Quantitative

- Test performance: multiple choice, true/false, matching, fill-in-the-blank, concept tests, final exams, cumulative finals
- Results from national, standardized licensing/certification exams (e.g., GRE)
- Results from classroom clicker data on tests or quizzes
- Course grades and grade distributions
- Admission rate into graduate school of graduating students
- Participation rate of students as research assistants, conference presenters, publication coauthors

- Course-based group work
- Written products: term papers, lab reports
- Performance on essay questions
- Capstone experiences
- Employer/internship supervisor ratings of student skills
- Classroom assessment techniques (one-minute papers, free-writing, concept maps)
- Student portfolios
- Credit for class participation
- Student research papers, conference presentations, senior theses
- Online activities summarized and assessed (discussion boards, chat rooms)
- Self-reflection, student journals, self-critiques
- Senior exit interviews

Subjective Assessments—Tend to Be More Qualitative

- Placement rates and starting salaries of new graduates
- End-of-semester course evaluation items
- National Survey of Student Engagement (NSSE) data
- Year-to-year retention rates, graduation rates
- Library use statistics/web hits
- Transcript analysis

- Alumni satisfaction and career perception/preparation surveys
- Focus groups comprising students, alumni, or employers
- Student and alumni recognition via honors, awards, scholarships received
- External examiner reviews (from departmental self-study process)
- Performance reviews by employers, graduate school advisors
- Departmental syllabus audit

Indirect Method: Perception-Based Evidence About Students

Notes: The items listed in this 2 × 2 matrix appear in multiple sources, including McConnell et al., 2006; Passow (2011), Pusateri (2009), and Suskie (2009). The positioning of the entries within the figure represents the authors' opinions.

Objective-Subjective Dimension

Although placement of items along this artificial dimension is debatable, this organizational scheme helps teachers comprehend the assessment literature. Objective assessments are those that possess absolutely correct and incorrect answers, for example, an objective test accompanied by a scoring key that allows the test to be machine scorable (Ericksen, 2009), although there are many variations on this theme (Wright, 1994). There is only one correct answer for an objective test item. Examples of objective assessment items include multiple-choice, true-false, and matching questions (Suskie, 2009). Objective assessments tend to yield quantitative outcomes.

According to Suskie (2009), the advantages of objective assessments are that (a) they are efficient, with the capability of delivering a large amount of information about student knowledge using little time; (b) large-scale, some-what mechanized approaches can be used (e.g., bubble sheet scoring), although objective assessments do not typically assess deep processing skills like subjective assessments can; (c) they are easy and quick to score, although their creation is neither easy nor quick; and (d) a singular score (e.g., performance indicator) can be calculated from objective assessments, making this approach popular for summarizing outcomes to third parties such as administrators, lawmakers, or the general public.

Alternatively, subjective assessments produce data where a machine-scorable answer solution is not feasible, and skilled judgments are needed to determine whether students have achieved corresponding LOs. Subject assessments often yield a qualitative rather than a quantitative outcome. Rubrics aid the assessment of student work that falls to the subjective side of the continuum. Multiple resources exist to aid teachers who want to use rubrics to facilitate subjective assessments (e.g., Arter & McTighe, 2001; Stevens & Levi, 2011; Suskie, 2009).

The advantages of subjective assessments are numerous, including (a) the ability to measure many important skills that objective tests cannot measure, including organization, synthesis, problem-solving, creativity, and originality; (b) skills can be assessed using subject assessments, such as having a student actually write a literature review on a research topic (rather than asking a student multiple-choice questions about how to write a literature view); (c) subjective assessments are thought to promote deep learning and help establish skills that outlast the rote memorization of textbook information; and (d) nuanced scoring can be used in subjective assessments, such as giving partial credit. To see the usefulness of the objective-subjective continuum, compare the right side to the left side of Figure 3.2.

The matrix shown in Figure 3.2 may be useful for future reviews of the assessment literature as well as for providing a conceptual framework for empirical assessment results such that multiple measures from multiple perspectives can yield insights to the extent that LOs are achieved, either at the course level or program level. However, some existing SoTL scholarship may not fit neatly into this 2 x 2 matrix. For instance, Min Yang, Beverley Webster, and Michael Prosser (2011) conducted a qualitative study in China on the variation among first-year undergraduates' induction into different academic disciplines. Authors collected data from focus groups with students from different disciplines at a university in Hong Kong. The authors' content analysis showed cognitive skills, professional skills, and study skills to be the important disciplinary skills for these students. Students' varying conceptions of problem-solving and critical-thinking skills implied qualitative differences in understanding about the nature of disciplinary problems. Other researchers have integrated both behavior-based and perception-based approaches into a single study (e.g., Sizemore & Lewandowski, 2009). It may be that these research designs provide better efficiency compared with other research that addresses only one of the matrix cells. More systematic research that chronicles successes and failure to enhance engagement would provide a valuable resource for teachers looking to match a pedagogical approach with a desired learning outcome—these are clearly the ultimate goals of SoTL research.

Conclusion

Teachers around the globe are conscientiously examining their students' learning. This research on one's own classroom, published and peer-reviewed, contributes to a growing knowledge base of scholarship of teaching and learning. Whether you are a teacher in a classroom in Saudi Arabia, Nigeria, Mumbai, Shanghai, New York, or Bali, it is important to consciously and methodologically examine the effects of one's teaching on student learning. After all, teaching is more than just the delivery of content. In this chapter, we described the basic fundamentals of doing SoTL with a particular emphasis on determining and assessing course learning outcomes. Starting with clearly defining learning outcomes and then designing classroom instruction to best achieve those outcomes is critical to successful teaching and optimal learning.

References

Alfi, M. Y. (2004). An applied linguistics approach to improving the memorization of the Holy Quran: Suggestions for designing practice activities for learning and teaching. *Journal of King Saud University, 16,* 1–32.

Angelo, T. A., & Cross, K. P. (1993). *Classroom assessment techniques: A handbook for college teachers* (2nd ed.). San Francisco, CA: Jossey-Bass.

Arter, J., & McTighe, J. (2001). *Scoring rubrics in the classroom: Using performance criteria for assessing and improving student performance.* Thousand Oaks, CA: Corwin Press.

Bender, E. (2005, September/October). CASTLs in the air. *Change, 37*(5), 40–49.

Berliner, D. C. (2006). Educational psychology: Search for essence throughout a century of influence. In P. A. Alexander & P. H. Winne (Eds.), *Handbook of educational psychology* (pp. 3–28). Mahwah, NJ: Lawrence Erlbaum.

Boyer, E. L. (1990). *Scholarship reconsidered: Priorities of the professoriate.* San Francisco, CA: Jossey-Bass.

Buskist, W., & Smith, R. A. (2008). The scholarship of teaching and learning in psychology. *Teaching of Psychology, 35,* 247–248. doi:10.1080/00986280802418737

Chick, N., Haynie, A., & Gurung, R. A. R. (Eds.). (2012). *Exploring more signature pedagogies.* Sterling, VA: Stylus.

Connor-Greene, P. A. (2002). Problem-based service learning: The evolution of a team project. *Teaching of Psychology, 29,* 193–197.

Dewar, J., Dailey-Hebert, A., & Moore, T. (2010). The attraction, value and future of SoTL: Carnegie affiliates' perspective. *Transformative Dialogues: Teaching & Learning Journal, 4,* 1–15.

Dewey, J. (2009). *Democracy and education: An introduction to the philosophy of education.* New York, NY: WLC Books. (Original work published in 1916)

Diamond, R. M. (2008). *Designing and assessing courses and curricula. A practical guide* (3rd ed.). San Francisco, CA: Jossey-Bass.

Dunn, D. S., McCarthy, M. A., Baker, S. C., & Halonen, J. S. (Eds.). (2011). *Using quality benchmarks for assessing and developing undergraduate programs.* San Francisco, CA: Jossey-Bass.

Enhancing Teaching and Learning Project. Retrieved from http://www.etl.tla.ed.ac .uk/publications.html

Entwistle, N. (2009). *Teaching for understanding at university: Deep approaches and distinctive ways of thinking.* New York, NY: Palgrave Macmillan.

Ericksen, S. C. (2009, April 14). *Testing and grading* [E-mail newsletter]. Available from http://cgi.stanford.edu/~dept-ctl/cgi-bin/tomprof/posting.php

Fink, L. D. (2003). *Creating significant learning experiences: An integrated design approach to designing college courses.* San Francisco, CA: Jossey-Bass/Wiley.

Goodburn, A., & Savory, P. (2009). Integrating SoTL into instructional and institutional processes. *MountainRise, the International Journal of the Scholarship of Teaching and Learning, 5,* 1–14.

Gurung, R. A. R., Ansburg, P. I., Alexander, P. A., Lawrence, N. K., & Johnson, D. E. (2008). The state of scholarship of teaching and learning in psychology. *Teaching of Psychology, 35,* 249–261.

Gurung, R. A. R., Chick, N., & Haynie, A. (Eds.). (2009). *Exploring signature pedagogies: Approaches to teaching disciplinary habits of mind.* Sterling, VA: Stylus.

Gurung, R. A. R., & Schwartz, B. M. (2009). *Optimizing teaching and learning: Practicing pedagogical research.* Malden, MA: Wiley-Blackwell.

Gurung, R. A. R., & Schwartz, B. M. (2010). Riding the third wave of SoTL. *International Journal for the Scholarship of Teaching and Learning, 4*(2). Retrieved from http://academics.georgiasouthern.edu/ijsotl/v4n2/invited_ essays/_GurungSchwartz/index.html

Hutchins, P. (Ed.). (2000). *Opening lines: Approaches to the scholarship of teaching and learning.* Menlo Park, CA: The Carnegie Foundation for the Advancement of Teaching.

Irons, J. G., & Buskist, W. (2008). The scholarship of teaching and pedagogy: Time to abandon the distinction? *Teaching of Psychology, 35,* 353–357.

Iverson, A., & Espenschied-Reilly, A. (2010). Made in America? Assumptions about service learning pedagogy as transnational: A comparison between Ireland and the United States. *International Journal for the Scholarship of Teaching and Learning, 4*(2). Available from http://academics.georgiasouthern.edu/ijsotl

Jonas-Dwyer, D., & Sudweeks, F. (2007). Informing students on using virtual microscopes and their impact on students' approach to learning. *Informing Science Journal, 10.* Retrieved from http://inform.nu/Articles/Vol10/ISJv10p 061-070Dwyer395.pdf

Kernahan, C., & Davis, T. (2010). What are the long-term effects of learning about racism? *Teaching of Psychology, 37,* 41–45. doi:10.1080/00986280903425748

Landrum, R. E., & Dietz, K. H. (2006). Grading without points: Does it hurt student performance? *College Teaching, 54,* 298–301.

Maclean, M. S., & Mohr, M. M. (1999). *Teacher-researchers at work.* Berkeley, CA: National Writing Project.

Mager, R. F. (1962). *Preparing objectives for programmed instruction.* Palo Alto, CA: Fearon.

Maki, P. L. (2011). *Assessing for learning: Building a sustainable commitment across the institution.* Sterling, VA: Stylus.

Marzano, R. J. (2009). *Designing & teaching learning goals & objectives.* Bloomington, IN: Marzano Research Laboratory.

McConnell, D. A., Steer, D. N., Owens, K. D., Knott, J. R., Van Horn, S., Borowski, W., & Heaney, P. J. (2006). Using concept tests to assess and improve student conceptual understanding in introductory geosciences courses. *Journal of Geoscience Education, 54,* 61–68.

McKernan, J. (1991). *Curriculum action research: A handbook of methods and resources for the reflective practitioner.* London, UK: Kogan Page.

McKinney, K. (2007). *Enhancing learning through the scholarship of teaching and learning.* Bolton, MA: Anker.

Mills, G. E. (2007). *Action research: A guide for the teacher researcher.* Upper Saddle River, NJ: Pearson.

Moore, T., & Gayle, B. M. (2010). Student learning through co-curricular dedication: Viterbo University boosts faculty/student research and community services. *Transformative Dialogues: Teaching & Learning Journal, 4,* 1–7.

Obaidat, I., & Malkawi, E. (2009). The grasp of physics concepts of motion: Identifying particular patterns in students' thinking. *International Journal of the Scholarship of Teaching and Learning, 3*(1). Available from http://academics.georgiasouthern.edu/ijsotl/

Olson, K. M. (2009). Assessing student learning and perceptions in an upper-level general education requirement argumentation course. *International Journal of the Scholarship of Teaching and Learning, 3,* 1–16.

O'Meara, K., & Rice, R. E. (2005). *Faculty priorities reconsidered: Rewarding multiple forms of scholarship.* San Francisco, CA: Jossey-Bass.

Pan, D. (2009). What scholarship of teaching? Why bother? *International Journal for the Scholarship of Teaching and Learning, 3*(1). Available from http://academics.georgiasouthern.edu/ijsotl

Passow, H. J. (2011). *Assessment handbook.* Available from http://www.engin.umich.edu/teaching/assess_and_improve/handbook/

Pusateri, T. (2009, November). *The assessment cyberguide for learning goals and outcomes.* Washington, DC: American Psychological Association Education Directorate. Retrieved from http://www.apa.org/ed/governance/bea/assessment-cyberguide-v2.pdf

Richlin, L. (2006). *Blueprint for learning: Constructing college courses to facilitate, assess, and document learning.* Sterling, VA: Stylus.

Russell, A. (2010). A mode for undergraduate research in statistics education. *International Journal for the Scholarship of Teaching and Learning, 4,* 1–4. Retrieved from http://academics.georgiasouthern.edu/ijsotl/v4n2/essays_about_sotl/_Russell/index.html

Savory, P., Burnett, A. N., & Goodburn, A. (2007). *Inquiry into the college classroom: A journey toward scholarly teaching.* Bolton, MA: Anker.

Seybert, J. A. (2002). Assessing student learning outcomes. *New Directions for Community Colleges, 117,* 55–65.

Sizemore, O. J., & Lewandowski, G. W. (2009). Learning might not equal liking: Research methods course changes knowledge but not attitudes. *Teaching of Psychology, 36,* 90–95. doi:10.1080/00986280902739727

Smith, R. A. (2008). Moving toward the scholarship of teaching and learning: The classroom can be a lab, too! *Teaching of Psychology, 35,* 262–266. doi:10.1080/00986280802418711

Smith, R. (in press). Benefits of using SoTL in picking and choosing pedagogy. In B. M. Schwartz & R. A. R. Gurung (Eds.), *The psychology of teaching: An empirically based guide to picking, choosing, and using pedagogy.* Washington, DC: American Psychological Association.

Stenhouse, L. (1975). *An introduction to curriculum research and development.* London, UK: Heinemann Education.

Stevens, D. D., & Levi, A. (2011). *Introduction to rubrics: An assessment tool to save grading time, convey effective feedback, and promote student learning.* Sterling, VA: Stylus.

Suskie, L. (2009). *Assessing student learning: A common sense guide* (2nd ed.). San Francisco, CA: Jossey-Bass/Wiley.

Tait, H., & Entwistle, N. J. (1996). Identifying students at risk through ineffective study strategies. *Higher Education, 31,* 99–118.

Valter, K., & Akerlind, G. (2010). Introducing students to ways of thinking and acting like a researcher: A case study of research-led education in the sciences. *International Journal of Teaching and Learning in Higher Education, 22*(1), 89–97. Available from http://www.isetl.org/ijtlhe/

Vines, A. (2010). Productive horizontal learning: A study of law students' engagement in informal peer colloquia. *International Journal of the Scholarship of Teaching and Learning, 5.* Retrieved from http://academics.georgiasouthern.edu/ijsotl/v4n1/articles/PDFs/Article_Vines.pdf

Walvoord, B. E. (2004). *Assessment clear and simple: A practical guide for institutions, departments, and general education.* San Francisco, CA: Jossey-Bass.

Weimer, M. (2006). *Enhancing scholarly work on teaching and learning: Professional literature that makes a difference.* San Francisco, CA: Jossey-Bass.

Weldy, T. G., & Turnipseed, D. L. (2010). Assessing and improving learning in business schools: Direct and indirect measures of learning. *Journal of Education for Business, 85,* 268–273. doi:10.1080/08832320903449535

Wiggins, G., & McTighe, J. (1998). *Understanding by design.* Upper Saddle River, NJ: Merrill/Prentice Hall.

Wolff, K., & Wahde, M. (2010). Balancing theory and practical work in a humanoid robotics course. *International Journal of Teaching and Learning in Higher Education, 22*(1), 80–88. Available from http://www.isetl.org/ijtlhe/

Wright, D. L. (1994). Grading student achievement. In K. W. Pritchard & R. M. Sawyer (Eds.), *Handbook of college teaching: Theory and applications* (pp. 439–449). Westport, CT: Greenwood Press.

Yang, M., Webster, B., & Prosser, M. (2011). Exploring the variation in first year undergraduates' induction into their academic disciplines. *International Journal of the Scholarship of Teaching and Learning, 5*(1). Retrieved from http://academics.georgiasouthern.edu/ijsotl/v5n1/articles/PDFs/_YangWebsterProsser.pdf

CHAPTER 4

From Document to Practice

Application of Outcome-Based Assessment in the Curricula of Police and Border Guard Service

KÄTLIN VANARI AND EINIKE PILLI

In recent years, European higher education has undergone many changes that are more revolutionary than evolutionary, and Estonian higher education is continually adapting to them. Paradigmatically, the emphasis of these new approaches may be described as a learner-centered outcome-based reform of the curriculum, accompanied by several changes in the targeting and assessment of study and management of the learning process.

In Estonia, the transition to outcome-based curricula has been conducted in two phases. Since the 2008–2009 academic year, all higher education curricula have been described by the members of higher education institutions and employers on an outcome basis (Standard of Higher Education, 2008). Since the 2010–2011 academic year, university teachers have been using a new system of assessment (Uniform Marking System, 2009). These changes have also occurred in the Estonian Academy of Security Sciences, which was one of the first higher education institutions in Estonia to start implementing learning outcomes in its curriculum related to police education.

Outcome-based curriculum is a student-centered model focused on assessing the knowledge and skills acquired by students using observable or empirical measures. The goals of this model identify specific knowledge or skills that students are expected to learn and demonstrate by the end of the learning process. We call student-centered learning goals *learning outcomes*. After identifying the learning outcomes, the next step is to align assessment with these outcomes to ensure that expected and promised learning goals are achieved.

At the heart of outcome-based curriculum reform are particular changes in the assessment of students' acquired knowledge and skills. The knowledge, skills, and attitudes described in learning outcomes are best achieved when teaching and assessment are guided by them. Assessment, in particular, is key to effective curriculum reform because it produces feedback to students, faculty, and administrators regarding the adequacy of the proposed learning outcomes, the effectiveness of selected teaching methods, and the preparedness of graduates to compete in the job market. Assessment also reveals how well teachers have understood the central principles of development of an outcome-based curriculum and broadly characterizes what they value the most in their subject matter, or what they deem as the most appropriate study goals for their students.

A central issue of educational reform is whether reform is perceived as a formality or as an actual change in mind-set for all involved parties, consequently bringing about genuine change in educational practices. This issue is particularly important in a country such as post-Communist Estonia, where opposition to the changes coming from "above" has resulted in documents being prepared in accordance with reform ideals, but in reality, the parties involved continue to be guided by the existing concepts. Such disconnects between reform ideals and actual practices often produce less than optimal results—for example, when assessment practices fail to accurately measure student achievement with respect to learning outcomes. To determine the extent to which educational reform is successful in producing meaningful change in education practices, we conducted a study in 2010 to analyze the congruence of assessment with planned learning outcomes of two curricula of the Estonian Academy of Security Sciences (EASS) as part of the Primus Program (2008–2013), which aims to support the quality development of higher education and increase the competitiveness of its graduates. The program is implemented by the Archimedes Foundation and supported by the European Union, European Social Fund (the preparation of this article was supported by a Primus grant number 30.3–7.5/364 and cofinanced by the European Union, European Social Fund).

Methodology

We analyzed two curricula of professional higher education of the EASS. We chose to examine the Police and Border Guard Service curricula because they were recently merged into a common curriculum; until the 2010–2011 academic year, they existed as separate and distinct entities.

The competencies of learners in the Police curriculum had already been described and evaluated in the 2004–2005 academic year, and the Border Guard Service curriculum had been described and evaluated in the 2008–2009 academic year. Blending these two curricula into a common curriculum leads to a practical need for developing appropriate learning activities for students.

We developed our methodology for this study based on work by Will Robley, Sue Whittle, and Deborah Murdoch-Eaton (2005). We conducted empirical research in two phases: (1) analysis of course syllabi and (2) interviews with lecturers, based on the course syllabi.

The course syllabi provided primary information on planned learning outcomes and on the assessment of student learning outcomes (Bers, Davis, & Taylor, 2000; Drew, 1998; Holsgrove, Lanphear, & Ledingham, 1998; Robley et al., 2005). We collected course syllabi of the fourth year of Police specialty (4 courses) and of the first year of the Border Guard Service specialty (12 courses) for the 2009–2010 academic year from the Study Information System of EASS. Two members of the research team read and analyzed all documents using content analysis. During content analyses, we coded and categorized learning outcomes, assessment methods, and criteria based on theoretical starting points (Biggs & Tang, 2008; Muldoon & Lee, 2007). The theoretical approach we used is called *constructive alignment*, and its central idea is to logically connect the various parts of the study process. John Biggs and Catherine Tang (2008) emphasized that assessment drives learning, and therefore, assessing all learning outcomes is crucial from the point of view of achieving these aims.

Previous studies (Bers et al., 2000; Drew, 1998; Lucas, Cox, Croudace, & Milford 2004) on learning outcomes and assessment have demonstrated the need for using additional methods besides the analyses of course syllabi. In the second stage of data collection, we used a semistructured interview of lecturers (Laherand, 2008). The questionnaire we used for the interview consisted of three parts: (1) the lecturer's explanation of the course, (2) the lecturer's explanation of course assessment, and (3) the lecturer's general understanding of the assessment.

Learning outcomes refer to the basic expected knowledge and skills of the learner at the end of the learning process. To provide a sharper focus on learning outcomes, we used the concept of the determining element of content mastery in the subject area. We expected lecturers to tell us what they valued as the primary knowledge or skills they expected learners to acquire by taking their courses. The first two central variables of this study were learning outcomes and assessment. The third variable was the element of content mastery. Introduction of such a third variable is also used in other studies (Feldman, 2007) to better understand the relationship between two key variables. Alignment of assessment with the proposed outcomes was evaluated, comparing the determining element of content mastery with the learning outcomes and assessment. In the analyses, we were interested in whether the central aspect of students' learning was also represented in the syllabi's described learning outcomes and assessment methods. As a result, our methodological approach moved from syllabi to interviews, and from interviews back to syllabi. These three concepts—the determining element of content mastery, the described learning outcomes, and assessment—formed three central variables of the research, and the basis of our analyses of syllabi and interviews.

We conducted the interviews with four lecturers of the Police specialty and four lecturers of the Border Guard Service specialty. We based our selection of interviewees on the principle of purposive sampling, and our selection included staff lecturers of specialty subjects. In purposive sampling, the researchers choose the sample based on who would be appropriate and who has expertise in the area for the study (Cohen & Manion, 1994; Punch, 2009). In our purposive content analysis, we used the code model of content analysis for the course syllabus (Cohen & Manion, 1994; Laherand, 2008) and supplemented the codes and categories with additional information from the interviews.

During our research, we developed a triangular model, which we call the congruence model of learning outcomes and assessment (see Figure 4.1). A course is well prepared and its basic components aligned if the determining element of content mastery is well aligned with learning outcomes and assessment.

In the case of congruent learning outcomes and assessment, the teacher has clearly stated the determining element of content mastery in the learning outcomes, which is assessed by the teacher. The teacher formulates assessment criteria in such a way that it is not possible to pass a course without students acquiring the determining element of the content mastery. Ideally, the assessment of the determining element of content mastery also contributes the highest percentage of the final mark in any course.

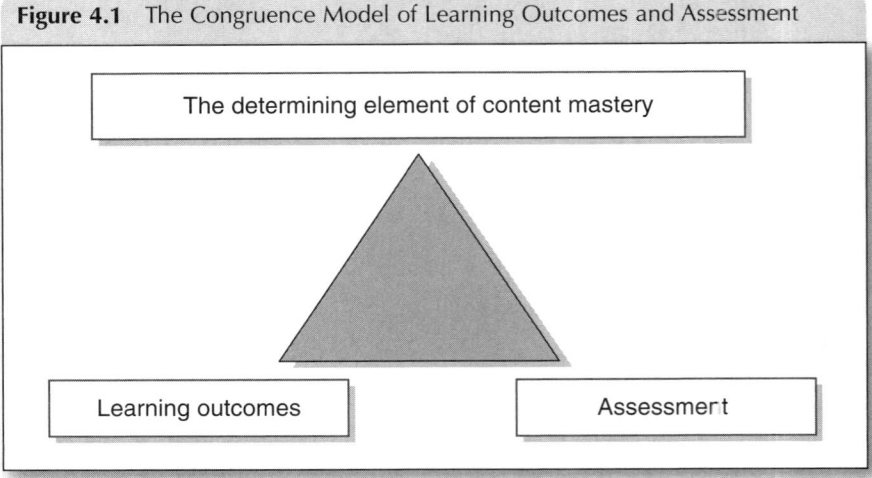

Figure 4.1   The Congruence Model of Learning Outcomes and Assessment

The determining element of content mastery

Learning outcomes

Assessment

In the following section, we present analyses of the relationship of the determining element of content mastery with the two central components of outcome-based curriculum: learning outcomes and assessment. Following our analyses, we provide a model of implementation of an outcome-based curriculum, which enables one to assess syllabi of other courses and the implementation of what is described therein.

Results

The Determining Element of Content Mastery and Learning Outcomes

Our respondents identified thinking skills as being especially important for students to acquire. Several interviewees mentioned these skills as being a component of "the determining element of content mastery." One respondent noted

> Some are afraid, at the beginning of legal subjects, that we will have to start to memorize the norms, but it is not so. The student must understand the norms, to interpret them by themselves, and to apply them in practice. Because higher education is to teach people to think and to think about what he or she does and why he or she does it.

A second distinct category of learning that respondents mentioned was that learners should have an overview of how different aspects of the subject matter function and the relationships between them. As one respondent noted, "I think the most important is that after the completion of the subject, he knows why something is done the way it is done, and if it is not done this way, what the consequences are."

A third category that respondents deemed to be crucial in learning was the development of specific action skills. One respondent expressed the importance of this category as follows:

> Awareness of direct heightened risks and the ability to behave in situations so that they do not increase the risk . . . that he or she is able to perform the duties for which the country has given to him or her a weapon and special equipment.

If one compares "the determining element of content mastery" described by each lecturer with the learning outcomes described in his or her syllabus, then at the highest generalization level, these two elements overlap. For example, one lecturer stated

> Handles safely firearms in a firing position in accordance with the purpose and masters the firing techniques . . . The worst is when he

injures himself doing that; I'd rather he didn't touch the weapon at all. This is a zero place; from here we will start, and then we will continue growing. The most important thing is that he is not dangerous to himself and his companions.

During our purposive content analysis of course syllabi, we identified differences between what was described in the syllabi and what lecturers told us during the interviews. For example, descriptions of learning outcomes were often much more varied and at times more idealistic than what lecturers described during the interviews as "the determining element of the content mastery." Consider, for example, these examples of learning outcomes:

- "Has knowledge for a comprehensive and complete application of the procedure"
- "Has a thorough and comprehensive knowledge of the various possibilities of implementation of the procedural law at both national and international level"

At the same time, however, lecturers described "the determining element of content mastery" in a more basic level as what all the students should really know and be able to do. The comparison of what was described in the interviews and in the documents revealed that the practical skills based on the theory were described as "the determining element of content mastery," whereas the learning outcomes were almost entirely theoretical.

In some instances, the overabundance of learning outcomes may potentially hinder the clarity of the goals set for the students. For example, one lecturer had 18 learning outcomes for one of the subjects. A second example of overabundance of learning outcomes hindering clarity of goals is evident in the title of one of the courses: Implementation of the Requirements and Recommendations of Procedural Methodology in Criminal Investigation. Such a title may make it difficult for students to focus on the core of the subject because the title involves several large, complex concepts and because students are new in the area.

The Determining Element of Content Mastery and Assessment

Biggs and Tang (2008) suggested that assessment significantly affects the students' learning. The more the planned learning outcomes match assessment, the more likely students will acquire what is expected of them.

The teaching practices of lecturers can also be differentiated into two layers: what is assessed and what is believed to be assessed (Dillon, Reuben, Coats, & Hodgkinson, 2007). The clearer and more transparent the description of the assessment in the course syllabus is in the lecturer's mind, the more likely students will achieve the intended learning outcomes. Nonetheless, studies show that there is a scanty link between learning outcomes and the assessment criteria (Quality Assurance Agency, 2006).

The connection between learning outcomes and assessment was not clear to the lecturers interviewed. The analysis of the syllabi revealed that these documents were not reliably sufficient to determine the alignment of learning outcomes and assessment. On the one hand, lecturers have the opportunity to prepare different forms of course syllabi (Estonian Academy of Security Sciences, 2010). On the other hand, while preparing their syllabi, the lecturers were influenced by subjective factors such as the following:

- Lack of knowledge of description of outcome-based assessment ("Because actually this is such a new thing, among us there are very few who have studied it directly. Everybody does it the only way they know how.")
- Insecurity in the field of instruction ("I personally do not even know how to exactly explain why it must be stated as a core value that a policeman must be human. We talk about it, but I think that there is no reason to ask it separately.")
- Absence of the possibility of elaboration of assessment ("In my head I have ideally all these ideas, maybe sometime I will be able to put them all down on paper as well and maybe I will even be able to implement them all in real practice. But I just do not know where to take time for this.")
- Fear of misinterpretation of the students ("This is one reason why the lecturers are in this unfortunate situation, they have all the assessment criteria in their heads; however, it is difficult to put them down on paper. As soon as you put them down on paper, it will be possible to oppose them.")
- Lack of cooperation between the lecturers who teach the same subject ("Everyone compiles their own final test at the end of their block . . . I guess it has not been written down in detail. They have been written by another teacher. Something could be really reviewed here.")

These factors, along with others, such as the lack of technical skills to implement the new assessment, may make transition to outcome-based assessment difficult (Ecclestone, 2001). Biggs & Tang (2008) described outcome-based assessment through the result model in which the subject of assessment is the extent to which students have achieved the learning outcomes. The result model is based on the understanding that it is important for the student's performance to correspond as closely as possible to the results necessary to succeed in real life.

In contrast, the central idea of the paradigmatically different measurement model is selection of students, with little or no connection of assessment to learning outcomes. Some researchers (e.g., Maclellan, 2001) have shown that the transition of lecturers from using the measurement model to using the result model is first expressed in the perceptions of assessment and only then are the actual assessment activities amended. This tendency was also evident in our research.

Achievement of learning outcomes is described here through assessment methods and criteria. The sequence of learning outcomes, assessment methods, and criteria is not always similar. Some teachers find it clearer to connect learning outcomes to assessment criteria first and then find methods for measuring the learning outcomes. Other teachers begin by choosing assessment methods that align with the learning outcomes, and then complete the assessment criteria. In Estonia, we usually use the second sequence (Pilli, 2010; Rutiku, Valk, Pilli, & Vanari, 2009). Accordingly, we analyzed both course syllabi and interviews with the lecturers as three subtopics: assessment methodology, assessment criteria, and formation of the final grade (Biggs & Tang, 2008; Pilli, 2010; Rutiku et al., 2009).

Assessment Methods

The lecturers mentioned many interesting assessment methods: essays, case studies, testing, video training, report writing, case-based homework, practical tasks, practical exercises, and practical work. In most cases, however, a student's final grade was predominantly affected by a written examination paper completed at the end of the course. In some cases, these types of examinations include assignments requiring students to use analytical thinking. One lecturer commented

> The course ends with an assessment, which includes a couple of theory questions and a case study. In the case study, a solution model has been provided, on the basis of which the learner must be able to highlight . . . and write how they understand it, and how they are trying to resolve this situation in a humane way.

In comparing what lecturers described in their syllabi and the interviews, we found that the lecturers sometimes had difficulty defining their assessment methods. For example, one lecturer commented

> I have set as a condition that all the homework and seminar tasks must be completed; in addition, students must participate in the seminar. And it is a prerequisite for access to the exam. . . . I consider their intermediate activities to be learning activities.

Lecturers noted that, formally, it is the final test score that primarily affects the final grade, and beside it, in several cases, also performing practical work at the basic level that serves as the requirement for completing the course. Some lecturers conveyed the impression that completion of the practical work is a more important assessment tool than the final examination.

One lecturer stated, "The practical part is very important; it clarifies how they understood the theory. At work, they should do what they were doing in the practical session." This attitude links the determining element of content mastery to assessment. However, the described practical central aspect of the subject was not represented in the marked exam, which gave the determining element of content mastery secondary value. From the point of view of the congruence model described previously, assessment is not well aligned with the determining element of content mastery.

Assessment Criteria

In reviewing the syllabi, it became evident that assessment criteria were usually left out or poorly described, and therefore difficult to identify. During the interviews, the lecturers described only a portion of the criteria they used in determining marks. Although quantitative assessment criteria are not encouraged any more, and not easily connectable to the learning outcomes, lecturers still sometimes use them. One of the lecturers explained the assessment criteria as follows: "I have all the time written in the syllabi that the grade will be shaped by the knowledge in the exam . . . I still use this 51 percent rate as a basis." This example shows possible lack of alignment, or poor clarity, among the determining element of content mastery, learning outcomes, and assessment.

The interviews also revealed the implementation of the result model within their assessment methods. Some assessment criteria related to learning outcomes included "(the student) is able to boldly state their position . . . You need to think with your own head . . . How to humanely deal with this situation . . ."

In addition, we found a shallow connection among the learning outcomes of the course, the determining element of content mastery, and lecturers' assessment criteria. For example, one lecturer considered the determining element of content mastery to be "that [the student] is able to distinguish between good and bad." However, this lecturer's assessment was based on the following:

When I see that he or she goes deep into the problem and understands . . . and he does not touch upon what we have been discussing in the class, and what I have been talking about, concerning how the things should be, but he or she is boldly able to point out their position.

This lecturer's comment shows only a vague connection between what is expected and what is said to be the assessment criteria. Although the determining element of content mastery and described assessment criteria were a bit similar, written learning outcomes did not correspond closely with assessment criteria described in the interview.

Assessment Criteria Formation of the Final Grade

Course syllabi or interviews did not provide clarity about how the final grade is derived from assessment methods that the lecturers used in their course. Although lecturers described different assessment methods they used including assessing practical skills, the final grade nevertheless consisted of theoretical knowledge, which resulted in diminished alignment between the determining element of content mastery and the assessment, especially with respect to the final grade.

One possible reason lecturers assessed only theoretical knowledge may be because of the use of differentiated assessment regarding the final grade: Each student's level of achievement is reflected by a letter or number grade. Several lecturers expressed that the practical skills are neither necessary nor possible to evaluate with a grade. For example, one lecturer noted

No, such things cannot be measured with a number. It is important that you think on your own. If he dares to write what he really thinks, then that is a great thing also. Not what they assume that I want them to write. Some of the students ask: what do you want me to write—the way I have to, the way my boss wants me to, or the way I think is right?

At the same time, lecturers invoked a wide range of arguments in favor of differentiated assessment. One such argument highlighted the risk that the learners may face if students are evaluated nondistinctively (pass or fail rather than alpha or numerical ranges of assessment) as simpler. For example, one lecturer observed

If it were nondistinctive, then maybe they would not do things the way they do them now. This makes them acquire the subject. Their attitude for the subjects which have the assessment of passed or not passed is more relaxed.

Some lecturers argued that differentiated assessment is justified by the students' interest to be distinguished. For example, one lecturer stated

For the student, the fact that if he or she has a perspective in which work he or she wants to do in the future, it makes them want to achieve the best possible grade, in order to win in the competitive environment to get access to the job.

Other arguments presented by the lecturers were related to the measurement model of assessment—they emphasized the importance of comparing the results of students. A number of lecturers' assertions showed that they did not yet connect learning outcomes and assessment together because both differentiated and nondifferentiated assessment require achieving all learning outcomes.

Continuous feedback to students throughout the course is fundamental to students' ability to learn the subject matter. When we asked the lecturers how they provided feedback to their students, they highlighted giving feedback to the entire class in cases of serious mistakes, although they also noted giving individual feedback to students. One lecturer opined

> These pieces that they have written, if there are very big blunders, I will never mention the names, but I generalize. Or maybe I have pulled the student aside and asked what happened. We have discussed things in the class and I have kept the essays, but those who have wanted them back have received them back.

Some lecturers reported feeling tired, or in some cases, frustrated because the university implemented a number of changes in faculty work with regard to developing learning outcomes and assessment procedures. These feelings were particularly present when they felt that they had just begun to feel comfortable with a new procedure only to have the university change it again. However, all the lecturers we interviewed, despite their emotions about the process, showed a sincere willingness to understand the matter and to evaluate their disciplines on an outcome basis.

The Congruence Model of Learning Outcomes and Assessment

Based on our results, it appears that the teaching of courses in the Police and Border Guard curricula does not fully comply with the congruence model of learning outcomes and assessment. Among the courses in both the curricula examined, there were anomalies from the congruence model (see Figure 4.2.). The most salient of these anomalies relates to assessment, but not to the learning outcomes per se (Option A). For example, according to the lecturers, the determining element of content mastery of the course is "to make a difference between good and bad." However, there is no congruence with the learning outcomes, which describe the knowledge and awareness of the basic principles of ethics, professional ethics, and values of the organization.

Additionally, there were courses where the determining element of content mastery was related to learning outcomes, but not to the assessment (Option B). Based on the learning outcomes, by the end of the course the student should be able to prepare official correspondence, to know the document management systems, and to have general knowledge of the legislation of records management. However, lecturers identified the determining element of content mastery as "the skill to prepare documents."

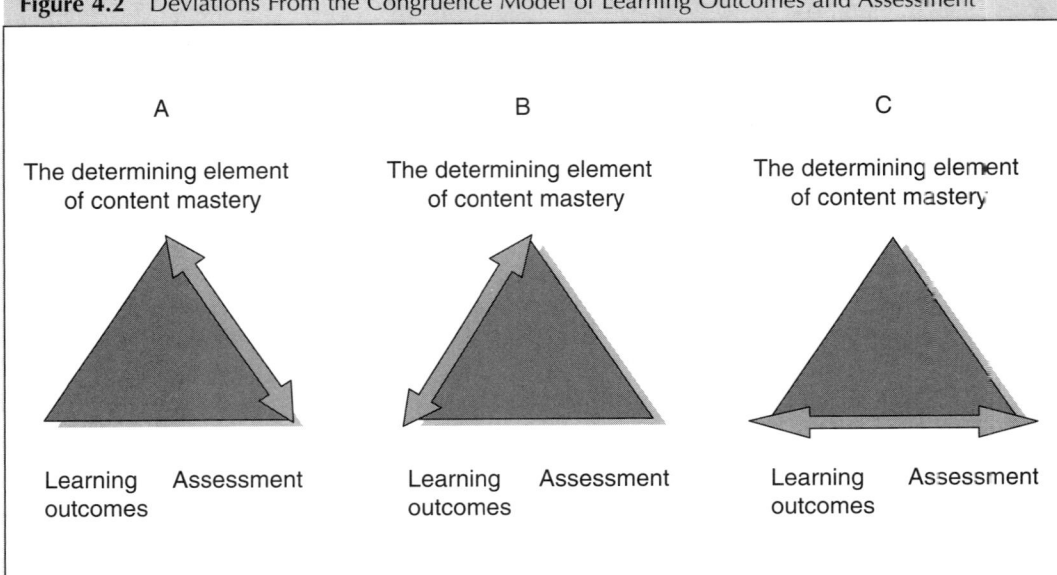

Figure 4.2 Deviations From the Congruence Model of Learning Outcomes and Assessment

A third deviation from the congruence model occurred in instances in which the learning outcomes were related to the assessment, but not to the determining element of content mastery (Option C). For example, during the interview, one lecturer identified the determining element of content mastery to be safety in handling weapons and in other activities of border guard tactics. Nevertheless, the learning outcomes and the assessment lacked this aspect and pointed to different kinds of competences.

There were also versions of the congruence model where focus on learning outcomes was more theoretical and the determining element of content mastery was more practical, but the final assessment of the subject pointed to a stronger link between assessment and learning outcomes, whereas the determining element of content mastery remained in the background. In these sorts of cases, the triangle representing the congruence model becomes rather lopsided, although, the process of aligning learning outcomes and assessment is still occurring.

Conclusions

In this chapter, we analyzed the congruence of assessment with the planned learning outcomes on the basis of syllabi and interviews with lecturers. We assessed lecturers' compliance of assessment with the planned learning outcomes through lecturers' views on the determining element of content mastery using the congruence model of learning outcomes and assessment. We found the signs of incongruence between learning outcomes and how lecturers assessed student learning in their courses. Nonetheless, our examination found partial alignment of the determining element of content mastery, learning outcomes, and the assessment. Comparing learning outcomes to the determining element of content mastery showed that learning outcomes in the syllabi were more idealistic and less focused than the determining element of content mastery lecturers identified in their interviews. Comparing assessment to the determining element of content mastery, we discovered a lack of congruence in how lecturers determined students' final grades.

Our most important conclusion is not whether the intended study outcomes were manifest from the syllabus to the actual learning process. On the contrary, the central issue is how the lecturer's understanding of the determining element of the mastery was described in the syllabus.

References

Bers, T. H., Davis, B. D., & Taylor, B. (2000). The use of syllabi in assessments: Unobtrusive indicators and tools for faculty development. *Assessment Update, 12*, 3, 4–7.

Biggs, J., & Tang, C. (2008). *Õppimist väärtustav õpetamine ülikoolis*. Tartu, Estonia: Tartu Ülikooli Kirjastus.

Cohen, L., & Manion, L. (1994). *Research methods in education*. New York, NY: Routledge.

Dillon, C. R., Reuben, C., Coats, M., & Hodgkinson, L. (2007). Learning outcomes and their assessment: Putting open university pedagogical practices under the microscope. In S. Frankland, (Ed.), *Enhancing teaching and learning through assessment: Deriving an appropriate model* (pp. 280–289). Dordrecht, Netherlands: Springer.

Drew, S. (1998). Students' perceptions of their learning outcomes. *Teaching in Higher Education, 3*(2), 197–217. Available from http://search.epnet.com

Ecclestone, K. (2001). I know a 2:1 when I see it: Understanding criteria for degree classifications in franchised university programmes. *Journal of Further and Higher Education, 25*, 301–313. Available from http://search.epnet.com

Estonian Academy of Security Sciences. (2010). *Regulation of organisation of studies*, confirmed 14.07.2010 with the decision of council No 1.1-6/25. Retrieved from http://www.sisekaitse.ee/public/Oppeosakond/OKE_kinnitatud_14.06.2011.pdf

Feldman, K. (2007). Identifying exemplary teachers and teaching. In R. P. Perry & J. C. Smart (Eds.), *The scholarship of teaching and learning in higher education: An evidence-based perspective* (pp. 93–143). Dordrecht, Netherlands: Springer.

Holsgrove, G. J., Lanphear, J. H., & Ledingham, I. (1998). Study guides: An essential student learning tool in an integrated curriculum. *Medical Teacher, 20*(2), 99–103.

Laherand, M.-L. (2008). *Kvalitatiivne uurimisviis*. Tallinn, Estonia: Infotrükk.

Lucas, U, Cox, P., Croudace, C., & Milford, P. (2004). "Who writes this stuff?": Students' perceptions of their skills development. *Teaching in Higher Education, 9*(1), 55–68. Available from http://search.epnet.com

Maclellan, E. (2001). Assessment for learning: The differing perceptions of tutors and students. *Assessment and Evaluation in Higher Education, 26*(4), 307–318. Available from http://search.epnet.com

Muldoon, N., & Lee, C. (2007). Formative and summative assessment and the notion of constructive alignment. In S. Frankland (Ed.), *Enhancing teaching and learning through assessment* (pp. 98–108). Dordrecht, Netherlands: Springer.

Pilli, E. (2010). *Väljundipõhine hindamine kõrgkoolis*. Tartu, Estonia: Archimedes.

Punch, K. F. (2009). *Introduction to research methods in education*. London, UK: Sage.

Quality Assurance Agency for Higher Education. (2006). *Code of practice for the assurance of academic quality and standards in higher education: Student assessment*. Retrieved from http://www.qaa.ac.uk/Publications/InformationAndGuidance/Documents/COP_AOS.pdf

Robley, W., Whittle, S., & Murdoch-Eaton, D. (2005). Mapping generic skills curricula: A recommended methodology. *Journal of Further and Higher Education, 29*, 221–223. Available from http://search.epnet.com

Rutiku, S., Valk, A., Pilli, E., & Vanari, K. (2009). Õppekava arendamise juhendmaterjal, Retrieved from http://primus.archimedes.ee/sites/default/files/ppekava%20arendamise%20juhendmaterjal.pdf

Standard of Higher Education. (2008) Passed 18.12.2008 with the Regulation of the Government of the Republic No 178—SG I 2008, 57, 322. Available from http://www.riigiteataja.ee

Uniform Marking System on the Level of Higher Education, Complete with the Conditions of Issuing of a Diploma with Honors (Cum laude). (2009). Passed 27.10.2009 with the Regulation of the Minister of Education and Research No 71—Appendix to SG 2009, 82, 1190. Available from http://www.riigiteataja.ee

PART III

Understanding Students

CHAPTER 5

Optimizing Adaptive Student Behaviors

Jacquelyn Cranney and Helen Dalton

The concept of "adaptive behavior" implies particular goals that must be obtained, which then begs the question: whose goals—the student's, the teacher's, or the university's? The university's primary goals need to be somewhat utilitarian to provide training for students to ensure appropriate remunerated postgraduation careers. However, can the goals of university education include more than the transformation of a novice into a professional? For example, should universities prepare their graduates to contribute more widely to society, possibly through service to their communities, with little direct personal benefit? Should a goal of university education be to transform naïve individuals into learned citizens, where citizenship implies not only rights, but also broadly individual responsibilities (e.g., "giving back" to the society that supported their education)? Inherent in such intent is the assumption that graduates will be better equipped than nongraduates will to understand societal issues from multiple perspectives, and thus be more effective leaders and citizens.

Authors' Notes: The authors thank Sue Morris and Eleni Andreou for their contributions to the study and positivity strategies materials. We also thank Jun Mo Jeong and Duya Zhou for their assistance in preparing this manuscript. Support for this publication has been provided by the Australian Learning and Teaching Council, an initiative of the Australian Government Department of Education, Employment and Workplace Relations. The views expressed in this chapter do not necessarily reflect the views of the Australian Learning and Teaching Council.

In considering the general goals of university education, there are likely to be national and individual university differences based on historical, economic, social, political, and environmental factors. For example, is one sociopolitical goal to produce graduates who question the status quo? Chinese and Korean universities traditionally emphasize didactic lectures and uncritical engagement by students (http://edu.sina.com.cn/l/2010-05-03/1633187881 .shtml; Gow, Balla, Kember, & Hau, 1996; Kim, 2001), although some Chinese universities are shifting from this approach (http://www.hebust.edu .cn/xwzx/Article_Show.asp?ArticleID=2731). Socioeconomic factors have implications for the employability of graduates. If the unemployment rate of graduates with generalist degrees is high, then employers may demand graduates with specialist knowledge and work-readiness (http://edu.sina.com .cn/l/2010-05-03/1633187881.shtml).

Teachers' goals will be influenced by (a) the culture of their university, particularly their discipline departments, which may place differential emphasis on the importance of their various roles (teaching, research, administration, community leadership) and (b) their personal philosophical approach to education. Finally, students are likely to come to the university with different expectations and goals, influenced by the aspirations of those supporting their study (e.g., parents; Kember & Gow, 1990). These goals may change as a result of personal growth including that attributable to university experiences.

The goals of "adaptive student behaviors" can be placed on two dimensions: instrumental and citizenship. A minimalist goal would be to do only what is necessary to obtain the degree, with no engagement with the cocurricular university culture. Such students are interested in learning only what is necessary to pass the course (a single academic offering will be referred to as a *course* [i.e., unit, module, subject], and a number of core or elective courses usually make up the degree *program* [i.e., degree course]) assessments and thus, the degree program (Biggs, 1987, 1990; Biggs & Tang, 2007; Case & Marshall, 2009); their learning is likely to be primarily extrinsically motivated.

Alternatively, students may have *broad education aspirational* goals (tapping into both citizenship and instrumental dimensions), in which they are intrinsically motivated to benefit from learning opportunities offered by the university, both curricular and cocurricular, leading to well-rounded graduates. Such students attempt to learn as much as possible of the material that interests them and are not overly driven by assessment requirements (Biggs & Tang, 2007). This goal requires high levels of cognitive and financial resources, and may be risky for students without those resources.

In general, which goal on the instrumental and citizenship dimensions students aim to achieve will depend on many factors, including whether they (a) have time for cocurricular involvement (if available), (b) are aware of the opportunities that involvement may afford, and (c) are academically capable of taking an approach other than a minimalist approach. It has been noted that in Chinese universities, even when extracurricular activities are available, students are unlikely to take up the opportunities (http://www .chinaedunet.com/jcjy/mxft/2009/12/content_183898.shtml). This outcome may be influenced by students needing to expend limited resources on the immediate vocationally oriented goal of obtaining the degree. In considering adaptive student behavior, the dimensionality of student goal-striving is acknowledged, as is the powerful transformative effect of even the minimalist instrumental approach.

Agents of student learning, with distinct roles and responsibilities, can contribute to the optimization of adaptive student behavior. Universities, to varying extents, aim to facilitate student adaptive behavior to achieve their goals through specific infrastructure (e.g., policies and procedures, centralized student learning support). The role of the university in optimizing adaptive student learning behavior is influenced by many factors, including government policy and funding (e.g., Kang, 2005). Nevertheless, the university has a responsibility to deliver what it promised to deliver to enrolling students.

The department delivering degree programs similarly has responsibilities in supporting students' behavior toward achieving their degree-related goals, for example, appropriate staffing to deliver educational programs. Many factors influence this departmental role, including faculty funding and curriculum policies. Individual teachers have a more direct role to play with specific responsibilities. For example, the nature of the course assessments should be clearly stated and discussed at the beginning of the course. Finally, students have a responsibility to engage in the program and course material according to the university's expectations and to seek additional information and assistance when needed.

Douglas Bernstein and Dominic Upton (2010) described the relationship between teachers and students in terms of parenting styles, arguing that the most productive learning relationship is when teachers adopt an authoritative style (i.e., authoritarian, permissive, and uninvolved; Bukatko & Daehler, 2004). Teachers, as subject experts, guide students toward gaining knowledge, and although there is attention to how students learn (i.e., a student-centered perspective), it is the students' responsibility to intentionally and actively construct their learning within the teacher-set boundaries. In contrast to the authoritative approach, the permissive educator provides fewer boundaries, allowing students to have an easy time, possibly resulting in positive student evaluations but little sustained learning. This approach reflects the tension between students wanting to "get their money's worth" and not wanting to work too hard to obtain their degree. The authoritative approach contrasts with the authoritarian approach, in which teachers maintain a high level of control, with little regard for learner needs, leading to less effective student learning. Finally, the uninvolved teacher does as little as possible to "get the job done." (For a review of university teachers' conceptions of teaching, which acknowledges motive and strategy components, see Kember, 1997.)

In considering adaptive student behavior, one needs also to consider the nature of modern students, the challenges and opportunities they face, and their specific needs. Fifty years ago, university students were generally male and from more well-to-do families. Teachers "transmitted" knowledge through teacher-centered methodologies with little use of technological resources. Today, in countries with a robust university system, men and women have relatively equal access to higher education and there is usually financial support and other resources in place for highly capable students from disadvantaged backgrounds. The expectation that one should go to university may be overly ambitious in some countries, in terms of whether students are capable of benefiting from the experience, compared with being more suited to careers that result from other educational systems that, for example, support apprenticeships. In other countries, the expectations may not be high enough, reflecting a lack of economic capacity or political motivation to provide a robust university system In general, five aspects of present-day university students' current and future lives differ from the past:

1. The influence of technology on learning (e.g., through online instruction, students can obtain a degree offered by a university in another country, which necessitates teachers delivering significant learning experiences through this medium, and students' capacity and willingness to engage with it)

2. The likelihood that graduates will change jobs and careers several times during their lifetimes, necessitating the capacity for lifelong learning

3. The explosion in the creation and communication of information, necessitating the skills to find, select, and evaluate information

4. The possibility that students and graduates will need to study and work across cultural boundaries, necessitating the need for cultural awareness and competency

5. The merging of economic and social systems worldwide, necessitating the capacity to take a global perspective (Halpern & Butler, 2011; Lantz, 2010).

Ronald Barnett (in press) refers to the transformation of students into "liquid learners," who have certain dispositions and qualities to allow them to thrive in an "age of supercomplexity," which defines an environment where there are multiple frameworks for understanding, action, and self-identity brought about by "dissolving boundaries, of uncertain and competing currents, and of turbulence"; this age is where "the world of work is coming to resemble the wider world of life itself" (Barnett, 2000, see pp. 72–95). He warned that universities must respond to the needs of such liquid learners. Similarly, Se-yeoung Cheon and Soonghee Han (2006) argued that universities need to evolve to serve the "life-long learning society."

In this chapter, we present categories of adaptive student behavior, under the broad classifications of general academic behavior, socio-emotional behavior, and finally, global citizenship behavior. For each category, we consider how the corresponding behaviors may be optimized by different agents of student learning, with an emphasis on teachers as custodians of content and its delivery.

Academically Related Behavior

Organizational and Time-Management Skills

To attain complex behavioral goals, one needs planning, organizational, and time-management skills (e.g., Lipnevich, MacCann, & Krumm, 2011). Achieving or improving these skills can be assisted at any agency level, but at the very least, through the university's student learning center offering courses on the topic. Moreover, pedagogy within individual courses could support students' time-management capacity, for example: (a) in the course syllabi distributed during the first class, descriptions of assessments including milestones and deadlines should be clearly stated; (b) teachers could question students during class about when their next assessment is due and check on their progress (social comparison among students about their relative progress may then be a motivator); (c) assessments could be staged, in the sense that a penultimate assessment could be preceded by a number of smaller assessments that lead up to or build into the final assessment. Such strategies assist students in engaging in adaptive behaviors toward successfully completing their assessments. Nevertheless, it is ultimately each student's responsibility to meet course requirements.

General Academic Skills

General academic skills include skills that most university students need for educational success, such as general inquiry skills (e.g., researching library databases), writing, oral communication, and numeracy skills. The university needs to provide "enabling" skill programs to support disadvantaged students, such as those from low socioeconomic or nonnative language backgrounds. Teachers should be aware of such issues and the need for university and departmental policies and procedures to assist students who (a) need enabling skill training and (b) need assistance in learning about the "hidden curriculum" (Snyder, 1971), in the sense of assumed academic cultural values and procedures, such as Western notions of plagiarism.

For example, the university's student learning center should offer generic skill training in essay writing, and the library should offer courses and support in finding relevant material on book shelves and online. Teachers could assist in this process by making it clear in their course documents that these services are available and that it is adaptive for students to acquire these skills as soon as possible. Additionally, teachers could schedule tutorial time to introduce students to the generic resources required (e.g., introduction to the student learning center). Nevertheless, it is ultimately each student's responsibility to acquire the general academic skills necessary for successful completion of their studies.

Effective Technology Use

Universities often assume that students arrive with general computer literacy; however, this assumption may not hold true for all students. Thus, universities should have methods in place to detect this need early in students' programs of study, and then provide training to help them rapidly gain these skills. Similarly, universities usually manage course materials through a web-based learning management system and may assume capability where social media and mobile technologies are used to support educational experiences. Universities need to assist teachers and students in accessing these technologies effectively.

Discipline-Specific Academic Skills

There are national and university differences in the extent to which programs are narrowly discipline-specific or allow study in other disciplines (http://edu.sina.com.cn/l/2010-05-03/1633187881.shtml). Subsequently, the extent of focus on discipline-specific skills varies across programs. Most university degree programs have explicit prerequisites or assumed knowledge specific to the discipline. To address the needs of disadvantaged groups, departments could provide opportunities to improve skills; for example, offer remedial tutorials (face-to-face or online) to help at-risk students and support "peer-assisted" tutorial schemes (Fitzsimmons, Kozlina, & Vines, 2007). Teachers could provide an overview of assumed knowledge at the beginning of each course, offering students opportunities to catch-up before moving on to core material. These efforts should be focused primarily on the first year of the program. To help develop specific academic skills for all students during the program, departments could develop, in consultation with university support units, discipline-specific resources, such as guides on information literacy, and written and oral communication. An introduction to such material could be integrated into students' preparation for a specific assessment during a tutorial (e.g., Cranney Morris, Spehar, & Scoufis, 2008). Again, it is ultimately each student's responsibility to take advantage of opportunities to strengthen and benchmark the acquisition of these discipline-specific academic skills.

Engaging With the Academic Material and Assessments

Adaptive student behavior such as timely study and completion of assessments is likely to be facilitated if teachers present course content in an engaging manner. The curriculum, how it is enacted, and its relevance to current and future student needs play a significant role in engaging students in academic work. Factors identified as providing conditions to facilitate students' desire to learn are that it must have value for students and students must expect to be successful when studying (Biggs & Tang, 2007; Feather, 1982).

Students favorably rate instructional methods such as problem-based learning (PBL) in active learning attitude, self-directed learning, motivation to study, improved problem solving, and integrated learning (Kim et al., 2004). The use of technology such as electronic response systems is reported to benefit student participation and learning and engender positive in-class emotion (Draper & Brown, 2004; Stowell & Nelson, 2007). In addition, assessment drives student study behavior. Thus, assessment strategies should be used to help motivate student engagement with the course content (Biggs, 2003; Ramsden, 2003). Although self-assessment should be developed throughout the program, particularly given the role it plays in lifelong learning, teachers should be aware of the mismatch between self-assessment and expert assessment at early stages of education (e.g., Huh, Han, & Im, 2008).

Encouraging Effective Study Skills

Specific behaviors related to learning course materials in preparation for examinations or other assessments would normally be considered adaptive, given the minimal student goal of passing the course. There has been much research in this area, although only a proportion is systematic, methodologically sound, and applied in classroom contexts (Worrell et al., 2010). Teachers (and students) should be aware of which strategies are most effective given the desired learning outcome because teachers can play a critical role in facilitating students' adaptive use of effective study strategies. For example, early in the academic term, teachers could challenge their students to share those strategies they think are most effective, then ask students to undertake a literature search on the effectiveness of the strategy, and to share their findings in an oral presentation or handout. Alternatively, teachers could occasionally spend 5 to 10 minutes during a class discussing these issues with students. The student learning center should also focus on helping students implement effective study strategies—acknowledging that such strategies, similar to medical treatments, work for most people most of the time, but not for all people all of the time. Students should be encouraged to systematically try different strategies and to reflect on their effectiveness. This sort of metacognitive monitoring has been conceptualized as a high-level adaptive student behavior (Worrell et al., 2010). Some strategies are outlined here briefly.

Strategy 1: Time on task, and organizational and time-management skills.

The amount of time students spend on a particular assessment (e.g., studying for an exam, writing an essay) is associated with the grade received for that assessment (Gibbs & Simpson, 2004). Teachers could encourage students to schedule weekly periods to study and complete assignments. It is not as simple as that, however: Students need to be in the right frame of mind (i.e., have positive attitudes toward attaining a high course grade and hence putting in the effort—see Strategy 2); then they need to be able to plan for the necessary "time on task" (i.e., organizational and time-management skills), and optimize that time (appropriate study conditions and study skills—see Strategy 3). In addition, there may be specific barriers to students being able to study effectively (see Strategy 4).

Strategy 2: Positive but realistic attitudes toward study and the concept of "desirable difficulties."

Students have different attitudes toward university study. Thus, the distinction between extrinsic and intrinsic motivation (Deci, Koestner, & Ryan, 1999) is relevant to student study habits. Intrinsically motivated students would be concerned about their grades. The goal of other students may be to acquire a particular degree that might require only passing grades, and so these students make specific strategic decisions about their study to help ensure a passing grade. Still other students may be unsure of their motivations to study a specific course or profession. Indeed, there may be national differences regarding when students need to decide on their career choice. For example, U.S. students are usually not required to choose a major until their second year, whereas in Chinese universities, this choice is usually made on enrollment (http://edu.sina.com.cn/l/2010-05-03/1633187881.shtml). If teachers become aware that students are unsure of the suitability of a program of study, they should encourage students to seek career advice.

For "desirable difficulties," Lindsey Richland, Marcia Linn, and Robert Bjork (2007) have suggested that for students to make the most of learning, they need to tackle difficult and unknown material. Learning new skills and attitudes and acquiring university-level knowledge is difficult—and students need to put in the effort and time to master it. Moreover, strategies such as interleaving rather than blocking practice on separate topics, and varying how to-be-learned material is presented, may appear to slow learning during a particular study period, but leads to better long-term retention (Bjork, 1999). Teachers could repeatedly make explicit for students the connection between making the effort to tackle difficult tasks and the subsequent sense of achievement and encourage perseverance.

Strategy 3: Improving the quality of study time.

Sometimes conscientious students spend a great deal of time studying, but achieve poor results. There are several explanations for this outcome, including a lack of general or specific skills. Two suggestions may help students avoid disappointment and improve the cost-benefit ratio for their study time and results. First, teachers can help students know *what* they need to learn and do. For example, teachers can encourage students to understand the requirements of the task before they start an assignment or exam study. Second, once students know what is needed, several techniques will improve study time. For example, it is well established through research on the "testing effect" that, after an initial focused reading of the material, testing oneself is a better strategy for remembering the material in the long term than is simply rereading the material (Cranney, Ahn, McKinnon, Morris, & Watts, 2009; Roediger &

Karpicke, 2006). Thus, students should be encouraged to construct questions from the material, and then construct and learn the answers. For exam study, if previous examination papers are available, teachers should encourage students to determine those questions that may be relevant to this year's material, construct answers, and learn them. Finally, research on the "spacing effect" has shown that, given an equal amount of total time spent studying, it is better to distribute multiple study periods over days or even weeks than to study a large amount in one or two periods (e.g., just before examinations; Cepeda, Pashler, Vul, Wixted, & Rohrer, 2006). Teachers could encourage students to schedule exam study throughout the time leading up to the exam by having the occasional pop quiz during lectures, particularly when the lecturer indicates that similar questions will be in the exam.

Strategy 4: Dealing with barriers and keeping healthy.

In class, teachers should explicitly advise students that during their university studies, it is likely that they will encounter barriers to their ability to perform to their full academic potential, and that they need to seek help to overcome such barriers. Specific barriers that may be encountered by students include fear of public speaking, test anxiety, housing and financial issues, disabilities, personal and interpersonal issues, and physical and emotional health. Relevant university services such as student counseling and student learning centers are generally "free" to students. Ultimately, it is the students' responsibility to take advantage of these opportunities.

Socio-Emotional Aspects of Adaptive Student Behavior

General Socio-Emotional Adaptation to the University Context

University degree programs often have little structure, which is challenging for many students. Hence, organizational skills are extremely important to students' success in achieving their goals. Another important aspect of the university experience, as Lev Vygotsky (1978) asserted in his constructionist approach to knowledge acquisition, is social interaction. Some degree programs have as few as 8 hours of formal contact each week, where there may be almost no course requirement to interact with others. At the very least, departments should encourage their teachers to regularly structure small group discussions whereby each small group is expected to report back to the class on the outcome of the group's discussion. This simple strategy increases socially enhanced learning within the classroom as well as the formation of friendships that will provide social support for students, and thereby increase the likelihood of surviving the rigors of university study (Halpern, 2004). Unfortunately, this strategy is not common practice in many universities.

Another strategy that departments can implement to increase social interaction among students is peer mentoring (e.g., Leidenfrost, Strassnig, Schutz, Schabmann, & Carbon, 2010), which may involve senior undergraduate students mentoring first-year students. Although usually an optional cocurricular activity, peer mentoring could be attached to a compulsory introductory course where some tutorial time could be devoted to the mentoring scheme. Peer mentoring is associated with increased satisfaction with university studies experienced by international students (Leask, 2009).

Effective Group Work

Many courses require students to work in face-to-face or online groups. As indicated previously, socio-emotional benefits can flow from working together. Nevertheless, we know from student feedback that group work can have negative consequences, such as below-standard output resulting from interpersonal conflict, uneven workloads caused by social loafing, or individuals dominating proceedings (Cranney et al., 2008). Often group work is not adequately introduced and supported by teachers, who may assume that students are able to work together constructively without specific guidance. Disciplines that realize the necessity of teamwork skills in graduate professional life, such as engineering, have developed strategies to scaffold the development of group work skills (e.g., http://www.engsc.ac.uk/nef/events/project_groupwork2.asp; for generic group-work guidelines, see http://www.learningandteaching.unsw.edu.au/content/userDocs/groupwork_WebV1_Jan2006.pdf). Structured group projects have been found to be more effective for building communication, problem-solving, and self-directed learning ability than traditional lecturing formats (Kim, Yoon, Choi, Park, & Bae, 2008).

Diversity Issues

University program delivery is naturally culture-specific and usually reflects the values and norms of the dominant cultural group; for example, in the England, United States, and Australia, the dominant group would be Anglo-Saxon, Christian, heterosexual, and nondisabled. These societies, however, are becoming increasingly multicultural, and there is pressure on universities to be inclusive of diverse staff and students, reflecting the increased diversity in the culture at large (Leask, 2009).

There are enormous challenges for university educators to address diversity and diversity-related issues. For example, structural changes need to be made to accommodate wheelchair access. More challenging is the accommodation of students with serious information-processing disorders, such as hearing and visual impairments. Who will pay for the extra support needed for such students—the government, the university, the department, or the student? China, for example, has special institutions for disabled students (http://www.14edu.com/jiaoxue/qitajx/10201006222010.html). To what extent should teachers attempt to accommodate students with severe psychological disorders that interfere with the student's capacity to meet course deadlines or to the religious practices of different students? Clearly, there should be policies and procedures in place that strike a fair balance between the needs of students and the resources available to support diversity (Craig & Zinkiewicz, 2010; Lantz, 2010). For example, increased government pressures on universities to enroll students from low socioeconomic backgrounds should be accompanied by funding to provide centrally delivered support for such students (e.g., Bradley, Noonan, Nugent, & Scales, 2008).

Ultimately, it is the university's and department's responsibility to make clear what their diversity policies and procedures are, and then it is the responsibility of prospective and current students to know their rights and responsibilities. Universities should build the capacity of individual teachers, both for the resources available to them for diversity planning and for their ability to implement appropriate policies and procedures.

From an extracurricular perspective, good practice by universities includes infrastructure or activities supporting nonmainstream students with respect to ethnic background (e.g., Vietnamese student group), religious background (e.g., prayer room), or sociopolitical orientation (e.g., gay and lesbian student lounge). Diversity should be celebrated at the university level (e.g., multicultural or harmony festivals) or the departmental level (e.g., weekly cultural lunches organized by faculty and students). It would then be adaptive for individual students to seek and take advantage of such opportunities if they felt a need for support from those with similar backgrounds and interests.

Socio-Emotional Well-Being Skills

There is an increased emphasis on student well-being driven by several factors, including (a) financial incentives to attract students through offering services or opportunities over and above academic pursuits, and to retain students once they are in the system; and (b) the broader altruistic incentive to provide students with skills that will help them to survive and to thrive during their study and beyond graduation. Whatever their motivation, students should gain from evidence-based well-being strategies, which are mostly derived from research in positive psychology. The field of positive psychology at an individual level centers on the subjective experiences that one values including well-being, contentment, satisfaction (in the past), hope and optimism (in the future), and happiness (in the present) (Seligman & Csikszentmihalyi, 2000). At a collective level, positive psychology has been described as being about civic virtues and institutions that move individuals toward better citizenship, responsibility, and work ethic (Seligman & Csikszentmihalyi, 2000).

Psychological research has identified several strategies as being effective in improving socio-emotional well-being. So called positivity strategies—such as "three blessings," writing a "gratitude letter," engaging in acts of kindness, controlling negative thoughts, and responding actively and constructively to others' expressed good or bad news—have been shown to decrease depression and increase socio-emotional well-being (Gable, Gonzaga, & Strachman, 2006; Kurtz & Lyubomirsky, 2008; Seligman, Steen, Park, & Peterson, 2005). A strengths-based approach (Park, Peterson, & Seligman, 2004) to curricular and extracurricular goal achievement has been adopted broadly within the educational contexts of primary and secondary schools (Haesler & Spitzer, 2011) and perhaps it is time to consider integrating this approach at the tertiary level. Practicing meditation has also been linked to decreased stress (Clifton & Chambers, 2010) and has been incorporated into medical training programs (e.g., http://www.monash.edu.au/health-wellbeing/events/meditation-classes-resources.html). The question of whether socio-emotional well-being strategies should be within the extra-curricular domain (e.g., counseling units), or should be officially integrated into the curriculum, has received little debate at the higher education level. Nevertheless, it is acknowledged that socio-emotional adjustment increases students' capacity to focus on study-related adaptive behaviors.

Optimizing Behaviors for Global Citizenship and Sustainable Learning

There is a renewed emphasis on the "citizenship" dimension of student goals for university achievement (Cranney & Morris, 2011; McGovern et al., 2010; Rhoads & Szelenyi, 2011), with three contributing factors. First, a graduate capability commonly defined by universities is global citizenship, reflecting what Barnett (2010) referred to as the outward-looking tendency of modern universities. For example, Australia's University of New South Wales recently defined *global citizens* as having an appreciation of (a) relevant applications of their discipline to solving problems in local, national, and international contexts and (b) the need to respect diversity, be culturally aware, be socially just and responsible, and be environmentally responsible (UNSW, 2010). This definition pushes strongly into the "values" arena and contrasts with conceptualizations of global citizenship as being equivalent to the completion of a study abroad experience, or as reflecting the capacity to communicate with people from around the world through web-based social media (although it is acknowledged that these experiences and capabilities can have immense positive impact on students). The University College London has explicit policies and programs to facilitate integration of global learning experiences for its students, offering a range of discipline-specific and cross-university curricular and cocurricular programs (see http://www.ucl.ac.uk/global_citizenship/Global_Citizenship.pdf).

    Second, there has been recent emphasis on values education and the notion of character development in school settings (Lovat, 2010), which has been extended into the university arena (Sokol, Hammond, & Berkowitz, 2010). Third, Barnett (in press) has recently defined "life-*wide* learning" as learning in different spaces simultaneously, whether curricular, extracurricular, or noncurricular, and has challenged universities to contribute to students' capacity to integrate their multiple simultaneous learning experiences as students develop their self-identity (Barnett's concept of "being").

A likely outcome of global citizenship experience is increased cultural awareness and enhanced cultural competence. As economic and social globalization increases, it becomes more important for students to gain at least some cultural awareness during their program of study. Whether this heightened awareness should become a core component of the curriculum or be situated more in extracurricular programs such as study abroad is an issue that every university should seriously consider.

Barnett (2010) has proposed that, in an age of supercomplexity, students need particular personal dispositions and qualities as they learn across "life-wide" boundaries. Knowledge and skills will take a back seat to the ability to assimilate, accommodate, and thrive in this increasingly complex and turbulent globalized world. Sustainable life-wide learning will require management of the self as a learner inhabiting (or rejecting) the dimensions of multiple learning environments (Barnett, in press). The role of all agents of student learning in capitalizing on the benefits of life-wide learning is a discussion that should be a priority for all universities.

Conclusion

Although we have emphasized the importance of optimizing adaptive student behavior, teachers also need to consider the many reasons why their students sometimes *fail* in reaching their minimalist goals. One reason is that students sometimes lack the knowledge, skills, or motivation to engage in behaviors that will lead to the acquisition of their goals. Universities, departments, and teachers need to be aware of the common and discipline-specific factors that lead to failure, and to provide reasonable structures, policies, and procedures to remove barriers to students' success. Nevertheless, there is a limit to what academic institutions can do to help students and these limits need to be made explicit. Many universities have in place strategies to permit students to withdraw without failure, thus allowing students the opportunity to return to study when they have dealt with the factors that are impeding their success. Again, having central support services such as a counseling center can provide students with the opportunity to discuss their issues with a professional who may be able to help them reach a solution. All levels of learning agents can play a role in helping students either to persist or find a "way out" that will not involve "burning their bridges" for the future.

Finally, we need to reexamine the role of teachers in supporting student learning goals, given the changing nature of learning environments and subsequent needs (Barnett, in press). It is tempting for teachers, particularly those in research-intensive universities in which the pressure to publish is primary, to take an "academic Darwinist" approach to their teaching (Bernstein & Upton, 2010): Only the best students deserve to "survive" the program, and these students do not need the care and attention inherent in a student-centered approach (i.e., they should be smart enough to learn in a minimal teacher-centered environment). However, we are no longer living in such times, and there is recognized value to the future of our species in educating more students than only the elite among them. Inherent in the "massification" of higher education is the adaptive attitude that all capable students, regardless of their socioeconomic background, deserve to have the opportunity to contribute to and benefit from our global society. To extend Barnett's (in press) terminology, we propose that teachers need to become "ecological educators," in the sense that they need to balance (a) supporting the learning goals of their current and future "liquid learner" students, which may involve a reorientation of their teaching approach, (b) managing their own multiple goals inherent in an age of supercomplexity (Barnett, 2000), and (c) striving themselves to be agents of adaptive global change. A whole-university approach is required to support such a transformation.

References

Barnett, R. (2000). *Realizing the university in an age of supercomplexity.* Buckingham, UK: Open University Press.

Barnett, R. (2010, November). Liquid learners. Invited address at *The Future of Undergraduate Psychology Conference*, Chicheley Hall, Milton Keynes, UK.

Barnett, R. (in press). The coming of the ecological learner. In P. Tynjala, M-L. Stenstrom, & M. Saarnivaara (Eds.), *Nothing is permanent but change: Transitions and transformations in learning and education*. London, UK: Elsevier.

Bernstein, D. A., & Upton, D. (2010). Bravery and creativity through the curriculum. In D. Upton & A. Trapp (Eds.), *Teaching psychology in higher education* (pp. 105–133). Chichester, West Sussex, UK: BPS Blackwell.

Biggs, J. B. (1987). *Student approaches to learning and studying*. Hawthorn, Victoria: Australian Council for Educational Research.

Biggs, J. B. (1990, July). *Asian students' approaches to learning: Implications for teaching and learning*. Paper presented at the 8th Australasian Tertiary Learning Skills and Language Conference, Queensland University of Technology, Australia.

Biggs, J. B. (2003). *Teaching for quality learning at university: What the student does* (2nd ed.). Buckingham, UK: Society for Research into Higher Education and Open University Press.

Biggs, J. B., & Tang, C. (2007). *Teaching for quality learning at university: What the student does* (3rd ed.). Buckingham, UK: Society for Research into Higher Education and Open University Press.

Bjork, R. A. (1999). Assessing our own competence: Heuristics and illusions. In D. Gopher & A. Koriat (Eds.), *Attention and performance XVII: Cognitive regulation of performance: Interaction of theory and application* (pp. 435–459). Cambridge, MA: MIT Press.

Bradley, D., Noonan, P., Nugent, H., & Scales, B. (2008). *Review of Australian higher education: Final report.* Retrieved from www.deewr.gov.au/he_review_finalreport

Bukatko, D., & Daehler, M. W. (2004). *Child development* (5th ed.). New York, NY: Houghton Mifflin.

Case, J. M., & Marshall, D. (2009). Approaches to learning. In M. Tight, J. Huisman, K. H. Mok, & C. Morphew (Eds.), *The Routledge international handbook of higher education* (pp. 8–21). New York, NY: Routledge.

Cepeda, N. J., Pashler, H., Vul, E., Wixted, J. T., & Rohrer, D. (2006). Distributed practice in verbal recall tasks: A review and quantitative synthesis. *Psychological Bulletin, 132,* 354–380.

Cheon, S. Y., & Han, S. (2006). Meaning of higher education in lifelong learning societies. *Journal of Lifelong Learning, 12,* 127–144.

Clifton, J., & Chambers, R. (2010, July). *Mindfulness for academic success in a tertiary setting.* Paper presented at the Fourth International Conference on Psychology Education, Sydney, Australia.

Craig, N., & Zinkiewicz, L. (2010). *Inclusive practice within psychology higher education.* York, UK: Higher Education Psychology Network. Retrieved from http://www.psychology.heacademy.ac.uk/docs/pdf/Inclusive_Practice_within_Psychology_Higher_Education.pdf

Cranney, J., Ahn, M., McKinnon, R., Morris, S., & Watts, K. (2009). The testing effect, collaborative learning, and retrieval-induced facilitation in a classroom setting. *European Journal of Cognitive Psychology, 21,* 919–940.

Cranney, J., & Morris, S. (2011). Adaptive cognition and psychological literacy. In J. Cranney & D. S. Dunn (Eds.), *The psychologically literate citizen: Foundations and global perspectives.* New York, NY: Oxford University Press.

Cranney, J., Morris, S., Spehar, B., & Scoufis, M. (2008). Helping first-year students think like psychologists: Supporting information literacy and team-work skill development. *Psychology Learning and Teaching, 7,* 28–36.

Deci, E. L., Koestner, R., & Ryan, R. M. (1999). A meta-analytic review of experiments examining the effects of extrinsic rewords on intrinsic motivation. *Psychological Bulletin, 125,* 627–668.

Draper, S. E., & Brown, M. I. (2004). Increasing interactivity in lectures using an electronic voting system. *Journal of Computer Assisted Learning, 20,* 81–94.

Feather, N. (Ed.). (1982). *Expectations and actions.* Hillsdale, NJ: Lawrence Erlbaum.

Fitzsimmons, D., Kozlina, S., & Vines, P. (2007). Optimising the first year experience in law: The law peer tutor program at the University of New South Wales. Retrieved from http://www.austlii.edu.au/au/journals/UNSWLRS/2007/7.html

Gable, S. L., Gonzaga, G., & Strachman, A. (2006). Will you be there for me when things go right? Social support for positive events. *Journal of Personality and Social Psychology, 91,* 904–917.

Gibbs, G., & Simpson, C. (2004). Does your assessment support your students' learning? *Journal of Learning and Teaching in Higher Education, 1,* 3–31.

Gow, L., Balla, J., Kember, D., & Hau, K. T. (1996). Learning approaches of Chinese people: A function of socialisation processes and the learning. In M. H. Bond (Ed.), *The handbook of Chinese psychology* (pp. 109–123). Hong Kong: Oxford University Press.

Haesler, D., & Spitzer, K. (2011, April). *Depression proofing: Preventing depression by using positive psychology to redefine education.* Paper presented at the Second Australian Positive Psychology in Education Symposium, Sydney, Australia.

Halpern, D. F. (2004). Creating cooperative learning environments. In B. Perlman, L. I. McCann, & S. H. McFadden (Eds.), *Lesson learned: Practical advice for the teaching of psychology* (Vol. 2., pp. 165–173). Washington, DC: Association for Psychological Science.

Halpern, D. F., & Butler, H. A. (2011). Critical thinking and the education of psychologically literate citizens. In J. Cranney & D. S. Dunn (Eds.), *The psychologically literate citizen: Foundations and global perspectives.* New York, NY: Oxford University Press.

Huh, J., Han, J., & Im, H. (2008). Medical students' goals, methods and opinions on self-directed learning and analysis of self-assessment. *Korean Journal of Medical Education, 20,* 123–132.

Kang, B-W. (2005). Policy suggestions for university structure reforming plan of government. *The Journal of Educational Administration, 23,* 421–446.

Kember, D. (1997). A reconceptualisation of the research into university academics conceptions of teaching. *Learning and Instruction, 7,* 255–275.

Kember, D., & Gow, L. (1990). Cultural specificity of approaches to study. *British Journal of Educational Psychology, 60,* 356–363.

Kim, H-G. (2001). Crisis of the humanities and the response of history: Calling for reformation of required courses in college educational system. *The Korean History Education Review, 80,* 31–52.

Kim, J-H., Kim, J. Y., Son, H. J., Choi, Y-H., Hong, K-P., Ahn, B-H., . . . Seo, J-D. (2004). A qualitative evaluation of problem-based learning curriculum by students' perceptions. *Korean Journal of Medical Education, 16,* 179–193.

Kim, K. K., Yoon, J., Choi, K. Y., Park, S. Y., & Bae, J. H. (2008). The effect of interdisciplinary cooperation project learning on communication, problem-solving, and self-directed learning ability of university students. *Learning, Communication, Problem Solving, 14,* 252–261.

Kurtz, J. L., & Lyubomirsky, S. (2008). Towards a durable happiness. In S. J. Lopez (Ed.), *Positive psychology: Exploring the best in people: Vol. 4. Pursuing human flourishing* (pp. 21–36). Westport, CT: Greenwood.

Lantz, C. (2010). Those we serve? Student issues and solutions. In D. Upton & A. Trapp (Eds.), *Teaching psychology in higher education* (pp. 22–53). Chichester, West Sussex, UK: BPS Blackwell.

Leask, B. (2009). Using formal and informal curricula to improve interactions between home and international students. *Journal of Studies in International Education, 13,* 205–221.

Leidenfrost, B., Strassnig, B., Schutz, M., Schabmann, A., & Carbon, C-C. (2010, July). *Teaching (by) mentoring: Cascaded blended mentoring: Support for first-year students.* Paper presented at the Fourth International Conference on Psychology Education, Sydney, Australia.

Lipnevich, A. A., MacCann, C. E., & Krumm, S. (2011, April). *Measuring attitudes towards mathematics: A theory of planned behavior-based approach.* Paper presented at the annual meeting of the American Educational Research Association, New Orleans.

Lovat, T. (2010). The new values education: A pedagogical imperative for student well-being. In T. Lovat, R. Toomey, & N. Clement (Eds.), *International research handbook on values education and student wellbeing* (pp. 3–18). New York, NY: Springer.

McGovern, T. V., Corey, L., Cranney, J., Dixon, Jr., W. E., Holmes, J. D., Kuebli, J. E., . . . Walker, S. J. (2010). Psychologically literate citizens. In D. F. Halpern (Ed.), *Undergraduate education in psychology: A blueprint for the future of the discipline* (pp. 9–27). Washington, DC: American Psychological Association.

Park, N., Peterson, C., & Seligman, M. E. P. (2004). Strengths of character and well-being. *Journal of Social and Clinical Psychology, 23,* 603–619.

Ramsden, P. (2003). *Learning to teach in higher education.* London, UK: Kogan Page.

Rhoads, R. A., & Szelenyi, K. (2011). *Global citizenship and the university.* Palo Alto, CA: Stanford University Press.

Richland, L. E., Linn, M. C., & Bjork, R. A. (2007). Instruction. In F. T. Durson (Ed.), *Handbook of applied cognition* (2nd ed., pp. 555–583). New York, NY: Wiley.

Roediger, H. L., III, & Karpicke, J. D. (2006). The power of testing memory: Basic research and implications for educational practice. *Perspectives on Psychological Science, 1,* 181–210.

Seligman, M. E. P., & Csikszentmihalyi, M. (2000). Positive psychology: An introduction. *American Psychologist, 55,* 5–14.

Seligman, M. E. P., Steen, T., Park, N., & Peterson, C. (2005). Positive psychology progress: Empirical validation of interventions. *American Psychologist, 60,* 410–421.

Snyder, B. R. (1971). *The hidden curriculum.* New York, NY: Knopf.

Sokol, B. W., Hammond, S. I., & Berkowitz, M. W. (2010). The developmental contours of character. In T. Lovat, R. Toomey, & N. Clement (Eds.), *International research handbook on values education and student wellbeing* (pp. 579–603). New York, NY: Springer.

Stowell J. R., & Nelson, J. M. (2007). Benefits of electronic audience response systems on student participation, learning, and emotion. *Teaching of Psychology, 34,* 253–258.

University of New South Wales (2010). UNSW Graduate Attributes. Retrieved from http://teaching.unsw.edu.au/sites/default/files/upload-files/groupwork_compre hensive_resource_2006_1.pdf

Vygotsky, L. S. (1978). Interaction between learning and development. In M. Cole, V. John-Steiner, S. Scribner, & E. Souberman (Eds.), *Mind in society: The development of higher psychological processes* (pp. 79–91). Cambridge, MA: Harvard University Press.

Worrell, F. C., Casasd, B. J., McDaniel, M., Messer, W. S., Miller, H. L., Prohaska, V., & Zlokovich, M. S. (2010). Promising principles for teaching and learning. In D. F. Halpern (Ed.), *Undergraduate education in psychology: A blueprint for the future of the discipline* (pp. 129–144). Washington, DC: American Psychological Association.

CHAPTER 6

Preparing Middle Eastern Students for the Future

Saudi Arabia as a Case Study

SALEH H. ALWASAL AND SOLAIMAN M. ALHADLAQ

E ducation in the Arab peninsula goes deep into history. A principle motivator for learning comes from the Islamic philosophy (620s CE) that
learning is an obligation of every Muslim man and woman. Young pupils
used to learn at the Kutabs, which were private-ungraded religious schools
associated with mosques. At Kutabs, boys and girls learn, separately, a variety of Islamic subjects such as history and basics of calculation. Kutabs were
usually run by one teacher with some help from an advanced student.
Memorization and recitation were central skills for students in such schools.

Public education in Saudi Arabia is relatively new compared with other
Middle Eastern countries. The rise of public education in Saudi Arabia is at
least partly the result of its rapid population and economic growth relative
to other countries in the region. The population of Saudi Arabia is about
24 million people, with more than 37 percent of Saudis younger than 15 years
old (Kingdom of Saudi Arabia Central Department of Statistics and
Information, 2007). Indeed, its educational system is expanding extremely
rapidly in both its size and diversity.

Since the foundation of the Kingdom of Saudi Arabia in September 1932,
the national government has devoted vast resources to programs aimed at
improving primary, intermediate, secondary, and tertiary levels of education.

All of the kingdom's development plans consider the educational aspirations of the Saudi people, providing free education to all students. The educational system has been continuously and systematically expanded to accommodate the ever-growing demand for educational services. Using this approach, the kingdom has been able to guarantee equality of opportunity for all its citizens and to ensure that the government sector's need for an educated and trained national workforce can be fulfilled to carry forward the Kingdom's future development.

The educational system in Saudi Arabia entails gender-segregation at all levels with exception of a few colleges. Public education for boys started in the 1940s, whereas the first school for girls in Saudi Arabia was established in 1956. Before that time, boys and girls could only be educated at Kutabs or at home by private tutors. Shortly after the founding of Saudi Arabia, few boys and girls were able to join these schools because they had to spend much time helping their families with daily work. Thus, the Saudi government established new schools in major regions of the country and encouraged education by giving monetary gifts or monthly stipends for poor students to help their families to send their children to school. Accordingly, the number of students in primary, intermediate, and secondary schools increased enormously.

From a few hundred students and several dozen teachers in 1940s, the Ministry of Education now is responsible for about 5,303,451 students (2,727,859 male and 2,575,592 female) and about 444,644 teachers (212,144 male and 232,500 female) in public schools. The gross enrollment ratio for boys is 95 percent, the gross enrollment ratio for girls is 92 percent, and the gross enrollment ratio for both males and females is 94 percent (King Saud University Central Department of Statistics and Information, 2007).

The dramatic increase in student numbers created a huge demand for new and well-equipped buildings and qualified teachers. To meet these demands, the Saudi government established the Ministry of Knowledge (now known as Ministry of Education) in 1959. The Ministry of Education tackled the problem of teacher shortages using two strategies. First, it employed distinguished individuals who finished intermediate and secondary schools to teach students in primary and intermediate schools, respectively. Second, it hired tens of thousands of teachers from other Arabic countries on annual contracts. This strategy changed, of course, when sufficient university-level Saudi teachers became available. However, some long-term educational problems, such as memorization-oriented education, that were created during earlier stages of managing the teacher shortage persist.

The Saudi Higher Education System began in 1957 with a 2-year Intermediate College for Teachers comprising 21 students, 5 teaching staff, and 4 administrative officers. A few years later, a 4-year college that offered the first degree in education was established in Riyadh and was called Riyadh University (it is known now as King Saud University) to provide secondary schools with well-prepared teachers. In the 1960s, more colleges (for literature, arts, and science) were established in the large cities of Riyadh and Jeddah. The number of graduates from education colleges and teachers colleges was not sufficient, though, to meet the demands of the dramatic growth in school numbers. Thus, other graduates from noneducational colleges such as agriculture, science, arts, and business were hired to teach in the public schools without proper preparation in teaching. Although this strategy was effective in providing a quick solution to the problem of teacher shortage in public schools, it led to a long-term problem for Saudi universities: Public schools teachers without educational background, combined with increased student numbers within public schools classes, resulted in a teaching system that focuses principally on memorization. These conditions produced public school graduates who are considered by Saudi university faculty as not being properly prepared for college level study. To address this matter, the Ministry of Higher Education has recently initiated a national exam for secondary school graduates who seek admission to institutions of higher learning. In addition, most universities and colleges have established preparatory year programs to increase learning skills level for new students.

The Higher Education Department within the Saudi Arabian Ministry of Education was established in 1957 with one university (Riyadh University as it was known then). One year later, this department broke away, formed the Ministry of Higher Education, and established six universities during the following 22 years. Although the number of universities remained unchanged until 1998, the number of undergraduate students increased dramatically from less than 500 in 1957 to more than 450,000 in 1998. Between 1998 and 2010, the number of universities increased to 24 governmental universities and 8 private colleges or universities. The number of students attending governmental universities continued to increase to reach 758,000 (including more than 200,000 female students) by 2010 (Kingdom of Saudi Arabia Ministry of Higher Education Statistics Center, 2010). As an example, King Saud University (KSU) started with 21 enrolled students and 9 staff in 1957, but the number increased to more than 80,000 students and 5,000 staff in 2007 (Kingdom of Saudi Arabia Ministry of Higher Education Statistics Center, 2010).

Modern higher education in the kingdom results from a mix of social, cultural, political, and technological interactions during the past 30 years as the nation has undergone massive development in each of these areas. The National Strategic Development Plan (Kingdom of Saudi Arabia Ministry of Planning, 1995, p. 21) expressed the expected role of the Saudi higher education system in national development as follows:

> To continue the development of manpower through the meticulous evaluation of educational curricula and training programs and implementing the development or modifications suggested by this education in conformity with Islamic Shari'a, the changing needs of society and the requirements of the development process.

To fulfill the requirements of the National Strategic Development Plan, the Saudi government established an extensive program to provide opportunities for excellent graduates to continue their studies and obtain master's and PhD degrees in various subjects at universities in North America and Europe. This program has been successful in providing Saudi universities with highly qualified faculty in their respective fields. However, only a small percentage of them had received formal training in teaching before entering their academic careers.

Current and Future Challenges to Saudi Higher Education

The Saudi higher education system is currently faced with many challenges and anticipates continued challenges in the future. In addition to the traditional higher education issues concerned with teaching methodology, overworked faculty, and shortage of qualified faculty, many of the challenges confronting higher education result from social, economic, and globalization factors.

Saudi universities are not immune to global trends in higher education, particularly in increased demand for qualified teaching staff. This matter is complicated by a number of aggravating historical and current issues. Economic pressure in the mid-1980s caused by reduced oil revenues forced the government to undertake severe austerity measures that affected all government sectors including higher education, which was exclusively public at that time. Reduction in spending resulted in reduced numbers of new university graduates (bachelor degree holders) awarded with scholarships to pursue academic degrees to become university professors. During this period, universities lost many good potential faculty to other economic sectors that offered better pay and more predictable opportunities for career advancement. This trend continued for almost two decades, resulting in many university professors retiring without replacements.

Fortunately, the recent oil-based economic boom in Saudi Arabia combined with a new political leadership has shifted governmental emphasis on education—especially higher education. The result has been an expansion in the number of public universities and increased hiring of hundreds of new faculty. However, the speed with which this shift has occurred has resulted in the unchecked hiring of new junior faculty, many of whom may not be well suited for academic work. On their return from their government-funded scholarships to pursue advanced graduate degrees, some of them have not been trained for teaching.

In addition, the rapid demand for college education among young Saudis has placed tremendous strain on universities to fulfill their education role. As early as 25 years ago, the Saudi government responded to the increasing number of high school graduates who wanted to pursue higher education by increasing the number of students admitted each year by universities with only nominal changes in human and physical resources. This increase was most drastic in 2000, in which the government increased higher education admissions by 50 percent. This rapid increase in students' numbers combined with inexperienced teachers using traditional methods of teaching essentially led to a drop in the quality of university education.

Like many other countries in the Gulf region, an undergraduate education is generally considered the minimum level of education for all young people to achieve. In Saudi Arabia, this notion is rooted in the fact that most Saudis seek office-based careers that require the bachelor degree. Expatriates occupy the majority of labor-intensive jobs (expatriates constitute about 30 percent of the Kingdom's population). Saudis highly regard certain disciplines such as medicine, engineering, and computer sciences, among others, and many parents exert pressure on their children to pursue careers in these areas. Thus, students often capitulate to pressure to seek study in areas in which they have little interest or ability. In the past, little was done in the educational system to help students make informed decisions about which topics to study at university or which career trajectory might best fit their inclinations and interests.

However, in the past decade, the Saudi government has implemented a new strategy to address the increased demand for university education by increasing the number of universities from 8 (public) to more than 30 (public and private). The government moved in this direction to reduce pressure on existing universities and spread the locations of universities across the nation. This move has been successful in creating multiple career options for students and has provided numerous opportunities for them to pursue their interests. This strategy has also been successful in addressing significant shortages of personnel in certain highly skilled disciplines such as health sciences.

Nonetheless, the rapid increase in the number of universities has not been without drawbacks. Although there is a dramatic increase in the amount of government spending on education in public schools, and higher education in particular, the rapid expansion in the number of universities has contributed further to the shortage of qualified faculty and teaching staff. Even with aggressive recruitment of international faculty, higher education has not been able to keep pace with its ravenous demand for faculty. Thus, faculty tend to be overworked with heavy teaching loads and student advising.

Another major challenge facing leading Saudi universities is the rapid shift from teaching-intensive to research-intensive priorities, which presumably will help Saudi Arabia improve the global standing of its higher education system. Saudi universities seek to establish scientific communities that focus on acquiring research funding, producing high-quality research publications, and contributing to the growing knowledge economy. For example, in the past 3 years, King Saud University has established more than 100 research chairs, established a number of research excellence centers, and initiated a large series of international collaborations focusing on advancing all academic fields in an effort to realize its vision as a research intensive and globally competitive university. As a result, though, this rapid transition from a teaching-centered to a research-centered institution has led many faculty and administrators to regard teaching as a secondary duty.

Teaching methods at most Saudi universities are typically traditional—indeed, PowerPoint lecture-based teaching is the standard of mode of instruction. Student-centered approaches to teaching have been largely ignored on many campuses. The shift in teaching methodology to meet modern standards of teaching, learning, and assessment has been slow because of many of the factors mentioned earlier, particularly high student enrollment, expanding obligations of faculty members, and the shift in focus from teaching to research.

However, the recent surge in higher education funding in the kingdom has been used by many universities to provide faculty development opportunities in the field of programs related to teaching, learning, and assessment. In addition, many faculty are now attempting to integrate course management systems (e.g., Blackboard) and smart classrooms into their teaching.

Efforts to Improve Saudi Higher Education ———

For decades, curricula and teaching practices in many Saudi universities were chosen in a way that reflects the interplay between the requirements of governmental departments and academic professionals. However, the governmental sector can no longer absorb all university graduates as a part of its workforce. At the same time, the growing private sector resists employing graduates from many academic departments because, according to business leaders, they do not have sufficient skills required to work in the private sector. Thus, Saudi universities are facing increased pressure to enhance their curricula and teacher practices to prepare students with job-ready skills upon graduation.

Curricular Reform,
Teaching Practices, and Employability

Higher education curricula around the world are increasingly involving stakeholder needs as a driving force for change. This focus, of course, brings with it the employability of graduates as key consideration in reforming higher education and emphasizes the growing worldwide trend for higher education working in collaboration with business and industry to produce a capable and workforce.

King Fahd University for Petroleum and Minerals has successfully implemented this idea, and many of its students receive job offers even before they graduate. At King Saud University, there have been some calls to reshape student study plans and curricula to improve the quality of teaching and learning processes and to provide students with skills suitable for the job market. Although there has been some resistance to this idea, the Ministry of Higher Education continues to address criticisms raised by the private sector about the employability of university graduates. This effort requires continuous evaluation of market needs as well as continuous reform of undergraduate curricula to ensure the development of practical job-related skills and increases in graduate employment rate.

Indeed, serious weaknesses exist in the curricula of many Saudi Universities. Some Saudi researchers have argued that the performance of Saudi universities has been unsatisfactory because of outdated curricula and because the quality of graduates' job-related skills fall short of those of graduates who have matriculated from Western universities (e.g., Al-Baker, 2002; Al-Turkestani, 1998). Twenty years ago, Ali Alghafis (1992) emphasized the need for comprehensive restructuring of undergraduate curricula, teaching methods, and administration to overcome the problems facing the Saudi higher education. He highlighted the importance of investigating issues related to the quality of curricula, the need for continuous evaluation, and the need to increase flexibility in regulations regarding curricula changes. Unfortunately, only now are Saudi universities making serious attempts to heed Alghafis's advice.

Recently, KSU and several other Saudi universities have revised and updated study plans, including curricula. These institutions are now considering the importance of the employability of their graduates in developing modern curricula. KSU, for example, has initiated curricular reform by organizing workshops to help staff construct curricula according to modern standards.

Reforming Teaching Practices

KSU has developed several strategic objectives, one of which is "to provide students with the best education and opportunities that will enhance their knowledge, skills and relevant experience" (King Saud University, 2011). Clearly, this objective cannot be achieved without continuous efforts to enhance teaching and learning practices. There is a general agreement among Saudi universities, including KSU, that teaching staff should implement teaching methods that improve job skills of graduates. However, in reality, numerous challenges may seriously impede the implementation of these strategies and decrease student achievements.

Generally speaking, and as we noted earlier, most instructors and students at KSU limit the process of teaching and learning to traditional lecture: The instructor talks and students memorize what is being taught. The majority of faculty members at many Saudi universities, including KSU, have not received any training in teaching that has introduced them to or otherwise familiarized them with teaching methods other than the lecture. Most faculty did not receive any formal training in teaching before they became college professors. Their only experience with "learning" how to teach was observing the professors who taught them. Unfortunately, faculty are resistant to trying more active and engaging teaching methods because they reduce the amount of class time that can be devoted to delivering content, especially in those courses that involve heavy course content and large student enrollments. For example, consider a comment from one of our colleagues: "How can I use the role-play method when I have a heavy content that I need to deliver? How can I explain cell structure, for example, in 50 minutes, if I waste the class time with unnecessary activities?" In addition, in our experience, many KSU students prefer lectures as a method for learning, probably because this is the only method of instruction to which many of them have been exposed.

Of course, now a great deal of evidence criticizes traditional lecturing and emphasizes its inefficiency in promoting deep learning (Chaudhury, 2011). For example, R. F. Edlich (1993) described lecturing as an outdated instructional method. Other writers have emphasized lecturing as being one-way communication that facilitates little or no student engagement—it ignores variations in students' learning style and inculcates a passive attitude to learning (e.g., Davis, 2009). Evidence suggests that the incorporation of active learning into the traditional large group lecture enhances the learning experience (e.g., Svinicki & McKeachie, 2011).

Traditional Lecturing and Student Engagement

However, switching from the traditional lecture to an alternative teaching format may not be an easy task for many Middle Eastern professors. It requires them to acquire a considerable knowledge about education in general, and teaching and learning processes in particular. Making this shift also requires intellectual consideration, enthusiasm for teaching and learning, and reflection on what sorts of changes are needed in each teacher's approach to instruction. Indeed, some Saudi university professors are not convinced that other teaching methods are more effective than the common traditional lecture. For example, one of our colleagues stated:

> I do not see in the near future an alternative to the lecture method. Teaching staff, students, and managers in most KSU humanitarian and science departments are happy with lecturing. However, I appreciate other efforts to implement technologies that make my lectures more effective.

Thus, at least some faculty members are satisfied using lecturing practices and see no need for change. Such faculty point to the success of their past students' success in their education and careers as evidence that lecturing is an effective teaching method. However, students, context, knowledge resources, educational purposes, and intellectual demands of the workplace nowadays are different from what they were 20 or even 10 years ago. In the past, the students' success was measured by the amount of factual knowledge they had accumulated from their courses (Knight & Wood, 2005), but the success of modern students must be measured by their ability to gather and analyze information, solve problems, and successfully adapt to rapidly changing work and life changes. Other teaching methods, alone or in combination with lecturing, have been shown to be superior to the traditional lecture method (Buskist & Groccia, 2011). Thus, one step in helping students become more successful learners and more successful in the workplace is to decrease lecturing and increase student engagement in class activities.

Simply put, student engagement in classes enhances students' meaningful learning and the development of problem-solving skills (Svinicki & McKeachie, 2011). Student learning also depends on the nature of the institution and quality of the instruction. Both contribute to creating an educational environment that promotes high quality learning, although, of course, the final responsibility for learning rests with the students (Davis & Murrell, 1993). Fostering engagement in introductory courses is a crucial means of establishing the foundations for success in more advanced courses (Astin, 1993). Even a small window of student engagement via active learning techniques can make a large difference in enhancing learning. For example, Jennifer Knight and William Wood (2005) found that switching from a traditional lecture format to a more interactive teaching technique (including group discussion and cooperative problem solving) increased student learning and conceptual understanding of course content.

Despite such evidence of the effectiveness of student engagement in the class, some Saudi teachers remain unconvinced that active learning strategies and other methods of student engagement will work in their classrooms. In addition to this worry, some faculty fear losing control of their classes when group discussion or other active learning strategies are introduced.

Resistance to change from the traditional lecture to a more interactive learning format also comes from students. Some students may dislike and distrust the interactive classes and group activities because it takes them out of their comfort zones as passive learners (Buskist & Groccia, 2011). Before coming to the university, Saudi students spend 12 years of almost pure passive learning in public schools because "spoon feeding" is common in Saudi public schools.

In addition, there are other reasons for why Middle Eastern university students may dislike class engagement. One is lack of confidence. As one of our students told us, "Sometimes I feel that I knew the answer to the teacher's question but I fear the response of my teacher or classmates if it was wrong . . . I don't want to embarrass myself." Some faculty members use such student perspectives as an excuse to continue with traditional lectures and stay away from active learning.

A closely related issue common among Saudi students is they do not want to take responsibility for their learning. In fact, many students want to place this responsibility on their teachers' shoulders, so that their success or failure reflects their teachers' success or failure to transmit knowledge to them. As teachers familiar with active learning techniques and their success in enhancing student learning and engagement, we believe that once teaching through active learning becomes the norm, students will become more comfortable with assuming responsibility for their learning.

Content Coverage

Instructors continue to be ensnared in the attempt to define what aspects of knowledge are essential for undergraduates to learn, and thus, how much content to cover in any given class remains a controversial issue. Some courses that are designed by professors with no education background are heavy on factual knowledge. Because content coverage is a top priority in many academic departments in Saudi universities, teachers overload their courses with content to the extent that there is no or little room for activities that focus on increasing thinking and problem-solving skills related to that content.

Despite the importance of factual knowledge content for students, it is not the only benefit, and perhaps not the most important benefit, that students may gain from their university experience. Developing critical-thinking and problem-solving skills as well as learning to understand the importance of various academic, social, economic, and world issues related to their chosen fields of study are important, too. Reducing content coverage in class and replacing it with outside-of-class assignments is one strategy that would seem likely to free class time for engaging students in active learning and placing responsibility for learning squarely on students' shoulders. In the long term, students will need to know how to find out essential information for themselves and accommodate it within the context of their future working and life environments. Teachers should help them gain these skills by improving their instructional practices.

Assessment and Accreditation

The surge in Saudi government spending on higher education has been driven by the need to improve the quality of higher education. Similar to other countries in the Middle East, the notion of ensuring quality in higher education is a relatively new concept in Saudi Arabia. However, the establishment of the National Commission for Academic Assessment and Accreditation (NCAAA) in 2004 is a clear indicator of the shift toward striving for quality in higher education.

The NCAAA started with international help to establish the standards for accreditation of academic institutions. The accreditation system is based on 11 standards that cover a wide array of factors ranging from governance to community services. However, the focus of the accreditation system is on standards for teaching and learning. Institutions seeking NCAAA accreditation must demonstrate a well-structured system with clear educational strategy for graduating competent students and provide evidence that they continuously strive to improve educational practices.

Along these lines, two key elements in the accreditation process are the program specification, which describes the details of the program, and the course file. The course file, which must be provided for every course in all departments, must contain descriptions of course objectives, intended learning outcomes for each educational session, and methods of assessment that measure all the required skills students should acquire as a result of taking the course. In addition, a course report must be provided at the end of each academic semester that includes suggestions for improving the course that should be implemented in the next offering of the course. Student feedback about the course is an integral part of monitoring the quality of the educational process and a major source for ideas about how to foster course improvement. These NCAAA requirements are intended to produce an educational system that will ensure continuous improvement based on student and faculty feedback and integration of new knowledge relevant to each department's curriculum.

The NCAAA requirements also provide for creating a properly structured course description that offers well-documented course materials in an effort to enhance consistency of content and course objectives among various sections of the same course. These requirements also provide new faculty both the resources necessary to teach their courses and the opportunity to contribute substantially to course improvement. Departments also use surveys of graduates to gauge student achievement of intended learning outcomes in their courses relative to the requirements of their employment.

In addition to attempting to achieve international standards in higher education through the NCAAA accreditation process, there is a general trend among Saudi universities to establish benchmarking with international reputable and comparable institutions of higher education to establish and fine-tune standards for specific academic programs. Saudi universities encourage individual academic programs to demonstrate their international standing by obtaining accreditation or recognition from international bodies such as the Accreditation Board for Engineering and Technology (ABET) and the Association for Dental Education in Europe (DentEd). Each institution of higher learning usually designs its key performance indicators (KPIs) to facilitate comparison with benchmark institutions. Thus, KPIs are used to monitor performance within specific institutions and as a measure to demonstrate relative standing to international standards.

The Preparatory Year

Saudi universities also have undertaken other initiatives to improve teaching and learning. One of these initiatives is the mandatory preparatory year for all new university undergraduate students. During this year, students receive training in computer skills; English; and communication, learning, research, and critical-thinking skills to ensure better preparation of high school graduates relative to contemporary requirements of higher education students.

Faculty Development

Faculty development programs to help academic institutions and faculty members achieve the new goals set forth by administrative policymakers and to achieve, or preferably surpass, NCAAA accreditation standards have been established at several Saudi universities. Universities often seek international support in consultation services, twining programs with similar academic goals, and joint degree programs. University administrations encourage their faculty to attend international conferences to develop their teaching (as well as research) skills. In addition, specialized units within Saudi universities are being established to promote excellence in teaching and learning. For example, the Deanship of Skills Development (DSD) was established at King Saud University in 2007 to provide training programs and workshops to promote excellence in teaching, learning, and leadership skills. These academic staff development units provide a wide range of local and international training activities for faculty—training is often provided by prominent international figures in teaching and learning and academic leadership. The DSD also provides peer consultation services for individual faculty across campus to receive feedback about their teaching as well as recommendations for how it might be improved.

Revision of the Governance Structure

One major obstacle to the process of controlling the quality of education in universities in the region is that teaching faculty are government employees and are governed by the same general rules and regulations as other government agencies are. In essence, Saudi faculty are tenured as soon as they are employed. Thus, it is difficult to practically link performance to promotion or reward and even harder to remove faculty members who fail to meet the standards of their teaching institution. University professors are generally treated equally with the same salary and benefits package regardless of their area of specialty and accomplishments.

Fortunately, higher education authorities have recognized the detrimental effect of this situation on the quality of higher education, and corrective measures have been initiated that impart incentives for distinguished faculty members. Universities have begun to offer financial incentives to faculty members with rare specialties and accomplishments in research and patent development. Universities now also offer different awards to distinguished individuals in teaching and research and to colleges that exhibit stellar accomplishments or that develop effective strategic plans for improving faculty performance.

Leaders in Saudi higher education are also considering revising the tenure system as well as the relationship between universities and faculty regarding contract terms. For example, currently under consideration is a proposed tenure track dedicated to teachers, in which promotion criteria will rely more on innovations and improvement in the educational processes rather than on research as is the case with the current system. The implementation of these proposed changes in the tenure and promotion system will resolve many current issues with monitoring faculty performance and is likely to dramatically enhance the quality of teaching and learning.

Conclusions

Saudi Arabia is currently focusing on improving the quality of its university graduates. It is undertaking tremendous efforts to bridge the gap between current educational strategies and what are considered the state-of-the-art teaching strategies. It is working relentlessly to integrate "best practices" in university teaching and undergraduate education (Chickering & Gamson, 1987; Hatfield, 1995). It is making a concerted attempt to place the student at the center of the educational process (Weimer, 2002). Although only time will tell if these strategies will result in achieving all of the noblest aims of the Saudi government to improve the quality of undergraduate education and students' preparation for the job market in an increasingly competitive global economy, it is a safe bet, based what has been discovered to enhance higher education in other nations, that, at the very least, the efforts are aimed in the right direction.

References

Al-Baker, F. B. (2002). Difficulties faced by new female students at the university level and their effect on university life satisfaction at the Girl Centre, King Saud University, Riyadh. *Journal of King Saud University (Educational Sciences & Islamic Studies), 14,* 353–396. [In Arabic]

Alghafis, A. N. (1992). *Universities in Saudi Arabia: Their role in science, technology and development.* New York, NY: University Press of America.

Al-Turkestani, H. M. (1998, February). *The role of higher education in meeting the requirements of Saudi job market.* Symposium on higher education in the Kingdom of Saudi Arabia: A vision of the future. Part 1 (pp. 201–218). Riyadh, Saudi Arabia: Ministry of Higher Education. [In Arabic]

Astin, A. (1993). *What matters in college? Four critical years revisited.* San Francisco, CA: Jossey-Bass.

Buskist, W., & Groccia, J. E. (Eds.). (2011). *Evidence-based teaching.* New Directions in Teaching and Learning, No. 128. San Francisco, CA: Jossey-Bass.

Chaudhury, S. R. (2011). The lecture. In W. Buskist & J. E. Groccia (Eds.), *Evidence-based teaching.* New Directions in Teaching and Learning, No. 128. San Francisco, CA: Jossey-Bass.

Chickering, A. W., & Gamson, Z. F. (1987). Seven principles for good practice in undergraduate education. *AAHE Bulletin, 39*, 7, 3–7.

Davis, B. G. (2009). *Tools for teaching* (2nd ed.). San Francisco, CA: Jossey-Bass.

Davis, T., & Murrell, P. (1993) A structural model of perceived academic, personal, and vocational gains related to college student responsibility. *Research in Higher Education, 34*, 267–289.

Edlich, R. F. (1993). My last lecture. *Journal of Emergency Medicine, 11*, 771–774.

Hatfield, S. R. (Ed.). (1995). *The seven principles in action: Improving undergraduate education*. Bolton, MA: Anker.

Kingdom of Saudi Arabia Central Department of Statistics and Information. (2007). Retrieved from http://www.cdsi.gov.sa/yb45/Pages/English_Main_Page.htm

Kingdom of Saudi Arabia Ministry of Higher Education Statistics Center. (2010). Retrieved June 14, 2011, from http://www.mohe.gov.sa/ar/pages/default.aspx

Kingdom of Saudi Arabia Ministry of Planning. (1995). General objectives and strategic bases of the sixth development plan. 1415–1420 A.H. (1995–2000 A.D.). Riyadh, Saudi Arabia: Ministry of Planning.

King Saud University. (2011). *Strategic plan*. Retrieved from http://www.ksu.edu.sa/AboutKSU/Pages/visionmissionold.aspx

Knight, J. K., & Wood, W. B. (2005). Teaching more by lecturing less. *Cellular Biology Education, 4*, 298–310.

Svinicki, M., & McKeachie, W. J. (2011). *McKeachie's teaching tips: Strategies, research and theory for college and university teachers* (13th ed.). Belmont, CA: Wadsworth.

Weimer, M. (2002). *Learner-centered teaching: Five key changes to practice*. San Francisco, CA: Jossey-Bass.

CHAPTER 7

Culture and Disability in the Classroom

DENNIS B. GALVAN AND JEREMY L. BRUNSON

T he opportunities for success for students with disabilities are compromised when the appropriate accommodation allowing them to participate as much (or as little) as they would like in the learning process are not provided. Effectively accommodating students with a disability is contingent on both parties—faculty and students—crossing cultural boundaries successfully. The diagnosis of, and thus the response to, a disability is a culturally situated event (Monk & Frankenberg, 1995) and can have a tremendous impact on a student's journey through higher education. In this chapter, we discuss the role that culture plays in accommodating students with disabilities and students' openness in discussing their disabilities. We thus will focus on a cultural model of disability rather than a medical model (Leigh & Brice, 2003).

Disabilities and Groccia's Model for Understanding Teaching and Learning

Disability affects every level of James Groccia's model of teaching and learning (Chapter 1, this volume; St. Clair & Groccia, 2009) but probably none more so than learner variables. For example, students can have a wide variety of disabilities including sensory, dexterity or mobility, and learning or psychological disabilities, among others. Many of these disabilities will directly affect learning processes. A student with low vision would need visual information presented verbally, and a student with a learning disability might need to listen to an audiotape of a book rather than reading it.

Learning contexts can also interact with disability. Students who are deaf and are using a sign language interpreter often have difficulty knowing who is speaking, and when it is appropriate to interject their thoughts into the discussion. A clear example of disability interacting with course content would be a student with a learning disability such as dyscalculia (a wide range of learning disabilities involving math) taking a statistics or math course. The attitude of the teacher about making accommodations for students with disabilities can also have both positive and negative impacts. If a teacher feels imposed upon for having to make handouts in larger fonts for a low-vision student, that attitude will likely be conveyed to the student through that teacher's actions. However, if the teacher is enthusiastic about doing whatever needs to be done to help students with disabilities have access to course content and to participate in course activities, then teacher variables can have a positive impact.

In short, the interaction of all the variables in Groccia's model influences a teacher's choices for deciding on and implementing the best instructional practices for students with disabilities. To complicate the matter, the same instructional process may not be successful for students with different disabilities. A student in a wheelchair and a student with low vision will need very different accommodations in instructional processes.

Disability and Culture

Discussing disability and an accommodation can be a difficult endeavor for both the instructor and the student, which is caused, in part, because many cultures still hold on to beliefs of disabled individuals as inferior human beings, even though the disability rights movement has gone global (Rembis, 2010). Culture is so entwined with one's identity that it is difficult, if not impossible, for someone to shed culturally bound behaviors. Likewise, it is often difficult for individuals to identify their culturally bound ideologies, which is an issue of particular importance to accommodating students with disabilities in the classroom. As Sylvia van Maastricht (1998) surmised, culture informs who is "classified as (in)competent, and the consequences of that classification" (p. 125).

Cultures socialize students with disabilities to behave in particular ways in response to their own and others' disabilities. In essence, their culture dictates what it means to have a disability. In U.S. culture, students have learned how to deal with their disabilities in interacting with teachers and negotiating accommodations. However, students who study abroad may encounter difficulties because of the way teachers from different cultures might view their disabilities and the accommodations necessary to address those disabilities. Thus, because disability is personal and one's response to it is contextual (Barton & Armstrong, 2001), having a foreign student with a disability in the classroom requires special consideration.

Disability is often associated with people's ability to participate in their country's economy (Barnartt, 1992); although more industrialized nations may deemphasize an individuals' ability to participate in the economy, it is nevertheless still present. This notion can influence how people react to their disability. In the United States, for example, where the idea of asking for help is often equated with weakness, some students may deny that they need accommodation. And, after failing several tests, they may feel it best to withdraw from the course. This situation may occur even when students are familiar with their legal rights to accommodations or when syllabi explicitly state how to go about getting an accommodation.

One factor that influences how a particular culture responds to a disability is the prevalence with which the disability occurs. For example, Nora Ellen Groce's (1985) study of the inhabitants of Martha's Vineyard from the 17th century to the 20th century found that because of the high prevalence of deafness among the islanders, the inhabitants did not recognize deafness as a disability; rather, they considered it "normal."

It is impossible to discuss all of the various cultures of the world here and how each of those cultures defines, interprets, and reacts to disability as it applies to higher education. Instead, we have chosen a few countries and a select number of disabilities for illustration.

Disability and Culture in the United States

According to the U.S. Department of Education's National Center for Education Statistics (2006), approximately 11 percent of undergraduate students in the United States reported having a disability during the 2003–2004 academic year. Of the students who reported having a disability, 25 percent reported having a mobility impairment, 22 percent reported mental illness or depression, and 17 percent reported a physical health impairment. With more than 1 in 10 students reporting a disability, it is likely that most, if not all, faculty members in the United States have taught or will teach students with disabilities. Severe visual impairments, deafness, and orthopedic or mobility disabilities are often obvious when a student with one of these disabilities first appears in class. Students with learning disabilities, psychiatric diagnoses, or chronic pain, however, may not be as obvious but will need accommodations, nonetheless.

In 1990, the United States adopted into law the Americans with Disabilities Act (ADA). This law mandates that "reasonable accommodations" be made for individuals with disabilities. The act defines a disability as a "physical or mental impairment that substantially limits one or more major life activities of such an individual, a record of such an impairment, or being regarded as having such an impairment" (ADA, 1992, 12102–3 [2]; cited in Johnson, 2006). This law makes it illegal to discriminate against anyone with a disability.

U.S. colleges and universities have established offices for students with disabilities to help ensure that these students receive reasonable accommodations.

Documentation of the disability in U.S. higher education is usually coordinated by the college or university office for students with disabilities. The decision of what "reasonable accommodations" might entail for a course should be made by the faculty member in consultation with the student and the campus office for students with disabilities. In some cases, a reasonable accommodation is easy for all, such as providing handouts written in large font in class for a low-vision student. Other times, accommodations are much more elaborate, such as providing a sign language interpreter for a deaf student in a lecture hall or an assistant for a visually impaired student in a chemistry class. Colleges and universities do not have to make accommodations that fundamentally alter the academic program in any way, and they are expected to maintain academic requirements, such as grade point average (GPA), and technical requirements, such as dental students having manual dexterity with their hands (Grossman, 2001).

Because of the legally mandated framework for providing access for students with disabilities to higher education in the United States, faculty may contact the campus office for students with disabilities for information about a student's disability, the disabled community on campus, and the services available for these individuals. Teachers can also find information on disability resources on the Internet from organizations such as the Association on Higher Education and Disability (http://www.ahead.org/) or the Center on Postsecondary Education and Disability (http://www.cped.uconn.edu/). For any teacher, it is helpful to learn as much as possible about students with disabilities on campus (Boyd, 2008; Johnson, 2006). It is appropriate to ask students about their disability in the context of the learning process. Hazel Denhart (2008) reported that students with learning disabilities (LD) often feel misunderstood and misjudged by their peers and professors. They feel that they work hard but have that effort go largely unrecognized by their professors. In a study of 400 faculty at a large U.S. university, Anne Thompson, Leslie Bethea, and Jennifer Turner (1997) discovered that only 18 percent of faculty were familiar with Section 504 of the Rehabilitation Act of 1973 and only approximately 50 percent were familiar with the ADA. Thompson, Bethea, and Turner also found that most faculty were not fully aware of their students' rights regarding accommodations and their responsibilities for providing students with those accommodations. Clearly, there is still a need to educate U.S. faculty members about reasonable accommodations for students with disabilities.

Most people are not aware of the ways in which disability and culture can interact with each other. In the United States, the majority culture is individualistic. One of the goals of higher education is to help students achieve independence financially and intellectually, so that they can analyze issues and make informed decisions independently of others. Given the structure of most colleges and universities, this intellectual work must be produced within a specific time frame (e.g., a semester). There is also a sense of competition for grades among students in many classes along with the need for fairness by the instructor so that no one student has unfair advantages. Students also should be able to use their intellectual skills learned in college to compete in the marketplace after graduation.

U.S. cultural values regarding independence, competition, and fairness influence how teachers perceive and deal with students who have disabilities. Students who are deaf, have visual impairments, or have orthopedic disabilities need access to the information provided in the course but once they have access to the information, they should be able to learn and process that information like any other student. Providing an interpreter for a deaf student, or audiotape books for a visually impaired student, or a ramp to get into the building for a student in a wheelchair are seen as fair and reasonable accommodations by most professors. However, giving a student with a learning disability more time on a test, or to complete assignments, seems unfair to other students. Moreover, teachers may feel that such students are not being adequately prepared for competition in the marketplace if they are given unfair advantages in college. Will employers be so generous? The U.S. values of independence, competition, and fairness seem to disadvantage students with a learning disability compared with other disabilities.

As a group, Mexican Americans have worked hard to hold onto their culture and language while attempting to acculturate into the U.S. mainstream. These borders, or moments where these two goals converge, in which Mexican Americans exist within the United States, has been well articulated (Anzaldua, 1987) and lay out acceptable behavior for members of the culture relative to sexuality, religion, and masculinity and femininity, among others. Within the Mexican culture, physical disabilities are more accepted than mental and psychological disabilities are (Santana-Martin & Santana, 2005). Shame and guilt are associated with mental and psychological disorders. Therefore, a teacher discussing an accommodation for blindness, deafness, or a mobility disability that a Mexican American student needs may not require much more than simply explaining that accommodations are available. Discussing an accommodation for a mental or psychological disability such as a learning disability with a Mexican American student, however, will require much more finesse. As with all accommodations, the teacher should wait until the student broaches the subject. When the student is having difficulties in the course, and the teacher suspects that these difficulties are linked to a mental or psychological disability, teachers should attempt to frame the discussion around a student's success rather than a "dealing with your disability" approach.

Disability and Culture in China

Often responses to disabilities reflect a culture's history. In China, the history of Confucianism, which emphasizes homogeneity, and Maoist ideologies, which emphasize a productive body, have led to a complex stigmatization of people with disabilities. The traditional terms for disability in Chinese reflect these views. Gloria Zhang Liu (2005) reported that the Chinese word *canfei* translates as "handicapped and useless" whereas *canji* translates as "handicap and illness." Liu noted that the term for "individuals with disabilities" is rarely used and that disability is often viewed as a punishment for the sins in one's past life or for the sins of one's parents. In addition, Evelyn Lee (1996, cited in Liu 2005) reported that mental health is a result of self-discipline and the avoidance of negative thoughts and that emotional problems are the consequences of weak character. Stigma, guilt, and shame for disability are attached to disabled persons and to their families.

Despite these cultural beliefs, living conditions and social status of people with disabilities in China has improved remarkably since the 1980s (International Disability Rights Monitor [IDRM], 2005). The first national sampling survey on disability reported that there were 60 million people with disabilities, or 5 percent of China's total population. Although many barriers exist for students with disabilities in higher education in China, by law no institution of higher education can discriminate against an individual based on a disability. Students with disabilities are gaining access to higher education in China. In 2003, 3,899 students with disabilities were enrolled in Chinese institutions of higher education. These colleges and universities are starting to provide accommodations for these students given the new antidiscrimination laws (IDRM, 2005). Unfortunately, it is not known if these institutions of higher education have offices that coordinate services for students with disabilities. There are approximately 38,000 grassroots disability rights organizations that work under the umbrella organization called China Disabled Person Federation (IDRM, 2005).

Teachers in universities and other Chinese institutions of higher education will need to work with students with disabilities and grassroots organizations and government organizations if their school does not have an office that coordinates services for these students. Addressing the needs of students with disabilities who have been acculturated into believing their disabilities are a punishment or that they cannot contribute as much as their nondisabled counterparts requires teachers to set aside their "naive realism" (McCurdy, Spradley, & Shandy, 2005) or the belief that everyone sees the world the same way they do. Rather than addressing the disabilities of specific students, teachers should attempt to make their entire class accessible to all students regardless of disability (e.g., reducing the amount of information on a PowerPoint slide or eliminating moving animation that may be distracting to students with intellectual disabilities. This approach can enable all students to participate in class without anyone being singled out.

Disability and Culture in the United Kingdom

According to the United Kingdom 2001 national census, 18.2 percent of the population has disabilities (IDRM, 2007), whereas only 3.1 percent of the students in higher education have disabilities (Organisation for Economic

Co-operation and Development [OECD], 2003). It is illegal for institutions of higher education to discriminate against people with disabilities according to the Disability Discrimination Act (DDA) of 1995 (IDRM, 2007). The Special Education Needs and Disability Act (SENDA) of 2001 amended the DDA made it illegal for any college or university to discriminate against individuals because of a disability. Colleges and universities must make reasonable accommodations for students with disabilities (IDRM, 2007). Examples cited in the *IDRM: Regional Report Europe* include allowing blind students to use guide dogs on campus when there is a no dogs policy, providing British Sign Language interpreters for deaf students as needed, and "providing services by alternative methods" to "overcome obstacles."

UK institutions of higher education implement support services in a variety of ways. Although all colleges and universities must designate special staff members to advise students with disabilities, the law does not dictate how this process should be done (OECD, 2003). Some coordinators are housed in special disability units, whereas others may be in the campus counseling center or in the student services offices.

Common services for students with disabilities include British Sign Language (BSL) interpreters, note takers, library support, and readers and scribes, among others. It appears that services for students with disabilities in UK colleges and universities are generally good but may depend on the institutional commitment to support staff for students with disabilities (OECD, 2003). The OECD report cited the University of East London for having what appears to be a well-established office for students with disabilities: It offers awareness programs such as deaf awareness month, provides a handbook for students with disabilities, and information for faculty.

Disability and Culture in the Switzerland

Although Switzerland provides disability insurance to people who were born with disabilities and to those who acquired a disability through illness or accident to reduce the consequences of being disabled, it has not focused on the civil rights of those individuals. It appears that people with disabilities are to be cared for and not expected to go on to higher education. Consequently, institutions of higher education are not required to provide reasonable accommodations for students with disabilities (OECD, 2003). The OECD report provided no data on the number of students with disabilities in Swiss universities. According to the European Agency for Development in Special Needs Education's (2009) website, the Swiss government passed a strong antidiscrimination law for disabled people in 2004, but the implementation of services at different Swiss universities remains highly variable. Of course, Swiss faculty will need to work with each student with a disability, their institution, and possibly grassroots or public agencies that focus on improving the educational and work environments for individuals with disabilities.

Disability and Culture in Jordan

In 2009, Jordan's population was approximately 6 million (U.S. Department of State, 2011). If one assumes 5 percent of the population (using the lowest percentage reported for countries we review), that would mean approximately 300,000 Jordanians have a disability. There are currently 23 universities in Jordan, and more than 94 percent of Jordan's high school graduates go on to college (Rutherford, 2007). Kenneth Rutherford noted that Jordan is becoming a leader in the Arab world on disability rights. Jordan has created its own disability rights law modeled after the ADA in the United States (Placidway, 2010). Institutions of higher education are prohibited from discriminating against people with disabilities but who are otherwise qualified for academic work. According to the University of Jordan website (http://www.ju.edu.jo/Pages/Offices/osscc.aspx), its Office of Student Support was established to provide assistance for students with special needs including those with mobility, visual, hearing, and other disabilities that affect learning. Teachers at the University of Jordan have the same level of support found at universities in the United States and United Kingdom.

Traditionally, people with disabilities in Arab cultures have been seen as something to be ashamed of by family members. Nonetheless, the new disability rights laws are beginning to make a difference in both Jordan and Lebanon (Nagata, 2008). In such an environment where tradition is being countered with new laws, university teachers will meet students with disabilities who have a wide variety of attitudes toward their disability ranging from shame to a new sense of being entitled to equal rights.

Culture also interacts with disability in Muslim communities. Mosques are not only for prayer but are a place of socializing for men (women often stay home to pray). Prayer is conducted with physical movements and mental concentration (Al-Oraibi, 2010). A man in a wheelchair would not be able to pray in a mosque and would have to pray at home with the women, thus affecting his ability to socialize with other men (Ai-Oraibi, 2010).

People with disabilities must deal with the way their culture views them as part of their daily lives. When a culture marginalizes people with disabilities by classifying them as dependent, incomplete, or in the case of a person in a wheelchair in Jordan, as something less than a human, they must deal with this perception and find ways to develop a healthy self-image. Of course, some individuals will be more successful in this regard than others. It is important for teachers to be sensitive to these kinds of issues.

Teaching Students With Disabilities

It is not difficult to make a course accessible for students with disabilities. Teachers may start by including a generic paragraph in their syllabus stating that the course is accessible to students with disabilities and describing how the students can arrange for accommodations. It is impossible to list all possible accommodations in the syllabus, thus the need for a generic paragraph. Each student with a disability is unique and will need a specific set of accommodations. Often these accommodations have worked for the student in the past. When meeting with a student who is requesting an accommodation, the teacher will need to bring knowledge of the course to the discussion with the student because reasonable accommodations in, for example, an introductory psychology course would be very different than would those made in a statistics or chemistry course. The final decision regarding any accommodations should be agreed on between the faculty member and the student, sometimes with consultation from the students with disabilities office. The key is making sure that the accommodations are reasonable and fair, and they do not put an undue burden on the teacher or other students.

Disability is a sensitive subject to many faculty and students. Faculty may be uncomfortable talking about disabilities and may have preconceived notions about students with disabilities that could interfere with a productive discussion about reasonable accommodations for students in their courses. It is always best to approach these situations with an open mind. As mentioned earlier, students are often the best source of information regarding their disabilities, what accommodations they have been given in the past, and what they are presently requesting.

Just as culture shapes views on disability, it also shapes the language one uses to discuss disability. Scholars in the social sciences, particularly within disability studies, have dropped various terms that were once considered appropriate. Words such as *handicap*, *impaired* (e.g., hearing-impaired), *challenged*, or *retarded*, have all fallen out of favor within the United States and other countries. New, more neutral, wording that does not have the same history, such as *intellectual disability*, *disability*, or *deaf*, is preferred because they carry with them less stigma. It is important for teachers to recognize the impact of their word choice in helping students feel comfortable about talking about their disability and accommodations.

It is beyond the scope of this chapter to discuss all disabilities that faculty might encounter in their teaching. Instead, we will focus on some common disabilities among college and university students.

Teaching Students With Learning Disabilities

Students with LD have normal intelligence but have information-processing deficits in one or more academic areas (e.g., reading, writing, or math). Students with LD are difficult to characterize as a group because they are so varied; however, the following characteristics can be attributed to students with LD (Hardman, Drew, & Egan, 2011):

- Above average or near average intelligence
- Perceptual problems
- Visual and auditory discrimination problems
- Attention problems

- Uneven skill levels in different areas
- Cognitive deficits (memory, organizational skills)
- Hyperactivity

Most students with LD also have a reading or writing disorder of some kind (Lindstrom, 2007). A common accommodation for students with learning disabilities is extended time on exams and other assignments. Research has suggested that although extended time on tests also helps normally achieving college students, students with LD make significantly greater gains when given more time on tests (e.g., Ofiesh, Mather, & Russell, 2005). In addition, as reading scores for students with LD decrease, the probability that they will benefit from extended time increases (Ofiesh & Hughes, 2002).

Other accommodations for students with LD can include

- frequent and prompt feedback on assignments;
- frequent meetings with the teacher to discuss progress;
- clear organization of the course (e.g., syllabus, exams, PowerPoint slides, handouts);
- consistent test organization (e.g., grouping multiple-choice questions over the same topic together);
- careful administration if Scantron forms are used; and
- extra paper provided for preparing answers (e.g., outlines) to essay questions.

Some students with LD, dyslexia, and visual disabilities are not able to read effectively so they must use audio recording. Teachers who have these types of students in their classes often need to order books well in advance so that audiotapes of these materials can be completed before the first day of class. Thus, these students often contact their teachers well in advance of the beginning in class to obtain a list of books and other reading materials that will be used in class.

Teaching Students With Attention Deficit/Hyperactivity Disorder (ADHD)

Students with ADHD have many problems that may appear similar to the problems of students with learning disabilities, including difficulties reading, writing (including organizational errors), and frequent errors in math calculation. In addition to memory problems, students with ADHD may have serious problems with time-management, organization, completing tasks, and metacognitive skills. Many of the same strategies used with working with students with LD can be effective when working with students with ADHD. Thus, to help students with ADHD (along with other students in the class), it is important for teachers to provide clear expectations for student performance, deliver clearly organized lectures and activities, and frequently repeat specific dates regarding impending deadlines.

Students with ADHD are easily distracted, so teachers should encourage these students to sit near the front of the class. Teachers should provide descriptions of all assignments both orally and in writing to help students with ADHD understand and remember them. Tests should be administered in relatively distraction-free environments. Because ADHD students also have problems with time management, it is beneficial for teachers to help them break down longer assignments into its component parts by setting deadlines for each major segment of the assignment (e.g., outline, summaries of articles reviewed, integration of reviewed articles into a review of the literature, first draft, final paper).

Teaching Students Who Are Deaf or Hard of Hearing

Students who are deaf or hard of hearing face many challenges in college revolving around communication issues. Faculty members often feel awkward working with sign language interpreters, talking about this disability with affected students, and discussing issues relating to deafness and communication within the classroom. Although deaf and hard of hearing individuals are hugely diverse (Leigh, 2009), the following suggestions can help to improve any teacher's communication with students who are deaf or hard of hearing:

- Speak to the student, not to the sign language interpreter.
- During class discussions, try to make sure that only one person speaks at a time so that the student who is deaf or hard of hearing knows who is talking. This process may slow down the class discussion until everyone gets used to working with the sign language interpreter.
- Students who are deaf or hard of hearing should sit near the front of the class.
- Students using an interpreter may need the teacher to slow the pace when using PowerPoint slides to enable these students to see each slide and then look to the interpreter to see what is being said about it.
- When using videos in class, teachers should make sure they are captioned and that the technology supports captions.
- It is helpful to provide the interpreter with advance copies of the PowerPoint presentation or other materials to be used in class.
- During the presentation, teachers should check to see that the deaf or hard of hearing student is following the presentation and is able to move his or her attention between the presentation and the interpreter.

Students who are deaf or hard of hearing, like all people with disabilities, are a heterogeneous group. Some deaf people identify themselves with the deaf culture of their country and will communicate primarily through sign language and socialize with other deaf sign language users. Others will not identify with the deaf culture and will communicate primarily through lip reading and speech and will associate largely with hearing people (Leigh, 2009).

Aside from sign language interpreters, a whole host of technologies and communication modalities are used by deaf and hard of hearing students. These include low-tech solutions such as writing back and forth on paper to state-of-the-art real-time captioning, which provides a transcription of what is being said in the classroom and displayed on a computer monitor. The person actually typing may be in the classroom or at a remote location connected electronically. Still others will rely on their residual hearing or rely on hearing aids, or a hearing loop that uses Induction Loop Technology (also called FM loops) to transmit sounds directly to a hearing aid's built-in wireless T-coil receiver. When a student uses some of these technologies, the teacher may be asked to wear a small lapel micro-transmitter that broadcasts a "cleaner" sound to the student's hearing aid.

Teaching Students With Visual Disabilities

Students with visual disabilities also face difficult, but not insurmountable, challenges in college, especially considering that today's modern classrooms are so visually oriented. Indeed, many tools used for transmitting information to students and measuring their retention of information is visual (e.g., smart boards, PowerPoint slide shows, streaming video, student response systems or "clickers"). Unless teachers work very closely with their students who are visually disabled in accommodating their needs, the experience will be a negative one for students. It is simply unrealistic to expect students who are visually impaired to benefit from today's modern teaching technologies without first working with these students in advance of the academic term (Fichten, Asuncion, Barile, Ferraro, & Wolforth, 2009).

Like students with hearing disabilities, students with visual disabilities are a highly diverse group. Although some students with visual disabilities have no vision at all, others can read simple sans serif fonts that are larger than normal sizes or simply printed on a particular colored (often yellow) paper. Some students with visual disabilities prefer handouts copied at an increased percentage of the original document (e.g., 175 percent); other students with visual disabilities may prefer to receive an electronic file via e-mail so they can open it in a special program that will enlarge its contents on their computer (Farmer & Morse, 2007; Fichten et al., 2009). Many students with visual impairments will use computers to convert printed material to Braille or read the text on a computer screen aloud using text-to-speech software (Fichten et al., 2009). Studies of technology used by students with visual impairments in Canada show that most students who are blind tend to use Braille, text-to-speech software, and audiocassettes, whereas most students with low vision tend to use screen magnification and large-screen monitors (Fichten et al., 2009). The following suggestions should help teachers in setting the stage for working with students with visual disabilities:

- Many students with visual disabilities will need extra time for exams and other assignments. They may also need a reader or specially prepared exams.
- Seeing eye dogs are working dogs. If others want to interact with the dog, they should ask the student's permission.
- Students with visual disabilities may need to be seated where they can hear clearly.
- Students with low vision may be able to see large PowerPoint slides.
- If students with a visual disability use recorded textbooks, they should contact the teacher for a list of required texts so that these can be ordered in time.
- Students with visual disabilities need the instructor to read everything aloud that is written on the blackboard or in the PowerPoint presentation.

Teaching Students With Limited Manual Dexterity and Mobility Impairments

Limited manual dexterity can also create a serious academic challenge in this technological age. The inability to type or write quickly can put students at a severe disadvantage on tests and other assignments, and thus students with limited manual dexterity will need extended time on all their written work. Students who have upper body limitations may need note takers, extended exam time, audiotape recorders to record exam answers, or a special exam room where they can dictate responses to questions. They also may not be able to raise their hands to participate in class discussion. Meeting with students with such disabilities before the academic term and discussing with them how best to accommodate their needs will put these students at ease, and will help ensure the opportunity for the student to participate fully in discussions and other classroom activities.

Delar Singh's (2003) national survey of 137 randomly selected U.S. colleges and universities concluded that only 7 percent of institutions of higher learning offer complete accessibility for students with orthopedic disabilities. Complete accessibility in this study meant structural accessibility (e.g., ramps and automatic doors for all buildings on campus, reserved parking, wheelchair accessibility to all campus rooms), academic accessibility (e.g., note takers, time extensions for tests), accessibility of dorm living (e.g., wheelchair accessible dorm rooms, laundry facilities, on-campus repair of mobility equipment, and help in arranging personal care attendants), and availability of recreational opportunities (e.g., availability of on-campus wheelchair sporting activities).

Concluding Thoughts

Students with disabilities are a diverse group of individuals with diverse needs. They often arrive at college with diverse perceptions of their disability as well as the disabilities of others. In this sense, it is important for teachers to realize that disability is another way that our students can differ from one another.

As teachers, we want to accurately measure what our students have learned and not what the impact of their disability might be on what they have learned. Providing a reasonable accommodation for students with disabilities, which is largely a Western conception (Devlieger, 1995), enables teachers to have a better picture of these students' genuine academic abilities. However, for teachers to truly understand what a reasonable accommodation is, they must discuss disabilities with students, and this strategy may sometimes require teachers to consider cultural issues.

Teachers who are unsure about what kinds of accommodations they should provide to their students with disabilities should ask these students questions about what kind of accommodations have worked for them in the past to facilitate their learning. In U.S. colleges and universities, the students with disabilities office provides medical documentation of disabilities and suggestions for how teachers can make reasonable accommodations in their classrooms for students with disabilities. It is always a good practice for teachers to get documentation of the disability before any accommodations are made. If teachers feel uncomfortable with the recommended accommodations, they should discuss the matter with a representative from this office or talk with their departmental chair or other knowledgeable colleagues about the situation. Most of the time, common sense and understanding will prevail, and reasonable solutions can be worked out to everyone's—the student, the teacher, and the institution—satisfaction.

References

Al-Oraibi, S. (2010, April 27). People with disabilities and social life in Jordan. *Disabled World* (Editorial). Retrieved from http://www.disabled-world.com/editorials/disability-jordan.php

Anzaldua, G. (1987). *Borderlands/La frontera: The mestiza.* San Francisco, CA: Aunt Lute Books.

Barnartt, S. (1992). Disability policy issues in developing countries. *Journal of Disability Policy Studies, 3,* 45–65.

Barton, L., & Armstrong, F. (2001). Disability, education and inclusion. In G. Albrecht, K. Seelman, & M. Bury (Eds.), *Handbook of disability studies* (pp. 693–710). Thousand Oaks, CA: Sage.

Boyd, D. R. (2008). Teaching students with disabilities: A proactive approach. In B. Perlman, L. McCann, & S. McFadden (Eds.), *Lessons learned: Vol. 3. Practical advice for the teaching of psychology* (pp. 99–108). Washington, DC: Association for Psychological Science.

Denhart, H. (2008). Deconstructing barriers: Perceptions of students labeled with learning disabilities in higher education. *Journal of Learning Disabilities, 41,* 483–497. Available from Education Module, http://journaloflearningdisabilities .sagepub.com

Devlieger, P. (1995). Why disabled? The cultural understanding of physical disability in an African society. In B. Ingstad & S. Reynolds Whyte (Eds.), *Disability and culture* (pp. 94–106). Berkeley, CA: University of California Press.

European Agency for Development in Special Needs Education. (2009). *Disability and higher education in Switzerland.* Retrieved from http://www.european-agency.org/agency-projects/heag/country-pages/switzerland/disability-and-higher-education

Farmer, J., & Morse, S. (2007). Project Magnify: Increasing reading skills in students with low vision. *Journal of Visual Impairment and Blindness, 101,* 763–769.

Fichten, C., Asuncion, J., Barile, M., Ferraro, V., & Wolforth, J. (2009). Accessibility of e-learning and computer information technologies for students with visual impairments in postsecondary education. *Journal of Visual Impairment and Blindness, 103,* 543–558.

Groce, N. E. (1985). *Everyone here spoke sign language: Hereditary deafness on Martha's Vineyard.* Cambridge, MA: Harvard University Press.

Grossman, P. (2001). Making accommodations: The legal world of students with disabilities. *87 Academe: Bulletin of the American Association of University Professors, November–December,* 41–46. Retrieved from http://www.aaup.org/AAUP/pubsres/academe/2001/ND/Feat/gross.htm

Hardman, M., Drew, C., & Egan, W. (2011). *Human exceptionality.* Belmont, CA: Wadsworth/Cengage.

International Disability Rights Monitor. (2005). *Regional Report of Asia.* Washington DC: International Disability Network/Center for International Rehabilitation. Available from http://www.idrmnet.org/content.cfm?id=5E5A75&m=3

International Disability Rights Monitor. (2007). *Regional Report of Europe.* Washington D.C.: International Disability Network/Center for International Rehabilitation. Available from http://www.idrmnet.org/content.cfm?id=5E5A75&m=3

Johnson, D. E. (2006). Students with disabilities. In W. Buskist & S. F. Davis (Eds.), *Handbook of the teaching of psychology* (pp. 153–158). Malden, MA: Blackwell.

Leigh, I. (2009). *A lens on deaf identities.* Oxford, UK: Oxford University Press.

Leigh, I., & Brice, P. (2003). The visible and invisible. In J. Robinson & L. James (Eds.), *Diversity in human interactions* (pp. 175–194). New York, NY: Oxford University Press.

Lindstrom, J. (2007). Determining appropriate accommodations for postsecondary students with reading and written expression disorders. *Learning Disabilities Research and Practice, 22,* 229–236.

Liu, G. Z. (2005). Best practices: Developing cross-cultural competence from a Chinese perspective. In J. Stone (Ed.), *Culture and disability: Providing culturally competent services* (pp. 65–86). Thousand Oaks, CA: Sage.

McCurdy, D., Spradley, J., & Shandy, D. (2005). *The cultural experience: Ethnography in complex society* (2nd ed.). Long Grove, IL: Waveland Press.

Monk, J., & Frankenberg, M. (1995). Being ill and being me: Self, body, and time in multiple sclerosis narratives. In B. Ingstad & S. R. Whyte (Eds.), *Disability and culture* (pp. 107–134). Berkeley, CA: University of California Press.

Nagata, K., (2008). Disability and development: Is the rights model of disability valid in the Arab region? An evidence-based field survey in Lebanon and Jordan. *Asia Pacific Disability Rehabilitation Journal, 19*, 60–78. Retrieved from http://www.aifo.it/english/resources/online/apdrj/apdrj108/diability_lebanon_jordan.pdf

Ofiesh, N., & Hughes, C. (2002). How much time? A review of the literature on extended test time for postsecondary students with learning disabilities. *Journal of Postsecondary Education and Disability, 16*, 2–16.

Ofiesh, N., Mather, N., & Russell, A. (2005). Using speeded cognitive reading, and academic measures to determine the need for extended test time among university students with learning disabilities. *Journal of Psychoeducational Assessment, 23*, 35–52.

Organisation for Economic Co-operation and Development (OECD). (2003). *Disability in higher education.* Paris, France: OECD Publications.

Placidway. (2010). Jordan encourages education and rehabilitation for disabled. *Disabled World.* Retrieved from http://www.disabled-world.com/news/africa/jordan.php

Rembis, M. (2010). Yes we can change: Disability studies—Enabling equality. *Journal of Postsecondary Education and Disability, 23*, 19–26.

Rutherford, K. (2007). Jordan and disability rights: A pioneering leader in the Arab world. *Review of Disability Studies: An International Journal, 3*, 23–36.

Santana-Martin, S., & Santana F. (2005). An introduction to Mexican culture for service providers. In J. Stone (Ed), *Culture and disability: Providing culturally competent services* (pp. 161–186). Thousand Oaks, CA: Sage.

Singh, D. (2003). Students with disabilities and higher education. *College Student Journal, 37*, 367–379.

St. Clair, K. L., & Groccia, J. E. (2009). Change to social justice education: Higher education strategy. In K. Skubikowski, C. Wright, & R. Graf (Eds.), *Social justice education: Inviting faculty to transform their institutions* (pp. 70–84). Sterling, VA: Stylus.

Thompson, A., Bethea, L., & Turner, J. (1997). Faculty knowledge of disability law in higher education: A survey. *Rehabilitation Counseling Bulletin, 40*(3), 166–181.

U.S. Department of Education, National Center for Education Statistics. (2006). *Profile of undergraduates in U.S. postsecondary education institutions: 2003–04* (NCES 2006–184). Washington, DC: U.S. Department of Education. Retrieved from http://nces.ed.gov/fastfacts/display.asp?id=60

U.S. Department of State, Bureau of Public Affairs, Electronic Information and Publications. Background Note: Jordan (March 21, 2011). Retrieved from http://www.state.gov/r/pa/ei/bgn/3464.htm

Van Maastricht, S. (1998). Work, opportunity and culture: (In)competence in Greece and Wales. In R. Jenkins (Ed.), *Questions of competence: Culture, classification and intellectual disability* (pp. 125–152). New York, NY: Cambridge University Press.

PART IV

Understanding Teachers

CHAPTER 8

Developing Faculty for the 21st Century in South Africa

Building Capacity Through Collaborative Preparation Programs

Stacey C. Nickson

Ian Scott succinctly establishes the argument for systemic reform in the curricular framework of higher education in South Africa:

> The need to address the shortcomings and inequalities of South Africa's primary and secondary schools is not in dispute; but the question is whether higher education can and should make a substantial contribution toward a solution through its own curricula and practices ... The central challenge is to enable talented students from very different educational backgrounds, with very different levels of preparedness, to realize their potential ... In the interests of equity and growth in high-skills areas, we must recruit students with good potential from all sectors of the population into all categories of institutions, as long as their potential is consistent with the demands of the programs in question. (Scott, 2010, p. 240)

However, my recent research interviewing a number of faculty members, administrators, and faculty developers at the University of Stellenbosch and the University of Cape Town during the summer of 2010 suggests that a broader view and approach to higher education reform needs to be developed.

Central to the success of students within the South African higher education system is the quality of teaching and teachers that students depend on to maximize their academic success. The need for an expanded pool of professorial candidates, qualified to meet the instructional needs of academia, specifically in South African universities is paramount. The expansion of higher education in postapartheid South Africa, coupled with the aging (and emigrating) professoriate has created a severe shortage deemed to have "reached crisis proportions" (Lindow, 2009, p. 1). In addition, private sector competition for these high quality recruits to support the country's economic development has exacerbated an already difficult situation. Although academia accommodates a stratified employment system including master's degree level "lecturers," the prestige of the South African academic profession in an international context (in both teaching and research) relies on the significant presence of graduates with doctoral degrees (Wolhuter, Higgs, Higgs, & Ntshoe, 2010). As such, the preparation strategies discussed in this chapter assume the end goal of developing doctoral level faculty to support and sustain the quality of South Africa's 23 tertiary universities.

The current dearth of professors available to meet the expanded needs of higher education in South Africa has its roots in numerous complex issues. This chapter focuses on providing answers to the following questions: What is the status and impact of the lack of professors in South Africa and the relationship to graduation throughput statistics? What is the assessment of recent trends in producing doctorates in South Africa including challenges and solutions? How do higher education national expectations/government objectives and economic development trends relate to issues of equity, social justice, and mobility? How can programs deliberately promoting professional socialization support the preparation of future academics? What is the role of systemic curricular reform in raising the level of graduate output to support the well-being of the nation? And what are the characteristics of collaborative postgraduate and preparation programs that build capacity for the development of future faculty in South Africa?

Shortage of Professors and Qualification (Graduation) Rates

According to Megan Lindow (2009), South African estimates include the need for 6,000 new PhDs per year. Half of South Africa's research output is produced by scientists older than 50 (Mouton, 2007), supporting concerns for the nation's ability to produce new knowledge, supervise and mentor young scholars, and staff tertiary universities. Lindow (2009) contends, "With a raft of professors in their 60s and about to retire . . . the dearth of qualified academics has reached crisis proportions at a number of African universities" (p. 1). A survey of vacant posts for professors and lecturers revealed 372 total combined vacancies at the Universities of Johannesburg, Pretoria, and Cape Town during one academic year (Govender, 2008).

Emigration also contributes to the professorial shortage. The United States and Europe compete for South African academics by offering expanded opportunities for teaching and research in addition to enhanced salaries (Higher Education in Sub-Saharan Africa, 2010). The commonly reported "brain drain" has significantly affected the teaching profession according to Jonathan D. Jansen (2010): "The largest percentage of expatriate teachers from Commonwealth countries in the United Kingdom comes from South Africa" (p. 134).

The expansion of higher education in South Africa, a significant national goal, has contributed to this shortage. In 1990, 395,700 students were enrolled in higher education. By 2005, this number had increased almost twofold to 732,000 (Lange, 2007). According to Pierre de Villiers and Gert Steyn (2009), the change in ratios of staff and student numbers between 1986 and 2003 indicates full-time equivalent (FTE) students at technikons (technical universities) increased 345 percent whereas FTE instructor/ researcher staff increased only 129 percent. This trend was consistent with university ratios where FTE students increased 96 percent whereas FTE instructors/researchers increased only 31 percent. In 2004, these numbers were affected further when the number of tertiary schools was reduced from 36 to 23 by government-mandated mergers resulting in a reduction of teachers but not an equivalent reduction of students (de Villiers & Steyn, 2009).

Although access is an ongoing focus of the postapartheid South African constitution, governmental policymakers and institutions of higher education, changes in throughput (graduation) rates, and the conditions surrounding them are an emphasis of current concern, especially regarding postgraduate degree completion (necessary to qualify for work in academia). The ratios of degrees awarded per FTE staff increased in every sector between 1986 and 2003 (de Villiers & Steyn, 2009). This trend held true for technikons, undergraduate university qualifications, and master's and doctoral degrees. However, national undergraduate cohort data (2000–2004) indicated only a 50 percent graduation rate for traditional universities (those whose primary activity is conducted in a classroom with teachers and students present and not online) and an overall rate of 30 percent for all higher education institutions, including technikons and online (which comprise 32 percent of total cohort enrollments) (Scott, Yeld, & Hendry, 2007). The increased ratios of students to teachers raises a number of questions: Have larger class sizes impeded teacher' ability to offer the highest quality instruction? Are students able to get the necessary additional academic support to enhance their success? Are overall graduation rates indicative of an imbalance between the preparedness of the influx of new students and the curricula reform required to accommodate them? These questions require additional research and data.

Even though the number of doctoral degrees awarded nearly doubled between 1986 and 2003, from 524 to 1,024 (de Villiers & Steyn, 2009), South Africa has since produced an average of 1,000 doctoral graduates annually (Mouton, 2007). This plateau in the growth of doctoral degrees awarded is of significant concern, given the anticipated need of the higher education sector. As the qualification data are disaggregated, implications for national development, equity, and social justice paint a bleaker picture than the numbers suggests.

National Expectations

The Department of Education (DoE) Annual Report (2009/10) offered a statement of priorities that read in part, "The strategic objectives and associated plans are based on the ministry's commitment to support the core work of higher education, i.e., teaching and learning as well as research and community service, via quality improvement of the higher education system, as well as enhanced efficiency and effectiveness" (p. 129). This document identifies three strategic objectives:

- The internationalization of higher education
- The strengthening of planning to support production of quality graduates, required for the social and economic development of the country
- The achievement of institutional diversity

Even partial realization of these priorities and objectives evoke challenges on many fronts. The statement of priorities offers support of the undeniable, traditional "core work of higher education," as the goals of "efficiency and effectiveness" elicit comparisons with business models, especially when combined with objectives of "internationalisation and globalisation." The consistent "production of quality graduates" is deemed by many to be at odds with "institutional diversity," including the diversity of faculty and students (DoE, 2009/10, p. 129). These views reflect concerns of governmental pressure (political and funding structures) to extend access to underprepared students and graduate them. In the face of increased class sizes and lack of support for systemic curricular reform necessary to alter national qualifications structures, teaching approaches and institutional schemes to accommodate the majority population, the task is daunting. The interpretation, application, and achievement of these priorities and objectives can have a decided impact on the preparation of future faculty.

Johann Mouton (2007) argues the DoE has infused the terms *efficiency* and *effectiveness* into its documents as an accusation of higher education's inefficiency in graduating more doctoral students and ineffectiveness in stemming undergraduate dropout rates. Mouton further asserts the country's National Research Foundation (NRF) continued the promotion of "the myth" of higher education's inefficiency in its 2007 business plan. However, Mouton finds the doctoral production rate too low for the needs of South Africa and warns that framing the failures in terms of a business model of efficiency and effectiveness detracts from the real issue: the number and quality of South African doctoral students. Finally, Mouton suggests a number of proposals, including "a national doctoral or post-graduate academy to provide prospective doctoral candidates with a better foundation in research methodology and thesis management and also provide high-quality seminars and workshops to build the capacity of our supervisors" (p. 1090).

Economic Development Trends

C. C. Wolhuter, P. Higgs, L. G. Higgs, and I. Ntshoe (2010) document economic growth worldwide. Between 1995 and 2006, there was a 50 percent economic output increase, a 57 percent increase in international trade, and average growth in gross domestic product (GDP) right at 3 percent. These economic trends helped prompt a 50 percent enrollment increase in tertiary education. Fifty years of research (Wolhuter et al., 2010) indicate that higher education is valuable to individuals, societies, and economic growth, leading to increased investment in education and research. Wolhuter et al. (2010) state that South Africa's economic growth between 1990 and 2006 included increases in GDP of 3.1 percent, and 50 percent growth in university enrollment. However, unlike the worldwide trend, South Africa's student–instructor ratio declined and the 15 percent gross tertiary enrollment ratio (the numbers enrolled in higher education compared with a segment of the population) in 2006 placed the country in a less favorable position than comparable upper-middle income countries (2005 figures included Brazil and Mexico, 24 percent, and Malaysia, 32 percent). Wolhuter et al. (2010) further pointed to results of the Changing Academic Profession (CAP) survey that indicate professorial activities (patents, publishing articles or book chapters in a foreign country, authoring or coauthoring books) less than international norms.

South Africa lags behind comparable countries in the number of university graduates who are needed to produce needed technological and economic growth (Wolhuter et al., 2010). With South Africa producing only 700 engineers annually, well under the estimated need of 11,000 per annum, growth in technology manufacturing and other high tech sectors is increasingly difficult. Further, science and engineering doctoral graduates are 0.05 percent of the population aged 24 to 34; by comparison, European Union countries are 0.42 percent and Sweden is 1.24 percent of the same aged population (Wolhuter et al., 2010). These numbers may have implications for South Africa's diminished capacity to keep pace with similar countries in economic growth unless increases in the throughput of quality university graduates occur.

Equity and Social Justice

National expectations in general and economic development trends specifically highlight South Africa's current higher education needs. Scott (2010) recognizes the nation's well-being depends on graduate output; however, higher education must function beyond just to satisfy the needs of the South African economy. Scott suggests a threefold rationale for equity in higher education. First, the use of diversity enhances student learning and preparation for society. Second, the participation of all population groups is good for the country's maintenance of an educated and well-functioning populace. And third, South Africa's stability, both socially and politically, is enhanced through inclusive higher education. Scott views the successful addressing of tensions between equity and development as promoting a prosperous, socially just, and stable South African democracy.

The South African National Qualifications Framework (NQF) is an eight level education system with NQF Level 4 commencing after Grade 12 and NQF Level 8 reflecting the highest postgraduate, masters, and doctoral degrees. Although significant changes have occurred in the higher education system postapartheid, Scott (2010) describes the informal NQF stratification as characterized by considerable diversity in history and mission. Vocational training, academic education, disparate resources, and long-standing student intake profiles (aligned with race and class) continue to serve as trademarks of the status quo. In fact, South African's qualification system was adopted from one developed in Scotland almost 100 years earlier. The 3-year academic bachelor's degrees and national diplomas and 4-year professional bachelor's degrees have a highly structured curriculum of prescribed subjects and requisite specialization near the onset of the program. Scott suggests the system's structure has significant impact on student success (or lack of), including the advantage afforded those committing to their future careers during high school.

Participation Equity and Outcome Equity

The apartheid government made race a central feature of every aspect of life, from the workplace to the ballot box, the bedroom to the schoolroom. In framing the Bill of Rights in the aftermath of apartheid, South Africans felt the urgent need to advance whole groups toward equality. The South African constitution guarantees all individual citizens "the full and equal enjoyment of all equal rights and freedoms" and asserts that to achieve equality, "legislative and other measures designed to protect or advance persons, or categories of persons, disadvantaged by unfair discrimination may be taken" (Cantor & Thomas, 2010, pp. 111–112).

However, as reflective data are disaggregated, these goals are far from achieved. Ian Scott, Nanette Yeld, and Jane Hendry (2007) find participation rates informative for educational policy, though not indicative of higher education's success in promoting student learning or graduation. As gross participation rates of the four recognized racial groups reported for 2005 indicate, South Africa's overall participation rate is low for countries of comparable economic development. Despite the massive expansion of black participation in higher education, data indicate enrollment and gross participation ratios similar to those during the apartheid era: for the 20–24 age group, 60 percent of whites, 51 percent of Indians, 12 percent of coloureds (*coloured* is not a derogatory term in South Africa or other countries of Southern Africa; the coloureds, although with different mixtures—Khoisan, Bantu, Malay, and European—have developed into a distinct ethnic group that self-identifies even postapartheid), and 12 percent of blacks were enrolled in higher education (Scott et al., 2007). The low participation rates of the majority populations (black and coloured) raise numerous concerns according to Scott et al. (2007), including the system's inability to include an equitable proportion of the majority population and the implications this has on skill shortages and national development. In addition, the underrepresentation of blacks in science and economics is not aligned with national needs and goals.

According to Scott et al. (2007) available outcome equity data, assessed after a 5-year student enrollment period, based on the Classification of Educational Subject Matter (CESM) degree categories found that in tertiary programs, black student graduation rates were consistently half those of white students, regardless of CESM. In programs where black students' enrollment outnumbered that of white students, the actual number of white graduates exceeded black graduates. Tertiary technikon programs yielded the least successful numbers overall with a graduation rate (within 5 years of enrollment) of 32 percent compared with a graduation rate of 50 percent for other tertiary universities. However, these programs have significantly higher black student populations, so the lower completion rates indicated higher numbers of black students not completing programs as compared with other tertiary programs. Conclusions based on the equity of outcomes analysis were that South Africa's higher education system is not able to provide high-skill graduates to match its developmental goals, and furthermore, the stated social goals of redress and inclusion are not being met by any sector of higher education given the 12 percent participation rate of the majority population and high levels of attrition.

Social Mobility

South Africa's primary and secondary school system is the significant obstacle to greater participation rates in higher education by the majority population (Jansen, 2010). Jansen finds the school system unable to qualify significant numbers of black students for higher education, with only 50 percent of all students graduating from high school and only 16 percent of those qualifying for university entrance. As such, Jansen notes the "limits of higher education as a gateway for social mobility" (p. 129), especially for the black majority. Jansen does, however, identify what he terms *pull-in* factors that create an avenue for higher education to serve as a means of social mobility and conflicting *push-out* factors that limit higher education as an avenue for social mobility. Jansen's first pull-in factor is financial aid. The development of the National Financial Aid Scheme, combined with institutional and private sector financial aid and loans allows students to select the discipline of their choice (under apartheid, blacks were limited to state selected public service–oriented degree programs) and offers greater financial support than previously available. The second pull-in factor is the competition among universities to increase enrollments (for state funding eligibility) and diversify. Top-tier former white universities are now desegregated, admitting middle-class blacks with strong academic records. Other lower-tier universities, including historically black universities, are left to compete for lower-achieving students, some only qualifying with special exceptions. Jansen sees this as widening access but weakening the university talent base. The third pull-in factor is the response from institutions to government mandates and incentives (both financial and special programs) to provide access to black students and increase their overall numbers (both undergraduate and graduate) especially in the math, science, and engineering fields.

Jansen's push-out factors limit both access and social mobility associated with higher education. The first push-out factor is the high university drop-out rate, prompted by poor academic preparation in high school. Jansen faults careless admission policies that set the stage for likely failure when admitting students without the academic background to compete at the college level. The second push-out factor is financial because university education is cost prohibitive even with financial aid. This, combined with loss of potential income (often needed to support their families) during the college years, increases the likelihood poor black students will bypass the opportunity to attend university or drop out during the early stages of their University programs. The third push-out factor is one of accommodation: Universities are often unprepared to meet the needs of nontraditional students though they come from the majority population. Barriers at former white, and sometimes Afrikaner, universities include language (academic English or Afrikaans), culture, poverty, socialization, institutional environment and technology access, and skills, among others.

Production of Doctorates

Mouton (2007) assessed data provided by the South African DoE on the production of doctorates between 2000 and 2005. Some trends noted were the following:

- Doctoral enrollments grew 50 percent, from 6,000 to 9,000, but graduation rates grew by just under 20 percent.
- Women doctoral graduates represented the highest growth rate and will equal the number of male graduates in less than 5 years.

- Black doctoral graduates grew at a faster pace than did whites doctoral graduates and will equal the number of whites in less than 5 years.
- Doctorates in natural and social sciences have grown the fastest.
- Doctorates earned in the arts and humanities have declined the most.
- Health and engineering science doctorates have remained the same.
- Three fourths of all doctorates are granted by six universities.
- 77 percent of doctoral candidates complete their degree within 4.7 years.

Mouton notes, "The real problem and challenge in South Africa is that we have too few doctoral students in the system" (2007, p. 1088). Mouton suggests a number of systemic issues associated with the insufficient numbers of doctoral degrees that would benefit from increased national and institutional support and commitment. These include doctoral supervisors with untenable workloads and lacking experience, inadequate research preparation for doctoral students, lack of financial support for doctoral students from South Africa and individual institutions, and the need for more dedicated resources to support postgraduate students and programs. Mouton offers suggestions to alleviate these challenges:

- Increased financial support of well-managed PhD programs in attracting doctoral candidates
- More utilization of innovative and structured career planning as a part of institutional support system
- Increased funding from the NRF to support full-time doctoral students
- Creation of a national academy for doctoral and postgraduate students to enhance research skills

South Africa is estimated to need more than 6,000 doctorates per year to meet national demand. Systemic analysis, nationally funded responses, and institutional commitment are essential components in meeting this challenge. In addition, recognition of and attention to redressing deficiencies in areas of affective support and motivation to pursue higher education opportunities are also necessary to undergird critical needs of graduate students and enhance the possibility they will choose and commit to a career in academia.

Professional Socialization

The richness of faculty talent should be celebrated, not restricted. Only as the distinctiveness of each professor is affirmed will the potential of scholarship be fully realized (Boyer, 1990, p. 27). The South African DoE (2009/2010) has identified higher education as a support system for societal transformation as it bolsters the intellect, skills, and aptitude of individuals. Further, the DoE promotes higher education as a means to develop citizens for the labor market and to create and disseminate information though academic scholarship. Given these expectations and the documented shortage of scholars to help meet them, the development of future faculty to serve the South African population is imperative.

Becoming a successfully socialized member of a profession requires the opportunity to observe, interact, and learn from the members of that profession. A socialized academic must acquire knowledge of the discipline and be imbued with the values, behaviors, and beliefs of the professoriate. J. J. Cornelissen and A. S. van Wyk (2007) describe a process of professional socialization that when applied to academia, allows for an understanding of the steps to the professoriate. Combining the "distinctiveness" referred to by Ernest L. Boyer with the characteristics, knowledge, and skills required of faculty supports the need to develop the identity associated with the profession. Cornelissen and van Wyk identify "states of identity and commitment which overlap" and develop in a nonlinear manner (p. 828). However, within South African higher education, the structured academic program requires that graduate students make an early professional commitment. Therefore, the process of professional socialization concerning academia must be understood and transmitted early to potential faculty to enhance opportunities to identify with and internalize the values and behaviors of the professoriate. This includes anticipatory professional socialization, formal professional socialization, and their core elements (Cornelissen & van Wyk, 2007). Most future faculty in South Africa will likely be introduced to the profession via recruitment into specially designed, structured programs, where the opportunity to respond to anticipated stereotypes, expectations, and preconceived notions of the profession can be addressed. According to Cornelissen and van Wyk (2007), this can be a time for the program to gather information regarding the participants' "attitudes, aspirations, orientation and goals" (p. 829) to prepare them for the formal process of professional socialization. Opportunities to interact at this stage may be designed to occur near the onset of the academic career, perhaps as early as the second year of the 3-year bachelor's degree program.

The formal professional socialization process is a period of both identity formation and the development of the insider's perspective. The program should give students the opportunity to engage in formal instruction from an academic practitioner. This is also the time when students engage in a social compact with their professional instructors to participate in the rewards (or punishments) that support the learning of professional competencies and the means by which mentors convey the norms and values of academia to support professional conformity. Cornelissen and van Wyk (2007) suggest that students engage in the core elements of professional socialization (knowledge acquisition, investment, and involvement) to internalize role acquisition, identification, and commitment. Knowledge acquisition involves developing performance skills, affective knowledge (i.e., norms and expectations, awareness of ability to perform, and a sense others share that awareness), specialized knowledge, the characteristics of the profession, and their ability to participate in the social culture. The program participant would display an understanding of the performance tasks of the profession and the beginning development of the professional identity as an academic and would begin to display understanding of a commitment to the profession as an investment. As the nation's investment in the academic profession raises its profile and social status, individual investment of time and career commitment is enhanced.

The final core element of professional socialization is involvement (Cornelissen & van Wyk, 2007). Any program to prepare future faculty must offer significant opportunities for involvement to maximize effectiveness. Involvement allows participants to transform their self-identification from student to future faculty member. This transformation occurs through status identification, commitment, and attraction. Status identification involves the assumption of a professorial self-image based on knowledge, behaviors, values, and sense of competence that align with academia. A structured program to prepare future faculty offers the opportunity for commitment through continuous and repeated practice of various aspects of the role. As program participants are involved in the profession, self-identify, and are recognized by others as qualified "initiates," a sense of attraction occurs, from which they develop personal and sentimental ties to their chosen profession. As the core elements are interrelated and interdependent, an effective program recognizes and supports them as key to successful professional socialization.

Systemic Curriculum Reform

Despite major changes in student intake, particularly regarding their linguistic and educational backgrounds, the South African higher education system is still dominated by curriculum structures and teaching approaches that were established decades ago, for a very different and largely homogeneous student body.

Despite blacks occupying 60 percent of enrollment spaces, graduation rates are so low that they impede South Africa's quest to maintain its desired level of economic development and sociopolitical stability. Scott (2010) builds a case that South Africa's unique situation as a developed country with an embedded higher education system designed to serve the minority, is now faced with the task of using this established system to serve the majority population. For two decades, academic development (AD) programs have been developed and used to promote equity. These programs, according to Scott, have been successful, but their limited use has allowed them to affect only 10 percent of the students enrolled in higher education.

AD programs have been used in a variety of ways. In admissions, polices have been altered to accommodate the use of alternative performance measures to determine a student's potential for success. Extended programs allow students 4 years to complete the traditional 3-year degree program. High potential, underprepared students have the opportunity to engage in foundational courses to build academic capacity and promote success. Recognizing the diverse educational, linguistic, and cultural backgrounds of the majority student population, Scott finds the expansion of alternative curricula critical to promoting desired national outcomes. Scott calls for a reconceptualization of the mainstream and establishing a 4-year degree to promote inclusion and success for all.

As the nation invests in the development of future faculty to meet the needs of government, higher education institutions, and the private sector, a focus on systemic curriculum reform would enable an efficient use of resources dedicated to innovation. The training of future faculty inclusive of alternative curricula could have multiple effects. As higher education is viewed as responding to the needs of the country by accommodating diversity and inclusion, a career in academia would be seen as an opportunity to serve as a catalyst for change. As academic positions become occupied by scholars well informed in their disciplines and capable of high level research and able to use pedagogical skills proven effective in promoting the success of all students, equity of outcome should improve.

Postgraduate Preparation Programs

Although the majority of resources and attention have been rightfully directed toward undergraduate education, the role of postgraduate education in meeting the needs of the development of South Africa's economy and citizens has been documented, as reported previously in this chapter. According to Mouton (2007), "The state of postgraduate studies in South Africa has come under scrutiny in recent years . . . the slow growth in master's and especially doctoral graduates and so on are much more prevalent nowadays than even five years ago" (p. 1078).

A number of programs and initiatives have been established to train PhDs on the African continent (Lindow, 2009). Although their success in producing quality graduates is well documented, none are able to reach the scale that would support the numbers of graduates needed to meet demand. Most of the programs have been funded by private foundations with support from foreign governments, higher education institutions from around the world, and as possible, the governments of the countries served. Founded in 1996, the University Science, Humanities & Engineering Partnerships in Africa (USHEPiA) has served as one such model (Lindow, 2009). Funded by the Mellon Foundation and the Carnegie Corporation, the program produces graduates that serve African universities well. However, USHEPiA has produced only 41 graduates since its inception. The cost (around $100,000) and time of training a PhD has made "the scaling up" of this program difficult without significant financial support from other sources. The Regional

Initiative in Science Education (RISE) is another program whose aim is to expand the number of African doctoral and master's degree holders in science and engineering. Funded by the Carnegie Corporation (2010), the program is administered through a collaboration of the Science Initiative Group (Princeton University) and the African Academy of Sciences in Kenya.

Lindow (2009) also reports on a number of other models attempting to increase the output of PhDs. One such model finds universities from throughout the continent and pools their resources to allow postgraduate students to collaborate on research. Another model selects a location with existing expertise and brings students together from the same geographic area where foreign faculty are brought in for intensive sessions to assist with the presentation of content. The African Institute for Mathematical Sciences in South Africa uses this model for postgraduate training. One of the most ambitious programs is the African Institutes of Science and Technology (AIST), which proposes establishing three campuses (including South Africa) to train 5,000 scientists and engineers annually (Higher Education in Sub-Saharan Africa, 2010). Each campus will require more than $1 billion in start-up costs and endowment for future expenses. Distance learning is yet another model that allows students access to expert supervisors not in the students' locations and resources from libraries and centers at other institutions. Finally, there are models, referred to as "sandwich degrees" that bring students to the United States (or other Western nations) where part of their training takes place before being completed in their home country.

Although all of these programs support postgraduate training for the purpose of advanced degree completion, none offers a comprehensive program specifically to prepare future faculty. A number of universities in South Africa do offer support programs for PhD students in recognition of their need for assistance with research and other academic skills, but most of these come in the form of one- or two-day retreats, conferences, or workshops limited in scope.

Preparing Future Faculty Program

The Preparing Future Faculty (PFF) program (2002), begun in the United States in 1993 as a collaboration between the American Association of Colleges and Universities, the Council of Graduate Schools, and the Pew Charitable Trusts (Goldsmith, Haviland, Dailey, & Wiley, 2004), could serve as a model for South Africa for professional socialization into the professoriate.

PFF is designed to address the need for an alternative to the research apprenticeship model used in graduate education and to meet broader societal demands such as the growth and diversity of academia. Through a process of self-selection (some programs require advisor approval), graduate students are able to apply to most PFF programs based on their desire to understand and experience what it means to be an academic. PFF offers graduate students an opportunity to explore academic careers and the various higher education institutions (traditional universities, technikons, and comprehensive universities). Through PFF, graduate students learn about the roles and responsibilities of faculty, have an opportunity to network at the institution in which they are enrolled and, importantly, at other types of institutions of higher education, gaining valuable social professionalization skills that may otherwise not be available. The PFF program can enhance students' graduate school experience by simultaneously addressing disciplinary skills and the professional teaching skills required for success in academia. This increased competency builds on self-efficacy and can increase the attraction of an academic career.

Though PFF programs strive to attain common goals and missions, they are flexible to meet host institution and student participant needs. There are generally six common characteristics: (1) courses, seminars, and workshops; (2) student-developed materials; (3) collaborative partnerships; (4) experiential activities; (5) opportunities to be mentored; and (6) contemporary issues (Goldsmith et al., 2004).

Courses, seminars, and workshops vary from semester-long credit-bearing classes to single or multiday seminars and workshops. Graduate certificates in college teaching are offered by some universities for completion of a series of courses and activities. Pedagogical issues, teaching techniques, professional development, and academic career information are some of the topic areas usually covered. Students are expected to develop portfolios, webpages, teaching philosophies, curriculum vitas, and course materials (lesson plans and presentation materials)—all displaying their research and teaching preparation and experience.

Collaborative partnerships offer opportunities for expanded experiences in diverse settings. These could include multi-institutional visitations, guest lecturing, and committee observations, thereby providing an opportunity for institutions to share faculty resources and expertise. Use of distance technology can enable these experiences to be wide ranging and regional or international in scope, depending on student and institution needs. Linked to this are experiential activities that offer practice teaching opportunities, mock interviews, committee service, opportunities to lead undergraduates in research projects, and so forth. These activities can take place on campus, at other local institutions, or internationally via technology.

Mentoring is another important element of a PFF program. Students can be given the opportunity to work with one or more faculty to learn to negotiate the professoriate as a career. It is also an opportunity to network and gain extensive professional socialization exposure. Exploration of contemporary issues can serve as an ideal opportunity to focus on national and institutional issues affecting higher education. Curriculum reform, diversity, technology, social, and any other issues affecting teaching and learning can find a forum in this open category.

Such a structured, career-oriented program could increase faculty numbers and help provide an inclusive body of faculty trained for the 21st century. The flexibility of PFF programs allows for designs that cater to the academic and societal needs of institutions in South Africa. PFF programs could operate in conjunction with South Africa's existing graduate initiatives (e.g., USHEPiA, RISE, AIST) adding a dimension to the preparation of doctoral students that would further enhance their quality and viability as academics. PFF programs can also be suitable for master's level students (both those in terminal masters programs and those intending to pursue doctorates while serving as undergraduate lecturers). Given there is a 6-to1 ratio of masters to doctoral students in South Africa (Mouton, 2007), the availability of PFF programs could substantially increase the eventual ranks of the professoriate. These approaches could potentially expand and diversify South Africa's pool of qualified academics.

As part of a comprehensive 3-year study of PFF, 963 PFF participants and 498 faculty and administrators associated with PFF programs were surveyed, gathering outcome data evaluating value and impact of the PFF program (Goldsmith et al., 2004). Findings most significant to this chapter included the following:

- 98 percent of participants would recommend PFF to other graduate students.
- 56 percent of participants cited PFF-offered opportunities to interact with students and faculty from diverse backgrounds and disciplines.
- 40 percent of participants reported receiving enhanced faculty mentoring.
- 12 percent of participants found PFF encouraged them to stay and complete their degree.
- 60 percent of participants thought PFF gave them the skills and confidence for a successful career in academia.
- 78 percent of faculty felt PFF participants would have more successful careers in academia than would nonparticipants.
- 88 percent of faculty stated PFF had improved graduate education at their institutions.
- 63 percent of faculty reported PFF changed the culture of graduate preparation for future faculty in their department.
- 76 percent of faculty found PFF made graduate students better classroom teachers.
- 63 percent of new tenure-track faculty that were PFF participants as graduate students stated PFF helped them secure their current faculty positions.

Many of the most critical issues regarding the growth of the professoriate as documented in this chapter could be addressed through the development and institutionalization of a PFF program, designed specifically for higher education in South Africa.

Funding is required to support any endeavor in higher education, so post-graduate training and the preparation of future faculty will require coordinated investment by various elements of the South African government (e.g., DoE, NRF), institutions of higher education, industry, and private foundations. International collaborations can also allow for a sharing of resources and expertise while supporting self-sufficiency and capacity building in South Africa.

Conclusion

Increasing the capacity to meet social, economic, intellectual, and political needs of South Africa is in great part a function of higher education. South Africa, as the most prosperous and successful country on the African continent, is a beacon for the nearly one billion inhabitants on its shores. As such, higher education in South Africa is critical for the continued growth and development of the entire African continent.

Increasing the graduation rates of the majority population (and the population in general) and meeting stated national needs and expectations for equity, social justice, and mobility can be linked to expanding the numbers, quality, and inclusivity of graduate degree holders and future faculty. A collaboratively developed and financed PFF initiative, with a national focus and local institutional control could contribute significantly to the higher education goals in South Africa. Sustaining and improving the most comprehensive network of higher education on the continent, and one of the premier higher education systems in the world, will require an investment of financial and social capital, national focus prioritization, and innovative programs to attract and produce an effective professoriate. Building capacity of faculty for the 21st century in South Africa is in the best interest of the country, the continent, and the international community.

References

Boyer, E. L. (1990). *Scholarship reconsidered: Priorities of the professoriate.* New York, NY: Carnegie Foundation for the Scholarship of Teaching and Learning.

Cantor, N., & Thomas, J. (2010). Affirmative action and higher education in the United States and South Africa. In D. L. Featherman, M. Hall & M. Krislov (Eds.) *The next 25 years: Affirmative action in the United States and South Africa* (pp. 111-112). Ann Arbor: University of Michigan Press.

Carnegie RISE. (2010, November 29). Regional initiative in science and education. Retrieved November 30, 2010, from http://www.arp.harvard.edu/AfricanHigher Education/Teaching.html

Cornelissen, J. J., & van Wyk, A. S. (2007). Professional socialization: An influence on professional development and role definition. *South African Journal of Higher Education, 21*, 826–841.

Department of Education (South Africa) Annual Report 2009/2010. Retrieved September 9, 2011, from http://www.education.gov.za/LinkClick.aspx?fileticke t=8mm2QuDyiuw%3D&tabid=358&mid=1263

De Villiers, A. P., & Steyn, A. G. W. (2009). Effect of changes in state funding of higher education on higher education output in South Africa: 1986–2007. *South African Journal of Higher Education, 23*, 43–68.

Goldsmith, S., Haviland, D., Dailey, K., & Wiley, A. (2004). *Preparing Future Faculty Initiative final evaluation report*. San Francisco, CA: WestEd Publishing.

Govender, P. (2008, November 21). South Africa: Skills shortage cripples universities. *Sunday Times*. Retrieved December 16, 2010, from http://www.universityworld news.com/article.php?story=2008112015620688

Higher education in Sub-Saharan Africa. Retrieved December 16, 2010, from http:// arp.harvard.edu/AfricanHigherEducation/Teaching.html

Jansen, J. D. (2010). Moving on up? The politics, problems, and prospects of universi- ties as gateways for social mobility in South Africa. In D. L. Featherman, M. Hall, & M. Krislov (Eds.), *The next 25 years: Affirmative action in the United States and South Africa* (pp. 129–136). Ann Arbor: University of Michigan Press.

Lange, L. (2007). Foreword. In I. Scott, N. Yeld, & J. Hendry, *A case for improving teaching and learning in South African higher education* (HE Monitor No. 6). Pretoria, South Africa: The Council on Higher Education.

Lindow, M. (2009, February 18). Africa's new crisis: A dearth of professors. *Chronicle of Higher Education*. Retrieved February 18, 2009, from http:// chronicle.com/article/Africa-s-New-Crisis-a-Dearth/2742

Mouton, J. (2007). Post-graduate studies in South Africa: Myths, misconceptions and challenges. *South African Journal of Higher Education, 21*, 1078–1090.

National Research Foundation. (2007, September). *The strategic plan of the National Research Foundation, National Research Foundation Vision 2015*. Retrieved December 1, 2010, from www.nrf.ac.za.

The Preparing Future Faculty Program. (2002). Retrieved December 17, 2010, from http://www.preparing-faculty.org

Scott, I. (2010). Who is "getting through" in South Africa? Graduate output and the reconstruction of the formal curriculum. In D. L. Featherman, M. Hall, & M. Krislov (Eds.), *The next 25 years: Affirmative action in the United States and South Africa* (pp. 229–243). Ann Arbor: University of Michigan Press.

Scott, I., Yeld, N., & Hendry, J. (2007). *A case for improving teaching and learning in South African higher education* (HE Monitor No. 6), Pretoria, South Africa: The Council on Higher Education.

Wolhuter, C. C., Higgs, P., Higgs, L. G., & Ntshoe, I. (2010). How affluent is the South African higher education sector and how strong is the South African aca- demic profession in the changing international academic landscape? *South African Journal of Higher Education, 24*, 196–210.

CHAPTER 9

Sustaining and Championing Teaching and Learning

In Good Times or Bad

Shelda Debowski, Lorraine Stefani, Margaret W. Cohen, and Angela Ho

A s universities put more focus on improving teaching and learning processes, outcomes, and strategies, the stakes have become higher for those working as academic, educational, and faculty developers. Universities are expecting increasing levels of performance, accountability, and strategic interaction from their academic development groups as competition for students escalates. Financial and policy shifts have influenced the environment in which teaching and learning operates, and by implication, the positioning of academic development. In some cases, the academic development center is seen as critical to the university's strategy, whereas in others, whole centers have been disbanded, based on the judgment that they have been of little value.

The Need for Academic Development ———

The first decade of the 21st century has seen a significant shift in the higher education teaching and learning context and related expectations of academics in promoting quality learning. The impacts of globalization have been far-reaching, with greater harmonization occurring across national boundaries, particularly in curriculum structures and design. National higher education systems have also become more cognizant of political and economic interventions that are being used by their international counterparts, demonstrating alacrity in adopting elements of those approaches if they are seen to be more effective or in tune with the current sociopolitical climate. The global financial crisis (GFC, 2008–2010) added additional urgency to the need to review the ways in which universities operate and to explore whether funding invested in university systems and structures is well spent. The ease of communication across national boundaries has also encouraged greater exchange of knowledge regarding university strategy and practice and increased opportunities to benchmark. At the same time, universities are facing considerable pressure from their stakeholders to achieve better educational outcomes and to more strongly influence educational practice across their universities.

A major focus of these debates relates to effectiveness and efficiencies in higher education teaching and learning. Education of students is a primary function of higher education institutions. Students who come to universities anticipate a quality education that will prepare them for their future roles and successful adaptation to their evolving world. They expect to be taught by teachers who are knowledgeable, passionate about their subject matter, and capable of designing and applying a quality learning experience. The Groccia model of teaching and learning (see Chapter 1, this volume) exemplifies the holistic experience that students anticipate when they enter a university setting. Unfortunately, many students find that expectations fall far short of reality, as they encounter variable teaching quality and in many cases, adjunct or casual teachers (academic staff employed on short-term, teaching-only contracts) who carry a large part of the teaching load.

Although students' consequent dismay may have been largely hidden in the past, there is increasing exposure as international ranking systems extend beyond research to consider the entire nature of university practice. The Times Higher Education World University Rankings, for example, have begun to influence the thinking of many universities regarding their reputation and issues that need to be addressed (see http://www.timeshigher education.co.uk/world-university-rankings/).

National assessments of student engagement are similarly promoting greater awareness of the comparative impact of institutional strategies. The National Survey of Student Engagement (NSSE) has been operating since 1998 in the United States, highlighting the importance of reviewing the ways in which students experience the learning environment. Key factors examined relate to the level of academic challenge, the degree to which students participate in active learning and collaborations with others, student interaction with teachers, the types of complementary learning activities that are generated, and the ways in which student needs are supported across the campus. (http://nsse.iub.edu/html/about.cfm). In Australia, the Australasian Survey of Student Engagement (AUSSE) explores similar issues to the NSSE across the university sector (http://ausse.acer.edu.au/).

Another public quality metric, the Course Experience Questionnaire (CEQ) designed for use in British and British-oriented educational systems measures the quality of students' educational experiences and satisfaction, and graduate outcomes. (See http://www.itl.usyd.edu.au/sceq/ for an example of how the CEQ is used in one university.). Although surveys such as the NSSE and CEQ remain somewhat contested (Hardy & Bryson, n.d.), particularly if used for competitive or funding purposes, they are helpful in exploring student learning experiences and outcomes. As students and potential students become more vocal and better informed when making choices about their educational options, universities around the world are taking these public metrics seriously.

As major agencies of change in universities, academic development centers can be critical forces for influencing these outcomes and ensuring the attainment of a high-quality educational experience. These centers operate in many different formats, with some solely supporting teaching and learning functions, whereas others also support additional areas of academic need, such as leadership development, organizational change, and in some cases, research development and academic career management (Debowski, 2010). For the purposes of this chapter, we will focus on the elements of academic development work that relate to teaching and learning and will use the term *TLC* to denote centers that support teaching and learning.

For some universities, the changing face of higher education has provided a positive and exciting opportunity for repositioning or consolidating the TLC as a critical hub for educational excellence. For other universities, it has created a political maelstrom where centers have been disbanded, restructured, or absorbed into larger entities (Chism, 2010; Schroeder, 2010). There has been recognition within the wider academic development community that TLCs may become "marginalized," "neutralized," or "on the fringes" of the core business of the university (Schroeder, 2010). Emerging evidence highlights the vulnerability of TLCs to being held accountable for the larger performance of their university educational practices. This raises an important question for those working in academic and faculty development: How can academic developers best position their centers to survive and thrive in these dynamic but uncertain times?

The International Context for Teaching and Learning

The 2010 Organisation for Economic Co-operation and Development (OECD) report of education investment and student participation in higher education highlights a changing dynamic in the international sector. As resources have become more limited, some nations have adapted their funding and priorities to push for tighter accountabilities and management of public funds whereas others have invested more heavily in their educational processes.

The United States of America

The vast array and number of higher education institutions in the United States have necessitated a range of organizational structures and practices. Unlike higher education institutions in the other nations discussed in this chapter, public universities, liberal arts colleges, and community colleges in the United States may be governed by state and in some cases, municipal authorities. Private institutions, on the other hand, do not report to a public government office but, instead, are responsible to a board of governors or trustees. The target student populations and the scope of educational activities vary considerably across these different forms of institution and have resulted in highly variable approaches to educational practice. The variations in governance and structural arrangements have also limited the scope of national initiatives or large-scale collaborations, which are often initiated by national organizations that attract participation from only similar institutions (e.g. public, research, or liberal arts). Sally Kuhlenschmidt (2011) analyzed the prevalence of TLCs in the 4,390 institutions of higher education in the United States that are in the data set of the Carnegie Foundation for the Advancement of Teaching. Her findings reveal that only 933 institutions, less than 22 percent, have TLCs. Although Kuhlenschmidt notes that some institutions support more than one TLC unit, the small overall percentage is a reflection of the different ways in which universities and colleges have organized their structures and activities and the varied requirements of regional accreditation bodies. Her data reveal that TLCs are more likely to be located in institutions "with a balance of arts and sciences versus professional degrees and some overlap between graduate and undergraduate programs" (p. 284).

In the United States, TLCs often reflect the character, history, and mission of the institution. Likewise, the work of each center reflects the teaching and learning needs of its academic programs. As the needs and resources of the institution demand, the center may also be responsible for technology integration, assessment, civic engagement, and leadership and organizational development. Mary Deane Sorcinelli, Anne E. Austin, Pamela L. Eddy, and Andrea L. Beach (2006) and Kay J. Gillespie, Douglas L. Robertson, and Associates (2010) compile the history, explain the context, and suggest a future vision of the growing place of academic development in the United States. As resources tighten and institutions reassess their priorities, TLCs in the United States are clarifying their institutional alignments and positioning themselves to reaffirm their value. An example of this is in the growing recognition of the need to focus more on leadership and organizational development (Schroeder, 2010). As the educational and economic landscape changes in the United States, those who work as academic developers look to two national organizations for support, mentoring, networking, and resources: the Professional and Organizational Development (POD) Network in Higher Education (see http://www.podnetwork.org) and the Historically Black Colleges and Universities Faculty Development Network (see http://www.hbcufdn.org/).

The immediate impacts of the GFC on higher education in the United States have (1) accentuated the funding differences among institutions that depend on federal and state government funding, tuition and private endowments, or profitability *and* (2) heightened within institutions the internal tensions that surround the work and define the context within which TLCs operate. Although greater accountability and diminished resources may direct unwanted attention, or elimination, to institutional units that do not generate tuition dollars and increase enrollments, administrators may look increasingly to centers for teaching and learning to support the initiatives and efforts that are designed to retain and graduate students and sustain institutional accreditations.

Tensions arise when administrative imperatives do not align with faculty expectations of the TLC. For example, although an institution's NSSE data may offer compelling messages about students' experiences and learning, those data may not be received well by faculty colleagues who prize the institution's research mission above its teaching mission. Even though greater numbers of faculty are being employed to teach on a part-time basis, their increased presence may be resented and a reminder that full-time faculty positions remain unfilled. When a hiring exception is approved for a full-time faculty position, approval may be to hire a nontenure-track colleague whose responsibilities only relate to teaching, and possibly, for specific teaching activities.

Additionally, higher education teachers are facing increasing expectations regarding the ways they engage with their students—through face-to-face and virtual, online learning settings—and escalating requirements for quality teaching that can meet resistance from some faculty members. These tensions between institutional imperatives and collegial understandings are examples of the challenges that academic developers in the United States are experiencing.

Australia

Australia has only 39 institutions with university status and many more colleges that offer undergraduate or postsecondary education qualifications. As a federally funded sector, there has been high consistency in the systems and structures that have evolved in Australian higher education institutions. Students pay a small Higher Education Contribution Scheme (HECS) fee for their study, and the majority of their educational costs are met by the government. Universities receive direct government funding to support delivering teaching programs to undergraduate and graduate students. This has resulted in strong federal government oversight and guidance, including close monitoring of educational standards and outcomes, and all universities are reviewed on a 5-year cycle, with teaching and learning forming a central focus of those reviews.

University funding is also a strong driver in encouraging engagement with national educational reforms. The recent Bradley review (Bradley, Noonan,

Nugent, & Scales, 2008), for example, has promoted a stronger focus on educational equity issues. The federal government requires regular reporting of student participation statistics and directs a portion of its funding toward universities that are demonstrating increased inclusivity of students from low socioeconomic backgrounds.

Every Australian university hosts some form of academic development center, and TLCs were first established in the 1970s as a result of a small community of visionary leaders (Lee, Manathunga, & Kandlbinder, 2008). These centers have generally focused only on teaching support, although some are more broadly based to cover student learning and, rarely, broader elements of leadership and organizational learning. There is an increasing push by universities to ensure teaching staff are trained in basic teaching strategies, and this has been a major focus of TLCs for many years. Academic developers appointed to the centers have generally been recruited from a teaching position where they have demonstrated a passion for good teaching. They may or may not have a professional grounding in theories of teaching and learning. TLC directors play a key role in the implementation of university strategies relating to teaching and learning. However, they have experienced considerable diminution of power and authority during the last 10 years as pro vice chancellor and deputy vice chancellor roles in education have been established to provide oversight of educational outcomes. The shift from being a strategic, highly influential voice in the area to a more applied manager has been strongly evident as these structural changes have occurred.

The Australian academic development community has been strongly supported by the Australian Learning and Teaching Council (ALTC)—a government-funded agency that sponsored national teaching awards, teaching grants, and particular projects (see http://altc.edu.au). Many academic development leaders have contributed to projects that advance our understanding of teaching and learning. Collaboration and benchmarking have become strong hallmarks of the sector, with many grants awarded and several publications generated from this research. However, in 2011 the Australian government announced the phasing out of the ALTC as a coordinating body.

A particular benefit for Australian academic development centers has been the allocation of dedicated funding to universities based on measures of institutional excellence in teaching and learning (see http://www.deewr .gov.au/HigherEducation/Pages/IndicatorFramework.aspx). This has been a positive funding base on which learning and teaching centers have built many of their activities. A number of societies and groups also support teaching and learning, including the Higher Educational Research and Development Society of Australasia (HERDSA).

The Australian academic development sector has benefited from a very stable era in which teaching and learning has been regarded as a critical priority. Government funding has been directed toward recognizing teaching excellence and increasing research and scholarship of teaching. This has encouraged the ongoing development of teaching and learning centers and a strong traditional focus on promoting quality learning outcomes. However, the higher education sector's strong reliance on federal government sponsorship has also meant that academic development may be more vulnerable to shifts in national policy and funding strategies. A move to provide funding to universities for demonstrable improvements in teaching quality has increased institutional expectations regarding teaching and learning centers. As a result, the academic development setting has been quite volatile with a number of established staff, including directors, advised that they are not meeting the expectations of their employers. Although centers have generally remained open, they have sometimes had an entirely new staffing complement appointed. These trends possibly reflect poor alignment between academic development center functions and stakeholder expectations.

New Zealand

New Zealand has eight universities, four of which would describe themselves as research-intensive institutions. The competition between the universities is often fierce around research ratings, and a consequence of this is that teaching is, at the very least, perceived to be a lower priority than research. However, the international ranking systems and student surveys mentioned earlier are also common to NZ institutions and have tended to sharpen attention on to the student experience.

Until recently, all eight of New Zealand's universities had a defined academic development center, with different titles and a range of responsibilities. Some, for example, incorporate student learning functions, whereas others are more targeted toward academic staff support services. The naming of these centers may once have delineated the core function of any individual center, but in today's changing and unpredictable economic and political climate, some naming seems outdated and outmoded. However, one of these academic development centers has been disbanded and another has "reformed" with positions lost and services farmed out to the faculties (academic units) within the university. A third is undergoing a major restructure, and two have recently been reviewed with the intention of renewing or reaffirming their overarching purpose.

It could be argued that the economic climate after the global downturn is the reason for such apparent harsh treatment of academic development centers. However, New Zealand did not suffer as acutely during the downturn as some other countries have, and therefore there is more to the issue than national economics. Government funding policy is another source to examine because it is well known that NZ universities operate within very tight funding constraints. Any small shift downward in funding has a major impact on what universities can achieve. In New Zealand, the fate of TLCs has been vulnerable to these shifts in resources.

In recent years, a government-sponsored National Center for Tertiary Teaching Excellence (Ako Aotearoa) was set up in New Zealand (http://akoaotearoa.ac.nz). Ako Aotearoa provides funding for research on teaching and learning, sponsors the National Teaching Excellence Awards, and promotes good higher education practice. Where it differs from the Australian Teaching and Learning Council is that Ako Aotearoa embraces the whole of the tertiary sector and therefore its influence within individual universities tends to be more limited in scope.

New Zealand's small academic development community has been active in establishing its own support networks to assist its ongoing development. Academic developers in New Zealand have a branch of HERDSA (as detailed previously), the Tertiary Education Research Network (TERNZ), and the Academic Staff Developers of the Universities of New Zealand (ASDUNZ) to support dialogue and discussion on academic development matters.

Although the national activities and infrastructures offer one element of support for academic developers, many New Zealand developers strive to build a positive international reputation and to create opportunities for collaboration and interchange across national borders.

The United Kingdom

Higher education in the United Kingdom has operated from a government funding and sponsorship model, where universities receive significant funding from government grants. However, the recent economic downfall dealt a significant blow to this funding, resulting in extensive higher education budget cuts. In such a climate, academic development has been a target for cutbacks at the institutional level. A recent example of this was the reduction of protected funding for Centres for Excellence in Teaching and Learning (CETLs). In 2005, the Higher Education Funding Council UK agreed to fund more than 70 CETLs, distributed geographically and across all main subject areas for 5 years (http://www.hefce.ac.uk/learning/tinits/cetl/). The overarching purpose of the CETLs was to enhance learning and teaching across institutions. In 2010, CETL-protected funding was rolled back into base funding for the institutions, leading to the closure of many CETLs with subsequent job losses for many academic developers.

The United Kingdom has been very well served by a number of professional bodies that have provided strong support for teaching and learning networks, research, and scholarship. The Higher Education Academy (HEA, http://www.heacademy.ac.uk), for example, is an independent organization supporting higher education institutions with strategies for the development of research and evaluation to improve student learning experiences. Established as a charitable organization, it is jointly funded by universities as an independent means of encouraging good practice and knowledge sharing. With its network of discipline-based subject centers, the HEA has promoted academic development within the disciplines. However, it has recently been announced that the HEA is also to be restructured as a result of the government funding cuts.

The UK government has been moving toward stronger credentialing of university teachers, and most university academic staff are strongly encouraged or required to complete an accredited program relating to teaching and learning. To date, these programs have been accredited by the HEA. Like the ALTC, the HEA also provides development grants for teaching development projects.

Another professional body that has done much to develop academic developers is the Staff and Educational Development Association (SEDA, http://www.seda.ac.uk/home.html/). SEDA was established in 1993 by the merger of the Standing Conference on Educational Development and the Staff Development Group of the Society for Research into Higher Education (SRHE, http://www.srhe.ac.uk/). Many of the current leaders of academic development centers in the United Kingdom and internationally started their careers with SEDA's support. A strong relationship still exists between SEDA and SRHE, with the latter providing an excellent vehicle for research publication and dissemination. SEDA has offered accredited pathways for staff entering into the profession, including the SEDA fellowship, obtained through presentation of a portfolio of professional practice aligned with a set of core professional values. This rigorous program promotes sustainable models of academic and educational development. SEDA has more recently offered other development programs such as Leading Educational Change and Supporting Educational Change to better prepare its academic developers for expanded roles in curriculum and academic reform (http://www .seda.ac.uk/?p=3_3). These programs are doing much to develop the academic development leaders of the future.

Thus, the United Kingdom has been gradually and consistently building academic development capability and capacity supported admirably by the academic development professional bodies and should be well placed to provide strong leadership in enhancing the student learning experience following the economic recovery. However, the folding of funding for teaching and learning into general university grants has opened challenges for TLCs to clearly show their value and contribution to the university's outcomes.

Hong Kong

In Hong Kong, the University Grants Committee (UGC) advises the government on funding and strategic development of higher education. Besides providing funding to institutions to support teaching, research, and professional activities, special grants such as teaching development grants and other earmarked funds are dispersed to promote the enhancement of teaching and learning.

All the eight UGC-funded higher education institutions have a TLC. Although the provision of staff development courses and workshops remains the core business of the centers, the provision of support to institutional education development initiatives such as the promotion of an outcome-based approach to teaching and learning has become an increasingly significant responsibility. This has resulted from the internal strategic development adopted by the centers as well as the external drive from the drastically changing context of the local education sector.

Hong Kong is currently undergoing major reform of the education system to introduce a new "3+3+4" academic structure with 3-year junior secondary, 3-year senior secondary, and 4-year undergraduate programs to be implemented in 2012. UGC is steering universities to change from the current 3-year curricula to a 4-year curricula structure with the goal of transforming undergraduate curriculum from a specialized focus to a more holistic all-round kind of education. At the same time, UGC urges universities to take the "3+3+4" curriculum reform as an opportunity to integrate an outcome-based approach into their curriculum design. This is an important large-scale curriculum and educational development initiative that involves a major shift in educational philosophy and development of new pedagogical knowledge and skills, and it is presenting both opportunities and challenges to TLCs.

Those centers that proactively assist university management in planning, promoting, facilitating, steering, and monitoring these initiatives and support academic departments and frontline teachers in their implementation are able to establish themselves in the eyes of key stakeholders as instrumental to institutional development. As a result, the perceived value of TLCs is strengthened. To this end, TLC directors and educational developers have to overcome numerous major challenges in workload and expertise.

Regarding workload, TLCs have to make immense efforts in supporting multiple sectors of the university through various stages of complex change processes in the institution-wide curriculum and educational development initiatives. This has become particularly difficult when additional resources are limited because of the GFC. Regarding expertise, these initiatives are relatively new to the local context, so center directors have to be aware of skill and knowledge gaps among their staff and address them strategically through recruitment, staff development for the existing academic developers, or the employment of external consultants. Supporting institution-wide educational development places much heavier pressure on academic developers than does promoting innovative teaching approaches where the developers enjoy the pleasure of working with motivated academics who participate at their own choice. With respect to institution-wide development, academic departments are compelled to be engaged and required to succeed; this therefore places much higher demands on the TLCs to deliver the right services and ensure high levels of successful change.

Navigating the Political
Context of Academic Development

The changing funding base for higher education and increasing expectations of academic developers have stimulated some major challenges for the field, particularly in recognizing the need for political acumen and strategic skills. In each of our national reviews, there is a sense of shifting sands—where TLCs have the potential to be key players in the new environment, or significantly marginalized, modified, or removed. The formulas and approaches that have operated well in the past are less likely to protect academic developers from being targeted in the future. Instead, directors of academic development need to cue into their sociopolitical context, to anticipate likely challenges that may emerge, and to respond to those challenges in creative and appropriate ways.

A first question to ask then is, Are current TLCs reflecting what is expected of them? A simplistic response is to suggest that centers may not be operating in a manner that is seen as effective by their constituents. When centers are disbanded, restructured, or otherwise redesigned, it is possible that they have not been regarded as effective or strategically focused. As Connie M. Schroeder (2010) notes, this does not mean the center staff were not working hard. In fact, staff may have been very active in supporting the development of individuals, and in the provision of programs to increase instructional capacity across the institution. However, they may have been largely invisible or underrecognized in their roles, and this may be one possible reason for the changing fortunes of TLCs. In nations where government influences are strong, a second issue might be that TLCs are not sufficiently adaptive in realigning their work to reflect government goals and agendas.

A second question to ask could relate to the marginal roles that TLCs sometimes play in supporting their institutional strategies for teaching and learning. Nancy Van Note Chism (2010) notes that many TLCs have been reluctant to be strongly allied to institutional change strategies that faculty may perceive as negative. However, this can mean that centers are largely inactive in either informing or guiding teaching and learning initiatives and may be relegated to merely implementing planned teaching initiatives, rather than influencing and shaping those agendas. With the growth of university administrators who are driving new priorities for teaching and learning, this lack of involvement generates a major risk for TLCs of being seen as disinterested, or even adversarial by those who determine the allocation of institutional resources.

Importance of Leadership

Center directors may not be nimble enough to adapt to a constantly changing internal and external landscape. The leadership of academic development centers is often central to the success or failure of the center. If the leader can both act as an advocate for the center and for change within the institution in accordance with the "big picture" of what is happening globally in higher education, perceptions of the efficacy of the center are likely to be positive.

The leader of the center also needs to be an individual with academic credibility to work in partnership with faculty across all disciplines and to develop the center staff to have such abilities. This suggests a need for a scholarly approach to academic development, taking on both a teaching and a learning role. Faculty do not want to be told what to do; they want the pedagogical literature, theories, and principles to be translated into their disciplinary context. Similarly, academic developers are expected to be research active, offering a scholastic approach to their roles and outcomes. This can be difficult for many developers who emerge from a specific disciplinary knowledge base (e.g., history or English) and move into the TLC and a new disciplinary sphere of practice. A further complicating leadership and identity issue is that some TLCs are staffed by nonacademic instructors. The lack of academic identity and role definition for academic development makes it difficult to clarify how this can affect the center and its outcomes.

The tools that academic developers have traditionally used to evaluate their practice may also fall short of clearly justifying the benefits of funding a TLC. Recent attempts to create a stronger evaluation framework offer a way to increase the accountability and visibility of TLC outcomes (Stefani, 2010). The regular assessment of center services by different stakeholders, for example, can provide evidence of the suitability of the TLC and its impact. Similarly, programs and services need to be regularly reviewed to ensure they remain relevant and responsive to the changing institutional and national needs.

Key Challenges to Be Addressed

TLCs face a number of major challenges in meeting the expectations of their stakeholders. They are expected to have high impact across the educational community, despite a relatively small resource base. Although many centers are modest in size, their mission is large: to influence and effect quality improvement across the entire university community. Although they are unlikely to do this in isolation, they provide professional guidance and support to the many teaching and academic leaders who work within the university. TLCs are the translators of university goals and mission; they encourage engagement with scholarship and research, and they are generally responsible for educating incoming teachers to their roles and responsibilities. Although the aforementioned core functions can consume considerable time and energy, they may be largely unrecognized by those in senior roles. University administrators tend to focus on strategic goals that are driven by the emerging context in which their universities sit. Administrators are looking to achieve shifts in behavior and practice that can position their universities more favorably. These leaders are also held accountable for their demonstrable outcomes in achieving those goals. By implication, they will then seek support from their academic development centers to effect any desired changes. This can place considerable pressure on the center as it seeks to maintain ongoing, established services and roles and support these strategic changes in focus or priorities. Further, the director and center staff are likely to be the most knowledgeable in educational development matters. They are informed about the theory, practice, and international context in which their work operates. Thus, they need to ensure that their leaders are provided with the best possible information and guidance to inform their decisions and strategies.

An additional area that is challenging many TLCs and their directors relates to the academic development models that they are employing. The faculty developer as expert is a model that has been long established and successfully applied. However, the increasing prominence of excellent teachers across the community; a stronger strategic emphasis on educational matters in faculties, schools, and departments (Fullan & Scott, 2009); the dispersal of educational functions to different service areas; and the growth of school or college-based centers have increased the need for academic developers to work as strategic partners with a range of educational leaders. This has changed the range of partnerships that must typically be established and sustained. These relationships are predicated on trust and respect, emphasizing the necessity of the faculty developer being attuned to the particular challenges that are operating for those leaders, and in understanding how generic principles may need to be customized to suit the needs of those partners.

The faculty developer needs to be continually renewed, strengthened, and consolidated by participating in ongoing research, scholarship, and reflection. Although some of these projects and activities may be driven by outside funding and priorities, there is also considerable potential to undertake institutional research about teaching and learning to support emerging issues that have been identified. A recent OECD study (2010) highlighted a range of different approaches to building high-quality learning environments, but with little acknowledgement of the role that academic developers might play in creating innovative strategies. This research offers some interesting insights for academic developers as they think of their role and contribution to educational reform.

Figure 9.1 depicts four critical TLC functions and highlights that each academic development unit will be positioned within a university and particular political context. The location of academic development as a university-based service means that many different stakeholders will have expectations and requirements that must be either addressed or renegotiated. To survive and thrive, academic developers must be attuned to their particular contexts and ensure they are well placed to operate as strategic and effective contributors to the university strategy. This can be difficult, if the primary function remains linked to building effective entry-level teachers—a largely undervalued or invisible role.

Political setting and university context play significant parts in determining how successful the academic developer is perceived to be. It could be

Figure 9.1   The Strategic Functions of Academic Development

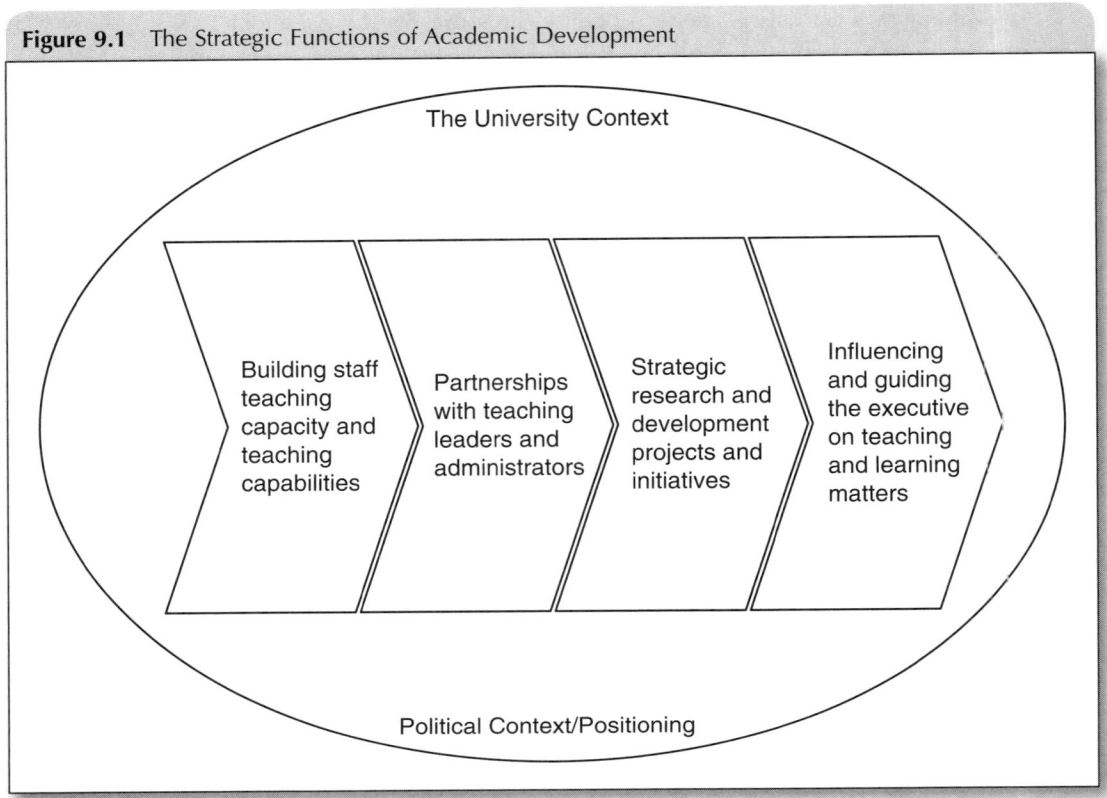

argued that centers that are closed, restructured, or remodeled by university leaders are perceived to be less effective than had been expected, regardless whether those expectations are unrealistic or unreasonable. We contend that academic developers need to actively manage expectations and build stronger support from key stakeholders to ensure they survive and thrive in their evolving contexts.

Sustaining Successful Academic Development

We suggest that the key to sustaining successful academic development is predicated on three elements:

1. Effective and well-managed academic development support to the university that reflects its evolving needs as well as maintaining established services that are core capacity-building functions

2. Active and respectful relationships with a range of stakeholders, from administrators to academics

3. Proactive and strategic positioning of the academic development service to ensure it is actively guiding university initiatives and strategies relating to teaching and learning

Within all national contexts, if academic development is to be valued and successful, it needs to be carefully positioned to be valuable to the majority, effective, and *visible*. These require effective management of the activities that are undertaken and of the marketing, partnerships, and value adding that is attributable to the center.

The following capabilities can assist academic developers in navigating through these complex times.

- Establish high credibility as a knowledgeable expert.

Academic developers need to be well positioned to provide helpful and accurate advice on matters as they arise. Developers must be able to draw on current literature and sources to offer an informed and scholarly perspective on issues being discussed. As this book illustrates, there is much to be understood about teaching and learning that needs to be integrated into university practice, particularly as our knowledge of students evolves (see Sharpe, Beetham, & de Freitas, 2010).

Academic developers need to operate proactively: anticipating likely issues and presenting cogent and well-positioned guidance to those who are making key decisions. Developers need to establish their credibility as a key source of knowledge on matters relating to teaching and learning. This credibility can be assisted by building a wide sphere of influence, expanding one's own skills in leadership, and anticipating emerging teaching and learning issues that may be relevant to the university. The latter is of great importance. The leader of a TLC needs to influence senior management on what shifts would best enable the institution to achieve teaching and learning excellence.

- Be flexible and adaptive.

A risk for academic developers is that they remain attached to the practices and methodologies that have been successful in the past. The shifting context for higher education requires adaptive responses in strategy, practices, and tactics as the environment alters (Tennant, McMullen, & Kaczynski, 2009). For example, the marketing and communication approaches employed by academic developers can benefit from better use of the many social media now in place. The mix of services may need to be adapted to better match user expectations, and the strategic goals of the university and its leaders will need to be supported and integrated into the development approaches. A stronger focus on institutional change and the development of effective academic leaders is also likely to be a major area of growth (Schroeder, 2010).

- Build strong partnerships with significant leaders.

Universities are political places, particularly when resources are tight and the stakes become larger. Academic developers need to build strong partnerships with a range of leaders—at executive administration, dean, and head levels. These collaborations ensure developers are in tune with the prevailing needs of the institution and that they have a number of sponsors across the community. This approach can also protect developers from the actions of less constructive or unsupportive administrators who might seek to marginalize the TLC and its director (Debowski, 2009). The development of professional partnerships and associations with colleagues beyond the institution also offer enrichment, support, and possible forums for innovation and exchange.

- Focus on the strategic needs of the university.

Although TLCs need to maintain their high-quality educational programs and established services, they must also operate at a strategic level (Chism, 2010). Despite burgeoning workloads, it is fatal to solely focus on daily operations. The center needs to be positioned as an influencing force that is enabling effective growth and development of teaching across the university, and in guiding future educational strategy. As a first step, this means maintaining a strong focus on the initiatives being developed within the university and developing new ideas for additional strategies (including those in place in other universities).

- Develop established credibility within your broader profession.

Another risk for academic developers occurs if they are invisible and undervalued in their professional community. Engagement with the broader professional community (e.g., HERDSA, SEDA, POD) confirms the worth of the individual and highlights the esteem in which he or she is held. It is important to contribute to the broader profession because it brings fresh perspectives back into the university and provides opportunities to be recognized more widely within the sector. This engagement also encourages the individual's university to recognize the respect garnered by its staff.

Additional Roles for Academic Development

Although the changing context for academic development has placed some strong pressure on each individual, it is also pushing professional societies to respond in similarly adaptive and responsive ways. The International Consortium for Educational Development (ICED) comprises the many teaching and learning societies and networks that operate around the world (http://www.osds.uwa.edu.au/iced/). The annual reports of these networks illustrate a strong focus on promoting the scholastic nature of teaching and learning and encouraging interchange through conferences and associated events.

Although these are extremely important functions, there is also considerable value in increasing the level of advocacy and strategic influencing that takes place. TLCs can use a number of potential roles to proactively address future fiscal and organizational challenges, including engagement and commentary on political agendas and policy before they are formed; increased lobbying capacity; advocacy relating to the function and contributions of academic development; industrial support for those who are experiencing difficulty; greater recognition of the evolving, political context in which academic development operates; formalized programs to provide preparatory training for developers and ongoing leadership development to support the changing role; and increased access to communities of practice that encourage sharing and exchange among colleagues.

Conclusion

The changing context of higher education worldwide has placed more emphasis on teaching and learning as a critical function that must be effectively supported and promoted. Academic development and TLCs are well positioned to take strong leadership of institutional, instructional, and individual capacity building. However, to be seen as both influential and effective, we need an ongoing evaluation of how well we reflect our constituent's expectations and consideration of the ways in which our centers might better reflect the changing context in which we are located. Although times are hard and will most likely remain so for the next few years, they are also exciting by allowing flexible and responsive centers to move into more central leadership roles that help take our institutions forward. Teaching and learning thrives on adaptive, creative, and strategic developers who can help shape a better future and, ultimately, sustain better outcomes for our learners.

References

Bradley, D., Noonan, P., Nugent, H., & Scales, B. (2008). *Review of Australian higher education, final report.* Canberra, Australia: Department of Education, Employment and Workplace Relations. Retrieved from www.deewr.gov.au/he_review_finalreport

Chism, N. V. N. (2010). Getting to the table: Planning and developing institutional initiatives. In C. M. Schroeder (Ed.), *Coming in from the margins: Faculty development's emerging organizational development role in institutional change* (pp. 47–59). Sterling, VA: Stylus.

Debowski, S. (2009). Pencilled in the margins: Dealing with bullies at work. In K. Naidoo & F. Patel (Eds.), *Working women: Stories of strife, struggles and survival* (pp. 65–78). Thousand Oaks, CA: Sage.

Debowski, S. (2010). Defining and locating academic development: The first step in evaluation. In L. Stefani (Ed.), *Evaluating the effectiveness of academic development*. New York, NY: Routledge.

Fullan, M., & Scott, G. (2009). *Turnaround leadership for higher education*. San Francisco, CA: Wiley.

Gillespie, K. J., Robertson, D. L., & Associates (2010). *A guide to faculty development* (2nd ed.). San Francisco, CA: Jossey-Bass.

Hardy, C., & Bryson, C. (n.d.). Student engagement: Paradigm change or political expediency? Retrieved October 25, 2010, from http://www.adm.heacademy.ac.uk/resources/features/student-engagement-paradigm-change-or-political-expediency/

Kuhlenschmidt, S. (2011). Distribution and penetration of teaching-learning development units in higher education: Implications for strategic planning and research. In J. E. Miller (Ed.), *To improve the academy: Resources for faculty, instructional and organizational development* (Vol. 29, pp. 274–287). San Francisco, CA: Jossey-Bass.

Lee, A., Manathunga, C., & Kandlbinder, P. (2008). *Making a place: An oral history of academic development in Australia*. Canberra, Australia: HERDSA.

Organisation for Economic Co-operation and Development (OECD). (2010). Supporting quality teaching in higher education. Retrieved from www.oecd.org/edu/imhe/qualityteaching/phase1

Schroeder, C. M. (2010). Faculty developers as institutional developers. In C. M. Schroeder (Ed.), *Coming in from the margins: Faculty development's emerging organizational development role in institutional change* (pp. 17–46). Sterling, VA: Stylus.

Sharpe, R., Beetham, H., & de Freitas, S. (2010). *Rethinking learning for a digital age: How learners are shaping their own experiences*. London, UK: Routledge.

Sorcinelli, M. D., Austin, A. E., Eddy, P. L., & Beach, A. L. (2006). Creating the future of faculty development: Learning from the past, understanding the present. Bolton, MA: Anker.

Stefani, L. (Ed.). (2010). Evaluating the effectiveness of academic development. New York, NY: Routledge.

Tennant, M., McMullen, C., & Kaczynski, D. (2009). *Teaching, learning and research in higher education: A critical approach*. New York, NY: Routledge.

CHAPTER 10

An Effective Model for the Professional Development of Middle Eastern Faculty

Mohammed A. T. Alsudairi

The progress of any nation has always been associated with knowledge and learning. Indeed, to promote the advancement of knowledge and to encourage learning at all levels, all nations have established systems of education. These systems generally include primary (elementary schools), secondary (middle and high schools), and tertiary (college and universities) schools. Shortly after it emerged as a nation in 1932, Saudi Arabia began developing and refining its educational system, a process that is ongoing throughout the Kingdom. Saudi Arabia established its first institution of higher learning in Riyadh in 1957. Known originally as Riyadh University, King Saud University (KSU) now enrolls more than 70,000 students annually and has a faculty numbering more than 5,000.

Like all public universities within the Kingdom, KSU receives ample government support to carry out its primary missions of teaching, research, and service. The government pays for students' tuition and provides job security for Saudi professors in the form of permanent positions upon hire. Non-Saudi faculty, most of whom are of Middle Eastern descent, are hired on a renewable contract basis. In addition to offering instruction across the traditional span of academic topics, KSU also offers programs in medicine, dentistry, law, pharmacy, and of course, petroleum and oil refining. As Saudi Arabia continues to emerge as a key player in the global economy, KSU and other public universities are increasing their emphasis on providing its graduates with the necessary practical knowledge and job skills to be competitive in the world market.

Most KSU faculty pursued their graduate education abroad, primarily in the United States or United Kingdom. While working on their doctoral degrees, relatively few KSU faculty received any formal training in pedagogy or gained experience as teachers of record or teaching assistants. In essence, these faculty return to the Kingdom prepared to conduct research but are not well prepared to teach. Because assistant professors teach especially heavy course loads (course loads are reduced when a faculty member becomes an associate professor, and reduced still further when they are promoted to full professor), they are often overwhelmed with teaching responsibilities. In addition, senior KSU faculty often use the lecture as their primary teaching tool and, following a long-standing tradition in the Middle East, expect their students to learn course content primarily through memorization.

Thus, there exists a strong need to provide support, guidance, and training in modern pedagogy and teaching among KSU faculty—and to create and support a culture that values teaching as an intellectual as well as a practical activity. To meet these needs, KSU established the Deanship of Skills Development (DSD) in 2007. The DSD also provides support for student, staff, and administrative development. In this chapter, I will provide an overview of the DSD's teaching and learning programs aimed at enhancing the quality of faculty teaching and offer it as a comprehensive model of faculty skills development.

Overview of the Deanship of Skills Development

The DSD exists as an independent unit of KSU. At the administrative level, the DSD is overseen by a dean, two vice-deans, and several directors responsible for the development and implementation of programs, creation of internally published print and electronic media, financial and budgetary duties, public relations, and quality assurance. In total, the DSD staff numbers almost 40 people.

Like most faculty development programs (Hussain, Sarwar, Khan, & Khan, 2010), the overarching mission of the DSD is to develop the teaching and learning skills of faculty, lecturers, teaching assistants, students, and academic and administrative leaders in an effort to strive for excellence in fulfilling KSU's instructional mission. Toward this end, the DSD has established clear objectives as a part of its strategic plan. These objectives include the following:

- Identifying the needs of KSU faculty, staff, and administrators in an attempt to identify areas of strength in teaching and academic leadership as well as identifying areas in need of improvement

- Training KSU faculty in cutting-edge instructional pedagogy and technology
- Training KSU faculty to design and develop course portfolios
- Training KSU faculty in assessment of teaching to help them improve the overall quality of their instructional effectiveness
- Providing professional consultation to KSU faculty to help them improve their teaching skills and enhance their overall level of professional instructional performance
- Organizing experience-sharing programs for maximizing the professional growth of KSU faculty
- Contributing to the development of students' self-learning skills in an effort to help student achieve excellence in academic, practical, technical, and social skills
- Publishing books, booklets, brochures, and newsletters that provide up-to-date information on teaching, learning, and academic leadership
- Supporting faculty and administrative regional and international travel for professional development
- Developing grants programs to support faculty in the scholarship of teaching and learning
- Evaluating and revising DSD programs in the attempt to improve their impact on faculty, staff, and administrative professional development

Thus, the DSD aims to improve the personal, teaching, research, technical, administrative, and communication skills of KSU faculty and administrators and the study and critical-thinking skills of KSU students. The DSD's ultimate goal is to provide for the professional development of KSU faculty so that KSU students benefit by becoming motivated and self-regulated lifelong learners.

In striving to accomplish these objectives, the DSD holds itself to the highest international standards for professional development. It regularly evaluates the quality of its programs and services, including inviting outside reviewers to campus to provide external assessment of its success in reaching its objectives and guidance in how to improve the quality of its performance relative to the objectives previously discussed. In addition, the DSD supports faculty travel to teaching and learning centers colleges and universities in the United States and United Kingdom in an effort to provide these faculty with additional training and experiences to improve their teaching.

The DSD sponsors a large number of programs in support of its work each year. Program activities and events include workshops, seminars, lectures, discussion circles, book groups, and one-on-one peer consultation for faculty. The DSD also publishes a large number of print and electronic resources for teaching. For example, for the 2011–2012 academic year, the DSD will publish 15 booklets (3,000–4,000 words each) on various topics related to teaching (e.g., preparing for the first day and first week of classes, teaching with active learning, assessment of student learning, and classroom management). For students, DSD sponsors seminars, lectures, and work-shops centered on developing both life and academic skills. In addition, the DSD holds seminars, lectures, and workshops for administrators to develop their leadership and management skills. Although the DSD has a wide vari-ety of programs in various stages of development and implementation, three of its programs—its faculty workshop series, the New Faculty Orientation Program, and the Peer Consultation program—are particularly noteworthy. Because space does not permit a detailed description of all DSD programs, I will only discuss the New Faculty Orientation Program and the Peer Consultation program in the remainder of this chapter.

Faculty Workshops on Teaching

The backbone of the DSD's weekly activities throughout the academic year is its extensive workshop series, which is based on principles of effective course design and teaching (e.g., Bain, 2005; Fink, 2003; Gurung & Schwartz, 2009). Workshops vary in duration from 1 day (typically 5 hours) to 4 days (or 20 hours). International as well as local scholars and peda-gogical experts lead these workshops. In addition, these experts often also lead book discussion groups (typically 3 hours) and visit specific on-campuses colleges (e.g., computer science, engineering, medicine, and dentistry) to give seminars and lectures on specific topics relevant to teaching topics, issues, and problems in these specialty areas.

These workshops, seminars, and lectures expand a wide variety of topics including, for example,

- active learning,
- assessment of student learning,
- classroom management,
- creating a teaching portfolio,
- critical thinking,
- generating and leading discussions,
- grading and feedback,
- problem-based learning,
- student motivation,
- teaching with technology,
- team-based learning, and
- writing a statement of teaching philosophy.

At the beginning of each new academic year, the DSD also sponsors the weeklong University Forum on Teaching and Learning. The forum begins with 2 days of invited "blended lectures" (lectures accented with active discussion and other activities) from well-known international experts in teaching and learning. Each lecture is 3 hours long with each guest speaker giving two lectures each day. On the remaining 3 days, these experts offer 5-hour workshops each day on specific topics. For example, for fall 2011, invited experts addressed workshop topics such as "getting the semester off to an excellent start," "making the most of class time," and "becoming a scholarly teacher."

New Faculty Orientation Program

To assist all new faculty (defined as faculty in their first 5 years of teaching) in getting off to a strong start in their academic careers, especially teaching, the DSD has developed its New Faculty Orientation Program (NFOP)—an extensive series of workshops and other activities designed to build specific faculty skills. The NFOP also helps acquaint new faculty with the policies, procedures, and regulations related to working at KSU and orients these faculty to the various services available to them as members of the KSU academic community. On a larger scale, the NFOP acquaints faculty newcomers with KSU's strategic vision, mission, and objectives.

Program Structure

The program consists of two parts, an orientation program and series of workshops. The orientation program spans 2 days and involves a series of lectures and seminars that focus on KSU campus life, including activities, facilities, and services that are available to all faculty (faculty rights and responsibilities, faculty development opportunities, other educational and community service opportunities, and opportunities for involvement in scientific research).

The workshop series involves 36 hours of training courses. These courses address course design and construction (9 hours), effective teaching (12 hours), learning outcomes and assessment (9 hours), and microteaching (6 hours). I will describe each of these courses in more detail.

Course design and construction. The goal of this course is to help participants acquire the basic knowledge and skills necessary to design and construct their courses in ways that achieve their specific academic programs' intended learning outcomes (e.g., Davis, 2009; Fink, 2003; Svinicki & McKeachie, 2011). Thus, in this course, participants learn the basic principles of sound course design, learn how to write student learning objectives (SLOs), choose the pedagogical tools most effective in helping students achieve those SLOs, and select assessment tools most appropriate to accurately measuring the extent to which students have achieved those SLOs. In addition, participants also learn how to (a) organize and deliver course content during class time, (b) integrate technology into their teaching, and (c) how to prepare a course syllabus and course portfolio.

Effective teaching. This course builds on the course design and construction course by providing more detail on effective teaching methods and developing an effective teaching style (e.g., Lowman, 1995; Palmer, 1998; Weimer, 2002). In particular, this course introduces participants to various active learning strategies and methods and how to implement active learning in both small and large classes. This course also introduces participants to the concept of self-regulated learning and offers participants suggestions for how to assist students in becoming lifelong learners. Finally, this course exposes participants to the scholarship of teaching and learning and some of its basic findings related to effective college and university teaching.

Learning outcomes assessment. The primary aim of this course is to provide participants an in-depth and hands-on experience with basic and advanced principles of student assessment design and practice (Suskie, 2009; Walvoord & Anderson, 2010). Participants receive instruction on a variety of student assessment techniques (e.g., multiple-choice examinations, quizzes, short answer essay questions, papers, group work), creating and using rubrics, and providing timely and appropriate feedback to students based on assessment technique used. As participants work through this course, they are given ample opportunity to practice writing test items, including essay questions. They also practice writing rubrics. The course instructor provides one-on-one feedback to participants regarding the quality of their test items and rubrics.

Microteaching. This course is entirely practical in nature and allows participants to present a short (i.e., 10 minutes) mini-lecture, after which the course instructor provides written and oral feedback to each presenter based on the quality of the mini-lecture. In addition, other course participants provide peer feedback to the presenter. Thus, participants in this course practice teaching and providing sound, constructive feedback to each other. Participants may either deliver a straight lecture, a PowerPoint–based lecture, a lecture blended with a demonstration or other class activity, or a discussion-based presentation. Following each presentation, the presenter generally takes questions from the course instructor and the other course participants.

Following each presentation, the course instructors gives participants the opportunity to gather their thoughts on the presentation, summarize them on paper, and then share them with the presenter in a brief and open feedback session. The role of the course instructor is to keep each presenter on time, moderate the feedback session, and provide feedback and suggestions for areas in which the presenter might improve his or her presentation skills.

Finally, this course provides the opportunity for all presenters to reflect individually on their strengths as teachers and the areas in which they need improvement. The underlying theme of this course is that teaching is a craft on which each teacher must continually tinker to work toward becoming an excellent teacher.

Program Assessment Activities

To assess the overall quality of the NFOP and the progress individual participants make across the four courses in their professional development as teacher-scholars, the DSD carefully monitors three assessment indices. The first is a pre-NFOP/post-NFOP questionnaire, which assesses participants' knowledge of basic pedagogical strategies and tactics. The intent of the questionnaire is for it to serve as a reliable gauge of how much participants learn about pedagogy as a result of their experience in the NFOP.

The second measure is a 1,000-word written statement due at the end of the NFOP in which participants reflect about their experience in the program and summarize what they perceive they have learned as a result of completing it. In this statement, participants describe what they learned throughout the program and on how they will use this information to improve their teaching.

The third assessment index is a teaching portfolio that each participant creates during the NFOP. In the teaching portfolio, each participant includes the following information: a copy of the participant's curriculum vita, a complete description of each course the participant teaches, copies of syllabi for those courses and sample materials, a statement of teaching goals and methods, evidence of student learning, copies of teaching evaluations, statement of teaching philosophy, and information regarding professional development as it relates to teaching.

Peer Consultation Program

Peer consultation, or peer review of teaching as it sometimes called, is a method for providing constructive feedback to faculty with regard to improving their teaching. In its most basic form, peer consultation involves only one individual observing another individual's teaching as it occurs in the classroom. However, because teaching involves more than an individual's classroom performance, authentic peer consultation entails examination of all aspects of teaching including (but not limited to) the course syllabus and learning objectives; preparation for classroom presentations; classroom activities; communication with students in and out of the classroom; assessment of student learning; and the individual's reflective assessment of his or her pedagogical knowledge, skills, and future goals. Authentic peer consultation, then, includes a comprehensive analysis of all aspects of any given teacher's approach to teaching and learning. Peer consultation may be either formative or summative, although theoretically, the ultimate purpose of peer consultation is purely formative—improvement of the individual's teaching for its own sake and for the benefit of his or her students.

The KSU Peer Consultation Program was initiated in spring 2010 with 16 faculty. In the past year, another 37 faculty have joined the program bringing the total number of faculty who have received DSD training for peer consultation to 53. These faculty represent all KSU colleges. The program is entirely voluntary, confidential, and aimed at the formative development of high-quality teaching skills. At present, there are no plans to use this program for summative assessment of teaching.

The DSD Peer Consultation Training Program involves 20 hours of training across four 5-hour workshops and is based on current best practices in college and teaching (e.g., Davis, 2009; Svinicki & McKeachie, 2011) and in peer review of teaching (Chism, 2007). The first 10 hours involves basic knowledge and skills training in key aspects of effective peer consultation, effective teaching practices, observation, learning, and feedback. These first workshops involve hands-on activities including role-plays, simulations, and mock feedback scenarios in which the faculty practice listening, observation, and feedback techniques. The first half of the training program also involves opportunities for participants to observe a microteaching demonstration given by the workshop leader and provide written and oral feedback to the leader on his or her classroom teaching strengths and areas in need of improvement.

The second half of the Peer Consultation Training Program (two more 5-hour workshops or 10 hours) involves participant microteaching (10–12 minute mini-lectures) and providing written and oral feedback to one another. As the process unfolds, the workshop leader provides feedback to participants on the substance and style of their observation and feedback to one another.

This second half of the training program also involves training participants in how to conduct focus groups with small groups of students to solicit their perspectives on the quality of their teacher's classroom teaching skills and the overall experience of being a student in his or her class. Thus, the peer consultant is trained to collect students' commentary on their teacher's classroom teaching, as well as the entire nature of students' learning experience in the class, which includes the organization and structure of the course, clarity of the course syllabus and learning objectives, communication style of their teacher, and the quality of assignments and examinations.

The actual KSU peer consultation process involves eight steps:

1. Faculty contact with the DSD—A teacher contacts the DSD to request a peer consultation.

2. DSD contact with the teacher—A trained peer consultant contacts a faculty member who wants to be observed to arrange for the observation and related meetings.

3. Pre-observation meeting—The peer consultant meets with the faculty member before the observation to introduce himself or herself and to learn more about the faculty member's approach to teaching.

4. Observation of faculty teaching—The peer consultant visits the faculty member's classroom and observes him or her teaching.

5. Discussion with students—After observing the faculty member teach for about 25 to 30 minutes, the teacher leaves the room, and the peer consultant meets for about 20 minutes with the students to gather their insights into their teacher's effectiveness. After this meeting with the students, the peer consultant will create a written, but anonymous, summary of the discussion with the students.

6. Writing the feedback report—Following the observation and student discussion, the peer consultant drafts a written report and gives it to the teacher in the post-observation meeting. Following this meeting, the peer consultant e-mails the teacher an electronic copy of the report and then deletes the report from his or her computer. This way, only the teacher has both a hard and soft copy of the document, which helps to ensure confidentiality.

7. Post-observation meeting and feedback—The peer consultant meets with the teacher to discuss the written report, which contains both a description of the teacher's strengths and areas for improvement.

8. Feedback to consultant/DSD—Finally, the teacher submits a written feedback report about the nature of his or her peer consultation experience to the DSD. This information is used to develop and refine the quality of the peer consultation process.

Peer consultation is having two important effects on the KSU campus. First, as faculty acquire stronger teaching skills, they develop professionally as more competent instructors. Second, as more and more faculty are improving their teaching skills, a new campus culture is being created that values and promotes effective teaching. Thus, the net result is that the overall quality of teaching at KSU is strengthened and a faculty culture is developing that truly cares about the quality of its instruction and student learning.

Two Challenges to Faculty Development at KSU

Although DSD faculty development programs are flourishing, there are nonetheless challenges that the DSD faces in maintaining its current programs and developing new ones. Chief among these obstacles is faculty resistance to changing the way they teach. As noted earlier, Saudi Arabia has a long and storied history of relying on lecturing and memorization as primary teaching and learning tools. As result, many students are used to learning only in this way, and many KSU faculty are not interested in learning about more effective teaching and learning skills. The sentiment among these faculty might be best expressed by noting these faculty got this far in their careers by using these tried and tested methods, and if it worked for them, why change?

Because faculty development is a purely individual and voluntary activity and guided by each faculty member's goals for his or her career, there is essentially nothing that the DSD can do to directly influence these faculty members' involvement in DSD programs. However, as more and more other faculty—those who feel that professional development as teachers is important to them and their students—become involved in DSD programs and improve their teaching, there is creeping pressure for these other faculty to improve their teaching. In addition, faculty who have attended DSD activities have been a strong source of endorsement for DSD-supported faculty development on the KSU campus, and through word of mouth, more and more faculty are becoming interested in participating in DSD activities. As a result, demand for DSD activities continues to grow, even the face of lingering resistance to professional development among some faculty.

A second challenge for the DSD, albeit a positive one, is having enough staff to meet the rapidly burgeoning need for KSU faculty development programming. Currently, the DSD depends on both Middle Eastern and foreign experts to lead workshops and seminars and to offer lectures. During any given week, there may be as many as 20 different workshops, seminars, and lectures available to KSU faculty and staff. Thus, there is a strong demand to locate teaching and learning leaders throughout the world to share their experience and expertise with KSU faculty. In response to this demand, the DSD has developed an aggressive recruiting program designed to attract new speakers and workshop leaders to campus. The program relies heavily on former workshop and workshop leaders and lecturers to identify and recommend new presenters to the DSD.

Fortunately, the DSD does not face the kinds of stiff challenges often faced by equivalent units (i.e., teaching and learning centers) on the campuses of many U.S. and U.K. institutions of higher education. For example, the DSD is well funded and enjoys the complete support of university administrators. Although budgets could always be larger, the DSD is able to fully fund all of its programs and develop new ones. Plans are currently underway to develop several new DSD activities, including expanding its workshop programming, establishing an international conference on teaching and learning to be held in Saudi Arabia, and creating a new international journal on teaching and learning that will be published by KSU.

Conclusion

Since its inception 4 years ago, the DSD has made significant inroads implementing, supporting, and expanding faculty development activities on the KSU campus. Indeed, hundreds of KSU faculty have attended its workshops, seminars, and lectures, and attended faculty development activities throughout the world. These activities focus on key aspects of teaching and learning, including course design and construction, developing syllabi, teaching using active learning, teaching for critical thinking, writing statements of teaching philosophy, and creating teaching and course portfolios, to name but a few DSD offerings. Two DSD programs that have had a particularly salient impact on faculty teaching are the New Faculty Orientation and the Peer Consultation Training programs. Both of these programs are having an especially strong influence on changing faculty attitudes about the role of teaching at the university. Faculty participants who have participated in these programs have remarkably strong positive attitudes about teaching and have become proponents, indeed ambassadors, across campus of DSD programs and, even more significantly, the importance of teaching well. Thus, DSD model of faculty development appears to be well on its way to achieving its overarching goal of providing support, guidance, and training in modern pedagogy and teaching among KSU faculty.

References

Bain, K. (2005). *What the best college teachers do.* Cambridge, MA: Harvard University Press.

Chism, N. V. N. (2007). *Peer review of teaching: A sourcebook* (2nd ed.). Bolton, MA: Anker.

Davis, B. G. (2009). *Tools for teaching* (2nd ed.). San Francisco, CA: Jossey-Bass.

Fink, L. D. (2003). *Creating significant learning experiences.* San Francisco, CA: Jossey-Bass.

Gurung, R. A. R., & Schwartz, B. M. (2009). *Optimizing teaching and learning: Practicing pedagogical research.* Malden, NJ: Wiley-Blackwell.

Hussain, S., Sarwar, M., Khan, M. N., & Khan, M. I. (2010). Faculty development programs for university teachers: Trainee's perceptions of success. *European Journal of Scientific Research, 44,* 253–257. Retrieved from http://www.euro journals.com/ejsr.htm

Lowman, J. (1995). *Mastering the techniques of teaching* (2nd ed.). San Francisco, CA: Jossey-Bass.

Palmer, P. J. (1998). *The courage to teach: Exploring the inner landscape of a teacher's life.* San Francisco, CA: Jossey-Bass.

Suskie, L. (2009). *Assessing student learning: A common sense guide* (2nd ed.). San Francisco, CA: Jossey-Bass.

Svinicki, M., & McKeachie, W. J. (2011). *McKeachie's teaching tips: Strategies, research, and theory for college and university teachers* (13th ed.). Belmont, CA: Wadsworth.

Walvoord, B. E., & Anderson, V. J. (2010). *Effective grading: A tool for learning and assessment in college* (2nd ed.). San Francisco, CA: Jossey-Bass.

Weimer, M. (2002). *Learner-centered teaching.* San Francisco, CA: Jossey-Bass.

PART V

Understanding Context

CHAPTER 11

Culture and Teaching

Lessons From Psychology

KENNETH D. KEITH

More than four decades have passed since, as a beginning graduate student, I taught my first university-level course in introductory psychology. I still have the textbook (Morgan & King, 1966) that I used for that course, and in recent years have from time to time (e.g., Keith, 2011b) gone back to consult it as I have tried to put into perspective the ways the field has changed during those four decades. One of the major changes, of course, is in the role that culture plays—in my own field of psychology, as well as in the broader enterprise of teaching in general. In this chapter, I attempt to show some of the ways the world has changed in the past generation, to illustrate some of the important challenges those changes present for those of us who call ourselves teachers, and to highlight some ways the field of cross-cultural psychology might contribute to the cultural competence of 21st-century teachers and students.

The Frog in the Well

I have often thought of our teaching in terms of a metaphor derived from an old Asian proverb, the story of the frog that lives in a well. The frog, as the story goes, cannot comprehend the ocean, and he assumes that the sun and the moon shining down upon his little well shine only for him. For the frog, his well is, for all practical purposes, the universe. His little bit of water and the patch of sky he can see are, as far as he knows, perfectly fine, and he does not, in fact, realize that he lives in a well.

I fear that for too much of our history, many of us have been quite like the frog in the well. Our little corner of the world, the college classroom, constituted a perfectly fine universe, and we saw little need to contemplate the world beyond its boundaries. I will also suggest that, while we were happily ensconced in our corner of the world, the larger world around us was (and is) dramatically changing. However, like the frog in the well, if we fail to get beyond our own little patch of sky, we may be ill equipped to cope with, or even notice, the change.

A Changing World

When I was teaching my first class in the faraway 1960s, I drove an automobile that sold new for about 1,900 American dollars, paid 55 dollars per month in rent, bought bread for 25 American cents per loaf, and ate instant soup at a cost of 10 cents per meal. We had no e-mail, no desktop (much less laptop or handheld) computers, and no mobile telephones. International travel was more a luxury than an everyday reality, and the incredible range of information engendered by the Internet and a vast array of cable television channels was not yet even a gleam in the inventors' eyes. In fact, some of the inventors were not yet alive!

The incredible growth of information availability, cross-cultural communication, and instant transmission of images, ideas, and personal data have combined to make the world a much smaller and very different place as we enter the second decade of the 21st century. And these changes have occurred *across* cultures and *within* the multicultural milieu of such complex nations as the United States (see, for example, Matsumoto & Juang, 2008, p. 2). Thus, the nations of the world are no longer isolated, and the diversity of cultural and subcultural groups within many nations has greatly increased as well. Unfortunately, as teachers, we have not always appreciated or acknowledged this great diversity. In my own field, this state of affairs has led critics to observe that we have taught a largely U.S. psychology, based on research conducted largely by Americans, using largely white Americans as research subjects. As Robert Guthrie (1998) famously pointed out in the title of a book on the subject, *Even the Rat was White*.

More recently, Jeffrey Arnett (2008) argued that the conclusions of psychological research are too often based on a small subset of the human population—that of the United States—and Americans have tended to treat their research results as if they were universally true, often in the absence of cross-cultural data to support many of those claims. The result, Michael Cole (1984) concluded, may be that "cross-cultural work is ghettoized" (p. 1000) and that students may learn little about other cultures. This lack of cultural context is not, of course, what we want in a changing world in which educators acknowledge the importance of teaching today's students about the relevance of an understanding of cultural diversity (e.g., Branche, Mullennix, & Cohn, 2007).

Why Culture?

Maybe, we might be tempted to say, it is true that psychological scientists have not been as sensitive to culture as they should have been, but what does that have to do with general knowledge of culture and the importance of teaching it? The answers to this question are both simple and complex. The simple answer is to say that intercultural literacy is important to us all if we want to understand our world, recognize cultural stereotypes, and appreciate the cultural diversity and differences around us (Hilferty, 2008). The complex answer lies in recognition that we live in a world fraught with political, religious, and governmental conflict; environmental challenges; inequitable resource distribution; and rapid technological change—and that solutions to these problems can come, at least in part, via improved understanding of cross-cultural psychology (Keith, 2011a).

Access to higher education for cultural and ethnic minorities is a universally recognized problem (e.g., Obua Ogwal, 1998), acknowledged by such international groups as the United Nations. And, as cultural subgroups gain access to higher education and become included in professional studies, cultural competence becomes increasingly important for the teachers providing that education (Leiper, Van Horn, Hu, & Upadhyaya, 2008). Dialogue with cultural groups is a foundation for the understanding necessary to teaching culture, and some authorities have asserted that cultural competence is an ethical imperative in teaching and research (Tracey, 2005). Clearly, culture matters in 21-century teaching, and cross-cultural psychology, I believe, has much to offer in support of teachers from all disciplines.

Cross-Cultural Psychology: What Is It?

Çigdem Kagitçibaşi and J. W. Berry (1989) provided a concise definition of *cross-cultural psychology*, calling it the "study of similarities and differences in individual psychological and social functioning in various cultures and ethnic groups" (p. 494). This definition suggests a foundation—in psychological and social processes—that should underpin the efforts of teachers striving to incorporate an understanding of culture in their work. A few organizing principles can aid teachers and students in their conceptualization of the field:

1. Culture consists of both objective and subjective components, but is essentially a psychological construct.

2. Although we tend to notice and focus on differences, people across cultures are more alike than different.

3. All people are likely to view and judge other cultures from the perspective of their own culture.

4. Cultures vary along important dimensions that are useful to understanding of cross-cultural issues.

5. Some psychological truths are universal; some are culture-bound (Keith, 2008, p. 484).]

Although cross-cultural issues have long interested researchers from several disciplines, the field has experienced a proliferation of research and an increase in interest in the past two or three decades. In the process, researchers have shown that cultural influences are powerful and that they run deep in shaping behavior and thought (e.g., Heine, 2008). What then, can teachers across disciplines gain from cross-cultural psychology as they work to improve pedagogy and learning in a diverse range of higher education environments?

Cross-Cultural Psychology and Teaching ———

Psychology teachers have long recognized the important role of culture in higher education (e.g., McGovern, Furumoto, Halpern, Kimble, & McKeachie, 1991). Like researchers and any other human beings, teachers bring to their work their own cultural understandings, expectancies, and biases. Each of the principles I enumerated earlier can help enlighten us as we set out to teach.

The Construct of Culture

Culture, as John Berry, Ype Poortinga, Marshall Segall, and Pierre Dasen (2002) stated, is "the shared way of life of a group of people" (p. 2). Such a shared way of life encompasses the behavioral norms and cognitions of the group, sets the group apart from other groups, and provides the means for conveying beliefs and behaviors to new members (Lehman, Chiu, & Schaller,

2004). Thus, culture, in contrast to such constructs as personality, passes from one generation to the next (Brislin, 2000). Some elements of culture are physical, tangible features such as tools or architecture, and others are subjective, such as attitudes, behaviors, and cognitions (Triandis & Brislin, 1984). The latter, the subjective elements of culture, most concern psychologists and teachers.

Awareness of the reality of culture and cultural diversity is essential for teachers. However, researchers interested in culture have long recognized a dearth of cultural content in teaching (e.g., Cole, 1984; Cushner, 1987). Nevertheless, there are appropriate approaches that teachers can use to improve cultural sensitivity and understanding. For example, Kenneth Cushner and Richard Brislin (1996) used a teaching technique involving presentation of scenarios depicting intercultural incidents. Students could choose among alternative ways of responding to incidents and receive constructive feedback to help them identify culturally sensitive alternative responses. The result was an improvement in cultural knowledge and empathy.

People Are More Alike Than Different

We live today in a global environment in which cultures have more frequent and varied kinds of interaction than at any time in our history. People of many countries have increasing access to common media and other sophisticated electronic communications, despite growing discrepancies between the lives of the rich and the poor in many parts of the world (Keith, 2011a). The result is a dynamic, intermingled mix that requires change in the ways we understand similarities and differences (Shiraev & Levy, 2007).

Despite a multitude of cultural differences in a variety of dimensions (e.g., social, psychological, economic, religious), the fact remains that all cultures have common needs to deal with the same problems—health, safety, reproduction, and, ultimately, survival (Matsumoto, 2009). Organizational leaders who work to solve these problems may differ in their particular styles across cultures (Singh & Pandey, 1986; Sinha, 1979), yet share many of the same leadership traits and levels of motivational strength (Tripathi & Cervone, 2008). Perhaps of more direct relevance to teachers is the finding that educators across cultures agree on the importance of several common sources of motivation for their students, including parental influence, student-teacher relations, and enjoyment of academic subjects (Hufton, Elliott, & Illushin, 2003). Thus, although our students differ in many obvious ways, including the role of such rewards as grades, praise, or goal attainment (Hufton, Elliott, & Illushin, 2002), their basic motivations may have important similarities.

Judging Cultures From Our Own Perspective

The human tendency to judge other cultures in relation to our own, and to see our own as superior, is perhaps universal (LeVine & Campbell, 1972). This phenomenon is known as ethnocentrism (Berry et al., 2002), an idea that Charles Darwin (1874) recognized, and that William Graham Sumner (1906) first named. Teachers are likely to encounter and experience ethnocentrism in a variety of ways. Researchers have, for example, studied ethnocentrism directed toward people with disabilities (Chesler, 1965), ethnic minorities in the United States (Gittler, 1972; Hraba, 1972; Mutisya & Ross, 2005; Prothro, 1952; Raden, 2003), and other nationalities (Beswick, 1972; Cashdan, 2001; Khan & Liu, 2008; Li & Liu, 1975).

As teachers, we want, of course, to find ways to overcome or to minimize ethnocentrism in ourselves and in our students. Here too, cross-cultural researchers can provide some possible direction. Higher education may play a role in reducing ethnocentrism (Hooghe, 2008), a possibility that Walter Plant (1958a, 1958b) investigated, finding that students became less ethnocentric following 2 and 4 years of college. Although Plant could not clearly specify the causes of the decrease in ethnocentrism, he suggested that personality and maturational changes associated with the college experience might play a role. There is also tentative evidence that a course with cross-cultural content (Pettijohn & Naples, 2009) or intercultural service requirements (Borden, 2007) may contribute to a reduction in ethnocentrism. Some writers (e.g., Allport, 1954) have discussed the possibility that creating contact between groups may reduce conflict between them, but teachers should know that this strategy may be successful only if we provide sufficient institutional and social support (Brewer & Brown, 1998).

The Importance of Cultural Dimensions

Geert Hofstede (1980; Hofstede & Hofstede, 2005) has identified five core dimensions that researchers have found useful to characterize cultures. Geert Hofstede and Gert Jan Hofstede defined these dimensions, and some of their implications for education, in the following way:

1. Power distance (PD)—the degree to which less powerful people in a culture expect and accept unequal power distribution. In a high PD context, students treat teachers with respect and education is teacher-centered. In a low PD situation, education is student-centered, students ask questions and may disagree or argue with teachers, and teachers may receive no special respect outside the educational environment.

2. Individualism-collectivism (IC)—the extent to which the interests of the individual or the interests of the collective prevail in a cultural

setting or group. Individualist teachers may be surprised to find that students from collectivist cultures, unless specifically addressed by the teacher, are reluctant to speak up in class without the consensus of the group. Teachers may overcome this tendency through use of smaller subgroups within the class. Collectivists may also place a premium on *how to do* things, whereas individualists are more likely to focus on the learning process—*how to learn* (Hofstede and Hofstede seem, here, to make a distinction between the active nature of skills and the cognitive aspects of learning).

3. Masculinity-femininity (MA)—the degree to which cultural gender roles are clearly distinct (masculine) or overlapping (feminine). According to Hofstede and Hofstede, teachers in feminine cultures are more likely to praise and encourage weaker students, in contrast to teachers in masculine cultures, where excellence (seen as a masculine concept) receives praise from teachers. Students from masculine cultures—who may see *average* as *below average*—are more likely to focus on grades and see failure as more disastrous than do students from feminine cultures.

4. Uncertainty avoidance (UA)—the level of tolerance of the ambiguous and unpredictable. Students from high UA cultures are likely to prefer highly structured learning environments: clear timelines, specific learning outcomes, and clearly detailed assignments. These students may see their teachers as expert and believe there is a single correct answer to important questions. Students from low UA countries prefer more informal structures, teachers and books that explain things in ordinary language, and experts who aren't afraid to say, "I don't know."

5. Long-term orientation (LTO)—the extent to which the culture fosters such future-oriented behaviors as perseverance and thrift (long-term) or past- and present-oriented virtues such as respect for tradition and saving face (short-term). Students from cultures ranking high in LTO tend to develop interest and ability in applied sciences, mathematics, and formal problem solving. They also see their academic success (or failure) as the product of their level of effort. In contrast, students from low LTO cultures are more likely to view success or failure as the product of luck, take an interest in more theoretical or abstract sciences, and be less skillful in mathematics and formal problem solving.

It is not, of course, invariably the case that individuals from cultures ranking high (or low) on these dimensions will follow the pattern for their culture. Thus, teachers must be wary of stereotyping individual students, and recognize that, for example, many cultures mix individualistic and collectivistic features or that not all people in a collectivistic culture will be collectivists (Triandis, 1994). Nevertheless, awareness of these culture-based patterns of behavior may well prove useful for teachers working in multicultural settings. Teachers may note, for example, that individualistic students find their motivation in personal goals or recognition, whereas collectivistic students are more attuned to the well-being of the group; or students from a background high in uncertainty avoidance may bring an expectation of a level of formality uncommon to many Western classrooms.

Universal and Culture-Bound Truths

Researchers have long searched for psychological principles that are universally valid or true. However, it is evident that many psychological research findings are limited, or at least significantly influenced, by their cultures. The concepts *emic* and *etic* derive from the work of linguist Kenneth Pike (1967) and denote principles or truths that vary from culture to culture (emics) or that seem pancultural or universal (etics). Just as psychological truth may differ across cultures, so too may views of education and teaching (Kemp, 2008). Recognition of this may be essential to those who teach in a multicultural or cross-cultural context.

For example, it is challenging to develop tests that measure skills that are valued in more than one culture (Cianciolo & Sternberg, 2004). Both teachers and students find it difficult to get beyond a single-culture (emic) perspective, to see the world from a broader etic viewpoint that allows understanding of multiple cultural perspectives. Teachers, like members of the helping and caring professions (see Zander, 2007), must realize that the reality of their students' lives can differ widely across the bounds of culture and that it is essential to bridge differences in communication, religion, and worldview. In a diverse world, an etic, one-size-fits-all perspective will well serve neither students nor teachers.

The Culture of the Classroom

Many university faculty members teach in settings that include a majority ethnic or cultural group and one or more minority groups. This situation, coupled with the fact that the faculty, too, often comprise majority and minority groups, has prompted some writers to question who should be responsible for teaching about cultural diversity. Should teaching about diversity be the role of majority faculty, minority faculty, or both? In a discussion of this issue, Loreto Prieto (2009) concluded, "We must engage in a joint, unified effort in which academicians from both majority and diverse cultures do their part" (p. 26). There is simply not, Prieto argued, a sufficient number of minority faculty to meet the immediate demands of teaching about culture, or to have a widespread impact on students' understanding of culture and diversity—it is a job for *all* faculty. In a similar vein, Kenneth D. Keith (2011a), writing about psychology, said, "We might imagine a future in which culture would be an integral part of all teaching and research in psychology" (p. 556).

Culture, then, might be embedded in all teaching, not necessarily as an explicitly taught addition to our courses, but as an implicit aspect of the regular culture of the classroom. Teachers' understanding of at least three areas of emphasis seems important to achieving such an integrated aim. These are the contribution of language and communication, the nature of acculturation, and conceptions of teaching and learning. I will briefly discuss each of these in relation to the role of college and university teachers.

Language and Communication

In a discussion introducing culture to the classroom, Karen Cone-Uemura (2009) described the communication factor of the Multicultural Counseling Inventory (Sodowsky, Taffe, Gutkin, & Wise, 1994) in terms of two key notions: an individual understanding that there are differences in people's ways of sharing meaning with each other, and recognition that there is not a single "right" way to communicate. Inevitably, as classrooms bring together people from different cultures, the importance of competent, flexible communication comes to the fore (Chung, 2011).

Unfortunately, cross-cultural misunderstandings and conflicts seem to occur regularly in academic exchanges between people of different cultures (Degen & Absalom, 1998). These difficulties may result in the inability of students to achieve learning objectives and may even cause them to drop out of educational programs (Slimmer, Highland, & Stout, 2009). In U.S. colleges, two interesting, related approaches have shown promise for alleviating some of the communication problems experienced by international students: the assignment of U.S. students as "buddies" for international students (Shigaki & Smith, 1997) and pairing of international students with English-speaking student, faculty, or staff conversational partners (Zhai, 2002).

Although many cross-cultural misunderstandings are directly related to language differences (rather than broader cultural differences; Roberts, Moss, Wass, Sarangi, & Jones, 2005), Thushari Welikala (2008) has proposed that language embodies particular approaches to knowledge and culture. Welikala argued that students from diverse cultures, studying in English, may feel disempowered in the face of apparent marginalization of their own cultural narratives and worldviews. According to Welikala, teaching and learning would be improved if English-speaking academics could work to overcome the disarticulation between the pedagogical perspective of the institution and that of students' native cultures. Thus, teachers need to make the effort to understand and be sensitive to the linguistic and cultural backgrounds of their students. Increased understanding can come from simple everyday efforts such as informal conversations with culturally diverse students, use of multicultural examples in teaching, or attendance at international student organizational activities. The result is likely to be improved communication and improved education.

Acculturation

People become competent members of their social group through experience with the normal institutions of their native cultures: parenting, education, religion, and the like, a process called *enculturation* (Cole & Packer, 2011). In contrast, a minority culture individual aspiring to become a competent member of the majority culture experiences acculturation (Miller, 2011). Colleges and universities are likely to support dominant cultural ideologies, and experience in the university exposes international or minority students to new aspects of culture, knowledge, and the majority society (Weiner-Levy, 2008), requiring them to become acculturated to the academic environment. In the process, they may well experience social isolation and a kind of transitional shock associated with accommodation to a different culture (McLachlan & Justice, 2009).

International students, then, may experience health and adjustment difficulties, especially within the first 6 to 12 months at a new university (McLachlan & Justice, 2009), suggesting the need for outreach to facilitate their adjustment. In addition to understanding the initial adjustment needs created by the transition to life in an unfamiliar university environment, teachers should be aware that students are also striving to become acculturated—trying to create an identity as a member of the majority university culture. Faculty members must also expect that minority students will sometimes withdraw and reject the majority culture, and that diversity can prompt backlash among majority students (Prieto, 2009). So, although it is true that people from various cultural backgrounds are more alike than different, it is also the case that teachers need awareness of the special acculturative challenges that students from such varying backgrounds may experience. Teachers can aid the process of acculturation by reaching out to students—in informal conversation; by inquiring about students' adjustment and well-being, or by remaining alert (and responding) to signs of academic difficulty.

Conceptions of Teaching and Learning

Teachers, like all people, have individual backgrounds and experiences that shape their perspectives on life and work—their worldview. Our worldviews influence our approach to broad social and cultural issues and affect our behavior in such environments as the classroom and in the inferences we make about the behavior of others (Robinson, 2009). Teachers from different cultures may therefore have different conceptions and beliefs about teaching (Kemp, 2008). Educators have, for example, characterized educational philosophies as "Western" or "Eastern" (Ryan & Louie, 2007, p. 404) and "teacher-centered" or "student-centered" (Kemp, 2008, p. 252)

Perhaps, as Darryl Mitry (2008) suggested, there was a time in Western cultures when the shared customs, beliefs, and practices of students allowed teachers to adopt a single-culture viewpoint and ignore a diversity of perspectives. That time, however, is past; today's teachers need to contemplate the cultural assumptions that underlie their methods and the corresponding difficulties those methods may present for students (Ryan & Louie, 2007). Teachers should also challenge their own worldviews, raising questions about their assumptions and their potential effects on student attitudes and learning. We must realize that, as teachers and researchers, we too, have our own biases and ethnocentrism. When considering the behavior of students from other cultures, we must be alert to the fact that they are products of their own experience. Accordingly, such judgments as "too reserved," "insecure," or "disengaged" may say as much about our own cultural biases as they do about the behavior of the student.

Concluding Thoughts

Much of the literature dealing with diversity and internationalization of curricula has discussed the importance of aiding the achievement and adjustment of international and minority students. However, as G. William Hill (2002) suggested, our students and our academic disciplines may suffer if we fail to excite the interest of diverse students because, he noted, students may simply choose not to pursue studies in fields they see as lacking ethnic and cultural diversity. It is therefore important that teachers not marginalize cultural content and viewpoints (Goldstein, 1995), but that they attempt to develop a "meta-cultural" awareness and be willing to attempt to meet the needs of all students, no matter what their cultural background (Ryan & Louie, 2007).

Clifford Geertz (1973) characterized cultures as webs of significance through which people seek meaning. We have seen that the search for meaning must extend beyond the knowledge deriving from culture-limited research and that the integration of culture and diversity is the job of all college and university teachers. As Regan Gurung (2009) concluded, "Culture is multifaceted, influencing every aspect of life. Healthy curricula need both specialty courses and the infusion of culture into standard courses" (p. 19). Unlike the frog in the well, we have a choice: We can move beyond the boundaries of our own cultural experience, and as we do so, we can provide our students a new, broader view of the world.

References

Allport, G. W. (1954). *The nature of prejudice.* Reading, MA: Addison-Wesley.

Arnett, J. J. (2008). The neglected 95%: Why American psychology needs to become less American. *American Psychologist, 63,* 602–614.

Berry, J. W., Poortinga, Y. H., Segall, M. H., & Dasen, P. R. (2002). *Cross-cultural psychology: Research and applications* (2nd ed.). Cambridge, UK: Cambridge University Press.

Beswick, D. G. (1972). A survey of ethnocentrism in Australia. *Australian Journal of Psychology, 24,* 153–163.

Borden, A. W. (2007). The impact of service-learning on ethnocentrism in an intercultural communication course. *Journal of Experiential Education, 30,* 171–183.

Branche, J., Mullennix, J., & Cohn, R. R. (Eds.). (2007). *Diversity across the curriculum: A guide for faculty in higher education.* Boston, MA: Anker.

Brewer, M. B., & Brown, R. J. (1998). Intergroup relations. In D. T. Gilbert, S. T. Fiske, & G. Lindzey (Eds.), *The handbook of social psychology* (4th ed., Vol. 2, pp. 554–594). New York, NY: McGraw-Hill.

Brislin, R. (2000). *Understanding culture's influence on behavior.* Fort Worth, TX: Harcourt.

Cashdan, E. (2001). Ethnocentrism and xenophobia: A cross-cultural study. *Current Anthropology, 42,* 760–765.

Chesler, M. A. (1965). Ethnocentrism and attitudes toward the physically disabled. *Journal of Personality and Social Psychology, 2,* 877–882.

Chung, L. C. (2011). Crossing boundaries: Cross-cultural communication. In K. D. Keith (Ed.), *Cross-cultural psychology: Contemporary themes and perspectives* (pp. 400–420). Malden, MA: Wiley-Blackwell.

Cianciolo, A. T., & Sternberg, R. J. (2004). *Intelligence: A brief history.* Malden, MA: Wiley-Blackwell.

Cole, M. (1984). The world beyond our borders: What might our students need to know about it? *American Psychologist, 39,* 998–1005.

Cole, M., & Packer, M. (2011). Culture and cognition. In K. D. Keith (Ed.), *Cross-cultural psychology: Contemporary themes and perspectives* (pp. 133–159). Malden, MA: Wiley-Blackwell.

Cone-Uemura, K. (2009). Pleased to meet you: Introducing multicultural competence and diversity awareness to your students. In R. A. R. Gurung & L. R. Prieto (Eds.), *Getting culture: Incorporating diversity across the curriculum* (pp. 259–268). Sterling, VA: Stylus.

Cushner, K. H. (1987). Teaching cross-cultural psychology: Providing the missing link. *Teaching of Psychology, 14,* 220–224.

Cushner, K., & Brislin, R. (1996). *Intercultural interactions: A practical guide* (2nd ed.). Thousand Oaks, CA: Sage.

Darwin, C. (1874). *The descent of man and selection in relation to sex* (2nd ed.). New York, NY: A. L. Burt.

Degen, T., & Absalom, D. (1998). Teaching across cultures: Considerations for Western EFL teachers in China. *Hong Kong Journal of Applied Linguistics, 3,* 117–132.

Geertz, C. (1973). *The interpretation of cultures: Selected essays.* New York, NY: Basic Books.

Gittler, J. B. (1972). Jews as an ethnic minority in the United States. *International Journal of Group Tensions, 2,* 4–21.

Goldstein, S. B. (1995). Cross-cultural psychology as a curriculum transformation resource. *Teaching of Psychology, 22,* 228–232.

Gurung, R. A. R. (2009). Got culture? Incorporating culture into the curriculum. In R. A. R. Gurung & L. R. Prieto (Eds.), *Getting culture: Incorporating diversity across the curriculum* (pp. 11–22). Sterling, VA: Stylus.

Guthrie, R. V. (1998). *Even the rat was white: A historical view of psychology* (2nd ed.). Boston, MA: Allyn & Bacon.

Heine, S. J. (2008). *Cultural psychology.* New York, NY: W. W. Norton.

Hilferty, F. (2008). Teacher professionalism and cultural diversity: Skills, knowledge and values for a changing Australia. *The Australian Educational Researcher, 35*(3), 53–70.

Hill, G. W., IV (2002). Incorporating cross-cultural perspectives into the psychology curriculum: Challenges and strategies. In S. F. Davis & W. Buskist (Eds.), *The teaching of psychology: Essays in honor of Wilbert J. McKeachie and Charles L. Brewer* (pp. 431–443). Mahwah, NJ: Lawrence Erlbaum.

Hofstede, G. (1980). *Culture's consequences: International differences in work-related values.* Beverly Hills, CA: Sage.

Hofstede, G., & Hofstede, G. J. (2005). *Cultures and organizations: Software of the mind.* New York, NY: McGraw-Hill.

Hooghe, M. (2008). Ethnocentrism. *International encyclopedia of the social sciences.* Philadelphia, PA: Macmillan Reference.

Hraba, J. (1972). The doll technique: A measure of racial ethnocentrism? *Social Forces, 50,* 522–527.

Hufton, N. R., Elliott, J. G., & Illushin, L. (2002). Achievement motivation across cultures: Some puzzles and their implications for future research. *New Directions for Child and Adolescent Development, 96,* 65–85.

Hufton, N. R., Elliott, J. G., & Illushin, L. (2003). Teachers' beliefs about student motivation: Similarities and differences across cultures. *Comparative Education, 39,* 367–389.

Kagitçibaşi, Ç., & Berry, J. W. (1989). Cross-cultural psychology: Current research and trends. *Annual Review of Psychology, 40,* 493–531.

Keith, K. D. (2008). Cross-cultural psychology and research. In S. F. Davis & W. Buskist (Eds.), *21st century psychology: A reference handbook* (Vol. 2, pp. 483–490). Thousand Oaks, CA: Sage.

Keith, K. D. (2011a). Cross-cultural psychology in perspective: What does the future hold? In K. D. Keith (Ed.), *Cross-cultural psychology: Contemporary themes and perspectives* (pp. 549–559). Malden, MA: Wiley-Blackwell.

Keith, K. D. (2011b). Introduction to cross-cultural psychology. In K. D. Keith (Ed.), *Cross-cultural psychology: Contemporary themes and perspectives* (pp. 3–19). Malden, MA: Wiley-Blackwell.

Kemp, S. (2008). Teachers' meanings: Transcending the cultural context. *Journal of Further and Higher Education, 32,* 251–262.

Khan, S. S., & Liu, J. H. (2008). Intergroup attributions and ethnocentrism in the Indian subcontinent: The ultimate attribution error revisited. *Journal of Cross-Cultural Psychology, 39,* 16–36.

Lehman, D. R., Chiu, C., & Schaller, M. (2004). Psychology and culture. *Annual Review of Psychology, 55*, 689–714.

Leiper, J., Van Horn, E. R., Hu, J., & Upadhyaya, R. C. (2008). Promoting cultural awareness and knowledge among faculty and doctoral students. *Nursing Education Perspectives, 29*(3), 161–164.

LeVine, R. A., & Campbell, D. T. (1972). *Ethnocentrism: Theories of conflict, ethnic attitudes and group behavior.* New York, NY: Wiley.

Li, W. L., & Liu, S. S. (1975). Ethnocentrism among American and Chinese youth. *Journal of Social Psychology, 95*, 277–278.

Matsumoto, D. (2009). Teaching about culture. In R. A. R. Gurung & L. R. Prieto (Eds.), *Getting culture: Incorporating diversity across the curriculum* (pp. 3–10). Sterling, VA: Stylus.

Matsumoto, D., & Juang, L. (2008). *Culture and psychology* (4th ed.). Belmont, CA: Thomson-Wadsworth.

McGovern, T. V., Furumoto, L., Halpern, D. G., Kimble, G. A., & McKeachie, W. J. (1991). Liberal education, study in depth, and the arts and sciences major—Psychology. *American Psychologist, 46*, 598–605.

McLachlan, D. A., & Justice, J. (2009). A grounded theory of international student well-being. *The Journal of Theory Construction & Testing, 13*, 27–32.

Miller, R. L. (2011). Multicultural identity development. In K. D. Keith (Ed.), *Cross-cultural psychology: Contemporary themes and perspectives* (pp. 509–523). Malder, MA: Wiley-Blackwell.

Mitry, D. J. (2008). Using cultural diversity in teaching economics: Global business implications. *Journal of Education for Business, 84*, 84–89.

Morgan, C. T., & King, R. A. (1966). *Introduction to psychology* (3rd ed.). New York, NY: McGraw-Hill.

Mutisya, P. M., & Ross, L. E. (2005). Afrocentricity and racial socialization among African American college students. *Journal of Black Studies, 35*, 235–247.

Obua Ogwal, B. (1998, October). *Opening the big door: Student declaration on equality, democracy and quality in higher education.* Paper presented at UNESCO World Conference on Higher Education, Paris, France.

Pettijohn, T. F., II, & Naples, G. M. (2009). Reducing ethnocentrism in U.S. college students by completing a cross-cultural psychology course. *The Open Social Science Journal, 2*, 1–6.

Pike, K. L. (1967). *Language in relation to a unified theory of the structure of human behavior* (2nd ed.). The Hague, Netherlands: Mouton.

Plant, W. T. (1958a). Changes in ethnocentrism associated with a four-year college education. *Journal of Educational Psychology, 49*, 162–165.

Plant, W. T. (1958b). Changes in ethnocentrism associated with a two-year college experience. *Journal of Genetic Psychology, 92*, 189–197.

Prieto, L. R. (2009). Teaching about diversity: Reflections and future directions. In R. A. R. Gurung & L. R. Prieto (Eds.), *Getting culture: Incorporating diversity across the curriculum* (pp. 23–39). Sterling, VA: Stylus.

Prothro, E. T. (1952). Ethnocentrism and anti-Negro attitudes in the Deep South. *Journal of Abnormal and Social Psychology, 47*, 105–108.

Raden, D. (2003). Ingroup bias, classic ethnocentrism, and non-ethnocentrism among American whites. *Political Psychology, 24*, 803–828.

Roberts, C., Moss, M., Wass, V., Sarangi, S., & Jones, R. (2005). Misunderstandings: A qualitative survey of primary care consultations in multilingual settings, and educational implications. *Medical Education, 35*, 465–475.

Robinson, T. N., III (2009). A metapedagogical approach to culture in the classroom. In R. A. R. Gurung & L. R. Prieto (Eds.), *Getting culture: Incorporating diversity across the curriculum* (pp. 41–51). Sterling, VA: Stylus.

Ryan, J., & Louie, K. (2007). False dichotomy? "Western" and "Confucian" concepts of scholarship and learning. *Educational Philosophy and Theory, 4*, 404–417.

Shigaki, I. S., & Smith, S. A. (1997). A cultural sharing model: American buddies for international students. *International Education, 27*, 5–21.

Shiraev, E., & Levy, D. (2007). *Cross-cultural psychology: Critical thinking and contemporary applications* (3rd ed.). Boston, MA: Pearson.

Singh, R. P., & Pandey, J. (1986). Leadership styles, control strategies and personal consequences. *Indian Journal of Industrial Relations, 22*, 41–58.

Sinha, J. B. P. (1979). The authoritative leadership: A style of effective management. *Indian Journal of Industrial Relations, 2*, 381–389.

Slimmer, L., Highland, D., & Stout, M. (2009). Communicating across cultures: Suggested teaching strategies. *Education for Health, 22*(3), 1–7.

Sodowsky, G. R., Taffe, R. C., Gutkin, T. B., & Wise, S. L. (1994). Development of the multicultural counseling inventory: A self-report measure of multicultural competencies. *Journal of Counseling Psychology, 41*, 137–148.

Sumner, W. G. (1906). *Folkways: A study of the sociological importance of usages, manners, customs, mores, and morals.* New York, NY: Ginn.

Tracey, M. D. (2005). Cultural competence: An ethical must in teaching and research. *Monitor on Psychology, 36*(11), 47.

Triandis, H. C. (1994). *Culture and social behavior.* New York, NY: McGraw-Hill.

Triandis, H. C., & Brislin, R. W. (1984). Cross-cultural psychology. *American Psychologist, 39*, 1006–1016.

Tripathi, R., & Cervone, D. (2008). Cultural variations in achievement motivation despite equivalent motivational strength: Motivational concerns among Indian and American corporate professionals. *Journal of Research in Personality, 42*, 456–464.

Weiner-Levy, N. (2008). Universities as a meeting point with new academic knowledge, society and culture: Cognitive and emotional transitions during higher education. *Cambridge Journal of Education, 38*, 497–512.

Welikala, T. (2008). Disempowering and dislocating: How learners from diverse cultures read the role of the English language in UK higher education. *London Review of Education, 6*, 159–169.

Zander, P. E. (2007). Cultural competence: Analyzing the construct. *The Journal of Theory Construction & Testing, 11*, 50–54.

Zhai, L. (2002). *Studying international students: Adjustment issues and social support.* San Diego, CA: Office of Institutional Research, San Diego Community College District.

CHAPTER 12

The Implications of Muslim Beliefs, Practices, and Traditions on University Teaching and Learning

SHAKEER ABDULLAH

This chapter will outline Muslim beliefs and practices as well as the importance of education in Islam. It will attempt to answer some frequently asked questions about Islam and Muslims and discuss student development theory and implications for counseling, teaching, and learning. It is important to understand that all of the information in this chapter is not universally applicable to every Muslim student, but it is designed to give some background information about Islam and Muslims.

It is important that faculty, administrators, and instructors have some understanding of Islam to better serve Muslim students inside and outside the classroom. Muslims have had a much higher worldwide profile since the tragedy of September 11, 2001, in New York City, Washington, D.C., and rural Pennsylvania. The investigation following that terrorist attack found that the hijackers and their associates claimed responsibility for their actions in the name of Islam. Their actions could not have been further from the teachings of Islam. There is a verse in the Qur'an that states, "Whosoever killeth a human being . . . (it as if) he had killed all mankind, and whoso saveth the life of one, it shall be as if he had saved the life of all mankind" (Qur'an 5:32).

Author's Note: It is Muslim tradition to include the notation PBUH (the peace and blessing of Allah be upon him) each time the Prophet Muhammad's name is mentioned, and this chapter reflects and respects that custom.

The Qur'an is the central guide for Muslim beliefs and practices and is used as a manual for Muslim life. Muslims use and quote the Qur'an to structure their lives and that tradition is followed in this manuscript.

If someone does not know the religion of Al-Islam, they may be open to believe that it encourages terrorism or the oppression of women and other faiths. The Prophet Muhammad is revered and honored as the ideal person and example for Muslims to follow. Islamic tradition holds that it is proper and expected to wish peace and blessings upon the Prophet Muhammad, Salli Allahualayhi Wa Salaam in Arabic or the peace and blessing of Allah be upon him (PBUH) in English. Muhammad (PBUH), said, "Whomsoever Allah intends to do good, He gives right understanding of religion." It is only with the proper understanding of Islam and the intention to learn the religion that one can truly be called a practicing Muslim. The overwhelming majority of Muslims do not personally know any terrorists and do not ascribe to the political beliefs that are at the root of many terrorist attacks. It should also be noted that Muslims suffer from the same range of mental and social disorders as the rest of humanity, and those disorders may make some Muslims susceptible to being influenced by people who would have them commit terrorist acts in the name of Islam.

Demographics

According to research by Darnell Cole and Shafiqa Ahmadi (2003), Muslims are overrepresented in colleges and universities compared with the general U.S. population. Islam, with about 1.6 billion followers, is the second largest world religion behind Christianity, which has about 2 billion followers. Judaism is the third largest of the Abrahamic faiths with about 14.5 million followers. Muslims live on every continent excluding Antarctica and make up the majority of the population in many countries in North Africa, the Middle East, and Southeast Asia. The Muslim population in the United States has been estimated to be between 3 and 8 million by Cole and Ahmadi (2010). The U.S. Census does not keep religious demographics, so there is no way to know for certain how many Muslims there actually are in the United States. The percentage of Muslims in countries around the world varies, but these numbers make clear the importance of getting to know more about your Muslim students: more about these students than just the rhetoric that surrounds the global war on terrorism, more than just the arguments that Islam oppresses women and others. The Qur'an speaks of the other Abrahamic faiths in reverent tones "nearest among them in love to the believers wilt thou find those who say, "We are Christians" (5:82). "O People of the Book! Come to common terms as between us and you" (Qur'an 3:64). This understanding belies the notion that Islam is exclusive and would seek to blot out other world religions.

Among Muslims, there are two main denominations, Sunni or orthodox Muslims and Shiite or Shi'a Muslims. These two sects are the dominant branches of Islam with more than 85 percent of Muslims identifying themselves as Sunni. The differences between Sunni Muslims and Shiite or Shi'a Muslims have their origins in the leadership succession of Muslims following the death of the Prophet Muhammad (PBUH). Sunni Muslims followed the wishes of the Prophet (PBUH) in electing his successor. Shiite Muslims believed that the caliphate, or leadership of the Muslim world, should have remained in the family of the Prophet (PBUH), and thus the rift was formed. The practical differences today have to do with additional holidays and beliefs because there is no longer an Islamic caliphate or central regulatory body of political and spiritual leadership. Many Muslims rely on their local Imams or spiritual leaders and other scholars or fiqh councils that set rulings or fatwas on religious interpretation.

Sufism and Wahhabism are two of the more famous Islamic reform movements. Sufism focuses on the spiritual side of Islam and on meditation and worship practices. The most famous proponents of Sufism remain the whirling dervishes from Turkey. Whirling dervishes dedicate their time to reflecting on God as they spin in circles in a dizzying fashion. Wahhabism strives toward taking Islam back to what it was like during the time of the Prophet (PBUH) and doing things exactly like they were done in the late 600s CE. Wahhabism has been most influential in Saudi Arabia, but has affected Muslims around the world.

Another offshoot of Islam is the Nation of Islam (NOI) established within the predominately African American population in the United States. The NOI has some Islamic references and practices, but for the most part does not align with orthodox Islam because of its nationalistic aims and its divergent theology. The Baha'i faith also borrowed some principles from Islam and has built an inclusive religious ideology without nationalistic tendencies.

There is a segment of the U.S. and world population that is not interested in learning more about Islam or Muslims because of preconceived notions. It is this author's desire to share more about Islam and Muslims for everyone and especially "for people who know the Qur'an's verses on violence but not its verses on mercy, who know the names of Muslim terrorists but not the names of Muslim poets or doctors or scholars" (Patel 2010, paragraph 4). It is to all educators who realize that the continuous acquisition of knowledge is the only way to keep from becoming stagnant that this chapter is dedicated.

Religious Practices and Beliefs

The root of Islam is the belief in the one true God, Allah. This belief in the oneness of God is known as taafsir in Arabic. *Allah* is the Arabic word for the one God. Jews refer to the one God in Hebrew as Elohim; Christians use the local language to refer to the one God as *God, Dios, Dieu*, and so on. Those who practice Islam are known as Muslims. Muslims believe that Allah has no partners or equals. There is no intercessor in Islam; Muslims pray directly to Allah. Muslims ask for forgiveness directly from God and do not worship the Prophet Muhammad (PBUH), or any other messenger of God. Muslims believe that the Islamic holy book, the Qur'an, does more than just share the origins and beliefs of Islam; it maps out their daily lives. "Islam is not just a religion; it is a way of life," Muslims are fond of saying. The Qur'an was originally revealed in Arabic and remains practically unchanged from the time of its revelation. The Qur'an has been translated as precisely as possible into many different languages, but has not been intentionally altered since its revelation. The Muslim holy book is supported in providing this guidance by the practice and habits of Islam's final messenger, Muhammad ibn Abdullah (PBUH), the Prophet of Islam.

The practice and habits of the Prophet Muhammad (PBUH) are known in Arabic as the Sunnah. Muslims often ask the question, "What would the Prophet Muhammad (PBUH) do?" about various situations, both personal and religious. Not every one of the questions that a Muslim could ask has been directly answered in the Qur'an. Many questions that Muslims had were answered directly by the Prophet (PBUH). The answers to the questions of religion and daily life given by the Prophet (PBUH) were collected and written down by his companions in volumes known as *Hadith*. These books, or Hadith, that share practices and habits of the Prophet Muhammad (PBUH) outline the Sunnah or habits and practice of the Prophet Muhammad (PBUH) and serve as guidelines for Muslims to follow in their religion and daily life.

The Qur'an, combined with the Sunnah, helps shape the daily lives and habits of Muslim students. An understanding of some of the traditions and history that bridge the multiple cultures that are represented by Muslim students can affect how they are taught and when and what lessons and cocurricular activities might be introduced in a class.

The Five Pillars of Islam

Islam is based on five pillars or requirements that all Muslims must follow. These five pillars, as outlined by the Prophet Muhammad (PBUH), are Iman (faith), Salat (prayer five times a day), Zakat (giving alms to the poor), Sawm (fasting during the Islamic month of Ramadan), and finally, Hajj (a pilgrimage to Mecca, Saudi Arabia, during the Islamic month of Dhul-Hijjah).

Iman (Faith)

To become a Muslim, one must have faith in one's heart, and one must make a declaration of faith: "I bear witness that there is no God but Allah and Muhammad (PBUH) was the final messenger." Once a person makes this declaration (Shahada), he or she is Muslim. There is no other requirement or ceremony that takes place; new Muslims are encouraged to learn more about the religion and practices of Islam. Muslims regularly make the declaration of faith during their prayers or Salat.

Salat

The second pillar of Islam is the requirement to make formal prayers (Salat) five times a day. These five prayers take place before sunrise, at midday, in the late afternoon, after sunset, and finally in the late evening. These prayers are of varying lengths and occur at different times throughout the year because the Islamic calendar is a lunar calendar and the sun rises and sets at varying times during the year. All Muslims around the world pray facing toward the Kaabaah or House of God in Mecca. The Kaabaah was originally built by Abraham and his son Ismail and reclaimed for Islam during the time of the Prophet Muhammad (PBUH). In addition to formal prayers, Muslims can petition God at any time in the form of reflective or supplicative prayers known as Du'aa.

Zakat

The third pillar of Islam is charity. Muslims are required to give charity to the poor in their community; this is known by the Arabic word *zakat*, which actually means purification (IslamiCity.com, 2011, para. 1). This duty requires Muslims to be considerate of the less fortunate in their community and encourages social justice. The duty of Zakat is upon every person regardless of how poor the person may be; every good deed is considered charity or Saadaqaa, and even a smile can be considered charity according to Hadith (Zakat.org, 2011). Much is discussed about Shari'a or Islamic law and how it imposes a tax on non-Muslims living in Muslim countries or communities. This tax exists and was imposed on non-Muslims living in Islamic lands so that those non-Muslims pay what is equivalent to the Zakat that Muslims are required to pay for the poor people in the community.

Sawm

Sawm refers to fasting during the month of Ramadan. Muslims fast or abstain from food or drink beginning shortly before sunrise until shortly after sunset for the entire month. This month is the holiest month of the Islamic calendar and is the month in which Muslims believe that the Holy Qur'an was revealed to the Prophet Muhammad (PBUH). During this month, Muslims are encouraged to read the entire Qur'an and to reflect on their faith. During fasting or daylight hours, in addition to abstaining from food and drink, Muslims are encouraged to refrain from foul language, ill thoughts, sexual relations, and bad habits such as smoking. During this month, Muslims are encouraged to give Zakat and other forms of charity (saadaqaa in Arabic) to their neighbors and community.

In addition to fasting during the month of Ramadan, Muslims also celebrate two multiple-day festivals known as *Eid*. The first Eid is known as Eid al Fitr, or feast of Fitr, is 3 days long, begins at sunset after the last day of Ramadan, and is marked by community prayer and celebrations expressed in varying degrees around the world. The other Eid is known as Eid al Adha or the Feast of the Sacrifice that marks the end of Hajj. This feast also commemorates Abraham's willingness to follow the command of God to sacrifice his son Ismail. These important holidays may fall on school days and Muslim students may ask to be excused from class on these days.

Hajj

The fifth and final pillar of Islam is Hajj or making a pilgrimage to Mecca for all Muslims who are physically able and can afford to make the trip. During Hajj, Muslims pray at the Kaabbaah and visit other holy sites. Muslims are forgiven for all of their sins if they successfully complete the pilgrimage.

The five pillars form the basis for the religion of Islam and are universal among Muslims. The differences that arise between Muslims beyond the five pillars and the Qur'an have to do with the practice of the religion and the cultural traditions that people have adopted during the last 15 centuries. It is important for Muslims to be educated so they know their religion. It is not enough to be able to recite and listen to Qur'an, Muslims must also be able to understand their faith and apply it to their everyday lives.

Muslims are required to believe in all the religious books including the Torah, the Bible, and the Gospel of David as well as all of the prophets that came before the final messenger of God, Muhammad (PBUH). This is a part of the first pillar of Islam, faith in all that has been revealed by God. Muslims believe that all of the messengers of God—from Adam, Abraham, Isaac, Ismail, Noah, Job, Jonah, Moses, Solomon, David, Jesus, John, to Muhammad—brought the same message, the message that humankind is supposed to believe in the one true God and submit to his will. Muslims believe the Muhammad was the final messenger of God and the Qur'an was the final revelation of God's message. "This day have I perfected for you your religion and completed My favor on you and chosen for you Islam" (Qur'an 5:3). Judaism and Christianity believe that their way is the true way to salvation; Islam believes that all of the righteous among the people of the book (Jews, Christians, and Muslims) who believe in the oneness of God (Tawheed), believe in the Day of Judgment, and practice good deeds will make it to paradise. Those who believe (in the Qur'an), and those who follow the Jewish (scriptures), and the Christians and the Sabians, "Any who believe in Allah and the Last Day and work righteousness shall have their reward with their Lord; on them shall be no fear, nor shall they grieve." (Qur'an 2:53)

"O mankind! We created you from a single (pair) of male and female, and made you into nations and tribes, that you may know each other (not that you despise each other)" (Qur'an 49:12). The Prophet (PBUH) in his last sermon said, "Your Lord is One, Allah the Almighty, and your Father is One, Prophet Adam, No Arab is superior than non Arab or non Arab over Arab, black over white, white over black, except in Taqwa (God fearing, piety)." Muslims were instructed to know their religion and practice it in the manner exemplified by the Prophet Muhammad (PBUH). There was to be no racism or classism in the practice of Islam, yet those things exist.

Impact of Islam on Student Behavior

Muslims are prohibited from eating pork and pork products, but there are few other dietary restrictions. Muslims are discouraged from being vegans or vegetarians because by doing so, one is making unlawful what has been declared lawful. The same idea applies to vows of chastity. Muslims are encouraged to remain chaste until marriage, but marriage and procreation are considered one's Islamic duty. The Qur'an also prohibits alcohol and gambling for Muslims. It is helpful to understand these prohibitions in Islam, but one should also understand that Muslim students may engage in all of these things, which can have an impact both in and out of the classroom. When teaching, advising, or counseling Muslim students who have issues related to alcohol violations, gambling, or premarital sex, it is important to be mindful that in addition to any institutional actions or sanctions that may occur, Muslim students may also feel internal religious as well as external family and community pressures related to these issues. Knowledge of the origins and practices of Islam may help give you some insight into the experience of Muslim students. All Muslims do not practice the religion in the same manner, but the shared roots and guidance found in the Qur'an provide basic fundamentals for all Muslims, regardless of their cultural, racial, global, or ethnic background.

The Importance of Education in Islam

According to Islamic tradition, one of the most blessed things that one can do is to learn and seek knowledge for the pleasure of Allah. "Whosoever treads any path in search of knowledge, Allah will make the path to Paradise easy for him, the Angels spread out their wings out of pleasure for the seeker of knowledge, those in the sky and the fish in the ocean seek forgiveness on behalf of the one seeking knowledge" (The Forty Hadith, 2011, para. 2). The Prophet (PBUH) says in the preceding Hadith that all of God's creation prays for those who are students and are in pursuit of knowledge.

"The ink of the scholar is worth 1,000 times (more than) the blood of the martyr." This quote has been a part of Islamic tradition for thousands of years, though its origin cannot be authenticated. What is clear though, is the importance that Islam places on education and improving one's self through learning about the religion of Al-Islam and struggling within one's self to be the best Muslim that one can be—in other words, performing Jihad. Many people take this word out of context and only think of Jihad in terms of holy wars against other faiths. Prophet Muhammad (PBUH) said, "Seeking knowledge is an obligation upon every Muslim." Wisdom is mentioned no less than 98 times in the Qur'an, and knowledge is mentioned 257 times. Jihad in any form is mentioned 28 times and fighting is mentioned 94 times. The internal or greater struggle known in Arabic as *jihad al-akbar* is the most important struggle and the way to fight that battle is to continuously learn more about Islam and the global society. The continuous pursuit of excellence in education and scholarship date back to the origins of Islam more than 1,400 years ago and continues in many parts of the vast Islamic diaspora.

The pursuit of knowledge and understanding has long been a part of the Islamic tradition. According to the Qur'an, *iqraa*, which in English means to read or recite, was the first command given to the Prophet Muhammad (PBUH) by the Angel Gabriel. The Prophet (PBUH) indicated that he could not read and he was commanded again to iqraa, or read. Gabriel told Muhammad (PBUH) that he had been chosen as the Messenger of God, or Rasul'Allah in Arabic, and that he was supposed to share the word of God with the world. "Proclaim! (or read) in the name of thy Lord and Cherisher, Who created man, out of a (mere) clot of congealed blood: Proclaim! And thy Lord is Most Bountiful, He Who taught (the use of) the pen; taught man that which he knew not" (Qur'an, 96:1–5).

Following this initial encounter, the Qur'an was then revealed during the next 23 years. The Islamic lunar calendar began several years after this initial revelation, around 622 CE. This beginning of the Muslim calendar is known as *hijraa*, and it marks the founding of the first Islamic state in Medina, in what is now known as Saudi Arabia. The year 2011 CE will encompass the years 1432 and 1433 of the Islamic calendar.

The command to read has taken on great significance in the Muslim world since the introduction of the Qur'an. Islamic tradition encourages the faithful to "seek knowledge from the cradle to the grave" and are encouraged to pursue knowledge from "here to China," though both of these exultations cannot be authenticated; they too have been used to encourage Muslims to learn more about themselves and the world around them.

Islamic Academic History and Tradition

During the height of the Islamic empires, science and architecture flourished. Many of the areas controlled by Muslims had great libraries and designed and built large mosques and hospitals (Esposito, 1999). Muslims have contributed much to world history and knowledge; from the use of Arabic numerals, which were originally Hindi numerals (Esposito, 1999) and the introduction of zero to some of the earliest institutions of higher learning. The Qur'an itself contains information about cells, human development, astronomy, and science that would not be proven for centuries after its introduction. The Qur'an outlines the process of aging from insemination to old age and does so in ways that were not proven by science for hundreds of years after the Qur'an was introduced.

Implications for Teaching

The tradition of learning has been highlighted through Islamic history and practice and rests on a strong tradition of discipline. Muslims must adhere to their daily prayer schedule and must avoid indulging in those things that are prohibited in Islam. This same discipline can manifest itself in the classroom and in Muslim students' academic work. Routine is related to discipline, and some Muslims may appreciate routine in the classroom and may be able to adopt classroom etiquette quickly. Traditional Islamic learning included reciting and memorizing the Qur'an, and some academic disciplines may value this type of learning more than others do and may therefore be more appealing to Muslims.

Muslim students may, because of the Islamic tradition of support for those who are less fortunate (Zakat), find service learning courses, community services efforts, global service trips, or any type of lesson that involves engaging people of varying economic means very appealing.

Muslims are required to pray five times at varying times throughout the day. These times vary throughout the year because the times of the sunrise and sunset change daily. Friday Jummaah prayer differs from regular Salat in that it is the communal prayer and weekly sermon or Islamic lesson for Muslims usually held at the local mosque or house of worship. Jummaah is required for Muslim men. Therefore, not scheduling Friday afternoon classes or meetings so that students can attend Friday prayers is helpful. Accommodations may need to be made for those students who are fasting and for those students who need to pray during class time. For students who are fasting, it is a good idea not to schedule lunch meetings, dinner meetings, or potlucks during fasting hours, sunrise to sunset. For students who need to pray, excusing them for a few minutes from class is helpful, as long as students are aware that they are responsible for any materials that they missed. A willingness on behalf of instructors and administrators to make these accommodations can show good will and open the path to further dialogue. Although these suggestions are specifically for Muslim students, it is important that instructors show flexibility for all students; these are just some suggestions to help manage classrooms that are becoming increasingly diverse and representative of a global society.

Muslim Student Identity Development Theory

Varying levels of Islamic identity can be described as falling within a Muslim student development framework or theory. This theory is based on other religious identity and student development theories. Even though little research has been done on Muslim identity development, some work is relevant to this idea, particularly the work of Cole and Ahmadi (2003, 2010) in their investigation of Muslim women and their practice of covering their hair and the work of Judith Klein (1980) and her research on Jewish identity. Klein highlighted the fact that Jewish people have an ethnic identity as well as a religious identity. Muslims are similar in that their religious identity is manifested in all that they do, even though all Muslims do not share the same ethnicity. It is important to note that both student development and religious development approaches are needed because Islam is both a religion and a way of life. This theory of Muslim student identity development is also rooted in racial identity development theory pioneered by Janet Helms (1990) and Joseph Ponterotto, J. Manuel Casas, Lisa Suzuki, and Charlene Alexander (1995) among others, and it is important to build on this new theory through additional research and practical application of the ideas shared here.

The five stages of Muslim student identity development presented here were developed by the author based on more than 10 years working at the university level in student and diversity affairs, more than 6 years of academic course work related to higher education, and from lifelong interactions with Muslims worldwide. The various stages of Muslim student identity development are not ordinal and can be manifested in different ways at different times in people's lives, much like Arthur Chickering's (1969) seven vectors of college student development, and students can move back and forth through the varying stages (Andreatta, 2009). Muslim student identity development has some similarities to both Cross's and Helms's models of racial identity development in that students will have life experiences, crises, and successes that can influence how and when someone might move from one stage to another.

Formative Stage of Muslim Student Identity Development

This stage considers that people who are raised Muslim in predominately Muslim environments adopt an understanding of Islam that is based on community involvement and community worship. They take their religious practices and identity for granted because everyone around them is Muslim and adheres to Islamic and local cultural traditions. This stage is evidenced by a lack of Qur'anic knowledge and knowledge of the tradition of the Prophet Muhammad or the Sunnah. People at this stage may take their religion for granted and may be unable to explain what they believe and why they believe it. They just know that they are Muslim. People at this stage may be uncomfortable practicing their faith outside of their community and may not actually know how to practice their faith outside of their community.

Passive Muslim Student Identity Development Stage

This stage is marked by a Muslim identity only in the nominal sense. Individuals functioning at this stage know they are Muslim and know how to practice their faith, but they only practice when it is convenient for them. They believe in Islam and aspire to be good Muslims, but they do not actively practice the faith. This stage can be brought on by life changes and other challenging personal times like moving away from your family to attend college or events such as 9/11. It can be evidenced in changes in behavior such as women no longer wearing the hijab or head covering or men no longer praying or observing chastity.

Dormant Stage of Muslim Student Identity Development

This stage is the phase where people who have been Muslim reject the practices of Islam and religion all together. People at this stage do not want to bother with belief or all of the things that go into being Muslim; they would rather just exist among fellow human beings without the guilt that may be felt by one not fulfilling religious obligations or without ritual prayers associated with their Islamic faith.

Reactive Stage of Muslim Student Identity Development

This stage comes about as a result of a life event, or events, that lead people who have abandoned their Islamic faith to return to the practice of their religion fervently. People in this stage tend to be hyper religious and attempt to follow Qur'an and Sunnah "to the letter." People operating at this stage tend to abandon all worldly interests and pursuits in their efforts to reconnect with Islam. Students at this stage may tend to ignore their academic responsibilities in the fervent quest to reclaim their Muslim faith. Faculty can help guide these students back to their studies by reminding them of the importance of education in Islam.

Proactive Stage of Muslim Student Identity Development

This stage can be termed as Islamic Enlightenment. Students at this stage are able to balance religious practice and tradition with the responsibilities and pursuits of everyday academic life and are engaged in the pursuit of the hereafter as well as the good in this world.

These stages of Muslim identity development are preliminary and need to be refined with additional research, but knowledge of these stages can help educators relate to students in their classes and may help educators reach Muslim students in ways that resonate with their religious values as they move through the various stages of identity development. It is important to understand that these stages are fluid, and people can fluctuate back and forth through them given their daily circumstances and choices. If students are failing academically, they may venture into the reactive stage as a way of avoiding the frustrations of their academic difficulties. At other times, students may be away from their families for the first time and venture into the passive or dormant stages and not practice their faith at all. There may be some cases where students, in the formative stage, find a teacher hard to relate to because that teacher is not Muslim and has not shared the traditions with which they are familiar. Muslim identity student development stages can provide a framework and another tool to help you understand Islamic students.

Muslim Student Diversity

Muslims are far from a monolithic community. There are many differences among Muslims based on historical and regional culture and practice. Instructors should refrain from making assumptions about students based on their names or appearances. It is imperative that instructors let students identify themselves and identify the cultural, religious, and educational perspectives from which they come. Assuming that a student with an Arabic name is Muslim or comes from another country can alienate that student and prevent the student from fully engaging in classroom or out-of-class learning activities. Asking students directly, in the presence of other non-Muslim students, about fasting or other religious practices can further isolate students. There may be circumstances where Muslim students in a given classroom are at different stages in their Islamic identity development and may give different answers to the same questions. It is a fallacy to think that all Muslims are the same and have the same perspectives or the same knowledge of historical or current events. Many Muslims are not aware of global political conflicts and cannot speak to those experiences, so it is important to remember this as faculty engage students.

Other Teaching
and Learning Considerations

Muslims have varying levels of faith as previously described by Muslim student identity development theory. These variances affect Muslim's understanding and practice of their faith, and it is possible that readers of this chapter have gained a better understanding of Islam than have Muslims who have not taken the time to learn their religion.

Cultural traditions around the world influence how Islam is practiced. In the many places where there are Muslim immigrants, differing cultural traditions come together at places of worship, mosques, or community centers and affect the way that Muslims pray, what they eat, how they interact with the opposite sex, and how they dress.

The tense climate surrounding Islam and Muslims around the world as a result of 9/11 and current changes in Middle Eastern and African politics can lead to the bullying of Muslim students during class discussions as well as exclusion from study groups or group projects. Issues can also arise in roommate situations as a result of accommodations not being made for prayer times or visitation of the opposite sex. Islam encourages the separation of the sexes to avoid inappropriate sexual contact. Modesty is encouraged among all Muslims including in their dress and talk, and it may be difficult to get Muslims to talk about themselves or reveal personal and family information in in-class discussion or written assignments.

Family is very important to most Muslims. Muslims are instructed to keep their ties with kinship, even the non-Muslim members of their families. The Muslim world considers every Muslim to be a brother or sister in faith. Islam allows intermarriage among the "people of the book": Christians, Jews, and Muslims. Although interfaith marriage is challenging for some, this flexibility in Islam allows interfaith dialogue to take place on intimate and global levels.

Some Muslims will not be native speakers of English or whatever the local language might be, and not all Muslims speak Arabic even though prayers are recited in Arabic. There is a good chance that many of your Muslim students will speak multiple languages.

An Islamic tradition encourages Muslims to only speak good things about other Muslims, and this tradition keeps Muslims from disparaging Muslims even if they know that other Muslims have done something wrong. This may explain why more Muslims do not denounce terrorist acts committed by Muslims. This tradition comes from the Prophet Muhammad (PBUH) and helps maintain intergroup harmony and keep people humble.

Conclusion

This chapter has outlined many of the important Muslim beliefs and practices as well as the importance of education in Islam. Not all of the information is universally applicable to every Muslim student, but it provides some background information about Islam and Muslims that can inform university teaching practices.

The Islamic faith and holy book are progressive in nature and leave room for interpretation with the understanding that knowledge will increase beyond what it was during the time of the Prophet (PBUH) and what exists today. It is imperative that Muslims and non-Muslims learn and know the religion of Al-Islam to break down the walls of hate and the barriers of misunderstanding that have been increasingly exploited in the past. It is true that Muslims have had a much higher worldwide profile since the tragedy of September 11, 2001, but it is also important to note that Muslims existed long before 2001, and they have been a productive part of many global societies. Islamic tradition holds that any knowledge passed on to future generations is considered beneficial to those who share it. It is the hope of this author that this chapter serves as a launching point for interfaith understanding and a resource for faculty, administrators, staff, and instructors to enhance their understanding of Islam so they can better serve Muslim students inside and outside the classroom. With better understanding will come more cross-cultural understanding, and university classrooms and campus communities can become models for the world to follow for social and cultural progress and enhanced learning.

References

Ali, A. Y. (1983). *The Holy Qur'an: Text, translation & commentary*. Brentwood, MD: Amana Corporation.

Andreatta, B. (2009). *Navigating the research university: A guide for first-year students*. Boston, MA: Wadsworth Cengage.

Chickering, A. W. (1969). *Education and identity*. San Francisco, CA: Jossey-Bass

Cole, D., & Ahmadi, S. (2003). Perspectives and experiences of Muslim women who veil on college campuses. *Journal of College Student Development, 44*(1), 47–66.

Cole, D., & Ahmadi, S. (2010). Reconsidering campus diversity: An examination of Muslim students' experiences. *The Journal of Higher Education, 81*(2), 121–139.

Esposito, J. L. (1999). *The Oxford history of Islam*. New York, NY: Oxford University Press.

The Forty Hadith. (2011). Twenty-sixth Hadith: On the pursuit of knowledge. Retrieved on May 1, 2011, from http://www.al-islam.org/fortyhadith/27.htm

Helms, J. E. (Ed.). (1990). *Black and white racial identity: Theory, research, and practice*. Contributions in Afro-American and African studies, No. 129. New York, NY: Greenwood Press.

IslamiCity.com. (n.d.). Zakat. Retrieved on May 1, 2011, from http://www.islamicity.com/mosque/zakat/

Klein, J. W. (1980). *Jewish identity and self-esteem: Healing wounds through ethnotherapy*. New York, NY: Institute on Pluralism and Group Identity, the American Jewish Committee.

Patel, E. (2010, November 22). On Islam, let's choose pluralism over prejudice. *USA Today*. Retrieved from http://www.usatoday.com/news/opinion/forum/2010-11-22-column22_ST_N.htm

Ponterotto, J. G., Casas, J. M., Suzuki, L. A., & Alexander, C. M. (Eds.). (1995). *Handbook of multicultural counseling* (pp. 93–122). Thousand Oaks, CA: Sage.

Zakat.org. Beyond Zakat. Retrieved May 5, 2011, from http://www.zakat.org/zakat_in_islam/faqs/category/beyond_zakat/

CHAPTER 13

The Context of Learning

Changes in UK Higher Education

ANNIE TRAPP

More students, less money. These four words alone are sufficient to describe the catalysts for the current transformation of UK higher education. Add a fifth word, *Bologna*, and the description can be extended to the transformation of higher education across Europe. In this chapter, I explore how recent policies are affecting teaching and learning in UK higher education with occasional references to further afield. I also discuss illustrative examples of the consequences of an emerging new model of higher education in the United Kingdom with Groccia's model of teaching and learning (see Chapter 1, this volume; St. Clair & Groccia, 2009).

The Transformation of Higher Education in Europe

European governments have introduced wide-ranging policies to reform university education. The anticipated outcome can be described as a shift from education as personal development and self-fulfillment to education as an investment for economic development. Gert Biesta (2006) traced this shift and concluded, "In about three decades, then, the discourse of lifelong learning seems to have shifted from 'learning to be' to 'learning to be productive and employable'" (p. 172).

Member states of the European Union have engaged with the European Commission's (EC) action and development plan known as the Lisbon Process to modernize universities through curricular, governance, and financial reforms. In 1999, ministers of education from 29 European countries signed the Bologna Declaration setting objectives for university curricular reform. These objectives included the establishment of a system of easily readable and comparable degrees, known as the European Credit Transfer and Accumulation System (ECTS), as a means of promoting student mobility. By 2010, the number of countries participating in the Bologna Process had risen to 46 nations, and the European Higher Education Area was launched through the Budapest-Vienna Declaration of March 2010 with universities offering three distinct cycles of university study—the bachelor (typically 3 years of study), master (typically 2 years of study), and doctorate (typically 2 years of study)—as opposed to one or two longer cycles. Although commonly described in terms of the length of time for each cycle, the actual determinant is the number of credits accrued, with the first cycle typically 180 to 240 credits, the second 90 to 120 credits, and the third cycle a doctoral degree where no range is provided by the ECTS.

This reform has brought the structure of higher education in European countries closer to the established degree structure in the United Kingdom. The long-term consequences of Bologna and the Lisbon Process are uncertain. Not all academics have accepted an educational model that provides a distinct "stepping off" point for students after the first cycle. One explanation for this skepticism is the misunderstanding that the new structure requires professional training to be condensed into 3 years whereas the intention is to equip students with an appropriate set of skills that allows them to enter the workforce earlier. For this possibility to become a reality, traditional courses cannot be neatly divided but need to be redesigned with distinctive learning outcomes at the end of the first and the second cycle.

UK Government Funding and Policy

The UK governmental response to recruiting a skilled workforce necessary to retain its economic competitiveness has been twofold. Successive governments have introduced policies to increase the number of people aged between 18 and 30 years attending a university and to provide further training for the existing workforce typically through encouraging the development of short courses offered in the workplace. As a result, participation in higher education has risen steadily from the late 1960s to 2010 with the number of 18- to 19-year-olds entering higher education increasing from 30 percent in the mid-1990s to 43 percent in 2010 (Chowdry, Crawford, Dearden, Goodman, & Vignoles, 2010). However, despite this increase, UK higher education participation rates have not grown as fast as have some of its European neighbors, such as Slovakia, Poland, the Czech Republic, and other countries (Organisation for Economic Co-operation and Development [OECD], 2009).

Alongside the *massification* (the term to describe the practice of making luxury products available to the mass market but here used to mean the process of broadening access to a larger and more diverse student population) of UK higher education have been gradual but radical changes in the way that university education is funded. In essence, these changes have shifted a greater proportion of the higher education costs from the government to the student and graduate. A tuition fee of as much as £1,000, for students with the ability to pay, was introduced in 1998 and maintenance grants were phased out in 1999 to be replaced by loans repayable after graduation and contingent on income. In 2004, English universities charged up to £3,290 per year tuition fees. In Scotland, though, universities do not charge tuition fees for Scottish students, although this policy is currently under review by the Scottish parliament. Following a review of higher education funding including tuition fees, loans, grants, and bursaries (Browne, 2010), the current English government plans to allow English universities to increase tuition fees to a maximum of £9,000 with the proviso that universities charging more expensive fees take compensatory measures to assist poorer students. Students will not be required to pay tuition fees upfront but will repay them with interest, after graduation, once their annual income exceeds £21,000. Alongside these changes, the government plans to withdraw public funding from all but "priority" subjects with state funding for teaching in the arts and humanities likely to be discontinued. These changes will make the cost of UK higher education more comparable with U.S. higher education but considerably more expensive than higher education in other European countries.

The Impact of Policy on University Teaching and Learning

Through changes to student participation and funding, UK government policy has reshaped the way in which universities go about their business. Unsurprisingly, such changes affect teaching and learning in higher education in a variety of ways. Groccia's model of college teaching (Chapter 1, this volume; St. Clair & Groccia, 2009) provides a helpful way of considering these effects through focusing attention on the learning context, teacher, learner, learning process, course content, instructional processes, and learning outcomes.

Learning Context

The reductions in university budgets coupled with rising costs, increased competitiveness, and reduced teaching budgets have led to greater emphasis on management and financial control within higher education institutions. William Locke and Alice Bennion (2008) described this shift in terms of "increased accountability and measurement of performance, management principles derived from the private sector, corporate-style governance arrangements, quasi-marketization and internationalization, the weakening of professional authority, and the growth of administrative and management personnel" (p. 1).

Two government initiatives have provided funding to support higher education institutions as they adapt to their changing environments. One initiative totaling £315 million pounds over 5 years provided selected universities with capital funding for building work ranged from £0.8 million to £2.35 million as well as recurrent funding £200,000 to £500,000 to establish 74 Centers of Excellence in Teaching and Learning (CETLs) in UK universities. The aim of the CETLS is "to reward excellent teaching practice, and to further invest in that practice so that CETLs funding delivers substantial benefits to students, teachers and institutions" (HEFCE, 2005, p. 1). Evaluation of this initiative reports that the most successful CETLS were those that had "active rather than rhetorical connections to, and support from, institutional policy makers and the strategic planning process" (Saunders et al., 2008, p. 6).

The second initiative was the formation of the Higher Education Academy in 2003. This body, with annual funding of approximately £15 million, focuses on quality enhancement through the identification, development, and dissemination of evidence-informed approaches; brokerage and encouragement of the sharing of effective practice; support for universities and colleges in bringing about strategic change; information, influence, and interpretation of policy; and raising the status of teaching. A unique feature of the Higher Education Academy has been its ability to work at discipline level through its 24 subject-based centers. With responsibility for a cognate group of discipline areas and led by academics from within those disciplines, the subject centers have been able to work closely with their relevant communities in the most appropriate way, for example, improving access to higher education in the sciences, good teaching practice around fieldwork for geography, improving the quality of placement supervision for nursing, and teaching research methods for psychology. Unfortunately, funding cuts will see the closure of these centers in 2011.

As stated previously, one of the consequences of shifting more of the cost of university education to the student has been an increased demand for public accountability and equitable standards. This emphasis is sometimes portrayed as a more consumer-oriented approach to higher education in which the student is viewed as the customer. Rankings of university performance are now taken more seriously particularly if they include data from the National Student Survey (NSS). This survey, introduced in 2005, is intended to provide a means for potential students to make more informed choices of what and where to study. The survey asks final-year undergraduates and students in their final year of a course to provide feedback on their courses. The 22 questions in the survey relate to the following aspects of the student learning experience: teaching of the course, assessment and feedback, academic support, organization and management, learning resources, personal development, and overall satisfaction. Since its introduction, the survey repeatedly reports that the majority of students are satisfied with the quality of their university education with the most recent figures (Higher Education Funding Council for England [HEFCE], 2010a) reporting that 82 percent of finalists at UK universities were satisfied with the quality of their course. Although the NSS survey results are included in a number of league tables (i.e., university rankings) for UK universities, it is not a valid indicator for making comparisons between universities or subject areas. The detailed results made available to participating universities are, however, a useful tool that allows university managers to identify areas of strength and weakness within an institution. As a result, many universities provide internal funding and support to enable departments to improve on areas where students have been given lower scores.

Other ways in which students are becoming involved in shaping higher education is through their involvement in the university audits conducted by the Quality Assurance Agency and representation on institutional teaching and learning committees. In Scotland, the Scottish Funding Council for Further and Higher Education provides funding for a dedicated student group to support effective student representation and student engagement in the management of quality assurance and enhancement in Scotland's Colleges and Higher Education Institutions (SPARQS, 2010).

The Teacher

In 2006, the National Professional Standards Framework for Teaching and Supporting Learning in Higher Education (Higher Education Academy, 2006) was introduced into the United Kingdom following government recommendations (Department for Education and Skills [DfES], 2003). The framework provides consistency and quality enhancement of teaching across higher education institutions and enables institutions to align their professional development courses for teachers within higher education to this framework. The Higher Education Academy also provides development activities for postgraduates who teach, graduate teaching assistants, and more experienced teaching staff. Mechanisms also exist within higher education institutions to develop teaching skills, for example, through peer observation of teaching. Academics are less accustomed to this practice than are teachers in pre-tertiary settings, but in theory the practice enables reflective, constructive, and analytical discussion with a peer about teaching practices, with the benefits often coming as much from observing as being observed (Chism, 2007). Peer-supported review can be improved by incorporating a broader range of topics such as e-learning, course design, assessment, and evaluation (Gosling & O'Connor, 2009).

In addition to demanding the professionalization of teaching in higher education, the government has also been influential, although to a lesser extent, in improving the reward structures for teaching. In recognition of the fact that academic status is usually defined more by research than teaching, a government white paper (DfES, 2003) stated

> In the past, rewards in higher education—particularly promotion—have been linked much more closely to research than to teaching. Indeed, teaching has been seen by some as an extra source of income to support the main business of research, rather than recognised as a valuable and high-status career in its own right. This is a situation that cannot continue. Institutions must properly reward their best teaching staff; and all those who teach must take their task seriously. (p. 51)

In response, the National Teaching Fellowship program was introduced in 2010 to reward and raise the status of learning and teaching in higher education. Each year as many as 55 awards of £10,000 are made to recognize individual excellence in teaching. Within institutions, there has also been an increase in the reward mechanisms for teaching. Many institutions offer teaching development awards and have improved their promotional criteria to give more weight to the applicant's teaching. Nonetheless, it is still relatively rare for promotion at the professorial level to be based solely on teaching, teaching improvement efforts, or research on one's teaching.

The number of academic staff employed in higher education has failed to keep pace with the large increase in the student population. In England, there has been a moderate increase of 8 percent from 2005–2006 to 2008–2009, with an increase in the proportion of senior lecturers from minority ethnic backgrounds rising from 3.9 percent in 1995–1996 to 6.9 percent in 2008–2009 (HEFCE, 2010b). The same source reports that the long-standing issue around the representation of women in academic posts persists, with women composing only 22 percent of permanent academic staff at head of department or professor rank. Initiatives to address this issue exist, for example, through the government-funded organization, the United Kingdom Research Staff Association (UKRSA), which provides advice, services, and policy consultation regarding the underrepresentation of women in science, engineering, and technology. This initiative also includes the Athena Scientific Women's Academic Network (SWAN) program for universities or research institutions, which is committed to the advancement and promotion of the careers of women in science, engineering, and technology.

The Learner

Government education policy to widen participation has resulted in increased student diversity that reflects students' academic backgrounds, as well as their "ability, disability, age, maturity, experience, commitment, motivation, study mode, class, sex, race, religion and the like" (Davis, 2003, p. 245). Indeed, the changing nature of the student body has demanded a response from higher education that goes well beyond the management of larger student numbers and increased class size. For example, in first-year courses, a more complex and diverse student body requires greater attention to induction processes, personal tutor systems, and student support. Academic timetabling (i.e., scheduling) also becomes more complex because most full-time students engage in part-time work and the boundaries between full-time and part-time studies become blurred. Differences in cultural background and students' previous learning habits as well as the increase in the number of international students developing their English language skills requires careful attention to course structure to ensure that lectures have a clear purpose, essential content is emphasized, turn-taking and participation in seminars is encouraged, and so on.

The combination of more, and more diverse, students is a major challenge for departments. Sheer numbers threaten student-tutor relationships, open-door policies that allow students access to their lecturers, and traditional forms of small-group teaching. Fortunately, the government initiatives described earlier have led to a wide range of publications, scholarship, professional development activities, and departmental innovations to innovate and adapt teaching practice. Illustrative examples are the diversity audit toolkit, developed by the psychology department at the University of Keele (Priest, Hale, & Jacobs, 2011) and the practical advice, around working with culturally diverse groups, offered by Judith Carroll and Janette Ryan (2005). Many other examples may be found by searching through the resource section of the Higher Education Academy website (www .heacademy.ac.uk).

Student diversity has also been tackled at the governmental level through the introduction of the Equality Act in October 2010. This law aims to harmonize existing equality legislation, including the Disability Discrimination Act (DDA) and the Special Educational Needs and Disability Act (SENDA). The legislation gives public sector organizations, including universities, a range of general and specific duties aimed at reducing discrimination and promoting equality. The key point about this legislation is that it requires universities to take anticipatory action in relation to the needs of students with disabilities in the way that learning and teaching and support services are organized. It is not sufficient to respond to needs as they are presented. Already university strategies reflect commitment to this legislation and professional development activities exist to support academics in their understanding and interpretation of the legislation.

One of the most significant changes in the skills and expectations of 21st-century students lies in their levels of computer literacy and their use of mobile and social networking technologies. However, a report commissioned by the Joint Information Systems Committee (JISC) and the British Library (Rowlands et al., 2008), though supporting the view that young people demonstrate an ease and familiarity with computers, states that in academic work they rely on the most basic search tools and do not possess the critical and analytical skills necessary to assess information that they find on the web. This problem illustrates the importance of higher education institutions ensuring that students possess the appropriate study skills either by developing their own support materials or alerting students to other sources, for example, the Virtual Training Suite (http://www.vts.intute.ac.uk/), a set of Internet tutorials on the use of the web (Intute, 2010).

The United Kingdom attracts many foreign students despite recent immigration regulations restricting the number of students from non-European countries. Unfortunately, however, although the benefits of studying abroad are well established (Davis, Milne, & Olsen, 1999; Kitsantas & Meyers, 2001; McCabe, 1994), only a small minority of UK students chooses to do so. Programs such as the European Erasmus staff and student mobility program provide opportunities for universities to build relationships overseas. With the rising cost of higher education, it is likely that more students will consider studying abroad where higher education is less expensive, for example, in Denmark, Sweden, and Norway where tuition fees are not levied. Language need not be a barrier because an increasing number of courses are offered in English. There are also examples of students choosing to study in franchised courses overseas or on UK campuses overseas.

The Learning Process

More academics than ever before in the United Kingdom are engaged in scholarship related to learning processes. This increase can be attributed partly to the increased recognition and rewards for teaching, reflective processes as part of professional development, the evaluation requirements of funded teaching projects, and a growing awareness of the global movement around the scholarship of teaching and learning (for example, the International Society for the Scholarship of Teaching and Learning). In addition, many CETLs have focused on particular aspects of the learning process, for example, assessment, integrative learning, work-based learning, inquiry-based learning, spatial literacy, and academic writing and have published widely, thereby contributing to the evidence base around teaching and learning practice. There is, however, no room for complacency. Many lecturers are content to build craft knowledge around teaching through experience and have little knowledge of, for example, the underlying psychological principles of learning or existing evidence relating to effective practice. This approach constrains the ability to conduct well-designed research that allows a better understanding of teaching and learning processes (Trapp, 2010). Nonetheless, my experience of building a European network focusing on quality enhancement in the teaching of psychology, European Psychology Learning and Teaching (EUROPLAT) (Trapp, 2009), indicates that there is more support for, and activity relating to, scholarship related to teaching and learning in higher education institutions within the United Kingdom than in most other European countries.

Course Content

The principal beneficiaries of good course design and curricular review are employers, researchers, and students, although designing the content of courses to be of maximum benefit to each group may be challenging because each of these groups may have different priorities and desired outcomes from a course. Increasingly, universities are coming under governmental pressure to provide courses that develop attributes and transferable skills that are of most value to employers. Most UK professors are also involved in research and therefore keen to ensure courses provide plentiful opportunities for students to develop good research skills and an interest in conducting their own research. Students have a growing awareness of employability and getting "value for money" from their courses. A National Union of Students (NUS/HSBC, 2009) survey showed a disconnect between how involved students feel they are in shaping the content of their courses and how involved they would like to be. Students indicated that the main way they would like to be involved in shaping the content of the course is through providing feedback on the course design

The thickness of any introductory undergraduate textbook is a constant reminder of the continual expansion of knowledge. For inexperienced teachers faced with large classes, the wealth of information to present can be both daunting—"How am I going to cover all this material in my course?"—and comforting—"I won't run out of things to say." More experienced and confident teachers, however, are well aware that trying to teach too much content can result in shallow learning and less critical student engagement. In the United Kingdom, there is now much more emphasis during course design on learning outcomes and desired competencies rather than a content-driven curriculum. This approach is concomitant with the aims of the European Higher Education Area to facilitate student mobility and enable comparisons between courses to be made more easily. Consequently, course designs are expected to follow the National Qualifications Frameworks (Qualifications and Curriculum Authority, 2006) that describe the learning outcomes expected at each of the described nine levels at which a qualification can be recognized in England, Northern Ireland, and Wales. There is also national guidance on the content of subjects studied through subject benchmark statements (Quality Assurance Agency, 2010) that established the academic characteristics and standards expected of UK programs. Some benchmark statements combine or refer to professional standards required by external professional or regulatory bodies in the discipline. These statements describe what gives a discipline its coherence and identity and define what can be expected of a graduate in the abilities and skills needed to develop understanding or competence in the subject. However, subject benchmark statements do not represent a national curriculum in a subject area; rather, they allow flexibility and innovation in program design, within an overall conceptual framework established by an academic subject community. An emerging problem with this approach, however, is that higher education institutions increasingly are developing interdisciplinary courses that are not covered by subject benchmarks.

As mentioned previously, it is now usual in the United Kingdom for courses to be designed as discrete modules. Modularization can constrain program design and lead to an examination for each module, resulting in over-assessment of students. Another disadvantage of modularization is that students do not have the opportunity to integrate knowledge across modules and may adopt surface learning approaches to the end of module assessments as evidenced by Stephen Newstead and Karen Findlay (1997, cited in Newstead, 2002) who presented students with the Approaches to Study Inventory (Entwistle & Tait, 1994) on a weekly basis throughout the semester. They found that deep approaches declined week by week until the surface approach dominated. Capstone courses can be an effective way of addressing this problem but such courses are not commonplace in the United Kingdom.

Another approach to ameliorate the effects of modularization and to provide students with the skills that enable them to apply their learning to new situations is to undertake more radical curriculum reforms. For example, the University of Aberdeen has undertaken curricular reform to enable students to take interdisciplinary programs, such as "Humans and Other Animals," "Health and Wealth of Nations," and "Science and the Media." This approach is novel within UK higher education but has been in place for much longer at universities such as Alverno College, Harvard University, and University of Melbourne. There are advantages to such an approach in that it gives students the opportunity to relate their study to today's issues and, by integrating and applying disciplinary knowledge, students can gain a broader and deeper contextual understanding. Unfortunately, this approach is resisted by teachers who prefer courses to have a narrower disciplinary focus. It is also likely that this approach to course design will become more difficult when government funding is prioritized for particular discipline areas.

With increasing pressure on staff resources and the need to give students access to a broad range of materials, the UK government has provided funding through the JISC to encourage open access to learning resources created in higher education institutions. This access has been made more viable through improvements in technology and new forms of licensing for digital content—for example, the Creative Commons licenses (Gourley & Lane, 2009). This approach is relatively new and, to my knowledge, no systematic evaluation of the uptake and usefulness of open access resources has been undertaken across the United Kingdom.

Instructional Processes

One of the most significant changes to instructional approaches within the United Kingdom has been the widespread integration of technology to support teaching and learning. To encourage greater efficiency in teaching while maintaining high quality standards for learning, the government introduced significant funding (£22.5 million pounds) for 108 projects through three phases of the Teaching and Learning Technology Programme (HEFCE, 1998). In addition, JISC receives substantial government funding to support technological innovation within higher education institutions. Many universities also encourage innovation through providing funding for the development of technology to assist teaching.

The use of technology is widespread across all aspects of UK higher education. There is considerable use of blended learning where valuable face-to-face contact with students is preserved through technology. For example, some departments digitally record lectures and make them available online to students, thereby freeing up time for professor-led seminars. Technology is also widely used to give students access to learning materials so that they are able to engage in learning off campus as described by Jane Holbrook and Christine Dupont (2008) and Alan Cann (2007). Other examples include the use of electronic slide projection (e.g., PowerPoint); online access to library catalogues, e-books, and e-journals; the use of virtual learning environments; audio or video lecture recordings; podcasts; plagiarism detection software; virtual world environments; simulation software; electronic submission of student work; and electronic forms of assessment. Of course, the availability of these technologies does not guarantee better teaching or more successful learning. It remains the responsibility of the course designer to harness these technologies in the most appropriate and effective ways.

Another noticeable shift within the United Kingdom is the increase in course design that takes an inquiry-based or problem-based learning approach where learning results from the process of working toward the understanding of, or resolution of, a problem (Barrows & Tamblyn, 1980). Course designers of medical programs have led the way, but there is growing interest in other, mainly postgraduate courses. In undergraduate courses in which large class sizes limit the amount of group work, there is more emphasis when designing courses to ensure students are engaged in active learning. In lectures, for example, students may be required to engage in short exercises, answer multiple-choice questions, respond to questions through personal response systems, and compare notes with neighboring students.

Learning Outcomes

Although there is much talk of harmonization of degrees across Europe to increase transparency, it should not be interpreted as standardizing the contents of degree courses in different countries. Instead, there has been a focus on learning outcomes as a means of making courses more compatible. The establishment of the Quality Assurance Agency (QAA) in 1997 led to the implementation of a National Qualifications Framework for Higher Education, subject benchmarking and program specifications, and institutional audit. Angela Maher (2004) described these developments as pushing "the HE sector as a whole towards a learning outcomes approach." (p. 47). The specific intentions of university courses are described in learning outcomes outlining what students should know, understand, or be able to do at the end of a program or module. Learning outcomes are intended to help students to know what is expected of them, help program managers plan exactly what they want students to achieve, and provide a useful guide to inform potential students and employees about the knowledge and understanding that a graduate will possess. In this way, learning outcomes can act as benchmarks for ensuring quality and efficiency in higher education and informing employers who argue that they are more interested in what students can "do" rather than what they "know" (Jackson, 2000). Critics of the learning outcomes approach argue that this approach constrains open-ended learning and may be detrimental to the student learning experience through stifling creativity and discussion outside of the set outcomes for the course (Hussey & Smith 2003; Maher, 2004). Such critics demand that learning outcomes should be used flexibly to guide rather than dictate student learning and curriculum development.

Conclusion

This chapter has focused on the role of the government in driving change within United Kingdom higher education and drawn attention to the ways in which government policies affect the context, process, and outcomes of teaching and learning in UK higher education.

The organization of UK higher education is very different from that of most other European countries. Traditionally, UK universities have had much greater autonomy than universities in other European countries have had, where governments may exert more control over university policies. The difference will extend yet further between English and other European universities if the government shifts a much larger part of the cost of university education from the state to the student.

The United Kingdom spends less money on higher education as a share of gross domestic product than is the average across the developed nations. Nonetheless, as evidenced in this chapter, the government has invested heavily in a wide variety of programs and initiatives to enhance higher education through innovation and training. It would be premature to suggest that there has been a radical transformation in teaching but there is certainly evidence of greater recognition and reward for teaching, improved teacher training courses for lecturers, and many excellent examples of innovation in curricular design and teaching practice. These changes have resulted from a mixture of university management (top-down) and individual academic interests and personal development (bottom-up) approaches.

As higher education in the United Kingdom hits a period of austerity, the level of funding to support quality enhancement is likely to decrease, leading to a greater emphasis on maintaining standards through enhanced quality assurance and audit measures. This change may have the undesirable consequence of constraining the creativity and innovation that has flourished over recent years. It will be interesting, therefore, to reflect on this chapter in say, 5 years time. By then, we will have a better understanding of the extent to which current changes in higher education have been sufficiently embedded to have a lasting impact. We will also see the results of students having more control over how and where they choose to study, which may lead to a greater understanding of which aspects of higher education students value. One can but hope that it will not be a case of fewer students as well as less money.

References

Barrows, H. S., & Tamblyn, R. N. (1980). *Problem-based learning: An approach to medical education.* New York, NY: Springer.

Biesta, G. (2006). What's the point of lifelong learning if lifelong learning has no point? On the democratic deficit of policies for lifelong learning. *European Educational Research Journal, 5*(3–4), 169–180.

Browne, J. (2010). *Securing a sustainable future for higher education.* Retrieved from www.independent.gov.uk/browne-report

Cann, A. (2007). Podcasting is dead. Long live video! *Bioscience Education Journal, 10,* c-1. doi:10.3108/beej.10.c1. Retrieved March 2, 2011, from http://www .bioscience.heacademy.ac.uk/journal/vol10/beej-10-c1.aspx

Carroll, J., & Ryan, J. (Eds.). (2005). *Teaching international students: Improving learning for all.* London, UK: Routledge.

Chism, N. V. (2007). *Peer review of teaching: A sourcebook* (2nd ed.). San Francisco, CA: Jossey-Bass.

Chowdry, H., Crawford, C., Dearden, L., Goodman, A., & Vignoles, A. (2010). *Widening participation in higher education: Analysis using linked administrative data.* IFS Working Papers (W10/04). London, UK: Institute for Fiscal Studies.

Davis, D., Milne, C., & Olsen, A. (1999). *Becoming internationally competitive: The value of international experience for Australian students.* Sydney, Australia: IDP Education.

Davis, M. (2003). Barriers to reflective practice: The changing nature of higher education. *Active Learning in Higher Education, 4,* 243–255.

Department for Education and Skills (DfES). (2003). *The future of higher education.* London, UK: DfES.

Entwistle, N. J., & Tait, H. (1994). *The revised approaches to studying inventory.* Edinburgh, Scotland: University of Edinburgh, Centre for Research into Learning and Instruction.

Gosling, D., & O'Connor, K. M. (Eds.). (2009). *Beyond the peer observation of teaching*. SEDA Paper (124). London, UK: Staff and Educational Development Association.

Gourley, B., & Lane, A. (2009). Re-invigorating openness at the Open University: The role of open educational resources. *Open Learning: The Journal of Open and Distance Learning, 24*, 57–65. doi:10.1080/02680510802627845

Higher Education Academy. (2006). *The UK Professional Standards Framework for teaching and supporting learning in higher education*. York, UK: Higher Education Academy.

Higher Education Funding Council for England (HEFCE). (1998). *TLTP Phase 3: Funded projects*. HEFCE Reference 98/10. Bristol, UK: HEFCE.

Higher Education Funding Council for England (HEFCE). (2005). *Centres for excellence in teaching and learning. Outcomes and funding allocations*. Bristol, UK: HEFCE.

Higher Education Funding Council for England (HEFCE). (2010a). *Trends in young participation in higher education: Core results for England*. Bristol, UK: HEFCE.

Higher Education Funding Council for England (HEFCE). (2010b). *The higher education workforce framework 2010*. Bristol, UK: HEFCE.

Holbrook, J., & Dupont, C. (2008). Profcasts and class attendance—Does year in program matter? *Bioscience Education Journal*. Retrieved November 16, 2010, from http://www.bioscience.heacademy.ac.uk/journal/vol13/beej-13-c2.aspx

Hussey, T., & Smith, P. (2003). The uses of learning outcomes. *Teaching in Higher Education, 8*, 357–368.

Intute (2010). *Virtual training suite*. Bristol, UK: University of Bristol. Available from http://www.vts.intute.ac.uk/

Jackson, N. (2000). Programme specification and its role in promoting an outcomes model of learning. *Active Learning in Higher Education, 1*, 132–151.

Kitsantas, A., & Meyers, J. (2001, March 28–31). *Studying abroad: Does it enhance college student cross-cultural awareness?* Paper presented at the combined annual meeting of San Diego State University and the U.S. Department of Education Centers for International Business Education and Research (CIBER), San Diego, CA. Available from ERIC database. (ED 456–648)

Locke, W., & Bennion, A. (2008, November 5–8). *The governance and management of higher education in "mature" higher education systems: The United Kingdom*. Paper presented at the Symposium, Association for the Study of Higher Education (ASHE) Annual Conference, Jacksonville, FL.

Maher, A. (2004). Learning outcomes in higher education: Implications for curriculum design and student learning. *Journal of Hospitality, Leisure, Sport and Tourism Education, 3*, 46–54.

McCabe, L. T. (1994). The development of a global perspective during participation in semester at sea: A comparative global education program. *Educational Review, 46*, 275–286.

Newstead, S. (2002). Examining the examiners: Why are we so bad at assessing students? *Psychology Learning and Teaching, 2*, 70–75.

NUS/HSBC (2009). *Students research experience report: Teaching and learning*. Retrieved November 16, 2010, from http://www.nusconnect.org.uk/resourcehandler/797d8465-c46d-48a8-93ed-979d508f4863/

Organisation for Economic Co-operation and Development (OECD). (2009). *Education at a glance*. Retrieved November 16, 2010, from www.oecd.org/edu/

Priest, H., Hale, R., & Jacobs, G. (2011). Diversity in the psychology curriculum: The development of a toolkit to audit, monitor and enhance responsiveness to diversity in an inclusive curriculum. *Psychology Learning and Teaching, 10*, 158–163.

Qualifications and Curriculum Authority. (2006). *The National Qualifications Framework*. London, UK: Qualifications and Curriculum Authority. Retrieved November 16, 2010, from http://www.courtauld.ac.uk/degreeprogrammes/documents/NQF.pdf

Quality Assurance Agency. (2010). *Subject benchmarks*. Gloucester, UK: Quality Assurance Agency. Retrieved from http://www.qaa.ac.uk

Rowlands, I., Nicholas, D., Williams, P., Huntington, P., Fieldhouse, M., Gunter, B., . . . Tenopir, C. (2008). The Google generation: Information behaviour of the researcher of the future. *Aslib Proceedings, 60*(4), 290–310.

Saunders, M., Machell, J., Williams, S., Allaway, D., Spencer, A., Ashwin, P., . . . McKee, A. (2008). *Centres of excellence in teaching and learning programme: Formative evaluation report to HEFCE*. Centre for Study in Education and Training/Institution of Educational Technology. Bristol, UK: Higher Education Academy Funding Council for England.

SPARQS. (2010). *Sparqs: Driving student engagement*. Retrieved November 16, 2010, from http://www.sparqs.ac.uk/

St. Clair, K. L., & Groccia, J. E. (2009). Change to social justice education: Higher education strategy. In K. Skubikowski, C. Wright, & R. Graf (Eds.), *Social justice education: Inviting faculty to transform their institutions* (pp. 70–84). Sterling, VA: Stylus.

Trapp, A. L. (2009, September). Thinking big, starting small: Addressing common challenges in teaching psychology in Europe. *The Observer, 2*(7). Retrieved from http://www.psychologicalscience.org/observer/getArticle.cfm?id=2549%20

Trapp, A. L. (2010). Teaching you to suck eggs? Using psychology to teach psychology. In D. Upton & A. L. Trapp (Eds.), *Teaching psychology in higher education*. Oxford, UK: Blackwell.

CHAPTER 14

Learning for Transformation in an International Context

The Implications of a Confucian Learning Model

QI SUN

This chapter focuses on learning for transformation of international students, particularly students from East Asia such as China (including Taiwan), Korea, and Japan, which have been strongly influenced by Confucianism (Sun & Cho, 2008; Yang, Zheng, & Li, 2006). It will first offer a context for understanding international students who confront issues and disharmony while studying abroad. Second, it will apply transformative learning theory (Mezirow, 1991; Mezirow & Associates, 2000) and Jarvis's (2006) lifelong learning model to illustrate the possibility and necessity of transformative learning and learning for transformation in an international context. Third, it will describe core values of the Confucian culture and explains how they have shaped and influenced East Asian students' ways of life and learning. Finally, it will review the Confucian multidimensional learning model and discuss its implication for holistic human development and transformation. In this chapter, I will argue that international students go through a series of phases, curves, and levels of adaptations and transformations while living and learning aboard. The Confucian learning model is likely to help readers understand that learning involves multidimensional processes of transformation, which is important for educators and administrators of host educational institutions to know in their attempt to help these students adjust to their new learning environments.

Contexts

With dreams to advance their knowledge and skills, enhance their career opportunities, and further their social mobility, more and more people pursue higher education in the United States. Ann Stock, Assistant Secretary of State for Educational and Cultural Affairs, recently expressed, "American colleges and universities have attracted a record number of international students" (Institute of International Education, 2010). In fact, the United States continues to host more international students than any other country in the world (Institute of International Education [IIE], 2010). The IIE (2010) reported that the number of international students at colleges and universities in the United States increased by 3% to 690,923 during the 2009/10 academic year.

International students, particularly students from countries and regions of East Asia such as China, South Korea, Japan, and Taiwan, have become an increasingly significant presence on U.S. university campuses. The growth of international students in the United States during the 2009/2010 academic year was driven by a 30% increase in Chinese student enrollment in the United States to a total of nearly 128,000 students, or over 18% of the total international student population, making China the leading sending country (IIE, 2010). The number of Chinese students coming to the United States to study is likely to continue to increase. U.S. ambassador Huntsman told Chinese reporters at a recent press meeting in China that "the United States will push for more student exchanges with China over the next several years," (Li, *China Daily*, Nov 12, 2009).

Other East Asian countries and regions number among the top sending places: South Korea, third place, Taiwan, fifth place, and Japan, sixth place. Among the four countries, China and South Korea comprise close to 30% of the total international enrollments in U.S. higher education. Taiwan and Japan each represents around 4% of the total international student population. Together these four top sending places comprise more than one third of the total international enrollment in U.S. higher education institutions.

On the one hand, these international students contribute substantially to the United States. They provide U.S. students with valuable knowledge and skills that will enable them to collaborate across political and cultural borders to address shared global challenges in the years ahead (Institute of International Education, 2010). At the same time, through their expenditures on tuition and living expenses, they contribute huge sums of money to the U.S. economy (Institute of International Education, 2010; Wang, 2006).

On the other hand, they also bring with them their own cultural values of living, learning, socializing, and communicating, which to varying degrees, mismatch the culture of the host country and campuses (Holmes, 2005). Different cultural values, teaching and learning mechanisms, and unique perspectives not only present challenges to the American educational system (Wang, 2006), but they also bring considerable amount of stress and difficulty to these international students' lives. Consequently, these students undergo challenges and struggles due to the complexity of language barriers, culture differences, new roles, and novel contexts (Gu & Maley 2008), constantly confronting adaptation and transformation of their former life with their new one.

The topic of transformative learning (TL; Cranton 1994, 2006; Mezirow, 1991, Mezirow & Associates, 2000; Taylor, 1998, 2006) is currently receiving even more attention than when Mezirow first introduced it in 1978. The theory of transformative learning that has been developed during the past three decades has evolved into a comprehensive description of how learners interpret, corroborate, and reformulate the meaning of their experience. Taylor (2006) observed a significant increase in peer-reviewed journal publications on TL and yet reported that there was "the lack of emphasis on identifying a transformative experience in a particular context (p. 392), in our case, the international context. Erichsen (2009) further confirmed that few authors discuss international students' transformative learning experience and its nature to inform our educators' understanding in order to effectively facilitate their learning in a foreign country.

In addition, numerous studies have explored challenges and barriers experienced by East Asian students abroad (Gu & Schweisfurth, 2006; Holmes, 2005, Signorini, Wiesemes, & Murphy, 2009), whose living and learning have been strongly influenced by Confucian culture. Yet, no study has ever used the Confucian perspective to illustrate and review learning as multidimensional transformations.

Given the fact that almost one-third of US international students are from East Asia, there is a growing need for educators, administrators, and even policymakers of host educational institutions to actively engage in learning about aspects of Eastern culture, particularly Confucian values that have shaped these international students' ways of thinking and life. Faculty members should increase their awareness of learning from the students' cultural perspective in order to help these learners adapt to the host culture and its novel learning environment.

Learning for Transformation in an International Context

Although we learn all the time, not all learning is transformative, and transformative learning happens only when we alter our beliefs or attitudes, or we change perspective or habit of mind (Mezirow, 2000). From this view, living and studying in the United States presents international students an environment that naturally requires them to adjust their feelings and attitudes, and even shift their philosophical and moral suppositions in their learning.

Merriam, Caffarella, and Baumgartner (2007) summarized Mezirow's 10-step model emphasizing four major components of the transformative learning process: experience, critical reflection, reflective discourse, and action. These processes may occur slow or fast depending on the particular individual's specific situation. "The learner must critically reflect on his or her experience, talk with others about his or her new worldview in order to gain the best judgment, and *act* on the new perspective" (Merriam et al., 2007, p. 137).

Having been an international graduate student in the United States, and now a faculty member at a U.S. university, my own learning journey, teaching and advising international students, most of whom are from East Asia have enabled me not only to experience, observe, share, and guide transformative learning, but also identify patterns of the complex process that loudly echo the above components of the model. These include, but are not limited to:

Experiencing disharmony:

- Discomfited by language barriers, though scoring high on the TOEFL and/or GRE,
- Experiencing the complexity of living—how things would normally get done does not work anymore,
- Misunderstanding others and being misunderstood due to regarding different ways of thinking and expression,
- Struggling with differences in classroom teaching and learning, and
- Feeling isolated—having lost key social support systems.

Reflecting on situations and self as emotional anxieties become intense:

- Unable to develop deep friendships—friendships considered from own cultural perspective: Why friends are so "superficial?"
- Feeling invisible—viewpoints, culture perspectives and even presence are often disregarded and ignored by others: What is wrong with me? Why do others treat me like this? and
- Becoming confused—surrounded by different identities, roles, and expectations: Who am I?

Discussing with people of same culture or others with similar experiences:

- Sharing fear, anger, guilt, and/or shame,
- Comparing with others on similar situations/feelings, and
- Exchanging ideas and thoughts on what one should do.

Taking action and feeling renewed:

- Stopping blaming self and beginning to re-navigate life,
- Learning to view things from host culture's perspectives,
- Looking for alternatives to resolve "problems," and
- Forming a new self-identity.

Reflecting on the above inventory, we see a pattern of disorienting situations and moments that kindle emotional, cultural, social, and critical reflections for transformative learning (Boyd & Myers 1988; Cranton 2006; Cranton & Roy, 2003; Illeris, 2004; Jarvis, 2006; Mezirow, 1991; Mezirow, 2003; Mezirow & Associates, 2000; Taylor, 1998, 2006). In this context, the conceptual frameworks of transformative learning theory (Mezirow, 1991; Mezirow & Associates, 2000) and Jarvis' lifelong learning model (2006) are particularly useful for understanding how international students adapt to their new environment and experience transformation in their perspective.

Applying transformative learning theory to learning in an international context suggests that international students must establish what Mezirow (2000) termed a new "frame of reference" and experience changes related to "meaning schemes" (points of view) and "meaning perspective" (habit of mind) in order to renegotiate their identities and roles within the new life world for success. As Mezirow and colleagues (2000) noted:

> Frame of reference is a 'meaning perspective,' the structure of assumptions and expectations through which we filter sense impression. It involves cognitive, affective, and conative dimensions . . . . It provides the context for making choice of what and how a sensory experience is to be constructed and/or appropriated. (p. 16)

Frame of reference may be viewed from two dimensions: habit of mind and point of view. A habit of mind is "a set of assumptions—broad, generalized, orienting predispositions that act as a filter for interpreting the meaning of experience" (Mezirow & Associates, 2000, p. 17). For instance, moral, ethical, aesthetic, philosophical, and psychological assumptions are examples of varieties of habit of mind (Merriam et al., 2007). A point of view is a "set of immediate, specific beliefs, feelings, attitudes, and value judgments" (Mezirow & Associates, 2000, p. 18). Point of view changes more easily than habit of mind.

For learners to change their point of view, they must engage in critical reflection on their experiences, which in turn leads to a perspective transformation. According to Mezirow (1991):

> Perspective transformation is the process of becoming critically aware of how and why our assumptions have come to constrain the way we perceive, understand, and feel about our world; changing these structures of habitual expectation to make possible a more inclusive, discriminating, and integrating perspective; and, finally, making choices or otherwise acting upon these new understandings. (p. 167)

Thus international students may often experience a transformation of perspective. The process may begin at any point in their transition to the host culture. My modest observation suggests it may start slowly as international students begin to reflect critically on their situation, but then the process intensifies as they begin to experience deep emotions in response to having to adjust to their new lives. Of course, I realize now that not all international students will undergo this transformative process, but many, perhaps most do. Jarvis's (2006) lifelong learning model helps explain the complex processes involved in the transformative learning of these international students.

According to Jarvis (2006), "learning occurs as a result of the person-in-the-world" . . . There are "four different relationships between the person and the world: Person to person; person to phenomenon (things/event); person to a future phenomenon; and person to self" (p. 17). He further noted that each relationship enables some kind of learning. Learning happens all the time and people change as a result. In the process of learning, people's interacts are also changed. This point has important implications for international students who have transplanted themselves in a new culture in which so many new relationships wait to be developed. Such relationships may be with the new living and learning environments, their fellow students, host universities' professors, administrators, and anyone who works or socializes with them in ways that facilitate learning. People seek harmony with the world in which they live, yet "disjuncture may appear via any relationship, or combinations of relationships that they may have with the world" (p. 24). In response to disjuncture, various types of learning may occur. Jarvis (pp. 10-31) categorized them into three types:

- Non-learning or pre-conscious learning: we are in harmony or experience disjuncture but we are at ease with it. "We may take our environment for granted and thus no need to learn in that situation,"
- Rejection and non-consideration, non-reflective learning, and/or thoughtful and reflective learning: When we experience "disjuncture we feel that the outside world is putting pressure on us," and
- Thoughtful and reflective learning or contemplation: When we experience "disjuncture as a result of our own learning, changed beliefs, values or changed aspirations and so on, we wish to change our world in some way."

Through the different types of learning, Jarvis further explained that relationships that we have with the world around us influence our learning, which highlights the social and emotional involvements in our learning. Illeris (2004) made a similar point: "all learning always includes three dimensions—the cognitive dimension of knowledge and skills, the emotional dimension of feelings and motivation, and the social dimension of communication and cooperation" (p. 84). Jarvis noted that the core of life-long learning is "the process of transforming episodic experience and internalizing it" (p. 22).

Thus, international students must make conscious changes in their previous frame of reference in order for perspective transformation. As they continue to become changed persons with increasing fitness and compatibility with their new world, they must keep negotiating their identities, adjusting to new roles toward other people from both their home and the host culture. Consequently, their learning for transformation becomes a cycle because they continually experience new disjunctures (Jarvis, 2006). In my view, the learning experiences of international students provide a particularly rich context for studying processes of transformative learning and learning for transformation.

From the host's side, to help East Asian students make a smooth transition to their new lives, educators and administrators must seek to understand how these students think, live, and learn. Indeed, understanding these students' culture backgrounds, social traditions, values, and norms, particularly those that have deeply shaped their way of life and learning is essential to helping them adapt to the host culture and enhancing their abilities to learn. In the following section, I will briefly review the Confucian culture and its values that have strongly influenced East Asian students' way of life and study.

Confucian Cultural Values and their Influence on Learning

Research shows that inadequate language skills have been found to mask other problems stemming from other causes, such as lack of familiarity with a new educational and social environment and with a new culture and its associated cultural norms, behaviors, background contexts (Gu & Schweisfurth, 2006; Huaung & Brown, 2009). Such findings help explain how these students' previous social and educational environment and especially their cultural norms and traditions have shaped the way they live and learn.

Cultural values are collective ideas that serve as standards of conduct. Jarvis (2006) noted:

> Culture is all the knowledge, skills, attitudes, beliefs, values and emotions that we, as human beings, have added to our biological base. Culture is a social phenomenon; it is what we as a society, or a people, share and which enables us to live as society. (p. 55)

Although culture is not the only factor that affects teaching and learning practices, personal preferences, and experience of international students (Gu & Maley, 2008), it significantly influences international students' lives and study in another country. Numerous researchers have shown that Confucian culture, the core of traditional Chinese values (Huang & Brown; Q. Zhang, 2009; Wang, Yong, Liu, & Tang, 2006), have had strong impact on Chinese and other East Asians' life and students' learning (Gan, 2009; Holmes, 2005; Huang & Brown, 2009; Mortenson, 2006; Nyuyen, Terlouw, & Pilot, 2006; Ryan & Louie, 2007; Yang et al. 2006).

Confucian Culture Values

Confucian culture emanates from Confucian philosophy, which is the ideology developed by Confucius and his followers (Huang, 2006; X. Zhang, 2009). It is a philosophical system that has evolved in Chinese society for over 2,500 years. It became the core of traditional Chinese culture values, and has long occupied a dominant position in Chinese history. In fact, it still has profound influence on almost every aspect of Chinese society (Sun, 2008; Huang & Brown; 2009).

Historically, Confucian values not only have the most enduring influence on China, but it also has exerted tremendous influence in other parts of East Asia such as South Korea, Japan (Sun & Cho, 2008; Yang et al. 2006), Vietnam (Tu, n.d.), and Taiwan. In fact, these societies share some common cultural values: harmony, filial piety, respect for the elderly, moderation, collectivism, hierarchical social structures, and family-centeredness (Huang & Brown; 2009; Yang et al. 2006), all values which evidently differ in some respects from those in Western societies (Nisbett, 2003; Nguyen et al., 2006; Wang, 2006).

"Ren," generally translated as humanity, morality, and righteousness, is the core value of Confucian philosophy. Confucius stressed that the virtue of humanity is meaningless unless it is involved in actual human relationships. Interestingly, the etymology of the word "Ren" is derived from the words "two" and "person" or "human being." The true manifestation of the quality of Ren is in the practice of human relationships. It is expressed only when there is more than one person involved, which is a necessary condition of the existence and exhibiting of Ren (Sun, 2008).

Thus, in the Confucian tradition, human relatedness is the primary given. Human beings exist in a social context. People learn from one another as they interact with each another. Confucian values view harmony among human beings necessary to achieve a harmonious society. Hence, emphasizing that relationship among people should fall into proper places and order, so that they can relate to and interact with each other in a supportive and harmonious way (Zhang, Lin, Nonaka, & Beom, 2005).

With respect to human relatedness through historical development, Wu Lu, which is based on the Confucian five basic human relationships (Xu, 2006), has long been practices by the Chinese. These human relationships include (a) ruler and subordinates (the relation of righteousness), (b) father and son (the relation of love), (c) husband and wife (the relation of chaste conduct), (d) elder brother and younger brother (the relation of order), and (e) friends and friends (the relations of faithfulness; Chang & Holt, 1991; Chen & Chung, 1994).

Resting on the five Confucian relationships, family in Chinese culture plays critical roles for each individual's development. Parents always have authority over their children and the children should respect their parents. This rule guides family but it also serves as the basis for social integration and societal stability. Confucian values emphasize that in order to seek harmonious relationships with others, one should respect and follow traditions and social hierarchy (rules, status, and authority).

For instance, in school, students should always respect teachers, who are regarded as the authorities. In society, younger people should always show respect for older people. Persons of lower social status should be loyal to the authority (Huang & Brown, 2009). Thus, "starting from the family as a center, when everyone is able to accord to his or her own role and treat others with propriety, the whole society can be well-regulated according to gender, age, generations and so on" (Chang & Holt, 1991, p. 254). In other words, regardless of with whom one interacts, one must follow the rules of order.

These values serve as standards and rules for social interactions of many East Asian countries. Understanding Confucian culture and values helps us to understand the struggles and barriers of East Asian students under the influence of Confucianism while studying abroad. It also clearly explains reasons why these international students learn in certain ways and perform differently than their fellow Americans in classrooms.

The Influence of Confucian Values on Learning and Socializing

The Confucian value of harmony and the emphasis on social hierarchy make Chinese and other East Asian students generally respect older people and people with higher social standing. They often follow their advice without questioning. Teachers, in particular, receive high honor and are considered as authorities for transmitting knowledge. They are generally expected to be experts and to pass on their knowledge and skills to learners, and care about and guide students' personal growth and career development. Teachers share knowledge with students but also help students choose their career paths. Thus, teachers are very influential figures in students' lives (Huang & Brown, 2009).

This value characterizes learning as an apprenticeship that is teacher centered and in which knowledge flows from the teacher to the student. Thus, within many East Asian countries, teaching is largely didactic and textbound with little time allowed for discussion (Yang et al., 2006). Influenced by the traditional educational system and the current highly competitive national entrance exam score required for entry into higher education (Huang & Brown, 2009), Chinese students have been shaped by the linear, competition-oriented, and authority-centered education throughout their educational histories. In Chinese classrooms, teachers carefully follow their texts and prepare their lectures to offer detailed point-to-point information that students write in their notes. Lectures and taking notes are main formats of teaching and learning in Chinese schools, which leave no room or little room for collaboration, creativity, or communication among students

(Holmes, 2005). The same is true of many schools in other East Asian countries. As a result, East Asian students have different perspectives on teaching and learning as it occurs on their host campuses, which is characterized by

- Too much student participation,
- Too much group work,
- Failure to follow the textbook,
- Poor lecture organization,
- Failure to summarize lectures and conclude the main points, and
- Broad and extensive blackboard writings compared with the "intensive, narrow, and detailed" information (Huang & Brown, 2009, pp. 648–650).

The Confucian emphasis on social hierarchy results in acceptance rather than questioning of knowledge, especially where such challenges might cause loss of face. Politeness and maintaining face, both one's own and that of others are important for group harmony. However in the United States, students often ask teachers questions or make jokes in class, students challenge teachers, and often interrupt their teachers to ask questions. All these behaviors may be considered rude and disrespectful in the eyes of East Asian students.

It is also shameful for Chinese students to say in front of the class that they do not understand the teachers' instructions and assignments Most East Asian students feel more comfortable following traditional ways of seeking alternative routes to addressing problematic question in class such as asking their same-culture peers rather than ask the teacher for explanation in class or during teachers' office hours (Holmes, 2005). This cultural difference helps us understand why so many East Asian students do not often ask teachers questions in class. However, not asking questions does not necessarily mean that these students do not actively think or learn (Huang & Brown, 2009).

Some researchers (Holmes, 2005; Liu 200l) found that Confucian collectivist values encourage students' desire to fit in, to be verbally reserved, and to avoid drawing attention to themselves. For example, using the class time to talk about one's own issues or questions is seen as selfish in the Confucian culture. In addition, the teacher is considered to be the center of the classroom not students. Thus, it is typical for students from East Asian countries to listen attentively, take notes, and expect that they may continue interactions with their teachers in warm social contexts beyond the classroom, which typically happen in their own cultures. In reality, however, the opportunities for teacher-student interaction on U.S. campuses are mainly in the classroom or during office hours (Holmes, 2005).

Family, as an enriching and nourishing support system, serves as a vehicle for the realization of the self. The self, in turn, must develop in its various roles as son or daughter, parent or sibling. Thus, family is the first and most direct support for one's growth and development regardless of age and marital status. Accordingly, one's success is also seen as the whole family's accomplishment and not just one's own. "A good education can bring honor to the family and even the community. Parents feel honored if their children can go to colleges and universities" (Huang & Brown, 2009, p. 646). Each family member has a responsibility to support others in the family for personal and familial achievements. As a whole, and together, everyone contributes to the welfare and success of the family.

Friends as well as leaders from one's working organization or learning institution are also seen as the extension of family support. An old Chinese motto says, "While staying with family, we have family members to help and support us. While living far away from home, we must mostly rely on friends." Nevertheless, for international students, family and friends are at a distance, and their new support system has to be established and developed. The fading of their previous support system from family and friends causes increasing feelings of uneasiness, fear, and helpless, and they must alone bear all the pressure and difficulties, which often prevent them from interacting with members of their host country.

Faculty Role in Facilitating Student Transition

Most research tends to examine difficulties and struggles in areas of teaching and learning that international students face, and how teachers feel about the performance of their international students (Gu & Maley, 2008; Holmes, 2005; Huang & Brown, 2009; Ryan & Louie, 2007; Wang, 2006; Yang et al., 2006). My teaching and working with international students has enabled me to experience that faculty can engage in several behaviors both in and outside classroom that seem particularly beneficial to facilitating the transition of international students from their native to host culture, particularly students from East Asia. In particular, teachers should (Sun & Erichsen, 2008)

- Try to learn to speak and greet them in their languages,
- Demonstrate respect and interest in their culture and ideas,
- Provide encouragement, emotional support, understanding, and appreciation for the ways in which they differ from them,
- Be patient with their ways of thinking and expressing ideas,
- Show genuine care, concern, and support for their well-being and family life,
- Create "connections" to their learning and life, such as asking about events or stories from their culture in order to help them feel more like an "insider" than an "outsider," and
- Develop true friendship with these students rather just superficial ones.

My experience clearly echoes learning theories and newer approaches that address the emotional, cultural, and sociological aspects of learning for holistic human development (Illeris, 2004; Jarvis, 2006; Taylor, 1998). In fact, international students not only long for academic achievements but also desire to live a successful life in the host culture. However, several characteristics of U.S. higher education institutions might be make it very difficult for international students to reach these goals. These barriers include

- The university environment and curriculum, which often encourage the separation of students' personal life and academic study,
- The focus on student academic progress at the expense of developing other areas of students' lives,
- Faculty's academic-only support role which prevents East Asian students from seeking other assistance and developing student-faculty relationships (as they expect in their own culture) that support their learning, and
- The support system of many colleges and universities, which does not match the experience and expectations or needs of these students, resulting in inefficient use of the institution's student services and resources.

These limitations disrupt the natural development of human beings as per Confucian values.

Clearly, Confucian cultural values greatly influence East Asian students' learning and life in the United States. However, oftentimes we miss seeing the whole picture of the Confucian educational practices, which may help promote a holistic view on human development and learning as transformation. In the next section, I present a Confucian learning model to illustrate the goal of Confucian education and describe the multiple areas and approaches of teaching and learning for the holistic development of becoming fuller human beings through lifelong learning.

A Confucian Learning Model

This Confucian learning model is developed from the Confucian perspective on learning. It is an extension of the Confucian ideal human model "Sage" and the realistic Confucian goal for the educated, "Jun Zi" who learned to strengthen self-cultivation and present Ren—humanity and righteousness towards the "world" in which we live (Sun, 2004, 2008).

Sage signifies multidimensional relationships that each human being holds within the world in which he or she lives. Sage is one who has reached the highest realm and become (a) the undivided "I" with the Universe, (b) the unity of "I" with other humans and other beings, and (c) the wholeness of "I" with self" (Sun, 2004). From all of these relationships, we learn accountability and to fulfill certain responsibilities.

Sun (2004) described and analyzed Confucian educational practice, which is exemplified in Jun Zi. "Jun Zi is commonly known as a moral exemplar of the Confucian educated, characterized by outstanding knowledge, multiple skills to access and practice Ren" (p.80). Jun Zi presents Ren toward a world with many dimensions: the natural world of universe, the social world of other human beings, and the inner world of self. People from the Confucian tradition understand, Jun Zi respects the Tao of Heaven and understands each human's fate. Toward society, Jun Zi has strong social responsibility, and toward other beings, Jun Zi follows "do not impose on others what you do not desire" (Sun, 2004, p. 80). Toward self, Jun Zi never ceases self-strengthening. Thus, Jun Zi is expected to illustrate a holistic development of a human being via an integration of learning and practice from multiple dimensions of the world they live and interact with.

I incorporated Jun Zi into a Confucian Learning Model (see Figure 14.1), which highlights a continuous transformative learning process that involves whole beings and their multiple life worlds and contexts. As human beings, we not only have physical bodies, rational minds, and emotional hearts, but also a spiritual inner self. The consciousness of the body, mind, heart, and inner self all perceive reality differently. However, all of these parts make up the whole of a person even though each part has its own unique needs and nature.

As human beings, we not only live in a cosmic, natural, and social world, but also in an inner and spiritual world. In this sense, we are not only natural and moral beings, but we are also social, political, and spiritual beings. These contexts naturally require human beings to learn and develop continuously in order to live in and interact properly with these different worlds.

Confucius emphasized that Jun Zi, living in and interacting with different contexts, we are required to learn and practice Ren accordingly. To become Jun Zi, one must remain in a continuous dialogue with the cosmic, natural, social, inner, and spiritual worlds. Human beings interact with and live in each of these worlds, which requires them to engage in various kinds of learning via manifold approaches and activities that help develop appropriate and necessary qualities related to knowledge and skills, socially accepted values, beliefs, and attitude, and emotional and psychological balance and capability to fulfill the roles they play in different worlds.

As Sun (2008) asserted

Confucianism recognizes the multidimensional nature of human beings, the various purposes of being human and their realization via lifelong learning, indicating a more holistic development encompassing the many capabilities and roles that human beings possess in the multiple worlds they belong to, live in, and interact with. (p. 573)

The purpose of Confucian education and learning is to self-cultivate and realize the full nature of human beings through lifelong learning. As we all

Figure 14.1   The Confucian Learning Model

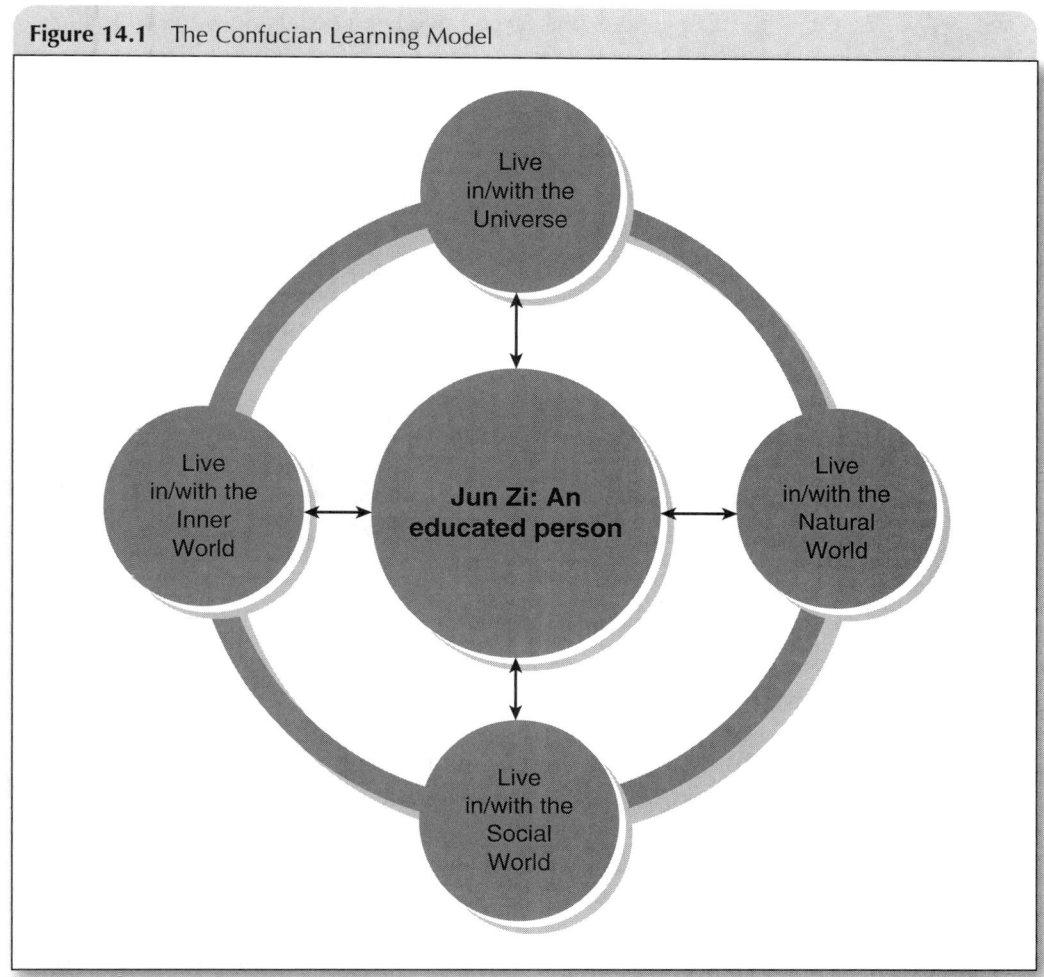

know, that although we were born human beings, we are not fully developed human yet. Each of us must still consciously learn to become fully human in its all dimensions.

In his own teaching practices, Confucius demonstrated that human learning is not only lifelong but also life wide (Sun, 2008). He selected and developed his own curriculum, the "Confucianized six arts" (Wang, Yong, Liu, & Tang, 2006; X. Zhang, 2009), consisting of "Poetry" (诗), "The Book of History or the Book of Documents" (书), "Yi" – I Ching (易), "Rites" (礼), "Music" (乐), and "Chun Quo Zou Zhuan" (春秋). The Confucian curriculum, through holistic approaches, emphasized learning from culture, history, and social political participation, and so on, which prepared learners to be able to actively participate in each world in which they live and interact.

Confucius applied extensive human experience and human concerns within the culture he had inherited to his teaching and learning (Tu, n.d.), including the classic texts that he compiled, studied, reviewed, and finalized: *"Shi Jing"* (*The Book of Odes*), *"Chun Quo Zou Zhuan"* (*The Spring and Autumn Annals*), and *"Yi Jing"* (*The Book of Changes*). Although each text has its own form, its own content, and, therefore, its own inner logic and function, together they frame a meaningful picture for us to see today that Confucian educational practices involve larger aspects of human experience, concern, and desires. Thus, we see, there is a poetic vision of being human, a ritual version of being human, a historical version of being human, a political version, and a cosmic version (Sun, in press).

There also is one more important version of being human, which is the international version—Confucius highly respected receiving foreign visitors and visiting other states. Confucius himself visited many states during 14 years of travel (Sun, 2011). Confucius believed that these occasions presented momentous opportunities for exchanging ideas, improvement, and transformation. "Is it not delightful to have friends coming from distance to share and exchange with?" (*The Analects of Confucius*, I, 1).

Tu (n.d.) insightfully expressed transformative learning and learning for transformation as follows:

> One also extends one's relationships beyond the familial structure, and so beyond nepotism, in order to be able to relate meaningfully to a larger community. By inference, to truly find one's roots, to find inspiration in one's ethnicity and cultural tradition, one must go beyond a closed ethnocentrism or a narrowly conceived culturalism. To truly realize one's commitment to one's own culture and to one's own nation, one must go beyond simple-minded cultural or national chauvinism. If we follow this line of reasoning, we have to transcend even anthropocentrism . . . It is, in this sense, a process of education for the creation of an open-minded character which can relate meaningfully to an ever-enlarging network of human relationships.

Conclusions

Studying abroad transplants international students into a new and multidimensional world. They face many physical and emotional challenges and issues, but also linguistic, cultural, socioeconomic, educational, as well as others. Thus, perspective transformation and conscious learning for transformation in various aspects are obvious goals for both host educators and international students to achieve.

The most well-known modern work that focuses on teaching for transformation may be Mezirow's theory of transformative learning as applied to adult education. This work emphasized that adults learn by critically reflecting on assumptions and changing their behaviors and meaning perspectives as a result of dealing with a disorienting dilemma. Mezirow (2003) believed that transformative learning is one of the key goals of adult learning and education. Hence, transformative learning may play a significant role in helping host educators to become more consciously aware of their roles in teaching in international students.

Similarly, Jarvis's learning model (2006) deliberately conveys that through different types of learning, we constantly change and establish different relationships with the world in which we live and interact. Thus learning for transformation is essential, particularly in an international context.

The Confucian learning model not only offers an insightful depiction of the goal of human learning, which is the realization of the full nature of being human beings. It also shows us how to become the Confucian Educated, *Jun Zi*, which helps us consciously revisit the purposes of contemporary education and critically ponder what we are missing—are we learning to become fully human or are we moving away from the whole of which we are a part, separating the connectedness of a holistic development of being human?

But more significantly, this learning model displays that learning occurs continuously over the life span (life-long), and that every aspect of social life (life-wide) is involved. Central to this model is that notion that continuous learning for transformation facilitates one to live in the world of multi-dimensions properly and successfully. By linking the Confucian learning model to learning as transformation in an international context, we see at least three significant implications for effective teaching and learning.

First, administrators and faculty members need to be sensitive to students' needs and identify issues and difficulties from their whole world rather than only academic study. Host educators and policymakers should help make meaningful connections of academic work to these students' personal lives and support their social, emotional, and spiritual well being by assisting them in acquiring the necessary knowledge and skills to easily interact with each world. Such efforts may be made through helping find proper host families from local communities and scheduling regular visits with students and their families beyond class activities.

Second, educators, administrators, and policymakers of host educational institutions should consciously improve their learning regarding their international students' culture. Appropriate offices on campus, such as the international student office or student learning center, may help by periodically organizing social and learning activities of various kinds to actively and purposefully learn from and interact with these students. In addition, the hosts must be willing to change their mindset that international students are here to learn from the United States. In fact, we must learn from each other in order to better facilitate these students' learning and well being. Such mutual learning will enable hosts to experience transformation as well.

Third, faculty members should become consciously aware of the fact that various kinds of learning are needed for these international students rather than just their own program of courses inside of the classroom. Teachers should try to mix the use of examples from North American culture with Eastern culture to help balance the group work/discussion. Faculty might consider altering the format of their office hours to meet the needs of their culturally different students. Faculty should be able to advise international students, and/or redirect them to proper campus or community offices if needed.

I have argued that international students go through a series of phases, curves, and levels of adjustment and adaptation while studying aboard. This process calls for learning for transformation as an important goal for host educators to strive for in teaching these international students. The Confucian learning model offers us an alternative lens through which to view learning for transformation, and offers important insights for teaching and learning that occurs within an international context.

References

Boyd, R. N., & Myers, J. G. (1988). Transformative education. *International Journal of Lifelong Learning, 7*, 261–284.

Chang, H. C., & Holt, R. (1991). More than relationship: Chinese interaction and the principle of kuan-hsi. *Communication Quarterly, 39*, 251–271. doi: 10.1080/01463379109369802

Chen, G., & Chung, J. (1994). The impact of Confucianism on organizational communication. *Communication Quarterly, 42*, 93–105. doi: 10.1080/01463379409369919

Cranton, P., & Roy, M. (2003).When the bottom falls out of the bucket: Toward a holistic perspective on transformative learning. *Journal of Transformative Education, 1*, 86–98.

Cranton, P. (1994). *Understanding and promoting transformative learning: A guide for educators of adults.* San Francisco, CA: Jossey-Bass.

Cranton, P. (2006). *Understanding and promoting transformative learning: A guide for educators of adults.* The Jossey-Bass higher and adult education series (2nd ed.). San Francisco, CA: Jossey-Bass.

Erichsen, E. A. (2009). *Reinventing selves: International students' conceptions of self and learning for transformation.* Unpublished doctoral dissertation, University of Wyoming, Laramie, WY.

Gan, Z. (2009). 'Asian learners' e-examined: An empirical study of language learning attitudes, strategies and motivation among mainland Chinese and Hong Kong students. *Journal of Multilingual and Multicultural Development. 30*, 41–58.

Gu, Q., & Maley, A. (2008). Changing places: A study of Chinese students in the UK. *International Journal of Bilingual Education and Bilingualism, 8*, 224–245. doi: 10.1080/14708470802303025

Gu, Q., & Schweisfurth, M. (2006). Who adapts? Beyond cultural models of "the" Chinese learner. *Language Culture and Curriculum, 19*, 74–89.

Holmes, P. (2005). Ethnic Chinese students' communication with cultural others in a New Zealand university. *Communication Education, 54*, 289–311. doi: 10.1080/03634520500442160

Huang, Z. (2006). 儒家德育学说论纲。 *[Confucian moral education theory review]*, *Wuhan*: Wuhan University Publisher.

Huang, J., & Brown, K. (2009). Cultural factors affecting Chinese ESL students' academic learning. *Education, 129*, 643–653.

Illeris, K. (2004) Transformative learning in the perspective of a comprehensive learning theory. *Journal of Transformative Education 2*, 79–89. doi: 10.1177/1541344603262315

Institute of International Education. (2010). *Open doors*. http://www.iie.org/en/ Who-We-Are/News-and-Events/Press-Center/Press-Releases/2010/2010-11-15-Open-Doors-International-Students-In-The-US

Jarvis, P. (2006). *Towards a comprehensive theory of human learning*. London & New York, NY: Routledge.

Li, China Daily @ http://www.chinadaily.com.cn/china/2009-11/12/content_8953810 .htm

Liu, J. (2001). *Asian students' classroom communication patterns in U.S. universities: An emic perspective*. Contemporary studies in second language learning. Westport, CT: Ablex.

Merriam, S. B., Caffarella, R. S., & Baumgartner, L. M. (2007). *Learning in adulthood*. (3rd ed.). San Francisco, CA: Jossey-Bass.

Mezirow, J. (2000). Learning to think like an adult: Core concepts of transformation theory. In J. Mezirow & Associates (Eds.), *Learning as transformation: Critical perspectives on a theory in progress* (pp. 329–358). San Francisco, CA: Jossey-Bass.

Mezirow, J. (1991). *Transformative dimensions of adult learning*. San Francisco, CA: Jossey-Bass.

Mezirow, J. (2003). Transformative learning as discourse. *Journal of Transformative Education, 1*, 58–63.

Mezirow, J., & Associates (2000). *Learning as transformation: Critical perspectives on a theory in progress*. San Francisco, CA: Jossey-Bass.

Mortenson, S. (2006). Cultural differences and similarities in seeking social support as a response to academic failure: A comparison of American and Chinese college students. *Communication Education, 55*, 127–146. doi: 10.1080/036345206 00565811

Nguyen, P. M., Terlouw, C., & Pilot, A. (2006). Culturally appropriate pedagogy: The case of group learning in a Confucian Heritage Culture context. *Intercultural Education, 17*, 1–19. doi:10.1080/14675980500502172

Nisbett, R. E. (2003). *The geography of thought: How Asians and Westerners think differently—and why*. New York, NY: The Free Press.

Ryan, J., & Louie, K. (2007). False dichotomy? 'Western' and 'Confucian' concepts of scholarship and learning. *Educational Philosophy & Theory, 39*, 404–417. doi:10.1111/j.1469-5812.2007.00347.x

Signorini, P., Wiesemes, R., & Murphy, R. (2009). Developing alternative frameworks for exploring intercultural learning: A critique of Hofstede's cultural difference model. *Teaching in Higher Education, 14*, 253–264. doi: 10.1080/13562510902898825

Sun, Q. (2008). Confucian educational philosophy and its implication for lifelong learning and lifelong education. *International Journal of Lifelong Education, 27*, 559–578. **doi:** 10.1080/01411920802343269

Sun, Q. (2011). *East meets west: Perennial wisdom for the ends/means issue of modern adult education*. Saarbrücken, Germany: VDM Verlag.

Sun, Q. (in press). The Confucian learning: Learning to become fully human. In P. Jarvis (Ed.), *The Routledge International Handbook on Learning*. London, UK: Routledge.

Sun, Q. (2004). To be Ren and Jun Zi: A Confucian perspective of the practice of contemporary education. *The Journal of Thought. 39*, 77–91.

Sun, Q., & Cho, S. R. (2008). From a Confucian tradition to the postmodern world: Korean middle-aged women's traditional roles and modern expectations in a globalized society. *International Forum for Teaching and Studies, 4*, 5–11.

Sun, Q., & Erichsen, A. E. (2008, November). *Transformative learning experiences of international graduate students: A qualitative study*. Paper presented at the 57th Annual Conference of American Association for Adult and Continuing Education, Denver, CO.

Taylor, E.W. (1998). *Transformative learning: A critical review*. Columbus, OH: ERIC Clearinghouse on Adult, Career, and Vocational Education.

Taylor, E. W. (2006). *Teaching for change: Fostering transformative learning in the classroom*. New directions for adult and continuing education, no. 109. San Francisco, CA: Jossey-Bass.

The analects of Confucius. (1992). (Bao, Shixing, Trans. into Modern Chinese & Lao An, Trans. into English). Shangdong, Ji Nan: Shandong Friendship Press.

Tu, W. *Core values in Confucian thought*. Retrieved from http://www.trinity.edu/rnadeau/FYS/Tu%20Wei-ming.htm

Wang, H. (2006). Teaching Asian students online: What matters and why? *PAACE Journal of Lifelong Learning, 15*, 69–84.

Wang, J., Yong, C., Liu, H., & Tang, M. (2006). 斯文在兹-儒学与中国传统文化. [*Confucianism and Chinese traditional culture*]. Ji Nan: Qi Lu Publishing Association.

Xu, R. (2006).人和论：儒家人伦思想研究。[*On human harmony: Study on Confucianism and human ethics]*, Beijing, China: People's Publisher.

Yang, B., Zheng, W., & Li, M. (2006). Confucian view of learning and implications for developing human resources. *Advances in Developing Human Resources, 8*, 346–354. doi: 10.1177/1523422306288427

Zhang, Q. (2009). 孔学今义。[*Confucianism and its contemporary meaning*. Beijing, China: Beijing University Publisher.

Zhang, Y. B., Lin, M. C., Nonaka, A., & Beom, K. (2005). Harmony, hierarchy and conservatism: A cross-cultural comparison of Confucian values in China, Korea, Japan, and Taiwan. *Communication Research Reports, 22*, 107–115. doi: 10.1080/0003681050013053

Zhang, X. (2009). 孔子的现象学阐释九讲：礼乐人生与哲学。[*Review and interpretation of the phenomenon of Confucius: Ritual and music in life and philosophy*]. Shanghai: China Eastern Normal University Publisher.

CHAPTER 15

Review of New University Education Policy Implementation in Croatia

VESNA KOVAČ AND MARKO TURK

The Croatian academic community will remember the last several years as marked by a strong tide of reforms in the higher education system in the context of the Bologna Process.[1] Becoming a part of the Bologna Process triggered a large number of radical and intensive changes in the Croatian higher education system. For example, the elimination of 4-year graduate studies to adopt a two-cycle higher education system of undergraduate and graduate studies in the 2004–2005 academic year caused the most intense stir in the academic community. However, these changes were only the beginning of changes—the implementation of the European Credit Transfer and Accumulation System (ECTS)[2] grading system, significant changes in the studying regime, and the implementation of a more rigorous teaching activities regulation are only some of the changes students and teachers faced in the past several years.

In this chapter, we will discuss how the Bologna Process affected the Croatian educational processes. We will present the national policy framework used to regulate teaching activities and analyze the new educational policy implementation using the example of one higher education institution: the University of Rijeka. This university was among the first institutions that implemented the new teaching system, which completely altered existing educational practices. The new regulation of studies of the University of Rijeka was adopted in 2008 and aimed to adjust existing educational practice at the university according to the principles of the Bologna Process. The new policy document, among other things, defined stronger regulation of the university education process, introduced the new grading system, and intervened more into issues of students' rights and responsibilities. The elementary provisions of the new university educational regulation will be presented in detail. We also will analyze the ways in which this regulation changes the academic practices of university constituents, their teachers, and students, and especially, the role of educational processes at the university.

To analyze the new university education regulation implementation, a theoretical framework to be used for the investigation of the education policy implementation was developed and applied. The actions of the new policy creators will be discussed as will the readiness of the academic community to accept and implement the changes. In addition, we identify the sources of the implementation process difficulties and problems. The conclusions of our review can be used as guidelines for decisionmakers who can implement them to improve the preconditions for successful regulation implementation. In addition, our conclusions can also provide a framework for individuals who are involved in planning the formulation of new higher education policies to predict the course and the preconditions of successful implementation.

Honig's (2006) Model: A Theoretical Framework for Understanding Educational Policy Implementation

Most policy implementation research emphasizes two dimensions of this sort of research: first, the success of the policy implementation, or the extent to which the policy has been implemented to suit the policy design, and second, the efficiency of the implementation, or the extent to which the policy implementation results in the desired improvements in practice (Ben-Peretz, 2009; Cooper, Cibulka, & Fusarelli, 2008; Fitz, Halpin, & Power, 1994; Fuhrman, Cohen, & Mosher, 2007; Honig, 2006; McLaughlin, 1987; Rizvi & Lingard, 2010). Educational policy researchers have observed two policy cycles in the recent past: policy formulation and policy implementation (e.g., Ben-Peretz, 2009; Rizvi & Lingard, 2010). At first, these cycles were thought to operate independently of each, but more recently, they appear to be strongly intertwined phases of a policy process.

Changes in trends can also be recognized in the adoption of dominant perspectives in implementation studies. Earlier research studies often viewed policy implementation as a top-down process in which policy decisionmakers and the policy instruments they used played the key role, whereas more recent research studies have viewed a bottom-up approach that emphasizes the role of policy implementation participants and their interaction.

Whereas the first generations of researchers emphasized determining the degree to which certain ideas were implemented in practice given the policy design, as well as the identifying factors that influenced its degree of success, more recent researchers have focused on detailed observation and explanation of how various factors interact during the policy process (e.g., Honig, 2006). Education policy implementation must be studied as a complex, dynamic phenomenon susceptible to contextual change. There is no unique pattern for analyzing educational policy implementation that suits every possible situation, which means that the results of any one research study cannot be used to indicate that certain experiences will generalize to other situations and contexts.

So far, attempts undertaken to sketch the theoretical framework for the investigation of educational policy implementation have resulted in the identification and grouping of key factors and their interactions that should be monitored during the policy process. These attempts have also resulted, on rare occasions, in discovering regularities that can direct the design phase of the policy process.

Meredith Honig (2006) introduced a useful theoretical model that allows for monitoring and analysis of the educational policy implementation. Honig singled out and described in detail three basic groups of factors that have a strong impact on the effectiveness and efficiency of educational policy implementation: (a) features of the policy under consideration, (b) people who are responsible for implementing the policy, and (c) the environment in which this policy will take effect. This model places a primary focus on people—those individuals who will be involved with any aspect of the implementation process. However, the model requires simultaneous monitoring of the interaction of all three factors. In this way, the capacity of the implementation structure to accept and implement policies can be determined in given policy environment and given circumstances.

Policies

The policy implementation process involves three general policy dimensions: policy objectives, targets, and tools. Policy objectives can be differentiated by several factors including scope, focus, the part of the system to be changed by new policy, the intensity of change that new policy will cause within the system, and the targets to be mobilized during the policy implementation. When the new policies change more than the existing policy, the implementation process will become more complex and thus susceptible to further departure from original policy design.

Targets include individuals and groups of people that a given policy system will most affect. It is important to monitor how the targets will interpret changes in policy and what role they will play in the implementation process. Thus, it is advantageous to be familiar with making policy decision processes (who the participants are and how they make decisions), and the ways in which the targets will be involved in the decision-making process.

A third policy relates to the tools or instruments and how they are applied to successfully achieve policy objectives. Although the type and efficiency of individual tools used by those who are introducing the new policies (e.g., giving or taking away the mandates, financial and other incentives, and capacity building tools) are easy to detect and monitor, several authors note that resources available to policy implementers should also be observed with equal attention (e.g., Fuhrman et al., 2007), stressing that, in particular, the strength of effect those resources have (e.g., dominant value orientations, interests, knowledge, and dispositions) on the new policy implementation process. Policy tools often vary in strength, or how they influence educational practice or how efficiently they support the achievement of policy objectives. Institutions should make the necessary resources readily available to policy implementers, and in turn, policy implementers should know how to use them to achieve intended policy outcomes.

People

In addition to those targets formally named in policy designs, implementers should attend to all those individuals and groups who nonetheless participate in and otherwise influence implementation.[3] The focus should be on the basic resources that these individuals or groups bring to the process that influence (a) the way these individuals or groups will interpret and reinterpret the policy message, (b) whether these individuals or groups will possess the capacities required for the successful implementation of policy objectives (e.g., motivation, knowledge, skills, time, power), and (c) what kind of role these individuals or groups will play in the implementation process. What may happen in actuality is that what was intended during policy design does not necessarily occur during policy implementation. Thus, the success of policy initiatives—even those that were planned, supported, and carefully thought through—often depend on the way individuals within the policy system interpret and execute them (McLaughlin, 1987).

People have a strong influence on the policy process dynamics because their positions and roles change over time. Participants may join in or leave the policy process of policy formulation and implementation. Likewise, political perspectives are also an important consideration in understanding policy development and implementation (Levinson, Sutton, & Winstead, 2009) because the influence participants in the policy arena have on each other strongly affects policy implementation activities and outcomes (Cibulka, 2001; Johnson, 2001; Mawhinney, 2001).

Places and Environments

This factor helps researchers explain why the same policy procedures are defined, understood, and implemented differently in different organizations, environments, or circumstances (McLaughlin, 1987). Places differ across many variables that strongly influence the policy process. In this vein, an organization's location within the educational system is one of the most important of characteristics (e.g., its interdependence with other institutions in the educational system), as is its historical and institutional context (i.e., the influence of traditions and its formal structure). The size and structure of the institutions that are influenced by educational policy also can affect the implementation process, as can the communication channels among different parts of the educational system (Fuhrman et al., 2007).

Identifying interactions among policies, people, and places and their characteristic dimensions offers a solid framework for understanding the new educational policy implementation process at the University of Rijeka. Based on the currently available data describing the roles and positions of various participants in the implementation process, we will identify and analyze several key interactions.[4] In the remainder of this chapter, we will give special attention to

- identifying relations among participants during decision making regarding new education policies together with understanding the configuration of participants in the implementation process,
- policy instruments used to provide successful execution of policy objectives,
- participants' relationship to the policy content, and
- necessary capacities that must be provided in advance by policymakers before the policy can be implemented as planned, which, in turn, will lead to anticipated practice improvements.

At this phase of our research and in the context of currently available information, we cannot make a thorough assessment whether and to what degree implementation of the new university education policy resulted in the improvements in quality and efficiency of the educational process at the University of Rijeka. Our aim in this chapter is to comment on several important aspects of the new university education policy implementation. We will note several key lessons stemming from the policy implementation and emphasize the importance of understanding policy context and its influence on direct educational practices.

Teaching Policy Background

In recent years, a series of policy initiatives has been initiated by the ministry and universities in the context of regulating the teaching activities at the Croatian universities.[5] These initiatives are especially visible when they are connected to the passing of fundamental documents (legislative and other) that regulate higher education and scientific-educational activities at each university (additional documents regulate educational activities of every institution of higher education). Our review and analysis of fundamental policy documents[6] will focus on the basic activities and changes teachers and students in Croatia are facing in the context of having to adjust higher educational process to meet the requirements of the Bologna Process.

Fundamental legislation determining the current higher education system in the Republic of Croatia is the Act on Scientific Activity and Higher Education in the Republic of Croatia passed by Croatian Parliament in July 2003 (n. d.). In the context of discussion about educational activities in higher education, the quality of education and the quality of graduate studies are not specifically mentioned anywhere in the act. The act does not define normative compliance, but it does contain specific indicators within its individual articles. For example, the act emphasizes students' rights regarding educational course quality and educational process quality consistent with the graduate study. The act also emphasizes students' right to state their opinions on the quality of their educational experiences and the quality of their teachers. In addition, the act specifies that students should be provided with the high-quality graduate studies. In the context of standardizing general regulations regarding the university, the act further stipulates that the university should provide continuous growth in the quality of students' work, as well as the continuous growth of educational, scientific, artistic, and expert work. Almost all Croatian universities adopted the regulations contained within this act to ensure their implementation, and consequently, to monitor and evaluate the educational system with regard to quality teaching. In addition, another act, the Act on Quality Assurance in Science and Higher Education (n.d.), regulates quality assurance and its improvement in science and higher education through initial accreditation, reaccreditation, thematic evaluation, and periodic external and independent review of the internal quality assurance system.

The *Strategic Development Framework for 2006–2013* (Dalič, 2006), adopted by the Croatian government in 2003, is another national level document influencing Croatian higher education. One particular segment of this document regarding higher education development (*Educational Sector Development Plan 2005–2010*) noted that one of its developmental goals is to establish a quality assurance system in the higher education system and to encourage continuous investment in the higher education quality. At a practical level, we can compare the goals of this plan with a number of key documents relating to higher education development in Europe, united under the common name of Trends Reports.[7] In Croatia, the Agency for Science and Higher Education and quality centers at every university play the key role regarding quality issues. In addition, all national universities have established quality offices or centers within their vice chancellors' office with the aim of creating institutional mechanisms for the systematic evaluation and coordination of initiatives and development programs. The long-range goal of these offices and centers is to promote high standards of professional development for its stakeholders in all operational areas.

With an aim to define clearly its mission and its activities and to respond to ongoing changes in higher education, the University of Rijeka prepared a common development document of all its constituents (schools and departments)—*University of Rijeka Strategy 2007–2013*. This document highlights the quality of the educational process as its strategic value.

The University of Rijeka has worked intensively on issues regarding educational process quality. In addition to the quality office that operates within the University of Rijeka, individual constituents have also been very active regarding educational process quality.[8] The National Foundation for Science, Higher Education, and Technological Development of the Republic of Croatia has financed 14 projects focusing on the investigation and analysis of higher education quality. As an additional way of supporting higher education quality and making sure it is continuously developed, the University of Rijeka has adopted the *Educational Quality Assurance Handbook of the University of Rijeka* (2010), which stemmed from one of the foundation's projects. The handbook closely follows the norms and guidelines of higher education quality assurance development proscribed by the European Association for Quality Assurance in Higher Education (ENQA) for those countries that have signed the Bologna Declaration.

The passing of the Regulation of Studies of the University of Rijeka by Senate of the University of Rijeka in July 2008 has caused significant change in the organization and focus of the educational system at the University of Rijeka. This document has exerted a strong influence on students and teachers and has contributed heavily to moving away from the university's long-established educational traditions. For example, previously autonomous (only slightly regulated teaching) is becoming strictly regulated and subject to constant control: Teachers no longer have dominant autonomy in making decisions regarding course duties and creating lesson plans, teachers must validate students accomplishments, examination processes have been redefined, and students' progress through the educational process is now more tightly regulated.

The regulation also increases teachers' scope of academic administration, regulates the manner in which teachers conduct examinations, and requires that students be constantly monitored and evaluated. For example, class work contributes a minimum of 70 percent of a student's grades whereas the final examination (according to the regulation it can only be in written form) may be worth only a maximum of 30 percent of a student's grades. These changes imply a significant distancing from the previous teaching practice, which did not require continuous monitoring of students and often based the bulk of students' success in their courses on their final examination results. Apart from the common numerical grading system (from 1 to 5), a new system of grading, based on percentages and letter grades (A, B, C, D, E, F, FX) has been implemented. The regulation also established cutoff grades for passing courses (40 percent of achieved grade for undergraduates and 50 percent for graduate students).

One particular provision of the new regulation provoked especially strong debate in the academic community. This provision requires teachers to assign grades according to a normal distribution: A = 10 percent, B = 25 percent, C = 30 percent, D = 25 percent and E =10 percent) in classes of 40 or more students. Thus, grading is standardized relative to the group. The implementation of this provision has provoked initial disagreement and resistance of the academic community and a large spectrum of variations in monitoring and evaluation practices because the teachers have (re)interpreted the provision in various ways.

Review of the New Educational Policy Implementation

Passing of the new education policy at the University of Rijeka is an example of a top-down model of decision making in which the educational policy process begins with the formulation of a policy message by university administrators and results in the implementation of policy at lower levels in the higher education system (Dyer, 1999). This process is based on three indicators.

First, the initiative for creating the new university education policy did not arise from university teachers and students (e.g., as a result of criticizing existing practices or identifying the need to improve the teaching processes). Instead, it emanated from university administrators who had only one motive in mind—adjusting the educational system to conform to the requirements of the Bologna Process. Media interviews with University of Rijeka administrators as well as official press releases from the university clearly reflect the strong ambitions of the University of Rijeka administration toward modernization and internalization. Those ambitions were also readily apparent in University of Rijeka administrators' public speeches to members of the academic community regarding the new regulation. Unfortunately, whereas most university teachers and students focused on anticipating real problems in educational practices that would be induced through implementation of the new regulation, administrators and others favoring the new regulation remained focused on broader higher education policy and the goals that would be accomplished once the new regulation was implemented. By and large, administrators disregarded warnings that local conditions were not adequate for implementing the regulation.

Second, during a public debate regarding the new regulation, which was initiated by the University of Rijeka administration as required by procedure, members of the university community voiced disagreement with the new regulation and showed resistance, even refusal to embrace some of the new regulation's provisions. Some of the provisions that members of the academic community viewed as unacceptable were (a) implementation of ECTS grading scale (e.g., grading students on the grounds of a relative criterion, determining a unique passing grade percentage ranging from 40 percent to 50 percent of achieved grade), (b) determining a unique system for the continuous monitoring of students, and (c) the evident increase in teachers' administrative duties. Unfortunately, University of Rijeka administrators failed to consider most of the academic community's perspectives in drafting the final version of the new regulation.[9] Thus, university administrators sent a clear message about the decision-making model they intended to use to achieve the new regulation's sociopolitical goals.

Third, University of Rijeka administrators have never created a projection showing how implementation of the new regulation will influence education given the local conditions in which the implementation will occur (Bardach, 2009). Although administrators addressed the importance of achieving excellent results, they have largely ignored quality of work issues for teachers as well as the role of teachers and students in the educational process.

Of course, during the public debate on the draft version of the new regulation, there was some agreement among administrators, faculty, and students regarding the possibility of some of the positive improvements that implementing the new regulation would bring. After all, the new regulation emphasized the importance of achieving high quality in all of the University of Rijeka's educational activities, which was especially welcomed given that the pre–new regulation educational process was ineffective along several dimensions (Kovač, 2001).

In Croatia, higher educational processes are no longer a "private" matter of individual teachers, but a highly public activity whose public tasks are being thoroughly examined in the public documents of the university's colleges. The education of students is becoming the focal point at universities, teachers are becoming increasingly responsible for the organization and quality of the educational process, and the entire educational system is becoming more focused on achieving specific learning outcomes. Nonetheless, both teachers and students have raised important questions about the practical means and consequences of implementing the new regulation.

However, neither teachers nor students think that the new regulation is an effective policy for improving the overall quality of higher education. Teachers and students—the key stakeholders in this process—do not see how the new regulation will achieve its goals. They also do not see how the new regulation will improve the working conditions at the university that are necessary to achieve these goals. Indeed, policy implementation research (e.g., Palmer & Snodgrass-Rangel, 2010) has shown that

> Teachers are not simply automatons who implement policies with no regard for their specific students' needs; rather, teachers make sense of the competing demands of formal and informal policy pressures on one hand, with what they believe to be authentic pedagogies on the other. (p. 4)

Thus, it is important to keep in mind that teachers—individually and collectively—will implement the policy as they think best for their students.

Facilitation and Accomplishment of Policy Goals

Successful policy implementation requires balance among various types of policy tools used by policymakers. Some policy tools can be used to provide additional support for implementers during the implementation process, and some can be used to create pressure for immediate implementation of new policy (McLaughlin, 1987).

The University of Rijeka's administrators created several additional instruments to facilitate the implementation of the new regulation. One of the instruments involved a plan for training all university teachers to implement the elements of the new regulation.[10] Expert trainers led training sessions, and teachers at that time exhibited a high level of interest and motivation to learn about it. However, the second phase of the plan did not arouse the same level of interest and motivation in learning about the implementation plan. Although the number of teachers who participated in the second phase was rather high,[11] we cannot say that all of them were motivated and willing to apply their training in the teaching of their classes.

As a part of the implementation plan, the University of Rijeka created and distributed a professional handbook as a part of the implementation program, and the program implementers were available for consultation. Nonetheless, when the university implemented the new regulation, it became clear that, as a whole, the institution was not prepared for the sorts of resulting changes that the new regulation produced. Thus, although the University of Rijeka approved and applied adequate support mechanisms to implement the new regulation, it was not sufficient to ensure its full and effective implementation.

Public forums involving University of Rijeka's administrators and teachers and students have allowed for some discussion of the issues surrounding implementation of the new regulation, but they have not stimulated any significant change in the implementation process. Instead, these discussions are focused primarily on explaining the importance of the new university policy in the context of the Bologna Process.

Interpretation and Reinterpretation of Policy During Implementation

During the implementation of any major educational policy, it is important to consider the capabilities and abilities of those individuals who are actively involved in the implementation process to interpret and reinterpret the policy in accordance with the knowledge, beliefs, and values they attribute to a given policy (Fitz et al., 1994; McLauglin, 1987): Practitioners are rarely comfortable executing orders from their superiors without being able to make adjustments to the policy based on any untoward effects that changes in policy might have on, in this case, teaching and learning.

Thus, it is extremely important to consider the practicalities of the situation at the University of Rijeka in which the implementation is taking place and to analyze to the extent to which the new regulation is being adequately implemented. For example, during the implementation period, it became obvious that student assessment practices varied from one teacher to another in defining the passing grade for their respective courses, choosing adequate examination procedures for continuous monitoring and evaluation, and determining the purpose of final exams in contributing to students' final grades. Although these indicators may not be so different from the teaching practices that existed before the implementation of the new regulation, faculty and administers had not anticipated the extent to which they would complicate the implementation process. The proof that these issues suddenly mattered during the process was evident during the public discussions of the implementation process when larger numbers of students and teachers vocalized their concerns about problems the new regulation was causing in their classrooms.

Teachers expressed dissatisfaction with the new education and examination practice. Part of their dissatisfaction was the result of their distrust in the new system because of the difficulties in identifying improvements in student learning relative to the system that that implementation of the new regulation replaced. Teachers claimed that students changed their approach to educational success and focused primarily on calculating scores they needed to pass and did not pay attention to important learning outcomes. Students reported using superficial approaches to learning course content and distributing their study time unrealistically in an effort to prepare for their exams or other forms of assessment. Teachers claimed that the University of Rijeka's resolution to increase the percentage of students who pass courses, an indicator of educational program quality, actually decreased the extent to which students learn course content and reduced the level of their skills and abilities at graduation.

Reviewing Preconditions for the New University Policy Implementation

Many of University of Rijeka's teachers noted problems of implementing the new regulation given large class sizes. Many teachers have more than 100 students in their courses (some teachers do not have teaching assistants), which makes it difficult to constantly monitor and provide high-quality feedback to individual students. University administrators did not plan for the added work that new regulation imposed on teachers, nor has the university hired additional teachers and staff to help ease these sorts of problems.

Other faculty objections regarded administrative and bureaucratic work in teaching because they did not receive adequate administrative support for this extra burden. Many faculty are worried that their teaching workload may negatively affect their academic advancement through research and research-related activities. Thus, many teachers view implementation of the new regulation as threatening their professional development and accomplishment.

Conclusions

We can draw several conclusions from this review. First, the new regulation was developed and implemented to adjust the Croatian national higher education system to the requirements of the Bologna Process. However, administrators excluded the academic community from critical aspects of the decision-making process during the planning and implementation of the new regulation. Second, the academic community did not receive adequate support and encouragement during the implementation of the new regulation. Third, administrators did not consider the importance of local conditions or provide the necessary resources necessary to achieve successful implementation of the new regulation. Thus, the extent to which the new policy can achieve fundamental objectives—increasing the quality and efficiency of higher education—remains uncertain. As university administrators prepare to implement the next phase of the Bologna process, we hope that they will involve members of the academic community in all stages of planning and implementation.

References

Act on Quality Assurance in Science and Higher Education. (n.d.). *Official Gazette, 45/2009.* Retrieved from: http://www.nn.hr

Act on Scientific Activity and Higher Education. (n.d.). *Official Gazette, 123/2003, 198/2003, 105/2004, 174/2004.* Retrieved from: http://www.nn.hr

Bardach, E. (2009). *A practical guide for policy analysis: The eightfold path to more effective problem solving.* Thousand Oaks, CA: Sage.

Ben-Peretz, M. (2009). *Policy-making in education. A holistic approach in response to global changes.* Lanham, MD: Rowman & Littlefield Education.

Cibulka G. J. (2001). The changing role of interest groups in education: Nationalization and the new politics of education productivity. *Educational Policy, 15,* 12–40.

Cooper, B. S., Cibulka, J. G., & Fusarelli, L. D. (2008). *Handbook of education politics and policy.* New York, NY: Routledge.

Dalič, M. (Ed.). (2006). *Strategic development framework for 2006–2013.* Zagreb, Croatia: Central Office for Development Strategy and Coordination of EU Funds. Retrieved from: http://www.strategija.hr/datastore/filestore/10/Strategic_Development_Framework_2006_2013.pdf

Dyer, C. (1999). Researching the implementation of educational policy: A backward mapping approach. *Comparative Education, 35,* 45–61.

Educational quality assurance handbook of the University of Rijeka. (2010). Rijeka, Croatia: University of Rijeka, Retrieved from http://www.uniri.hr/files/kvaliteta/PRIRUCNIK%20ZA%20KVALITETU.pdf

Educational sector development plan 2005–2010. (2005). Zagreb, Croatia: Ministry of Science, Education and Sport, Retrieved from http://public.mzos.hr/lgs.axd?t=16&id=14193

European Communities. (2009). *ECTS users' guide.* Luxembourg, Belgium: Office for Official Publications of the European Communities. Retrieved from http://ec.europa.eu/education/lifelong-learning-policy/doc/ects/guide_en.pdf

Fitz, J., Halpin, D., & Power, S. (1994). Implementation research and education policy: Practice and prospects. *British Journal of Educational Studies, 42,* 53–69.

Fuhrman, S. H., Cohen, D. K., & Mosher, F. (2007). *The state of education policy research: Theoretical concepts and research methods.* Mahwah, NJ: Lawrence Erlbaum.

Honig, M. I. (2006). *New directions in education policy implementation: Confronting complexity.* Albany: SUNY Press.

Johnson, L. B. (2001). Micropolitical dynamics of education interests: A view from within. *Educational Policy, 15*(1), 115–134.

Kovač, V. (2001). *Osposobljavanje i usavršavanje visokoškolskih nastavnika.* Rijeka, Croatia: Filozofski fakultet u Rijeci.

Levinson, B. A. U., Sutton, M., & Winstead, T. (2009). Education policy as a practice of power: Theoretical tools, ethnographic methods, democratic options. *Education Policy, 23,* 767–795.

Mawhinney B. H. (2001). Theoretical approaches to understanding interest groups. *Educational Policy, 15*(1), 187–214.

McLaughlin, M. W. (1987). Learning from experience: Lessons from policy implementation. *Educational Evaluation and Policy Analysis, 9,* 171–178.

Palmer, D., & Snodgrass-Rangel, V. (2010). High stakes accountability and policy implementation: Teacher decision making in bilingual classrooms in Texas. *Education Policy, 20,* 1–34.

Regulation of studies of the University of Rijeka. (2008). Rijeka, Croatia: University of Rijeka, Retrieved from http://www.uniri.hr/files/studenti/studiji/propisi_i_dokumenti/Pravilnik_o_studijima-2008.pdf

Rizvi, F., & Lingard, B. (2010). *Globalizing educational policy.* London, UK: Routledge.

Trends reports in European higher education. Available from http://www.eua.be/eua-work-and-policy-area/building-the-european-higher-education-area/trends-in-european-higher-education.aspx

University of Rijeka strategy 2007–2013. (2007). Rijeka, Croatia: University of Rijeka. Retrieved from http://www.uniri.hr

Notes

1. The overarching aim of the Bologna Process is to create a European Higher Education Area (EHEA) based on international cooperation and academic exchange that is attractive to European students and staff as well as to students and staff from other parts of the world. The envisioned EHEA will facilitate mobility of students, graduates, and higher education staff; prepare students for their future careers and for life as active citizens in democratic societies and support their personal development; and offer broad access to high-quality higher education, based on democratic principles and academic freedom. In each country of the Signatories of the Bologna Declaration, implementation of Bologna Process has performed in different ways and caused different interventions in higher education.

2. ECTS is the credit system for higher education used in the EHEA and is a cornerstone of the Bologna Process. Most Bologna countries have adopted ECTS by law for their higher education systems. Among other objectives, the Bologna Process aims at the establishment of a system of credits as a proper means of promoting the most widespread student mobility (European Communities, 2009).

3. McLaughlin (1987) identified and described the creation and operation of new organizations in the policy process, and he calls them intermediary and hybrid organizations.

4. At the time of writing this article, the Quality Office at the University of Rijeka was conducting a detailed evaluation of the Bologna Process implementation, and some new information regarding the implementation of this new regulation will soon be published. Data used in this article are the result of author's direct experience (VK) during the phase when the conditions for the new education regulation implementation were being created and later when the author, holding the position of vice dean for undergraduate education, acted as an intermediary between the policy creator and the policy implementer. Data used in this article were collected from different sources including public lectures on the new education regulation implementation, records from Centre for Studies' Professional Council meetings, information published in the media that reflect the opinions of various participants in the creation and implementation of the new university policy, and individual experiences and reflections of the implementation participants on the new university policy gathered during the first 2 years of implementation.

5. Croatia is a small academic community in which two types of higher education institutions coexist—university and non-university institutions. In this article, we discuss activities common in the university setting. In the 2010–2011 academic year, there are nine active universities in Croatia (seven public ones and two private ones).

6. At the national level, documents include *Act on Scientific Activity and Higher Education* (n.d.), *Act on Quality Assurance in Science and Higher Education* (n.d.), *Educational Sector Development Plan 2005–2010* (2005), and *Strategic Development Framework for 2006–2013* (Dalič, 2006), which was adopted by Croatian Government. At a local level (University of Rijeka), the following documents have been analyzed: *University of Rijeka Strategy 2007–2013, Educational Quality Assurance Handbook of the University of Rijeka,* and *Regulation of Studies of the University of Rijeka.*

7. Full name: Trends Reports in European Higher Education (Trends I, Trends II, Trends III, Trends IV, Trends V, Trends VI)

8. With that in mind, students' and teachers' evaluation has been conducted; workshops for students and teachers have been organized, as have practica for freshmen, public lectures, and so on.

9. Media analysis (daily newspapers) conducted in 2007 to 2008 clearly indicated the criticism by academic community; however, in the text of the new regulation, those provisions have remained intact. Thus, the regulation—only slightly changed—was adopted at the session of the University of Rijeka Senate in July 2008, and its implementation began at the beginning of the 2008–2009 academic year.

10. Education of teachers involved the selection of a group of participants comprising representatives from every university constituent and elected by the university administration, given their prior engagement in the education reform processes. In addition to being trained in educational content, participants were also trained to disseminate acquired knowledge to teachers and their constituents. The content of this knowledge centered on the rules of course design, formulation of learning outcomes, and establishing constructive relations among learning outcomes, educational methods, and student assessment methods. Special review was made of ECTS monitoring and the evaluation system implementation model.

11. Unfortunately, evaluations of education programs show that there was some significant resistance among teachers who say reasons for their resistance were lack of interest in participation, lack of faith in the entire process, and their unwillingness to invest additional time in educational process activities.

CHAPTER 16

The Impact of Organizational Culture on the Leadership of Higher Education Curriculum Development

Laurie Lomas

Organizational culture can be defined as the values, myths, heroes, and symbols that have come to mean a great deal to the people who work in a particular organization (Deal & Kennedy, 1988). It can also be considered as "the glue that holds an organization together" (Baron, 1994, p.64) and "corporate DNA" (Morgan, 2006, p.99). Organizational culture is a relatively new concept that developed from books published in the United States in the early 1980s such as Thomas Peters and Robert Waterman's (1982) *In Search of Excellence* and Terrence Deal and Allan Kennedy's (1988) *Corporate Cultures.* The ideas in these two books and others were then promulgated by business managers and consultants (Stanford, 2010). Although many academic staff and business people have found the notion of organizational culture helpful in understanding the functioning of their organizations, critics such as Maurice Kogan (1999) believe that the concept, when used in higher education, is simply "intellectual polyfiller" that is used to explain the inexplicable.

Simple definitions of organizational culture need to be applied with care because the notion is far from straightforward and uncomplicated. It is

Author's Note: Acknowledgement—The Higher Education Funding Council for England for funding the King's/Warwick Project.

necessary to avoid stereotyping and to separate rhetoric from reality. A reductionist approach is to be avoided because culture is dynamic and perverse (Schein, 2004), and it is better to think of "multiple cultural configurations" (Alvesson, 2002). For some, although the existence of numerous subcultures has been acknowledged (Peters & Waterman, 1982) and although organizations are a blend of cultures, often one or more cultures may be dominant (Dopson & McNay, 1996).

Nevertheless, a sound understanding of organizational cultures can help identify how basic assumptions, beliefs, and values within an organization shape its development. Karen St. Clair and James Groccia (2009) argued that learning does not occur in a vacuum because there is a clear context for learning at microlevels and macrolevels. St. Clair and Groccia stated that context is one of seven variables that need to be investigated fully if a clear perspective of university learning and teaching is to develop. They identified organizational culture as a key element of the macro context because it relates to issues such as university mission, purpose, priorities, and shared beliefs. It is possible to "measure" organizational culture through the use of quantitative methods such as surveys and qualitative approaches using interviews or focus groups (Stanford, 2010).

In this chapter, I will focus on just one area of organizational culture: its impact on the leadership of higher education curriculum development. Gareth Morgan (2006) highlighted the link between culture and leadership using numerous exemplars from organizations in the United States and the United Kingdom. One example he gave from the latter country is the leadership style of the late Anita Roddick who founded the Body Shop cosmetics chain. Her new corporate style of leadership was not based on the hierarchical management ideas of business schools but on feminine principles that emphasized caring and intuitive decision making.

Edgar Schein's (2004) model of organizational culture provides a helpful analytical framework both generally and particularly in relation to curriculum leadership at two case study English universities, which will follow later in the chapter. Schein's model identifies three levels of organizational culture. At the base are underlying assumptions. These are "taken-for-granted" beliefs, thoughts, and feelings. For example, an underlying assumption of Christians is that Jesus is the Son of God and there is no questioning of this belief. The second level represents espoused values or the explicit strategies, values, and principles that an organization claims to be trying to achieve. A university's mission statement espouses its strategies, values, and principles. The third and final level in Schein's model relates to an organization's artifacts. These are the visible structures and processes of a particular organization. An example of an artifact in the United Kingdom would be a portrait of Queen Elizabeth II, which hangs prominently in all police stations and evokes notions of order and tradition that are central to the operation of the police service.

Before I describe and examine recent empirical research at King's College London and the University of Warwick, I will use Schein's framework to highlight how national culture and traditions influence a particular organization's behavior. A brief examination of four national higher education systems will help to illustrate how national culture impacts its universities and colleges. I have conducted research with international colleagues into aspects of the Finnish, Dutch, and English higher education systems. I am also indebted to my PhD student, Fahdah Althanayan, for her insights into Saudi Arabian higher education.

The Saudi Arabian, Finnish, Dutch, and English Higher Education Systems ——————

Saudi Arabia

Higher education in Saudi Arabia is shaped by underlying assumptions and beliefs and values related to Islam. Islam is the only religion sanctioned by the government and, as with society as a whole, education is highly influenced by Islamic rules and values. National culture is based on the five fundamental pillars of Islam. There is belief in one and only God, Allah, and Muhammad his prophet. Muslims are to perform five prayers a day, fast during Ramadan and, if wealthy enough, pay a religious tax known as Zakat. Muslims are also, if capable, to perform Hajj, which involves a pilgrimage to Mecca to show submission to the one God (Akhter, 1998; Teece, 2003). The five pillars remind Muslims of Allah and are the basis of teachers' and students' study, actions, and interrelationships.

In 1950, Saudi Arabia established in Mecca its first college, and it taught Islamic studies. The setting of the first college in the Holy city of Mecca demonstrates how strongly Islam is embedded in Saudi culture. Later, in 1957, King Saud University opened, initially with just 21 students and 9 staff. It is now the largest university in Saudi Arabia with more than 70,000 students on its men's campus and more than 40,000 students on its women's campus. Currently, Saudi Arabia has a mix of state-funded and private universities. All these universities aim to achieve particular objectives that include, among other goals (Saleh, 1986),

- developing loyalty to Allah and providing Islamic education, which makes students responsible before Allah and puts their capabilities into useful actions;
- enabling the Saudi educational system to provide the highly trained human resources necessary to manage the country's increasingly sophisticated economy; and
- preparing competent and qualified citizens to perform their duties in the service of their country and for the progress of their nation in the light of Islamic principles and ideology.

Thus, the relatively recently formed and rapidly developing Saudi higher education system is profoundly influenced by a national culture based on Islam, which permeates all aspects of the economy and society.

Finland

Autonomy in Finnish higher education has been linked with the historical context of the country, which has significantly influenced its culture. The Royal Academy of Åbo (currently the University of Turku) was established in 1640 as the first university when Finland belonged to the Kingdom of Sweden. When Finland became part of Russia in the early 19th century, there were gains in autonomy in internal administration. During the period of Russian hegemony, the Royal Academy (now called the Imperial Alexander University) moved from Turku to Helsinki (Välimaa, 2001). However, both the expansion in the number of higher education institutions and greater autonomy did not begin until Finland gained independence in 1917. The Finnish higher education system now is a binary one consisting of 20 universities and 28 polytechnics (universities of applied sciences), and all these higher education institutions (HEIs) are controlled by central or local government.

Finnish culture has not been based overtly on performance management and the primacy of the student as a customer, as have those of some other western European countries. Consequently, there has been an emphasis on liberal ideals associated with the Humboldtian notion of a university, which has led to the continued dominance in the 20th and early 21st centuries of a collegial culture (Dopson & McNay, 1996) in its universities and colleges, and which together with their academics, have enjoyed a relatively high level of autonomy (Lomas & Ursin, 2009).

The Netherlands

As in Finland, there is a binary divide in the Netherlands. There are 14 research-intensive universities that concentrate on academic teaching and research, and 47 universities of professional education that are also known as "hogescholen." Some HEIs have a religious foundation, but the influence of religion is limited and has a minimal impact on life outside higher education unlike in Saudi Arabia.

Dutch academic staff have been determined to preserve their relatively high level of autonomy with research and teaching, and they have fought hard to resist central government's attempts to implement quality management systems. Again, as in Finland, efforts have been made to maintain the dominant collegial culture and the hegemony of academic staff in curriculum and pedagogical issues (Teelken & Lomas, 2009).

England

The English higher education system has been established far longer than have those in Saudi Arabia, Finland, and the Netherlands because it dates back to the Middle Ages with the establishment of University College, Oxford, in 1249 and Peterhouse College, Cambridge, in 1284. The 19th century was a major period of growth with the establishment of University College London (1826), King's College London (1829), and the Universities of Manchester (1851) and Bristol (1876). Further expansion came with the development of "redbrick" universities such as Leicester and Reading in the 1920s but the major impetus was given by the Robbins Report of 1963, which led to the creation of "plate glass" universities such as Sussex, Kent, Essex, Warwick, and York. The Further and Higher Education Act of 1992 ended the binary divide between polytechnics and universities with the former becoming universities, which led to the creation of a large number of modern universities such as Coventry, London South Bank, Leeds Metropolitan, Sheffield Hallam, Liverpool John Moores, and Birmingham City (Lomas & Ursin, 2009). There are now more than 80 universities in England, including one private university (Buckingham). A relatively small proportion of universities and colleges have religious foundations. Canterbury Christ Church University is an example.

Compared with the Finnish and Dutch systems, there is less autonomy in the English higher education system in which far greater compliance is required with codes of practice and subject benchmarks (Hodson & Thomas, 2003). David Billing (2004) noted that English HEIs are subject to more audit criteria than elsewhere in Europe, the United States, Australia, and South Africa. In part, this auditing has been the result of the centralizing, managerialist tendencies in England during the later part of the 20th and early part of the 21st centuries. These tendencies have been illustrated by the Jarratt Report (Jarratt, 1985), which strongly encouraged HEIs to adopt managerialist approaches such as action planning, mission statements, appraisal schemes, and performance indicators. The Croham Report (Croham, 1987) recommended performance indicators for teaching and research and finance and management. These codes of practice, benchmarks, and managerialist approaches have had a significant impact on culture and therefore the priorities of English HEIs.

Culture, in terms of beliefs and values, is strongly contested in English HEIs, which have great diversity of purpose as shown by their mission statements. Ronald Barnett and Nicholas Maxwell (2008) firmly believe in the general idea that universities should promote wisdom but the researchers are concerned that this is not what universities do. The official view of English universities (in their mission statements) is that they encourage intellectual inquiry that develops knowledge and they train students to become professionals in fields such as education, law, engineering, medicine, and dentistry. However, Barnett and Maxwell believe that mission statements do not accurately reflect their key purpose, which is now largely to attract research funds. Kathryn Hayes and Dennis Ecclestone (2008) also support the more traditional esoteric purpose of universities, arguing that higher education is an end in itself with students desiring to acquire knowledge for its own sake. These authors are concerned that this ideal is threatened by the high levels of instrumentalism in universities, which they consider to encourage students to be compliant in achieving stated learning outcomes that have a clear application, rather than expanding their knowledge and understanding. These authors argued for a liberal education rather than a basic form of vocational training. Davis Palfreyman (2007), director of the Oxford Centre for Higher Education Policy Studies, has also championed liberal education based on critical thinking and reflection. He argued that liberal education can also contribute to the economic well being of a country because it develops freethinking people able to undertake top leadership posts in commercial organizations and give direction to the technically qualified middle management "droids" who, assumedly, have not had the benefit of a liberal higher education (Reisz, 2008).

The previous writers are among a number of individuals who support the early 19th-century ideal of the Humboldtian university with its desire to produce the purest and highest form of knowledge. To ensure this knowledge, a university needs to be secluded to a large extent from the outside world (Theisens, 2004). Barnett (2008) contended that universities justifiably prize their autonomy, and there should be "epistemological distancing" from the economy and "epistemological openness." The main feature of the traditional Humboldtian ethos is the emphasis on three unities: the unity of teachers and learners, the unity of research and teaching, and the unity of knowledge (Pritchard, 2003).

Until the 1960s, the hegemony of this traditional ideal was rarely challenged. For example, the traditional ideal valued pure rather than applied or vocational knowledge (Inglis, 1985). A challenge to the "traditional ideal" came in the early 1980s with Thatcherism, which was associated with Prime Minister Margaret Thatcher. The "New Right" wanted the Universities Grants Committee (UGC) abolished because it was seen as restricting the operation of the market through "producer capture" and producer-led provision. Oliver Letwin and others forcefully expressed this view in the right-wing Institute of Economic Affairs in the late 1980s (Salter & Tapper, 2002). The polytechnics were freed from local education authority control in 1988, and then, when they became modern universities in 1992, they adopted a governance model based on business that relied heavily on nonexecutive directors (Knight, 2002).

Currently, English universities have to respond to the government's emphasis on public accountability, efficiency, effectiveness, and the measurement of performance (Henkel, 2000). Entrepreneurial universities have developed that have the commercial acumen to generate funds to enhance their academic position (Shattock, 2003). A growing number of entrepreneurial universities demonstrate institutional self-reliance. Burton Clark (2004) offered the universities of Warwick and Strathclyde as UK examples, and the University of Twente in the Netherlands, the University of Joensuu in Finland, and Chalmers University of Technology in Sweden as mainland European examples. The University of Warwick encouraged all its sectors to look outward for possible opportunities, aim to maximize their incomes, and to put in place managerial approaches that do not conflict with academic principles. The University of Warwick makes optimal use of its alumni and is prepared to take risks. It generates income through research grants and contracts, particularly through its business school (Clark, 2004).

A predominantly business culture prevails in many English universities with financial criteria largely determining policy, and consequently, there is less emphasis on critical thought (Taylor, Barr, & Steele, 2002). This culture has led to fear among many academic staff that enterprise will drive out and replace the more traditional and fundamental aspects of universities such as intellectual integrity, critical inquiry, and commitment to learning and understanding (Williams, 2003). There is also the worry that the academic ethos will be transformed from collegiality and cooperation to corporation and competition (Kinman, 1998).

Our Empirical Research

Our research, funded by the Higher Education Funding Council for England, was part of the King's College London/University of Warwick Project. The curriculum leadership development strand of this project examined the leadership needs of academic staff and senior administrators at these research-intensive English universities. King's College London and the University of Warwick are 2 of the 20 "Russell Group" universities in England, which, it is claimed, are "committed to maintaining the very best research, an outstanding teaching and learning experience and unrivalled links with business and the public sector" (Russell Group website, 2010).

We attempted to "measure" the organizational culture of the two research-led universities using statistical background information and qualitative, in-depth face-to-face interviews. From October 2009 to February 2010, we used semistructured interviews to explore the respondents' views on the most effective ways of leading curriculum change. We interviewed 10 staff from each institution. These 20 staff members included 3 school/faculty heads, 3 department heads, 10 program directors, and 4 senior administrators. We constructed a flexible interview schedule based on a review of recently published international literature on leadership, change management, and leadership development. Each interview lasted at least an hour and included questions such as, "What curriculum innovations are you or your staff involved with at present?," "What role do you take in the leadership of change?," "Is there a particular leadership style you adopt or leadership theories you apply?," "What strategies do you employ to bring about effective change?," "Have any barriers or blockages hindered change and, if so, how have these been overcome?" We also asked questions about what they considered to be the key skills in leadership related to curricular change, the knowledge and attitudes required to lead effective curriculum change, forms of training or development activities that have been particularly helpful, and what additional training and development would have helped them improve their leadership skills and knowledge? In addition to these questions, we asked appropriate supplementary questions to follow up the respondents' answers.

We analyzed the qualitative data using the constant comparative method (Strauss & Corbin, 1998). With this method, meaning is ascribed to a particular note in an interview and is then compared with other interview notes and, when similarities of meaning are found, they are grouped into themes. If no similar meaning is found during a comparison, a new theme category is created. The interviews led to the accumulation of rich qualitative data and deep insights into the respondents' perceptions of curriculum leadership development in higher education. The King's College London Education and Management Ethical Research Panel approved the research design and methodology we used in this study.

King's College London and the University of Warwick

King's College London was founded in 1829 by King George IV and the then prime minister, the Duke of Wellington, as a university college in the tradition of the Church of England, although it now welcomes staff and students of all faiths and beliefs. King's College has grown and developed through mergers with several institutions that have their own distinguished histories, including the United Medical and Dental Schools of Guy's and St. Thomas's Hospitals, Chelsea College, and the Institute of Psychiatry. King's College London is the fourth oldest university in England and has nearly 23,000 students, of whom more than 8,600 are graduate students from nearly 140 different countries. King's College London is now the largest center for the education of doctors, dentists, and other health care professionals in Europe and is home to six Medical Research Council centers. King's College has played a major role in many of the advances that have shaped modern life, such as the discovery of the structure of DNA. According to its mission statement, "King's College London is dedicated to the advancement of knowledge, learning, and understanding in the service of society" (King's College London website, 2010).

The University of Warwick received its Royal Charter of Incorporation in 1965. It is situated on a large 700-acre campus that straddles the boundary between the City of Coventry and the County of Warwickshire. In 1984, the

University of Warwick Science Park was opened on a site adjacent to the university as a joint venture between the university and the local authorities of Coventry City, Warwickshire, and West Midlands Enterprise. The park is now home to 85 high technology companies with an income of £4.4million per annum. More recently the university has invested in and successfully won government support for a series of initiatives to develop a culture in which academic inventions can be exploited either through licensing or as spin-off companies. Warwick Ventures was founded in 1999 jointly with the University of Warwick Science Park. University of Warwick has 21,598 students, of which 9,088 are postgraduates. Twenty percent of the student body comes from overseas, and more than 125 countries are represented on the campus. The university has 29 academic departments and more than 50 research centers and institutes in four faculties: arts, medicine, science, and social sciences. The University of Warwick's mission is

> to become a world leader in research and teaching; through research of international excellence, to increase significantly the range of human knowledge and understanding; to equip graduates to make an important contribution to the economy and to society; to serve our local region—academically, culturally and economically; and to continue to make a Warwick education available to all those able to benefit from it, regardless of economic or social circumstances. (University of Warwick website, 2010)

Both universities are research-led and strive for excellence in research and teaching. As members of the Russell Group of universities, they are rated highly by students and academic staff throughout the world. In broad terms, their general organizational cultures differ. King's College London is well established, having been founded in 1829. Its particular strengths lie in various forms of medical education. The University of Warwick is a "plate glass" university founded in the 1960s, and from the outset, it has established its reputation through its links with industry. Its culture is far more business-orientated than is the more traditional King's College London.

Underlying Assumptions From the Research Findings

In terms of underlying assumptions related to organizational culture, 15 of the 20 respondents mentioned without any prompting that the culture of their school or faculty within their institution was predominantly collegial. Support for this view was based on the observation that their colleagues were generally helpful and cooperative, and one person said, "Often this led to academic staff learning together as if through osmosis." Another noted, "The collegial culture is very strong at Warwick and there is firm resistance to any form of managerialism, primarily because managerialism suggests a lack of trust of professionals such as ourselves."

However, two respondents made the point that as universities were becoming larger and more complex, it was more difficult for a collegial culture to thrive because universities were generally moving away from being collegial academies toward being corporate enterprises. Although there was an underlying assumption among most of the 20 respondents that the organizational culture of their schools, faculties, and departments was largely collegial, some identified pressure from the senior management of their institutions or central government for cultural change. There were major concerns about this apparent shift to a more corporate culture because it was generally associated with managerialism, which was widely regarded as being anti-intellectual.

Espoused Beliefs and Values

Given the general view that the two institutions had a predominantly collegial culture, it is not surprising that when asked about their beliefs on the appropriate leadership style respondents favored a democratic approach that tried to gain consensus. It was felt to be important to "take people with you" and, as one person warned, you cannot force staff in research-led universities to do something they do not want to do as they will find ways of resisting. To gain commitment, a leader should draw on others and allow them a high degree of autonomy to maximize their contributions. Also, it was necessary to "sell" an idea to members of their team and members of senior management such as deans, pro–vice chancellors, and the principal or vice chancellor. However, some respondents pointed out that although an inclusive style in which everyone's voice was heard would usually bring success in the change management process, there were occasions when leaders need to be more directive. Their style was contingent largely on the individual because subtle changes in approach are required to trigger the enthusiasm and effort of particular staff members.

Respondents considered that specific knowledge, skills, and attitudes are required to become a successful curriculum leader. Emotional intelligence was thought to be important as leaders needed to know their staff as individuals and be aware of their strengths and weaknesses so that weaknesses could be addressed and strengths used to the best advantage. Institutional knowledge was essential so that a curriculum leader could make effective use of the university's systems (e.g., academic regulations) and structures, such as how various committees operate. The use of shadowing, secondments, delegation, and mentoring were viewed as means of increasing the general level of institutional knowledge among all academic staff. Communicating effectively was a required skill mentioned by all respondents. Other skills that respondents often highlighted were organizing, networking, and being an active listener. As bringing about and embedding change was a major challenge for curriculum leaders, it was important that leaders are able to inspire their staff. Empowering them was also a way of gaining their commitment and helping staff to fulfill their potential.

As well as identifying the knowledge, skills, and attitudes required to be an effective curriculum leader, we explored how the respondents thought these attributes could be acquired. Six respondents referred to the value of leadership development courses in providing a framework for analysis and the time provided on these courses to consider and reflect on their leadership roles. A faculty head argued that these courses were greatly enhanced when a coach was also made available. She felt that if at all possible, several members of a department could undertake leadership development courses together so that they could learn as a group. Change and development would more likely be embedded using this strategy. Support from senior managers was needed if curriculum leaders were to be funded for in-house or external leadership development courses. Respondents particularly appreciated assistance with financial and legal matters. However, leadership development on its own was not considered to be adequate because, although it was most helpful, development courses needed to be supplemented with opportunities to gain new experiences such as through shadowing and delegation. Leadership development courses are generally provided by staff development departments, but rather than using a central department, a department head firmly believed,

> It would be more appropriate for the university's business school/management department to provide the courses as then the participants would be exposed to cutting-edge research and consequently they would be more intellectually challenged.

Underlying assumptions and beliefs largely determined the strategies that curriculum leaders adopted. The assumption that collegiality was the dominant culture in a research-intensive university meant that there was significant support for a distributive approach to leadership whereby the role was largely shared among members of the department. One respondent argued that a shared approach to leadership encouraged creativity because it acknowledged that the formal leader did not have all the best ideas. Because of the inclusivity, distributive leadership was more likely to gain the commitment and engagement of all those involved in a curriculum innovation. A program director made the point that now there was so much that had to be done in higher education that it made sense to share the responsibility for leadership through delegation. In any team of academics, there is likely to be a very good skill mix, and if a curriculum leader is aware of colleagues' strengths and weaknesses, then leadership tasks can be distributed appropriately. Another strategy that found favor among respondents was making use of "champions" whose enthusiasm and teaching skills were a model for others. Ideally, department heads should be "champions." There are times when it is appropriate to use external experts to inspire academic staff but generally "insider champions" are more effective than those from outside the organization.

By far the most commonly expressed belief was the primacy of research at both King's College London and the University of Warwick. Seventy-five percent of the respondents stated this perspective, and the following two comments from a program director and a department head, respectively, illustrate this view:

> Curriculum leadership and its importance do not seem to be recognized and appreciated. The influence of research is all pervading. Research articles and grants are what is valued.

> Without question, research is the priority.

Respondents felt that teaching was the "poor relation" of research, and success in research was the main criterion for promotion in a research-led university. Respondents also acknowledged that there had been attempts by senior management to increase the status of teaching but some respondents felt that much more needed to be done, particularly because teaching earns a university a significant proportion of its income. A university's drive for "research superstars" meant that fewer staff were prepared to invest time in teaching-based leadership roles such as director of undergraduate studies when their time could be more profitably spent improving their career prospects by gaining research grants and publishing academic papers. Respondents noted that it was possible to concentrate on teaching and research and be successful in both these areas, but that doing so was an ideal that was most challenging and very difficult to achieve.

Artifacts

The two universities' artifacts included committee rooms where teaching and learning committees met regularly, a teaching and learning forum, and a leadership center. However, these artifacts could also be found in many other universities in England, so they were not regarded by the respondents as having any special impact on the organizational culture in either institution.

Discussion

Several key points related to organizational culture emerge from the research findings. Using Schein's (2004) framework, respondents' beliefs and values provide most of the issues for discussion. However, the major underlying assumption of the respondents was that the culture of King's College London and the University of Warwick was predominantly collegial. Ian McNay (1995) and Lee Harvey (1995) characterized a collegial culture as one that has three elements: the process of shared decision making that relates to academic matters, adherence to the notion of academic integrity, and the intense desire to protect and preserve a particular field of specialist knowledge and practice. Academic autonomy and the freedom of the individual are highly prized.

The preference for a collegial culture can be seen in the desire for a democratic approach to leadership that is based on finding consensus and empowering colleagues so that they have a significant part in the decision-making process and the implementation of curricular innovations. An extension of this democratic approach is distributive leadership, which respondents mentioned on several occasions. Paul Ramsden (1998) supported this idea by arguing that leadership should be the shared responsibility and the concern of all academic and support staff in a university. John Cowan and John Heywood's (2001) empirical research supported Ramsden's view by suggesting that academic leadership is not based on hierarchy and that transformative change to universities occurs through a multilevel approach at institutional, departmental, and individual levels. Henry Mintzberg, James Brian Quinn, and Sumantra Ghoshal (1998) also advocated for this distributive approach, arguing that organizational members will take leadership responsibility at one, two, or even three levels. At the individual level, a leader motivates, coaches, and mentors colleagues. At the group level, the main task is to build high-performing teams, and at the institutional level, the goal is to develop a culture conducive to cooperation, change, and goal setting. Jean Hartley (2000) argued that traditional individual leadership skills alone are not adequate, and distributive leadership involving numerous university staff in the management of change is necessary if goals are to be achieved. Developmental, influencing, and negotiating skills are now essential in an environment of flux and uncertainty.

Twenty percent of the respondents were disappointed to report that they considered the dominance of a collegial culture to be under threat. They supported McNay's (1995) belief that universities in general and their university in particular were shifting from a "collegial academy to a corporate enterprise." Concern for collegiality being superseded by corporatism, sometimes referred to as *managerialism*, can be traced back to 1989 when the Universities Funding Council replaced the UK Universities Grants Council. This change led to particular subjects being favored by the government and attracting larger amounts of funding at the expense of less favored subjects such as sociology (Theisens, 2004). The change in funding arrangements for universities was a step on the path toward managerialism that strengthened the control of the government at the expense of institutional autonomy (Hodson & Thomas, 2003). Managerialism, characterized by the three "Es" of economy, efficiency, and effectiveness (Morley, 2003), has grown and gained a hold in English universities because of the influence of government values such as public accountability, the efficient use of resources, and the measurement of performance (Henkel, 2000). The development of an audit culture, with the greater regulation of work (Brehony & Deem, 2005), has involved closer supervision of academics' professional activities and a reduction in their autonomy (D'Andrea & Gosling, 2005). Rosemary Deem (2003) argued that managerialism is an international phenomenon affecting universities throughout the world. Managerialism was not so necessary when universities were well-resourced, elite organizations. However, pressure by world governments since the 1980s on universities to achieve more with less (Salter & Tapper, 2002) reduced public expenditure on teaching and research (Sporn, 2003) to ensure efficient and effective governance (Dearlove, 1998). The UK government's promotion of market competition, its emphasis on the importance of customer choice, together with the tightening of accountability through quality assurance procedures, performance indicators, and publishing of league tables (Naidoo, 2005) also have led to the growth of managerialism in universities at the expense of collegiality.

Although there is ample evidence of the rise of managerialism, the respondents' commitment to the notion of collegiality was nevertheless apparent. Sue Dopson and Ian McNay (1996) noted a link between a collegial culture, liberal education, and the Humboldtian ideal. The importance respondents placed on research in their subject areas and the desire to produce the purest and highest form of knowledge typified the purpose of the traditional Humboldtian university (Theisens, 2004) with its liberal education curriculum, high levels of academic autonomy, and what Barnett (2008) referred to as "epistemological openness and distancing." However, as Rosalind Pritchard (2003) noted, the Humboldtian ethos emphasizes the unity of research and teaching, but generally, there was a concentration on research at the expense of teaching in both the universities. Respondents illustrated their belief in the primacy of research through numerous references to the pressure to gain research grants and publish in high-impact peer-reviewed journals to enhance their promotion prospects. Teaching was regarded as the junior partner in the research-teaching nexus because it was considered to offer far fewer promotion opportunities.

Conclusion

The broader national culture of higher education in England establishes the parameters for the organizational culture of particular universities. Russell Group universities such as King's College London and the University of Warwick are research-intensive, so the dominance of research comes as no surprise. Similarly, King's College London is one of England's older universities, so its link to traditional Humboldtian ideals is to be expected. The University of Warwick is a "plate glass" university founded more recently. Nevertheless, the emphasis on academic autonomy associated with the Humboldtian ideal was just as strong there, although a greater element of entrepreneurial culture was seen in the literature and identified by University of Warwick respondents.

The analysis of the impact of organizational culture on the leadership of higher education curriculum development at King's College London and the University of Warwick suggests that organizational culture is still predominantly collegial despite the rise in managerialism. There was generally a desire for the liberal education and academic autonomy associated with the ethos of the Humboldtian university among respondents, but there was not the unity of research and teaching that one would expect. Research was dominant, and a career based largely on teaching was considered a poor career choice. Consequently, it was not an attractive prospect to take on curriculum leadership roles. An emphasis on research was strongly encouraged by senior managers and academics and appropriately rewarded. Although senior management in both institutions were attempting to enhance the promotion prospects for curriculum leaders, a culture fuelled by further rewards is required to redress the balance and strengthen the nexus between research and teaching.

References

Akhter, A. (1998). *The essence of Islam according to the Qur'an and traditions.* Chicago, IL: IQRA International Educational Foundation.

Alvesson, M. (2002). *Understanding organizational culture.* London, UK: Sage.

Barnett, R. (2008). Coda: Towards the university of wisdom. In R. Barnett & N. Maxwell (Eds.), *Wisdom in the university* (pp.101–102). London, UK: Routledge.

Barnett, R., & Maxwell, N. (Eds.).(2008). *Wisdom in the university.* London, UK: Routledge.

Baron, A. (1994, October). Winning ways with culture. *Personnel Management,* (October), 64–68.

Billing, D. (2004). International comparisons and trends in external quality assurance of higher education: Commonality or diversity? *Higher Education, 47,* 113–137.

Brehony, K., & Deem, R. (2005). Challenging the post-Fordist/flexible organization thesis: The case of reformed educational organizations. *British Journal of Sociology of Education, 26,* 395–414.

Clark, B. (2004). *Sustaining change in universities.* Maidenhead, UK: SRHE/Open University Press.

Cowan, J., & Heywood, J. (2001). Curriculum renewal in an institution of higher education. In J. Heywood, J. Sharp, & M. Hides (Eds.), *Improving teaching in higher education* (pp. 7–18). Manchester, UK: University of Salford.

Croham, L. (1987). *Review of the University Grants Committee, Cmnd 81.* London, UK: Her Majesty's Stationery Office.

D'Andrea, V., & Gosling, D. (2005). *Improving teaching and learning in higher education.* Maidenhead, UK: Society for Research in Higher Education/Open University Press.

Deal, T., & Kennedy, A. (1988). *Corporate cultures.* London, UK: Penguin.

Dearlove, J. (1998). The deadly dull issue of university administration, good governance, managerialism and organising academic work. *Higher Education Policy, 11*(1), 59–80.

Deem, R. (2003). New managerialism in UK universities: Manager-academic accounts of change. In H. Eggins (Ed.), *Globalization and reform in higher education* (pp. 55–67). Maidenhead, UK: SRHE/Open University Press.

Dopson, S., & McNay, I. (1996). Organization culture. In D. Warner & D. Palfreyman, (Eds.), *Higher education management* (pp. 16–32). Buckingham, UK: Open University Press.

Hartley, J. (2000). Leading and managing the uncertainty of strategic change. In P. Flood, S. Carroll, L. Gorman, L., & T. Dromgoole, (Eds.), *Managing strategic implementation* (pp. 109–122). Oxford, UK: Blackwell.

Harvey, L. (1995). Beyond TQM. *Quality in Higher Education, 1*(2), 123–146.

Hayes, D., & Ecclestone, K. (2008). *The dangerous rise of therapeutic education.* London, UK: Routledge.

Henkel, M., (2000). *Academic identities and policy change in higher education.* London, UK: Jessica Kingsley.

Hodson, P., & Thomas, H. (2003). Quality assurance in higher education: Fit for the new millennium or simply year 2000 compliant? *Higher Education, 45,* 375–387.

Inglis, F. (1985). *The management of ignorance: Political theory of the curriculum.* Oxford, UK: Blackwell.

Jarratt, A. (1985). *Report of the steering committee for efficiency studies.* London, UK: Committee of Vice Chancellors and Principals (CVCP).

King's College London website (2010). Retrieved February 9, 2010, from http://www.kcl.ac.uk

Kinman, G. (1998). *Pressure points: A survey into the causes and consequences of occupational stress in UK academic and related staff.* London, UK: Association of University Teachers.

Knight, M. (2002). Governance in higher education corporations: A consideration of the constitution created by the 1992 Act. *Higher Education Quarterly, 56,* 276–286.

Kogan, M. (1999). The culture of academe (review of P. Maassen, *Governmental steering and the academic culture*). *Minerva, 37,* 63–74.

Lomas, L., & Ursin, J. (2009). Collegial or managerial? Academics' conceptions of quality in English and Finnish universities. *European Educational Research Journal, 8,* 447–460.

McNay, L. (1995). From the collegial academy to corporate enterprise: The changing cultures of universities. In T. Schuller (Ed.), *The changing university* (pp. 105–115). Buckingham, UK: Open University Press.

Mintzberg, H., Quinn, J., & Ghoshal, S. (1998). *The strategy process* (European ed.). Hemel Hempstead, UK: Prentice Hall.

Morgan, G. (2006). *Images of organization.* London, UK: Sage.

Morley, L. (2003). *Quality and power in higher education.* Maidenhead, UK: SRHE/Open University Press.

Naidoo, R. (2005). Universities in the marketplace: The distortion of teaching and research. In R. Barnett (Ed.), *Reshaping the university* (pp. 27–36). Maidenhead, UK: SRHE/Open University Press.

Palfreyman, D. (2007). Markets, models and metrics in higher education. *Perspectives: Policy and Practice in Higher Education, 11*(3), 78–87.

Peters, T., & Waterman, R. (1982). *In search of excellence.* New York, NY: Harper & Row.

Pritchard, R. (2003). Staff and students in German universities: Traditional values in a changing world. *SRHE International News* (53), 4, 5.

Ramsden, P. (1998). *Learning to lead in higher education.* London, UK: Routledge.

Reisz, M. (2008, January 17). Diversity challenge. *Times Higher Education*, pp. 30–35.

Russell Group website (2010). Retrieved February 7, 2010, from http://www.russell group.ac.uk/

Saleh, M. (1986). Development of higher education in Saudi Arabia. *Journal of Higher Education, 15*, 17–23.

Salter, B., & Tapper, T. (2002). The external pressures on the internal governance of universities. *Higher Education Quarterly, 56*, 245–256.

Schein, E. (2004). *Organizational culture and leadership* (3rd ed.). San Francisco, CA: Jossey-Bass.

Shattock, M. (2003). *Managing successful universities.* Maidenhead, UK: SRHE/ Open University Press.

Sporn, B. (2003). Trends relating to higher education reform in Europe: An overview. In H. Eggins (Ed.), *Globalisation and reform in higher education* (pp. 117–130). Maidenhead, UK: SRHE/Open University Press.

Stanford, N. (2010). *Organization culture: Getting it right.* London, UK: Economist/ Profile Books.

St. Clair, K., & Groccia, J. (2009). Change to social justice education: Higher education strategy. In K. Skubikowski, C. Wright, & R. Graf (Eds.), *Social justice education: Inviting faculty to transform their institutions* (pp. 70–84). Sterling, VA: Stylus.

Strauss, A., & Corbin, J. (1998). *Basics of qualitative research: Techniques and procedures for developing grounded theory.* Thousand Oaks, CA: Sage.

Taylor, R., Barr, J., & Steele, T. (2002). *For a radical higher education: After postmodernism.* Buckingham, UK: SRHE/Open University Press.

Teece, G. (2003). *Islam.* London, UK: Franklin Watts.

Teelken, C., & Lomas, L. (2009). How to strike the right balance between quality assurance and quality control in the perceptions of individual lecturers: A comparison of UK and Dutch higher education institutions. *Tertiary Education and Management, 15*, 259–275.

Theisens, H. (2004). *The state of change: Analysing policy change in Dutch and English higher education.* Enschede, Netherlands: CHEPS/UT.

University of Warwick website: http://www2.warwick.ac.uk

Välimaa, J. (2001). A historical guide to Finnish higher education. In J. Välimaa, (Ed.), *Finnish higher education in transition: Perspectives on massification and globalisation* (pp 13–53). Jyväskylä, Finland: Institute of Research, University of Jyväskylä.

Williams, G. (Ed.). (2003). *The enterprising university: Reform, excellence and equity.* Buckingham, UK: SRHE/Open University Press.

CHAPTER 17

Leading Higher Education Teaching, Learning, and Innovation

Shelda Debowski

The effective enactment of higher education teaching and learning relies on the efforts of many individuals. Although the final interface with the student may be the teacher, many other influences will also play a major part in determining the overall experience that a student encounters. This chapter examines the different roles that key teaching and learning leaders play in constructing and promoting a quality learning environment. This chapter highlights the criticality of building consistent and synergistic messages and practices across the many layers of higher education activity, and argues for a more proactive role by academic developers to achieve that goal.

The conditions for successful learning operate across a range of dimensions, from the preparedness, capabilities, and dedication of the teacher through to the overall outcomes that a student ultimately derives from each learning experience (see Chapter 1, this volume). At one level, these dimensions are highly contingent on the particular learning experience an individual student will receive (Gibbs, Knapper, & Piccinin, 2008; Yorke & Longden, 2004). However, the broader institutional and cultural context in which that instructional activity operates also plays a major part in determining how rich and meaningful that learning experience will be (Bradley, Noonan, Nugent, & Scales, 2008; Koljatic & Kuh, 2001; Markwell, 2007).

Teachers, no matter how committed, can lose heart and energy if they operate in an unsupportive educational community. Their capacity to transfer new skills and learning or willingness to take risks in testing new teaching strategies will be strongly affected by critical colleagues, unsupportive heads, or conflicting messages from senior university leaders (Fullan & Scott, 2009). An individual teacher, no matter how dedicated and committed to making a student feel valued and respected, needs to operate within a community that is also similarly focused on creating a holistic and seamless quality educational experience (Henard, 2010). Students can experience an indifferent educational experience through exposure to variable teaching quality, poor teaching facilities, limited or indifferent student services, and myriad other influences (Henard, 2010). Richard Light (2001) noted that student experiences are a composite of in-class and out-of-class encounters. Each person in the university has the capacity to influence that overall outcome.

In the last decade, there has been increasing recognition of the role of teaching and learning leadership in guiding, shaping, and challenging instructional and administrative practices within higher education (Fullan & Scott, 2009; Henard, 2010; Tennant, McMullen, & Kaczynski, 2010). There is also greater understanding of the need to develop an educational environment that is constructive, supportive, and innovative for both teachers and students. These changing expectations have placed greater focus on the roles leaders assume in guiding and promoting optimal learning contexts for students (Scott, Coates, & Anderson, 2008).

Teaching and Learning Leaders

Within a university, there will be a diversity of leaders who variously influence teaching and learning. As Table 17.1 illustrates, these leaders operate across a range of levels within the university. Some are highly influential in guiding broader policy and infrastructure while others are more influential in shaping the local culture and learning environment.

University Executive

The evolution of university leadership has rapidly changed the way in which learning and teaching is guided and structured within our system. There has been an increasing consolidation of executive roles that provide strategic oversight of the educational direction and process. Provosts and pro-vice chancellors are two common roles now found in many Commonwealth nation university structures. These positions are focused on strategic design of the academic community to create a suitable environment where learning and teaching can flourish (Scott et al., 2008). External pressures and requirements must also be reflected in the planning and review processes that these senior leaders undertake.

Table 17.1   Leading Higher Education Teaching, Learning, and Innovation

Position	Focus	Consistent valuing of teaching and learning	Student-oriented focus and support	Scholastic, evidence-based approach	Effective and Responsive Academic Development Support
University executive	Strategic oversight of the educational agenda Vision Institutional messages about teaching Policy development and oversight Educational systems Funding arrangements Infrastructure and support (including the provision of e-services, faculty development centers, etc.)	⇑	⇑	⇑	⇑
Deans, associate deans	Translation of the strategic agenda Quality assurance of programs and college/faculty practices Consistent policy implementation Development and maintenance of standards Collaboration and articulation across levels Knowledge exchange Facility development				
Heads of school, departments	Promoting a strong culture around quality teaching and learning Teacher preparedness Oversight of governance and management of educational practice Quality assurance of teachers and teaching outcomes Student liaison, communication Learning outreach and engagement				
Program coordinator	Program design Course context review and development Instructor consistency and quality Innovation and review	⇓	⇓	⇓	⇓
Teacher	Well-prepared Quality assurance Student-oriented Knowledgeable Effective				

The interpretation of the university's educational goals is often driven by a strong vision of how the institution will position its identity. Some universities will have a strong focus on ensuring students are highly employable. Others will aim for a research-intensive experience, and an international presence might be the focus of others (Henard, 2010). This setting of a strong vision and conveying those messages are part of the role of these executive members.

Strategic planning within universities has become a guiding focus, with learning and teaching strongly emphasized. In many universities, major curriculum reform has been enacted in an attempt to create a more responsive educational program that better prepares students for their future. Critical thinking, service learning, a research-intensive experience, and stronger links with employers are but a few of the recurring themes that can be found in many university strategies.

Executive leaders play a strong role in both establishing and promoting these priorities. They set the vision for the university and oversee the development of the associated policies and systems that will support the achievement of those goals (Clegg, 2003). The determination of funding allocations and rewards for teaching innovation all stem from the strategic deployment of funds to those groups that best reflect these expectations. However, leaders at this level largely operate through influence more than through direct management of other leaders and, thus, rely strongly on the commitment of many other educational leaders across the community. This means that they need to be articulate, persuasive, and effective in conveying their strategic vision and promoting its enactment. And they need to build a strong coalition of committed partners throughout the university. Conversely, weak or dispersed leadership of educational matters has a profound impact on the consistent enactment of the key priorities and emergent strategies. This can result in highly variable student experiences, inconsistent standards and rules, and inadequate development of the different services that a student may require to achieve effective outcomes.

To achieve their outcomes, executive leaders will rely on a number of knowledgeable experts who can spread the message and share the load of building that organizational focus. A number of service agencies may support this role, ranging from those supporting undergraduate or postgraduate students, through to the academic and faculty development services that assist staff in building stronger capabilities. These services fill an important function in translating the strategic vision and goals into strategies that can be implemented and promoted to the wider university community. Those directing these services need to be strongly attuned to the executive priorities. They will operate at two levels: the maintenance of existing core services (which could include evaluative, support, or educational activities) and the oversight of new initiatives that are intended to consolidate or strengthen the university's educational focus.

As with other teaching and learning leadership roles, executive members are drawn from a range of backgrounds and levels of experience. Although some may have operated as deans or in other senior administrative roles, an increasing number are selected because they themselves were judged to be outstanding teachers. Their knowledge and experience of institutional leadership of teaching and learning may be limited, as may their knowledge of instructional theory and practice. They may have little understanding of academic development and the potential ways in which good developers could assist with strategic positioning of teaching and learning (Boylen, 2005).

This poses both opportunity and risk for teaching and learning centers (TLCs). Their relative effectiveness has been strongly debated, with some key writers suggesting that the focus on individual and instructional support (Schroeder, 2010), rather than organizational development and influencing more senior layers of the institution, has resulted in a marginal or peripheral role (Chism, 2010). There is recognition of the need for directors of TLCs to be strongly linked to institutional priorities and to contribute in a number of ways to emerging issues and strategies. Effective TLC leaders can be highly influential facilitators and change agents when actively working to support the institutional goals in tandem with building capacity of individual teachers or academic groups. Thus, the goals of the executive to enhance teaching and learning and the need of academic developers to increase their influence and impact can be mutually supportive if enacted correctly.

Deans and Associate Deans

Faculties (*faculty* in this chapter represents the British-origin term for school or college as used in the North American context) generally operate as multidisciplinary hubs that draw together a number of educational communities. Deans carry strategic responsibility for the full range of activities that occur within disciplinary areas under their jurisdiction (Del Favero, 2006). Deans may interpret the institution's broader educational agenda in terms of their more specific context. A medical faculty, for example, might focus on problem-based learning as a particularly important educational strategy, whereas an engineering faculty could see links to industry and project management as important educational frameworks. The dean is responsible for quality assurance and ensuring appropriate systems and activities have been implemented *and are adhered to*. Monitoring student well-being, assessing emerging risks, and addressing of issues likely to compromise the student experience are part of this role. Rewarding excellence and promoting good practice across the different disciplinary groups, planning, and resource allocation also fall under this role. Provision of an effective and seamless student support and advisory service is something a dean should monitor and strongly promote. The chairing of the faculty teaching and learning committee commonly operates through this role, or that of the associate dean. Monitoring educational standards and student feedback on their experience may also be undertaken by the dean. Thus, the dean can have a major impact on the learning context, policy, and standards and messages delivered to both students and teachers. A challenge for many deans is that they are increasingly spending considerable time overseas as they seek to build new student markets and collaborations with other institutions, reducing the time many can spend within their faculties or colleges in promoting necessary standards and emergent strategies.

In response to these pressures and the increasing recognition of learning and teaching as critical activities for university well-being, a new position of associate dean has emerged at many institutions. This delegated role reports to the dean, acting as the channel through which the dean's oversight of educational matters can be accomplished. An effective associate dean is one who has a strong grasp of the educational agenda, the profiles of the constituent discipline areas, and the systems that support sound educational outcomes. Associate deans can bridge the different disciplines, encourage knowledge exchange, and may be particularly helpful in guiding schools or departments toward improved understanding of the university strategy. They are also key agents for promoting innovation and excellence. Commonly filled by excellent teachers who are committed to promoting learning outcomes, these roles are variously defined—often by the individuals themselves! This fluidity can lead to reduced effectiveness, in that few know what the role entails, and those in the roles often fill the function of go-between more than strategic influencer. The frequency of turnover of this role may also limit its efficacy. In some instances, these individuals function in a full-time capacity, but others are given a small reduction in teaching load. The resultant variability in role deployment has made this position more difficult to effectively establish as a bone fide formal leadership role, despite its important focus on bridging different communities within the faculty or college.

The roles of deans and associate deans are sometimes undervalued because their function in translating the university mission into a contextualized framework may be largely invisible to many. However, this strategic role in planning for the ongoing strengthening of instructional outcomes is an important educational leadership role.

Academic developers can provide significant support to deans, associate deans, and other senior administrators in their efforts to promote quality outcomes and positive student experiences (Lieberman, 2010). Partnerships between these individuals can result in significant shifts in whole communities and in stronger alignment of colleges and faculties with the broader institutional goals for quality learning. Roles at this level will commonly focus on major cultural and systemic shifts in practice, values, and systems. As such, they can encourage widespread engagement with the principles of quality learning and its implementation. Without the support of "co-constructors of institutional change" (Lieberman, 2010), senior leaders face a much more difficult path in achieving strong staff engagement with change agendas and quality enhancement efforts.

Heads of School or Department

Within each faculty or college, there are likely to be a number of schools or departments, presided over by a head. These roles are interesting, in that they have been consistently structured across the international community as rolling appointments, filled by academics who accept the responsibility of guiding their communities for a 3- to 5-year term. This creates some very large challenges for those heads in gaining a full sense of the many different priorities they must fulfill and how that might be accomplished (Knight & Trowler, 2001). In some cases, heads will only possess a limited understanding of larger university educational goals and priorities. They may have little experience of teaching and learning committees, curriculum rules and regulations, and the emergent issues for their disciplines. They may know little about the community and its enactment of teaching and learning: Who are the excellent teachers? Which courses are students unhappy about and why? How effectively are new teaching staff being inducted into teaching practices? Is teaching evaluation well managed? What are current teaching strengths and weaknesses? Is the school well connected with its relevant constituents (e.g., industry) and do students have good forums to give feedback? How is the school rated compared with other comparable schools? Are classes viable, that is, cost effective, in terms of student demand? The head needs to be conversant with these and many other issues, and it is at this school level that many fine educational strategies fail. Heads are faced with many conflicting demands, and this can lead to educational matters being relegated to a lower priority. When this occurs, they are likely to operate as crisis managers more than as strategic guides.

Effective heads play a critical role in building the environment in which teaching and learning excellence will thrive (Ramsden, Prosser, Martin, & Trigwell, 2007; Viskovic, 2007). Teachers operate at this institutional level: They mingle with their colleagues regularly, they are likely to attend staff meetings and other forums to hear about university initiatives; they report on their performance and outcomes to the head or a delegated school member. The head therefore has the most powerful opportunity to promote and cultivate a strong culture around teaching and learning.

Various strategies send a strong message about the importance of teaching and learning. First, the head's own modeling and visible commitment to teaching excellence conveys its importance to others. Second, the positioning of educational matters into formal discussions, strategic planning, and regular reviews and monitoring cycles all integrate regular quality assurance into the ongoing fabric of the community. Third, the head can play an influential role by insisting that all staff demonstrate they are sufficiently skilled and prepared for their teaching roles. The requirement that they undertake a formal training program to ensure they are knowledgeable about current educational practice sends a powerful cue to all faculty members.

Regular professional development sessions for all staff on teaching and learning also promote a culture that says teaching matters. An important element of the head's role is monitoring and evaluating the individual performance of teachers (Smith, 2008). Traditionally, teaching performance has been regarded as the private business of the teacher. Student reviews of teaching can therefore create concern, depending on the teacher's willingness to seek, accept, and learn from feedback. In institutions where student feedback is at the teacher's discretion, students may have no forum for influencing their curriculum, and the head may have little knowledge of the quality of the program that is being offered. In other institutions, there is an increasing recognition of the need to monitor, review, and respond in a more structured manner. Heads need to know and acknowledge who is performing as an excellent teacher and who they need to more actively guide to perform better. Students have a right to an excellent education, and the head's ability to articulate and guide educational quality assurance creates a strong message to the entire community that teaching matters.

Two other areas fall within the head's role: student liaison and communication. The inclusion of student representation in decision-making groups and project teams offers an important mechanism for increasing the student voice and ensuring the quality learning experience is supported by planned innovations or changes. The head also plays a key role in linking the school with its relevant constituents: alumni, parents, the media, prospective students, schools, and many other groups. Although the head may not be the direct connector, the role is pivotal in building staff engagement with this work.

This brief overview of the head's role highlights the critical nature of this leadership in preparing and connecting the individual teacher to the broader institutional strategies and expectations about teaching. Strong and innovative educational cultures can be formed at this level around colleagues with whom one interacts regularly. Heads need to model, plan, monitor, and communicate the various messages that underpin educational quality and ensure that teaching is not seen as the poor relation in the school's activities.

Heads need to be comfortable with leading change to create the right environment for student learning. Unfortunately, many heads are poorly equipped to handle these complex roles—and it can show. In 2009, I gave a keynote address on the student experience at the Higher Education Research and Development Society of Australasia (HERDSA). The 350 participants, who comprised both faculty members and academic developers from a range of nations, were asked to identify any of the following statements that reflected the ways their academic leaders were approaching educational reform.

My Academic Leaders:

- Have sufficient skills to lead academic change
- Are well supported when leading change

- Encourage staff participation in change
- Believe in academic reform
- Promote innovation
- Are strategic thinkers
- Plan ahead to address challenges
- Look after their community

About 30 percent of the audience indicated that *none* of the descriptors applied to their leaders. A second question then asked them to identify any ways in which their community embraced opportunities to improve the student experience through new initiatives.

My Academic Community:

- Welcomes change
- Explores how it can contribute to change
- Discusses change issues regularly
- Seeks continuous improvement
- Encourages newcomers to engage with the change process
- Celebrates innovation and creativity
- Looks for ways to improve the student experience

Again, many were unable to pick any of these characteristics as symptomatic of their own communities. This is concerning because it highlights the challenges a head may face in bringing the community toward new and improved ways of thinking, acting, and responding to the changing learning environment.

Given the ways in which heads emerge into their roles, and the complexity of the work they undertake, there is a significant need to provide effective support for building teaching and learning expertise, leadership skills, and understanding of organizational change (Debowski & Blake, 2007; Wright, Cook, & O'Neal, 2010). The complexity of this leadership role and the challenge of bringing whole communities toward a new direction or set of values require considerable support from experienced facilitators and developers who can complement the skills of the head and provide a safe and supportive backup as they take risks in challenging existing values and beliefs. This is critical organizational influencing and will have a major impact on the communities that are the primary interface with students.

Program or Course Coordinator

Within each school or faculty there will be many coordinators who oversee programs or courses of study or instructional teams. This is largely undervalued and under-recognized work. Good coordinators put vast amounts of time and creativity into their role, focusing on the improvement of the curriculum, guiding instructors to ensure consistency and quality, and monitoring the student feedback on the program or course. Their direction of planning, implementation, monitoring, and evaluation is a major contribution to the student experience.

A challenge for highly committed coordinators can be the impact of their extensive curriculum leadership activities on their career progression. Good coordinators are valued by their heads, as they translate quality assurance into practice and reduce the need for crisis management. However, the broader recognition of these roles is generally quite limited. When an academic seeks promotion, effective coordination is commonly under-recognized as a major service contribution to the university. The limited valuing therefore makes many academics reluctant to assume roles of this nature. The U.S. model where graduate teaching assistants are hired to assist with some of those coordination activities offers a valuable model for other nations to consider. Alternatively, a skilled administrative officer who can assist with the management practices would also reduce the demands on busy academics. An important issue not yet well addressed is the overreliance on junior teaching staff to coordinate large undergraduate units. A role of this nature when they are still learning to teach, research, and work within a university can be quite deleterious to career management and well-being.

The Teacher

The final teaching leader who influences the student experience is, of course, the teacher. As the face-to-face instructor who interacts with students, teachers need to be knowledgeable about their subject matter, well-prepared, engaging, and committed to providing a quality learning experience. They need to ensure that student outcomes reflect the agreed upon learning goals, that the broader student capabilities have been enhanced and that student needs are understood and reflected in the teaching processes. Undergraduate students, for example, benefit from learner-centered classroom practices (Blumberg, 2009) and increasingly rely on online support, even when attending on-campus classes.

The modeling of good practice is an important leadership role played by teaching practitioners (Horii, 2010) along with ongoing quality enhancement through reflection, scholarship, and research. There is increasing recognition of the need to integrate regular reflection on the effectiveness of the teaching and its impact on students (Black, Ray, & Villa, 2010). Evidence of teaching effectiveness can be drawn from many sources, including mid-term feedback (McGowan & Osguthorpe, 2011), peer review of teaching (Bell, 2005; Young, 2010), student outcomes, and regular end-of-course evaluations. Students can be actively engaged in critiquing their learning experiences, offering a particularly important "insider" view (Cook-Sather, 2010). Inexperienced teachers will largely focus on how their practice is achieving the desired results, but more experienced teachers should be moving toward critiquing whether those results are the correct goals to be emphasized and whether more innovative approaches will lead to better educational outcomes. The shift from engaged practitioner to expert model and guide is an important leadership role that is assumed by experienced teachers. However, the emergence of new technologies and theory around higher education learning also requires experienced teachers to reengage with their learning and knowledge base regularly.

Teachers also maintain broader responsibilities to ensure they are connected with their wider educational community: as continual learners, in sharing their own experiences and innovations with other teachers, in mentoring new teachers, and in contributing to educational reform. Teachers are the critical link in the whole educational strategy. It is unfortunate that many academics are disconnected from their institution's goals and priorities. This is an increasingly critical aspect of academic know-how that needs to be cultivated as the rate and impact of change becomes more strongly experienced within all elements of our universities.

In enacting the instructional role, some conflicting loyalties will likely influence a teacher's willingness to allocate time to teaching and its enhancement. The differential messages conveyed about teaching and research and their relative valuing by the institution can necessitate careful consideration of where time and energy should be allocated (Lucas, 2007). Although a teacher may be keen to build stronger teaching commitment and focus, institutional priorities, promotion requirements, and cultural expectations will all influence this decision. In effect, we have returned to the importance and influence of executive and senior leadership levels, where many of these organizational cues are established and reinforced.

Conditions for Success

As Table 17.1 also illustrated, throughout all leadership levels, the first condition of success is encouraging consistency in the philosophy, strategy, systems, and processes that are followed. That is not to say that there cannot be customization and adaptation from those principles, but these should operate from an informed and considered base, not by default. This can be challenging—it means that everyone from the executive to the individual teacher needs to be clear about the university's intentions and how they should be enacted. This is an achievable ambition, but it will rely heavily on groups such as academic developers to act as facilitators and message brokers.

A second condition relates to the focus on the student. Each activity and person that students encounter makes a difference to their impressions, responses, and motivations, and this needs to be well understood by all university members. Although teachers are a major determinant of student satisfaction, learner assessments of their experience will also be based around the administrators, facilities, service groups, other teachers, and infrastructure that they have encountered.

Third, there is a need to build a strong evidence base around university educational practice. Institutions can draw on a number of educational data sources, including student engagement (National Survey of Student Engagement [NSSE], Australasian Survey of Student Engagement [AUSSE]), outcome measures (e.g., Course Experience Questionnaire [CEQ]), and other national assessments. Institutions can also explore more fine-grained feedback from course reviews, unit evaluations, and other statistical tools. Student feedback, focus groups, industry advisory groups, and many other sources of input and evaluation are possible. These are going to be increasingly important sources of evidence as we progress to escalating teaching quality to its rightful strategic position. Evidence also assists in highlighting groups that need more assistance or stronger leadership. The encouragement of academic scholarship around teaching and learning also raises the professionalism attached to this work. We need to better understand how our teaching affects students and which factors are likely to be most influential in engaging or disconnecting them from learning.

Finally, the enhancement of teaching and learning leadership is unlikely to be accomplished by simply learning through trial and error. Each leadership role requires ongoing development by the individual to achieve more effective outcomes. This is emergent and highly strategic work for academic developers. However, it is likely to require an expanded repertoire of capabilities that enable a stronger focus on institutional and leadership capacity building in conjunction with instructional and individual development, which has been the major focus for many developers in the past (Schroeder, 2010).

Implications for Quality Student Learning

This discussion has argued for stronger understanding and articulation of the different roles that academic leaders play in our universities and has highlighted the need to promote greater strategic awareness of the teaching and learning environment and the roles leaders should enact. Looking again at Groccia's model of teaching and learning, some new questions have surfaced in reviewing these roles. Table 17.2 highlights some issues for further consideration.

Table 17.2　Leadership Issues Relating to Groccia's Model of Teaching and Learning

Dimension	Issues
Teacher	Are our teachers well prepared for their roles?
	Who inducts new teachers?
	Do teachers participate in ongoing learning?
	How do they evaluate their teaching quality? Who knows about the quality? What is done if a teacher is performing poorly?
	Does the environment encourage sharing and learning from other teachers?

Dimension	Issues
Learner	Are the students sufficiently well supported to accommodate their particular learning needs?
	Does the curriculum offer variety and challenge to reflect their evolving maturity as learners?
Learning process	How well developed is the institutional understanding of learning?
	Are those in leadership roles well informed of the principles and research relating to learning and its transfer?
Learning context	How much do teachers know about their sector's trends and emergent teaching and learning issues?
	Who is funding education and what do they expect from that funding?
	What is the institutional mission and vision relating to teaching and learning?
	Is teaching appropriately funded?
	Does teaching matter in this institution? How do we know? What stories do we hear about this?
	Are the facilities conducive to learning?
Course content	How are courses reviewed and evaluated? How often? Who by?
	How do these courses rate against comparable courses taught elsewhere?
	Does the curriculum challenge students? Is it suitable to their vocational, critical thinking, and other needs?
	How can students give feedback on these matters?
	Who reviews that feedback? What is done when a course is poorly scoped?
Instructional processes	Are teachers well equipped to offer variety, engaging learning activities, good levels of interactive learning, supportive learning settings?
	What skills are students acquiring?
	Do different courses encourage a range of student learning experiences?
Learning outcomes	How are learning outcomes determined?
	Is there any peer review of outcomes?
	How are outcomes measured and reported?
	Is there an institutional approach to assessment? How was it determined? Does it draw on the evidence?

The questions in Table 17.2 challenge a number of assumptions around how we manage and guide our learning communities. The questions highlight the need for leaders throughout our universities to be actively engaged in debating, cultivating, and evaluating the nature of a quality learning context. This is a role for all teaching leaders, although certain issues may be more related to a particular position where influence is more strongly established. A key issue emerging from this review is the need for greater clarity around who carries responsibility for what. It is in a university's interest to build some accountability around roles for teaching and learning to achieve higher levels of synergy and integration. Quality learning is everybody's business, but it needs to be explicit, not assumed.

Conclusion

One hopes most of us can recall a quality learning experience—where content, process, outcomes, teacher, and all of the other factors coalesced into that feeling of well-being that comes from an optimal learning encounter. The sad thing is that these experiences normally stand out because they are so rare. It is well past time for universities to professionalize their teaching and learning activities: ensuring teachers are well prepared and capable and that their work is recognized and valued. A major first step in that direction is the clarification of roles that each individual plays in achieving that goal. Academic leaders are critical factors in building and promoting a quality learning environment. However, they cannot build the necessary capabilities through osmosis. Academic developers have much to contribute in building institutional capacity to realize the ideal learning context for our students.

References

Bell, M. (2005). Peer observation partnerships in higher education. Canberra, Australia: HERDSA.

Black, L. J., Ray, T., & Villa, J. (2010). Survivor academe: Assessing reflective practice. *To Improve the Academy: Resources for Faculty, Instructional and Organizational Development, 28*, 341–358.

Blumberg, P. (2009). Practical tools to help faculty use learner-centered approaches. *To Improve the Academy: Resources for Faculty, Instructional and Organizational Development, 27*, 111–134.

Boylen, E. (2005). Translating teaching skills to leadership roles. *Academic Leaders, 21*(7), 3.

Bradley, D., Noonan, P., Nugent, H., & Scales, B. (2008). *Review of Australian higher education: Final report.* Canberra, Australia: Commonwealth Government. Retrieved from http://www.deewr.gov.au/HigherEducation/Review/Documents/PDF/Higher%20Education%20Review_one%20document_02.pdf

Chism, N. V. N. (2010). Getting to the table: Planning and developing institutional initiatives. In C. M. Schroeder (Ed.), *Coming in from the margins: Faculty development's emerging organizational development role in institutional change* (pp. 47–59). Sterling, VA: Stylus.

Clegg, S. (2003). Learning and teaching policies in higher education: Mediations and contradictions of practice. *British Educational Research Journal, 29*(6), 803–819.

Cook-Sather, A. (2010). Teaching and learning together: College faculty and undergraduates cocreate a professional development model. *To Improve the
Academy: Resources for Faculty, Instructional and Organizational Development,
29*, 219–232.

Debowski, S., & Blake, V. (2007). Collective capacity building of academic leaders:
A university model of leadership and learning in context. *International Journal
of Learning and Change, 2(3)*, 307–324.

Del Favero, M. (2006). Disciplinary variation in preparation for the academic dean
role. *Higher Education Research and Development, 25(3)*, 277–292.

Fullan, M., & Scott, G. (2009). *Turnaround leadership for higher education.* San
Francisco, CA: Wiley.

Gibbs, G., Knapper, C., & Piccinin, S. (2008). Disciplinary and contextually
appropriate approaches to leadership of teaching in research-intensive academic departments in higher education. *Higher Education Quarterly, 62(4)*,
416–436.

Henard, F. (2010). *Learning our lesson: Review of quality teaching in higher education.* Paris, France: Organisation for Economic Co-operation and Development.

Horii, C. V. (2010). Transforming teaching cultures: Departmental teaching fellows
as agents of change. *To Improve the Academy: Resources for Faculty,
Instructional and Organizational Development, 28*, 359–378.

Knight, P., & Trowler, P. (2001). *Departmental leadership in higher education.*
Buckingham, UK: Society for Research into Higher Education.

Koljatic, M., & Kuh, G. D. (2001). A longitudinal assessment of college student
engagement in good practices in undergraduate education. *Higher Education,
42(3)*, 351–371.

Lieberman, D. (2010). Nurturing institutional change: Collaboration and leadership
between upper-level administrators and faculty development. In C. M. Schroeder
(Ed.), *Coming in from the Margins: Faculty development's emerging organizational development role in institutional change* (pp. 60–73). Sterling, VA: Stylus.

Light, R. J. (2001). *Making the most of college: Students speak their minds.*
Cambridge, MA: Harvard University Press.

Lucas, L. (2007). Research and teaching work within university departments:
Fragmentation or integration? *Journal of Further and Higher Education, 31(1)*,
17–29.

Markwell, D. (2007). *A large and liberal education: Higher education for the 21st
century.* Melbourne: Australian Scholarly Publishing.

McGowan, W. R., & Osguthorpe, R. T. (2011). Student and faculty perceptions of
effects of midcourse evaluations. *To Improve the Academy: Resources for
Faculty, Instructional and Organizational Development, 29*, 160–172.

Ramsden, P., Prosser, M., Martin, E., & Trigwell, K. (2007). University teachers'
experiences of academic leadership and their approaches to teaching. *Learning
and Instruction, 17*, 140–155.

Schroeder, C. M. (2010). Faculty developers as institutional developers. In
C. M. Schroeder, (Ed.), *Coming in from the margins: Faculty development's
emerging organizational development role in institutional change* (pp. 17–46).
Sterling, VA: Stylus.

Scott, G., Coates, H., & Anderson, M. (2008). *Learning leaders in times of change: Academic leadership capabilities for Australian higher education.* Sydney: University of Western Sydney and Australian Council for Educational Research.

Smith, C. (2008). Building effectiveness in teaching through targeted evaluation and response: Connecting evaluation to teaching improvement in higher education. *Assessment and Evaluation in Higher Education, 33*(5), 517–533.

Tennant, M., McMullen, C., & Kaczynski, D. (2010). *Teaching, learning and research in higher education: A critical approach.* London, UK: Routledge Kegan Paul.

Viskovic, A. (2007). Becoming a tertiary teacher: Learning in communities of practice. *Higher Education Research and Development, 25*(4), 323–339.

Wright, M. C., Cook, C. E., & O'Neal, C. (2010). Developing and renewing department chair leadership: The role of the teaching center in administrative training. *To Improve the Academy: Resources for Faculty, Instructional and Organizational Development, 28,* 278–291.

Yorke, M., & Longden, B. (2004). *Retention and student success in higher education.* Buckingham, UK: Society for Research into Higher Education.

Young, N. (2010). The value of the narrative teaching observation to document teaching behaviours. *To Improve the Academy: Resources for Faculty, Instructional and Organizational Development, 28,* 98–114.

PART VI

Understanding Content

CHAPTER 18

Internationalizing the Curriculum

RICHARD S. VELAYO

As the world becomes more complex and interconnected, it is critical that universities and colleges internationalize their curricula. There is an increasing need to pursue strategic ways to prepare students to become more knowledgeable and respectful of different cultures, to be more informed about international and global matters, and to become effective citizens able to function well in our increasingly interconnected world. The effort to internationalize the curriculum should focus on affecting the spectrum of fundamental activities at the institutional, departmental, and faculty levels, each contributing distinctive and significant ways toward curricular reform. Although higher education recognizes the need to internationalize, particularly at the undergraduate level, there is a considerable gap between the rhetoric of internationalizing education and the reality of institutional activities and priorities.

An Internationalized Curriculum: Definition and Relevance

Various academic disciplines and professional schools have begun efforts to internationalize their curricula. Janet Knight (2004) proposed a working definition of "internationalization" as "the process of integrating an international, intercultural or global dimension into the purpose, functions or delivery of post-secondary education" (p. 7). In contrast, the term *multicultural* generally refers to domestic racial or racial diversity, and the term *intercultural* describes an encounter with cultures of other nation states or diasporas (Green & Olson, 2003). Internationalization of the curriculum involves varied internationalization activities including foreign language courses, study abroad programs, interdisciplinary programs, and the development of courses or programs with an international, intercultural, or comparative focus (Bremer & van der Wende, 1995). The primary goal of internationalizing the curriculum is to transform students' national perspectives into a broader and more informed view of the world in which students understand and appreciate the interdependence among nations and among world cultures. Thus, an internationalized curriculum is critical to prepare students to work, live, and interact in a global society.

Knight (2000) pointed out that the curriculum is the most important element of internationalization in higher education. Josef Mestenhauser (1998) also noted that universities are required to reform their curricula if students are to have an international education. Persuasive arguments are made within the literature why internationalized curricula are integral to any process of internationalization in higher education (Bond, 2003a; Burn, 2002; Ellingboe, 1998; Harari, 1992). Ideally, an internationalized learning environment, whether it be in a classroom or the broader academic environment within an institution, should recognize, value, and accommodate students' cultural differences and worldviews and reflect the diverse cultures, perspectives, and experiences of students.

Suggestions for Internationalizing the Curriculum

Methods to internationalize curricula vary among institutions. Research has stressed that an effective implementation to curricular transformation requires a dedicated involvement of various constituencies within an institution (Bonfiglio, 1999; Edwards & Tonkin, 1990; Ellingboe, 1998; Green & Olson, 2003; Harari, 1992; Schoorman, 1999, 2000a, 2000b; Schuerholz-Lehr & van Gyn, 2006; Taylor, 2000). Deciding how best to internationalize and the extent of the internationalization process may be based on an institution's resources, mission, goals, context, and unique history. Curricular reform needs to occur at the institutional level, the departmental level, and at the faculty level for students' experiences with an internationalized curriculum to be effective.

Institutional Initiatives

When reform initiatives originate from top-level administrators, initiatives can focus on modifying college missions and policy documents, diversifying language requirements and internationally related courses for students, establishing study abroad programs, and implementing intercultural competence training and incentives for curriculum planning and development for faculty. In creating collegewide reforms, it is essential to ensure that support for international education does not remain in the hands of a select few (e.g., institutional administrators) but, rather, be distributed throughout the college. To ensure programmatic continuity, colleges must constantly mentor new generations of leaders and educators with respect to efforts to continue and refine efforts to internationalize.

To develop meaningful international initiatives, a clearly stated institutional mission statement must develop globally engaged students and be supported by the institution's leadership (Wood, 2007). Faculty will be obliged, or perhaps encouraged, to think thoughtfully about their personal global perspectives and how they will expose their students to different worldviews. They may effectively redesign courses that entice students' interest in world events and inspire them to think about solutions to global problems. There have been strategic efforts by many U.S. colleges and universities to produce mission statements and international programs that focus on developing citizens who possess the language and cultural skills necessary to help sustain U.S. leadership in the world and be competitive in a global society (e.g., Byers-Pevitts, 2008; Griffiths & Chieffo, 2007; Rubin, 2009). Implementing a strong mission statement sets the tone for all subsequent international initiatives.

Another institution-based approach to internationalization is to diversify language requirements and internationally related courses. Although this step is in the right direction, developing and sustaining global educational goals is not easily accomplished by merely offering a few introductory courses. Many institutions require students to take a minimum number of internationally related courses as part of their undergraduate experience (Siaya & Hayward, 2003). An example is to link language acquisition to graduation requirements by requiring students to minor in at least one foreign language.

Arcadia University is one of several forward-thinking institutions that offer creative ways to increase the number of globally educated students, requiring them to enroll in two "global connections" courses, an international experience at home or abroad, and a reflection course (Rubin, 2009). Examples of such experiences include working with Latino immigrants and then traveling abroad to better understand the work of nongovernmental organizations (NGOs) in an international context. The university also offers stipends to faculty to become involved in internationalizing its curriculum.

Institutions can also aggressively promote education abroad programs by establishing partnerships with foreign government, industry, and other academic institutions to increase the number of graduates who demonstrate global awareness and competency. Only 108 institutions (of more than 4,200 U.S. colleges and universities) account for 50 percent of all the students abroad (Commission of the Abraham Lincoln Study Abroad Fellowship

Program [CALSAP], 2005). With almost 18 million students in higher education, only 1 percent study abroad every year (Goodman, 2009). CALSAP suggested that the profile of students studying abroad does not match the demographic profile of the U.S. undergraduate population. An approach to minimize this gap is for institutions to create programs that seek and financially support underrepresented students, nontraditional students, students with disabilities, community college students, and others. Daniel Obst, Rajika Bhandari, and Sharon Witherell (2007) noted efforts to provide and promote education abroad opportunities in less traditional locations such as the Middle East, China, and India. Notably, the availability of financial aid and timing of education abroad programs are relevant factors in determining whether students have the resources to study overseas. Lois DeFleur (2008) pointed out two institutions as examples. The State University of New York at Binghamton places a priority on creating programs during winter and summer breaks when students are not generally enrolled in classes. Michigan State University's (MSU) Freshman Seminars Abroad provides travel abroad opportunities for students through a 2-week summer program by taking students, led by MSU professors, to destinations such as Canada, Ireland, Japan, and South Africa.

Institutions can also implement intercultural competence training and incentives for curriculum planning and faculty development. Educators who have the necessary knowledge, skills, and experience can better design and conduct programs or teach courses that will result in positive intercultural learning outcomes. A helpful approach is to offer workshops for faculty to help them determine ways to internationalize their courses. These workshops may be led by other faculty members who have internationalized their courses or by departments committed to this objective. Faculty may also be provided with incentives (through grants, stipends, release time, sabbatical leaves, and awards) to help them contribute to internationalizing efforts. McGill University is a successful example of a flexible model for curriculum redesign that facilitates faculty efforts to integrate newly developed intercultural and interdisciplinary perspectives into the curriculum by offering workshops for faculty to help them redesign their course curricula and instructional approaches (Saroyan & Amundsen, 2004).

Departmental Initiatives

Academic departments can play a crucial role in internationalizing discipline-specific curricula. Course offerings and departmental initiatives can highlight the relevance of an international perspective as a goal within the major. For example, there is growing recognition of the importance of exploring ways to internationalize the psychology curriculum (Power & Velayo, 2006; Stevens & Gielen, 2007; Stevens & Wedding, 2004; Velayo, 2000). Departmental initiatives to help internationalize the curriculum include using the experiences of international students in the major to secure international literacy, sponsoring talks and collaborative projects with those abroad, introducing new course content, and partnering with student affairs professionals.

Departments can use the experiences of international students to bring cross-border perspectives to the major and contribute to the diversity of a department, and indeed, the institution. Specific programs can be developed to take advantage of the learning opportunities that these students bring with them to the classroom. Departments can involve international students to help the departments become more internationalized through international students' interactions with faculty, staff, and other students. For example, international students, along with other students, can be invited to become actively involved in departmental committees and student-led committees. They may also be encouraged to participate in meetings in which faculty and students meet to discuss research and to join research teams. Departments can ask international students to participate in panel discussions and other public venues to offer their perspectives on issues relevant to the particular discipline represented by the department. Thus, international students can become key resources for on-campus internationalization efforts, although it is important to note that not all international students possess the necessary skills to teach others, and international students' worldviews may not always represent their country's mainstream culture (Raby, 2007).

Departments can also sponsor talks and collaborative projects with those from abroad. One way is to invite visiting foreign scholars to give talks, presentations, and perhaps even teach courses to provide the faculty and students with an international perspective. Additionally, using Internet-based technologies (e.g., e-mails, websites, podcasts, YouTube videos, videoconferencing, blogs, and wikis) and social media sites (e.g., Facebook) allows opportunities for scholars and students from different countries to collaborate on course projects and discussions on course topics. Such technologies can be relevant and effective pedagogical devices in internationalizing the psychology curriculum, or for that matter, just about any curriculum (Takooshian & Velayo, 2004; Velayo, Oliva, & Blank, 2008). Departments can also facilitate collaborative work between their faculty and faculty from other countries on projects that are beneficial for faculty scholarship for students' projects such as presentations in international or domestic conferences as well as publications in foreign journals and other forms of media.

Academic departments may also propose introducing new, specifically designed international courses in the major. The addition of new courses sets a context for in-depth internationalization that the infusion approach (incorporating international content within existing courses) lacks. Rosalind Raby (2007) pointed out that new classes can be general (world literature or introduction to global studies), specific (films of Latin America or global environmental agriculture), or thematic (Spanish for nursing or Chinese in business). Some examples of new classes are Culture and International Business: Kiss, Bow, or Shake Hands (Santa Ana College); Introduction to Global Studies (Mission College); International Trade, Marketing, and Management (Long Beach City College); and International Politics (Santa Barbara City College). Although there are several benefits to adding new international courses, the process of doing so can be expensive and potentially time-consuming, especially if it requires curriculum committee approval. Generally, courses with a comparative focus (e.g., religion, literature, political science) or those that address cross-border issues (e.g., cultural anthropology, cross-cultural psychology, ethnic studies, intercultural communications) can be easily internationalized. Both faculty and administrators often attempt to internationalize their campuses through these types of courses (King & Fersh, 1992). However, any discipline can be easily internationalized by asking faculty to reconceptualize the curriculum. For example, if a biology course includes a section on infectious diseases, a discussion of pandemics will help infuse international considerations into class discussion.

Academic departments may also consider establishing partnerships with the student affairs professionals in the college to provide practical learning experiences that increase college students' level of global awareness. Examples of such partnership goals include creating language learning opportunities, international programs in campus housing, overseas internships and work experiences through career services, and campuswide programs that support internalization efforts. In addition, advising student majors by departments in conjunction with student affairs office can include information regarding education abroad opportunities. New student orientation programs, with the help of departmental representatives, may provide breakout sessions to help students learn about other cultures, as well as study aboard travel and internship possibilities abroad.

Faculty Initiatives

Faculty are ultimately responsible for internationalizing the curriculum. Sheryl Bond (2003b) noted that most faculty believe that the curriculum falls into their domain of responsibility. Faculty tend to incorporate both new content and pedagogy in their attempt to internationalize the courses they teach.

Infusing international content into a course is viable and cost-efficient and requires little more than faculty initiative and commitment to add international content, ideas, and themes in their class presentations. To infuse the curriculum, faculty can rely on life experiences, such as international travels, participation in internationally themed seminars, and even discussion of internationalized components of the textbooks used in the course. Although Mestenhauser (1998) suggested that merely adding pieces of international content to courses may not be sufficient to internationalize curriculum, it may be an appropriate way for some instructors to begin the process of slowly adding international content and themes to their courses.

Relative to pedagogy, some useful strategies that instructors can use to internationalize their courses include the following:

- Having visiting scholars, international students, and study-abroad returnees (and those who have simply traveled and stayed in another country) as guest speakers
- Discussing faculty international experiences during class and informally during advising sessions or office hours
- Facilitating interaction between domestic and international students by providing more opportunities for collaborative student projects and structured activities
- Including contributions of non-U.S. authors on course reading lists and in class lectures (e.g., discussion of the history of a subfield or content area)
- Showing videos that enhance an international perspective and critical thinking pertaining to course concepts
- Adopting critical questioning and cross-national comparisons of course content as a means of helping students examine and challenge their own assumptions, beliefs, values, and practices regarding international perspectives (e.g., students learn that the perspectives common in their country are not the only possible perspectives from which to view life and that basic assumptions about the essential nature of course material may be questioned by others in some parts of the world)
- Encouraging students to attend international events and conferences on and off campus (providing extra credit when relevant)
- Discussing world events and current issues whenever possible and recommending good international news outlets
- Using Internet-based technologies (e.g., Facebook and other social media sites, blogs, wikis, virtual worlds, videoconferencing) while integrating international issues and ideas in teaching, training, and research

Individual faculty members, instead of working in isolation to internationalize their courses, can also collaborate with and use the services of study abroad programs, the international student office, and student international organizations on campus. They may also collaborate with other faculty members who have internationalized their courses to gain knowledge and share strategies with each other. Whatever teaching strategies are used, it is best to outline explicitly the expectations in an internationalized course and to guide students in understanding the reasons and goals for using particular teaching strategies in the classroom.

Conclusion: A Perspective on the Challenges to Internationalizing Curriculum ——

Joan Stark and Lisa Lattuca (1996) noted that the critical major barriers to internationalization include the lack of background knowledge by faculty in the international aspects of their discipline, the lack of institutional incentives that entice faculty to be involved in international work on curriculum development, and a narrow view of education by the university. Although these comments were made 15 years ago, they still apply to faculty and institutions that have not made a concerted effort to include international and global issues in their curriculum.

An institution's task is not to impose curriculum change but to provide ways for its constituents to acknowledge the need for change, value it, and agree to move toward a more comprehensive approach to internationalization. Sociopolitical forces within the institution may also prevent internationalization of the curriculum (Hill, 2001). Development, refinement, and maintenance of the curriculum operate within institutional sociopolitical constraints (e.g., departments competing for space and other resources). Thus, the crucial task is for faculty committed to internationalization of the curriculum to negotiate for the changes to the curriculum that would benefit all the key players: students, faculty, administrators, and in some cases, perhaps even boards of trustees. A useful faculty tactic along these lines is for faculty to seek membership on institutional committees that directly shape the nature of the curriculum (Ross, 2005). Similarly, in those cases in which the administration is primarily involved in making curricular decisions, faculty committed to internationalizing the curriculum should offer their support to administrators seeking faculty support for internationalization.

Faculty often play a critical role in curriculum design and reform, although some faculty may be uninterested, or worse, resistant to internationalizing the curriculum. Faculty interest, motivation, and lack of involvement are three likely key factors in limiting faculty contributions to internationalizing the curriculum (Labi, 2009). A key method to begin acculturating the institution toward internationalization is to hire new faculty who demonstrate interdisciplinary competence and who show international and global interest in their teaching and research.

Internationalization of the curriculum must be an institution-wide effort. Leadership for internationalization must be demonstrated at the highest levels of the institution, and mission statements must be global and inclusive. Academic departments must engage in curriculum reform to achieve international education objectives. Faculty participation must be inherent in recommendations for the future of global education. Faculty who are supported and encouraged by administrators to explore new internationally focused courses, or provide global perspectives in existing courses, will contribute significantly to curriculum reform. One hopes that a more international perspective will eventually permeate curricula in institutions worldwide and that the day will come when students will be able to acquire relevant knowledge and perspectives about cultures other than their own. This goal is certainly one we can all strive to achieve.

References

Bond, S. (2003a). *Engaging educators: Bringing the world into the classroom: Guidelines for practice.* Ottawa, ON: Canadian Bureau for International Education.

Bond, S. (2003b). *Untapped resources: Internationalization of the curriculum and classroom experience: A selected literature review* (CBIE Research Millennium Series No. 7). Ottawa, ON: Canadian Bureau for International Education.

Bonfiglio, O. (1999). The difficulties of internationalizing the American undergraduate curriculum. *Journal of Studies in International Education, 3,* 3–18.

Bremer, L., & van der Wende, M. (Eds.). (1995). *Internationalising the curriculum in higher education: Experience in the Netherlands.* The Hague, Netherlands: Organisation for International Co-operation in Higher Education.

Burn, B. (2002). The curriculum as a global domain. *Journal of Studies in International Education, 6,* 253–261.

Byers-Pevitts, B. (2008). Innovative education for an interconnected world. *The presidency: Meeting the challenges of 21st century globalization, 11*(3), 24.

Commission on the Abraham Lincoln Study Abroad Program (CALSAP). (2005, November). Global competence & national needs: One million Americans studying abroad. Retrieved from NAFSA: Association of International Educators, http://www.aplu.org/NetCommunity/Document.Doc?id=190

DeFleur, L. B. (2008, Fall). A visible commitment to global education. *The presidency: Meeting the challenges of 21st century globalization. 11*(3), 20–21.

Edwards, J., & Tonkin, H. (1990). Internationalizing the community college: Strategies for the classroom. In R. Greenfield (Ed.), *Developing international education programs: New directions for community colleges* (pp. 17–26). San Francisco, CA: Jossey-Bass.

Ellingboe, B. J. (1998). Divisional strategies to internationalize a campus portrait: Results, resistance and recommendations from a case study at a U.S. university. In J. A. Mestenhauser & B. J. Ellingboe (Eds.), *Reforming the higher education curriculum: Internationalizing the campus* (pp. 198–228). Phoenix, AZ: Oryx Press.

Goodman, A. (2009). Foreword. In P. Blumenthal, & R. Gutierrez (Eds.), *Meeting America's global education challenge: Expanding study abroad capacity at U.S. colleges and universities* (pp. 4-6). New York, NY: Institute of International Education.

Green, M. F., & Olson, C. (2003). *Internationalizing the campus: A user's guide.* Washington, DC: American Council on Education.

Griffiths, L., & Chieffo, L. (2007). *Best practices in international education.* Retrieved from the Institute of International Education, http://iienetwork.org/page/96758/

Harari, M. (1992). The internationalization of the curriculum. In C. B. Klasek (Ed.), *Bridges to the future: Strategies for internationalizing higher education* (pp. 52–79). Carbondale, IL: Association of International Education Administrators.

Hill, I. (2001). Curriculum development and ethics in international education. *Disarmament Forum, 3,* 49–57.

King, M. C., & Fersh, S. H. (1992). *Integrating the international and intercultural dimension in the community college.* Washington, DC: Association of Community College Trustees and Community Colleges for International Development.

Knight, J. (2000). *Taking the pulse: Monitoring the quality and progress of internationalization including tracking measures* (CBIE Research Millennium Series No. 2). Ottawa, ON: Canadian Bureau for International Education.

Knight, J. (2004). Internationalization remodeled: Definition, approaches, and rationales. *Journal of Studies in International Education, 8,* 5–31.

Labi, A. (2009, September). Priorities in internalization shift from research to preparing students. *The Chronicle of Higher Education.* Retrieved from http://cge.cua .edu/res/docs/Priorities-in-Internationalization.pdf

Mestenhauser, J. A. (1998). Portraits of an international curriculum: An uncommon multidimensional perspective. In J. A. Mestenhauser & B. J. Ellingboe (Eds.), *Reforming the higher education curriculum: Internationalizing the campus* (pp. 3–39). Phoenix, AZ: Oryx Press.

Obst, D., Bhandari, R., & Witherell, S. (2007, May). Current trends in U.S. study abroad & the impact of strategic diversity initiatives. *Meeting America's Global Education Challenge, 1,* 1–25.

Power, F., & Velayo, R. (2006). Hello world!: The case for internationalizing the psychology curriculum. *International Psychology Reporter, 10*(1), 10–11.

Raby, R. L. (2007). Internationalizing the curriculum: On- and off-campus strategies. *New directions for community colleges, 138,* 57–66. Available from www.inter science.wiley.com. doi:10.1002/cc.282

Ross, B. (2005). *Internationalization of higher education: A case study of the University of Regina* (Unpublished master's thesis). University of Regina, Saskatchewan, Canada.

Rubin, K. (2009, September). Globalizing general education. *International Educator, 28*(5), 20–29.

Saroyan, A., & Amundsen, C. (2004). *Rethinking teaching in higher education.* Sterling, VA: Stylus.

Schoorman, D. (1999). The pedagogical implications of diverse conceptualizations of internationalization: A U.S.-based case study. *Journal of Studies in International Education, 3,* 19–46.

Schoorman, D. (2000a). *How is internationalization implemented? A framework for organizational practice.* Boca Raton: Florida Atlantic University. (ERIC Document Reproduction Service No. 444426)

Schoorman, D. (2000b). What really do we mean by "internationalization"? *Contemporary Education, 71,* 5–11.

Schuerholz-Lehr, S., & van Gyn, G. (2006, March). *Internationalizing pedagogy or applying pedagogy to internationalism? The journey of a professional development workshop.* Paper presented at Internationalizing Canada's Universities:

Practices, Challenges, and Opportunities symposium. Retrieved from http://www.yorku.ca/yorkint/global/archive/conference/canada/papers/Sabine-Schuerholz-Lehr.pdf

Siaya, L., & Hayward, F. (2003). *Mapping internationalization on U.S. campuses.* Washington, DC: American Council on Education.

Stark, J., & Lattuca, L. (1996). *Shaping the college curriculum: Academic plans in action.* Toronto, ON: Allyn & Bacon.

Stevens, M. J., & Gielen, U. P. (Eds.). (2007). *Toward a global psychology: Theory, research, intervention, and pedagogy.* Mahwah, NJ: Lawrence Erlbaum.

Stevens, M. J., & Wedding, D. (Eds.). (2004). *Handbook of international psychology.* New York, NY: Brunner-Routledge.

Takooshian, H., & Velayo, R. (2004, Spring). Internationalizing our psychology curriculum. *Newsletter of the Society for Teaching of Psychology*, 8–9.

Taylor, F. (2000). *Canadian university efforts to internationalize the curriculum.* Ottawa, ON: Association of Universities and Colleges of Canada.

Velayo, R. (2000, Winter). The globalization of psychology via the Internet: Anticipating the not-too-distant future. *International Psychology Reporter, 4*(1), 18–19.

Velayo, R. S., Oliva, J., & Blank, D. (2008, Winter). Using the Internet: A call to internationalize the psychology curriculum. *International Psychology Bulletin, 12*(1), 22–26.

Wood, V. R. (2007). *Globalization and higher education: Eight common perceptions from university leaders.* Retrieved October 25, 2010, from the Institute of International Education http://www.iienetwork.org/page/84658/

Cultural Contexts and Curricular Design in Saudi Arabia and Other Middle Eastern Nations

EMAD A. ISMAIL AND MOHAMMAD M. HASSAN

Curriculum design is an important process that is shaped by many factors. For example, according to Groccia's model of teaching and learning (St. Clair & Groccia, 2009), course content directly affects curricular design. Indirect factors such as culture also may affect curriculum design. Thus, effective curriculum development requires, among other things, understanding both content and cultural diversity (Bixler, 2010).

In this chapter, we will discuss the relationship between curriculum and instruction from a global perspective and the factors that affect curriculum design processes. In particular, we will focus on culture and how religious, gender, social-economic, political, and environmental forces influence curriculum design in higher education in Saudi Arabia and other Middle East countries.

Defining Culture and Curriculum

Culture entails patterns of thought and behavior that include values, beliefs, rules of conduct, political organization, economic activity, and communication

---

Author's Note: It is Muslim tradition to include the notation PBUH (the peace and blessing of Allah be upon him) each time the Prophet Muhammad's name is mentioned, and this chapter reflects and respects that custom.

styles that have been developed over time by groups of people and passed from one generation to another so that they can survive in particular environments (Banks & Banks, 1995). Research has established that culture can have powerful effects on learning and academic achievement (e.g., Cano, 1999; Joy & Kolb, 2007; Smith & Renk, 2007). Culture determines how people learn because it affects the way the people think, behave, and respond to their environments (Dunn & Marinetti, 2006). Culture can also be considered "as the epistemology, philosophy, observed traditions, and patterns of action by individuals and human groups" (Branch, 1997, p. 38) and as a "set of attitudes, values, beliefs, and behaviors shared by a group of people, but different for each individual, communicated from one generation to the next" (Matsumoto, 1994, p. 548, cited in Kitayama & Cohen, 2007). In his study of 50 different countries, Geert Hofstede (1991) noted that a key aspect of culture was whether a culture is individualistic or collectivistic. *Individualism* refers to an emphasis on individual independence and accomplishment, whereas *collectivism* centers more on accomplishing the group goals. For example, U.S. culture tends to be more individualistic than collectivistic, whereas Arab cultures tend to be more collectivistic than individualistic.

Curriculum is the course of study offered by an educational institution. The curriculum establishes the learning content, activities, and the educational experiences that teachers provide their students (Beach & Reinhatz, 1989; Marshall, 2004; Tanner & Tanner, 1995). Curriculum determines what instructors are expected to teach and what students are expected to learn. Curriculum content includes knowledge, skills, and attitudes that teachers expect students to acquire in a particular learning domain at a particular year or grade level. Several essential questions to ask when planning and developing a curriculum at any educational level (Cook & Doll, 1973) include the following:

- What are the primary overall objectives of the curriculum?
- What should the subject matter of the curriculum include?
- What function do these subjects serve within the curriculum?
- How should the courses within the curriculum be organized?
- Where, when, and how should the curriculum be delivered?
- What resources are needed to deliver the curriculum?
- What factors other than the subject matter should drive the curriculum (e.g., culture)?

Why Consider Culture When Designing Curricula?

A person's cultural background can result in different interpretations of concepts, meanings, images, symbols, colors, and sounds, and thus affect how that individual learns (Chen, Mashhadi, Ang, & Harkrider, 1999). If such differences are not considered when designing a course, difficulties for students in understanding and learning may result. For example, Catherine McLoughlin (1999) emphasized that three important factors should be considered when designing culturally appropriate instructional materials for Indigenous Australians: "cultural awareness of the target group, instructional design, and the provision of educational flexibility in an online environment" (p. 234). Betty Collis (1999), Catherine McLoughlin (1999), and Martyn Wild and Lyn Henderson (1997) each noted the importance of teachers using multiple cultural models of interactive multimedia instructional design, which incorporates different cultural issues and perspectives in the curriculum so that members of different cultures may retain their ties to their native cultures.

In some cases, cultural values may not be well considered in curriculum design: Pedagogical values in one culture can be culturally inappropriate in another. For example, in many parts of the world, a student questioning a teacher's knowledge or point of view is considered inappropriate (Reeves & Reeves, 1997), especially at the precollege level. In some cases, even talking to teachers (or other adults) without addressing them with the appropriate title (e.g., "Dr.") may be considered a sign of disrespect. Arguing with teachers in the classroom or doubting their knowledge would be considered especially inappropriate in these types of cultures.

Types of Curriculum Design and Their Relationship to Culture

Curriculum development usually does not explicitly address the social context in which learning takes place, nor does it consider the underlying cultural processes by which the content is acquired and used. Ray Barnhardt (1981) divided curriculum design into three different types—subject-oriented, process-oriented, and project-centered approaches to curriculum design— and related each of these types to culture background.

Subject-oriented curricula focus on content and are deeply rooted in the classical Western tradition of categories of knowledge: humanities, social sciences, natural sciences, mathematics, languages, and aesthetics. Their primary focus is on transmitting a predetermined body of knowledge or a particular set of skills from teacher to student. The knowledge or the content is often separated from the situational framework for students and is usually culturally biased and not applicable to wider range of cultural conditions. Thus, this approach is not generally sensitive to minority and ethnic students, but it has the inertia of tradition behind it and serves many functions compatible with the needs of the society at large and, as such, cannot be disregarded when thinking about curriculum design.

Unlike the subject-oriented approach, the *process-oriented* approach focuses more on the question of how students learn rather than on what should be taught. The emphasis is on process and students rather than on content and institutions. A curriculum design centered on process is potentially less culture-bound, and thus may be more readily adapted to alternative settings without intruding on students' cultural and situational variability. Unfortunately, this approach does not address the second-level question of how students learn process skills. Although the process-oriented approach has greater potential for adapting curricular content to fit varied cultural settings, it does not adequately place that content into an everyday experiential framework in which it can be tested against reality and put to practical use.

As a means of integrating the useful features of the subject and process orientations and putting them into a functional experiential framework for minority students, John Bransford, James Brown, & Rodney Cocking (2000), explored a project-centered approach to curriculum design. In this case, the term *project* referred to an activity that involved communication, diagnosis, problem definition, planning, and taking actions to solve problems systematically. A project can take almost any form. It can be a lesson plan, a unit, or a yearlong effort. It can take place inside or outside the classroom. It can involve one student, a small group of students, or the entire class, and it can be incorporated into nearly any course or learning activity. Some examples of educational projects are field trips, work/travel/study programs, internships, practica, and apprenticeship programs.

In Middle Eastern countries, such as Egypt and Saudi Arabia, the most common models for curriculum design seem based around subject-oriented and project-oriented approaches. In both pre–higher education and higher education, the focus is what schools and teachers should teach more than what students should learn. Memorization is the primary learning skill characterizing education in both countries: Students' ability to store and retrieve massive amounts of information is the primary criterion for passing most examinations. Curriculum design in these countries reflects this. In this context, Sheble Badran (1993), in his assessment of quality of science curricula in seven Arabian Gulf States, found that science teaching was based on the subject-oriented approach and that projects that help students' develop important cognitive skills (processes) such as critical thinking and problem solving were seldom integrated into teaching. Although it is not a particularly useful learning strategy for students relative to understanding and analyzing information, memorization is key to learning the Holy Qur'an (the Muslim holy book) and poetry (Vassall-Fall, 2008). The use of memorization as a teaching and learning strategy is commonplace throughout Saudi Arabia and can be found on other continents such as Asia and Africa as well (Al Rashudi, 2002).

Cultural Factors Affecting Curriculum Planning and Design

Several factors within culture can affect curriculum planning and design. These factors include religion, gender, social grouping, and societal expectations. Catalina Bixler (2010) argued that other important factors influencing students should also be considered when planning and developing the curriculum, including the following:

- Politics—local, state, and national government policies and procedures that may influence the interpretation of curricular materials and the approval of examination systems
- Economics—employability and the expected benefit of educating a nation's students in terms of their contributions to its economy
- Technology—the ability of students to learn and use technology in accomplishing their educational goals and competing in the global market place
- Learning theories—understanding current theories of student learning to select content and delivery strategies to teach the subject matter, interactive activities, and experiences to maximize learning
- Environment—encouraging awareness and action toward conservation and reversing and ending pollution continues affecting curriculum development

In what follows, we discuss these and other factors and describe how they can affect curriculum planning and design in Saudi Arabia and other Middle Eastern countries.

Political Factors

Until very recently in the Arab world, there were neither institutional nor national mechanisms to assess quality of higher education, and terms referring to external standards such as *benchmarks* and *key performance indicators* did not exist. Currently, the biggest challenge for Arab institutions of higher education is to implement newly mandated policies, practices, and measures for improving teaching and learning quality and to ensure their practical application to daily life practices. Accordingly, developing curricula in Arab institutions of higher education have received much attention by ministries of higher education.

Ministries of higher education in most Arab universities have recently mandated quality enhancement and accreditation. Efforts have been made to establish independent quality assurance and accreditation associations focusing on higher education in Bahrain, Egypt, Jordan, Libya, Oman, Palestine, Saudi Arabia, Sudan, Tunisia, United Arab Emirates, and Yemen (Al-Abedi, 2009).

Initiatives of several world organizations also have been directed toward enhancing higher education in Middle Eastern countries. For example, the Arab Network for Staff Development (ANSD) in higher education was established in 1993 at Alexandria University, Egypt, with support from the United Nations Educational, Scientific, and Cultural Organization (UNESCO) to help university professors to integrate the latest technologies into their courses (UNESCO, 2003). Since ANSD was established, numerous pedagogical and learning technology training programs for all member universities have been launched, with more emphasis on computer-aided instruction, student-instructor interaction, and enjoyment of teaching and learning (El Hares, 1994).

In Egypt, government-backed higher education reform initiatives have been launched based on the national conference on Globalization and Internationalization of Higher Education: The Need for Change, in February 2000 (The World Bank Report, 2002). Among the initiatives was the Higher Education Enhancement Project Fund (HEEPF) to provide funds for higher education developmental projects. Most of these projects centered on improving educational curricula and establishing new e-learning courses to address local and international job market needs (Higher Education Enhancement Project [HEEP], 2009).

Simultaneously in Egypt, educational reformers and policymakers pushed for educational development and refinement, particularly after a free trade treaty with the European Union had been signed by Egyptian political leaders. This treaty led to increased ease with which foreign workers could move in and out of Egypt—leading to heightened fear that foreign labor flow into the Egyptian market would increase competition for jobs. In turn, this situation accelerated calls for massive educational reform to prepare Egyptian students for stiff competition in that market. For example, some initiatives targeted improving the skills and quality of agriculture education graduates (AERI, 2004), whereas other initiatives focused on helping agricultural faculty become more effective teachers by incorporating more skill-building activities in the curricula. Similarly, a major part of the 2007 HEEPF report also addressed the enhancement of agricultural education and improving curriculum in Egypt (Abdellah, Taher, & Ismail, 2007).

At the same time, similar initiatives for improving higher education in Saudi Arabia took place. For example, quality assurance and accreditation initiatives at King Saud University and many other Saudi universities began in earnest and continue to take place on an ongoing basis (King Saud University, 2008).

Social and Economic Factors

As noted by Gawdat Saadate and Mohamed Abdullah (1997), social principles that reflect community values often affect higher education. For example, in Egypt and other Middle Eastern countries, students face increasing family and societal pressure to perform well in school, so they can compete in local economies and compete in the larger global economy as well. Because of large numbers of students seeking higher education, the limited number of seats at universities, and limited job opportunities, students face increasing pressure to graduate at the top of their classes at both secondary and tertiary levels.

Likewise, economic factors can be an obstacle in designing curricula, particularly when teaching and learning activities are costly. For example, in some countries such as many African nations, incorporating e-learning, distance learning, or any Internet-based learning platform in the curricula is impossible or nearly impossible because Internet technology is still prohibitively expensive in these countries. Fortunately, in some Middle Eastern countries such as Saudi Arabia, Egypt, and Libya, the annual cost for an Internet connection is becoming less than 10 percent of the average income (UNESCO, 2005). Nonetheless, public perception in these countries is not favorable of e-learning relative to formal classroom-based education (Ali, Sait, & Al-Tawil, 2003). Even with the development of centers for e-learning and distance education, public perception of non-classroom-based approaches to higher education remains negative.

Religion

Islam, of course, is the main religion among Arab nations. Islam views education as a form of worship (*ibadah*) in which Muslims share a common set of values based on the Holy Qur'an and Sunnah (the teachings of the Prophet Muhammad [Peace and blessings be upon him PBUH]; Hashim & Langgulung, 2008). Norlain Dindang Mababaya and Mamarinta Omar Mababaya (2005) observed that Islamic education and its curriculum have developed over many centuries starting with Prophet Muhammad (PBUH) in Makkah until the end of Umayyad period (750 CE). During this period, the curriculum for all students was based on the Prophet's (PBUH) teachings, and Arabic and foreign languages. Over time, Middle Eastern scholars and teachers introduced Western educational values, content, and practices slowly into their respective educational curricula.

Today, religious curricula exist only in public and religious schools throughout the Middle East. For example, in Egypt, there exists a religious educational system, the Al-Azhar system, which runs parallel to the public educational system. In this system, all students are Muslims, and males and females are segregated at all levels of education. The bulk of the curriculum consists of religious subjects (Ministry of Higher Education, 2007). However, with increasing globalization of social and economic norms, religious schools such as Al-Azhar (Al-Azhar University was acknowledged as the oldest religious university in the world (Ministry of Higher Education, 2007]) have had to incorporate newly emerging educational issues into their curricula by creating new courses. In Saudi Arabia, at least two universities—the Imam Muhammad Ibn Saud Islamic University, and Umm al-Qura University—originally founded for religious instruction, have integrated secular subjects and practical training into their curricula. The latter was originally a college of Shari'a (jurisprudence) with an institute to teach Arabic to non-Arabs (Metz, 1992).

After the September 11, 2001, attacks on the United States, Middle Eastern countries have attempted to increase the availability of modern basic education in Arab (Egypt, Yemen, Jordan, Iraq, Lebanon, and Morocco) and predominantly Muslim countries such as Afghanistan, Pakistan, and Bangladesh. These attempts included the U.S. commitment of millions of dollars to general (and indirectly higher) education reform in these countries (Blanchard, 2008). As a result, strong pushes have been made by ministries of higher education throughout the Middle East to provide a more religious-secular balance in education. Indeed, universities have redesigned their curricula from preschool through graduate study to include modern instructional pedagogy, subject matter, and technology without sacrificing Islamic values.

Gender

In Saudi Arabia, and to a lesser extent in other Islamic nations, religion directly affects gender issues related to societal customs and educational practices. For example, in Saudi Arabia, the goal of education for women is stated in official government policy:

> The purpose of educating a girl is to bring her up in a proper Islamic way so as to perform her duty in life, be an ideal and successful housewife and a good mother, ready to do things which suit her nature such as teaching, nursing, and medical treatment . . . [and that] women's right to obtain suitable education [is] on equal footing with men in light of Islamic laws. (Al Sheikh, Al Saad, & Al Omer, 2008, p. 185)

In Saudi Arabia, educational policies regarding gender require that men and women be educated in separate schools from kindergarten through college. Thus, some colleges have separate campuses for men and women and others accept only men (e.g., King Fahd University for Petroleum and Minerals) or only women (e.g., Princess Nora bint Abdulrahman University). There are some exceptions to this general segregation rule—for example, in the dental and medical colleges at King Saud University and others, men and women take classes together, although they are required to sit on separate sides of the classroom (Al-Mengash, 2010)

Gender segregation has had an effect on curriculum design. Although the majority of the curriculum is similar for boys and girls at college level, at many Saudi universities almost no engineering curricula exists for women on the premise that an engineering career would not be possible to pursue in the context of gender segregation practices. In other Arab countries, the picture is very different. According to the UNESCO Institute for Statistics Database (2010; see also AlSisi, 2010), in contrast to Saudi Arabia, which has the lowest percentage of females studying engineering (2%), countries such as

Jordan (30%), United Arab Emirates (29%), and Qatar (24%), have much higher percentages of women studying engineering.

Strategies for Content Delivery

In the Middle East, college students from different countries perceive various teaching techniques differently, so it is important for teachers to carefully choose their approach to teaching before academic term begins. Some pedagogy is universally accepted among Arab educators, including lectures, lecture outlines and handouts, multiple-choice questions, essay questions, and so on. These approaches can be simply incorporated in most curricular design regardless of students' cultural background. In contrast, more active approaches appear to be culture-sensitive. For example, many Middle Eastern teachers rarely teach using group work, role playing, and case studies (Mahrous &Ahmed, 2009) because their students seem unprepared, indeed, resistant to accept the requirements of active learning (e.g., participation, speaking in front of others; Johnson, Monk, & Swain, 2000). Nasser Mansour (2007) noted that the current academic environment in Middle Eastern countries does not accept the basic principles on which some active learning strategies such as cooperative learning are based. In addition, in instances in which Mansour discovered faculty using cooperative learning, he also discovered that this method of active learning often lacked the features recommended in the literature for its effective use.

Some notable exceptions exist, however. Mara Al Mugren (2009) found that cooperative language learning was more effective compared with traditional teaching methods such as the lecture in improving composition writing for students in the College of Languages and Translation at Imam Muhammad Ibn Saud Islamic University (Riyadh, Saudi Arabia), particularly in the areas of grammar, punctuation, spelling, and word choice. Latifa Saleh Al-Semairi (2004) found that cooperative learning was effective in developing leadership, participation, communications, and teamwork skills for female students in King Saud University's College of Education. Al-Semairi recommended that cooperative learning strategies be adopted so all teachers can develop these skills. Likewise, Dona Vassall-Fall (2008) found that cooperative learning increased critical thinking skills of students enrolled in a techniques in language teaching class at King Saud University in processing, analyzing, understanding, and retaining course ideas and concepts.

Abdel-Salam AbdelSalam (1999) suggested that instructional methods other than traditional lecture—for example, role playing, forums, individual projects, cooperative groups, report writing, and field experiences—should be used to teach science curricula and recommended these approaches for developing teaching skills within Egyptian academic communities driven by science and technology. In particular, he recommended that students in colleges of education specializing in the teaching of science content should be trained during their internships on how to teach science courses using these methods.

Catherine McLoughlin and Ron Oliver (2000) argued that curricular design also should reflect the multiple cultures in the society and incorporate ways of teaching and learning that consider culture and promote equity among all learning outcomes. As Ronald Doll (1996) noted, because instruction is the creation and implementation of purposefully developed plans for the teaching curriculum content, both pedagogy and curriculum should be compatible to achieve the best learning outcomes.

Nonetheless, some authors think that cultural background may have a limited effect on choosing teaching methods or the way course content is delivered to students. For example, Sefa Bulut (2010) argued that cultural background for graduate students' experiences with collaborative learning strategies in different countries does not affect the ways they perceive the application of these strategies because the basic nature of cooperative tendencies are universal: All cultures support some degree of cooperation among their citizens (Armstrong, 2002).

Environmental Factors

Concern about the quality of the natural environment has become an important factor influencing aspects of curriculum development in Arab countries. For example, in Qatar, a team of authors has suggested infusing environmental issues into the curriculum (Al Malki, Shehata, & Al Agha, 2001). Madalla Alibeli and Abdul Fattah Yaghi (2011) found that college students' concern about water problems in five developing Arab countries (Bahrain, Jordan, Kuwait, Saudi Arabia, and Qatar) was influenced by whether students had a major or a minor in public affairs or in one of the natural sciences. This study recommended policymakers design all curricula in higher education so that students are provided opportunities to learn about environmental issues.

In the same context, Saeed Al-Saeed (1993) investigated the development of environmental awareness among education students in Saudi Arabia. He found that environmental awareness was higher for senior-level students than for first-year students. He attributed this finding to the fact that students took an environmental education course later rather than earlier in their course work and argued for moving such courses to earlier stages of the college curriculum. In an attempt to link environmental education courses to moral, social, and political values across Arab nations, many faculty and administrators have argued for the incorporation of water scarcity and pollution subject matter into the curriculum (e.g., Al Domyati, 2009). For example, Abass Allam (2003) proposed a comprehensive program dealing with important water problems in the 21st century in Arab countries generally, and in Egypt particularly, within social studies courses.

Conclusions

Culture is the outcome of several interrelated factors that can influence and control curricular design in higher education. The most influential factors include politics, social trends, economics, religion, gender, content delivery strategies, and environmental issues. Because culture includes a set of attitudes shared by a group of people and curriculum content often contributes to the development of student attitudes about all realms of life, culture, and curriculum may mutually affect each other.

In Saudi Arabia and other Middle Eastern countries, competition in the global economy has been an important driving change in higher education, including curricular design. To ensure that these changes are in line with international standards for quality higher education, many Middle Eastern universities have developed quality assurance programs and sought accreditation through independent agencies. Thus, compared with even a few decades ago, the subject matter, teaching strategies for delivering that subject matter, and learning outcome assessment methods for measuring student learning have undergone substantial change.

References

Abdellah G. A., Taher, S. E. M., & Ismail, E. A. (2007). Enhancing agricultural education in Egypt through competitive mechanisms. Cairo, Egypt: Ministry of Higher Education. Retrieved from http://academic.research.microsoft.com/Publication/11305232/enhancing-agricultural-education-in-egypt-through-competitive-mechanism

AbdelSalam, A.-S. (1999). Developing physics course of high school students in light of science, technology and society interaction. *Journal of Scientific Education: Egyptian Society for Scientific Education, 2*, 1–33.

Agriculture Export for Rural Income (AERI). (2004). *Agriculture export for rural income report: A USAID-funded project.* Cairo: Arab Republic of Egypt.

Al-Abedi, S. G. (2009, December). *Quality assurance of higher education outcomes in alignment with community needs.* Paper presented at the 12th Conference of Higher Education and Scientific Research Ministers in Arab World, Beirut, Lebanon.

Al Domyati, M. A. (2009). The role of educational institutions in water awareness development. *Journal of Education, 38*, 292–303.

Ali, S. H., Sait, S. M., & Al-Tawil, K. M. (2003, April). *Perceptions about e-learning in Saudi Arabia.* Paper presented at ICASE World Conference on Science & Technology Education, Penang, Malaysia.

Alibeli, M. A., & Yaghi, A. (2011). Exploring students' concern about water problems in five Arab states: A study on college students. *Asian Journal of Social Sciences, 2*, 1–24. Retrieved from http://onlineresearchjournals.com/aajoss/art/58.pdf

Allam, A. R. (2003). Proposed perspective for social studies curricula of general education in the light of water issues. *Journal of Studies in Curriculum and Instruction Methods, 90*, 94–139.

Al Malki, A. K., Shehata, M. A., & Al Agha, N. K. (2001). Perspective proposal for incorporating environmental awareness concepts into high school curriculum in Qatar. *Journal of Studies in Curriculum and Instruction Methods, 76*, 127–182.

Al-Mengash, S. A. (2010). The degree of achieving the factors of successful women's university in Nora Bent Abdurahman University for girls in Riyadh and Nara Women University in Japan from the perception of their students: A comparative field study. *Journal of Faculty of Education, 72*, 3–54.

Al Mugren, M. (2009). *The impact of cooperative language learning on improving the writing competency of third-year English majored college students* (Unpublished master's thesis). Department of English Language and Literature of College of Languages & Translation. Al Imam Muhammad Ibn Saud Islamic University, Riyadh, Saudi Arabia.

Al Rashudi, M. H. (2002). *Evidence of rote memorization as a learning strategy by female Saudi students of the Department of English, King Saud University* (Unpublished master's thesis). King Saud University, Riyadh, Saudi Arabia: King Saud University.

Al-Saeed, Saeed M. M. (1993). Towards the environmental concepts of education college students at Abha. *Studies in Curricula and Instruction Methods* (22), 23–42. [In Arabic]

Al-Semairi, L. S. (2004). *The effect of using the cooperative learning strategy on developing the social skills of students in College of Education, King Saud University in Riyadh* (Unpublished master's thesis). College of Education, King Saud University, Riyadh, Saudi Arabia.

Al Sheikh, A. W., Al Saad, N. K., & Al Omer, A. M. (2008). *Message to the West: Perspective from Saudi Arabia* (2nd ed.). Riyadh, Saudi Arabia: Ghainaa Publications.

AlSisi, A. H. (2010, January). *Adapting higher education of Saudi female to fulfill development requirements.* Seminar on Female's Higher Education: Dimensions and Perspectives. Madena, Saudi Arabia: Taibah University.

Armstrong, N. (2002). *Learning strategy preferences of international graduate students at Oklahoma State University* (Doctoral dissertation). Oklahoma State University, Stillwater, OK. Retrieved from *Dissertation Abstract Internationals.*

Badran, A. (1993). The status of science teaching in the Gulf countries. In M. Debs (Ed.), *Proceedings of the first scientific conference on the future of science and math teaching and the needs of Arab society* (pp. 154–172). Beirut, Lebanon: Arab Development Institute.

Banks, J. A., & Banks, C. A. M. (Eds.). (1995). *Handbook of research on multicultural education.* New York, NY: Macmillan.

Barnhardt, R. (1981). *Culture, community and the curriculum.* Retrieved from http://www.ankn.uaf.edu/curriculum/Articles/RayBarnhardt/CCC.html

Beach, D. M., & Reinhatz, J. (1989). *Supervision: Focus on instruction.* New York, NY: Harper & Row.

Bixler, C. (2010). Factors that affect the curriculum design process. Retrieved from http://www.ehow.com/list_6529581_factors-affect-curriculum-design-process.html#ixzz13MF1958k

Blanchard, C. M. (2008). *Islamic religious schools, "Madrasas": Background.* Washington, DC: Congressional Research Services, Congress Library, RS 21654.

Branch, R. M. (1997). Educational technology frameworks that facilitate culturally pluralistic instruction. *Educational Technology, 37*, 38–41.

Bransford, J., Brown, A., & Cocking, R. R. (2000). *How people learn: Bridging research and practice.* Washington, DC: National Research Council and National Academy Press.

Bulut, S. (2010). A cross-cultural study on the usage of cooperative learning techniques in graduate level education in five different countries. *Revista Latinoamericana de Psicología, 42,* 111–118.

Cano, J. (1999). The relationship between learning style, academic major, and academic performance of college students. *Journal of Agricultural Education, 40,* 30–37.

Chen, A.-Y., Mashhadi, A., Ang, D., & Harkrider, N. (1999). Cultural issues in the design of technology-enhanced learning systems. *British Journal of Educational Technology, 30,* 217–230.

Cook, R., & Doll, R. (1973). *The elementary school curriculum.* Boston, MA: Allyn & Bacon.

Collis, B. (1999). Designing for differences: Cultural issues in the design of WWW-based course-support sites. *British Journal of Educational Technology, 30,* 201–215.

Doll, R. C. (1996). *Curriculum improvement: Decision making and process* (9th ed.). Boston, MA: Allyn & Bacon.

Dunn, P., & Marinetti, A. (2006). *Cultural adaptation: Necessity for global e-learning.* Retrieved from *LINE Zine* at http://www.linezine.com/7.2/articles/pdamca.htm

El Hares, H. (1994). University teaching networks: The Arab network for staff development. In M-L. Kearney (Ed.), *Higher education staff development: Directions for the 21st century* (pp. 93–106). Paris, France: United Nations Educational, Scientific and Cultural Organization (UNESCO). Retrieved from http://www.usc.es/ceta/recursos/documentos/barnes.pdf

Hashim, C. N., & Langgulung, H. (2008). Islamic religious curriculum in Muslim countries: The experiences of Indonesia and Malaysia. *Bulletin of Education & Research, 30,* 1–19.

Higher Education Enhancement Project (HEEP). (2009). *Final report, Ministry of Higher Education, Egypt.* Retrieved from www.heep.edu.eg

Higher Education Enhancement Project Fund (HEEPF). (2007). *Academic development in higher education enhancement.* Retrieved from http://www.heepf.org.eg/Publication.php

Hofstede, G. (1991). *Cultures and organizations: Software of the mind.* New York, NY: McGraw-Hill.

Johnson, S., Monk, M., & Swain, J. (2000). Constraints on development and change to science teachers' practice in Egyptian classrooms. *Journal of Education for Teaching, 26,* 9–24.

Joy, S., & Kolb, D. A. (2007). Are there cultural differences in learning style? *International Journal of Intercultural Relations, 29,* 521–548.

King Saud University. (2008). *Annual report.* Riyadh, Saudi Arabia: King Saud University Press.

Kitayama, S., & Cohen, D. (Eds.). (2007). *Handbook of cultural psychology.* New York, NY: Guilford Press.

Mababaya, N. D., & Mababaya, M. O. (2005, September). *Religious curricular offerings in the Muslim world: Challenges and prospects in the light of strategic planning, social networking, modern technological advancement and globalization of Islamic knowledge.* Paper presented at the International Seminar on Religious Curricular in the Muslim World: Challenges and Prospects, Kuala Lumpur, Malaysia.

Mahrous, A. A., & Ahmed, A. A. (2009). A cross-cultural investigation of students' perceptions of the effectiveness of pedagogical tools: The Middle East, the

United Kingdom, and the United States. Available from *Journal of Studies in International Education Online,* http://jsie.sagepub.com

Mansour, N. (2007, September). *Cooperative learning in Saudi Arabia schools: Teachers' understanding and intentions.* Paper presented at the British Educational Research Association (BERA) annual conference at Institute of Education, University of London, London, UK.

Marshall, K. (2004, September). Let's clarify the way we use the word "curriculum." *Education Week, 24*(1), p. 43.

McLoughlin, C. (1999). Culturally responsive technology use: Developing an online community of learners. *British Journal of Educational Technology, 30,* 231–243.

McLoughlin, C., & Oliver, R. (2000). Designing learning environments for cultural inclusivity: A case study of indigenous online learning at tertiary level. *Australian Journal of Educational Technology, 16,* 58–72.

Metz, H. C. (Ed.). (1992). *Saudi Arabia: A country study.* Washington, DC: GPO for the Library of Congress.

Ministry of Higher Education. (2007). *Annual report, Arab Republic of Egypt.* Cairo, Egypt: Ministry of Higher Education.

Reeves, T., & Reeves, P. (1997). Effective dimensions of interactive learning on the World Wide Web. In B. Khan (Ed.), *Web-based instruction* (pp. 59–66). Englewood Cliffs, NJ: Educational Technology Publications.

Saadate, G. I., & Abdullah, M. (1997). *Educational curricula in the 21st century.* Kuwait: Al Falah Publishing House.

Smith T., & Renk, K. (2007). Predictors of academic-related stress in college students: An examination of coping, social support, parenting, and anxiety. *NASPA Journal, 44,* 405–431.

St. Clair, K. L., & Groccia, J. E. (2009). Change to social justice education: Higher education strategy. In K. Skubikowski, C. Wright, & R. Graf (Eds.), *Social justice education: Inviting faculty to transform their institutions* (pp. 70–84). Sterling, VA: Stylus.

Tanner, D., & Tanner, L. (1995). *Curriculum development: Theory into practice* (3rd ed.). Englewood Cliffs, NJ: Merrill.

The World Bank Report. (2002). *Project appraisal document on a proposed loan in the amount of US$50 million to the Arab Republic of Egypt for a higher education enhancement project.* Published by the World Bank, Human Development Sector, Middle East and North Africa Region. Report No: 23332-EGYT. Available from http://www-wds.worldbank.org

UNESCO. (2003). *Higher education in the Arab Region 1998–2003.* Paris, France: UNESCO.

UNESCO. (2005). *Towards knowledge societies.* Paris, France: UNESCO.

UNESCO Institute for Statistics Database. (2010). *EFA global monitoring report.* Retrieved from http://gmr.uis.unesco.org

Vassall-Fall, D. A. (2008, March). *No memorization: Helping students to understand, process, analyze and retain information.* Paper presented at the International Institute on Muslim Unity's Conference Higher Education in the Muslim World: Challenges and Prospects, International Islamic University of Malaysia, Kuala Lumpur, Malaysia. Retrieved from http://www.learninglinkco.net/files/MalayHandout.pdf

Wild, M., & Henderson, L. (1997). Contextualizing learning in the World Wide Web: Accounting for the impact of culture. *Education and Information Technologies, 14,* 179–192.

CHAPTER 20

Strategic Curriculum Change

CAMILLE B. KANDIKO AND PAUL BLACKMORE

T he curriculum is at the heart of learning and teaching in all institutions of higher education. The curriculum can be considered at several different levels, from the microenvironment of the module through to program, degree, and up to university, national, and supra-national curricula. There has been a recent global trend of large-scale, university-level curriculum change. This chapter uses data collected from a yearlong project exploring university-level curriculum change at research-intensive universities around the world to develop a dynamic model of curriculum change, exploring the forces for change, curriculum structures, and goals and outcomes.

There are convergent and divergent influences on curriculum change. For example, national policies may regulate and standardize the curriculum, whereas disciplinary and professional organizations may contradict national agendas. The introduction of strategic curriculum change needs to account for national and international policies and trends, the local context, and disciplinary differences. University-wide curriculum change often cedes control of disciplinary content to the local level, but works across schools and faculties to enhance student learning experiences through broader and interdisciplinary content, more innovative pedagogies, and integration with the cocurriculum.

This chapter draws on a number of sources. Curriculum change sits at the intersection of national and university policy, educational research, and academic practice, which creates a complicated literature. Institutional policy can be challenging to research: Often the curriculum is decided among university committees, and working papers are constantly changed and proposals amended, creating a vast, and usually inaccessible, grey literature. Final curriculum plans tend to be distilled into a small number of general and aspirational sound bites (e.g., academic excellence) and detailed sets of course requirements for students. Much of the academic literature focuses on the broad nature and purposes of higher education, often with little reference to the implementation of such designs (Barnett & Coate, 2004; Bridges, 2000; Knight, 2001; Parker, 2003). Finally, academic practice may differ at a departmental-level or an individual instructor–level from institutional policy.

Methodology

The sources of information about curriculum change are varied, often restricted-access, in addition to being sensitive and often work-in-progress. Therefore, to discover the heart of curriculum change—the intersection of the purposes of change, the forces affecting it, and the intended goals and the actual outcomes—we visited a number of universities that conducted or were conducting curriculum change initiatives. To begin this process, we conducted a Web-based survey to uncover what major initiatives were occurring in undergraduate curriculum change, which included checking hundreds of institutions' websites and reviewing the informal higher education literature. To narrow the scope of the project, and best reflect the nature of the institutions leading on the project, we limited our research to university-wide undergraduate curriculum change at research-intensive universities. We concentrated on institutions recently active in curriculum change initiatives, from the beginning of the project in 2009.

As a result of this work, we discovered a group of institutions that were leading international trends in undergraduate curriculum change. We selected a subset of these institutions for comprehensive site-visits, which allowed us to have in-depth conversations about four main areas: the policies, purposes, processes, and outcomes of curriculum change. We met with senior administrators, disciplinary-based academics, and staff involved in curriculum change. In this chapter, we often speak about changes generally rather than directly citing institutions. Curriculum change is often a contentious and political endeavor, and we were fortunate to have very candid conversations about change processes and have respected their sensitive nature. Our chapter draws on data from institutions on four continents, six countries, and from more than 20 site visits. Although higher education is a global business, it is always contextualized by national and local variables. Although there is much to learn from institutions elsewhere, each university has its own context, including its mission, vision, goals, staff, students, location, and history.

We use Groccia's (St. Clair & Groccia, 2009) model of teaching and learning (see Chapter 1, this volume) as a starting point for a discussion of curriculum change. The model depicts the teaching and learning processes that feed into learning outcomes, and vice versa. This chapter works to develop a "mirror" model of how learning outcomes can be facilitated through curriculum structures and features, and what forces can be used to achieve curriculum change.

Background

We conceptualize the curriculum as all student learning, including that beyond what is taught (Bridges, 2000). The *curriculum* may be defined as a set of policies, or requirements, but it may also be seen as a process that students move through. However, the relative importance of content and process may change over time. Kathryn Dey Huggett, Nora Smith, and Clifton Conrad (2010) highlighted the shift in the mid-1980s from a content focus in curriculum discussions to interest in educational processes (Lattuca & Stark, 1994), which mirrors a broader move from teacher-focused to student-focused learning (Barr & Tagg, 1995).

Undergraduate curriculum change in research-intensive universities can be understood in relation to global shifts in society, politics, economics, and education. In the competitive global knowledge economy, nations and institutions compete to attract the best and brightest staff and students. There is a worldwide trend toward mass enrollment in higher education, knowledge and skill specialization, and credentialing. Employers expect students to graduate with various skills, attributes, and aspects of knowledge, many of which did not exist a generation ago. Many universities have concluded that the curriculum in place does not meet, or could better meet, the needs of society and students, which has led to a general broadening of education at all levels, as well as to increased levels of specialization in some curricula. For example, the former is seen in the move to putting majors in a wider context at the University of Aberdeen and the latter in the explosion of molecular biology subfields. Lisa Lattuca (2010) outlined this tension in contemporary curriculum development between broader liberal arts approaches and more specialized majors and degrees, which is played out at the department, school/college, and university levels in battles for space, content, and process in the curriculum.

In analyzing global practices in curriculum development, we looked at various curriculum characteristics, which were implemented in three main ways. First, they could be infused in the existing curriculum or embedded in new modules (e.g., communication skills). Second, they could be required elements, again through existing courses or through new developments (e.g., foreign language requirements). Last, they could be structured, such as in core modules for all students or through distributed elective elements (e.g., Solving World Problems courses). We saw that institutions often placed the responsibility to meet such requirements on students, although some provided more support to embed these in the curriculum and assist students in meeting them.

Many broad influences shape a curriculum, set its scope, and provide a sense of coherence throughout the educational experience. Some of these are seen across a number of countries, but although there are similarities across the globe, the curriculum is always shaped by the local context. All of the institutions that we visited grappled with these issues in different ways. The next section discusses how issues of competition, scope, and coherence, among other issues, can drive curriculum change.

Forces Driving Curriculum Change

Deborah Dezure (2010) noted four broad collections of forces for change in U.S. higher education, including external critiques, focused largely on graduates' attributes; calls for accountability from government and for greater attention to student assessment; greater variation in incoming student preparation, along with demographic changes within the student body, and declining interest in science and technology subjects; and new developments in pedagogy and learning technologies. External forces included national reports such as *A Nation at Risk* (National Commission on Excellence in Education, 1983) and the Boyer report (1998), along with pressure from business and industry for graduates with a broad range of skills, and critiques of graduates' disengagement from society and citizen groups.

In the United Kingdom, the central government has worked over many years to create a market environment for higher education (Brown, 2010; Molesworth, Nixon, & Scullion, 2010). Other external forces can be seen in recent arguments for universities to make an increased contribution to economic prosperity, reflected in a series of reports (Browne, 2010; CBI, 2009; DIUS, 2009; Leitch, 2006; Sainsbury, 2007).

Similarly, in our research, we identified six general drivers for curriculum change: financial and marketing concerns; university restructuring; a focus on educational aims and learning outcomes; change through a strategic planning process; crises, including natural disaster, budget, social and political change; and external agencies. However, some drivers, particularly financial ones, are often hidden in the discourse, whereas others, such as learning outcomes and goals, are widely promoted internally and externally. There are always many drivers for curriculum change, with various university constituencies more responsive to some than others. Overall, positive drivers, such as widening the breadth of the curriculum, increasing student choice, and simplifying and streamlining degree options, seem to be more successful in achieving change than are negative drivers, such as low student satisfaction or financial crisis.

Finance and Marketing

Financial and marketing drivers can provide the motivation for change but are often seen by staff and academics as part of a hidden agenda. Marketing efforts (or "branding" initiatives) can be drivers, done as part of public relations efforts afterward, or more commonly some combination of both approaches. For example, one of our participant institutions changed its curriculum partly to market the institution, although the stated intention was a desire to ensure that all the students felt "connected" to other students and the history of the institution.

Restructuring

Restructuring, such as changing how disciplines and departments are organized, internal reporting relationships, and how degree-levels are defined, can be a driver internally or externally (e.g., through the Bologna Process or institutional mergers). We found that for some institutions, restructuring was mainly a bureaucratic streamlining process, and for others, it became the impetus for a major curriculum overhaul. For one institution, a key driver for change was the excessive number of degrees, programs, choices, and requirements for students. Thus, the change was largely an administrative process that moved into deeper curricular and pedagogical issues including articulation with postgraduate degrees. From the student and faculty point of view, there was a need to simplify rules, procedures, and definitions for teaching responsibilities to free time for research. The institution also wanted to ensure student mobility, especially within the bachelor's degree. Several other universities discussed attempts to reduce the number of options within majors—there were instances where more course units were in the catalogue than there were students at the university, creating massive administrative burdens and confusion for students.

Educational Aims

For some institutions, a force for change was a wish to develop structured learning outcomes and the broad purposes of a degree. At one institution, the senior academic staff felt that the core values of a democratic society were not present in the curriculum and that these ideals might have been lost in the marketization of the university. In addition, the university recognized that both it and its students often face moral and societal dilemmas. It thus saw a need for students to develop critical intellectual inquiry and moral and ethical values.

One institution noted that externally, particularly from the government and employer groups, there is a desire for generic, less-specialized skills among graduates, and thus an emphasis on broader training. Another university began the change process by spending several months discussing the nature and purpose of the curriculum to reach agreement on a set of educational principles. The changes agreed upon included a focus on understanding disciplines in a wider context and free space in the curriculum for the development of new courses. In many institutions, the need for particular learning outcomes was not the initial driver for curriculum change, but became prominent during the change process, offering an example of the way in which a positive driver for change can be used strategically to gain support and build momentum for change.

Strategic Planning

Other curriculum change forces include the increasing use of institutional strategic planning through which some institutions link the undergraduate curriculum with the mission, vision, and aims of the institution. Questions about what constituted the distinctiveness of a higher education curriculum were often voiced at an institutional level, and were sometimes a matter of national debate. Institutions that had less success did not seem to have a firm grasp of the strengths and weaknesses of their current curriculum. Some of this problem resulted from institutional challenges but for many institutions, this issue reflected uncertainty at a national level. Tension can also exist between the need to respond to local drivers, particularly social inclusion, and the desire to compete internationally for academic staff and students. However, the greatest challenge is often in balancing external drivers with internal ones because faculty often take a strong position that is at odds with the institution's strategic direction. For example, one disciplinary academic noted,

> There are economic and social drivers. There is much attractive higher education discourse but a lot is bad too. I am skeptical of policy-driven curriculum change; the drivers should be disciplines and professions . . . The change needs to come from within the disciplines. I see educational development/academic development and teaching and learning as mediators of change. I see that there is a danger of bypassing knowledge in the curriculum.

Such perspectives were common in discussions with discipline-based academics, and created tension with leaders of curriculum change, an issue we discuss further later.

Crises

Crises, including natural disasters, budget cuts, social upheaval, and political changes, can be drivers to motivate an institution into action and bring attention to the need for curriculum change. South African universities in the postapartheid era are a key example of this process. Across many different countries, professional and accrediting bodies were often drivers of curriculum change within specific schools or disciplinary areas, particularly when there is a direct link with employment, such as in pharmacy or medicine.

External Agencies

In contrast to internal discussions about educational aims and purposes, external agencies, such as quality assurance bodies, accrediting agencies, and professional societies, were the primary driver for curriculum change in many universities. Whether these external forces were actually the main impetus or whether they made it easier to "sell" change within the institution is debatable. One senior academic said that an institution needs to make use of any and all external drivers, whether it is competition, budgets, students, or Bologna processes. He believed that institutions need to use their situation strategically to make change happen.

Governments had a significant role in driving several change initiatives. For example, across Hong Kong, the government's move from 3- to 4-year degrees was the driver for re-thinking the curriculum. In one institution in the Netherlands, a university-wide curriculum change initiative with a model for small-scale education was driven largely by the Bologna restructuring.

One of the most interesting findings from the site visits was the role that employers, professional, and accrediting bodies played in curriculum change initiatives. We heard repeatedly from institutions that had not done a full-scale curriculum change, or failed in such efforts, that these bodies made change difficult or impossible because of their standards and requirements. However, several institutions that had successfully conducted curriculum changes found these sorts of bodies to be very supportive. As one institution noted, talk about accreditation as a reason not to change provides a shield for inactivity. One senior administrator claimed that academics often use professional and accrediting bodies as barriers to change, as a means of safeguarding disciplinary autonomy. Another institution bypassed academic staff: Central administrators went to professional bodies and accrediting councils to gain their opinion, and eventually their support, for curriculum changes they desired to see implemented within the university.

Careful research needs to be done with external agencies to gather opinions and data about what is necessary in a curriculum and what graduates should be capable of doing. This process can include general skills as well as discipline-specific and professionally mandated attributes. Similar linking can be done with the secondary school curriculum, and what skills and experiences incoming students bring with them. These ideas feed into the structures and features of curriculum change initiatives, which we discuss in the next section.

Structuring Curriculum Change

As noted, we focused on institutions that conducted university-wide curriculum change. Many of these universities sought a set of common learning experiences for all students, including features such as experiential learning, common core courses, interdisciplinary exposure, and research opportunities. For some institutions, these modifications required (or were a consequence of) changing degree lengths. Some institutions moved portions of disciplinary knowledge, particularly professional and vocational aspects, to the postgraduate level and thus dedicated more space in their undergraduate curricula to innovative curriculum content and processes. However, for most institutions, curriculum change meant adding features to existing discipline-based curricula, and thus risking a loss of coherence for students and staff. Some institutions, however, took the opportunity to reconsider the basis of coherence.

Coherence

> The notion of coherence is parasitic upon that of subjects as forgiveness is parasitic upon sin. (Dancy, 1982, p. 21)

Coherence, or "connectedness," indicates the need to link, sequence, and structure various curricular elements and help students connect what they study with their lives and work. For many institutions, coherence is managed within the disciplines. However, coherence becomes a particular concern when institutions offer unstructured elective options. The question then arises: What is the relationship between electives and majors? How electives relate to the degree is of both theoretical and practical concern. If students have free choice in electives, it can be hard for them to experience the curriculum as a coherent whole. One institution that introduced significant flexibility and choice in elective modules has subsequently introduced themed pathways to provide students with a sense of coherence.

There are also challenges for coherence with options for joint degrees (and joint majors, both structured and unstructured), minors, and their various combinations. Some universities opt for more student choice, allowing double majors both within schools and across disciplines. Students can structure how broad (akin to a liberal arts degree) or discipline-specific they wish their education to be. For other universities, dual degree options are built into the curriculum and structured dual degrees are already available.

Although the tradition of defining coherence in terms of the discipline remains strong in research-led institutions, there are other possible foci. Some curricula aim to ensure vocational and professional competence and a more general preparedness for work. Most curriculum changes aspire to equip graduates with the abilities to succeed both as workers and as members of society. For example, the underpinning aim of the Harvard University General Education curriculum is to navigate the tension between general education and applied education while recognizing the need to provide connections between educational experience in the university and the demands of life outside of it. As another institution noted, there is a need to develop graduates with an education that is "fit for purpose."

For some institutions, curriculum coherence involved incorporating changes from the secondary-schooling system as well. In South Africa, this strategy was made necessary because of the postapartheid revised school curriculum, the first cohorts from which are now enrolling in universities. In Hong Kong, the governmental education commission has restructured the entire education system, including primary, secondary, and tertiary levels. This change represents a particular challenge to faculty because they do not know the learning histories of the incoming students, a point underscored by medical and science faculties.

Features

We identified a number of distinctive curriculum features that universities adopted as a focal point for their change efforts. These features often arose from a number of differing forces, and following extensive discussion, resulted in a particular initiative. Perhaps as a consequence, these features often have multiple purposes and goals. For example, an institution might undertake a first-year initiative to help with retention efforts or final-year projects to link with postgraduate opportunities. All curriculum initiatives had some articulation of what a major means and all retained the major structure, although some opted to have interdisciplinary general education courses included as requirements for graduation. A common approach to curriculum change is through general education requirements, which allow an institution to retain traditional disciplinary degree structures while offering exposure to other ways of thinking. A broad intellectual base rather than a narrow disciplinary one is the foundation of any institution's general education requirements. After all, most students do not go on to become disciplinary-based academics or to do postgraduate research, so they need a broader education that prepares them for a work environment in which they are likely to change jobs and careers and in which the conditions of their work are likely to change. However, space has to be found within the curriculum to accommodate these goals. The three primary means for freeing such space is through (a) condensing disciplinary knowledge, in either time or content; (b) lengthening a degree, often from 3 to 4 years; and (c) moving some disciplinary knowledge to the masters level.

Universities structured elective units in many ways, some of which focused on content and others on structures. These included

- focusing core courses on exploring "Canon" texts and "Great Books,"
- exploring major questions and ways of thinking about the world,
- using a distribution model of general education requirements,
- completing student choice within an elective framework,
- focusing on disciplines in greater depth,
- developing interdisciplinary modules for learning, and
- exploring disciplines in a wider context.

First-year seminars may be completed in a semester or a full year. One institution conducts a first-year experience program online that has an institutional focus to it. Another institution offers a spring capstone seminar that challenges first-year students to expand on the knowledge and skills acquired during the first two quarters of the year and to complete a substantive project of their own. To help engage students early on, one institution conducts first-year interest groups (FIGs) in which students enroll in a cluster of three classes organized around a central theme (i.e., literary imagination). This format helps students make the transition to learning at the university. Other institutions adopted senior (final-year) capstone courses, which were either a stand-alone research project or a research project incorporated into a regular course.

Some universities offer curriculum enhancement for select students, such as advanced research opportunities, which are often pathways for students intending further academic study or an academic career. Imperial College runs a well-regarded Undergraduate Research Opportunities Programme (UROP). It functions as a flagship and landmark program, but it is challenging to create opportunities for students to link with research centers and to make the initiative more widely embedded across the institution.

Another option is to offer an alternative or separate honors curriculum. For example, the University of Western Australia plans to offer a bachelor of philosophy degree based on elite entry for the top 2 percent of the age cohort. It will be a 4-year honors degree that can be taken in any discipline. It is likely to contain small cohorts, around 100 students, divided into small groups, each of which will conduct a joint multidisciplinary research project. The degree includes major and elective units, a 2-week residential time before the semester begins, and a guaranteed study abroad scholarship, and students can study or pursue scholarship abroad or participate in a summer-time experience. Students must take at least one foreign language unit. This program is offered as a signature degree that focuses on research throughout.

Utrecht University (UU) offers an alternative curriculum through its University College Utrecht (UCU) that is geared for elite students and is small and selective. UCU offers a broader education than the traditional degree option and is a residential-based program. UCU encourages students to enroll in a different field or attend a different institution for master's degrees, whereas most UU students continue on from the bachelor to master's at the same institution in the same degree program. Students choose a major and a minor, which can be in different faculties, although most students stay within one faculty.

Several institutions included work experience, internships, placements, or community volunteering experience in the curriculum. To link with the academic curriculum, this structure has to be organized by administrators and academics at the local, school, department, or discipline level, and it can be very difficult to "universalize" across the student body. Such activities are standard in some fields and disciplines, but not in line with others. In part, this situation relates to the purpose of degree and the level of vocational and professional training versus a more liberal arts "learning how to learn and think" perspective. It is very challenging to accomplish for all students, and some institutions have preferred to create opportunities for interested students only. For example, the University of Chicago has developed a largely student-run Community Service Center, which has more than 3,000 students involved in credit-bearing and volunteering activities.

Intentions for Learning

The overall intentions for students' learning are often the most publicized and featured elements of a curriculum change. All change initiatives involved an expression of what the institution intends that its students learn. Sometimes the initiatives were set out by the university as very general statements. In other cases, university leaders paid attention to the outcomes or goals that were reflected in curriculum statements. Another focal point has been the articulation and development of sets of graduate attributes—characteristics that individuals would develop through the course of study. All attributes are somewhat culturally bound, both at a national and local level. For example, at institutions we visited in the United States, and as noted previously, there was an emphasis less on the utility of employability and more on the role of universities in educating graduates who were equipped for social responsibility and citizenship. Institutions sometimes very generally express intentions as educational aims and principles, or more specifically as student learning outcomes, curriculum goals, or graduate attributes or skills. Universities varied in whether these intentions were strict requirements for students, structured in the formal curriculum and assessed, or offered as guides and signposts, and such intentions could be met through both the formal academic curriculum and the cocurriculum.

Outcomes and *goals* have the advantage of being relatively neutral terms. However, the idea that the learning outcomes either can or should be expressed in advance is contestable, and some terms acquire particular connotations. Although we note an important difference, institutions often link graduate attributes with employability and skills. This shift in the purpose of higher education is reflected in critiques that universities have moved "from understanding to skill, from knowing that to knowing how" (Bridges, 2000, p. 46), and this tension surfaced often in discussions we had with faculty and administrators. The issue of language about outcomes arose in discussions with several institutions. For example, one academic suggested that although learning was clearly central to a higher curriculum, the term *learning to learn* might be interpreted to be a competence approach to learning, and therefore be resisted. Institutions that were successful with a focus on outcomes appeared to have guiding principles, pathways for students to meet objectives, and achievable curriculum outcomes for students. Only with faculty support would they become embedded in the formal curriculum.

Goals and Aims

A number of universities adopted specific university-wide curriculum goals. However, it can be challenging to achieve agreement on cross-institutional outcomes because disciplinary groupings often seek autonomy in goal setting (Lattuca & Stark, 1994). The University of Western Australia developed disciplinary-based curriculum goals. At the exit from the bachelor degree, the goal is for all graduates to "think like (Major X)" in terms of methodologies, applications of methodologies, and skill sets, and to be able to communicate like "an X" within the discourse of the discipline. The goal is to give students the skills to solve interdisciplinary world problems from a disciplinary perspective. At Temple University, there is a strong commitment to the importance of a general education curriculum that meets employability goals such as analysis and critical thinking without being too narrow or prescriptive.

The new Harvard General Education curriculum has four overarching goals for a general education that

- prepares students for civic engagement;
- teaches students to understand themselves as products of—and participants in—traditions of art, ideas, and values;
- prepares students to respond critically and constructively to change; and
- develops students' understanding of the ethical dimension of what they say and do.

Learning Outcomes

The University of Wisconsin–Madison (UW–M) provides a link between educational aims and learning outcomes. These are supported in the curriculum by a series of essential learning outcomes that were developed through the Association of American Colleges and Universities (AAC&U) in consultation with employers, faculty, staff, and alumni regarding the simple question, "What qualities and skills do you want in college graduates?" UW-M identified four core areas under which the essential learning outcomes fall for students:

- *Knowledge of human cultures and the physical and natural world.* This outcome is achieved through an engagement with major questions that are both contemporary and enduring.
- *Intellectual and practical skills.* This outcome is achieved across the curriculum by providing increasingly more challenging problems, projects, and standards of performance.
- *Personal and social responsibility.* This outcome is achieved through students' active involvement with diverse communities based around real-world challenges.
- *Integrative learning.* This outcome is demonstrated through knowledge, skills, and responsibilities developed in one context applied in new settings to meet complex problems.

The Hong Kong government requires student learning outcomes in its new education system across the course, program, and degree level. There are a number of approaches to meeting these outcomes at the universities in Hong Kong. In one university, outcomes are a key element in the teaching and learning strategy, and there is pressure for the outcomes to be integrated in a process of program design, reflection, and development. Assessment within the university is geared for outcomes, and they are built in at the course and program levels. Another Hong Kong institution took an outcomes-based approach for the whole curriculum. The learning outcomes stem from the educational aims and are expressed in faculty-based learning outcomes and then course-based outcomes. These outcomes are also tied to assessment modes and types of learning as well as pedagogies. At all institutions, there was a navigation of the tension between learning for learning's sake and an outcomes-based instrumental employability agenda.

Graduate Attributes

Graduate attributes were the most discussed aspect of curriculum change. Several institutions preferred to adopt the term *attribute* rather than *capability, skill,* or *competence* because it refers to a personal quality or characteristic that is broader and more flexible in its definition and application. Some institutions felt that a focus on graduate attributes, because they could be communicated quite readily and interpreted flexibly, could be a driver for curriculum change. However, graduate attributes approaches are also a very contentious subject, particularly for many discipline-based academics, who sometimes believe that they represent a mechanistic, overly prescriptive, and instrumental view of university learning. In one university, graduate attributes approaches were seen by the humanities as "ridiculous and irrelevant." Some faculty felt that there had been a managerialist approach to developing attributes, without faculty input. The faculty felt the attributes needed to come from departments and be put into the curriculum, rather than the other way around. Or as one disciplinary academic put it, graduate attributes are "fine" in themselves, but she wanted her chemistry students to be able to do chemistry.

There were many different approaches to articulating, defining, requiring, and assessing graduate attributes. At the University of Stellenbosch, the Centre for Teaching and Learning offers seminars on the scholarship of teaching and learning, as well as functional workshops on developing attributes. There are also generic skills modules, such as study skills and thinking skills, which represent an effort to infuse writing and other attributes into the curriculum. This initiative is grounded in a metaphor of building a "brick wall." The "bricks" are the disciplines and the "mortar" is provided by generic skills. When learning is at its most successful, mortar is said to "infuse within the bricks" as well.

One institution felt that its adoption of graduate attributes had been a success and had gained influence within the university, based on feedback from academics and students. It was noted that the relationship between graduate attributes and their expression in degree programs and assessment had been a weakness. However, attributes offer a focal point outside individual faculty specialty and can be helpful in thinking about the larger university-wide curriculum. Another institution was introducing e-portfolios as a vehicle to embed the attributes in the curriculum by giving students a medium to self-report their attributes. However, across the university, how graduate attributes are implemented varies.

As one academic summarized graduate attributes, some can "be taught," but most are "absorbed," so paying attention to the environment for learning is essential. However, this possibility then raises the question of how to measure the "embeddedness" of attributes—both to the scope the attributes are infused in the curriculum and to the extent students are engaged with them. Graduate attributes were also conceptualized by academics as links— not just between the curriculum and students but also between staff and students. For example, the University of Aberdeen considered the use of trained and mentored postgraduate students as a means of teaching graduate attributes.

Putting It All Together

This view of university-wide curriculum change, derived from many interviews across a large number of institutions, highlights many of the issues that arise when a broad review of the purposes and processes of teaching and learning is undertaken. Through analyzing policies, we looked at who was involved and how they affected outcomes in curriculum change efforts. We also looked at the scope of change initiatives and how students developed a sense of coherence through their degree programs. Our study found six major drivers for curriculum change and analyzed how drivers were used strategically to build support for change. We noted how structures and features were used to create a curriculum that students progress through in their course of study. Finally, we found numerous ways institutions were trying to capture the intentions of learning, both for students' educational benefit and for external reporting. Based on this view, we have developed a model that "mirrors" Groccia's model of teaching and learning (St. Clair & Groccia, 2009; see Figure 20.1). This model signals that learning outcomes are a key feature of teaching and learning processes as well as broader curriculum change.

Groccia's model (see Chapter 1 this volume) shows the ways in which contextual aspects for learners can be considered through teaching processes to result in outcomes for learners. We believe that our approach complements

Figure 20.1   Model of Strategic Curriculum Development

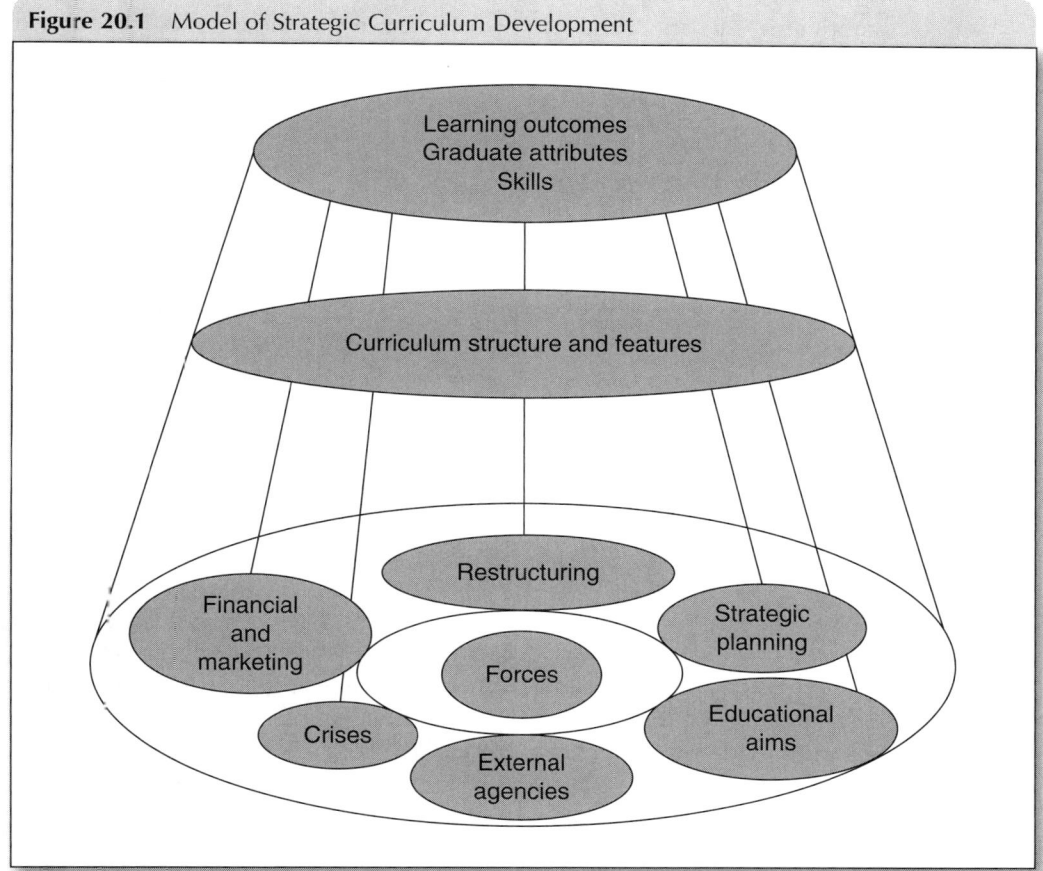

Groccia's by showing ways in which system and institutional concerns influence decisions on curriculum and, in turn, on the outcomes of learning. The model indicates how forces operating on curriculum change are enacted through curriculum structures and features to lead to outcomes of learning. We now finally turn to comments on several other aspects of curriculum change that emerge from this model.

Curriculum Change in a Wider Context

Curriculum change indicates other aspects of the university beyond the disciplines that need to be considered to meet desired goals and outcomes. For many institutions, further work included liaising with secondary school leaders about what students were learning before university entrance. Institutions also had to engage with employer and professional bodies to know what attributes and skills they were looking for in graduates. All institutions found that even a narrow attempt at curriculum change had far-reaching consequences. Internally, these issues included assessment, evaluation, quality issues, the cocurriculum, staff, and resources. Externally, issues arose over local, national, and international student recruitment; access and widening participation concerns; and graduates' attributes for continuing education and employment. Many of these issues were raised earlier, and several of these that emerged across a number of institutions are discussed here.

Quality and Assessment

Several other important aspects of curriculum change emerge from our model of strategic curriculum development. First, how do institutions address issues of support and quality? We discussed this question through a number of examples, often in the context of national quality assurance frameworks. In several countries, there has been a move from standards and the idea of "fitness of purpose" to "fitness for purpose" as the overarching educational goal. Thus, the focus of concern for quality assurance becomes not "what" is being done but "how well" it is being done.

A second issue that emerged was how institutions address evaluation and assessment. This issue included assessment schemes for students at the module and degree level. Several institutions dropped honors degrees and moved to a U.S.-style grade point average (GPA) system. We also uncovered issues about the evaluation of the change process and the impact of new curricula. Several institutions worked throughout the change process to merge the new curriculum with standard university evaluation schemes. However, many institutions found the change process so challenging that there was little drive left to evaluate the change process. As one academic noted, "We have gone too far to go back now, we all will just have to live with it."

Academic and Staff Development

A third issue that emerged was academic and staff development, which includes initiatives to use postgraduate students in teaching, advising, and mentoring capacities. In one institution, although there are formal academic development courses, academic leaders found that teaching circles were an effective means of developing new ideas about the connection between teaching and learning and the curriculum. The teaching circles involved meeting once every 2 weeks for one semester to discuss particular teaching goals. There is usually some incentive for membership of the group, such as additional pay or time release. Faculty from different departments compose these teaching circles, hence facilitating connections across disciplines.

Another institutional approach to academic development and curriculum change is the team approach. To facilitate curriculum innovation, faculty meet with teams including academic developers, student representatives, and library staff to develop courses and assignments. This strategy enhances links among support staff, students, and teaching staff, enabling new perspectives and making the process of change a supported and collaborative one. Further considerations in relation to administrative structures include issues related to academic staff, either in developing current staff to teach a new curriculum or in appointing new staff to teach or support a new curriculum.

The Curriculum and Society

Finally, there are issues about how a new curriculum might have implications for the local community, for incoming students and outgoing graduates. Equality and access structures are important, particularly for access to honors programs, as are considerations about who could be excluded or underrepresented. There are also issues about pathways to and from degrees. Numerous times we heard about the importance of linking with secondary school systems, particularly if there were changes to the school curriculum as happened in South Africa and Hong Kong.

Conclusion

All too often in discussing higher education, little attention is paid to curriculum issues, even though they have a profound effect on what is taught and learned. We showed that, for many different reasons, universities have embarked on fundamental reviews of their curricula of a kind that have rarely been attempted in the past. The situation is a highly complex one, characterized by many voices and by tensions in conceptions of the purposes of universities and the desired outcomes of university learning.

Parallel discussions are taking place in institutions worldwide and in many cases institutions are learning from one another. What seems clear is that the higher education curriculum, for so long a "given" in universities that have tended to favor incremental change in their development of academic provision, has now become very much a "live" issue, presenting challenges but also opportunities for beneficial change.

References

Barnett, R., & Coate, K. (2004). *Engaging the curriculum in higher education.* Maidenhead, UK: Society for Research into Higher Education and the Open University Press.

Barr, R. B., & Tagg, J. (1995). From teaching to learning: A new paradigm for undergraduate education. *Change, 27*(5), 13–25.

Boyer Commission on Education Undergraduates in the Research University. (1998). *Reinventing undergraduate education: A blueprint for America's research universities.* Stony Brook: SUNY at Stony Brook for the Carnegie Foundation for the Advancement of Teaching.

Bridges, D. (2000). Back to the future: The higher education curriculum in the 21st century. *Cambridge Journal of Education, 30,* 37–55.

Brown, R. (2010). *Higher education and the market.* Abingdon, UK: Routledge.

Browne, J. (2010). *Securing a sustainable future for higher education.* Retrieved from www.independent.gov.uk/browne-report

CBI. (2009). *Stronger together—Businesses and universities in turbulent times.* Available from http://highereducation.cbi.org.uk/press_release/00231/

Dancy, J. (1982). The notion of coherence in the curriculum. *Oxford Review of Education, 8,* 21–26.

Department for Innovation, Universities and Skills (DIUS). (2009). *Building Britain's future—New industry, new jobs.* Retrieved September 12, 2011, from http://www.bis.gov.uk/files/file51023.pdf

Dey Huggett, K., Smith, N. C., & Conrad, C. F. (2010). *Traditional and contemporary perspectives.* Retrieved from http://education.stateuniversity.com/pages/1896/Curriculum-Higher-Education.html

Dezure, D. (2010). *Innovations in the undergraduate curriculum.* Retrieved from http://education.stateuniversity.com/pages/1896/Curriculum-Higher-Education.html

Knight, P. T. (2001). Complexity and curriculum: A process approach to curriculum-making. *Teaching in Higher Education, 6,* 369–381.

Lattuca, L. R. (2010). *National reports on the undergraduate curriculum.* Retrieved from http://education.stateuniversity.com/pages/1894/Curriculum-Higher-Education-NATIONAL-REPORTS-ON-UNDERGRADUATE-CURRICULUM.html

Lattuca, L. R., & Stark, J. S. (1994). Will disciplinary perspectives impede curricular reform? *Journal of Higher Education, 65,* 401–426.

Leitch, L. (2006). *Prosperity for all in the global economy—World-class skills.* Retrieved from http://www.hm-treasury.gov.uk/leitch_review_index.htm

Molesworth, M., Nixon, L., & Scullion, R. (2010). *The marketisation of higher education: The student as consumer.* Abingdon, UK: Routledge.

National Commission on Excellence in Education. (1983). *A nation at risk: The imperative for educational reform.* Washington, DC: Author.

Parker, J. (2003). Reconceptualising the curriculum: From commodification to transformation. *Teaching in Higher Education, 8,* 529–543.

Sainsbury, D. (2007). *The race to the top: A review of government's science and innovation policies.* Retrieved from http://www.hm-treasury.gov.uk/sainsbury_index.htm

St. Clair, K. L., & Groccia, J. E. (2009). Change to social justice education: Higher education strategy. In K. Skubikowski, C. Wright, & R. Graf (Eds.), *Social justice education: Inviting faculty to transform their institutions* (pp. 70–84). Sterling, VA: Stylus.

PART VII

Understanding Learning

Visualizing Knowledge Structures of University Teaching to Relate Pedagogic Theory and Academic Practice

IAN KINCHIN

> *"To be knowledgeable in some area is to understand the inter-relationships among the important concepts in that domain"*
>
> (Goldsmith, Johnson, & Acton, 1991, p. 88)

In this chapter, higher education is considered from a knowledge structures perspective that focuses on the qualitative arrangement of elements of understanding rather than on the quantitative assessment of acquired information. These knowledge structures have been elucidated through the application of concept mapping as developed by Joseph Donald Novak (2010). This chapter draws on a diverse literature considering the importance of knowledge structures from a range of theoretical viewpoints and draws on the author's direct observations made on several thousand concept maps during the past decade. From these observations has emerged a qualitative typology of knowledge structures based on the gross morphology of concept maps (Kinchin, Hay, & Adams, 2000), which has been shown to be a good indicator of students' learning success (Gerstner & Bognor, 2009), and has been used to distinguish between *competence* and *understanding* in professional education settings (e.g., James, Davies, Kinchin, Patel, & Whittlesea, 2010).

The qualitative interpretation of concept maps also offers a perspective on the wider consideration of the scholarship of teaching (Kinchin, 2009).

The concept mapping tool originated from Novak's work in the United States (Novak & Cañas, 2007) and has been successfully applied to studies in various learning contexts and cultural settings, including studies in the Middle East (e.g., Elhelou, 1997) and the Far East (e.g., Chiou, 2008). The success of concept mapping as a learning tool has occurred despite the evident clash between the explicit constructivist epistemology of its origins and the persistence of the positivist leanings of university education where teaching still relies heavily on lectures, rote learning, and dictation with examinations depending on the memorization of facts (as described in Western, Middle Eastern, and Far Eastern cultures, Chiou, 2008; Kinchin, 2001; Mahrous & Ahmed, 2009). The passive nature of student learning is often bemoaned by

Figure 21.1 A Concept Map Showing How the Main Ideas Presented Within This Chapter Interrelate

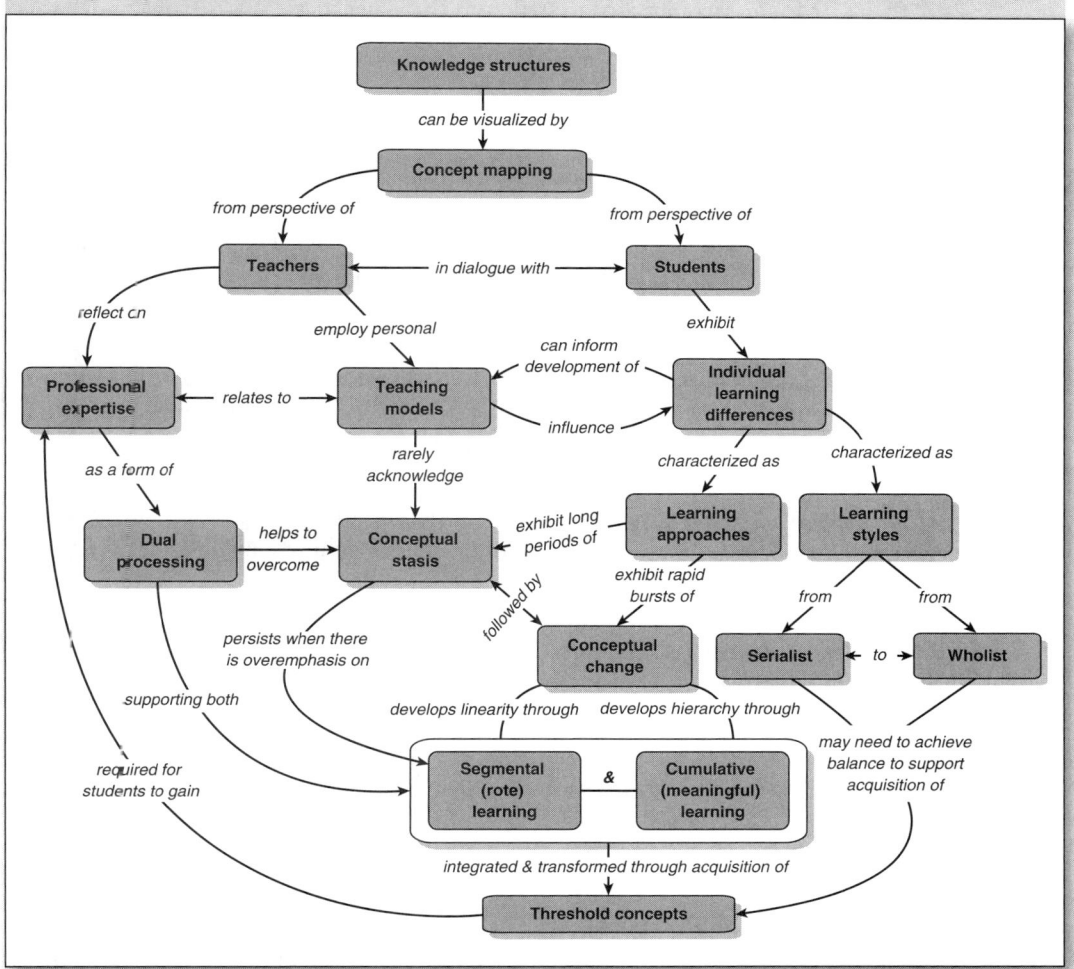

university teachers who would like to wean students away from the status quo of "spoon-feeding," and the way in which students fail to question their role in the learning process (e.g., Lord, 1999). Concept mapping is a tool to enhance student metacognition and encourages students to question alternative perspectives in their learning (Ritchhart, Turner, & Hadar, 2009).

Underlying Structure

Figure 21.1 illustrates the foundation for the structure of this chapter. This figure can be used as a map to navigate and highlight the links between the theoretical concepts that follow—concepts that are usually described in the literature in isolation from each other. To set the trajectory for this chapter further, consider three deceptively simple statements drawn from the literature. The first is from Joseph Donald Novak and David Symington (1982, p. 8):

1. Moving from a linear structure to a hierarchical structure and back again is in some ways the fundamental educational problem.

This comment is taken from a rarely cited paper that expands the potential of concept mapping from a simple study-aid tool to a heuristic device that can be used to demonstrate the links between elements of pedagogic theory and to link theory with practice. In the years since this statement was written, this wider potential of concept mapping has emerged as a result of a qualitative analysis of map structures (i.e., morphology) rather than as an exclusive focus on the content expressed within the map (Kinchin et al., 2000). Within studies of student and teacher knowledge structures, the widespread occurrence of linear and hierarchical concept maps has stimulated analysis of the affordances (i.e., the range of learning behaviors that are initiated by certain teaching actions; Kinchin & Cabot, 2007) of these structures and the contribution they may make to higher education. Particular structures can be seen to populate different sections of a knowledge transformation cycle that underpins teaching episodes—alternating between linear and hierarchical (Kinchin & Hay, 2007).

The second quotation (Norman, 2005, p. 418) refers to the significance of the transformation of knowledge structures in the development of professional expertise:

2. Expertise lies in the availability of multiple representations of knowledge.

For the expert within a discipline, the translation of information from one format to another is second nature. For example, a clinician often compares a patient's case notes with a radiograph or a scientist translates a table of data into a graphical representation. Such multiple representations are taken for granted within certain contexts, but are often overlooked in the classroom environment. To fulfill the demands of the first two quotations, I include several figures to complement the inevitable linearity of the text and help expose the underlying networks that might be otherwise overlooked.

The third quotation is from Shoshanah Keiny's (2002, p. 208) work on educational change where she offers a definition of learning that stresses the key notions of engagement, development, and community:

3. To learn is to participate in and contribute to the evolution of the communal practice.

If learning is defined as being participatory and evolutionary within a community of practice, traditional models of teaching as transmission of information immediately become redundant. To contribute to the evolution of communal practice, the student voice has to be heard—with faculty acknowledging students as active producers of knowledge rather than as passive consumers of information (Gamache, 2002). Taken together, these three quotations point to the importance of the cyclical transformation of knowledge structures within the process of higher education.

I next will look at the value in visualizing knowledge structures to link four areas of contemporary education theory (models of expertise, punctuated learning models, student learning differences, and threshold concepts). In the final part of the chapter, I will then consider the implications for current practice (offering an analysis of e-learning as an exemplar) before concluding by briefly considering implications for faculty development.

Theory

Models of Expertise

Ian Kinchin and Lyndon Cabot (2010) claimed that development of university pedagogy needs to consider the nature of professional expertise and how this can be modeled for students. Kinchin and Cabot's dual processing model of expertise builds on the understanding that experts are able to oscillate meaningfully between linear knowledge that comes from experience and hierarchical knowledge that comes from understanding (see Figure 21.2). Whereas expert practitioners make the transitions from one knowledge structure to another in a seemingly automated manner, expert teachers need to be able to reflect on these transitions and model them for their students. The conscious reflection needed to move between these knowledge structures is seen as one of the distinctive qualities of expert teachers and has been described by Amy Tsui (2009) as the complementary capabilities of "theorizing practical knowledge" and "practicalizing theoretical knowledge." The visualization of understanding in this way has been considered a threshold concept in the development of university pedagogy (Kinchin, Cabot, & Hay, 2010).

Figure 21.2   Summary of a Dual-Processing Model of Expertise Relating Linear and Experiential Chains of Knowledge Indicating Competence to Hierarchical and Conceptual Networks Indicating Understanding

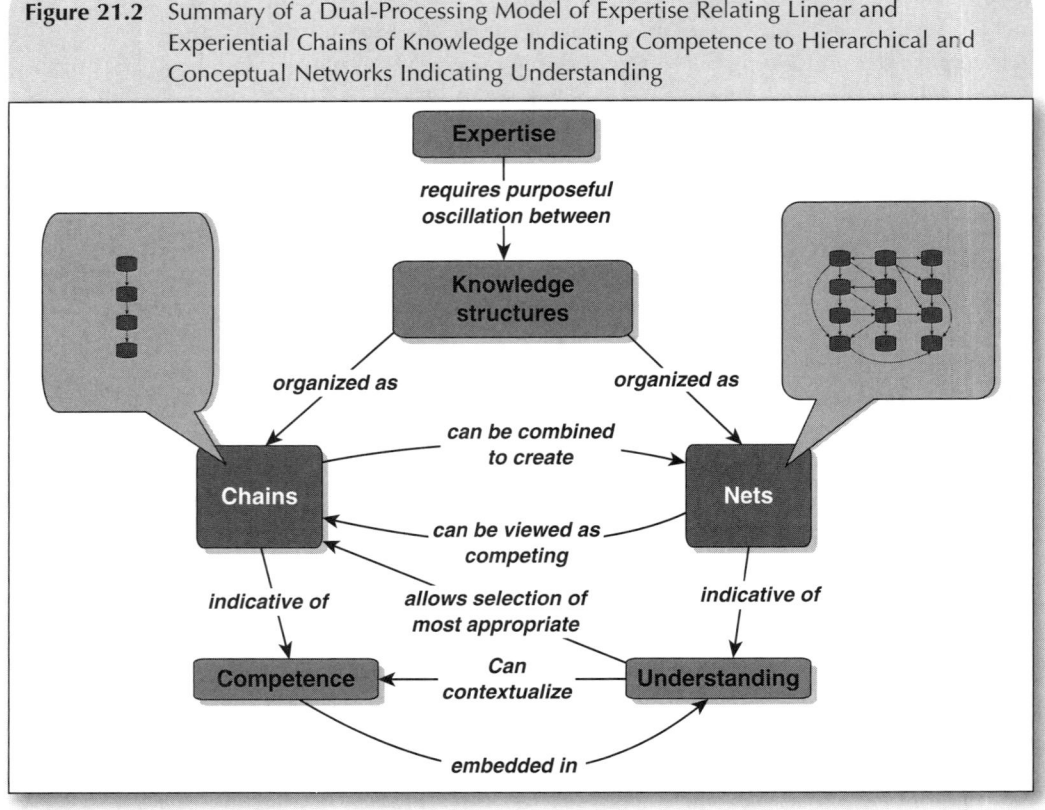

Source: Kinchin & Cabot, 2010.

Punctuated Learning

In conversation with teaching colleagues, I find a common recognition that students seem to spend long periods during which they appear to make little or no progress in their understanding of course content. These periods are punctuated by "aha" moments when things seem to fall into place. A punctuated model of learning may help explain this observation. Although curriculum documents persist in representing curricula as long lists of content in which the underlying expert structure is obscured from view, students have a tendency to view the elements within the lists of content as being of equal importance even though several decades of research has shown, as Joel Mintzes and Heather Quinn (2007, p. 301) have noted, "All knowledge is not of equal value, that some propositions take precedence over others in the knowledge frameworks of experts, and that teachers and students should focus their efforts on those fundamental concepts that are critical to understanding."

Coupled with the punctuated nature of learning is the recognition of the qualitatively different ways in which students learn various aspects of the curriculum. This separation is most pronounced within clinical subjects (e. g., medicine and dentistry) where the experiential learning of the clinic has to be related to the hierarchical, conceptual learning of the underlying basic sciences. This distinction exists in a more subtle, nuanced form in other academic disciplines. When one of these complementary knowledge structures is afforded undue dominance in the curriculum (typically the linear structures), students are not helped in making the link between the experiential and the conceptual learning. Students are then impeded in their progression toward expertise and so may exhibit conceptual stasis, where no development in understanding is observable despite the acquisition of more information (Kinchin, 2010).

One of the most developed conceptual frameworks for the generic consideration of the variation in knowledge structures is that based on Basil Bernstein's (2000) sociology of education. When elaborating on horizontal knowledge, Bernstein (p. 159) referred to a "segmental organization" in which "there is no necessary relation between what is learned in different segments." This view resonates with the recognition of rote learning of content without understanding (Kinchin et al., 2010; James et al., 2010). In contrast to horizontal structures, Bernstein (2000, p. 161) viewed hierarchical knowledge structures as attempting "to create very general propositions and theories, which integrate knowledge at lower levels, and in this way shows underlying uniformities across an expanding range of apparently different phenomena," which resonates with the view of integrated expert knowledge structures that are often hierarchical in structure (Bradley, Paul, & Seeman, 2006). Bernstein's framework has been developed by Karl Maton (2009, p. 44) to consider how "curriculum structures play a role in creating conditions for students to experience cumulative learning, where their understandings integrate and subsume previous knowledge, or segmented learning, where new ideas or skills are accumulated alongside rather than built on past knowledge." Such segmented learning equates to a surface approach that on its own would result from the serial acquisition of chains, and ultimately leads to cycles of non-learning (Kinchin, Lygo-Baker, & Hay, 2008).

Student Learning Differences in Styles and Approaches

Appreciation of student learning differences (whether developed from the learning styles tradition or from the approaches to learning tradition; Cuthbert, 2005) has encouraged moves toward greater student-centeredness in university teaching. This perspective adds uncertainty to the teaching process (Kinchin, 2009), particularly where a variety of terms (e.g., learning styles, learning differences, learning approaches, learning patterns, learning dispositions) suggests a fragmentation of the field, which as Bernstein (2000, p. 171) described, may "shatter any sense of underlying unity."

Various studies have tried to categorize students according to their learning differences and then consider optimization of curriculum structures to support learning (see, e.g., Rayner & Cools, 2011). Studies that look at the influence of matching learning styles with teaching styles generally omit consideration of the underlying structure of the discipline, with the result that some studies have offered support for a balanced use of thinking styles but others have not (e.g., Zhang, 2005). A greater focus on disciplinary structure supports M. David Merrill's (2002) assertion that the priority should be to match teaching strategies with the subject being taught rather than to the students' learning style.

Analyses of the validity of the evidence supporting learning styles theory have tended to adopt an experimental approach. Researchers in this field have indicated dissatisfaction with purely positivist and experimental approaches, calling for more longitudinal and mixed methods approaches (e.g., Peterson, Rayner, & Armstrong, 2009). Experimental studies have sought to isolate a linear relationship between two factors within a complex system of classroom activity—adoption of the theory and an improvement in examination results (e.g., Pashler, McDaniel, Rowher, & Bjork, 2008)—with the frequent observation that little evidence is found to support the application of theory. However, such studies fail to consider the more nuanced observations of student or teacher behaviors, or that individuals may be operating within more than one style for portions of their teaching and learning. It is also evident that cultural differences exert an influence on learning styles (e.g., Yamazaki, 2005), although more research is needed before links between culture and learning style could be exploited within the classroom.

The commercial activity that often follows research into styles (i.e., selling inventories for use by teachers in the classroom) tends to be perceived as offering a "quick fix," providing teachers with a pathway to success, and may pose a problem if teachers are encouraged to employ tools and interventions uncritically. The learning styles research community has commented on the negative effects of commercialization on scholarship (Peterson et al., 2009). Just because some learning characteristics can be measured does not necessarily mean that teachers should be focusing on the process of measurement. Harold Pashler et al. (2008) concluded that the existence of study preferences does not by itself suggest that administering learning-style tests would be a good use of limited teaching resources to support learning. Leonora Ritter (2007) has noted how learning styles inventories can be employed simply to categorize learners into a manageable number of groups with the effect that discourses of student diversity get subverted by institutions to promote increased commonality and homogeneity. The response to critiques of the learning styles literature given by Carol Evans, Eve Cools, and Zarina Charlesworth (2010, p. 468) in calling for educational institutions to "consider how they can use styles research in an expansive (to analyze learning situations) rather than a restrictive (focus on types) way," seems to offer the most helpful direction for future studies.

Threshold Concepts

Jan Meyer and Ray Land (2006) have described threshold concepts as those key ideas within a discipline that open a portal, giving access to a previously inaccessible way of thinking about something and represent a transformed interpretation of the subject matter, without which the learner cannot progress to higher levels of understanding. These thresholds are not just important ideas within a discipline. They also play a fundamental role in integrating and transforming students' understanding in such a way that their appreciation of the subject changes qualitatively and irreversibly. The crossing of thresholds may be supported by making reference to a range of content such that the curriculum could be reconceptualized from "content to be covered" to "thresholds to be crossed" (Mintzes & Quinn, 2007). If so, then assessment will need to shift in focus from the refinement of single knowledge structures toward a focus on *change within* meaning structures and the relationship among them (Dall'Alba & Sandberg, 1996).

A strength of the threshold concepts perspective is that it places subject specialists at the center of curriculum inquiry (Cousin, 2008), and may therefore help provide a safe trading zone between disciplinary language and the language of educational research. Indeed, Noel Entwistle (2008, p. 30) has commented that introducing the notion of threshold concepts to teachers seems to "open up their thinking about the nature of knowledge, so that threshold concepts act as a threshold concept about teaching and learning" and may therefore act to integrate the first three theoretical positions described earlier (models of expertise, punctuated learning, and learning styles), especially when visualized from a knowledge structures perspective (see Figure 21.1). Threshold concepts may also act as a focus for critical dialogue on the structure of the curriculum between students and teachers (Irvine & Carmichael, 2010).

Uncovering the network of threshold concepts as suggested by Peter Davies and Jean Mangan (2007) would make explicit the underlying conceptual skeleton of a discipline that would be invisible to the novice, but self-evident to disciplinary experts. To do so, the role of the curriculum is paramount, and teachers need to exploit it as a tool to create an appropriate learning environment: "Because knowledge structures tend to remain implicit to those working in the field of production, they usually only become visible and explicit as deliberate attempts are made to reveal them when the knowledge gets recontextualised into a curriculum" (Luckett, 2009, p. 442). However, we need to recognize the variation in underlying knowledge structures when comparing one discipline with another. In her pioneering work, Janet Donald (1983, 1987) showed that science courses tend to operate within a hierarchical structure of key concepts whereas arts and humanities courses tend to be arranged in a more linear structure. In addition, the strength of connections between key concepts varies between disciplines such that

> In the sciences, key concepts appear to be tightly structured with more links between them, which would support an all-or-none learning pattern. Courses in the social sciences, on the other hand, appear to be more loosely structured with certain key concepts acting as pivots or organizers. (Donald, 1983, p. 37)

These disciplinary variables should be considered when exploring the application of threshold concepts within any given curriculum.

Application and the E-Learning Exemplar

The application of educational theory can be explained best through discussion of a concrete example. E-learning or learning that is enhanced with digital technologies is currently an important growth area in university provisions and offers an interesting exemplar of the influence of knowledge structures on developing practice because it is of generic interest across academic disciplines. The relative newness of digital technologies forces faculty to ask fundamental questions about pedagogy—something that experienced academics may not have done for a long time (Peruski & Mishra, 2004). However, Glenn Brand (1997) considers the traditional methods of technology training for teachers, consisting of workshops and short courses, to be ill-suited to develop the expertise that can assist faculty in becoming intelligent users of pedagogical technology (see also Mishra & Koehler, 2006). More generally, the focus on linear discourses is seen to encourage an emphasis on segmented, context-dependent learning, as described earlier (Bernstein, 2000).

Most of the software tools and digital devices that are used to support teaching in universities (either face-to-face or by distance learning) were designed for business, not education. Therefore, the conversion of these general tools for use in the classroom requires teachers to engage with the affordances of the particular packages and devices to repurpose them to meet pedagogic goals (Mishra & Koehler, 2006; Laurillard, 2009). This problem has been demonstrated in the case of Microsoft PowerPoint (Kinchin & Cabot, 2007) where the affordances of the software can be moderated by the complementary affordances of concept mapping to help align PowerPoint with a more student-centered, constructivist pedagogy (see Figure 21.3).

Figure 21.3 The Author Giving a Lecture to Colleagues at King Saud University About the Value of Presenting Complementary Knowledge Structures Within PowerPoint Presentations

The alignment of pedagogy and technology is not a trivial undertaking, and failure to recognize the mismatch between software design and pedagogic goals can result in a diminished student experience. As Sandi Mann and Andrew Robinson (2009) have noted, "The most important teaching factor contributing to student boredom is the use of PowerPoint slides" (p. 243).

Meta-analyses of numerous studies of the effectiveness of e-learning have concluded that online materials should not simply be an electronic copy of paper-based materials (Bernard et al., 2004) with faculty believing that the online environment changes the way they approach and think about the way they teach and relate to students (Major, 2010). However, there seems to be a difference between aspirations and observed practice. According to Marco Alfano, Nicola Cuscino, and Biagio Lenzitti (2009),

> Unfortunately, most of the existing e-learning platforms offer just a single way to organize the course content (book structure). Whoever is interested in organizing course contents in a different way (e.g., with a concept map) must use specific tools that are external to the e-learning environment and are often difficult to use. (p. 51)

The replication of "book structure" within e-learning materials is an example of what Gavriel Salomon (2002, p. 72) has described as "the domestication" of innovative technology so that it "does more or less what its predecessors have done, only a bit faster and a bit nicer." Whereas Diana Laurillard (2009, p. 6) has called for a robust consideration of the nature of formal learning to avoid the risk of technology being used "merely to enhance conventional learning designs, rather than generate designs that are much more effective and innovative," Lorenzo Vigentini (2009) showed that whatever the level of technology, human behavior will dominate so that nontechnical, student traditions (such as cramming in the 2 weeks before final examinations) continue within digital learning environments.

Building on Lee Schulman's (1987) notion of pedagogical content knowledge (PCK), Matthew Koehler, Punya Mishra, and Kurnia Yahya (2007) argued that bringing technology into the mix requires thinking of PCK as just one component of technological pedagogical content knowledge (TPCK): A model that offers three components (content, pedagogy, and technology) with the intersection of the three requiring a sensitivity to the dynamic, transactional relationship among content, pedagogy, and technology.

Mishra and Koehler (2006, p. 1029) described how "TPCK . . . would not typically be held by technologically proficient subject matter experts, or by technologists who know little of the subject or of pedagogy, or by teachers who know little of that subject or about technology." Therefore, there needs to be a sharing of knowledge and expertise between e-technologists and teachers that will encourage a dialogue between "the analogue and the digital experience of staff and students" (Watling, 2009, p. 96). Colleagues may commonly seek support with technical aspects of teaching from computer specialists (e-technologists) because the computer is a far more seductive object than is a new approach to teaching (Salomon, 2002). However, the same colleagues tend to be more reluctant to seek advice on pedagogy from specialists in education (academic developers) because academic developers are likely to engage faculty in dialogue about PCK and direct colleagues away from the "safe systems" that dominate university teaching (Canning, 2007). Tackling a new pedagogy arouses uncertainty (Salomon, 2002; Kinchin, 2009) and is likely to employ terminology that is alien and promotes a defensive reaction among faculty (Green, 2009). E-technologists are less likely to ask questions about pedagogy, but rather concentrate on delivery of content through discussion of technological content knowledge (TCK), which does not threaten teachers' core knowledge.

As a result of the dislocation of the linear, segmented discourse of e-learning and the hierarchical discourse of pedagogy, there is a danger that inappropriate application of digital technologies may take university teaching back toward its medieval origins, where the teacher is seen as the sole authority and holder of knowledge (e.g., Bodner, Metz, & Tobin, 1997; Novak, 1977)—the only difference being that now the teacher dispenses information online rather than from the lectern at the front of the class. If virtual learning environments (VLEs) act only as repositories for PowerPoint slides or information management systems, then there is the likelihood that e-learning is simply the high-tech transmission of content. Indeed, Sue Watling (2009, p. 84) has commented on how the managerial pressure to participate in the digital revolution has encouraged the replication of traditional transmission models of teaching, so that "In the first decade of this century, it appears that they [VLEs] may have not only failed to live up to their early promise but actively contributed to growing evidence of digital resistance."

In curricula that are focused on the transmission of content, Tony Harland, Jules Kieser, and Alison Meldrum (2006, p. 158) commented,

> Teachers typically collude with the students and protect them by ensuring that they have the correct and authorized knowledge, but this is nearly always the product of someone else's thinking. The culture of the curriculum then becomes anti-reflection and possibly even anti-learning.

Kinchin, Lygo-Baker, and Hay (2008) have developed this notion to show how the predominant knowledge structures within such a teaching framework are linear chains of information—the exchange of which between teachers and students leads to cycles of non-learning. E-technologists are viewed by faculty as providing solutions to problems with the familiar context of non-learning cycles, whereas faculty development may be more concerned about examining the underlying pedagogic problem, which may suggest solutions that would interfere with established cycles of non-learning. A way out of these non-learning cycles may be afforded by making explicit the knowledge structures that are embedded within digital media (e.g., Chen, Kinshuk, Wei, & Chen, 2008; Thorpe, 2008).

The evolution of Internet pedagogy appears to have mirrored the evolution of university pedagogy as a whole as a progression in three broad steps, from a focus on content to a focus on students toward a more nuanced focus on the dialogue required to develop expertise within disciplinary contexts (Kinchin, Baysan, & Cabot, 2008). In the digital environment, the Web 1.0 phase of Internet development consisted mainly of text and still images (resembling an online version of the textbook). The Web 2.0 phase became more student-centered with growing emphasis on the development of the student voice through the application of blogs and wikis. Web 3.0 will likely offer the potential for even greater interactivity and dialogue. The challenge then is to build models of teaching that bridge the analog-digital divide, so that the pedagogic discourses of face-to-face and online learning become part of a coherent whole. Thus, pedagogy and technology need to evolve together (i.e., in parallel rather than in series). Pedagogy cannot be added to e-learning materials as an afterthought as the implicit values and beliefs required to construct a pedagogy will already inhabit the digital media and will underpin the pedagogic discourse that inevitably preempts the linear discourse of teaching methods (see Figure 21.4). There is evidence in the literature of consideration of the intercultural aspects of e-learning, which is concerned with the underlying pedagogic network described in Figure 21.4. For example, Catherine McLoughlin (2006) focused on learners' values and belief systems in her consideration of e-learning across cultural boundaries. In so doing, she opened discussion of the underlying pedagogy of e-learning.

Figure 21.4   Juxtaposing the Linear Knowledge Structure of Teaching Discourse (the Chain of Practice) With the Hierarchical Knowledge Structure of Pedagogic Discourse (the Network of Understanding) to Illustrate the Need for a Linking Concept to Develop a Dual-Processing Model of Teacher Expertise

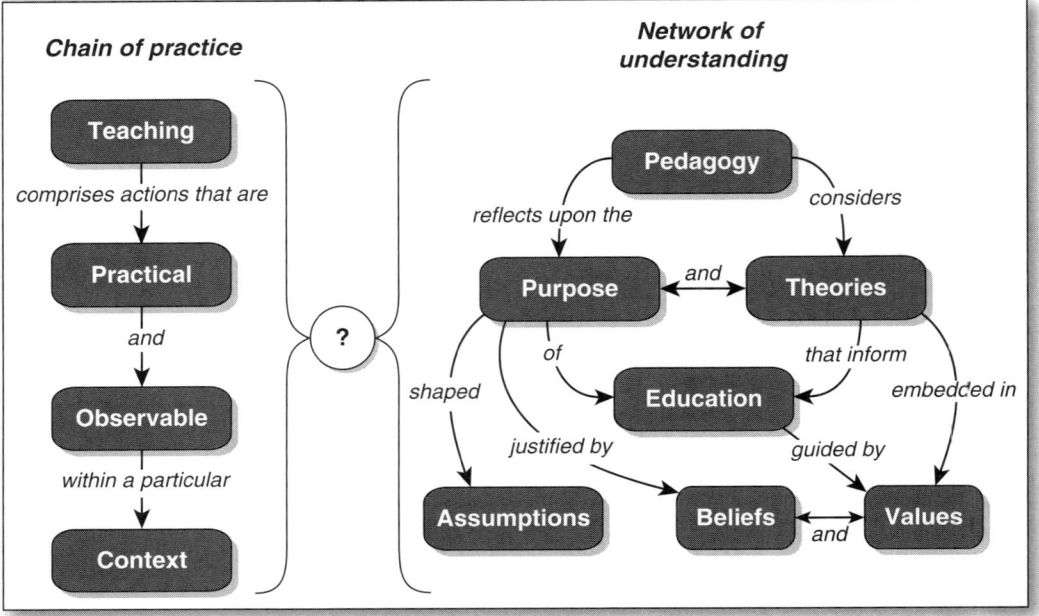

Implications for Faculty Development

Although lectures will probably remain the lynchpin of undergraduate teaching, the affordances for learning within the lecture format remain open for debate and development (e.g., Jones, 2007). Even within the most precise of disciplines, such as mathematics, where there are clearly occasions in which there is a single correct answer, Leigh Wood, Sabhbh Joyce, Peter Petocz, and Melissa Rodd (2007, p. 907) noted that "a central purpose of lectures is to be a natural venue for the links between different representations of mathematics experienced by learners."

The pedagogy of the lecture theater needs to evolve and exploit the potential of new technology such as audience response systems (commonly known as clickers; e.g., Trees & Jackson, 2007), and to reappraise the use of embedded technologies such as PowerPoint (Kinchin, Chadha, & Kokotailo, 2008). Whether in analog or digital environments, a balanced consideration of knowledge structures (the teaching and the pedagogy illustrated in Figure 21.4) and their role in the developing pedagogy of higher education can help add coherence to the field (e.g., Ryan, Scott, & Walsh, 2010).

It seems inevitable that digital technologies will have an increasing role in university education—both in face-to-face teaching and in distance learning.

If digital technology is to fulfill its early promise and enhance student learning, e-learning materials need to reflect the underlying structures of the discipline (rather than adopting a default linear/book structure), and demonstrate awareness of the ways in which students' prior knowledge will interact with it (i.e., expert knowledge structures may not be the most conceptually accessible structure for students). The sequencing of materials should acknowledge that learning is a punctuated process that needs to prepare students to cross conceptual thresholds. This process can be supported by curriculum structures that promote complementary elements of segmented and cumulative learning that facilitate the expert practice of linking experiential and conceptual knowledge. The development of these perspectives in parallel with the development of innovative technology-enhanced learning will put TPCK at the center of e-learning provision—bridging the digital-analog divide that is currently a feature of the student experience.

Some challenges to existing models of faculty development (such as competency-based training) can also be visualized and further explained with the aid of the framework depicted in Figure 21.4. For example, Leesa Wheelahan (2007) concluded that competency-based training fundamentally transforms the nature of knowledge by *dislocating* the experiential knowledge from conceptual understanding, which in the case of faculty development, involves separating teaching practice from pedagogic theory (Figure 21.4). This idea is reflected in the literature that describes experienced teachers' general conceptions of teaching and learning and a range of practical classroom strategies that they employ, for example,

> The good ones (i.e., proficient teachers) usually possess knowledge of content-specific pedagogy—a special form of knowledge which develops through the apprenticeship model of observation and experience. Their experience usually relates to behaviours, strategies and instructional techniques—the "how" of teaching—but few understand the basic principles, theories and concepts of the teaching process—the "why" of pedagogic behaviours. (McLeod, Steinert, Meagher, & McLeod, 2003, p. 638)

Unless teachers are granted access to the conceptual knowledge that underpins experience, they will be denied access to what Wheelahan (2007, p. 639) has termed the "yet-to-be-thought." In the absence of the necessary understanding, faculty cannot participate in the evolution of the communal practice of teaching, and so in Keiny's (2002) view, are denied access to learning. A linear perspective on teaching will encourage faculty to perceive teaching as unproblematic (Kinchin, 2009), whereas greater recognition of teaching as a complex, nonlinear system will help learners (and teachers) to function within the predictable unpredictability that is inherent within the process (Fromberg, 2010).

Additionally, Scott Reeves, Ann Fox, and Brian Hodges (2009) considered that competency-based approaches restrict mechanisms to support the introduction of new and innovative ideas that offer contrasting perspectives for practice. Linear curriculum structures may be seen as sterile sequences that have been "purified from networks of interdisciplinary connections" (Matusov, 2009, p.183) that can result in cycles of nonlearning in which students are rewarded by simply repeating the teachers' comments back to them (Kinchin et al., 2008). It is therefore important that teachers are involved in discussions about the underlying theories that support university teaching, which will enable faculty to be informed participants in the evolution of higher education pedagogy by participating in the construction of contextually appropriate networks of pedagogic understanding, and not just behave as the passive recipients of decontextualized chains of teaching practice in the form of "tips for teachers." The key to opening up discussion about these issues is the visualization of embedded knowledge structures within both digital and analog environments, with concept mapping providing the tool to achieve this critical goal.

References

Alfano, M., Cuscino, N., & Lenzitti, B. (2009). Structuring didactic materials on the web (STRUCT). *Communication & Cognition, 42*(1–2), 51–62.

Bernard, R. M., Abrami, P. C., Lou, Y., Borokhovski, E., Wade, L., Wozney, L., . . . & Huang, B. (2004). How does distance education compare with classroom instruction? A meta-analysis of the empirical literature. *Review of Educational Research, 74*(3), 379–439.

Bernstein, B. (2000). *Pedagogy, symbolic control and identity*. Lanham, MD: Rowman & Littlefield.

Bodner, G. M., Metz, P. A., & Tobin, K. (1997). Cooperative learning: An alternative to teaching at a medieval university. *Australian Science Teachers' Journal, 43*(1), 23–28.

Bradley, J. H., Paul, R., & Seeman, E. (2006). Analyzing the structure of expert knowledge. *Information and Management, 43*, 77–91.

Brand, G. (1997). What research says: Training teachers for using technology. *Journal of Staff Development, 19*(1), 10–13.

Canning, J. (2007). Pedagogy as a discipline: Emergence, sustainability and professionalisation. *Teaching in Higher Education, 12*, 393–403.

Chen, N-S., Kinshuk, Wei, C. W., & Chen, H. J. (2008). Mining e-learning domain concept map from academic articles. *Computers & Education, 50*, 1009–1021.

Chiou, C-C. (2008). The effect of concept mapping on students' learning achievements and interests. *Innovations in Education and Teaching International, 45*(4), 375–387.

Cousin, G. (2008). Threshold concepts: Old wine in new bottles or new forms of transactional curriculum inquiry? In R. Land, J. H. F. Meyer, & J. Smith (Eds.), *Threshold concepts within the disciplines* (pp. 261–272). Rotterdam, Netherlands: Sense Publishers.

Cuthbert, P. F. (2005). The student learning process: Learning styles or approaches? *Teaching in Higher Education, 10*(2), 235–249.

Dall'Alba, G., & Sandberg, J. (1996). Educating for competence in professional practice. *Instructional Science, 24*, 411–437.

Davies, P., & Mangan, J, (2007). Threshold concepts and the integration of understanding in economics. *Studies in Higher Education, 32*(6), 711–726.

Donald, J. G. (1983). Knowledge structures: Methods for exploring course content. *The Journal of Higher Education, 54*(1), 31–41.

Donald, J. G. (1987). Learning schemata: Methods of representing cognitive, content, and curriculum structures in higher education. *Instructional Science, 16*, 187–211.

Elhelou, M-W. A. (1997). The use of concept mapping in learning science subjects by Arab students. *Educational Research, 39*(3), 311–317.

Entwistle, N. (2008). Threshold concepts and transformative ways of thinking within research into higher education. In R. Land, J. H. F. Meyer, & J. Smith (Eds.), *Threshold concepts within the disciplines* (pp. 21–35). Rotterdam, Netherlands: Sense Publishers.

Evans, C., Cools, E., & Charlesworth, Z. M. (2010). Learning in higher education—How cognitive and learning styles matter. *Teaching in Higher Education, 15*, 467–478.

Fromberg, D. P. (2010). How nonlinear systems inform meaning in early education, *Nonlinear Dynamics, Psychology, and Life Sciences, 14*(1), 47–68.

Gamache, P. (2002). University students as creators of personal knowledge: An alternative epistemological view. *Teaching in Higher Education, 7*(3), 277–294.

Gerstner, S., & Bognor, F. X. (2009). Concept map structure, gender and teaching methods: An investigation of students' science learning. *Educational Research, 51*(4), 425–438.

Goldsmith, T. E., Johnson, P. J., & Acton, W. H. (1991). Assessing structural knowledge. *Journal of Educational Psychology, 83*(1), 88–96.

Green, D. A. (2009). New academics' perceptions of the language of teaching and learning: identifying and overcoming linguistic barriers. *International Journal of Academic Development, 14*(1), 5–18.

Harland, T., Kieser, J., & Meldrum, A. (2006). Cultural fragmentation of knowledge in clinical teaching. *Teaching in Higher Education, 11*(2), 149–160.

Irvine, N., & Carmichael, P. (2010). Threshold concepts: A point of focus for practitioner research. *Active Learning in Higher Education, 10*(2), 103–119.

James, K. L., Davies, J. G., Kinchin, I. M., Patel, J. P., & Whittlesea, C. (2010). Understanding vs. competency: The case of accuracy checking dispensed medicines in pharmacy. *Advances in Health Sciences Education.* doi:10.1007/s10459-010-9234-7

Jones, S. E. (2007). Reflections on the lecture: Outmoded medium or instrument of inspiration? *Journal of Further and Higher Education, 31*(4), 397–406.

Keiny, S. (2002). *Ecological thinking: A new approach to educational change.* Lanham, MD: University of America Press.

Kinchin, I. M. (2001). If concept mapping is so helpful to learning biology, why aren't we all doing it? *International Journal of Science Education, 23*(12), 1257–1269.

Kinchin, I. M. (2009). A knowledge structures perspective on the scholarship of teaching and learning. *International Journal for the Scholarship of Teaching and Learning, 3*(2). Available from http://www.georgiasouthern.edu/ijsotl

Kinchin, I. M. (2010). Solving Cordelia's dilemma: Threshold concepts within a punctuated model of learning. *Journal of Biological Education, 44*(2), 53–57.

Kinchin, I. M., Baysan, A., & Cabot, L. B. (2008). Towards a pedagogy for clinical education: Beyond individual learning differences. *Journal of Further and Higher Education, 32*(4), 373–387.

Kinchin, I. M., & Cabot, L. B. (2007). Using concept mapping principles in PowerPoint. *European Journal of Dental Education, 11*(4), 194–199.

Kinchin, I. M., & Cabot, L .B. (2010). Reconsidering the dimensions of expertise: From linear stages towards dual processing. *London Review of Education, 8*(2), 153–166.

Kinchin, I. M., Cabot, L. B., & Hay, D. B. (2010). Visualising expertise: Revealing the nature of a threshold concept in the development of an authentic pedagogy for clinical education. In J. H. F. Meyer, R. Land, & C. Baillie (Eds.), *Threshold concepts and transformational learning* (pp. 81–95). Rotterdam, Netherlands: Sense Publishers.

Kinchin, I. M., Chadha, D., & Kokotailo, P. (2008). Using PowerPoint as a lens to focus on linearity in teaching. *Journal of Further and Higher Education, 32*(4), 333–346.

Kinchin, I. M., & Hay, D. B. (2007). The myth of the research-led teacher. *Teachers and Teaching: Theory and Practice, 13*(1), 43–61.

Kinchin, I. M., Hay, D. B., & Adams, A. (2000). How a qualitative approach to concept map analysis can be used to aid learning by illustrating patterns of conceptual development. *Educational Research, 42*(1), 43–57.

Kinchin, I. M., Lygo-Baker, S., & Hay, D. B. (2008). Universities as centres of non-learning. *Studies in Higher Education, 33*(1), 89–103.

Koehler, M. J., Mishra, P., & Yahya, K. (2007). Tracing the development of teacher knowledge in a design seminar: Integrating content, pedagogy and technology. *Computers & Education, 49*, 740–762.

Laurillard, D. (2009). The pedagogical challenges to collaborative technologies. *Computer-Supported Collaborative Learning, 4*, 5–20.

Lord, T. (1999). Are we cultivating "couch potatoes" in our college science lectures? *Journal of College Science Teaching, 28*, 59–62.

Luckett, K. (2009). The relationship between knowledge structure and curriculum: A case study in sociology. *Studies in Higher Education, 34*(4), 441–453.

Mahrous, A. A., & Ahmed, A. A. (2009). A cross-cultural investigation of students' perceptions of the effectiveness pedagogical tools: The Middle East, the United Kingdom and the United States. *Journal of Studies in International Education.* doi:10.1177/1028315309334738

Major, C. (2010). Do virtual professors dream of electric students? College faculty experiences with online distance education. *Teachers College Record, 112*(8). Retrieved from http://www.tcrecord.org/content.asp?contentid=15946

Mann, S., & Robinson, A. (2009). Boredom in the lecture theatre: An investigation into the contributors, moderators and outcomes of boredom amongst university students. *British Educational Research Journal, 35*(2), 243–258.

Maton, K. (2009). Cumulative and segmented learning: Exploring the role of curriculum structures in knowledge building. *British Journal of Sociology of Education, 31*(1), 43–57.

Matusov, E. (2009). *Journey into dialogic pedagogy.* New York, NY: Nova Science.

McLeod, P. J., Steinert, Y., Meagher, T., & McLeod, A. (2003). The ABCs of pedagogy for clinical teaching. *Medical Education, 37*, 638–644.

McLoughlin, C. (2006). Adapting e-learning across cultural boundaries: A framework for quality learning, pedagogy, and interaction. In A. Edmundson (Ed.),

Globalized e-learning cultural challenges (pp. 223–238). Hershey, PA: Information Science.

Merrill, M. D. (2002). Instructional strategies and learning styles: Which takes precedence? In R. A. Reiser & J. V. Dempsey (Eds.), *Trends and issues in instructional design and technology* (pp. 99–106). Upper Saddle River, NJ: Merrill Prentice Hall.

Meyer, J. H. F., & Land, R. (2006). Threshold concepts and troublesome knowledge: An introduction. In J. H. F. Meyer & R. Land (Eds.), *Overcoming barriers to student understanding: Threshold concepts and troublesome knowledge* (pp. 3–18). London, UK: Routledge.

Mintzes, J., & Quinn, H. J. (2007). Knowledge restructuring in biology: Testing a punctuated model of conceptual change. *International Journal of Science and Mathematics Education, 5*, 281–306.

Mishra, P., & Koehler, M. J. (2006). Technological pedagogical content knowledge: A framework for teacher knowledge. *Teachers College Record, 108*(6), 1017–1054.

Norman, G. (2005). Research in clinical reasoning: Past history and current trends. *Medical Education, 39*, 418–427.

Novak, J. D. (1977). *A theory of education.* Ithaca, NY: Cornell University Press.

Novak, J. D. (2010). *Learning, creating and using knowledge: Concept maps as facilitative tools in schools and corporations* (2nd ed.). Oxford, UK: Routledge.

Novak, J. D., & Cañas, A. J. (2007). Theoretical origins of concept maps, how to construct them and uses in education. *Reflecting Education, 3*(1), 29–42.

Novak, J. D., & Symington, D. J. (1982). Concept mapping for curriculum development. *Victoria Institute for Educational Research Bulletin, 48*, 3–11.

Pashler, H., McDaniel, M., Rowher, D., & Bjork, R. (2008). Learning styles: Concepts and evidence. *Psychological Science in the Public Interest, 9*, 105–119.

Peruski, L., & Mishra, P. (2004). Webs of activity in online course design and teaching. *ALT-J, Research in Learning Technology, 12*(1), 37–49.

Peterson, E. R., Rayner, S. G., & Armstrong, S. J. (2009). Researching the psychology of cognitive style and learning style: Is there really a future? *Learning and Individual Differences, 19*, 518–523.

Rayner, S., & Cools, E. (2011). *Style differences in cognition, learning and management: Theory, research, and practice.* London, UK: Routledge.

Reeves, S., Fox, A., & Hodges, B. D. (2009). The competency movement in the health professions: Ensuring consistent standards or reproducing conventional domains of practice? *Advances in Health Sciences Education, 14*, 451–453.

Ritchhart, R., Turner, T., & Hadar, L. (2009). Uncovering students' thinking about thinking using concept maps. *Metacognition Learning, 4*, 145–159.

Ritter, L. (2007). Unfulfilled promises: How inventories, instruments and institutions subvert discourses of diversity and promote commonality. *Teaching in Higher Education, 12*, 569–579.

Ryan, J., Scott, A., & Walsh, M. (2010). Pedagogy in the multimodal classroom: An analysis of the challenges and opportunities for teachers. *Teachers and Teaching: Theory and Practice, 16*(4), 477–489.

Salomon, G. (2002). Technology and pedagogy: Why don't we see the promised revolution? *Educational Technology, 42*(2), 71–75.

Schulman, L. S. (1987). Knowledge and teaching: Foundations for a new reform. *Harvard Educational Review, 57*(1), 1–22.

Thorpe, M. (2008). Effective online interaction: Mapping course design to bridge from research to practice. *Australasian Journal of Educational Technology, 24*(1), 57–72.

Trees, A. R., & Jackson, M. H. (2007). The learning environment in clicker classrooms: Student processes of learning and involvement in large university level courses using student response systems. *Learning, Media and Technology, 32*(1), 21–40.

Tsui, A. B. M. (2009). Distinctive qualities of expert teachers. *Teachers and Teaching: Theory and Practice, 15*(4), 421–439.

Vigentini, L. (2009). Using learning technology in university courses: Do styles matter? *Multicultural Education and Technology Journal, 3*(1), 17–32.

Watling, S. (2009). Technology-enhanced learning: A new digital divide? In L. Bell, H. Stevenson, & M. Neary (Eds.), *The future of higher education: Policy pedagogy and the student experience* (pp. 83–96). London, UK: Continuum International.

Wheelahan, L. (2007). How competency-based training locks the working class out of powerful knowledge: A modified Bernsteinian analysis. *British Journal of Sociology of Education, 28*(5), 637–651.

Wood, L. N., Joyce, S., Petocz, P., & Rodd, M. (2007). Learning in lectures: Multiple representations. *International Journal of Mathematical Education in Science and Technology, 38*(7), 907–915.

Yamazaki, Y. (2005). Learning styles and typologies of cultural difference: A theoretical and empirical comparison. *International Journal of Intercultural Relations, 29*(5), 521–548.

Zhang, L-F. (2005). Does teaching for a balanced use of thinking styles enhance students' achievement? *Personality and Individual Differences, 38*, 1135–1147.

CHAPTER 22

Culture and Learning Styles

Maria Martinez Witte and James E. Witte

Thomas Friedman (2006) revealed that the flattening or globalization of the world will prompt individual workers to become more responsible for managing their own career, risks, and economic security, and the role of government and business will be to assist workers in doing so. A skilled workforce is needed to support our society. In addressing the importance of a strong economic local, regional, and global position, it is beneficial to address obstacles that may hinder adults from engaging and continuing educational goals and interests. Economic globalization has changed the nature of work so that it is now emerging as flexible and accessible. "The resulting intensification of global economic competition and hyper-volatility in labor markets demand a constant reorganization and readjustment of national economic structures and work patterns" (Anderson, Brown, & Rushbrook, 2004, p. 236).

Roland Robertson (1992) defined globalization as a concept that "refers both to the compression of the world and the intensification of consciousness of the world as a whole" (p. 8). The use of the word *globalization* is relatively new and increased in usage in the late 1980s. Although this term has been used in a loose manner, it has become considered part of a worldly consciousness. In 1991, the *Oxford Dictionary of New Words* actually included the definition of *global* as "receptiveness to and understanding of cultures other than one's own, often as part of an appreciation of world socio-economic and ecological issues" (as cited in Robertson, 1992, p. 8).

As indicated in James Groccia's model (see Chapter 1, this volume), to understand the teaching and learning dynamic and facilitate successful learning opportunities for individuals, we must know the learner. Knowing the learner can include information about his or her personality and cultural values. According to Pat Guild (2001), the learner is a product of nature and nurture. Each of us is born with a predisposition for learning in certain ways and should acknowledge the external, cultural influences that have imprinted their learning patterns and resulting learning style preferences.

Culture

The concept of culture is multifaceted and complex. It has been regarded as the central organizing base for social anthropology, which in the early 1900s was referred to as *cultural anthropology*. It was considered a major object of study in sociology and political science and was associated with terms such as *subculture, counterculture, organizational culture, civic culture*, and *political culture* (Smelser, 1992). Social philosophers and historians considered culture as an idea that provided a basis for characterizing a society. "Needless to say, such an approach almost dictated the corollary assumption that each civilization's culture possessed a coherent unit or pattern that encompasses its religious, philosophical or aesthetic underpinnings" (Smelser, 1992, p. 4).

Culture has been popularly described as one of the most complicated words in the English language. Initially, it was considered an individual habit of mind, the state of intellectual development of a whole society, the arts, and the whole way of life of a group or people (Milner & Browitt, 2002). Andrew Milner and Jeff Browitt offered a nondefinition of *culture* that refers to an entire range of institutions, artifacts, and practices that make up the symbolic universe. The term includes art and religion, science and sport, education and leisure; however, it does not include the range of activities considered economic or political.

According to Michael Apple (1982), culture has a dual form. It includes the lived experiences that are developed from day-to-day lives and interactions, and it allows specific societal groups to transform their culture into a commodity and accumulate cultural capital. Culture is context-specific and takes meaning from the particular context, both historical and conceptual. "The operative definition of culture is inseparable from the type of critique being pursued, as the two constantly interact with and influence one another" (Surber, 1998, p. 4).

William Sewell (1999) explained that culture can be considered as an aspect of social life that is contrasted to some other equal aspect or category of social life, such as politics or the economy. However, when culture is considered in a plural context, such as cultures, then it should be considered a concrete and explicit set of beliefs and practices. Cultures can then be specific and clearly identifiable subsocietal groups such as U.S. culture, middle-class culture, or Latino culture. The contrast is then made between the separate cultures. Sewell (1999) referred to concepts of culture that are either a system of symbols and meanings or cultural practices. Culture as a system of symbols and meanings has been the prominent definition since the 1960s. Culture as practice refers to activities that are subjected to power relations, struggle, change, or contradiction. These are considered complementary concepts. Cultural practices require the use of cultural symbols, and the use of these symbols can be expected to accomplish a particular goal only because they have designated meanings. Therefore, practice implies the use of symbol system, and this system implies the use of practices. "System and practice constitute an indissoluble duality or dialectic: the important theoretical question is thus not whether culture should be conceptualized as practice or as a system of symbols and means, but how to conceptualize the articulation of system and practice" (Sewell, 1999, p. 47).

Paul Bohannan (1995) acknowledged rules of matter, life, and culture:

> Culture is as natural as life. . . . In the course of growing up, we learn culture as ways to exercise our genetic capacities. When we finally learn to deal with culture . . . we can question it, ask how it works, take advantage of parts of it, and learn to avoid some of its manifestations . . . (p. 2)

There are biological conditions that facilitate matter and life organizes matter. Yet, the rules of culture are considered extensions of the rules of matter and life just as the rules of life are extensions of the rules of matter. This is an interesting perspective because living matter can be transformed by culture because culture transcends and enriches matter and life. Cultural rules are so complex and

> hampered by the irony that people cannot even think about culture except through the categories of thought that we have learned from the culture we grew up in and the one in which we have been trained. We must make gigantic efforts to step outside our culture-laden views. (Bohannan, 1995, p. 4)

If we are examining our own culture, we should use the same framework as would be used in understanding another culture. Examining other cultures would be easier because differences are more apparent when viewed from our own culture. Guild (1994) indicated that the individual's culture, family background, and socioeconomic level will affect his or her learning. The environment in which someone grows up in will affect his or her learning.

Culture is not just a specific behavior or mannerism; it pertains to the beliefs, attitudes, and values of individuals and in turn how those experiences are interpreted and eventually guide future individual actions. Recognizing the need to globalize market opportunities, organizations strive to improve what they know about cultural differences and how nations differ when working with cross-cultural business issues. Geert Hofstede's

(1980, 2001) cultural consequences research established cultural dimensions from individuals in 66 countries. The five cultural dimensions were power distance, uncertainty avoidance, individualism, masculinity, and long-term orientation (Fougere & Moulettes, 2007). For the purpose of this chapter, Hofstede's (1980, 2001) consideration of cultural layers will be used to frame this discussion. The term *culture* is designated as the basic norms and values, the collective beliefs and values shared by a specific group of people, and an individual's unique experience of people and things. Individuals' background will influence their behavior when approaching a new learning situation. The resulting learning style preferences will transfer to the learning environment.

Learning Styles

Learning styles refers to the variety of ways individuals use, store, and retrieve information (Sonbuchner, 1991). Learning styles can assist in identifying specific ways that information can be acquired and retained. Individuals often show a preference for a given learning style, and instructors who acknowledge these varying strengths and abilities will be able to structure successful learning experiences for their students. Lynne Baldwin and Khaled Sabry (2003) stressed that learners are different and will approach learning tasks differently and those individual differences will affect an individual's learning processes. Being aware of the variety of learning styles in classrooms can strengthen connections between preferred learning styles and instructional methods. "The differences among learning styles have become more striking as our learning communities in higher education have become more diverse" (Sarasin, 1998, p. 2). Higher educational institutions are no longer bound by specific geographic boundaries. With more global accessibility and increased ease in pursuing academic endeavors, there will be a greater diversity of learners and learning styles among the student population.

Learning Style Definitions

Waynne James and William Blank (1993) identified learning style as the "complex manner in which, and conditions under which, learners learn most efficiently and most effectively perceive, process, store, and recall what they are attempting to learn" (p. 47). This term generally refers to the way in which learners will react to the learning environment. It can also be used to describe an individual's preferred way of understanding experiences and converting those experiences into knowledge (Cuthbert, 2005; Kolb, 1984).

Another definition of *learning style* refers to a student's consistent way of responding and using stimuli in the learning environment. David Kolb (1984) indicated that learning styles relate to an individual's preference of methods to perceive and process information. Barbara Given (2000) stated,

"Learning styles pertain to rather consistent ways humans interact with new and difficult information including ways they select, take in, make sense of, remember, recall and use input from all that is available to them both internally and externally" (p. 3).

Gregory Krätzig and Katherine Arbuthnott (2006) stressed that an individual's memory will be stimulated through various sensory learning styles. Lynn Curry (1991) considered learning styles as a combination of an individual's motivation to learn, engagement in the learning process, and cognitive processing habits. R. J. Riding and Stephen Rayner (1998) included the individual's preferences for instruction in their learning styles definition and the differences along intellectual and personal psychology lines. In earlier research, the term *cognitive style* was used in place of the term *learning styles*. Cognitive style was recognized as the cognitive characteristics modes of functioning as discovered through perceptual and intellectual activities or the intrinsic information processing patterns an individual uses when perceiving, thinking, problem solving, or remembering (Swanson, 1995).

There has been some controversy about the use of learning styles and lack of empirical evidence (Fridley & Fridley, 2010; Pashler, McDaniel, Rohrer & Bjork, 2009; Riener & Willingham, 2010; Scott, 2010); however, to be an instructor who creates optimal learning conditions requires knowledge of self and students. How an individual approaches learning situations can affect the performance and achievement of learning outcomes (Cassidy, 2004). An instructor would also benefit from developing an awareness of student learning styles to organize course content for improved academic success. Bo Heffler (2001) also reinforced the notion that it would be advantageous to know one's own learning style when approaching a new learning situation to optimize the outcome.

Learning Styles Frameworks

Historically, the discussion and use of learning styles terminology and research did not become well known until the 1970s (American Association of School Administrators, 1992). Learning styles taxonomies are usually type theories and classify people into distinct groups instead of assigning them graded scores on different dimensions (Pashler et al., 2009). Benjamin Bloom's (1976) taxonomy, pinpointing interdependent factors that affect student learning differences, comprised three key learning factors:

1. What students bring to a learning task—the "cognitive entry behaviors" that they already have learned, or their learning history

2. What factors make a student want to learn—"affective entry characteristics," or motivation

3. What learning techniques are most appropriate for the student, or the quality of instruction (p. 9)

Learning style theories are based on conceptual frameworks that can be categorized as cognitive, affective, and physiological (Keefe, 1979, 1987). Mark Tennant (1988) agreed that there have been numerous attempts to categorize the ways in which cognitive or learning styles vary; however, these approaches should not be considered mutually exclusive. Frameworks stressing the cognitive aspects of learning include those of Kolb (1976), Charles Claxton and Patricia Murrell (1987), Tennant (1988), Shirley Griggs (1991), and Judith Reiff (1992). Cognitive styles are the preferred ways in which an individual perceives, organizes, uses, and retains information. There is a relationship to intellectual abilities; however, cognitive styles relate more to process and how the information is being used as abilities to measure specific capacities (Keefe, 1987). Geoffrey Squires (1981) observed that cognitive styles are typically represented as polar opposites of a single dimension so that a person is described as field dependent or independent, reflective or impulsive, serialist or holist, or a converger or a diverger. Reiff (1992) considered cognitive styles as those that encompass brain theories, field dependence/field independence, context in learning, impulsive versus reflective responses, mindstyles, modalities, and multiple intelligences. Robert Sternberg and Elena Grigorenko (1997) regarded cognitive styles as cognition, personality, or activity centered.

Some of the instruments that assess the cognitive learning styles are the Kolb Learning Styles Inventory (Kolb, 1976) and the Gregorc Style Delineator (Gregorc, 1982a).

The Kolb Learning Styles Inventory identifies an individual's perception and processing preferences. Perception preferences can be concrete or abstract and processing preferences can be through active experimentation or reflective observations. Based on the results, individuals would be classified in one of four types: divergers (concrete and reflective), assimilators (abstract and reflective), convergers (abstract and active), and accommodators (concrete and active) (Kolb, 1984, 1985).

The Gregorc Style Delineator (Gregorc, 1982a) was created as a self-analysis instrument and was based on Kolb's learning style inventory. The Gregorc Style Delineator is designed to reveal two types of mediation abilities: perception and ordering. Perception abilities, comprising abstractness and concreteness, are means through which one grasps information. The abstractness quality enables one to grasp, conceive, and mentally visualize data and intuitively register and deal with inner and subjective thoughts and ideas. The concreteness quality enables one to grasp and mentally register data through the direct use and application of the physical senses. Ordering abilities, composed of sequence and randomness, indicate arrangement, systematization, reference, and disposition of information. The sequence quality allows the mind to grasp and organize information in a linear, step-by-step, methodical, predetermined order. The randomness quality allows one to grasp and organize information in a nonlinear manner (Gregorc, 1982b).

O. J. Harvey, David Hunt, and Harold Schroder (1961); Hunt (1978); and Samuel Messick and Associates (1978) describe affective conceptual learning style frameworks. Affective styles entail aspects of personality including attention, emotion, valuing, and the motivational process. Affective style characteristics include the ability to impose structure on the environment through a conceptual systems perspective, persistence, curiosity, level of anxiety, locus of control, risk taking, competition versus cooperation, and social motivation (Hunt, 1978; Keefe, 1987). Two instruments that assess affective learning style are the Myers-Briggs Type Indicator and Peter Honey and Alan Mumford's Learning Styles Questionnaire.

The Myers-Briggs Type Indicator is based on Carl Jung's theory that explains human personality. The Myers-Briggs psychological types were patterns of the way people prefer to perceive and make judgments. All mental activity can be classified into four mental processes or functions including two perception processes (sensing and intuition) and judgment processes (thinking and feeling). The four dimensions of type are sensing and intuition, thinking and feeling, extraversion and introversion, and judging and perceiving (Lawrence, 1995).

The Honey and Mumford Learning Styles Questionnaire (1992) was originally developed to apply learning style theory to the context of work and behavior in organizations. It is also based on Kolb's work and identifies four types of learners: Activists—those who are active, enjoy new experiences, and tend to make decisions intuitively; Theorists—those who focus on ideas and logic and plan systematically; Pragmatists—those who like down-to-earth approaches, group work, and risk-taking; and Reflectors—those who observe and describe processes and try to predict outcomes, and focus on trying to understand meaning. Individuals will tend to rely naturally on one of these approaches when they are in the learning mode (Swailes & Senior, 1999).

Russell French (1975), Clarence Edwin Cherry (1981), and Rita Dunn, Jeffrey Beaudry, and Angela Klavas (1989) focused on physiological styles of learning that are biologically based, such as gender-related differences, personal health, or accustomed responses to the physical environment. Environmental factors include temperature, light, design, posture, sound levels, or preferences for specific time of day (Dunn & Dunn, 1978; Hunt, 1978; Keefe, 1987). Instruments that assess the physiological learning style are Albert Canfield's Learning Styles Inventory (1980) and Rita Dunn and Kenneth Dunn's Learning Style Instrument (1993).

Canfield's Learning Style Inventory (1980) identifies scales in four areas:

1. Conditions of learning—the students' need to develop personal relationships with other students or the instructor; their need for structure, organization, and detail; and their need for goal-setting and achievement

2. Content—students' preferences for numerics and logic, their need for working with words or language, their need to work with tangible items, and their need to work with others

3. Mode—students' preference to listen, read, and to be directly involved

4. Expectations—the actual grades students think they will receive for their work

The Dunn and Dunn Learning Style Instrument contains 21 items within five element areas. The five elements are environmental, emotional, sociological, physiological, and psychological. The environmental stimuli reflect the sound, light, temperature, and design preferences. Emotional stimuli preferences consist of motivation, persistence, responsibility, and structure preferences. The sociological stimuli preferences are self, pair, peers/team, adult, and varied preferences. The physiological stimuli preferences refer to perceptual, intake, time, and mobility preferences. The psychological stimuli preferences consist of global/analytic styles, hemisphericity preferences, and impulsive/reflective preferences. The purpose of this learning styles model is to improve the effectiveness of instruction through the identification and matching of student learning styles with the most appropriate learning opportunities (Dunn & Dunn, 1993).

Different learning styles highlight the importance of the learning process rather than actual teaching techniques. The differences between and among learners can be used and should not be interpreted as either all positive or all negative. Each learner is just different and will have different learning styles. Because of their own internal motivation and drive, some will have clearer expectations for personal, academic, or career goals (Baldwin & Sabry, 2003).

Culture and Learning Styles Research

Peter Kennedy (2002) found that Chinese culture may influence Chinese students' learning styles. Chinese culture has been typically characterized as low on individualism and high on collectivism, which is a strong sense of belonging to a social group and a preference to work together to solve problems (Kennedy, 2002; Nield, 2009; Sayers & Franklin, 2008). Kennedy (2002) shared that the learning styles adopted by Chinese students can be attributed to the Confucian values and heritage, which is adherence to strict discipline and proper behavior. The Confucian code of social conduct requires respect and obedience to be shown in the five cardinal relationships: ruler and minister, father and son, husband and wife, older and younger brother, older and younger friends. Respect for age, teachers, and rank are a must and so is conforming to the interests of the group and maintaining harmonious relationships.

Contrary to the Chinese stereotype, Chinese learners reported a stronger preference for high-level, meaning-based learning strategies and preferred to avoid rote-learning (Kennedy, 2002). Chinese learners preferred an orientation to active and communicative modes of learning and were receptive to modes that may have been quite different than they had previously experienced. Chinese students can adopt new learning styles when the context of learning changes and new learning approaches are needed. "The successful adoption of such approaches will depend on factors such as language proficiency, the assessment system and teachers' expectations" (Kennedy, p. 442). Li-fang Zhang and David Watkins (2001) stressed that students will approach their learning tasks based on how they will be assessed. Janet Sayers and Trish Franklin (2008) used their research findings about the importance of understanding how Chinese and other international students learn to make adjustments to their teaching and assessments.

Donald Tucker (2003) found that cultural values determined the form and style of communication along with interpersonal behavior and interaction. The Korean college students' cultural variations were evident in writing assignments, rules of classroom interaction, the style of learning and taking tests, essays, papers, and expected roles of teacher and student. The contrast between U.S. and Korean students can provide helpful differences in cultural values and learning behaviors. Regarding classroom interaction and behavior, U.S. students were categorized as informal and casual and Korean students as formal with rules of proper behavior. With U.S. students, there was individual work, competition, independence of thought and judgment, whereas with Korean students, there was group work, cooperation, and interrelatedness and the quality of relationships was stressed. Tucker suggested a balance, not total adaptation, in accommodating students from different cultures and countries. Another important finding was that orienting foreign students to the U.S. system can be challenging. Faculty orientation and assistance are essential and include building basic knowledge about the cultural differences; being self-aware of one's attitude, personal thinking, and learning style; and the development of a battery of alternative teaching methods to supplement instruction.

Shu-hua Wu and Sulaiman Alrabah (2009) conducted a cross-cultural study of Taiwanese and Kuwaiti English as a foreign language (EFL) students' learning styles and multiple intelligences. *Multiple intelligences* refers to abilities in the following areas: spatial intelligence, musical intelligence, bodily-kinesthetic intelligence, interpersonal intelligence, intrapersonal intelligence, and naturalist intelligence (Chen, Moran, & Gardner, 2009). The Taiwanese group were considered to have a Confucian, Mandarin orientation, and the Kuwaiti group had a Muslim, Arabic cultural background. The Taiwanese group's dominant learning style preferences were visual followed by global. The Kuwaiti group preferred mostly a global learning style followed by an intuitive style. For the multiple intelligences, the Taiwanese group was mainly visual, interpersonal, musical, and linguistic. The Kuwaiti group was mainly interpersonal, visual, kinesthetic, and logical-mathematical. The results from this study could be used to suggest some appropriate teaching strategies for these groups of learners.

Two learning styles inventories, Kolb's (1976) experiential learning and Richard Felder and Barbara Soloman's Index of Learning Styles (1991), were used with Greek university undergraduate students from a variety of disciplines (education, psychology, polytechnics, and pre-teacher education) (Platsidou & Metallidou, 2009). The sample preferred the accommodative and divergent learning styles; however, there were no differences in terms of discipline. There was also a preference for visual and sensing learning styles. The results of this study could be used to encourage self-development "but not as a tool for grouping them according to given learning styles" (p. 324).

The learning styles of Indian students, enrolled in a master's program in Hyderabad, India, were examined to eventually improve delivery of management courses (Gantasala & Gantasala, 2009). A questionnaire combined the Honey and Mumford (pragmatist, reflector, activist, theorist) and Dunn and Dunn's (visual, auditory, kinesthetic) learning style theories. Learning style preferences were found to be independent of gender and year of study but no other preferences were ascertained.

Turkish and American graduate students were compared for their learning preferences (Kovach, 2009). Turkish students were not comfortable with teaching methods that were participative, interactive, and reflective. When asked about the learning methods, students indicated that the Turkish culture is more aligned with an authoritarian approach in the classroom. Four cultural student groups (15–16 years of age) were examined to see if there were any cultural differences in cognitive learning and study styles at international schools (de Nooij & Riedel, 2010).

The cultural groups were categorized as Northern Europe, North America (United States and Canada), Southern Europe, and Southeast Asia (China and Taiwan). All students, except the Southeast Asia group, preferred auditory learning when processing information. The least preferred learning style was tactile/kinesthetic. All groups preferred step-by-step learning when perceiving information. Northern European students had the greatest tendency to use a combined style of information processing that included auditory, visual, and tactile and kinesthetic. North American (American and Canadian) students had the most preference for using music as an aid for studying and would listen to background music while studying. The Southern European group had the largest number of abstract learners and preferred information to be presented in a step-by-step manner. They also had the highest scores in relating to others in classes. Relating to others refers to connecting to individuals through conversations or similar experiences. Southeast Asian students also showed a preference for abstract learning and step-by-step learning approaches. This group also preferred the visual learning mode. In the education setting, Madzy de Nooij and Marian Riedel strongly urged the continued identification of individual learning and study styles to strengthen techniques and opportunities for students to be successful.

Learning styles, as measured by Felder and Soloman's Index of Learning Styles (1991), and cultural conditioning of students in a multicultural international business management class were examined by Glauco De Vita (2001). The Felder and Soloman learning styles instrument categorizes preferences by type and mode of information perception (sensing or intuitive, visual or verbal), and approaches for the organization and processing of information (inductive or deductive, active or reflective) (Felder & Spurlin, 2005). More than 75 percent of the international business students, from 19 different nationalities, preferred visual rather than verbal inputs. Overall, the wider array of learning styles variations in this study may be attributed to the different cultural influences operating within this sample. "The scores reported by international students on the active-reflective, sensing-intuitive and sequential-global learning style dimensions display substantially greater values of absolute and relative dispersion compared to the scores reported by home students" (De Vita, 2001, p. 170).

Native Canadian adult students' learning styles were compared against multicultural adult students (Fraser, 1996) in the areas of family, holism, humanism, culture and voice, school, technology, employment, politics, assimilation, and acculturation. The results of this study reflected the need to be culturally sensitive about the similarities and differences in heritage and learning styles. Doing so will enhance curriculum and learning outcomes, personal development, mutual trust, and respect.

In the United States, demographic trends predict minorities will become a larger percentage of the population (National Center for Education Statistics, 2010). Cross-cultural research within Mexican American cultural groups identified differences and value conflicts (Creason, 1992; Swanson, 1995). Mexican American students were more likely to be field dependent learners—work well in groups, be motivated by group competition and achievement, and be influenced more by affective variables in learning. Anglo-American students were more likely to be field independent learners—work well alone; be motivated by individual competition and achievement and not be affected as much by outside stimuli such as the instructor or the environment.

Hani Morgan (2010) and Linda Swanson (1995) also reported variations in learning style and how students from different cultures learned differently. African American, Latino, Native American, and Alaska native students were reported to do better with cooperative learning methods and preferred to work together. Anglo-Americans preferred to work alone and tended to be field-independent: goal-oriented, competitive, analytical, and logical. Asian Pacific-American students may refrain from answering questions in a group or expressing their feelings in creative writing or speech because their culture emphasizes humility and modesty.

Guild (2001) revealed that learning styles are not equally valued in schools. "Most schools do a more effective job with learners who are reflective, linear, or analytic than those who are active, holistic, personal, or practical. Learners whose styles are accommodated more frequently in school achieve more immediate success. Students who struggle to adapt to an uncomfortable way of learning often underachieve" (p. 15). If students are deficient in specific skills or there is a possibility of them failing specific tasks, it should not preclude developing these skills within the classroom setting. Students will benefit from exposure to different ways and values of other cultures. Accepting that students learn in different ways will raise issues of uniformity and diversity, but it also might motivate an instructor to try a new method or technique to target reaching a select group of learners.

Conclusion

Bohannan (1995) revealed that human beings are hardwired to learn culture; however, culture is not hardwired into people. Humans can make choices, and these choices are made based on their biological capacities to choose, act, and reason. Culture can be a tool to navigate a variety of settings because the selected behavior patterns also create meaning for group and society members. "The immense human capacity for choice leads to many different satisfactory solutions to the challenges of living. . . . An act can have a different meaning in different contexts or to different peoples" (p. 9).

Learning styles assessments can be used to match instructional delivery or to enhance a learner's abilities and accommodate a variety of instructional approaches. Although some learning style theorists strive to identify personal preferences that are consistent throughout a variety of learning situations, other learning style theorists find that learners use a variety of methods to assist in their learning. The varied approaches to learning styles are not mutually exclusive, but illustrate the concept that individuals differ in their learning styles in a number of ways. Heffler (2001) also stressed that each individual's learning style has its strengths and weaknesses based on what has to be learned and how it should be learned. Simon Cassidy (2004) indicated that the general acceptance of the manner in which individuals choose or are inclined to approach a learning situation will ultimately affect performance and achievement of learning outcomes.

Instruments designed to identify an individual's learning style are primarily based on theoretical perspectives such as "self-report questionnaires, preferences for structure, environment, climate, complexity, sensory modality, philosophical orientation, cognitive organization and so on" (Smith & Associates, 1990, p. 47). Instrumentation is helpful within a learning environment because it provides learners with the ability to describe themselves and others. This ability includes an objective and nonemotional response when describing behavior and is especially useful within the professional development environment.

Instrumentation that is objective and uses common language provides learners standardized responses that are quantifiable. Nahla Aljojo, Carl Adams, Abeer Alkhouli, Tineke Fitch, and Huda Saifuddin (2009) reported the challenges of using an English language version instrument to measure learning styles of non-English speaking learners. An Arabic version of Felder and Soloman's Index of Learning Styles was developed, and validity and internal reliability calculations were made on the translated instrument (Aljojo et al., 2009). Efforts such as this contribute to future research in developing appropriate instruments in various languages and cultures.

If individuals know about their preferences, they could attempt to match learning activities with their preferred style or to try to extend their range of styles and use the less preferred style as a form of trial and error or as a discovery process. Guild (2001) considered that learners will bring their own individual approach, talents, and interests to the learning situation so it is important to not assume that all members of a group have the same style preferences. It is detrimental to use stereotypes of specific cultural groups because this would limit educational possibilities.

Swanson's (1995) recommendation that higher education institutions conduct professional development activities on the use of learning styles to improve teaching and student learning is still valid. Kimberlee Kovach (2009) suggested that when instructors work in foreign educational institutions, accommodating student learning preferences is critical. Using learning styles information can be helpful because it serves as a reminder to create engaging and rich learning environments. Using examples from the community to develop lessons that account for various cultural settings can provide useful and accessible learning cues.

Demetrios Kinshuk, Tzu-Chien Liu, and Sabine Graf (2009) investigated how students handled courses that were mismatched with their learning styles, as measured by the Felder and Soloman's Index of Learning Style instrument (1991). The results of this study found that reflective, intuitive, and sequential learners (with high scores) spent more time in the course material and visited more technology-related learning objects. Global learners (with high scores) did not seek additional learning objects. There was a correlation between students' behavior and their abilities to perform in the course. These findings suggested that students can be provided adaptive supports and given suggestions about how to overcome difficulties with other learning strategies that were successful for learners with the same learning style.

To overgeneralize culture-based learning strategies and learning styles would be detrimental in the teaching and learning environment. Sociocultural insights will promote understanding and awareness in providing culturally sensitive instruction in higher education institutions. Generalizations can foster discrimination and weaken culturally responsive teaching. "The sheer number of cultures represented in a classroom can make it difficult or even impossible to address each one adequately. Although no easy answers can be offered for such concerns, knowledge of cultural differences will certainly avert many conflicts" (Morgan, 2010, p. 117).

References

Aljojo, N., Adams, C., Alkhouli, A., Fitch, T., & Saifuddin, H. (2009, January). A study of the reliability and validity of the Felder-Soloman Index of Learning Styles in Arabic. *Proceedings of the European Conference on e-Learning*, 715–724. Available from http://academic-conferences.org/ecel/ecel2010/ecel09-proceedings .htm

American Association of School Administrators (AASA). (1992). *Learning styles: Putting research and common sense into practice.* Arlington, VA: Author.

Anderson, D., Brown, M., & Rushbrook, P. (2004). Vocational education and training. In G. Foley (Ed.), *Dimensions of learning: Adult education and training in a global era.* Berkshire, UK: Open University Press, McGraw-Hill Education.

Apple, M. (1982). *Education and power.* Boston, MA: Routledge & Kegan Paul.

Baldwin, L., & Sabry, K. (2003). Learning styles for interactive learning systems. *Innovations in Education & Teaching International, 40(4),* 325–340.

Bloom, B. (1976). *Human characteristics and school learning.* New York, NY: McGraw-Hill.

Bohannan, P. (1995). *How culture works.* New York, NY: Free Press.

Canfield, A. (1980). *Learning styles inventory manual.* Ann Arbor, MI: Humanics Media.

Cassidy, S. (2004). Learning styles: An overview of theories, models, and measures. *Educational Psychology, 24(4),* 419–445.

Chen, J., Moran, S., & Gardner, H. (2009). Multiple intelligences around the world. San Francisco, CA: Jossey-Bass.

Cherry, C. E. (1981). The measurement of adult learning styles: Perceptual modality (Doctoral dissertation, University of Tennessee, Knoxville, TN). *Dissertation Abstracts International, 42(09A),* 3852.

Claxton, D., & Murrell, P. (1987). *Learning styles: Implications for improving educational practices* (Report No. 4). Washington, DC: Association for the Study of Higher Education.

Creason, P. (1992, January). *Changing demographics and the importance of culture in student learning style.* Retrieved from ERIC database. (ED361270)

Curry, L. (1991). Patterns of learning style across selected medial specialties. *Educational Psychology, 11(3/4),* 247–277.

Cuthbert, P. (2005). The student learning process: Learning styles or learning approaches? *Teaching in Higher Education, 10(2),* 235–249.

de Nooij, M., & Riedel, M. (2010). Cultural differences in cognitive learning at international schools. *International Schools Journal, 24(2),* 36–41.

De Vita, G. (2001). Learning styles, culture and inclusive instruction in the multicultural classroom: A business and management perspective. *Innovations in Education and Teaching International, 38(2),* 165–174.

Dunn, R., Beaudry, J., & Klavas, A. (1989). Survey of research on learning styles. *Educational Leadership, 46(6),* 50–58.

Dunn, R., & Dunn, K. (1978). *Teaching students through their individual learning styles: A practical approach.* Reston, VA: Reston.

Dunn, R., & Dunn, K. (1993). *Teaching secondary students through their individual learning styles: Practical approaches for grades 7–12.* Boston, MA: Allyn & Bacon.

Felder, R., & Soloman, B. (1991). *Index of learning styles questionnaire.* Retrieved from http://www4.ncsu.edu/unity/lockers/users/f/felder/public/ILSpage.html

Felder, R., & Spurlin, J. (2005). Applications, reliability, and validity of the Index of Learning Styles. *International Journal of Engineering Education, 21(1),* 103–112.

Fougere, M., & Moulettes, A. (2007). The construction of the modern west and backward rest: Studying the discourse of Hofstede's culture's consequences. *Journal of Multicultural Discourses, 2(1),* 1–19.

Fraser, J. (1996, March). *How learning styles of native students are different from multicultural students*. Paper presented at the Conference on Urban Ethnography. Philadelphia, PA. Retrieved from ERIC database. (ED415338)

French, R. (1975). *Teaching style and instructional strategy*. Unpublished paper, Department of Curriculum and Instruction, University of Tennessee, Knoxville, TN.

Fridley, W., & Fridley, C. (2010). Some problems & peculiarities with the learning styles rhetoric & practice. *Journal of Philosophy and History of Education, 60*, 21–27.

Friedman, T. (2006). *The world is flat: A brief history of the twenty-first century*. New York, NY: Farrar, Straus & Giroux.

Gantasala, P., & Gantasala, S. (2009). Influence of learning styles. *The International Journal of Learning, 16*(9), 169–184.

Given, B. (2000). *Learning styles: A guide for teachers and parents*. Oceanside, CA: Learning Forum.

Gregorc, A. (1982a). *An adult's guide to style*. Columbia, CT: Gregorc Associates.

Gregorc, A. (1982b). *Gregorc style delineator: Development, technical and administration manual*. Columbia, CT: Gregorc Associates.

Griggs, S. (1991). *Learning styles counseling*. Ann Arbor, MI: ERIC Counseling and Personnel Services Clearinghouse.

Guild, P. (1994). The culture/learning style connection. *Educational Leadership, 5*(8), 16–21.

Guild, P. (2001). Diversity, learning style and culture. *New Horizons for Learning*. Retrieved from http://education.jhu.edu/newhorizons/strategies/topics/Learning%20Styles/diversity.html

Harvey, O., Hunt D., & Schroder, H. (1961). *Conceptual systems and personality organization*. New York, NY: Wiley.

Heffler, B. (2001). Individual learning style and the learning style inventory. *Educational Studies, 27*(3), 307–316.

Hofstede, G. (1980). *Culture's consequences: International differences in work-related values*. Beverly Hills, CA: Sage.

Hofstede, G. (2001). *Culture's consequences: Comparing values, behaviors, institutions and organizations across nations* (2nd ed.). London, UK: Sage.

Honey, P., & Mumford, D. (1992). *The manual of learning styles* (3rd ed.). Maidenhead, UK: Honey.

Hunt, D. (1978). Conceptual level theory and research as guides to educational practice. *Interchange, 8*(4), 78–90.

James, W., & Blank, W. (1993). Review and critique of available learning-style instruments for adults. *New Directions for Adult and Continuing Education, 59*, 47–57.

Keefe, J. (1979). Learning style: An overview. In *Student learning styles: Diagnosing and prescribing programs* (pp. 1–17). Reston, VA: National Association of Secondary School Principals.

Keefe, J. (1987). *Learning style theory and practice*. Reston, VA: National Association of Secondary School Principals.

Kennedy, P. (2002). Learning cultures and learning styles: Myth-understandings about adult (Hong Kong) Chinese learners. *International Journal of Lifelong Education, 21*(5), 430–445.

Kinshuk, D., Liu, T., & Graf, S. (2009). Coping with mismatched courses: Students' behaviour and performance in courses mismatched to their learning styles. *Education Tech Research Development, 57,* 739–752.

Kolb, D. (1976). *Learning style inventory.* Boston, MA: McBer.

Kolb, D. (1984). *Experiential learning.* Englewood Cliffs, NJ: Prentice Hall.

Kolb, D. (1985). *Learning styles inventory.* Boston, MA. McBer.

Kovach, K. (2009). Culture, cognition, and learning preferences. In C. Honeyman, J. Coben, & G. De Palo (Eds.), *Rethinking negotiation teaching: Innovations for context and culture* (pp. 343–355). St. Paul, MN: Dispute Resolution Institute Press.

Krätzig, G., & Arbuthnott, K. (2006). Perceptual learning style and learning proficiency: A test of the hypothesis. *Journal of Educational Psychology, 98*(1), 238–246.

Lawrence, G. (1995). *People types and tiger stripes* (3rd ed.). Gainesville, FL: Center for Application of Psychological Type.

Messick, S., & Associates. (1978). *Individuality in learning.* San Francisco, CA: Jossey-Bass.

Milner, A., & Browitt, J. (2002). *Contemporary cultural theory: An introduction* (3rd ed.). New York, NY: Routledge.

Morgan, H. (2010). Improving schooling for cultural minorities: The right teaching styles can make a big difference. *Educational Horizons, 88*(2), 114–120.

National Center for Education Statistics. (2010). Status and trends in the education of racial and ethnic minorities. Retrieved from http://www.nces.ed.gov/pubs2010/2010015/chapter1.asp

Nield, K. (2009). The problems of applying labels of learning style to national cultures. *The International Journal of Learning, 16*(7), 426–434.

Pashler, H., McDaniel, M., Rohrer, D., & Bjork, R. (2009). Learning styles: Concepts and evidence. *Psychological Science in the Public Interest, 9*(3), 105–119.

Platsidou, M., & Metallidou, P. (2009). Validity and reliability issues of two learning style inventories in a Greek sample: Kolb's learning style inventory and Felder & Soloman's index of learning styles. *International Journal of Teaching and Learning in Higher Education, 20*(3), 324–335.

Reiff, J. (1992). *Learning styles: What research says to the teacher series.* Washington, DC: National Education Association.

Riding, R., & Rayner, S. (1998). *Cognitive styles and learning strategies.* London, UK: David Fulton.

Riener, C., & Willingham, D. (2010, September/October). The myth of learning styles. *Change, 42*(5), 32–35.

Robertson, R. (1992). *Globalization: Social theory and global culture.* London, UK: Sage.

Sarasin, L. (1998). *Learning style perspectives: Impact in the classroom.* Madison, WI: Atwood.

Sayers, J., & Franklin, T. (2008). Culture shock! Cultural issues in a tertiary course using reflective techniques. *Reflective Practice, 9*(1), 79–88.

Scott, C. (2010). The enduring appeal of learning styles. *Australian Journal of Education, 54*(1), 5–17.

Sewell, W. (1999). The concept of culture. In V. Bonnell & L. Hunt (Eds.), *Beyond the cultural turn* (pp. 35–61). Berkeley, CA: University of California.

Smelser, N. (1992). Culture: Coherent or incoherent. In R. Munch and N. Smelser (Eds.), *Theory of culture* (pp. 3–28). Berkeley, CA: University of California.

Smith, R., & Associates. (1990). *Learning to learn across the life span.* San Francisco, CA: Jossey-Bass.

Sonbuchner, G. (1991). *Help yourself: How to take advantage of your learning styles.* Syracuse, NY: New Readers Press.

Squires, G. (1981). *Cognitive styles and adult learning.* Nottingham, UK: University of Nottingham.

Sternberg, R., & Grigorenko, E. (1997). Are cognitive styles still in style? *American Psychologist, 52,* 700–712.

Surber, J. (1998). *Culture and critique: An introduction to the critical discourses of cultural studies.* Boulder, CO: Westview Press.

Swailes, S., & Senior, B. (1999). The dimensionality of Honey and Mumford's learning styles questionnaire. *International Journal of Selection and Assessment, 7*(1), 1–11.

Swanson, L. (1995, July). *Learning styles: A review of the literature.* Retrieved from ERIC database. (ED387067)

Tennant, M. (1988). *Psychology and adult learning.* New York, NY: Routledge.

Tucker, D. (2003, March). *Understanding learning styles and study strategies of Korean students in American colleges and universities: A research study with recommendations for faculty and academic advisors.* Retrieved from ERIC database. (ED478616)

Wu, S., & Alrabah, S. (2009). A cross-cultural study of Taiwanese and Kuwaiti EFL students' learning styles and multiple intelligences. *Innovations in Education and Teaching International, 46*(4), 393–403.

Zhang, L., & Watkins, D. (2001). Cognitive development and student approaches to learning: An investigation of Perry's theory with Chinese and U.S. university students. *Higher Education, 41,* 239–261.

CHAPTER 23

Metacognitive Learning
and Culture

Kevin Downing and Kristina Shin

Metacognition is among the most actively investigated cognitive processes in contemporary psychological research generally, and in the study of learning specifically. The term *metacognition* became part of the lexicon of higher education in the1970s when John Flavell (1971) introduced the term *metamemory*, but the concept is much older than that drawing on the work of ancient philosophers from around the globe including Plato, Aristotle, Confucius, Solomon, Buddha, and Lao Tzu (King, 2004). The importance of developing metacognitive skills was recognized long before the term came into common use, with John Locke commenting in 1690, that most children gradually develop the ability to "reflect" on their own thinking processes. For example, when young children are asked if they understand something, they often simply nod in agreement or fail to ask questions (Brown, 1973). However, by adulthood most of us have a better understanding of the complex processes involved in knowing what we do and do not know (Piaget, 1972). Amanda Brown (1987) and Neville Hatton and David Smith (1995) report that as early as 1917, Edward Thorndike was testing metacognition by asking his students to problem-solve by answering questions on texts they had read. Consequently, when Flavell (1963) published a text on the developmental psychology of Jean Piaget, the as-yet-unnamed *metacognition* caught the attention of researchers and by 1975 had come into common use.

Metacognition is best defined as "thinking about thinking" (Bogdan, 2000; Flavell, 1999; Metcalfe, 2000) but also involves knowing how to reflect and analyze thought, how to draw conclusions from that analysis, and how to put what has been learned into practice. To solve problems, undergraduates need to perceive how they perform important cognitive tasks such as remembering, learning, and problem solving. This is akin to Rainier Kluwe's (1987) concept of metacognition whereby thinkers know something about their own and others' thought processes, and thinkers can pay attention to and change their own thinking. Douglas Hacker (1998) pointed out the difference between *cognitive tasks* (remembering things learned earlier that might help with the current task or problem) and *meta-cognitive tasks* (monitoring and directing the process of problem solving), stressing the importance of learning more about thinking as a process. Cesare Cornoldi (1998) emphasized the role of learners' beliefs about think-ing and made the point that if students feel confident that they can solve problems, they tend to do better work. In his definition of *metacognition* as "thinking about thinking" or "second-order cognition," Franz Weinert (1987) acknowledges that purpose, conscious understanding, the ability to talk or write about tasks, and generalizability to other tasks are also impor-tant factors in determining whether a given task is metacognitive. This view-point is supported by Brown (1987), who agrees that metacognition requires the thinker to use and describe the process of mental activity. Many others also make the point that *metacognition* is best defined by acknowledging that it is both knowledge about, and control of, thinking processes (Allen & Armour-Thomas, 1991). Vimla Vadhan and Philip Stander (1993) make the distinction between ordinary thinking and awareness and understanding of thinking, and this is elaborated by Hacker (1998), who gives the most com-prehensive description of metacognition by dividing it into three types of thinking: (1) metacognitive knowledge—what one knows about knowledge; (2) metacognitive skill—what one is currently doing; and (3) metacognitive experience—one's current cognitive or affective state. Therefore, cognition focuses on solving the problem and metacognition focuses on the process of problem solving (Marchant, 2001). In addition to the knowledge people have about how they use their thoughts and strategies (Brown, 1987), knowledge about how much they will be able to learn, and what kinds of strategies they use (Gleitman, 1985; Weinert, 1987; Kluwe, 1987), people also have a set of general heuristics—for example, how they plan, set goals, and process feedback (Frese, Stewart, & Hanover, 1987). The assumption is that these general heuristics can be either conscious or automatic (Brown, 1987; Flavell, 1987), and they may be highly generalized or specific. Consequently, the study of metacognition is a fruitful area for those inter-ested in potential gender differences, learning processes, motivation, self-efficacy, undergraduate development, and an almost limitless range of other variables (Downing, 2009; Ning & Downing, 2010a, 2010b).

Metacognition and the Learning and Study Strategies Inventory (LASSI)

One of the most popular ways to assess metacognition is through questionnaires that require students to report perceptions about their thinking and problem-solving strategies. Claire Ellen Weinstein and David Palmer (1988) suggest that poor grades rebound when students learn the tricks of pinpointing key points in lectures and assert that learning is more effective when engaging in thinking about the process of learning, thinking, and problem-solving. The Learning and Study Strategies Inventory (LASSI), contains 10 scales and 80 items to assess students' awareness and use of learning and study strategies related to the skill, will, and self-regulation components of strategic learning (Weinstein, 1987). Research has repeatedly demonstrated that these factors contribute to successful study and can be learned or enhanced through educational interventions such as study skills courses (Hanley, 1995; King, 1991; Letteri, 1992; Weinstein, 1994a, 1994b). The LASSI measures three main areas of strategic learning:

Skill component of strategic learning

These scales examine students' perceptions (metacognition) of their learning strategies, skills, and the thought processes related to identifying, acquiring, and constructing meaning for important new information, ideas, and procedures. The LASSI scales related to the skill component of strategic learning are as follows:

- Information processing: ability to process ideas by mentally elaborating on them and organizing them in meaningful ways
- Selecting main ideas: ability to identify the important information in a learning situation
- Test strategies: ability to prepare effectively for an examination and to reason through a question when answering it

Will component of strategic learning

These scales measure students' perceptions of their receptivity to learning new information; their attitudes and interest in college; their diligence, self-discipline, and willingness to exert the effort necessary to successfully complete academic requirements; and the degree to which they worry about their academic performance. The LASSI scales related to the will component of strategic learning are as follows:

- Attitude: perceived motivation and interest to succeed in their study and willingness to perform the tasks necessary for academic success
- Motivation: extent to which the student accepts responsibility for performing those tasks by using self-discipline and hard work
- Anxiety: degree of anxiety perceived by the student when approaching academic tasks

Self-regulation component of strategic learning

These scales measure students' perceptions of how they manage, self-regulate, and control the whole learning process through using time effectively, focusing attention, and maintaining concentration over time; checking to see if they have met the learning demands for a class, an assignment, or a test; and using study supports such as review sessions, tutors, or special features of a textbook. The LASSI scales related to the self-regulation component of strategic learning are these:

- Concentration: perceived ability to focus one's attention, and avoid distractions, while working on school-related tasks such as studying
- Time management: perception of the extent to which students create and use schedules to manage their responsibilities effectively
- Self-testing: awareness of the importance of self-testing and reviewing when learning material, and use of those practices
- Study aids: student's perceived ability to use or develop study aids that assist with the learning process

There is a wealth of research, making use of the LASSI as a measure of metacognition, that identifies the value of learning to learn interventions (Loomis, 2000). This chapter extends this investigation of metacognition by looking at two studies that identify factors outside the learning institution that affect the development of metacognitive skills.

Study 1: Undergraduate Metacognition and Moving to University Residence

Methods

The LASSI is administered within weeks 3 to 5 of the first semester to all freshmen to help them monitor and develop appropriate learning attitudes and strategies, and maximize the opportunity to enjoy a successful learning experience during university and beyond. An interim test follows around the middle of the undergraduate program, and a posttest is administered toward completion of their program. Each undergraduate takes the LASSI three times during his or her degree program. Longitudinal data provide evidence of growth in metacognitive ability over the time spent in undergraduate study, and the interim test allows the university to correct any problems with this development early. It takes approximately 25 minutes to compile the inventory, which can be completed online.

Materials

The Learning and Study Strategies Inventory (Weinstein & Palmer, 2002) and demographic entry data collected by the university during the student admission process.

Participants

We collected LASSI data from 1,821 first-year students, from a wide range of countries, who were studying in Hong Kong and correlated with variables taken from their demographic data. Students were distributed into four groups for analysis, and data related to LASSI score and background information were obtained:

Group A—Full-time Universities Grants Committee (UGC-government-funded place) students ($n = 984$)

Group B—Part-time non-UGC (self-financed) students ($n = 343$)

Group C—Foundation-year students (all from the Chinese mainland/self-financed) ($n = 134$)

Group D—Students not belonging to any of the previous 3 groups ($n = 360$) (for exceptions, see Table 23.1)

Table 23.1   Category of Students

		Frequency	Percent	Valid Percent	Cumulative Percent
Valid	Exception	360	19.8	19.8	19.8
	Foundation	134	7.4	7.4	27.2
	UGC-funded	984	54.0	54.0	81.2
	Non-UGC funded	343	18.8	18.8	100.0
	Total	1821	100.0	100.0	

Procedure

To investigate correlations between LASSI scores and other demographic and academic factors, a number of correlations were attempted with the four groups. Six cases were omitted because of incomplete or confounding data, therefore operationally $N = 1815$.

Results

A range of data for correlation was collected and analyzed, but the results presented relate primarily to Group C and have been selected because they were unexpected. Analysis of variance (ANOVA) on the relationship between LASSI scores and housing yielded highly significant results ($p < .001$) demonstrating a significant relationship between LASSI score and whether a student is living in the home environment (family home or FH) (see Table 23.2). Mainland Chinese students coming to Hong Kong to study (moving away from home) with unidentified housing type obtained the highest overall LASSI scores ($n = 127$, mean = 619.73) with those students living in City University's accommodation on campus producing the second highest LASSI scores ($n = 45$, mean = 580.58). Those living in private housing produced ($n = 621$, mean = 435.83) the third highest LASSI scores (see Table 23.2).

When the total LASSI score is broken into the three major components of the inventory, "will," "skill," and "self-regulation," the following results are obtained (see Tables 23.3 to 23.6).

Table 23.2 Mean Total LASSI Score According to Type of Housing (FH vs. NFH)

		N	Mean LASSI Score
LASSI	Staff quarters (FH)	5	369.8000
	HOS/PSPS (FH)	269	419.3494
	Private housing (FH)	621	435.8293
	Public housing (FH)	748	418.4238
	Student halls (NFH)	45	580.5778
	From Chinese mainland (NFH)	127	619.7323
	Total	1815	442.4887

Key: FH—Living in family home. HOS—Home ownership scheme. NFH—Living away from family home. PSPS—Private sector participation scheme

Table 23.3 Mean Will Component Score According to Type of Housing (FH vs. NFH)

		N	Mean "Will" Score
Will Component	Staff quarters (FH)	5	83.2000
	HOS/PSPS (FH)	269	98.9182
	Private housing (FH)	621	104.7536
	Public housing (FH)	748	98.9184
	Student halls (NFH)	45	157.4667
	From Chinese mainland (NFH)	127	159.0945
	Total	1815	106.5339

Key: FH—Living in family home. HOS—Home ownership scheme. NFH—Living away from family home. PSPS—Private sector participation scheme

Table 23.4 Mean Skill Component Score According to Type of Housing (FH vs. NFH)

		N	Mean "Skill" Score
Skill Component	Staff quarters (FH)	5	150.0000
	HOS/PSPS (FH)	269	136.7993
	Private housing (FH)	621	142.0177
	Public housing (FH)	748	133.6484
	Student halls (NFH)	45	181.6889
	From Chinese mainland (NFH)	127	199.3307
	Total	1815	142.8110

Key: FH—Living in family home. HOS—Home ownership scheme. NFH—Living away from family home. PSPS—Private sector participation scheme

Table 23.5 Mean Self-Regulation Component Score According to Type of Housing (FH vs. NFH)

		N	Mean "Self-Regulation" Score
Self-Regulation Component	Staff quarters (FH)	5	136.6000
	HOS/PSPS (FH)	269	183.6320
	Private housing (FH)	621	189.0580
	Public housing (FH)	748	185.8570
	Student halls (NFH)	45	241.4222
	From Chinese mainland (NFH)	127	261.3071
	Total	1815	193.1438

Key: FH—Living in family home. HOS—Home ownership scheme. NFH—Living away from family home. PSPS—Private sector participation scheme

Discussion

These results raise the question of the extent to which the metacognitive skills assessed by LASSI are influenced or associated with moving away from the home environment. In other words, does a significant change in the social context positively affect metacognitive development? Jean Piaget (1929, 1954, 1977) describes the process of intellectual development in terms of movement from "egocentrism" to "decentration," but, since L. S. Vygotsky

Table 23.6 ANOVA

		Sum of Squares	df	Mean Square	F	Sig.
Will Component	Between Groups	531261.269	5	106252.254	40.561	.000
	Within Groups	4738756.397	1809	2619.545		
	Total	5270017.666	1814			
Skill Component	Between Groups	546883.932	5	109376.786	31.883	.000
	Within Groups	6205872.248	1809	3430.554		
	Total	6752756.180	1814			
Self-Regulation Component	Between Groups	785366.094	5	157073.219	31.249	.000
	Within Groups	9093021.373	1809	5026.546		
	Total	9878387.468	1814			
LASSI	Between Groups	5478997.128	5	1095799.426	45.101	.000
	Within Groups	43952864.391	1809	24296.774		
	Total	49431861.518	1814			

(1975) highlighted the role of social interaction in cognitive development, contemporary researchers (Lynch, Leo, & Downing, 2006; Lourenco & Machado, 1996; Rogoff & Chavajay, 1995; Serpell & Boykin, 1995) have focused on the role of culture and social interactions in cognitive development. This view posits that young adults develop by internalizing and absorbing knowledge from their social context.

Metacognitive Development, Culture, and Social Context

Piaget recognized the importance of a challenging environment so it should not be surprising that metacognitive development progresses as a result of significant life events such as leaving home. It seems likely that this will involve the internalization of new experiences and subsequent increases in metacognitive activity. The overall LASSI scores presented in Table 23.2 demonstrate that students who have moved from the Chinese mainland to Hong Kong score significantly above the mean LASSI score. Additionally, students from Hong Kong who had moved into student residence halls on campus, and so had moved away from home (although not quite so far in geographical terms) also scored well above the mean LASSI score. The first of these findings suggests some element of cultural difference in metacognitive development (Serpell, 2000). However, the fact that the group of students living in halls, from the very different cultural context of Hong Kong also score much more highly than their Hong Kong counterparts living in the family home suggests that there is something about the changed social context that affects metacognitive development. Analysis of the component scores for will, skill, and self-regulation casts some light on this process.

Skill, Self-Regulation, and Social Context

The differences from the mean scores ($N = 1815$) for the will component are 52.56 for the Chinese mainland students and 50.93 for students living in halls of residence are not great but look more interesting when we consider the skill and self-regulation components. Differences from mean scores for the skill component are 56.52 for the Chinese mainland students and 38.88 for students living in halls of residence. For the self-regulation component, these figures are 68.16 and 48.28, respectively, suggesting that these two components are differentially influenced in the two groups. Students from mainland China are geographically distant from their home culture, and so the requirement to self-regulate and think about this process (metacognition) is likely to be more pressing than for those students living in their own culture but away from the family home. For both groups, the changed social context is likely to influence their perceived ability to concentrate and focus attention positively because they are not subject to the often considerable demands of living in the family home, and this will no doubt impact the sense of control they perceive in relation to their time-management abilities. For the perceived use of self-testing and study aid strategies, the changed social context gives students everyday opportunities to try out different problem-solving strategies (skill component) and eliminate those that do not work as well, gradually evolving new strategies depending on changes in the situation in the same way as Robert Siegler (1996) describes for cognitive development.

Challenges emerging from new social contexts provide fertile environments for the development of metacognition. The highest meta-level of cognition is usually not implicated when we receive an outside task and when the task solution is known. The meta-level tends to be consulted when things go wrong or when the situation is new. Therefore, the meta-level will come into play when we move to other housing, or we consider our life goals in a more general sense, something we are surely disposed to do when moving away from home environment and culture. The challenging new social context of living away from home in a different culture increases the use of metacognition because the student cannot call on routinized or automatic cognition. There is almost a requirement in these circumstances to have knowledge about and control over thinking processes (Allen & Armour-Thomas, 1991).

According to Marcy Perkins Driscoll (1994), Piagetian (cognitive) theorists generally agree on three basic instructional principles: (1) the learning environment should support the activity of the learner (i.e., an active, discovery-oriented environment), (2) the learner's interactions with peers are an important source of cognitive development (i.e., peer teaching and social negotiation), (3) instructional strategies that make learners aware of conflicts and inconsistencies in their thinking promote cognitive development (i.e., conflict teaching and Socratic dialogue). Why then should metacognitive strategies such as planning, monitoring, and evaluating one's own learning evolve more effectively when undergraduates are away from their home environment and culture? Vygotsky's (1986) view was that to subject a function to intellectual and voluntary control, we must first possess that function. In other words, metacognition and self-reflection will develop first as a skill before it can be used as a series of consciously controlled strategies. The emphasis on social interaction as a precondition for the training of reflective skills is today shared by many approaches to instruction (Von Wright 1992).

In terms of social constructivist theory, metacognitive processes begin as social processes and gradually become "internalized" (Downing, 2001). The social context of living in an environment outside what might be termed your *comfort zone* will undoubtedly provide an action- and discovery-oriented learning environment, and the scope for peer interaction and social negotiation is considerably widened. Finally, Socratic dialogue is a method widely used in Europe, which allows for in-depth understanding of various issues concerning everyday life. Through rigorous inquiry and consensus, students start to unravel some of their basic assumptions and develop metacognitive skills and knowledge. This approach has long valued everyday life as a formidable teacher of self-reflection.

Thomas E. Scruggs, Margo A. Mastropieri, Jay Monson, and Cheri Jorgensen (1985) suggest that direct instruction in metacognitive strategies (e.g., learning to learn courses) leads to increases in learning, and independent use of these strategies develops only gradually. Although there is a wealth of research in support of Scruggs (Bogdan, 2000; Driscoll, 1994; Hanley, 1995), it is essential that educators not neglect the crucial role of experience outside of the classroom in the development of metacognitive skills. Independent use of metacognitive strategies is a by-product of coping with everyday new social contexts and cultures. It seems likely from the data presented in this paper that the experience of moving away from home creates a metacognitive environment that fosters the development of "thinking about thinking" and provides students with more opportunities to become successful problem solvers and lifelong learners.

Study 2: Gender and Metacognitive Development

In recent years, policymakers and researchers have given much attention to what is described as an emerging gender gap in terms of educational attainment (Van de gaer, Pustjens, Van Damme, & De Munter, 2004). The pattern of academic performance on achievement tests and public examinations that has emerged since the mid-1980s is of females outperforming males on almost all areas of the curriculum (Arnot, David, & Weiner, 1999; Cole, 1997; Gorard, Rees, & Salisbury, 2001; Kleinfeld, 1999; Rowe & Rowe, 2003; Yates, 1997). The public examination that provides the gateway to higher education in Hong Kong and the United Kingdom is the A-level, and our review of entry scores by gender for this sample suggests that these countries reflect this trend. In Hong Kong "A" level (AL) scores are calculated on a point basis with AL subjects or one AL subject plus two advanced-supplementary (AS) level subjects being counted. For AL subjects, grade A = 10 points, B = 8 points, C = 6 points, D = 4 points, E = 2 points; for AS level subjects, grade A = 5 points, B = 4 points, C = 3 points, D = 2 points, E = 1 points. Thus, the maximum score for each student should not exceed 20 points. Table 23.7 shows mean AL scores for both genders on entry to the university. These results were subjected to a t test for equality of means and found to be highly significant at $p < 0.004$.

Table 23.7   A-Level Scores of Participants

A-level score	Overall	N	Percentage
Male	9.48	1025	58.305%
Female	9.95	733	41.695%
Total		1758	100%

In contrast, gender researchers have long argued that cognitive functioning and achievement do not always favor one sex (Halpern & LaMay, 2000; Marsh & Yeung, 1998; Royer, Tronsky, Chan, Jackson, & Marchant, 1999; Wigfield, Battle, Keller, & Eccles, 2002) with males outperforming females on tests of visuospatial ability and mathematical reasoning (Gallagher, Levin, & Cahalan, 2002; Halpern, 2004; Lawton & Hatcher, 2005; Skaalvik & Skaalvik, 2004;), whereas females do better on tests involving memory and language use (Huang, 1993; Lowe, Mayfield, & Reynolds, 2003; Temple & Cornish, 1993). Study 2 investigated relationships between gender, AL scores, and scores on the LASSI at a university in Hong Kong and suggests that the significant gender differences in AL scores provide limited practical information at a cognitive level. In contrast, LASSI data allow a detailed and practical metacognitive analysis suggesting gender differences in certain areas of self-perceived performance, with females demonstrating significantly higher levels of self-regulation and a more positive attitude to academic study than their male counterparts have.

Methods

Participants for this study were selected at random from an overall LASSI sampling exercise, and males and females were compared using their LASSI. Data were then subjected to t test analysis for equality of means to determine the significance of the results.

Materials

The measure of metacognition used for this study is the Learning and Study Strategies Inventory (Weinstein & Palmer, 2002).

Participants

First year, entry cohort undergraduates from a university in Hong Kong participated in this study ($N = 1,758$). The male group was larger than the female group at $n = 1,025$ and $n = 733$, respectively.

Procedure

Participants were grouped according to self-identified gender with all participants identifying as either male or female. AL scores on entry to university were calculated according to the Hong Kong convention described earlier.

Results

The results are presented as tables beginning with the overall LASSI mean scores and then by each of the three components and composite items. Levels of significance and standard deviations are also presented in Tables 23.8 to 23.11.

Table 23.8 Overall LASSI Scores

	Gender	Mean	Std. Deviation	Std. Error Mean	t test for Equality of Means
Overall	Male	47.325	14.676	0.459	0.596
	Female	47.697	14.378	0.531	

Table 23.9 Self-Regulation Component Scores

	Gender	Mean	Std. Deviation	Std. Error Mean	t test for Equality of Means
Self-Regulation	Male	52.184	17.951	0.561	0.027
	Female	54.034	16.716	0.618	
CON	Male	51.573	23.240	0.727	0.032
	Female	53.913	21.941	0.811	
TMT	Male	50.586	20.586	0.644	0.033
	Female	52.702	20.508	0.758	
SFT	Male	49.717	25.157	0.787	0.704
	Female	49.264	24.214	0.895	
STA	Male	56.390	26.054	0.815	0.005
	Female	59.762	23.875	0.882	

Note: CON–Concentration, TMT–Time management, SFT–Self-testing, STA–Study aids

Table 23.10 Skill Component Scores

	Gender	Mean	Std. Deviation	Std. Error Mean	t test for Equality of Means
Skill	Male	52.833	18.365	0.574	0.006
	Female	50.410	18.027	0.666	
INP	Male	57.387	24.071	0.753	0.000
	Female	51.031	24.324	0.899	
SMI	Male	53.101	22.061	0.690	0.402
	Female	52.216	21.599	0.798	
TST	Male	48.001	24.103	0.754	0.977
	Female	47.967	23.942	0.885	

Note: INP–Information processing, SMI–Selecting main ideas, TST–Test strategies

Table 23.11 Will Component Scores

	Gender	Mean	Std. Deviation	Std. Error Mean	t test for Equality of Means
Will	Male	34.838	15.662	0.490	0.144
	Female	35.955	15.899	0.588	
ANX	Male	53.698	24.180	0.756	0.021
	Female	51.036	23.493	0.868	

Note: ANX–Anxiety

Table 23.12

	Gender	Mean	Std. Deviation	Std. Error Mean	t test for Equality of Means
ATT	Male	18.028	19.381	0.606	0.000
	Female	23.343	20.546	0.759	
MOT	Male	32.771	23.860	0.746	0.496
	Female	33.551	23.498	0.868	

Note: ATT–Attitude, MOT–Motivation

Discussion

There are no significant differences on overall mean scores for LASSI, but results reveal significant differences on all three components, with female participants scoring significantly higher for self-regulation and will components than did males who score significantly higher on one item from the skill component. If the self-regulation component is broken down into its constituent items, it is evident that female participants rate themselves as significantly more adept than their male counterparts for three of the four items. They perceive themselves to be better at focusing attention and avoiding distractions when studying, better at creating and using schedules to manage responsibilities effectively, and better at using and developing study aids that assist with learning. There is no significant difference between male and female participants in awareness of the importance of self-testing when learning material and using these strategies. This is broadly in line with results reported by Richard Felder, Gary Felder, Meredith Mauney, Charles Hamrin, and Jacquelin Dietz (1995) although in their study females also scored more highly than male counterparts did for self-testing. However, it should be noted that the current study involves students from all disciplines offered by the university rather than just the engineering discipline studied by Felder et al.

Social Interaction and Self-Regulation

Identifying the central role played by social interaction in cognitive development, Vygotsky (1975) demonstrated the impact of environmental challenges on this process, and many contemporary researchers have tended to focus on the role of culture and social interactions when investigating gender differences in cognitive development. However, this study raises the specific question of why females differ from males in their self-evaluations of key aspects of self-regulatory abilities. Vygotsky's (1986) conclusion was that self-regulation develops first as a skill before it can be used as a series of consciously controlled strategies, so how does self-regulation develop as a skill, and why might female participants rate themselves more highly than males on this component? Mieke Van Houte (2004) suggests that differential levels of social interaction resulting from the gender-specific cultures adolescents experience influence cognitive and metacognitive development. Carole Beal (1994) quotes a number of studies that suggest that young males and females create separate social worlds based on different styles and interests and that qualitative differences emerge in the nature of their friendships, with females tending to associate with one or two "best friends" nurturing and maintaining relationships in which both parties have equal status. To maintain this sort of relationship requires the exercise of self-regulatory skills and contrasts with the male equivalent, which is dominated more by the external "rules" of a dominance hierarchy (Pettit, Bakshi, Dodge, & Coie, 1990) and less homogenous networks. These early female social behaviors are not directly related to study skills and strategies but nonetheless create opportunities for females to develop and practice self-regulation that might be expected to carry over into other areas with practice. Duane Burhmester and Wyndol Furman (1987) point out that intimate friendships are formed earlier for teenage females than for their male counterparts, and this requires hard work and restraint to cultivate trust and mutual support. This emphasis on social interaction as a precondition for the development of self-regulatory skills is shared by many approaches to instruction (Von Wright, 1992) and is consistent with social constructivist theory that suggests metacognitive processes begin as social processes and gradually become internalized (Downing, 2001; Downing, Ho, Shin, Vrijmoed, & Wong, 2007).

Self-Perceived or Metacognitive Skill

For the skill component of LASSI scores, the situation for self-regulation is reversed, with males perceiving themselves as doing better than females. However, a closer look at the results indicates that the significant difference on this component results entirely from one item, with males scoring significantly higher on information processing, the ability to process ideas by mentally elaborating and organizing them in meaningful ways. Some researchers (Baron-Cohen, 2004; Geake & Cooper, 2003) have suggested that this might be explained by how the male and female brains communicate, whereas others (Biddulph, 1997; Gurian, 2002) claim that male and female brains are wired differently. However, these claims are largely discounted by neuroscientists (Northen, 2004), who point out that the brain is a tensile organ and responds to external stimuli. For example, the differences in information processing scores might equally be a result of females not wishing to overrate themselves in an area that is stereotypically masculine. Despite this, evidence suggests that in general males tend to perform better in cognitive tasks that depend heavily on information processing ability. A number of studies suggest that males and females process information differently

(Gilligan, 1982; Meyers-Levy, 1986) with males generally encoding fewer details than females. If females process more details than males, then males must use heuristics in their processing of information (Meyers-Levy, 1986; Meyers-Levy & Maheswaran, 1991), and this tendency might be explained in two ways. First, the amount of information stored in long-term memory depends on the amount of information processed. Because males encode fewer details (Meyers-Levy, 1985), they would recall less information for decision making, so they would have to resort to heuristics to compensate for the lack of stored information. Second, the presence of contrasting information in the data set causes cognitive strain (Kahneman, 1973). When faced with contrasting information, normative decision theories suggest that people pay greater attention to details to reconcile the contrasting information. Females pay greater attention to details (Meyers-Levy, 1986), so this suggests that the genders do not react to contrasting information in the same way. Females deal with contrasting information by increasing processing effort whereas males make greater use of heuristics (Chung & Tang, 1998). Both explanations are consistent with our results, suggesting that males perceive themselves as being better at information processing because they make greater use of heuristics to process ideas in meaningful ways. The downside of this approach is that some detail is inevitably lost in the processing.

Self-Perceived or Metacognitive Will

There are no significant differences overall on the will component, but there are significant differences between males and females for both attitude and anxiety items. Differences between genders on the anxiety scale was also observed by Felder et al. (1995), who identified higher levels of anxiety from females when approaching academic tasks. Depending on the degree of anxiety experienced by females, this could either improve academic performance by maintaining optimum levels of stress for efficient functioning, or damage performance by exceeding these levels and so become a debilitating factor. The former possibility is more likely with our sample given their more positive reflections about their attitude to academic study. A developing body of research (Cupchick & Leventhal, 1974; Cupchick & Poulos, 1984; Darley & Smith, 1995; Leventhal & Cupchick, 1975; Meyers-Levy, 1989; Tversky & Kahneman, 1973) supports the view that males use more heuristics when processing information than females do. The picture that emerges from this study is of a characteristically different approach to learning strategies taken by males and females. The male approach seems to result in poorer attitudes to study and less anxiety but suffers from potential loss of information in comparison with females. The reasons for these observed differences in metacognition remain elusive and return us to arguments about the relative impact of nature and nurture on metacognitive development that are beyond the scope of this study. However, females would be expected to develop heightened abilities in concentration, use of schedules, developing study aids, and higher anxiety levels if they perceive themselves to be suffering from information overload as a result of their different approach to information processing.

Following a review of the literature in relation to cognition, intelligence testing, and AL achievement scores, this study takes a different approach to the gender differences in cognitive functioning and achievement debate, preferring to focus on metacognitive differences between male and female undergraduates. Analysis of data produced by the LASSI indicates that there are significant differences in self-perceived metacognition between the genders, and these are a potentially fruitful area for further research given the differential pattern of functioning identified by our male and female participants. We are not arguing that females do not engage in the use of rules of thumb or heuristics, but results suggest that, as late adolescents or young adults, there are differences in the extent and patterns of this usage. Females appear focused on attempting to process more details than do their male counterparts, who in turn tend to make more use of heuristic devices to information process "effectively." A combination of biological, social, and psychological factors might predispose differential cognitive abilities but we are likely to see more clearly the outcomes of these factors in the fascinating area of metacognition.

Conclusion

Both studies reported in this chapter highlight the importance of social interaction in the rapid and continuing development of metacognition in undergraduates. Whether the challenge is moving away from home to study or maintaining relationships, social interaction is a critical component in metacognitive development in undergraduates. These findings support and confirm Vygotsky's (1986) view that various key aspects of metacognition (e.g., self-regulation) develop first as skills before they can be used as a consciously controlled set of strategies for dealing with challenges from our environment.

References

Allen, B.A., & Armour-Thomas, E. (1991). Construct validation of metacognition. *Journal of Psychology, 127*(2), 203–211.

Arnot, M., David, M., & Weiner, G. (1999). *Closing the gender gap: Postwar education and social change.* Cambridge, UK: Polity Press.

Baron-Cohen, S. (2004). *The essential difference.* London, UK: Sage.

Beal, C. R. (1994). Boys and girls: The development of gender roles. New York, NY: McGraw-Hill.

Biddulph, S. (1997). *Raising boys*. London, UK: Thorsons.

Bogdan, R. J. (2000). Minding minds: Evolving a reflexive mind by interpreting others. Cambridge, MA: MIT Press.

Brown, A. (1987). Metacognition, executive control, self-regulation, and other more mysterious mechanisms. In F. Weinert, & R. Kluwe (Eds.), *Metacognition, motivation, and understanding* (pp. 65–116). Hillsdale, NJ: Lawrence Erlbaum.

Brown, R. (1973). *A first language: The early stages*. Cambridge, MA: Harvard University Press.

Burhmester, D., & Furman, W. (1987). The development of companionship and intimacy. *Child Development, 58*, 1101–1113.

Chung, J., & Tang, K. (1998). Inherent gender differences as an explanation of the effect of instructor gender on accounting students' performance. In B. Black & N. Stanley (Eds.), *Teaching and learning in changing times* (pp. 72–79). Proceedings of the 7th Annual Teaching Learning Forum. Perth: University of Western Australia.

Cole, N. J. (1997). *The ETS gender study: How females and males perform in educational settings*. Princeton, NJ: Educational Testing Service.

Cornoldi, C. (1998). The impact of metacognitive reflection on cognitive control. In G. Mazzoni & T. Nelson (Eds.), *Metacognition and cognitive neuropsychology* (pp. 139–159). Mahwah, NJ: Lawrence Erlbaum.

Cupchick, G. C., & Leventhal, H. (1974). Consistency between expressive behavior and the evaluation of humorous stimuli. *Journal of Personality and Social Psychology, 30*, 429–442.

Cupchick, G. C., & Poulos, C. X. (1984). Judgments of emotional intensity in self and others: The effects of stimulus context, sex, and expressivity. *Journal of Personality and Social Psychology, 46*(2), 431–439.

Darley, W. K., & Smith, R. E. (1995). Gender differences in information processing strategies: An empirical test of the selectivity model in advertising response. *Journal of Advertising, 24*(1), 41–56.

Downing, K. (2001). Information technology, education and health care: Constructivism in the 21st century. *Educational Studies, 27*(3), 229–235.

Downing, K. (2009). Self-efficacy and metacognitive development. *International Journal of Learning, 16*(4), 185–200.

Downing, K., Ho, R., Shin, K., Vrijmoed, L., & Wong, E. (2007). Metacognitive development and moving away. *Educational Studies, 33*(1), 1–13.

Driscoll, M. P. (1994). *Psychology of learning for instruction*. Needham Heights, MA: Allyn & Bacon.

Felder, R. M., Felder, G. N., Mauney, M., Hamrin C. E., Jr., & Dietx, E. J. (1995). A longitudinal study of engineering student performance and retention. III. Gender differences in student performance and attitudes. *Journal of Engineering Education, 84*(2), 151–163.

Flavell, J H. (1963). *The developmental psychology of Jean Piaget*. New York, NY: Van Nostrand Reinhold.

Flavell, J. H. (1971). First discussant's comments: What is memory development the development of? *Human Development, 14*, 272–278.

Flavell, J. H. (1987). Assumptions on the concept metacognition and on the development of metacognitions. In F. Weinert & R. Kluwe (Eds.), *Metacognition, motivation and understanding* (pp. 1–19). Hillsdale, NJ: Lawrence Erlbaum.

Flavell, J. H. (1999). Cognitive development: Children's knowledge about the mind. *Annual Review of Psychology, 50*, 21–45.

Frese, M., Stewart, J., & Hanover, B. (1987). Goal-orientation and planfulness: Action styles as personality concepts. *Journal of Personality and Social Psychology, 52,* 1182–1194.

Gallagher, A., Levin, J., & Cahalan, C. (2002). *GRE research: Cognitive patterns of gender differences on mathematics admissions tests.* ETS Report No. 02–19. Princeton, NJ: Educational Testing Service.

Geake, J. G., & Cooper, P. W. (2003). Implications of cognitive neuroscience for education. *Westminster Studies in Education, 26*(10), 7–20.

Gilligan, C. (1982). *In a different voice: Psychological theory and women's development.* Cambridge, MA: Harvard University Press.

Gleitman, H. (1985). Some trends in the study of cognition. In S. Koch & D. E. Leary (Eds.), *A century of psychology as science: Retrospections and assessments* (pp. 420–436). New York, NY: McGraw-Hill.

Gorard, S., Rees, G., & Salisbury, J. (2001). Investigating the patterns of differential attainment of boys and girls at school. *British Journal of Sociology of Education, 27,* 125–139.

Gurian, M. (2002). *Boys and girls learn differently!* San Francisco, CA: Jossey-Bass.

Hacker, D. J. (1998). Definitions and empirical foundations. In D. Hacker, J. Dunlosky, & A. Graesser (Eds.), *Metacognition in educational theory and practice* (pp.1–23). Mahwah, NJ: Lawrence Erlbaum.

Halpern, D. F. (2004). A cognitive-process taxonomy for sex differences in cognitive abilities. *Current Directions in Psychological Science, 13*(4), 135–139.

Halpern, D. F., & LaMay, M. L. (2000). The smarter sex: A critical review of sex differences in intelligence. *Educational Psychology Review, 12*(2), 229–246.

Hanley, G. L. (1995). Teaching critical thinking: Focusing on metacognitive skills and problem solving. *Teaching of Psychology, 22*(1), 68–72.

Hatton, N., & Smith, D. (1995). Reflection in teacher education: Towards definition and implementation. *Teaching and Teacher Education, 11*(1), 33–49.

Huang, J. (1993). An investigation of gender differences in cognitive abilities among Chinese high school students. *Personality & Individual Differences, 75,* 717–719.

Kahneman, D. (1973). *Attention and effort.* Englewood Cliffs, NJ: Prentice Hall.

King, A. (1991). Improving lecture comprehension: Effects of a metacognitive strategy. *Applied Cognitive Psychology, 5,* 331–346.

King, K. (2004). Just don't make me think: Metacognition in college classes. In J. Chambers (Ed.), *Selected papers from the 15th International Conference on College Teaching and Learning* (pp. 145–165). Jacksonville: Florida Community College at Jacksonville, Center for the Advancement of Teaching and Learning.

Kleinfeld, J. (1999). Student performance: Male versus females. *Public Interest, 134,* 3–16.

Kluwe, R. H. (1987). Executive decisions and regulation of problem solving behaviour. In F. Weinert & R. Kluwe (Eds.), *Metacognition, motivation, and understanding* (pp. 1–19). Hillsdale, NJ: Lawrence Erlbaum.

Lawton, C. A., & Hatcher, D. W. (2005). Gender differences in integration of images in visuospatial memory. *Sex Roles, 53*(9–10), 717–725.

Letteri, C. A. (1992). Diagnosing and augmenting basic cognitive skills. In J. W. Keefe & H. J. Walbert (Eds.), *Teaching for thinking* (pp. 59–71). Reston, VA: National Association of Secondary Principals.

Leventhal, H., & Cupchick, G. C. (1975). The informational and facilitative effects of an audience upon expression and the evaluation of humorous stimuli. *Journal of Experimental Social Psychology, 11*, 363–380.

Loomis, K. D. (2000). Learning styles and asynchronous learning: Comparing the LASSI model to class. *Journal of Asynchronous Learning Networks, 4*(1), 23–31.

Lourenco, O., & Machado, A. (1996). In defense of Piaget's theory: A reply to 10 common criticisms. *Psychological Review, 103*, 143–164.

Lowe, P. A , Mayfield, J. W., & Reynolds, C. R. (2003). Gender differences in memory test performance among children and adolescents. *Archives of Clinical Neuropsychology, 18*(8), 865–878.

Lynch, R., Leo, S., & Downing, K. (2006). Context dependent learning: Its value and impact for workplace education. *Education + Training, 48*(1), 15–24.

Marchant, G. J. (2001). Metateaching: A metaphor for reflective teaching. *Education, 109*(4), 487–489.

Marsh, H. W., & Yeung, A. S. (1998). Longitudinal structural equation models of academic self-concept and achievement: Gender differences in the development of math and English constructs. *American Educational Research Journal, 35*(4), 705–738.

Metcalfe, J. (2000). Metamemory: Theory and data. In E. Tulving & F. I. Craik (Eds.), *The Oxford handbook of memory* (pp. 197–211). New York, NY: Oxford University Press.

Meyers-Levy, J. (1985). *Gender differences in information processing: A selectivity interpretation* (PhD dissertation). Northwestern University, Evanston, IL.

Meyers-Levy, J. (1986). Gender differences in information processing: A selectivity interpretation. In P. Cafferata & A. M. Tybout (Eds.), *Cognitive and affective responses to advertising* (pp. 219–260). Lexington, MA: Lexington.

Meyers-Levy, J. (1989). Gender differences in information processing: A selectivity interpretation. In P. Cafferata & A. M. Tybout (Eds.), *Cognitive and affective responses to advertising* (pp. 39–54). Lexington, MA: Lexington.

Meyers-Levy, J., & Maheswaran, D. (1991). Exploring differences in males' and females' processing strategy. *Journal of Consumer Research, 18*(June), 63–70.

Ning, H. K., & Downing, K. (2010a). Connections between learning experience, experience, study behavior and academic performance: A longitudinal study. *Educational Research, 52*(4), 457–468.

Ning, H. K., & Downing, K. (2010b). The reciprocal relationship between motivation and self-regulation: A longitudinal study on academic performance. *Learning and Individual Differences, 20*(6), 682–686.

Northen, S. (2004, September 3). Why men aren't from Mars. *Times Educational Supplement*, p. 19.

Pettit, G. S., Bakshi, A., Dodge, K. A., & Coie, J. D. (1990). The emergence of social dominance in young boys' play groups: Development differences and behavioural correlates. *Developmental Psychology, 26*, 1017–1025.

Piaget, J. (1929). *The child's conception of the world.* New York, NY: Harcourt, Brace.

Piaget, J. (1954). *The construction of reality in the child.* New York, NY: Basic Books.

Piaget, J. (1972). Development and learning. In C. S. Lavatelli & F. Stendler (Eds.), *Readings in child behaviour and development* (3rd ed., pp. 38–46). New York, NY: Harcourt Brace Jovanovich.

Piaget, J. (1977). *The development of thought: Equilibrium of cognitive structures.* New York, NY: Viking Press.

Rogoff, B., & Chavajay, P. (1995). What's become of research on the cultural basis of cognitive development? *American Psychologist, 50,* 859–877.

Rowe, K. J., & Rowe, K. S. (2003, January 5–8). *What matters most: Evidence-based findings on key factors affecting the educational experiences and outcomes for girls and boys throughout their primary and secondary schooling.* Paper presented at the International Congress for School Effectiveness and Improvement, Sydney, Australia.

Royer, J. M., Tronsky, L. N., Chan, Y., Jackson, S. J., & Marchant, H., III. (1999). Math-fact retrieval as the cognitive mechanism underlying gender differences in math test performance. *Contemporary Educational Psychology, 24*(3), 181–266.

Scruggs, T. E., Mastropieri, M. A., Monson, J., & Jorgensen, C. (1985). Maximizing what gifted students can learn: Recent findings of learning strategy research. *Gifted Child Quarterly, 29*(4), 181–183.

Serpell, R. (2000). Intelligence and culture. In R. J. Sternberg (Ed.), *Handbook of intelligence* (pp. 549–577). Cambridge, UK: Cambridge University Press.

Serpell, R., & Boykin, A. W. (1995). Cultural dimensions of cognition: A multiplex, dynamic system of constraints and possibilities. In R. J. Sternberg (Ed.), *Handbook of perception and cognition: Vol. 2. Thinking and problem solving* (pp. 369–408). Orlando, FL: Academic Press.

Siegler, R. S. (1996). *Emerging minds: The process of change in children's thinking.* New York, NY: Oxford University Press.

Skaalvik, S., & Skaalvik, E. M. (2004). Gender differences in math and verbal self-concept, performance expectations, and motivation. *Sex Roles, 50*(3–4), 241–252.

Temple, C. M., & Cornish, K. M. (1993). Recognition memory for words and faces in schoolchildren: A female advantage for words. *British Journal of Developmental Psychology, 11*(4), 421–426.

Tversky, A., & Kahneman, D. (1973). Availability: A heuristic for judging frequency and probability. *Cognitive Psychology, 5,* 207–232.

Vadhan, V., & Stander, P. (1993). Metacognitive ability and test performance among college students. *Journal of Psychology, 128*(3), 307–309.

Van de gaer, E., Pustjens, H., Van Damme, J., & De Munter, A. (2004). Effects of single-sex versus co-educational classes and schools on gender differences in progress in language and mathematics achievement. *British Journal of Sociology of Education, 25*(3), 307–322.

Van Houtte, M. (2004). Why boys achieve less at school than girls: The difference between boys' and girls' academic culture. *Educational Studies, 30*(2), 159–173.

Von Wright, J. (1992). Reflections on reflection. *Learning and Instruction, 2,* 59–68.

Vygotsky, L. S. (1975). *Mind in society: The development of higher psychological processes.* Cambridge, MA: Harvard University Press.

Vygotsky, L. S. (1986). *Thought and language.* Cambridge, MA: MIT Press.

Weinert, F. E. (1987). Introduction and overview: Metacognition and motivation as determinants of effective learning and understanding. In F. Weinert & R. Kluwe. (Eds.), *Metacognition, motivation and understanding* (pp. 1–19), Hillsdale, NJ: Lawrence Erlbaum.

Weinstein, C. E. (1987). *LASSI user's manual.* Clearwater, FL: H & H.

Weinstein, C. E. (1994a), Strategic learning/strategic teaching: Flip sides of a coin. In P. R. Pintrich, D. R. Brown, & C. E. Weinstein (Eds.), *Student motivation, cognition and learning* (pp. 257–273). Hillsdale, NJ: Lawrence Erlbaum.

Weinstein, C. E. (1994b). Students at risk for academic failure: Learning to learn classes. In K. W. Pritchard & R. M. Sawyer (Eds.), *Handbook of college teaching* (pp. 375–385). Westport, CT: Greenwood Press.

Weinstein, C. E., & Palmer, D. (1988). *Learning and studies skills inventory.* Bloomington, MN: Pearson NCS Trans-Optic EP, 30–27841, 321.

Weinstein, C. E., & Palmer, D. R. (2002). *LASSI user's manual* (2nd ed.). Clearwater, FL: H & H.

Wigfield, A., Battle, A., Keller, L. B., & Eccles, J. S. (2002). Sex differences in motivation, self-concept, career aspiration, and career choice: Implications for cognitive development. In A. McGillicuddy-De Lisi, & R. De Lisi (Eds.), *Biology, society, and behaviour: The development of sex differences in cognition* (pp. 93–124). Westport, CT: Ablex.

Yates, L. (1997). Gender equity and the boys' debate: What sort of challenge is it? *British Journal of Sociology of Education, 18,* 337–347.

PART VIII

Understanding Teaching

CHAPTER 24

Emerging Evidence for Excellent Teaching Across Borders

Jared Keeley, Andrew N. Christopher, and William Buskist

W hen we think about the teachers we have had in our lifetimes, it is easy to think of which ones were "good" and which ones were "bad." However, it is difficult to define just what it was about the "good" teachers that made them so good. The elusive concept of "excellent teaching" has been the topic of much debate and study for many years (see e.g., Chism, 2004; Elton, 1998; Kreber, 2002). In this chapter, we will provide an overview of the most recent and consistent findings regarding the qualities of excellent teachers from an international, cross-cultural perspective.

What Is Excellent Teaching?

Currently, higher education is facing many different challenges. The world is fast becoming a global community, joined together by growing technology that makes it possible to be in instantaneous contact with just about anyone across the globe. As the world changes, so must the way in which we educate its citizens. In a world with immediate access to information, the ability to discriminate successfully between accurate and inaccurate information is imperative. More than ever, a modern citizen of the world must be able to quickly and effectively communicate ideas, think critically about new information, and adapt to changing circumstances. Hand-in-hand with these changes come increasing (and in our minds, reasonable) demands for higher education to be accountable for meeting these goals. Students, parents, alumni, business and industry, and government expect college professors to be competent in preparing college graduates to make positive and sustained contributions to the world of the future. Simply conveying information is no longer an adequate standard by which teachers should be evaluated, and so our concept of what it means to be an excellent teacher must change accordingly. As Alan Skelton (2009) argued, tradition is not an adequate criterion for defining what professors do and how they do it. Teachers must be challenged and guided to evaluate the efficacy of pedagogical practices in the context of effective and desirable outcomes, such as students' problem-solving abilities. However, in this postmodern world, what constitute the criteria for excellent teaching? What makes excellent teachers, and what qualities and skills do they possess? Recent research on the qualities and behaviors of these teachers has yielded an interesting picture of what excellent teaching appears to be.

Empirical Studies of Excellent Teaching

Researchers have long been interested in factors that contribute to excellent teaching. Early factor-analytic studies of student evaluations of teachers at both the high school and college levels revealed a short list of likely factors related to excellent teaching including fairness in grading, empathy, teaching skill (e.g., Smalzried & Remmers, 1943), clear explanations of course content, encouraging student participation, teacher-student rapport, and quality of feedback given to students (Isaacson et al., 1964). More recently, William Faranda and Irvine Clarke (2004) conducted interviews with undergraduate senior business students in a U.S. university to determine what these students considered "effective performance" for a professor. Faranda and Clarke found five major categories (with subcategories). In order of student-cited importance, these categories were (1) rapport (approachability, accessibility, personality, empathy), (2) delivery (communication, personal style, pedagogy), (3) fairness (performance evaluation, assignments), (4) knowledge/credibility (expertise, experience, intelligence), and (5) organization/preparation (clarity, thoroughness, instructional materials).

Using a different approach, Donald Barnes and colleagues (2008) found remarkably similar descriptions of the qualities of excellent teaching. To understand what makes an excellent teacher, these researchers gathered nine different teaching evaluation forms and used a panel of eight expert judges to define excellence inductively through distilling the essences of these instruments. The judges agreed on seven domains: preparedness, professionalism, fair and timely evaluation, rapport, enthusiasm, delivery, and a general "excellence" category that included overall global ratings. After further review, the judges combined the preparedness, evaluation, and professionalism categories into a higher-order factor they termed *teaching readiness*. The other categories of rapport, enthusiasm, delivery, and excellence were combined into a higher-order factor termed *teaching excellence*, designed to reflect the optimal teacher-student relationship. Barnes et al. used these categories as their definition of the construct of teaching excellence and developed a teaching evaluation instrument with items designed to assess all seven aspects. When the researchers subjected this instrument to confirmatory factor analysis, a two-factor structure of readiness and relationship-oriented excellence described the data well.

Other researchers have used college alumni as participants in studies trying to determine what makes for excellent teaching. Alumni have the important advantage of hindsight. Relative to undergraduates still in school, they are able to reflect on those aspects of their college experience with teachers who have made the most salient impact on their postgraduate lives. Sarah Moore and Nyiel Kuol (2007) surveyed University of Limerick (United Kingdom) alumni requesting descriptions of faculty they might recommend for a teaching award. These descriptions followed an interesting pattern. When alumni described general qualities of a teacher, they referred more often to student-centered aspects of the classroom such as a professor being warm, which made students feel comfortable. However, when alumni referred to specific teaching behaviors, they focused on subject-centered aspects of the classroom. For example, if participants referred to a professor's use of a particular teaching method, it was usually in reference to its effectiveness for learning a specific subject matter. Thus, this study also pointed to two factors underlying excellent teaching—one factor related to the student-teacher relationship and the other factor related to teaching skill or expertise. Actually, the literature on excellent teaching has been remarkably consistent regarding these two factors. Across a variety of modalities and study methods, these two major categories—technical and interpersonal aspects of teaching—have emerged as the primary components of excellent teaching (Addison, 2005; Keeley, Smith, & Buskist, 2006, Lowman, 1995).

In the context of James Groccia's model (St. Clair & Groccia, 2009; see Chapter 1, this volume), these findings emphasize particular teacher variables to the exclusion of others. Across all studies on excellent teaching, teacher variables such as gender, age, ethnicity, area of expertise, and so on do not bubble to the top, or even the middle, of the list of key factors involved in excellent teaching. The absence of these factors in the literature on excellent teaching is encouraging—it would appear that anyone, regardless of sex, race, or ethnicity, can be become an excellent teacher. If teaching excellence were bounded by static factors such as these, there would be minimal hope for most teachers to improve the quality of their teaching. We are not suggesting that these are not important variables to consider in higher education, but by themselves, these variables do not seem to serve as barriers or catalysts to excellent teaching.

Groccia (Chapter 1, this volume) correctly noted that it is important for teachers to understand themselves because it will help them maximize their strengths and minimize their weaknesses as classroom teachers. The literature on excellent teaching helps teachers focus on what it is that is important to understand about the teaching-learning environment: the specific skills one possesses as a teacher and the social context in which those skills are applied.

Other Perspectives on Excellent Teaching

Several studies have also attempted to compare differences in how teachers and students view excellent teaching. For example, Michael Dunkin (1995) compared the definitions of excellence in teaching of novice and expert faculty in Australian institutes of higher education. He classified faculty responses as belonging to one of four groups: "(a) teaching as structuring learning, (b) teaching as motivating learning, (c) teaching as encouraging activity and independence in learning, and (d) teaching as establishing interpersonal relations conducive to learning" (Dunkin, 1995, p. 24). Novice teachers, categorized as those in their first few years of university teaching, tended to focus on just one or two aspects of teaching, such as content delivery methods. On the other hand, expert teachers, defined as those who had won a university-wide teaching award, offered more complex and multidimensional definitions of teaching excellence that accounted for different aspects of teaching and learning, such as structuring the course effectively, providing opportunities for growth/independence, and providing a supportive interpersonal environment. Interestingly, the quality of the responses did not differ from novice to expert, only the quantity. Experts seem to have developed a more well-rounded appreciation of *all* components that go into excellent teaching, where novices, perhaps because of the challenge of adapting to university life, simplify the task by focusing on only a single dimension of excellent teaching.

Similarly, in the United Kingdom, Andrea Revell and Emma Wainwright (2009) investigated what constitutes an "unmissable lecture" by comparing the views of geography students and faculty. Qualitative interviews conducted by the researchers found remarkable consistency between students and teachers. Both agreed on the importance of providing a good structure to the lesson that incorporates student involvement (technical aspects), as well as adequate interpersonal interaction and passion on the part of the professor (interpersonal aspects).

A study in the United States mirrors the consistency cited previously but also found some interesting differences between students and teachers. We will discuss this study in some detail, because it forms the basis of new research presented later in this chapter. Bill Buskist, Jason Sikorski, Tanya Buckley, and Bryan Saville (2002) asked U.S. undergraduate students to list the characteristics that they believed were central to being a "master teacher." These students generated a list of 47 characteristics. The researchers then asked a separate sample of undergraduate students to list as many as three specific behaviors that corresponded to each characteristic. In several instances, the behaviors substantially overlapped between categories, and the researchers collapsed several categories, resulting in only 28 categories. The list of these qualities and the corresponding behaviors that reflect them has been termed the *Teacher Behavior Checklist* (TBC) and has served as the basis for a teaching evaluation instrument (see Table 24.1; Keeley, Furr, & Buskist, 2010; Keeley, Smith, & Buskist, 2006).

Table 24.1   The Teacher Behavior Checklist

Item	Teacher Qualities and Corresponding Behaviors
1	Accessible (Posts office hours, gives out phone number, and e-mail information)
2	Approachable/Personable (Smiles, greets students, initiates conversations, invites questions, responds respectfully to student comments)
3	Authoritative (Establishes clear course rules; maintains classroom order; speaks in a loud, strong voice)
4	Confident (Speaks clearly, makes eye contact, and answers questions correctly)
5	Creative and Interesting (Experiments with teaching methods; uses technological devices to support and enhance lectures; uses interesting, relevant, and personal examples; not monotone)
6	Effective Communicator (Speaks clearly/loudly; uses precise English; gives clear, compelling examples)
7	Encourages and Cares for Students (Provides praise for good student work, helps students who need it, offers bonus points and extra credit, and knows student names)
8	Enthusiastic about Teaching and about Topic (Smiles during class, prepares interesting class activities, uses gestures and expressions of emotion to emphasize important points, and arrives on time for class)
9	Establishes Daily and Academic Term Goals (Prepares/follows the syllabus and has goals for each class)
10	Flexible/Open-Minded (Changes calendar of course events when necessary, will meet at hours outside of office hours, pays attention to students when they state their opinions, accepts criticism from others, and allows students to do make-up work when appropriate)
11	Good Listener (Doesn't interrupt students while they are talking, maintains eye contact, and asks questions about points that students are making)
12	Happy/Positive Attitude/Humorous (Tells jokes and funny stories, laughs with students)
13	Humble (Admits mistakes, never brags, and doesn't take credit for others' successes)
14	Knowledgeable About Subject Matter (Easily answers students' questions, does not read straight from the book or notes, and uses clear and understandable examples)
15	Prepared (Brings necessary materials to class, is never late for class, provides outlines of class discussion)
16	Presents Current Information (Relates topic to current, real-life situations; uses recent videos, magazines, and newspapers to demonstrate points; talks about current topics; uses new or recent texts)
17	Professional (Dresses nicely [neat and clean shoes, slacks, blouses, dresses, shirts, ties] and no profanity)

Item	Teacher Qualities and Corresponding Behaviors
18	Promotes Class Discussion (Asks controversial or challenging questions during class, gives points for class participation, involves students in group activities during class)
19	Promotes Critical Thinking/Intellectually Stimulating (Asks thoughtful questions during class, uses essay questions on tests and quizzes, assigns homework, and holds group discussions/activities)
20	Provides Constructive Feedback (Writes comments on returned work, answers students' questions, and gives advice on test-taking)
21	Punctuality/Manages Class Time (Arrives to class on time/early, dismisses class on time, presents relevant materials in class, leaves time for questions, keeps appointments, returns work in a timely way)
22	Rapport (Makes class laugh through jokes and funny stories, initiates and maintains class discussions, knows student names, interacts with students before and after class)
23	Realistic Expectations of Students/Fair Testing and Grading (Covers material to be tested during class, writes relevant test questions, does not overload students with reading, teaches at an appropriate level for the majority of students in the course, curves grades when appropriate)
24	Respectful (Does not humiliate or embarrass students in class, is polite to students [says thank you and please, etc.], does not interrupt students while they are talking, does not talk down to students)
25	Sensitive and Persistent (Makes sure students understand material before moving to new material, holds extra study sessions, repeats information when necessary, asks questions to check student understanding)
26	Strives to Be a Better Teacher (Requests feedback on his/her teaching ability from students, continues learning [attends workshops, etc. on teaching], and uses new teaching methods)
27	Technologically Competent (Knows how to use a computer, knows how to use e-mail with students, knows how to use overheads during class, has a Web page for classes)
28	Understanding (Accepts legitimate excuses for missing class or coursework, is available before/after class to answer questions, does not lose temper at students, takes extra time to discuss difficult concepts)

The researchers next asked a new group of students and a group of teachers to rank the importance of the 28 qualities of "master teachers." Students and faculty agreed on 6 of their top 10 qualities: (1) teachers have realistic expectations and fair grading, (2) they are knowledgeable about the topic, (3) they are approachable and personable, (4) they are respectful, (5) they are creative and interesting, and (6) they are enthusiastic about teaching. In general, faculty members ranked the technical aspects of teaching (such as promoting critical thinking) higher than students did, but students emphasized the interpersonal aspects of teaching (such as a teacher being understanding) more than faculty did. Using the same procedure as Buskist et al. (2002), other researchers found almost identical results in U.S. community college and master's level school settings (Schaeffer, Epting, Zinn, & Buskist, 2003; Wann, 2001) as well as a public and primarily undergraduate

Canadian setting (Vulcano, 2007). Likewise, students in medical school in South Africa also emphasize the interpersonal aspects of teaching more than their professors, who emphasize the technical aspects (McLean, 2001).

Cross-Cultural Perceptions of Excellent Teaching

We wanted to examine the international generalizability of Buskist et al.'s (2002) results in two ways. First, we wanted to explore the perceptions of master teaching among U.S. students at a small 4-year liberal arts college. Including data from such a school would further test the extent to which Buskist et al.'s original findings based on students at Auburn University, a large research-oriented institution in the United States, generalize to other U.S. samples. Second, we wanted to compare these results with those of Japanese students attending a small liberal arts college in an attempt to expand current understanding of excellent teaching at a global level. We studied students at Albion College, a small liberal arts school of approximately 1,700 students in the United States and students at Miyazaki International College in Japan, a small liberal arts school of about 400 students, where all classes are taught in English.

Method, Sample, and Procedure

At Albion College, we stratified the student population by year in school (i.e., first-year, sophomore, junior, or senior) and took a random sample of 35 percent of students in each year. We sent e-mails to 622 students asking them to participate in a study that examined student "opinions about the behaviors of master teachers." Students selected a hyperlink that contained the survey. A total of 231 students (152 women and 79 men) participated (37.1 percent response rate). Participants ranged in age from 17 to 38 years ($M = 19.6$ years, $SD = 1.7$ years).

At Miyazaki International College, we recruited 111 students (54 women and 54 men, 3 unspecified) from a variety of classes. We gave these participants, who ranged in age from 18 to 29 years ($M = 20.3$ years, $SD = 2.1$ years), hard copies of the materials during normal class sessions and asked them to complete the survey during their own time and return the completed forms to a locked box placed in an accessible location for this purpose.

All participants completed the 28-item Teacher Behaviors Checklist (TBC) by rating the extent to which a "master teacher" displays each quality and its attendant behaviors using a 1 (*never exhibits this quality*) to 5 (*frequently exhibits this quality*) Likert-type scale. For example, the quality "approachable/personable," is defined as involving behaviors such as "smiles, greets students, initiates conversations, invites questions." Participants provided their age, sex, and year in school.

Results and Discussion

We first rank ordered the 28 teacher qualities based on their means (see Table 24.2, second and third columns). U.S. and Japanese liberal arts students largely agreed on 7 of the top 10 teacher qualities: knowledgeable, confident, approachable/personal, enthusiastic, effective communicator, prepared, and good listener. U.S. students also believed that master teachers are accessible, respectful, and intellectually stimulating, which Japanese students ranked 21st, 20th, and 25th, respectively. For Japanese students, being creative and interesting, strives to be a better teacher, and humble completed their 10 most important teacher qualities. U.S. students ranked these qualities 13th, 22nd, and 24th, respectively.

In comparing the U.S. liberal arts students to U.S. students at a research-intensive university (Buskist et al., 2002; see Table 24.2, column 4) and U.S. students at a community college (Schaeffer et al., 2003; see Table 24.2, column 5), these three samples agreed on 4 of the top 10 teacher qualities: knowledgeable, approachable/personal, respectful, and enthusiastic. Whereas U.S. and Japanese liberal arts students perceived master teachers to be confident, effective communicators, prepared, and good listeners, students at a research-intensive university and at a community college ranked such qualities as less important. In addition, U.S. students at a research-intensive university and community college ranked fair testing/grading, creative and interesting, happy/positive/humorous, encouraging, flexible, and understanding more highly than did the U.S. and Japanese liberal arts students.

Table 24.2   Rank Order of Importance of the 28 Teacher Qualities

	U.S.	Japanese	Buskist et al. (2002)	Schaeffer et al. (2003)
Quality	Student Rank	Student Rank	Student Rank	Student Rank
Accessible	1	21	12	12
Knowledgeable About Subject Matter	2	7	2	1
Confident	3	3	16	16
Approachable/Personable	4	1	4	2
Respectful	5	20	4	4
Enthusiastic	6	9	10	7
Effective Communicator	7	4	15	17
Prepared	8	10	20	19.5
Good Listener	9	5	18	19.5
Intellectually Stimulating	10	25	23.5	22

(Continued)

Table 24.2 (Continued)

	U.S.	Japanese	Buskist et al. (2002)	Schaeffer et al. (2003)
Punctual/Manages Class Time	11	18	23.5	23
Provides Constructive Feedback	12	17	13	11
Flexible/Open-Minded	13	16	9	9
Fair Testing/Grading	14	19	1	3
Understanding	15	15	3	10
Presents Current Information	16	22	23.5	18
Encourages and Cares for Students	17	11	8	8
Creative and Interesting	18	6	6	5
Establishes Daily and Academic Term Goals	19	24	23.5	24
Promotes Class Discussion	20	23	19	21
Rapport	21	12	11	14
Strives to Be a Better Teacher	22	8	17	16
Sensitive and Persistent	23	14	14	13
Humble	24	2	21	25
Authoritative	25	27	26	14
Happy/Positive Attitude/ Humorous	26	13	7	6
Technologically Competent	27	26	27	26.5
Professional	28	28	28	28

To compare the Japanese and U.S. liberal arts students on the relative importance of each teacher quality and their accompanying behaviors, we conducted a between-subject, two-group multivariate analysis of variance (MANOVA), with country of participant as the factor and each of the 28 teacher qualities serving as dependent variables. The multivariate effect was significant: Pillai's Trace = .48, $F(28, 307) = 10.33$, $p < .001$, $\eta^2 = .485$. We provide the univariate ANOVA results in Table 24.3. Regarding the top 10 qualities cited by our U.S. liberal arts respondents, significant differences emerged on four qualities: accessible, knowledgeable, respectful, and intellectually stimulating. With the exception of knowledgeable, these qualities

Table 24.3 Comparison of Japanese and U.S. Students on the 28 Teacher Qualities

	U.S. Students		Japanese Students			
Quality	M	SE	M	SE	F(1, 334)	η2
Accessible	4.83	.044	4.25	.066	54.02*	.139
Knowledgeable About Subject Matter	4.81	.037	4.59	.054	11.23*	.033
Confident	4.70	.044	4.65	.065	0.40	.001
Approachable/ Personable	4.68	.040	4.71	.059	0.24	.001
Respectful	4.65	.046	4.26	.069	22.53*	.063
Enthusiastic	4.63	.048	4.53	.071	1.21	.004
Effective Communicator	4.61	.042	4.63	.063	0.06	.001
Prepared	4.58	.043	4.53	.064	0.62	.002
Good Listener	4.56	.045	4.64	.067	0.99	.003
Intellectually Stimulating	4.54	.052	3.72	.077	76.57*	.186
Punctual/Manages Class Time	4.52	.047	4.31	.070	6.14*	.018
Provides Constructive Feedback	4.49	.061	4.30	.082	3.82	.010
Flexible/Open-Minded	4.48	.051	4.36	.075	1.59	.005
Fair Testing/Grading	4.45	.052	4.28	.078	3.44	.009
Understanding	4.41	.057	4.36	.085	0.23	.001
Presents Current Information	4.39	.053	4.15	.079	6.43*	.019
Encourages and Cares for Students	4.38	.053	4.49	.078	1.34	.004
Creative and Interesting	4.37	.052	4.63	.077	7.52*	.022
Establishes Daily and Academic Term Goals	4.35	.055	3.95	.081	16.67*	.048
Promotes Class Discussion	4.33	.057	4.01	.084	9.13*	.027
Rapport	4.32	.054	4.47	.080	2.42	.007
Strives to Be a Better Teacher	4.31	.056	4.53	.082	4.98*	.015
Sensitive and Persistent	4.31	.055	4.37	.081	0.43	.001

(Continued)

Table 24.3 (Continued)

	U.S. Students	Japanese Students				
Humble	4.27	.055	4.68	.082	16.57*	.047
Authoritative	4.20	.056	3.63	.082	33.49*	.091
Happy/Positive Attitude/Humorous	4.20	.054	4.45	.080	6.43*	.019
Technologically Competent	4.15	.060	3.70	.089	18.06*	.051
Professional	3.94	.060	3.39	.089	26.00*	.072

* $p < .01$

were the three qualities on which U.S. and Japanese students differed in their respective "Top 10" lists. Japanese students completed their top 10 list with creative and interesting, strives to be a better teacher, and humble, each of which Japanese students rated as significantly more important than did U.S. students. In sum, we found a reasonably high overlap between U.S. and Japanese students regarding the most important qualities constituting master teaching, and with few exceptions, these qualities do not seem to differ in their relative importance across the two groups of students.

It is interesting to note some of the similarities in lower-ranked items between our two samples and those of Buskist et al. (2002) and Gerald Schaeffer, Kimberly Epting, Tracy Zinn, and Bill Buskist (2003). In particular, "professional" and "technically competent" were consistently lower-ranked qualities. This finding is particularly noteworthy given that students do not value the technical aspects of teaching as much as faculty do (Barnes et al., 2008; McLean, 2001).

In a comparative study of U.S. and Japanese classrooms, Kayoko Inagaki, Eiji Morita, and Giyoo Hatano (1999) found that U.S. teachers tended to make more evaluative remarks to student comments in class than did Japanese teachers. If indeed the tendency to evaluate student comments is common in U.S. classrooms, students may expect or hope that such evaluations will be done in a manner that respects their comments. Likewise, these same researchers found that Japanese teachers, more so than U.S. teachers, tended to ask the class for feedback on other students' contributions to class discussions. In Japan, it was also the students' responsibility to evaluate their classmates' contributions and perhaps this responsibility explains why Japanese students rated the intellectually stimulating quality much lower than did U.S. students, who may look to the teacher for such stimulation.

In a study of fifth- to eighth-grade mathematics teachers in Japan and the United States, Clea Fernandez and Joanna Cannon (2005) found that Japanese teachers emphasized helping students develop their ability to learn. In contrast, U.S. teachers emphasized helping students learn specific mathematical content. To the extent such an emphasis is expected among college students in Japan, they will value teachers who strive to improve their work, which may be reflected in how creative and interesting class meetings are. U.S. college students will value teachers who are accessible to help them understand course content and are respectful in helping them achieve this outcome.

That Japanese students valued humility in their teachers attests to the value placed on this characteristic in the larger Japanese culture. R. A. Brown (2010) had U.S. and Japanese college students read a statement made by a fictitious target person and assess that person on 13 characteristics. This statement was one in which the target person expressed relatively high or low levels of self-esteem. In addition, participants rated the importance of self-esteem and completed a measure of their own level of self-regard. In addition to U.S. students rating self-esteem as more important than Japanese students did, U.S. students also held themselves in higher regard than Japanese students held themselves. U.S. students formed more positive impressions than did the Japanese students of the target person who expressed high levels of self-esteem. However, Japanese students formed more positive impressions of the target person who expressed a lower level of self-esteem than did U.S. students, thus underscoring the importance they place on humility.

In addition to cultural differences, the current study highlights the idea that different types of institutions may have different expectations for faculty and students. U.S. liberal arts students rated teacher accessibility as their most important master teacher quality; interestingly, this quality ranked only 12th in both Buskist et al.'s (2002) and Schaffer et al.'s (2003) research. We speculate that these results may result from the nature of differences among the institutions. Albion College is a small, selective school where alumni surveys consistently reveal the faculty-student relationship was the most important aspect of their undergraduate careers. Without accessibility to faculty, such relationships could not be developed. We ran a series of paired samples t tests on the U.S. sample to examine the extent to which the top two rated qualities exceeded the other qualities. We found that these students rated accessibility as significantly more important than all other qualities save knowledgeable, ts (230) > 2.57, ps < .02, and in turn, they rated knowledge significantly more important than all other qualities save accessibility, ts (230) > 2.46, ps < .02. Thus, it appears that these U.S. liberal arts students particularly value faculty accessibility and knowledge base. In addition, our U.S. liberal arts students, more so than Buskist et al.'s and Schaeffer et al.'s student samples, rated the qualities of confident, effective communicator, prepared, good listener, and intellectually stimulating as particularly important.

In a study comparing liberal arts colleges with research universities and regional institutions in the United States, Ernest Pascarella, Ty Cruce, Gregory Wolniak, and Charles Blaich (2004) assessed the extent to which each type of school engaged in good undergraduate educational practices as defined by the National Survey of Student Engagement. Compared with research universities and regional institutions, students at liberal arts colleges reported a higher level of contact with faculty. Although one can only speculate about the precise causal reason for this finding, perhaps students at liberal arts colleges expect their teachers to be freely and openly accessible. In addition, students at liberal arts colleges rated their teachers as more skillful and prepared than did students at research universities and regional institutions. Perhaps if students at liberal arts colleges have this expectation of their teachers, they likewise value qualities such as effective communicator, prepared, good listener, and intellectually stimulating.

For two reasons, it is premature at this point to claim that liberal arts students in the United States or Japan differ substantially from undergraduates at research-intensive universities or community colleges in their perceptions of master teachers. First, there was a methodological difference between the current study and those of Buskist et al. (2002) and Schaeffer et al. (2003) in that participants in our research judged the 28 qualities on an interval scale, whereas participants in Buskist et al.'s and Schaeffer et al.'s research rank-ordered the 28 qualities. Thus, in the current research, it was theoretically possible for all 28 qualities to be equally important. Second, we examined students at only one liberal arts college in the United States and one in Japan. It is almost a certainty that different types of liberal arts colleges will tend to attract different types of students. For example, some liberal arts colleges are politically conservative and others are liberal. Thus, our research needs to be extended to other liberal arts schools in the United States and across the world. Likewise, students at larger universities in Japan might perhaps value teacher qualities that more closely resemble those valued by students in Buskist et al.'s (2002) research.

Two Universal Principles of Master Teaching?

Research on the qualities and characteristics of master teaching is honing in on those few qualities that may represent universal principles of mastering teaching. At the very least, this research has reached the point where cautious speculation is warranted. The similarities in TBC-item ratings in this study in conjunction with TBC-ratings from previous student samples (e.g., Buskist et al., 2002; Schaeffer et al., 2003; Vulcano, 2007) strongly suggest that, from the students' perspective, there may be two universal principles of master teaching: (1) knowledge or technical competence and (2) enthusiasm and interpersonal competence (see also Lowman, 1995). These principles seem consistently to emerge regardless of educational or geographic setting. Some of the defining features of these principles as they appear on the TBC include the following:

- *Knowledgeable*: Easily answers students' questions; does not read straight from the book or notes; uses clear and understandable examples
- *Effective communicator*: Speaks clearly/loudly; uses precise English; gives clear, compelling examples
- *Enthusiasm*: Smiles during class; prepares interesting class activities; uses gestures and expressions of emotion to emphasize important points; arrives on time for class
- *Approachable/personable*: Smiles; greets students; initiates conversations; invites questions; responds respectfully to student comments

These behaviors represent clear starting points for teachers who want to become more effective teachers or who aspire to become master teachers. Most of the behaviors listed, regardless of the principle with which they are associated, are relatively simple behaviors to acquire as part of a repertoire of practical and effective teaching skills. For example, small adjustments in one's teaching behavior such as smiling more in class, arriving to class on time, and using clearer examples to help explain difficult concepts may yield huge benefits in student (and faculty) perceptions of the quality of one's teaching. Presumably, these behaviors increase student receptivity to both the teacher and the teacher's message (Benson, Cohen, & Buskist, 2005).

The research on these qualities, however, has been limited to only a handful of countries that may share particular aspects of the way in which education is approached and practiced. It is an open question how well these qualities will describe master teaching in other educational contexts across the world. However, based on TBC research to date in combination with other research on excellence in teaching (e.g., Addison, 2005; Lowman, 1995), it is our opinion that these qualities will likely hold to be near universal. In areas of the world where higher education is expanding fast but has yet to develop the infrastructure or traditions that accompany it, we imagine that focusing on these principles could be a useful guiding mechanism for developing and rewarding excellent teaching.

Developing, Promoting, and Rewarding Excellent Teaching

What can institutions of learning do to foster and reward excellent teaching? Reward contingencies for faculty do not always mesh well with conceptions of excellent teaching at many institutions (Harrison, 2002). For example, many institutions value research productivity more than (if not to the direct exclusion of) excellent teaching when considering tenure, promotion, or merit raises. Thus, many faculty members have no external incentive to improve their teaching. If university teaching stagnates or minimal emphasis is placed on it, then it seems unlikely that higher education will be able to meet societal demands for improving educational outcomes.

Harrison specifically reviewed the educational policies of several countries (Canada, United States, Australia, United Kingdom, Sweden, and Norway) and concluded that the emphasis on excellent teaching needs to be increased and substantially recognized if higher education in any nation is to meet the standards of today's evolving world. To do so will require several steps.

First, the evaluation of teachers needs to match definitions of excellent teaching by using well-researched and sound teaching evaluation instruments that represent key aspects of the construct. Many evaluation forms used in higher education are homegrown, with little consideration given to the reliability or validity of the measurement outside of the institution at which it was developed. Examples of some empirically derived and investigated instruments include two cited in this chapter (Barnes et al., 2008; Keeley et al., 2006). From a cross-cultural perspective, it is imperative that the properties of instruments to assess teaching be established in each context in which they are used. In addition, items to assess teaching must be relevant to those faculty members completing them and the instructional methods used. For example, items meant to assess the quality of classroom discussion might be irrelevant in lecture or laboratory courses.

Second, relative to research and service, institutional reward structures need to place more balanced emphasis on excellent teaching. Using psychometrically sound instruments, institutions may want to develop benchmarks for teacher performance or require faculty to document efforts to improve their teaching.

Finally, and perhaps most critically, research needs to continue on the concept of excellent teaching and how it relates to other variables in Groccia's (Chapter 1, this volume) model, especially learning outcomes. This step is necessary for demonstrating the meaningfulness of excellent teaching: To be useful, it must have a measurable impact on student learning. This step will also improve the case for any society anywhere in the world where higher education is a worthwhile endeavor.

Final Thoughts

We began this chapter by noting some of the current factors that contribute to the context within which college and university teaching takes place. In general, these forces have demanded greater accountability for the quality of education the academy provides its students. Thus, it becomes ever more important for higher education to have a solid understanding of the concept of excellent teaching and what sorts of actions and qualities lead to improved student outcomes. Although the research presented in this chapter underscores the consistency in the ways in which students from two different cultures view excellent teaching, much more research must be conducted to understand or demonstrate the link between the qualities/ behaviors of excellent teachers and desirable student outcomes. In other words, we know what teachers and students consider to be "excellent" teaching, but we have yet to demonstrate convincingly that these factors lead to greater learning, improved critical thinking, or other key student outcomes. In our opinion, although knowing that the perception of excellent teaching is bounded by both professional competency and interpersonal factors is useful, this knowledge is not sufficient to tell us how it affects student learning. The next step in this line of research is to manipulate these factors to determine the role they play in affecting both student motivation for learning and learning achievement.

References

Addison, W. E. (2005, August). *The multidimensionality of effective teaching: Evidence from student evaluations.* Paper delivered at the American Psychological Association convention, Washington, DC.

Barnes, D., Engelland, B., Matherine, C., Martin, W., Orgeron, C., Ring, J., . . . Williams, Z. (2008). Developing a psychometrically sound measure of collegiate teaching proficiency. *College Student Journal, 42,* 199–213.

Benson, T. A., Cohen, A. L., & Buskist, W. (2005). Rapport: Its relation to student attitudes and behaviors toward teachers and classes. *Teaching of Psychology, 32,* 236–238.

Brown, R. A. (2010). Perceptions of psychological adjustment, achievement outcomes, and self-esteem in Japan and America. *Journal of Cross-Cultural Psychology, 41,* 51–61.

Buskist, W., Sikorski, J., Buckley, T., & Saville, B. K. (2002). Elements of master teaching. In S. F. Davis & W. Buskist (Eds.), *The teaching of psychology: Essays in honor of Wilbert J. McKeachie and Charles L. Brewer* (pp. 27–39). Mahwah, NJ: Lawrence Erlbaum.

Chism, N. V. N. (2004). Characteristics of effective teachers in higher education: Between definitional despair and uncertainty. *Journal on Excellence in College Teaching, 15,* 5–35.

Dunkin, M. (1995). Concepts of teaching and teaching excellence in higher education. *Higher Education Research and Development, 14,* 21–33.

Elton, L. (1998). Dimensions of excellence in university teaching. *International Journal for Academic Development, 3,* 3–11.

Faranda, W., & Clarke, I. (2004). Student observations of outstanding teaching: Implications for marketing educators. *Journal of Marketing Education, 26,* 271–281.

Fernandez, C., & Cannon, J. (2005). What Japanese and U.S. teachers think about when constructing mathematics lessons: A preliminary investigation. *The Elementary School Journal, 105,* 481–498.

Harrison, J. (2002). The quality of university teaching: Faculty performance and accountability. A literature review. *Canadian Society for the Study of Higher Education—Professional File, Spring*(21), 3–20.

Inagaki, K., Morita, E., & Hatano, G. (1999). Teaching-learning of evaluative criteria for mathematical arguments through classroom discourse: A cross-national study. *Mathematical Thinking and Learning, 1,* 93–111.

Isaacson, R. L., McKeachie, W. J., Milholland, J. E., Lin, Y. G., Hofeller, M., Baerwalt, J. W., & Zinn, K. L. (1964). Dimensions of student evaluations of teaching. *Journal of Educational Psychology, 55*, 344–351.

Keeley, J., Furr, R. M., & Buskist, W. (2010). Differentiating psychology students' perceptions of teachers using the teacher behavior checklist. *Teaching of Psychology, 37*, 16–20.

Keeley, J. W., Smith, D., & Buskist, W. (2006). The teacher behavior checklist: Factor analysis of its utility for evaluating teaching. *Teaching of Psychology, 33*, 84–90.

Kreber, C. (2002). Teaching excellence, teaching expertise, and the scholarship of teaching. *Innovative Higher Education, 27*, 5–23.

Lowman, J. (1995). *Mastering the techniques of teaching* (2nd ed.). San Francisco, CA: Jossey-Bass.

McLean, M. (2001). Rewarding teaching excellence: Can we measure teaching "excellence"? Who should be the judge? *Medical Teacher, 23*, 6–11.

Moore, S., & Kuol, N. (2007). Retrospective insights on teaching: Exploring teaching excellence through the eyes of the alumni. *Journal of Further and Higher Education, 31*, 133–143.

Pascarella, E. T., Cruce, T. M., Wolniak, G. C., & Blaich, C. F. (2004). Do liberal arts colleges really foster good practices in undergraduate education? *Journal of College Student Development, 45*, 57–74.

Revell, A., & Wainwright, E. (2009). What makes lectures "unmissable"? Insights into teaching excellence and active learning. *Journal of Geography in Higher Education, 33*, 209–233.

Schaeffer, G., Epting, K., Zinn, T., & Buskist, W. (2003). Student and faculty perceptions of effective teaching. A successful replication. *Teaching of Psychology, 30*, 133–136.

Skelton, A. (2009). A "teaching excellence" for the times we live in? *Teaching in Higher Education, 14*, 107–112.

Smalzried, N. T., & Remmers, H. H. (1943). A factor analysis of the Purdue rating scale for instructors. *Journal of Educational Psychology, 34*, 363–367.

St. Clair, K. L., & Groccia, J. E. (2009). Change to social justice education: Higher education strategy. In K. Skubikowski, C. Wright, & R. Graf (Eds.), *Social justice education: Inviting faculty to transform their institutions* (pp. 70–84). Sterling, VA: Stylus.

Vulcano, B. A. (2007). Extending the generality of the qualities and behaviors constituting effective teaching. *Teaching of Psychology, 34*, 114–117.

Wann, P. D. (2001, January). *Faculty and student perceptions of the behaviors of effective college teachers*. Poster presented at the National Institute for the Teaching of Psychology, St. Petersburg Beach, FL.

CHAPTER 25

Writing for the U.S. University

HELEN FOX

S everal of the contributors in this volume have described philosophies, religious traditions, and cultural values they would like us to understand so we can appreciate their influence on teaching and learning in the global community. Surely, readers have noticed some intriguing similarities among these traditions as well as some important differences. But I'd like to take us further than that. I'm going to make a huge generalization—backed up by evidence in the fields of cross-cultural communication, second language writing, and contrastive rhetoric—that the cultures of the world majority, that is, the people of color throughout the world, value similar styles of communication and human interaction, and that these styles are sometimes at odds with the values and expectations of the U.S. university. This cultural mismatch can result in attempts at academic writing that look different from what the university expects and desires, and can cause endless trouble for undergraduate and graduate students of color—and for the faculty who try their best to help them.

Diversity of World Majority Students

Culture and custom do not influence every individual in the same way or to the same degree. In other words, what we can say with confidence about groups we cannot say with the same assurance about any particular student who walks into our classroom. We might agree that on the whole, the United States is an individualistic society that values personal freedom over family loyalty and solidarity. Although many U.S. students do move away from home, travel widely, and keep in touch infrequently with their parents and home communities, I would not be terribly surprised if a high-achieving student told me he plans to return to his small town after graduation to join the family business, or if another student declined an opportunity to travel because it would take her too far away from her parents and old friends. In the same way, I can say that world majority students value certain communication styles that cause trouble in academic writing, but I cannot predict that every student from Korea or Sierra Leone or South Central Los Angeles will have difficulty in communicating with a U.S. academic audience.

Considered individually, world majority students are extremely diverse in terms of education, socioeconomic class, language background, nationality, upbringing, personality, and life experience. Many international students come from schools that are not English medium or even English oriented, where no writing is done in English outside of English class. When these students arrive at the U.S. university, they struggle to varying degrees with reading, making themselves understood, taking notes, understanding the professor, and so on. Such students fit the profile that might come to mind when we think of the typical international student.

But other newly arrived students have been educated in schools for the international elite, where flawless English is considered essential. I once had a first-year undergraduate from the Sultanate of Oman, where the high school class in creative writing had seven students and was taught by a U.S. instructor in prep school style, producing such writing as this: "Her scent woke me from my frustrating meditation on the square root of negative one. It was like a soothing balm on an unhealed wound." Sometimes U.S. instructors comment that their international students speak and write a more sophisticated English than many of their U.S. counterparts.

Not only do world majority students come with different skills, they have a variety of motivations for being in the United States. Although many have come voluntarily to the United States to study and perhaps to pursue professional jobs after they graduate, others could be termed "involuntary minorities" (Ogbu, 1989), that is, students who did not choose to come to this country for its advantages, but whose ancestors were enslaved, conquered, or colonized, or whose parents were forced to seek work in the United States when their small farms or businesses became unsustainable as a result of U.S. trade practices. These students, understandably, may have a more ambivalent attitude about becoming educated in the ways of those who have historically considered these inferior in intelligence and lifestyle. They want to succeed in the system, yet the system has not been kind to them, and they often have been treated dismissively, marginally, or condescendingly, which can make it hard to find the will and the courage to do their best. Because of the historical barriers holding them back, these "involuntary minorities" are also the "underrepresented minorities" in U.S. universities: African Americans, Native Americans, Native Hawaiians, and some Latino groups such as Puerto Ricans, Central Americans, and some Mexican Americans.

Adding to the complexity of this huge "world majority" category are the many second generation immigrants who were born in the United States or who immigrated as children or young teens—the "1.5 generation" (Harklau, Losey, & Siegal, 1999). Some of these students may remain in touch with the cultural values, communication styles, and languages of their immigrant parents, immersing themselves in these ways of living and thinking and speaking at home or after class with friends. Other children of immigrants tend to reject their parents' influence and try to mainstream themselves as much as the majority culture will allow. These students may have been actively encouraged by their friends, teachers, and extended families, especially the young people in those families, to ignore or disparage their parents' cultures and languages, and adopt the lifestyles of those who have "made it." Yet even in these students, the parents' first languages and cultures may leave traces that are not so easily erased and forgotten.

Cultural Similarities Among World Majority Students

Despite their diversity, many world majority students share a core of assumptions and values and communication styles that are different from those that are expected and admired and called "smart thinking" or "good writing" by a tiny minority in world terms, the U.S. dominant culture. In my book, *Listening to the World: Cultural Issues in Academic Writing* (1994), I describe three fundamental differences between the ways world majority cultures and "mainstream" U.S. culture approach oral and written communication. First, world majority cultures often prefer indirect forms of discourse rather than the straightforward, focused, "logical" organization that teachers often call "good writing" or "clear thinking." Second, world majority cultures often assume that the solidarity or harmony of the group is more important than the goals or choices or ideas of the individual. And third, world majority cultures tend to value ancient or expert knowledge over novelty and creativity, especially in one's role as a student, but in other areas of life, as well.

These cultural values and communication styles are interlocking and very deep-rooted; they are learned in early childhood and thus may not be recognized as cultural values at all, but just what feels "normal" or "natural" or "reasonable." As many of us who have lived for a significant period in another country realize, we are not necessarily aware of our own cultural values, but we can easily recognize and, at times, feel quite negatively about values and practices that are unfamiliar to us, or are at odds with what we've been taught is right, or smart, or valuable.

Because of this tendency to see one's own point of view as natural and normal and the "other's" point of view as illogical or undesirable, world majority values of indirection, holism, collectivism, and deference to the authority and wisdom of others are often misunderstood, disparaged, or even caricatured in racist discourse in this country, which can make it difficult to talk about cultural differences at all. Just bringing up the subject can appear to be pointing out weaknesses of vulnerable students, or making their cultures seem bizarre or abnormal—"orientalizing" or "essentializing" in a negative way. My aim, however, is quite the opposite. Because I value all cultural styles as legitimate, interesting, and equally complex, I would like us to look closely at the logic behind these values and worldviews, rather than simply concentrating on our human similarities, of which there are many.

Indirection

The easiest difference for U.S. faculty to recognize is a preference, by many of the world majority, for subtle or discursive communication that puts the responsibility for interpretation and understanding on the audience, rather than on the speaker or writer. Many of us have seen this style in our international students' writing: the senior from Brazil, effortlessly bilingual, who writes in elegant language about issues that seem totally extraneous to her problem statement. Or the Japanese freshman who starts each paragraph with some abstract, general comments that lead gradually up to the point, with the expectation that the reader will not mind waiting patiently for the meaning to come into focus, and then, once it does, beginning again, slowly, with other general abstractions before getting to the gist of matter in the *next* paragraph, and so on.

In my own research and teaching, I have noticed several broad strategies for indirection in the writing of world majority students. Central ideas might be omitted, or packed into long, complex sentences, or tangled together in short paragraphs. Sometimes the most important analysis is relegated to a footnote when it seems more logical to the U.S. writer to put it in a prominent position in the text and expand upon it. Transitions, either the single word variety ("moreover," "nevertheless," "although," "additionally") or phrases that link ideas from paragraph to paragraph may be left out, leaving a series of free-standing statements that are baffling to the reader. Or, because "lack of transitions" is so often commented on by English teachers, transition words may be overused or blatant, stitching the prose together clumsily, so that it "doesn't flow."

Students who value indirection might also choose abstract words or generalities that smooth over or obscure their meaning, or use examples and quotes without explicit analysis. They may attempt an extended metaphor without showing clearly enough how it relates to their main point, or ask questions that are never answered. Although these choices may look to the U.S. instructor like second language difficulties, and indeed may have *something* to do with lack of vocabulary or ease with English phrasing, there is also an underlying cultural rationale. These writers are showing respect for the reader's ability to analyze or make meaning; they are trying to avoid saying things so directly that the reader is insulted. At the same time, they are displaying their own intelligence and sophistication in ways that they have learned are valuable.

This cultural propensity for indirection can make the directness of U.S. academic writing seem simplistic or illogical to world majority students. A Chilean graduate student told me, "When I read something written by an American it sounds so childish. It's because we don't see with these connections. It's just like, 'This is a watch, the watch is brown, da-da, da-da, da-da.' For us, that's funny. I think that for Americans, it must be funny, the way I describe things." A Japanese student spoke of U.S. academic writing as "just a skeleton: there's no juicy, meaty part in it." A student from Cote d'Ivoire told me with some exasperation, "In my country, you don't say 'Listen, I want to talk to you about this!' If you want to talk to me about something and you already said it, why should I listen any further? You try to make a sort of suspense, and as we say, 'It brings appetite to the conversation,' you know? The person is thinking, 'What is he or she going to tell me?' And you really pull him to listen to you, you see? And finally, you say it. And by the time you say it, you are also at the end of what you are going to say."

Another common strategy for indirection is almost the opposite: rather than leaving things out, the writer adds a great deal of contextual information that is only marginally related to the topic, a strategy that the U.S. university calls digressiveness, rambling, or beating around the bush. A world majority writer might begin a dissertation on curriculum reform with page after page of the history and geography of the country concerned, without making any direct connection to the problem statement—if there is a problem statement at all. This strategy is not simply "hot air" or excessive formality; it is meant to fill readers in with general background knowledge to give them a holistic sense of the topic and situate it within its proper context. When the reader is more responsible for the interpretation of the text than the writer, adding seemingly irrelevant contextual material is a way of showing respect for the reader's intellect and autonomy.

Collectivist Values

In addition to a preference for indirection, world majority students often come from cultures that have more of a collectivist than individualist orientation. Such values affect students' communication styles in a variety of ways (Bennett, 2004; Triandis, 2001). Students who come from cultures that value group solidarity or harmony over self-expression or self-actualization may have learned early to pay close attention to others' unexpressed thoughts and feelings. Because they in a sense, "know" what others are experiencing, they don't need to put everything into words. And because they expect others to pay attention to *their* unexpressed thoughts and feelings, they assign more responsibility for miscommunication to the reader or listener. To build solidarity they might scold their audience or ask a great many rhetorical questions that a U.S. reader might find strange or even insulting in a college essay. As their teacher, I might gently suggest that my world majority students are overgeneralizing, exaggerating to make a point, or not bringing in proper evidence, but to them, using mottoes or slogans or talking about "what everybody thinks" adds credence to their argument. In their world, people tend to say they agree for the sake of solidarity, and if they don't, they might be persuaded or exhorted with emotional appeals to come around.

In a group-oriented or collectivist society, questions about personal identity—who you really are or what you are becoming, what your true voice sounds like, or whether you can make your mark on the world before you retire—are less important than are your feelings of belonging and connectedness and agreement with what your group thinks, and does, and aspires to. Thus when you write, you are not so concerned about whose ideas are whose. Intellectual property isn't so much of an issue to you. The idea of plagiarism may seem curiously illogical. And though you have heard time and time again that copying an author's words without giving credit is wrong, or that following an author's established line of reasoning too closely is not what is expected at the college level, you are not convinced this is true. When people are assumed to be interconnected, or at least more connected than separate, why does it matter so much whose words are whose? And if someone important and skilled enough to write an academic book already said something highly intelligent, why should a mere student try to improve on that?

Valuing Authority and Wisdom of the Past

In addition to valuing group norms and respecting the reader's expectations for subtlety and context, many world majority students have learned to value the wisdom and authority of professionals, teachers, or revered historical figures over their own novel or creative ideas. Although citing authors and experts is of course expected in the U.S. university as well, U.S. students are also supposed to come up with an original thesis, and create their own unique arguments and rationale. This expectation for originality in academic writing is not explained to students in any detail, and this can cause cultural confusion that would be humorous if it were not so painful. One of my great friends in graduate school who was raised in Sri Lanka and then lived and taught throughout Africa and who had spoken English for 30 years, realized, through conversations and interviews with me for my research that she had been misunderstanding her professor's use of the word "original" for the first several years of her graduate program.

Kamala's professor had been unhappy with her work for some time, in fact, he had lost his temper on several occasions saying "This is not original! You can't just keep reproducing what others have done!" What the professor didn't realize was that the student's sense of the word *original* was "of the origin," the original texts, the original, ancient ideas. She told me that the way she was educated by her family and society, "you have to search, you have to understand what has happened there, in that time, in that original work. So by simply learning it, it becomes original to you."

So even this highly educated English speaker believed for years that her graduate advisor either was dim-witted, which was unlikely, or that he didn't like her, or that he believed her culture was inferior. "I wonder sometimes, what do professors here think of Buddhists?" Kamala asked me. "Do they think we are a stupid people?" Though I was sure this was not the case, Kamala was clearly suffering from her advisor's ignorance. Because when she wrote an "original" argument that carefully documented what others had done without expressing her own opinion, her advisor had belittled her work, and, by extension, had belittled her, as well. Kamala was finding it very hard to write under these circumstances and had developed a massive case of writer's block.

Teaching Writing to World Majority Students

I began to realize the significance of these differences and how they affect student writing when I was asked to develop and teach a writing course to graduate students from the Global South at the University of Massachusetts at Amherst's Center for International Education in 1987. As I taught different versions of the course, conducted interviews of students and professors, and worked intensively with students from every continent on their master's papers and PhD dissertations, I began to realize that the usual advice about writing improvement didn't seem to have the same effect on world majority writers as it did on mainstream U.S. writers. These world majority students did not seem convinced that going straight to the point makes sense, nor were they open to the idea that vague generalities, rhetorical questions, and ornamentation of the text with disembodied quotes would not be welcome in an academic paper. Their skepticism was very different from the reactions of my U.S. mainstream students, who might also have great difficulty making themselves clear, or pursuing a line of logical reasoning, or avoiding digressions. To my mainstream students, the advice, "Be clear, remove excess words, and hold your readers by the hand as you walk them through your text," was thoroughly familiar, given the number of times they had been told by parents or teachers or friends in the schoolyard, "I don't get it."

"What's your point?" "Can you give me an example?"—that is, that they should adhere to mainstream U.S. cultural expectations for "clear communication." As I got to know the international graduate students better, I began to realize that many of them were published writers in their own countries, some of them even in English, and that the negative feedback they had been receiving from their U.S. professors was confusing, hurtful, and frustrating to many of them.

You might think that such profound miscommunication across cultures would be relatively easy to clear up, once both sides understood the often-conflicting assumptions and values that affected their ideas of good writing. Yet I encountered resistance from U.S. professors, so sure were they that there is—or should be—one standard for "good writing" across cultures. Faculty consistently believed that clarity and directness, explicit analysis, and the use of particular kinds of evidence to support an original argument were features of skillful written expression. Any differences, they believed, must have more to do with the students' relative inexperience with writing, their difficulties understanding the reading, their poor schooling, their authoritarian political systems, or even their inability to think and reason. "Good thinking makes good writing," professors would say. "If you can think clearly you can write clearly." And because these students weren't writing in a transparent, step-by-step way, their thinking must be at fault.

Even the faculty who were open to the idea that cultural differences could account for some of the "poor writing" they were seeing would ask me to show them examples of writing styles from these students' home countries, thinking we should be able to discern cultural influences from texts alone. However, it was difficult to find clear examples to show them. Perhaps because I was not trained as a linguist, I could not clearly see rhetorical patterns at the paragraph level such as those described by Robert Kaplan in his seminal study that initiated the field of contrastive rhetoric, which has by now developed an extensive literature (Connor, 1996; Kassabgy, Ibrahim, & Aydelott, 2004; Panetta, 2000; Purves, 1988). Kaplan (1966) originally called these patterns the *Oriental spiral, Semitic parallelism, Romantic digressions*, and so on—terminology that by now is considered ethnocentric and derogatory. Yet Kaplan was on to something intriguing, I thought, even though I couldn't discern clear patterns in my students' texts. I could see *tendencies* toward Kaplan's styles of communication, but I didn't really understand what these students were trying to do until I talked to them at length, sometimes over a period of years, asking them to think about why their ways of organizing and expressing their ideas made sense to them.

Psychological Changes

As I talked and worked with students in both formal and informal contexts, I began to hear their stories of life in their home countries, the psychological changes they had been experiencing during their years in the United States, their resistance to these changes, and their anger, fear, and loss of confidence as they saw themselves changing, sometimes profoundly, as a result of having to learn to write differently. In this way, I began to understand that writing style is "more than just a technique." As one of my students from Chile told me,

> You said it was just a technique, but what I discovered was that it meant I had to look at things differently. Real differently. And in that sense, my world view has to change. You know, it's so powerful when you start to see things from a different perspective—the whole meaning of the world changes. So how am I going to change? Or would it make sense to me? All my life and everything is going to make sense in a different way. There is so much changing! And that's powerful. You see? I mean, that's incredible. That's so strong!

It's not that world majority students don't ever express themselves directly, or argue with authorities, or critique the political situation with friends and family. And it's not as if mainstream U.S. students don't ever speak indirectly out of politeness, or get good grades by repeating the wisdom of the professor, or try to achieve harmonious relations among their groups of friends. Directness and indirectness, individualism and collectivism, cherishing the past and idolizing the new are not fixed categories of experience. But they *are* tendencies, sometimes very strong tendencies, to interpret the world and communicate about it according to the ways that are passed down through families, schools, media, political institutions, artistic and musical traditions, health practices, religious ceremonies, and daily conversations. Individual differences in personality, gender, class background, fluency in English, degree of "Westernization," and experience with writing also play a role in how students express themselves, both orally and in writing. But underlying these differences is the deep stream of culture.

The most difficult thing for world majority students, the most painful, depressing, annoying, maddening thing, is that U.S. instructors so often confuse these legitimate and interesting cultural differences with poor preparation, faulty English language skills, difficulties with reading, lack of practice writing, or poor cognitive skills. Difference and deficiency are hard to separate, of course, and sometimes both may be occurring simultaneously. But faculty who have been carefully trained to succeed in the U.S. system are so used to seeing U.S. mainstream values as the norm, so used to thinking about "academic writing" as the best and only way to express one's self intellectually, so used to talking about traditions of writing and thinking in the dominant culture as "good writing" and "good thinking," that even when we try our hardest to respect our students, we may use deficit language rather than the language of difference. We might say, for example, that this Korean student's thoughts are "not adequately elaborated," or that this Mexican American student's ideas are "all over the place." We might even say that an Asian student's writing is "excessively polite, full of hyperbole and unnecessary rhetorical flourishes," as I once wrote on a Nepali student's paper before I understood the power and value of cultural rhetorical style. These are all reasonable observations and critiques from the point of view of the U.S. reader. But put this way, in deficit language, they assume a global standard for good writing that is not being met by students whose cultural assumptions and values are different from those of the U.S. mainstream.

African American Student Writing

An interesting exception to my argument, and one that may have some relevance for teaching writing to minorities in other countries, is African American student writing. Of course, African Americans are part of the great "world majority"—the people of color that inhabit most of the globe. But African American student writing does not differ markedly, at least at the college level, from the cultural style of writing expected by the U.S. university. After all, African American culture is a deeply American culture. African American history stretches back as far as British and European history on the North American continent. African Americans have been integral to the American experience, albeit on drastically unequal terms. African American Vernacular English (AAVE) is a U.S. dialect, a cultural form of the English language that influenced the British dialects of early America just as it has been influenced by them. So the values, and assumptions, and expectations about writing in college are about as familiar to African American college students as they are to white students. When African American student writing differs from academic writing in culturally specific ways, these differences are not as obscure or confusing to them as they are for many international students who have just arrived from abroad, or for some Native American students (Monroe, 2004) or for U.S.-born Latino, or Arab American, or Asian students who are deeply connected to their cultural communities.

Effects of Racism

Probably the most important cultural difference that affects African Americans when they write in college is the stress of living and learning in an environment where they do not feel entirely welcome. Social exclusion has various consequences, depending on the student's experience, emotional state, and attitude toward life. One strategy that some of my African American students adopt is to use an overly formal tone for even the most incidental writing: journal writing, responses to reading, or informal argumentative pieces. The grammatically faultless, scripted nature of the language sometimes leaves me wanting the writer to loosen up a little, be real, talk to me in a way that reaches me as a reader, rather than keeping me at such a distance. Of course, formal writing works for a wide variety of academic pieces, so I rarely ask these students to change their style. But it's a kind of cultural difference that I have noticed, and I understand it as a tactic that writers might use with an audience they don't fully trust. If your people historically have been ridiculed and disparaged for their intellect, their uses of language, and their potential as scholars and professionals, then you just might want to use a formal, scholarly tone even when your reader expects you to sound more casual.

Like most writing instructors, I try to create a safe space for all students in my classroom and a warm, personal relationship with each of them. But regardless of what we are able to accomplish in our classroom communities, our students spend most of their time outside of our classes—in large lectures where creating a safe space is more difficult, in their dormitories, in their social activities on campus, and in their forays into town. Even at a progressive university that emphasizes recruitment and retention of students of color, offers mandatory classes about race and racism for all students, multicultural celebrations, ethnic student clubs and performances, and safe spaces for dialogue about differences; students whose ancestors were, in John Ogbu's terms, "involuntary minorities" still face both overt and subtle racism on campus and in the surrounding community—as do international students and other students of color.

Racism on U.S. Campuses

Racism takes many forms on college campuses: a few students participate in blatant, nasty expressions of prejudice—especially when inebriated—yelling racial slurs from car windows, writing racial epithets on bathroom mirrors or on the dormitory doors of students of color, or dreaming up party "pranks" that demean students of various ethnicities. Other students who deride this behavior as juvenile may express their own more subtle racism through their difficulty seeing other cultural styles as "normal." They may find it humorous, for example, to imitate a Chinese teacher's accent (as a "joke"), or find the physical characteristics of an unfamiliar ethnic group "weird" or, perhaps, compellingly exotic. They may tap into the internalized racism of their friends and acquaintances of color, believing, for example, that their African American roommate is to be pitied for her "bad hair," or that a Korean friend who has an operation on her eyelids to make her eyes look rounder is only trying to become more beautiful. These students generally do not see their attitudes or remarks as racist. Racism to them is a violent act, a cross-burning, or a law that keeps African Americans out of an autoworker's union or seated in the back of a bus. They may recognize the racist stereotypes in their parents' or grandparents' remarks, but they certainly do not see racism in themselves or anyone in their generation, and this can make it difficult to talk about, much less eradicate (Fox, 2009).

Faculty and staff, too, can be purveyors of racism, sometimes intentionally, but more often without quite realizing it, and this can make campus life
painful for students of color. An African American football player who
attempts to get a standard signature on a form is treated with contempt by
the office manager, as if the student is somehow acting irresponsibly for
coming in at all. An academic advisor suggests to an African American student that she might be better off pursuing an easier major, despite her high
grade point average. A writing teacher expresses surprise when she receives
an outstanding paper written by a Latino student, or tries to complement
that student by telling him that he's "not like other Mexicans at this university." Faculty may unwittingly exasperate a Native American student by
asking her to tell the class about life on the reservation, or look to the only
African American student in the class to provide "the experience of living in
the inner city," believing, perhaps, that all students of an ethnic type live
under the same conditions and have similar opinions, experiences, skills, and
deficits. At the curriculum level, courses in U.S. literature often give short
shrift to writers of color. U.S. history classes erase the contributions of
Asians and Latinos to the building of the nation, and in a course that does
mention slavery, photos of impoverished people degraded by suffering and
despair might be projected on the huge lecture hall screen, while the noble
history of resistance and the stirring black oratory that inspired both blacks
and whites to speak out against that nefarious institution are ignored.

Though these displays of ethnocentrism and racism can be profoundly
discouraging and insulting to students of color, they may not be paid much
attention by white students or faculty. To white students in the lecture hall,
the lack of depictions of dignified resistance to slavery, or the absence of
Mexican American and Native American points of view, or the erasure of
the Chinese and Japanese and Filipino contributions to American life simply
confirm their view of history. The crude drawing of a noose on the bathroom
mirror is dismissed by well-meaning white students as an "isolated incident"
that almost never happens and certainly shouldn't frighten or upset anyone.
Yet to minority students, particularly "involuntary minority" students, these
are the kinds of daily indignities that wear away at their confidence and
affect their determination to do their best work.

Student writers are particularly vulnerable in an unwelcoming atmosphere. When we write, we lay our ideas bare for anyone to see. Sometimes
we are proud of those ideas, but more often, we fear that our awesome
thoughts haven't quite made it to the page. And that makes many students—
of any ethnicity—rush through the writing, working on it late at night,
sometimes not even reading it over when it comes off the printer. Hoping for
the best, yet fearing the worst, many of our students take one quick look at
their grade before throwing their paper into the trash.

Now imagine this same scenario for students who are reminded daily that
their presence is unwelcome. African American students, touchy about their
writing just as all students are, also have their confidence undermined by the
atmosphere of racism and exclusion. If they don't feel safe, if they feel that

at any moment they can be judged by their effort as well as for something about their identity, their will to write and even their ability to write may suffer. Unlike international students or any student whose first language is other than English, African American students cannot chalk up their poor writing to second language difficulties, which makes them even more vulnerable. Of course, many African American students, like many white students, are fine writers. Despite the atmosphere, some have discovered how to use writing to express powerful thoughts in elegant ways. But when African American student writing is insubstantial, we need to be aware of the factors that can lie behind it.

The Influence of "Stereotype Threat" on Writing

Stanford University psychologist Claude Steele (1997) has found that when students are reminded of a well-known stereotype about their social identity group before taking a test, they tend to underperform in a manner consistent with the stereotype. For example, when women are told that male students outperform them in math, they do worse on math tests. When African American college students take a difficult verbal test that reminds them of stereotypes about their ability, their anxiety is raised, they become more easily distracted, and their blood pressure soars, leading to diminished performance. This result is not limited to traditionally disadvantaged groups, Steele points out. When white male engineering students take a test after being told that Asian students generally outperform them, they do significantly worse than they would have otherwise.

The simple fact that a stereotype is in the air can negatively affect our students' performance. Actually, Steele says, the most achievement-oriented students, who are also the most skilled, motivated, and confident, are the most impaired by stereotype threat. When top students are subtly yet frequently reminded that they are not thought to be as worthy, as able, or as smart as other students, even when they know, intellectually, it is not true, their performance can suffer. These are some of the cultural differences—because prejudice and racism are aspects of U.S. culture—that may affect African American student writing in the U.S. context. And because prejudice is not unique to the United States, some of these factors may influence the writing of minorities in other countries as well.

Advice for Instructors

How should instructors teach students who are affected by all these factors I've outlined—some of which are central to their students' cultural backgrounds and experiences, and others that arise from pervasive attitudes in the dominant culture? The atmosphere of the classroom is probably easiest for teachers to control. Having high expectations for all students, making sure the classroom is a safe space for students to be themselves while respecting the dignity of others, and finding ways to create a close-knit classroom community are central to eliciting the best writing from all our students.

More difficult is deciding what to do about the differences in cultural expectations and values that can keep world majority students' writing from reaching their U.S. readers. Ideally, a truly global university would be skilled in all the myriad cultural styles that students bring to campus. Faculty and administrators would honor those styles, learn from them, and at the same time, teach all students how to meet the expectations of writing for a U.S. academic audience. But while most of us believe that diversity makes a more interesting campus, I think we also want an easy multiculturalism: "Let's just invite the world over to our place and expect our visitors to adapt to our cultural values and expectations. When in Rome, do as the Romans do, right? It would be too hard to learn *all* those cultural styles. Where would I find the time? This is not my area of expertise!" It can be hard, even for the most committed faculty, to find the courage and the will to begin.

Fortunately, there is a growing body of literature on second language writing (Selected, 2010; Swales & Feak, 2004), and for academics, reading is the usual place to start. I would also suggest that interested faculty learn as I do, from the students themselves. Instead of criticizing their rhetorical styles, ask them what they were trying to say, and what they value and want to keep in their writing. Explain your difficulties understanding their writing in terms of audience expectations, explicitly showing them the style that the U.S. academy values, but without laying down rigid rules about what "good writing" looks like. Ask them about their favorite authors, and read some of these books if they are accessible in translation, trying to grasp the different ways the writers choose to express themselves. Listen to the oral strategies your students use: their subtlety, their metaphors, their humor, their ways of telling a story or making a point. Communicate what you are learning to your colleagues, despite the inevitable resistance.

No doubt, it is hard for anyone from any culture to avoid being ethnocentric. But learning to see writing through a different cultural lens can be particularly challenging for those of us who have been socialized in the dominant culture. When assumptions about good writing and, by extension, good thinking, are connected to—even based upon—the political, social, economic, and psychological dominance of one culture (or set of cultures) over the rest of the world, the result is harmful, both for the dominant culture—the culture of the center—and for the cultures that are excluded—the cultures of the periphery. If the periphery cultures allow themselves to be assimilated, they lose their voice, their style, their individuality, their uniqueness. But if they resist being swept up into the mainstream, they forfeit connection with the dominant producers of knowledge and remain isolated in their own communities. In either case, the center loses the biodiversity, as it were, of world styles and strategies of communication.

By imposing a particular idea of what "good writing" looks like, and what "smart thinking" sounds like, the center loses a whole lot of good ideas, and it denies itself a full range of ways to be human. I want us—the teachers at the center—to reconsider this situation, not only for the sake of respect and fairness, but also for our own personal and intellectual growth.

References

Bennett, M. J. (2004). Becoming interculturally competent. In J. Wurzel (Ed.), *Toward multiculturalism: A reader in multicultural education* (2nd ed.). Newton, MA: Intercultural Resource Corporation.

Connor, U. (1996). *Contrastive rhetoric: Cross-cultural aspects of second language writing.* New York, NY: Cambridge University Press.

Fox, H. (1994). *Listening to the world: Cultural issues in academic writing.* Urbana, IL: National Council of Teachers of English.

Fox, H. (2009). *When race breaks out: Conversations about race and racism in college classrooms* (Rev. Ed.). New York, NY: Peter Lang.

Harklau, L., Losey, K. M., & Siegal, M. (Eds.). (1999). *Generation 1.5 meets college composition.* Mahwah, NJ: Lawrence Erlbaum.

Kaplan, R. (1966). Cultural thought patterns in inter-cultural education. *Language Learning, 16*(1), 1–20.

Kassabgy, N., Ibrahim, Z., & Aydelott, S. (Eds.). (2004). *Contrastive rhetoric.* Cairo, Egypt: American University in Cairo Press.

Monroe, B. J. (2004). *Crossing the digital divide: Race, writing, and technology.* New York, NY: Teacher's College Press.

Ogbu, J. (1989). *Cultural models and educational strategies of non-dominant peoples.* The Catherine Molony Memorial Lecture. New York, NY: City College School of Education, The Workshop Center.

Panetta, C. G. (2000). *Contrastive rhetoric revisited and redefined.* Mahwah, NJ: Lawrence Erlbaum.

Purves, A. C. (1988). *Writing across languages and cultures.* Newbury Park, CA: Sage.

Selected bibliography of recent scholarship in second language writing. (2010, December). *Journal of Second Language Writing,19*(4), 183–244.

Steele, C. M. (1997). A threat in the air: How stereotypes shape intellectual identity and performance. *American Psychologist, 52,* 613–629.

Swales, J. M., & Feak, C. B. (2004). *Academic writing for graduate students.* Ann Arbor: University of Michigan Press.

Triandis, H. C. (2001). Individualism-collectivism and personality. *Journal of Personality, 69,* 907–924.

CHAPTER 26

Culture Bump

An Instructional Process for Cultural Insight

Carol M. Archer and Stacey C. Nickson

> *Culture hides much more than it reveals, and strangely enough what it hides, it hides most effectively from its own participants. Years of study have convinced me that the real job is not to understand foreign culture but to understand our own. (Hall, 1959)*

Although Edward Hall's early insight into the dilemma of culture, communication, and understanding has underpinned much of the research in the fields of diversity, multicultural education, and cross-cultural and intercultural communication, James Groccia's (see Chapter 1, this volume) model of teaching and learning delineates the relationship between the variables in effective college teaching. This chapter clarifies Hall's two fundamental insights while applying culture bump theory using Groccia's typology regarding the instructional process. Hall's first insight that humans are unconscious regarding the influence culture has on their perceptions is nuanced by presenting the culture bump as an ontological shift in how we deal with differences, cultural and otherwise. His second conclusion that we must understand our own culture rather than foreign culture supports the use of the culture bump as an organizing principle in cross-cultural trainings.

Together these represent a paradigm shift consistent with Groccia's model of teaching and learning, specifically his awareness regarding instructional process. Indeed, by using the culture bump as the organizing principle in training about difference, the focus is shifted from acquiring cultural knowledge to the epistemological process of discovering and constructing knowledge. Using the culture bump approach to training means that the participant's experience rather than the content becomes explicit, and any culture-specific knowledge becomes part of the process rather than the product.

The culture bump theory and methodology emerges from an interpretivist framework of inquiry that assumes reality or realities are constructed by the knower. Culture bump theory thus approaches cultural differences assuming that a hermeneutic conversation between members of different cultures can construct a shared reality. To understand this approach to differences, we will summarize the theory of culture bumps and then describe how the methodology that has evolved from the culture bump theory is manifested in cross-cultural training designed to inform higher education instruction.

Culture Bump Theory

Culture bump theory essentially provides an explanation for the impact of a cultural difference on perceptions. Emerging from the understanding of the relationship between the difference and the resultant perception are the culture bump steps, a specific strategy for understanding and using cultural differences. Approaching cultural differences from the perspective of a culture bump allows an individual to view cultural differences not as problems to be solved but as opportunities to learn more about oneself and others.

Culture Bumps and Perceptions

The culture bump has been defined as a "cultural difference" (Archer, 1991). This phenomenon occurs when an individual has expectations of a particular behavior within a particular situation and encounters a different behavior when interacting with an individual from another culture. Expectations as used in this definition refer to the expectations of "normal behavior as learned in one's own culture" (Archer, 1991). This theory suggests that a number of ramifications emerge from encountering a culture bump. These include an emotional response, a knowledge dichotomy resulting in a search for information, and the formation of a perception.

A basic premise in culture bump theory is that culture bumps occur whether individuals are aware of them or not. Individuals are many times unaware of having culture bumps and simply experience a sense of disconnection that has an emotional component and a rational component, neither of which is usually conscious.

Emotional Component

Culture bumps can be experienced as negative, if the individual does not like them, positive if he or she does like them, or neutral if there is no strong emotional reaction. Furthermore, a culture bump that is experienced as positive on one occasion may be experienced as negative or neutral on another. Therefore, the affective quality of the bump reflects the emotional balance of the individual experiencing it at that particular point in time rather than being intrinsic to the behavior itself. It literally changes depending on the individual and the situation.

The importance of understanding this aspect of culture bumps is underscored by Kristine Fitch's (1986) assertion that even individuals with a great deal of intercultural experience, such as English as a second language (ESL) teachers, must be ever vigilant to manifestations of their own ethnocentrism given that the cultural differences merely change qualitatively over time rather than disappear.

Rational Component

The rational component is a concept that Carol Archer (1996) calls a *knowledge dichotomy.* Archer suggests that a knowledge dichotomy occurs as a result of a culture bump and is characterized by two phenomena that occur simultaneously: a "feeling of disconnectedness" that is accompanied by a sense of "not knowing."

Although the experience of disconnectedness is frequently confused with the sense of not knowing, it actually derives from a break in a primal sense of human bonding. Essentially, this sense of disconnectedness occurs because of a lack of awareness of how one's self fits into the worldview of the Other or vice versa. This is frequently accompanied by a loss of knowledge of an appropriate normative response(s) or interpretation. An innate response springs from the implicit assumption that the discomfort would be relieved if the reason for the different behavior were understood (Stoddard, 1986). Therefore, questions that focus on *why* something occurred seem to be an instinctive response. This type of question gains culture-specific information about the Other's culture and can lessen the discomfort that emanates from the sense of "not knowing" somewhat; however, it does little or nothing to explain increased awareness of the self in relation to the Other. The acquisition of culture-specific information, though satisfying the "need to know," sometimes reinforces the deeper discomfort of disconnection simply because the focus remains on difference, which intensifies the sense of anomie that resulted from the initial culture bump and out of which the *why* question originated. At this stage, there is a strong sense of *us* and *them.* Hall's quotation provides evidence that this very human response is inadequate. The reason for this inadequacy becomes clearer if the *why* question and the answer that it evokes are deconstructed as they are in Figure 26.1.

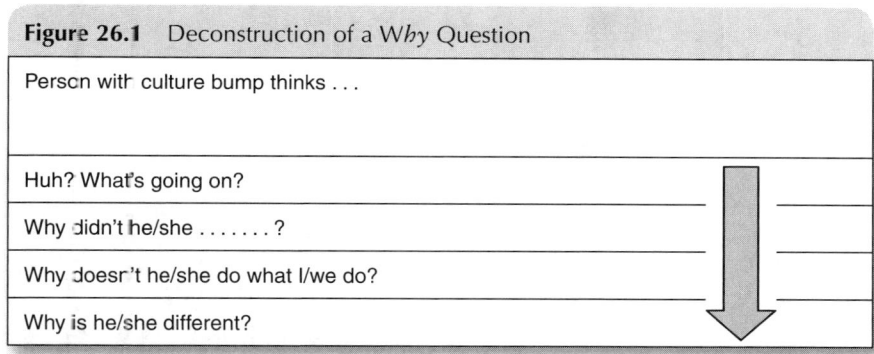

Figure 26.1 Deconstruction of a *Why* Question

Person with culture bump thinks . . .
Huh? What's going on?
Why didn't he/she . . . . ?
Why doesn't he/she do what I/we do?
Why is he/she different?

The *why* questions stimulate a particular kind of cross-cultural interaction that Archer terms *culture-bound* interactions.

In a culture-bound interaction, participants tend to adopt coping strategies in an attempt to alleviate their feelings of anomie. Some of the characteristics of these strategies include a tendency to focus on the contrast culture, to identify the attributes of one or the other of the cultures and ultimately, to perpetuate and replicate cultural differences. The precise form that the coping strategy assumed seems to depend on the circumstances and the individual's own proclivities. One phenomenon that frequently happens is what Archer (1991) calls *mirroring*. Mirroring occurs when individuals from the same cultural background discuss a previously experienced culture bump. Unwittingly, they generally reinforce one another's perceptions and become confirmed in their original impression of the Other. As a consequence, their bias is neither identified nor acknowledged and remains firmly embedded in their unconscious, intersubjective world. This can be seen in the closed cycle in Figure 26.2.

Culture Bump Approach

The culture bump approach gives individuals a conscious strategy for deconstructing their own experience with any type of difference. One of the most profound impacts of the culture bump approach is simply the use of the term *culture bump*. In using the term *culture bump* to refer to differences, learners from disparate backgrounds immediately create a shared frame of reference for conversing about a particular experience. It is at once accessible and nonconfrontational and provides immediate detachment. The term itself impersonalizes the incident and acknowledges two truths: (1) Each of us is more complex than a culture, and (2) each of us is empowered to respond to bumps, even those that are enormously complex, with confidence and authenticity.

By consciously identifying one's experience as a culture bump, an individual can amplify the instinctive process described earlier that inevitably

Figure 26.2   Diagram of a Culture-Bound Interaction

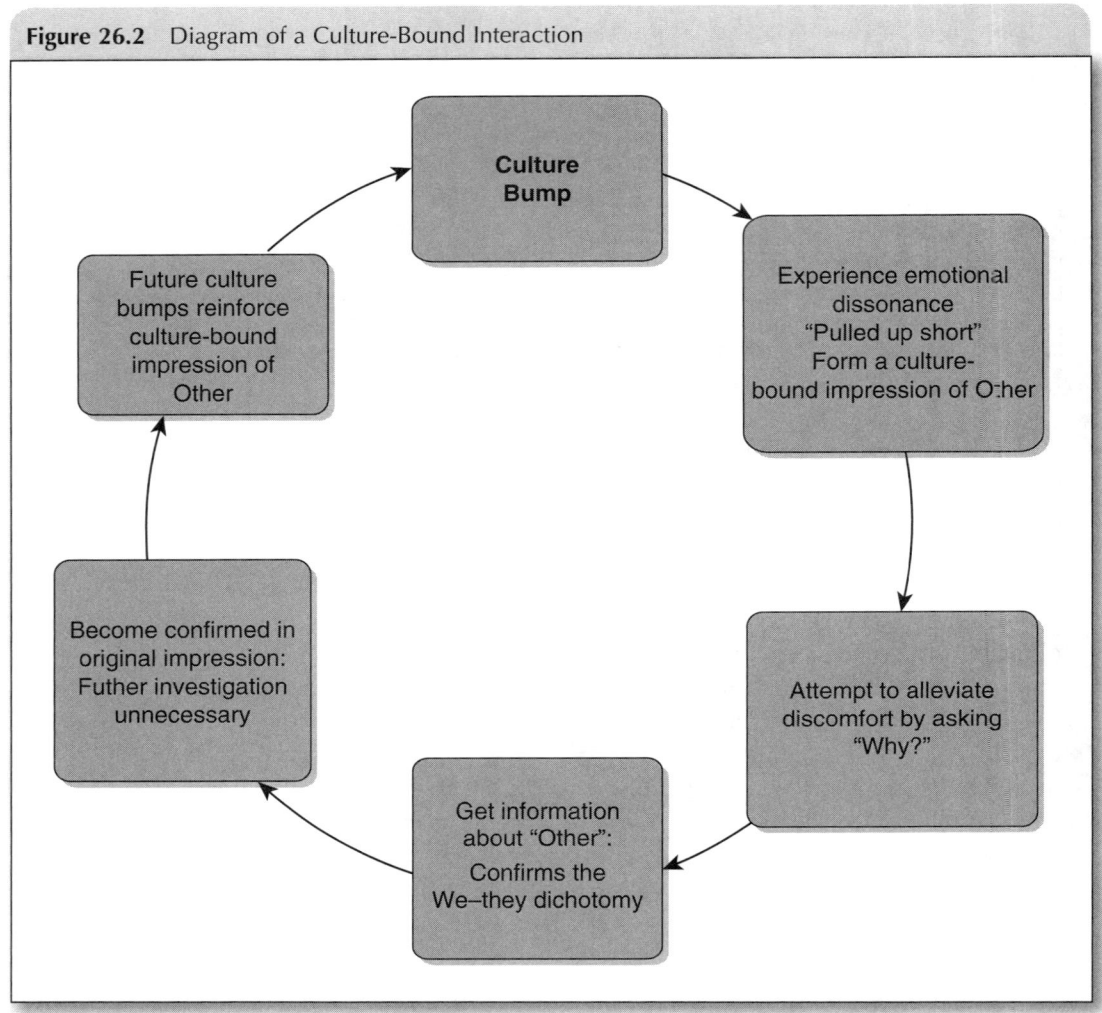

occurs when encountering a cultural difference. Awareness that a knowledge dichotomy is inevitable and normal allows an individual to continue beyond the *why* question with its resultant but necessary culture-specific, culture-bound information to a different, less instinctive level of knowledge. In the process, the primary difficulty, the disconnection from the Other, is resolved. The resolution occurs through an analysis guided by the culture bump steps that lead to a shift in the search for information and reconnection.

Connectedness

An unexamined culture bump frequently leads to a sense of disconnection, but a conscious examination of one's own culture bumps provides a sense of connection. *Connectedness* is the state of being that an individual experiences while in an interaction with another in which all the responses (even unpleasant responses) of all the actors are "known" within a normatively defined range that constitutes one's worldview (Archer, 1996). This largely unconscious state of comfort does not imply that the individual knows exactly how the Other will respond but, rather, that the Other's responses fall within a parameter of previously experienced responses. More importantly, in this state, an individual has a notion of how he or she fits into the worldview of the Other and vice versa. Clearly, by its very nature, this state of connectedness is rare with individuals who hold differing worldviews who generally maintain a sense of us and them. However, if they can "create" common ground, they can experience the quality of connectedness. This creation can occur through a particular type of conversation that Archer (1991) terms a *culture-free conversation* or *interaction*.

Culture Free

These culture-free interactions emerge from making culture bumps explicit. Acknowledgment of the culture bump corresponds to step one of the culture bump analysis. Following the culture bump steps leads inexorably through an analysis of a culture bump beyond that initial "why" question to a more complex question that, though not as instinctive as the "why" question, focuses precisely on commonalities. These resulting culture-free interactions are characterized by self-reflection and mutual exploration of individual and cultural characteristics as well as of universal themes.

Acknowledgment of the culture bump can be formal or informal. In formal acknowledgments, the individual having the culture bump reflects on it later and verifies his or her assumptions with respondents from the contrast culture. Informal acknowledgments occur within the context of a conversation where participants immediately explore their assumptions with one another. Both types of acknowledgement provide the possibility for relieving the original, frequently unconscious feeling of anomie because they include human commonalities as well as cultural differences. A diagram of this type of question can be seen in Figure 26.3.

Culture Bump Steps

The culture bump steps are a structured means of replicating a culture-free conversation at any time about any cultural difference. The steps of the culture bump are as follows:

Step One: Pinpoint a culture bump.

Step Two: Describe the behavior of the Other(s).

Step Three: Describe your own behavior.

Step Four: List your feelings during the incident.

Step Five: Extrapolate the universal situation out of the specific incident.

Step Six: Describe the behavior you would engage in yourself or that you would expect from someone from your own culture in that universal situation.

Step Seven: Identify and name the specific underlying "human" characteristic that you assign to that normal behavior when it occurs in your own culture or when you do it.

Step Eight: Reflect on how individuals in the Other culture might know if and when someone has or does not have that "human" characteristic? Ask yourself (or someone from that culture) about the precise criteria that they might use to evaluate the presence or absence of that characteristic in their culture? (Step Eight moves the individual beyond the question of why "they" are different into the question of how "we" are the same.)

Figure 26.3   Diagram of a Culture-Free Interaction

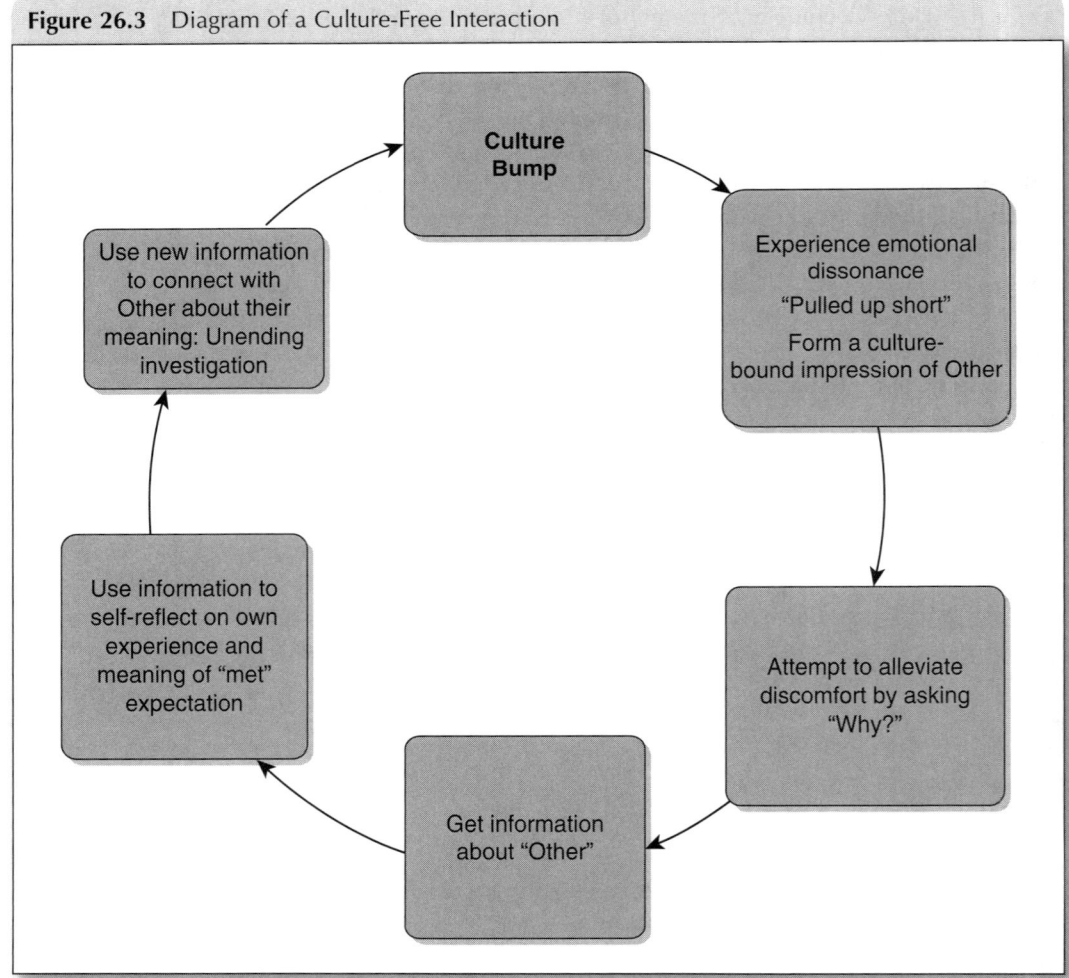

The affective connection with the Other simultaneously resolves the original sense of anomie and prompts a conversation that naturally leads to a common ground. Common ground and commonalities do not imply acceptance or even agreement; they simply imply a mutually understood category in which the individuals can hold opposite points of view. It is analogous to a brother and sister who disagree over the merits of vanilla ice cream versus chocolate ice cream yet never question their fundamental bond. Each knows where he or she stands in relation to one another. In these conversations, culturally distinct individuals examine various patterns of behavior, their individual beliefs and feelings associated with the behavior, and ultimately, the meaning they attach to such behavior. The addition of self-reflection about *meaning* moves the interaction into a transformative act. In this kind of conversation, meaning refers to that phenomenon that Jürgen Habermas (1984) calls "existential themes" and through which humans can connect because these "existential themes" exist in every culture. They include themes such as birth and death, need, guilt, love, and loneliness that "open equally primordial possibilities of 'making sense of human life'" (p. 59). A comparison of the culture bump steps with the hermeneutic circle clarifies this development.

Hermeneutics and the Culture Bump

Hans-Georg Gadamer's (1975) work with hermeneutics provides both a context with which to understand the culture bump process and an explanation for the efficacy of the culture bump steps. In *Truth and Method*, Gadamer (1975) seems to be describing a culture bump when he speaks of "being pulled up short" by a different usage in a text. Gadamer suggests that we can understand these "apparent absurdities" through a hermeneutic circle that leads to understanding in a cyclical manner. We understand the whole of a phenomenon by examining a detail, and we understand a detail by examining the whole. The hermeneutical rule is that "It is a circular relationship in both cases . . . understanding that the parts, that are determined by the whole, themselves also determine this whole" (pp. 258–259).

This hermeneutic circle is inherent in the culture bump analysis. The culture bump begins with a specific incident (detail) and proceeds to extrapolate a universal situation from the culture bump (whole). It then moves on to examine one individual's expectations of a specific cultural behavior (detail) and relates that to a worldview norm (whole). The entire process is repeated by questioning an individual from the Other culture as to how he or she perceives the universal quality (whole). This secondary process again begins with a whole and moves to a detail or the second individual's expectations of a specific cultural behavior.

Specifically, the process of moving back and forth between the "details" and the "wholes" of these two situations require an exploration of one's own cultural worldview. This exploration allows the individual to become cognizant of some of his or her own biases or "fore-meanings" about the criteria that the individual uses to evaluate a particular phenomenon. The individual simultaneously becomes conscious of his or her previous unawareness of how those behaviors would be evaluated by the Other. Overall, the eight steps became an exercise in training the participant's mind hermeneutically as well as a step-by-step approach for fulfilling the hermeneutic circle.

Gadamer (1975) identifies the cause of apparent absurdities as the "fore-meanings that determine my own understanding" (p. 237). These fore-meanings correspond to cultural expectations in culture bump theory. For Gadamer, the juxtaposition of contradictory behaviors provides a way of understanding one's own fore-meanings. He asserts that one's prejudices or biases are precisely that which allow any human being the possibility of understanding another human being. Culture bump theory builds on this perspective on prejudice by insisting not on the elimination but rather on the identification and acknowledgement of prejudices by removing them from the intersubjective, unconscious status in which they normally exist. This insight thereby provides the subtle shift that allows bias and ethnocentrism to become the key rather than a barrier to cross-cultural understanding.

Hall's seminal work on cultural differences focused on the influence of culture on its participants. This approach has been echoed by many in the field of education who clearly saw the need for educators to become aware of their hidden cultural values (Hannigan, 1990; Sparks, 2002; Whitfield, Klug, & Whitney, 2007). Hui-Lin Hung and Eunsook Hyun's (2010) study specifically cited the need for intercultural training for university faculty members. Others have focused on models for understanding cultural differences from David Hoopes and Paul Ventura's model of U.S. contrast values (1979); Carley Dodd's (1998) model of functional and dysfunctional intercultural communication; Kenneth Cushner, Averil McClelland, and Philip Safford's (2000) integrative approach; or Matthias Otten's (2009) ideal type of higher educational institution with its "new synergetic transcultural practices." All of these share a common paradigm in that they view individuals at a macro-cultural level leading to a focus on individuals being products of a culture.

However, culture bump theory approaches cultural differences at the point of individual difference and, by examining the minutiae encountered there, clarifies the process by which effective cross-cultural interactions do or do not occur. The steps that emerged with the theory provide that which Archer (2001) describes as a structured process by which "prejudice and ethnocentric 'blind spots' are not eliminated but are identified, acknowledged and become a part of the process itself. They are a necessary element for diverse individuals to truly connect with one another. In one sense, by using the culture bump, individuals, more than describing what happens as simple events, are actually accessing the domain of understanding of another's worldview—not as knowledge—but through an extension of his or her own horizon . . ." (p. 6) in a fusion that Richard Bernstein (1983, p. 143) describes as "our own horizon being enlarged and enriched." This approach has driven the development of a precise instructional process for cultural insight.

Culture Bump Methodology

The question of otherness arises less from a knowledge-based approach to labelling, categorization and description than from inter-subjective understanding. . . . The singularities that are wrongly explained using the term "differences" are more directly perceptible than universality, which requires analysis. In this sense, to talk of the learning of differences is to avoid a reflection, the object of which is to bring these singularities towards a subjacent universality. (Abdallah-Pretceille, 2006)

Groccia's model for understanding teaching and learning (see Chapter 1, this book) isolates instructional process as one of the seven elements in effective teaching, whereas Martine Abdallah-Pretceille's quote marks a shift in thinking about the instructional process for teaching about culture and cultural differences. An examination of the traditional process described by William Gudykunst, Stella Ting-Toomey, and Richard Wiseman (1991) provides a clear distinction as applied to course design.

Traditional Intercultural Instructional Design

Gudykunst et al. (1991) describes a culture-general approach to a course that includes two aspects: (1) a concept for explaining cultural differences such as Geert Hofstede's (1980) four dimensions of cultural variability or Florence Kluckhohn and Fred Strodtbeck's (1961) five value orientations, and (2) specific content areas such as theories about verbal and nonverbal communication styles, social cognitive processes, and the cultural adjustment cycle. In addition, Kluckhohn and Strodtbeck emphasized the importance of including experiential teaching techniques such as role-playing, simulations, and critical incidents along with culture-specific information. Gudykunst et al. (1991) provide a comprehensive overview of the development of intercultural training and teaching during the past four decades. Some programs have concentrated primarily on domestic issues in the United States, and others have concentrated on educational, business, or governmental exchanges between nations. All emanated from a macro view of culture as the focus of the learning and instructional process and therefore, even with cautions about stereotyping, individuals are viewed as products of their culture(s). Consequences of this macro view are the lack of a structured way in which participants could make the transition from recognition of different perceptions to an enlargement of their own world-view and the lack of recognition that courses have a unifying theme for all the disparate components.

Training for Cultural Traces

In contrast, in her critical analysis of the theoretical bedrock of multicultural or global education, Abdallah-Pretceille (2006) suggests that any paradigm should focus on process and relations rather than focusing on characteristics of groups, and she correctly identifies stereotyping or categorizing as a logical consequence of this approach. She argues that an individual is rarely in contact with the entirety of a culture but with an individual from that culture who may be considered a "concentrate" of the culture and terms these encounters *cultural fragments* or *cultural traces*. In addition, she points out that differences are easier to perceive than finding and practicing an analysis that leads to a common foundation. Yet she maintains that it should be an educator's goal for cultural training to lead themselves and their students to the universality that lies below the differences. Abdallah-Pretceille's (2006) perspective represents an ontological shift from a macro-cultural perspective to the perspective of a "cultural fragment" or a culture bump.

Culture Bump Methodology and Instructional Process

Culture bump methodology has developed an instructional process that actually combines Abdallah-Pretceille's (2006) perspective with Gudykunst et al.'s (1991) elements of an intercultural course. This has been accomplished by being cognizant of human reactions to differences, grounding training in the participants' experiences and using the culture bump as an organizing principle for incorporating components of traditional intercultural communication trainings.

Traditional Intercultural Components

These components are used in a multilayered design at the level of objective, normative, and intersubjective knowledge. Traditional subjects such as concepts about cultural perceptions, explanations of different communication styles, models of cultural values and behaviors, and descriptions of the cultural adjustment cycle are included, but two additional subjects are added. A unit about culture bump theory and about emotional intelligence is also part of the culture bump methodology content area. However, these units differ significantly from the course previously described by Gudykunst et al. (1991) in the instructional process. These subjects are both sequenced to follow the culture bump cycle within the overall training order, and each experiential activity within each unit is sequenced consistent with the cycle. In Figure 26.4, the types of content areas such as communication styles or values are presented cyclically in the first box (D1), the second box shows the cycles of sameness and difference (D2), and finally, in Figure 26.5, content overlays with sameness and difference (D3).

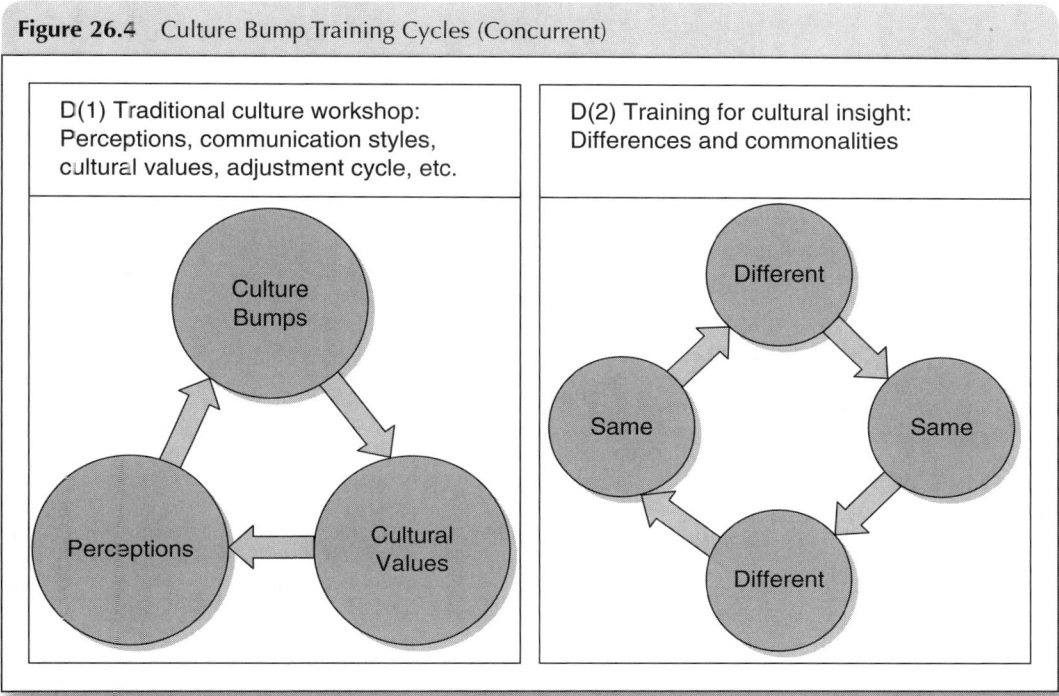

Figure 26.4   Culture Bump Training Cycles (Concurrent)

Culture Bump as Organizing Principle ————

Figure 26.4 demonstrates how culture bump training essentially interweaves the culture bump as both a concept and as an organizing principle strategy into an intercultural communication workshop framework. Three examples of content areas are represented on the left side D(1) of Figure 26.4, and the right side of the figure shows how the culture bump approach would sequence these content areas. With a culture bump approach, the sequencing of content consists of a consistent movement from differences to commonalities D(2). A closer examination of this cycle from sameness to difference reveals two elements of sameness and two elements of difference. The cycle begins with (1) the identification of a culture bump (*difference*) and (2) proceeds to extrapolate a universal situation from the culture bump (*same*), then (3) examines normative behavior regarding that situation (*difference*), and finally (4) relates that to a shared human theme (*same*). Each cycle must

Figure 26.5   Culture Bump Training: Content Overlays With Sameness and Difference (D3)

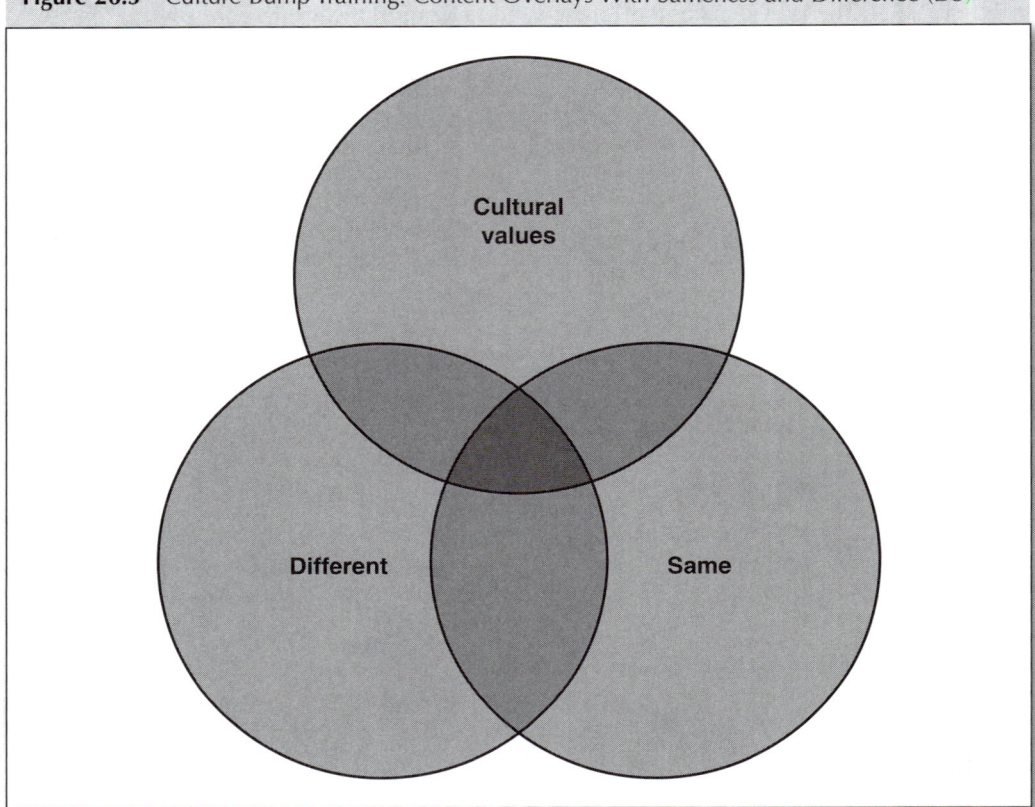

contain these four elements. By beginning with the culture bump, the instructional process is grounded in a concept of culture that differs significantly from a macro view to a view of culture as a collection of interpretative frames shared by groups of individuals to varying degrees along a continuum so that the participants define, create, and interpret their own cultural identity or identities and beliefs and criteria. This shifts the emphasis from viewing individuals as products of culture to viewing individuals as generators and interpreters of their culture. This, in turn, ensures that the content emerges from the cultural differences of the participants themselves.

An awareness of the knowledge dichotomy drives several aspects of the instructional process. To meet the rational need to know that emerges from a culture bump, units on cultural values and behaviors as well as communication styles are included. As explained earlier, these have been developed to a sophisticated level during the past decades and are of value in meeting that fundamental human reaction to a culture bump. However, the culture bump approach, cognizant of the need to recover relationships, ensures that the culture bump cycle is included in each of the traditional units. In other words, their design is altered to include a conscious movement of the participants to Abdallah-Pretceille's (2006) "subjacent universality" where reconnection occurs. In addition, a unit on culture bump theory and the culture bump steps is positioned early in the learning sequence to ensure that the participants and instructor have a common language with which to communicate about activities and information. This early contextualization provides a common thread throughout the entire course or training. The culture bump steps, each of which is an aspect of an analysis that guides a participant through a reflective practice leading to an insight as to the existential theme embedded in each culture bump, makes transparent the very process that leads to cultural insight. Thus, participants achieve self-awareness and awareness of self in relation to the Other along with objective, normative, and intersubjective knowledge of themselves and the Other. The instructional components and sequencing addresses the issue of changing personal awareness and, through the culture bump, has built in a modality for changing behavior. That is, once participants achieve new cultural and individual self-awareness, they then can self-select new, more effective communication patterns and behaviors (See Figure 26.6).

Figure 26.6 Self-Reflective Cycle

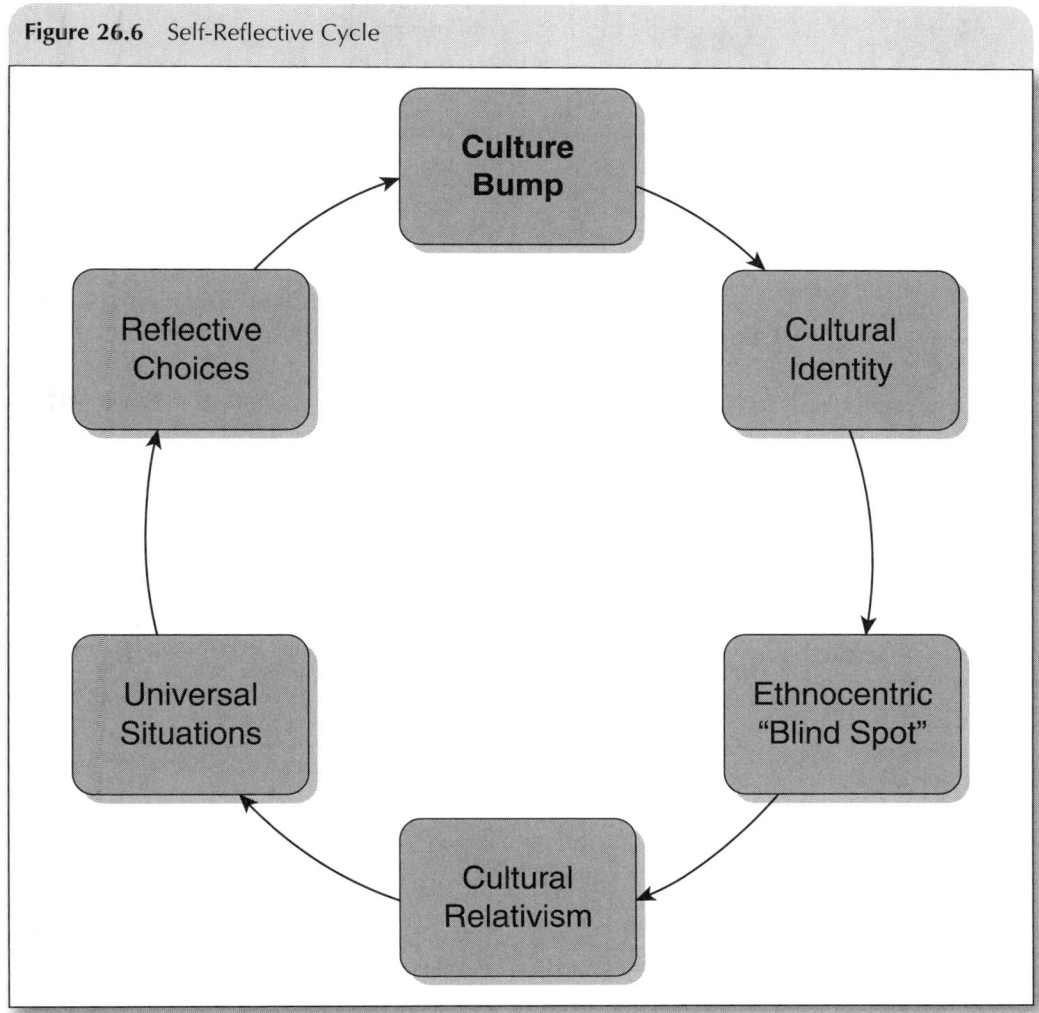

Example of Culture Bump Training

The Toolkit for Culture and Communication (Archer, 2004) is an example of the culture bump as an instructional process. It has elements of a traditional cultural training but is grounded in the epistemological process of understanding how to understand culture bumps and intertwines culture bump as an organizing principle in each unit and presents a unit on culture bump theory and practice. The toolkit contains six modules and has both cognitive and experiential components.

Module 1: Perception

The perception module is first in the sequence because it demonstrates the entire culture bump cycle in context. By using visual aids from the Middle East, Asia, and the United States, participants are presented with culture bumps that prompt different perceptions. Once this perceptual process is explored, culture-specific information is provided that explains the cultural context for each visual aid. This fulfills the "need to know" for the participants and in traditional trainings would mark the end of the activity. But by understanding that the learner is also motivated by the need for reconnection, a subjacent universality is revealed through stories about the characters in the visuals that consciously exposes existential themes such as love, aging, family, and solidarity. Thus, the learning process is extended beyond learning about specific cultural behaviors and values to the more complex question of how humans are the same. Once the participants experience this process, it is immediately and explicitly contextualized for them as being the culture bump cycle. This cognitive and affective experience lays the groundwork for each future activity in the toolkit.

Module 2: Culture Bump

The second module is the culture bump unit that replicates the cycle from culture bump to culture-specific information to underlying universality while providing both a model of a culture-bound conversation and a culture-free conversation. The basic culture bump theory is introduced by means of a video of a critical incident between U.S. and Middle Eastern cultures. The first part of the video presents a scenario in which two university classmates, one from the United States and one from the Middle East, attempt to form a relationship with one another; however, their numerous culture bumps cause them both to withdraw from one another and "mirror" (Archer, 1991) with individuals from their own background. The video is stopped at this point so that the bumps can be identified and traced to their logical culture-bound conclusion, the creation of stereotypes on both sides.

Once the culture bump steps are introduced, an alternative ending is presented in which both young men cyclically deconstruct their culture bumps and, in the process, demonstrate an authentic culture-free conversation.

Participants come to understand their own reaction to culture bumps by using the eight culture bump steps to analyze one of their own culture bumps. In learning the eight steps, the participants are actually acquiring three fundamental skills necessary for effective cross-cultural communication: (1) the skill of detaching, (2) the skill of identifying one's own cultural positioning as being relative, and (3) the skill of finding universal meaning in any situation. These skills are learned as follows:

Steps one, two, three, and four teach participants how to detach by first identifying the culture bump, giving a precise description of the difference, and finally by expressing one's emotional response to the incident. The self-reflection required in these steps results in a sense of "detachment."

Steps five and six teach the participant how to recognize cultural relativism in oneself by requiring a typification of the incident and a precise description of one's expectations in the matter. The result of the self-reflection or "mirroring" with members of one's own group in these steps is a conscious awareness that one's own expectations in the incident are culturally relative.

Steps seven and eight train the participant to look for and recognize universal meanings in any situation by requiring a determination of the meaning implicit in the fulfillment of the expectations described in step six. Finally, Step eight acknowledges that there is a lack of access to the contrast culture's criteria for determining that meaning. The combination of these two steps propels the process beyond cultural relativism into an existential domain. This conscious understanding of their own epistemological workings regarding cultural differences ensures that participants emerge with confidence in their ability to communicate across cultures.

With these two cornerstones in place at the beginning of the learning process, there is flexibility in choosing the remaining content areas—as long as they are presented with the culture bump cycle of culture bump, culture-specific information, followed by an underlying universality.

Each succeeding module then moves the learner along the process that culture bump theory suggests is necessary for expanding the learners' worldview. Each step from culture bump to culture-specific information to underlying universality is carefully choreographed.

Conclusion

Culture bump training essentially interweaves the culture bump as both a concept and as a strategy into an intercultural communication workshop framework with each step from culture bump to culture-specific information to underlying universality being carefully choreographed. In so doing, culture bump theory provides a template for an instructional approach that is hermeneutical in nature and leads to the development of a methodology for training that fulfills Abdallah-Pretceille's (2006) call to "learn to see to hear to be mindful of other people" (p. 476). This instructional process for cultural insight provides a structured way in which to access the learner's life experience in all its uniqueness and analyze it using a specific protocol. This methodology emerging from culture bump theory leaves aside the question about whether we learn about Others or about ourselves. Instead, with the training for cultural insight, the inquiry is more about learning how to learn. Culture bump training is less about content areas than about the conversations we have with one another in which we arrive at shared definitions of existential themes—conversations in which we walk on common ground.

References

Abdallah-Pretceille, M. (2006). Interculturalism as a paradigm for thinking about diversity. *Intercultural Education, 17*(5), 475–483.

Archer, C. M. (1991). *Living with strangers in the U.S.A.: Communicating beyond culture.* Englewood Cliffs, NJ: Prentice Hall.

Archer, C. M. (1996). *A qualitative study of the communicative experience of a Venezuelan and a North American* (Unpublished doctoral dissertation). University of Houston, Houston, Texas.

Archer, C. M. (2001). Training for effective cross cultural communication. Retrieved from http://culturebump.com/relatedmaterials.htm

Archer, C. M. (2004). *Toolkit for culture and communication.* Houston, TX: Department of Intellectual Property, University of Houston.

Bernstein, R. J. (1983). *Beyond objectivism and relativism: Science, hermeneutics, and praxis.* Philadelphia: University of Pennsylvania Press.

Cushner, K. H., McClelland, A., & Safford, P. (2000). *Human diversity in education: An integrative approach.* New York, NY: McGraw-Hill.

Dodd, C. H. (1998). *Dynamics of intercultural communication.* New York, NY: McGraw-Hill.

Fitch, K. (1986). Cultural conflicts in the classroom: Major issues and strategies for coping. In P. Byrd & J. C. Constantinides (Eds.), *Teaching across cultures in the university ESL program* (pp. 51–62). Washington, DC: NAFSA.

Gadamer, H. G. (1975). *Truth and method.* London, UK: Sheed and Ward.

Gudykunst, W. B., Ting-Toomey, S., & Wiseman, R. L. (1991). Taming the beast: Designing a course in intercultural communication. *Managing Multicultural Communication Education, 40,* 272–285.

Habermas, J. (1984). *The theory of communicative action: Reason and the rationalization of society* (Vol. 1). (T. McCarthy, Trans.). Boston, MA: Beacon Press.

Hall, E. T. (1959). *The silent language.* Garden City, NY: Anchor Press/Doubleday.

Hannigan, T. P. (1990). Traits, attitudes, and skills that are related to intercultural effectiveness and their implications for cross-cultural training: A review of the literature. *International Journal of Intercultural Relations, 14,* 89–111.

Hofstede, G. (1980). *Culture's consequences: International differences in work-related values.* Beverly Hills, CA: Sage.

Hoopes, D. S., & Ventura, P. (1979). *Intercultural sourcebook: Cross-cultural training methodologies.* LaGrange Park, IL: Intercultural Network.

Hung, H., & Hyun, E. (2010). East Asian international graduate students' epistemological experiences in an American university. *International Journal of Intercultural Relations, 34*(4), 340–353.

Kluckhohn, F., & Strodtbeck, F. (1961). *Variations in value orientations.* New York, NY: Row Petersen.

Otten, M. (2009). Academicus interculturalis? Negotiating interculturality in academic communities of practice. *Intercultural Education, 20*(5), 407–417.

Sparks, B. (2002). Epistemological and methodological considerations of doing cross cultural research in adult education, *International Journal of Lifelong Education, 21*(2), 115–129.

Stoddard, S. (1986). Cultural assumptions, frames, and the allowable economies of English: A cross cultural problem. In P. Byrd & J. C. Constantinides (Eds.), *Teaching across cultures in the university ESL program* (pp. 123–125). Washington, DC: NAFSA.

Whitfield, P., Klug, B. J., & Whitney, P. (2007). "Situative cognition": Barrier to teaching across cultures. *Intercultural Education, 18*(3), 259–264.

CHAPTER 27

Intercultural Pedagogy

Deep Cultural Issues and Challenges for Global Universities

PO LI TAN

Internationalization is not new to many universities, having been initiated decades ago with an agenda to recruit international students and to collaborate in cross-nation research and scholarly activities. It was not until about a decade ago that the internationalization agenda and philosophy broadened due to globalization. Today, institutions of higher education in both Western and Eastern nations regularly recruit international students and staff to increase their global profile. Although internationalization may be complex because each institution often conceptualizes it differently (Gacel-Avila, 2005), it has been one of the most important driving forces for change in higher education internationalization (Knight, 2007; Organisation for Economic Cooperation and Development (OECD), 2004).

The emphasis on internationalization is unsurprising considering the increase in the diversity of student populations in institutions of higher education across continents. For example, in the United States last year (2010), international students accounted for more than 18% of the total student enrollment and spent about 18 billion U.S. dollars In addition, some U.S. universities recruit heavily for international research and academic staff (Institute of International Education, 2010). Similarly, in the United Kingdom, international students account for 2.3 billion UK pounds or 13% of the total overall UK income (Universities UK (UUK), 2009). Policymakers in Asian nations such as China, Korea, Hong Kong, Taiwan, and Japan also are interested in internationalizing their institutions of higher learning (Mok, 2007). Other nations such as Malaysia and Singapore have been receiving international students from neighboring countries such as Vietnam, Africa, Indonesia, Thailand, and United Arab Emirates.

Although many universities have had much success in attracting international students and staff, many institutions once promoted agendas focusing on attracting international students and staff for financial purposes, the emphasis now is on developing global citizens, promoting sustainable development and global values, and providing inclusive education. Indeed, for over the last decade, many universities, particularly those in in the United Kingdom, Australia, and United States have reviewed their curricula in the attempt to embed international and global perspectives into them. However, even after a decade of curriculum reviews, debates, and change, many institutions still face difficult challenges in terms of internationalization.

For many institutions, internationalization of the curriculum tends to focus on developing intercultural knowledge of the academic disciplines. For example, the international business curriculum might entail increasing student knowledge on intercultural business structures, ethics, and values. However, whether teachers impart this knowledge, and assess it fairly, or are culturally sensitive to how it impacts a rapidly increasing number of diverse student populations, is often unclear or completely ignored. For example, consider Australia's newly initiated "Global Education," which aims to provide teachers the resources necessary to support the integration of a global perspective across the curriculum (http://www.globaleducation.edna.edu.au/globaled/page1.html); or The Development Education Association (DEA): Promoting Education for a Just and Sustainable World in the United Kingdom (http://www.dea.org.uk/). Both of these organizations provide excellent international and intercultural curriculum resources, *but* significantly ignore discussion of interculturally sensitive pedagogical issues such as learning philosophy or deep values related to learning.

Interculturally sensitive pedagogy is pertinent to ensuring the processes of teaching and learning are fair so that students from intercultural backgrounds are not marginalized. Indeed, there is an urgent need to explore these issues considering the poor academic performance of many students. For example, Higher Education Statistics Association's (HESA) analysis of the academic performance of international and local UK students from 1995–2000 found that students domiciled in the European Union, Asia, Africa, and the Middle East achieved fewer first or upper-second-class honors degrees than UK-domiciled students. These findings did not change after controlling for age, gender, discipline studied, and prior qualification (Morrison, Merrick, Higgs, & Le Métais, 2005). Despite a decade of discussing and implementing internationalization strategies both in UK and Australian universities, international students reported that they still feel marginalized (Caruana & Ploner, 2010). Likewise, Po Li Tan's (2006) investigation of Malaysian and Chinese adult learners further reinforces cultural pedagogical issues as being a key factor influencing lower academic performance.

Current debates on the complexities of higher education have questioned the appropriateness of Western learning theories (Case, 2007; Tan, 2010; Watkins, & Reghi, 1991). Thus, it becomes imperative for faculty to consider the complexity of cultural discrepancies in teaching and learning in light of the intensity of developing global perspectives for internationalization of the curriculum, and to address the possibility of cultural imperialism of teaching and learning in higher education. The goal of this chapter is to unpack some of these challenges in developing a culturally sensitive pedagogy for 21st-century universities.

Pedagogical Values and Global Perspectives

Research on internationalization emphasizes students' need for developing global perspectives and to increase their intercultural knowledge. Although institutions of higher learning have made some headway in revising their curricula to enhance their students' global perspectives and intercultural knowledge, it is important not to assume that academic faculty and staff at the universities are value-free agents who are professionally fair, non-judgmental, and culturally sensitive. For example, Douglas Barnes (1982, p.15) argued that

> No curriculum planning is neutral: every curriculum is imbued with values. These values embody a view of the kind of people we wish our students to become . . . and of the kind of society that such people could live in . . . under the rug of technique, there lies an image of man.

Hence, examining teachers' pedagogical values, which may be embedded in the curriculum, is of paramount importance for genuinely internationalizing the curriculum, especially in light of the recent call for universities to develop "globally-competent teachers"—teachers who adopt culturally sensitive pedagogy. Nevertheless, the lack of research focusing on university teachers and internationalizing the curriculum (Foote, Li, Monk, & Theobald, 2008) implies that faculty may not need training in interculturalism. This assumption has possibly led to the neglect of the pedagogical values that underpin important issues in curriculum design and revision. Harmon (2005, p. 131, cited in Sanderson, 2009) has noted that

> . . . there is almost complete absence of material on the active involvement of academics in internationalization, their perceptions of the other cultures and people, the value they place on internationalization, and their competence in speaking and reading other languages than English.

Pedagogical Issues Related to Deep Cultural Values

Although scholars have long debated the concept of culture (Hofstede, 1986), they generally agree that cultural values are a "deeply entrenched, unconscious framework of shared meaning within a cultural group" (Shaules, 2002, p. 27). Deep culture refers to "unconscious meanings, values, norms, and hidden assumptions that allow us to interpret our experiences as we interact with other people" (Shaules, 2002, p. 12). Thus, deep cultural values generally function at an intuitive level—as individuals, we usually remain unaware of them until we meet other people with different cultural assumptions. Even so, on occasion people may remain unaware of their deep cultural assumptions even when they are confronted by others with different cultural assumptions, unless they are directly prompted by a particular aspect of the situation. Hence, I argue that unless these unconscious assumptions are made conscious, many deeply embedded intercultural pedagogical issues could pose serious challenges to students' learning in globalized universities.

Varieties of Intelligence and Conception of Knowledge

Although much research has been published on varieties of intelligences, learning styles, and study approaches (see Kolb, 1976; Biggs, 2001; Pashler, McDaniel, Rohrer, & Bjork 2008), we know much less about how cultural values influence these important issues (Tan, 2006). Richard Nisbett (2010) advocated that cultural differences have significant influence on intelligence and academic achievement. He argued that current definitions of intelligence tend to omit aspects of intelligence that are important in some cultures. For example, he noted that social abilities and empathy (i.e., interpersonal intelligence) are particularly important in some East Asian and African cultures. Congruent with other studies on world values (e.g., Feather, 1986; Wink, Gao, Jones, & Chao, 1997), he observed that East Asian cultural values and intelligence stress pragmatic, utilitarian knowledge or outcome more so than Western cultural values. Differences in conceptions of intelligence could add insights to research on comparative world philosophies and belief systems. James Maffie (2001) argued globalization could potentially create a "philosophical monoculture by silencing, eliminating, and outright replacing non-Western philosophies with Western philosophy—just like it is silencing the world's indigenous cultures in favor of Disney, Barnes and Noble, and MacDonald's" (p. 263). He further argued that differences in philosophies have significant influence on how cultures conceptualize knowledge and truth. For example, he noted that Taoist and Confucian epistemologies are not concerned with truth, true belief, or truthful representation. Instead, they are concerned with identifying the proper way of life suitable for human beings. In many cultures influenced by Confucian philosophy, living a complete life would be to live in harmony with one's surroundings.

Ethnoepistemology stresses that understanding of epistemology should remain neutral so as to include as many world epistemologies as possible (Maffie, 2005). In some cultures, such as East Asian cultures, "to know" really means "know how," and not "know that." Thus, these cultures emphasize practical knowledge of the world rather than theoretical knowledge. Similarly, research on Native American philosophy cited by Maffie (2005) supports the notion that these cultures tend to focus on actions and practices, and adopt attitudes of non-belief (i.e., neither belief nor disbelief) towards these actions and practices. This perspective is rooted in the Native American idea that one is defined by one's actions, not one's beliefs. Such practicality is evident in Confucian teaching, which postulates that one learns not because one seeks learning merely for the sake of learning, but to achieve a specific purpose (Lee, 1996). Several researchers (e.g., Salili, 1996; Winter, 1996) have suggested that, culturally, Chinese learners are not similar to Western learners and view education as a means to an end. Asians, particularly overseas Chinese immigrants, often view education as a tool to combat discrimination and other barriers to obtaining high status jobs (Chan, 1999; Chen, Stevenson, Hayward, & Burgess, 1995; Rothstein, 2000). The same is true for University of Hong Kong Chinese students (Kember, Wong, & Leung, 1999).

Similarly, social psychological cross-cultural studies have consistently found that Chinese, more so than other cultures, tend to adopt more pragmatic perspectives in all aspects of life (Redding, 1990; Wink et al., 1997). For example, Paul Wink et al.'s (1997) cross-cultural value survey on Chinese American adult women and Euro-American adult women revealed that the Chinese Americans approached life in a more pragmatic orientation compared to Euro-Americans. This study also showed that the Chinese American women scored higher on measures of practicality and pragmatism, hierarchy, and traditionality whereas the Euro-American women scored higher on measures of voluntary pro-social behavior and philanthropy. Some studies have suggested that this pragmatic worldview may be responsible for the economic success of many Chinese living abroad (see, e.g., Chinese Culture Connection, 1987; Redding, 1990; Wink et al., 1997).

Thus, if different cultures conceptualize knowledge differently, then internationalizing the university curriculum adds a new dimension of complexity beyond its already intricate nature. Indeed, it may contribute additional layers of pedagogical complexities without acknowledging what Barnett (2000) called as the "supercomplexity of university": "Universities have a duty to encourage epistemological pandemonium . . . an openness and even rulelessness in the domain of knowing and understanding" (p. 132). By bringing these deeply rooted philosophies and epistemologies to light and breaking them into their component parts, we may then uncover the rich interwoven complexities of intercultural pedagogy.

Socratic vs. Confucian
Approach and Critical Thinking ——————————

The hidden pedagogical philosophy in most Western curricula draws from Socratic philosophy. Socrates (469–399 BCE) advocated that "I shall not teach him, only ask him, and he shall *share the enquiry* with me" and "I cannot teach anybody anything, I can only make them *think*" (Epistemology: http://en.wiki-quote.org/wiki/Epistemology). This strongly value-laden philosophy is evident in the UKCISA's (United Kingdom Council for International Students Affairs, 2010) web site for international students studying in the United Kingdom. In the United Kingdom, international students are generally expected to:

- *work independently*, studying on their own for significant periods of time;
- develop *critical judgment*, which means an ability to assess whether an argument is coherent and well supported by evidence; and
- adopt a *critical approach* to knowledge inquiry (italics in original).

Contrasting Eastern philosophies such as that of Confucius (55–479 BCE) who argued that "When we see men of a contrary character, we should turn *inwards and examine ourselves*," A superior man is *modest in his speech*, but exceeds in his actions" and "He who *speaks without modesty* will find it difficult to make his words good" (http://www.quotationspage.com/quote/3088.html, italics in original).

It is apparent that these two philosophies are situated at two ends of a paradox. Socrates argued that learning comes from the individuals because the teacher cannot make students learn but only make them think. It is individual learners who initiate thinking and learning in creating personal, independent knowledge. Individuals learn by engaging in debate. Hence, individuals are independent learners who constantly and openly raise questions and challenge what they know. In contrast, Confucius emphasized that learners should constantly look inward and reflect silently, exhibiting a certain humility in the process. Self-reflection and self-criticism in relation to the context and significant people (i.e., teachers and peers) are important in examining the meaning of learning, especially if new knowledge is appropriate for oneself and one's wider community.

Given the profound differences in Socratic and Confucian approaches to knowledge and learning, it is not surprising that many international students, particularly those from the East, feel disengaged and alienated in Western universities. These students often express frustration in working toward their education. For example, Viv Caruana and Josef Ploner (2010)'s study on internationalization in UK universities quoted Chinese students:

> . . . Chinese students are shy; their culture is more quiet, you don't have to answer everything . . . you are not the teacher . . . in our

Chinese culture if you want to ask questions they must be very deep . . . simple questions . . . waste time . . . Australians just want to share opinions . . . but they also just think this is the question I must solve . . . they don't think like we do . . . (p. 83).

Thushari Welikala (2008), who investigated scripts of international students in the United Kingdom, offered another expression of frustration among Chinese students: "We are not for this arguing, questioning, and critically reviewing others' points of view. That is our culture. In China we have self-criticism" (p. 6).

Welikala (2008) also noted that the epistemologies embedded in diverse cultural groups often contribute to making students feel inadequate as learners. He noted that the pedagogical values embedded in Western curricula suggest that

students from diverse backgrounds need to adapt to Socratic way of knowing, without allowing the opportunity to consider their way of knowing. It is not surprising that some students felt alienated and may eventually reject this notion way of knowing, as evident in the script of a PhD student from Bulgaria, "They talk about this global higher education. But, we only learn how to learn as they do . . . nothing global about it . . . ." (p. 9)

It is apparent that Western and Eastern pedagogical philosophies have marked differences, and it is not surprising that international students from Eastern educational backgrounds face challenges if they are not equipped with flexible learning attributes. Unfortunately, the study of how international students learn in Western university environments is largely superficial and focuses on issues such as learning styles (see Dunn, Dunn, & Price, 1975; Fleming & Baume, 2006), language issues and socialization (Dawson & Conti-Bekkers, 2002; Li, Fox, & Almarza, 2007) discrimination (Lee & Rice, 2007), and psychological and sociocultural adjustment (Spencer-Oatey & Xiong, 2006). There is little research that attempts to unpack international students' deeply embedded cultural values or philosophy. When research addresses cultural values and breaks them down into their component parts, even culturally similar collectivist Malay and Chinese learners display significant differences (e.g., Tan, 2006). In an attempt to understand why there is academic performance gap between Malay and Chinese learners in Malaysia, Tan (2006) investigated how cultural values such as "conception of self," "face," and "the practice of Middle Way" impacted Malay and Chinese adult learners' motivation and approaches to learning. For example, "face" can have both positive and negative influence on memorization as an approach to learning. But when memorization is a culturally ingrained approach (such as memorizing 5,000 Chinese characters for Chinese learners to function at daily activities), it can lead to meaningful learning and deep understanding, in particular for Malaysian Chinese adult learners as compared to their Malay counterparts.

High Context vs.
Low Context Communication ───────────

The ways in which we communicate with each other influence the ways we learn. Edward Hall (1981), an anthropologist, argued that communication exists along a continuum bounded on one end by low context and on the other end by high context. He noted that in high context communication, most of the information is either present in the physical context or is internalized in the person in the high-context culture. When information is embedded in cultural contexts, very little of it is coded, made explicit, or transmitted as part of the message. The context in which the information is exchanged gives that information meaning. Hence, in a high context communication culture, meaning is conveyed not only in words, but through the group's implicit understanding of voice tones, body language, facial expressions, eye contact, speech, and use of silence (Rosinski, 2007).

Hall (1981) used the Chinese language as an example of high context communication: In order to find a word in a Chinese dictionary, one must know the context in which the word is being used. Thus a reader who wants to look up for the Chinese word "star" (星) would have to know that this word comes from the word radical "sun"(日). Similarly, the Chinese phoneme (Ma) could mean either "mother" (妈) or "or not" in a question (吗), depending on the context in which the word is used. Similarly, the Japanese expression "hear one and understand 10" (ichi wo kite, juu wo) aptly emphasizes the notion of high context communication where one just has to hear one phrase and understand 10 times deeper the meaning of the one phrase heard based on context around. For example, Shaules (2002) discovered that a tenured Korean lecturer in a Japanese university found it difficult for her to decode some of the contextual meaning or hidden rules of the Japanese language even after living in Japan for over 10 years and being actively engaged in the culture there.

In contrast, low context communication involves messages conveyed primarily in explicit code. Communication is highly individualized, and tends to be separated from the cultural community and context. Low context communication is invested in explicit code, provides ample details, and instructions. Because of the lack of fluidity with the context, communication tends to be elaborated, with every idea and detail fully expressed. According to Hall (1981), American culture is located toward the low context end point of the communication continuum. For example, sales and purchase agreements in the United Kingdom consist of detailed information compared to sales and purchase agreements in Eastern countries like Malaysia (this observation is based on my personal experiences of having lived in both Malaysia and the United Kingdom).

Ways of knowing and learning in Western cultures involves encouraging learners to articulate clearly when engaging in a debate or argument and providing individual perspectives on the issues in question. In contrast, Eastern cultures, especially those rooted in Confucian philosophy, encourage learners to consider the context of learning and knowledge, and to reflect inwardly, adopting a high context communication approach. Thus, it is little wonder why Eastern students with strong Confucian cultural backgrounds struggle when attempting to learn in Western contexts: They are often confronted with incompatible ways of knowing and learning because they have little or no conscious knowledge of the context in which knowledge is being articulated.

A particularly challenging issue for Eastern students is the Western expectation of actively and explicitly articulating knowledge and presenting individualized and independent critical argument. If teachers do not make students aware that this highly individualized, Socratic way of learning is not superior to their contextual and modest way of knowing, instead of being merely another way of knowing, then these students may feel disengaged in the learning process and sense that their cultural identities and values are challenged or even "stripped off." As a consequence, struggling students may respond in one of two ways. Students may adopt the Western approach to knowledge and learning and abandon their native mode or they may become alienated from the learning process all together. Such alienation may cause students to underperform or even drop out from university system—thus, it is critically important that teachers identify and address this problem (Case, 2007).

As examples of the difficulties that many international students often face when attempting to learn in Western universities, consider the statements of several students (Welikala, 2008):

"Some discussion topics are vague and I found it difficult to talk about. In school days, we Japanese are not given many chances to discuss in classrooms. So every discussion was hard, especially presenting my idea first." (Student from Japan; p. 7)

"The self-directed, liberal learning they say they have here, [in British universities] is not true. You know, when I was doing MA . . . there was this gentleman who continuously disturbed the lesson. He went on telling his own experience which was not important for me at all. He would never stop. And the teacher didn't do anything to stop him. This happened every day during that lesson and for one whole year, I did not learn anything . . . none of us learned anything . . . those who can talk will always dominate the class." (Student from Ghana; p. 4)

Clearly, the low context communication style of Western cultures impairs some international students' ability to learn. These students have been labelled negatively as "passive learners" (Renshaw & Volet, 1995; Kember, 1991; De Vita, 2007) because of their high communication context style of learning. Indeed, Welikala (2008) noted that there is little or no opportunity for learners with different cultural scripts to negotiate their learning within the UK higher education system. The only recourse for these learners is to adjust to the host university's pedagogy, which retards the pace at which these students can learn what they came to the university to learn (Koehne, 2006).

Memorization

Despite decades of internationalization of many universities, many faculty view international students in Western university as ineffective "rote-learners" who regurgitate information without understanding its meaning or significance (Tan, 2010). Western learning theories disdain memorization as an approach to learning and discourage its use as a meaningful way of knowing. For example, one dominant Western pedagogical theory that has had a significant influence on universities in the United Kingdom and Australia is called the "Student Approach to Learning" (Case, 2007; Haggis, 2003) originally developed by Ference Marton and Roger Saljo (1976). Briefly, this theory holds that there are two broad, generic approaches to learning—surface approaches and deep approaches, and suggests that the ultimate aim of learning is for students to integrate old and new knowledge in ways that produce meaningful understanding of knowledge and not merely to recall information.

However, culturally sensitive investigation of memorization has been found to be a culturally internalized way of knowing based deeply embedded cultural values (Tan, 2010), which can lead to effective meaningful learning (Entwistle & Entwistle, 2003; Kember, 1991; Marton, Dall'Alba, & Kun, 1996). For example, using an indigenous conceptualization of memorization, Tan (2010) found that Malaysian adult learners adopted memorization strategies to enhance deep learning even while studying at the doctoral level. In fact she argued that memorization is closely related to learning the form or the structure of Chinese language and is expressed as the character or "the way of thinking." Like many languages based on ideograms, Chinese learners must invest enormous effort to memorize the 3,000–5,000 Chinese characters used in daily language. Hence, it is unsurprising that memorization has been a culturally ingrained learning approach to many Asian learners.

Emeritus Professor of general linguistics at the University of Oxford, Roy Harris has recently noted ". . . that rote learning, currently held in contempt most by European teachers, is still highly valued in the Far East" (Times Higher Education, 2008). He further argued that memorization may be a cultural epistemology—a culturally specific way of knowing. Similarly, Hall (1981) argued that culture represents a powerful force in shaping cognitive processes such as memory and thinking. He noted that in Iran, for example, schools emphasize verbal memory, and the government requires workers to possess the ability to recall large blocks of information to be employed even at low levels within organizations. Similarly, Kursat Cagiltay and Barbara Bichelmeyer (2000) noted a simple emphasis on rote memory in approaches to learning used in Turkey.

Plagiarism and Copying

If memorization requires learners to consistently recall and repeat information, then it is plausible that learners who have internalized memorization strategies for learning ideogram languages such as Chinese could potentially memorize and copy large amounts of information. For example, Pennycook (1996) related the experience of asking Chinese students to write essays and later discovered that her first-year university students could reproduce verbatim the same essay they had memorized a long time ago. Commenting on the complexity of plagiarism, she noted:

> Arguing that plagiarism cannot be cast as a simple black-and-white issue, the prevention of which can be achieved via threats, warnings, and admonitions, I suggest that it needs to be understood in terms of complex relationships between text, memory, and learning. (p. 201)

Hence, it is not uncommon for plagiarism to be a particular issue for many international students (Leask, 2006).

Although many Western universities have explicitly defined plagiarism, Leask (2006) argued that plagiarism often cannot be reduced to a simple definition because it is highly dependent on context. Plagiarism is so rampant among UK universities that in 2008 the United Kingdom held special conference on this topic. A key outcome of this conference was the acknowledgment that plagiarism is culturally complex and that "The notion of plagiarism is alien to Chinese culture, where there is no individual claim, no ownership over intellectual property, and it is hard for Chinese students to conceptualize the idea" and that "Knowledge is communal, everyone knows who says what and there is no question about the source" (Times Higher Education, April, 2008, p 11). Similarly, John Lake (2004), who investigated the academic writing of university Chinese students, found that more than half of the Chinese students surveyed had no previous experience of acknowledging an author in academic writing. He concluded that perceptions of "copyright" or "plagiarism" can be different between countries and cultures.

According to Professor Hiroaki Sato, Vice Director, Office of Education Planning and Research at Ehime University in Japan, a similar pattern is seen in Japanese culture (personal communication, June 2010). The Japanese word that connotes "to learn at a higher level" is "manebu" (学ぶ. The original meaning of manebu is "to imitate." The Japanese word connoting "studying at a lower level" is "benkyo-suru" (勉強する, which literally means "being forced to do something." He explained that in Japanese culture, before one can acquire deep knowledge, one needs to (in the Japanese expression) "swallow and vomit" it out first. Hence, copying is an accepted and encouraged art of learning both at lower and higher levels of learning.

Thus, when teaching Asian students, for example, Chinese and Japanese students, it is difficult to make culturally non-biased judgments about plagiarism and copying. Indeed overcoming the inertia of learning that is so deeply culturally based requires teachers in Western universities to do two things. First, teachers should be culturally sensitive to different ways of knowing and learning among these students, Second, teachers should provide a supportive environment for socializing them to alternative, nonnative ways of learning and knowing that are acceptable in Western cultures.

Conclusion

When cultural issues are unpacked relative to important pedagogical issues, it becomes apparent that key pedagogical concepts are not as clear cut as we assume they are. I believe that discussion and debates, regardless whether it is on developing an internationalized curriculum, about teaching strategies or assessment, cannot happen in a vacuum—they must take into consideration the understanding of some of the deeply embedded pedagogical values that pose challenges for students with different cultural backgrounds.

Discussion on deep cultural pedagogical values has always been difficult and limited. The metaphor of culture as an iceberg or an onion draws attention to the fact that there are deep and surface cultures. Shaules (2002) argued that it is very unusual for people to question the deep assumptions behind their norms and values as they are highly abstract and operate at a deeply intuitive level. Practicing culturally sensitive pedagogy requires university teachers to be conscious of pedagogical assumptions and values that they impose on their students. The literature on intercultural development argues that the most significant phase in becoming conscious is practicing "critical self-consciousness" or what Socrates described as "know thyself." The power of knowing oneself is also consistent with the early Chinese philosopher Lao Tzu (6th century BCE) who advocated that "He who knows other men is strong, He who knows himself is all-powerful" (知人者智,自知者强). Consistent with these views, intercultural authors such as Shaules (2007) have argued that "Knowing oneself is the starting point for intercultural learning" (p. 146). Likewise, Pedersen (1988) noted that "Harmony with others depends on knowing ourselves and our cultures" (p. 74). However, in a multicultural learning context, I take the stand that to be globally competent university teachers of the 21st century, not only do we need to be conscious of our pedagogical values, we also need to be culturally knowledgeable on diverse pedagogical beliefs, values, and philosophies; able to balance and juggle the cultural tensions that students bring with them to our classes; and most importantly, to be able to see diversity as "strength or a resource," rather than a "burden or hindrance."

References

Barnes, D. (1982). *Practical curriculum study*. London: RKP.

Barnett, R. (2000). Supercomplexities and the curriculum. *Studies in Education, 25,* 255–265.

Biggs, J. (2001). Enhancing learning: A matter of style or approach? In R. J. Sternberg & L. F. Zhang (Eds.), *Perspectives on thinking, learning, and cognitive styles* (pp. 73–102). Mahwah, NJ: Lawrence Erlbaum.

Cagiltay, K., & Bichelmeyer, B. (2000, April). Differences in learning styles in different cultures: A qualitative study. *Paper presented at the Annual Meeting of the American Educational Research Association,* New Orleans, LA.

Caruana, V. & Ploner, J. (2010). *Internationalization and equality and diversity in higher education: Merging identities.* Equality Challenge Unit, United Kingdom.

Case, J. M. (2007). Alienation and engagement: Development of an alternative theoretical framework for understanding student learning. *Journal of Studies in International Education.* Retrieved from http://www.springerlink.com/content/m51qgp07j4x8278w/fulltext.pdf

Chan, S. (1999). The Chinese learner—A question of style. *Education and Training, 41,* 294–304.

Chen, C. S., Stevenson, H. W., Hayward, C., & Burgess, S. (1995). Culture and academic achievement: Ethnic and cross-national differences. In M. L. Maehr & P. R. Pintrich (Eds.), *Advances in motivation and achievement: Culture, motivation and achievement* (pp. 119–151). London: JAI Press.

Chinese Culture Connection. (1987). Chinese values and the search for cultural-free dimensions of culture. *Journal of Cross-Cultural Psychology, 18,* 143–164.

Confucius (551–479 BCE) Retrieved from http://www.quotationspage.com/quote/3088.html

Dawson, J., & Conti-Bekkers, C. (2002). Supporting international students' transition to university. *Proceedings of the Learning and Teaching Forum 2002.* Retrieved from www.ecu.edu.au/conferences/tlf/2002/pub/docs/Dawson.pdf

De Vita, G. (2005). Fostering intercultural learning through multicultural group work. In J. Caroll & J. Ryan (Eds.), *Teaching international students: Improving learning for all.* Abingdon, UK: Routledge.

Development Education Association (DEA): Promoting Education for a Just and Sustainable World in the UK. Retrieved from http://www.dea.org.uk/

Dunn, R., Dunn, K., & Price, G. E. (1975). *Learning Styles Inventory.* Lawrence, KS: Price Systems.

Entwistle, N., & Entwistle, D. (2003). Preparing for examination: The interplay of memorising and understanding, and the development of knowledge object. *Higher Education Research and Development. 22,* 19–41.

Feather, N. T. (1986). Value systems across cultures: Australia and China. *International Journal of Psychology, 21,* 697–715.

Fleming, N., & Baume, D. (2006). Learning styles again: VARKing up the right tree! *Educational Developments, 7,* 4–7.

Foote, K., Li, W., Monk, J., & Theobald, R. (2008). Foreign-born scholars in US universities: Issues, concerns, and strategies. *Journal of Geography in Higher Education, 32,* 167–178.

Gacel-Avila, J. (2005). The internationalization of higher education: A paradigm for global citizenry. *Journal of Studies in International Education, 9,* 121–136.

Global education: Teacher resources supporting the integration of a global perspective across the curriculum. Retrieved from http://www.globaleducation.edna .edu.au/globaled/page1.html

Haggis, T. (2003). Constructing images of ourselves? A critical investigation into 'approaches to learning' research in higher education. *British Educational Research Journal, 29*, 89–104.

Hall, E. (1931). *Beyond culture* (2nd ed.). New York, NY: Doubleday.

Hofstede, G. (1986). Cultural differences in teaching and learning. *International Journal of Intercultural Relations, 10*, 301–320.

Institute of International Education. (2010). *International student enrollments rose modestly in 2009/10, led by strong increase in students from China.* Retrieved from http://www.iie.org/en/Who-We-Are/News-and-Events/Press-Center/Press-Releases/2010/2010-11-15-Open-Doors-International-Students-In-The-US

Kember, D. (1991). A challenge to the anecdotal stereotype of the Asian student. *Studies in Higher Education, 16*, 117–127.

Kember, D., Wong, A., & Leung, D. Y. P. (1999). Reconsidering the dimensions of approaches to learning. *British Journal of Educational Psychology, 69*, 323–343.

Knight, J. (2007). Internationalization brings important benefits as well as risks. *International Higher Education, the Quarterly publication of the Boston College Center for International Higher Education.* (46). Retrieved from http://123.202.171.126:2101/iau/internationalization/pdf/article_IHE.pdf

Koehne, N. (2006). (Be)Coming, (Be)Longing: Ways in which international students talk about themselves. *Discourse: Studies in the Cultural Politics of Education, 27*, 241–257.

Kolb, D. A. (1976). *The Learning Style Inventory: Technical manual.* Boston: McBer & Company.

Lake J. (2004) EAP writing: The Chinese challenge: New ideas on plagiarism *Humanising Language Teaching.* The School of Oriental and African Studies (SOAS), London, U.K. 6(1). Retrieved from http://www.hltmag.co.uk/jan04/ mart4.htm

Leask, B. (2006). Plagiarism, cultural diversity and metaphor—implications for academic staff development. *Assessment & Evaluation in Higher Education, 31*, 183–199.

Lee, J, & Rice, C. (2007). Welcome to America? International student perceptions of discrimination. *Higher Education, 53*, 381–409.

Lee, W. O. (1996). The cultural context for Chinese learners: Conceptions of learning in the Confucian tradition. In D. Watkins & J. Biggs (Eds.), *The Chinese learners: Cultural, psychological and contextual influences* (pp. 25–41). Melbourne, Australia: Australian Council for Educational Research.

Li, H., Fox, R. F., & Almarza, D. J. (2007). Strangers in stranger lands: Language, learning, culture [Electronic Version]. *International Journal of Progressive Education, 3.*

Maffie, J. (2001). The editor's introduction: Truth from the perspective of comparative world philosophy. *Social Epistemology, 15*, 263–273.

Maffie, J. (2005). *Ethnoepistemology. The internet encyclopaedia of philosophy (IEP). A peer-reviewed academic resource.* Retrieved from http://www.iep.utm .edu/ethno-ep/

Marton, F., & Saljo, R. (1976). Learning processes and strategies-II: On qualitative differences in learning: Outcome as a function of the learner's conception of the task. *British Journal of Educational Psychology, 46*, 115–127.

Marton, F., Dall'Alba, G., & Kun, T. L. (1996). Memorising and understanding: The key to the paradox. In D. Watkins & J. Biggs (Eds.), *The Chinese learners: Cultural, psychological and contextual influences* (pp. 69–83). Melbourne: Australian Council for Educational Research.

Mok, K. H. (2007). Questing for internationalisation of universities in Asia. *Journal of Studies in International Education, 11,* 433–454.

Morrison, J., Merrick, B., Higgs, S., & Le Métais, J. (2005). Researching the performance of international students in the UK. *Studies in Higher Education, 30,* 327–337.

Nisbett, R. (2010). *Intelligence and how to get it.* New York, NY: Norton.

Organisation for Economic Cooperation and Development (OECD). (August, 2004). Internationalisation of Higher Education. *Policy Brief.* Retrieved from http://www.oecd.org/dataoecd/33/60/33734276.pdf

Pashler, H., McDaniel, M., Rohrer, D. & Bjork, R. (2008). Learning styles: Concepts and evidence. *Psychological Science in the Public Interest, 9,* 105–119.

Pedersen, P. (1988). *A handbook for developing multicultural awareness.* Washington, D.C.: American Association for Counselling and Development.

Pennycook, A. (1996). Borrowing others' words: Text, ownership, memory, and plagiarism. *TESOL Quarterly, 30,* 201–230.

Renshaw, P. D., & Volet, S. E. (1995). South-east Asian students at Australian universities: Reappraisal of their tutorial participation and approaches to study. *Australia Educational Researcher, 22,* 85–106.

Redding, G. S. (1990). *The spirit of Chinese capitalism.* New York, NY: Walter de Gruyter.

Rothstein, R. (2000, October 11). *On culture and learning.* New York Times, p. B10.

Rosinski, P. (2007). *Coaching across cultures.* King's Lynn, Norfolk: Biddles .

Salili, F. (1996). Accepting personal responsibility for learning. In D. Watkins & J. Biggs (Eds.), *The Chinese learners: Cultural, psychological and contextual influence* (pp. 85–106). Melbourne, Australia: Australian Council for Educational Research.

Sanderson, G. (2009, June). The secret lives of internationalised lecturers: A detective's story. Invited address presented at *the Centre for International Curriculum Inquiry and Networking (CICIN) Conference: Internationalising the Home Student.* Oxford Brookes, Oxford.

Shaules, J. (2002). *Deep culture: The hidden challenges of global living.* Buffalo, Toronton: Multilingual Matters LTD.

Socrates (469-399 BCE). Retrieved from http://en.wikiquote.org/wiki/Epistemology.

Spencer-Oatey, H., & Xiong, Z. (2006). Chinese students' psychological and sociocultural adjustments to Britain: An empirical study. *Lanuguage, Culture and Curriculum, 19,* 37–53.

Tan, P.-L. (2010). Towards a culturally sensitive and deeper understanding of 'rote-learning' and memorisation of adult learners. *Journal of Studies in International Education, 15,* 124–145.

Tan, P.-L. (2006). *Approaches to learning and learning values: An investigation of adult learners in Malaysia.* Unpublished doctoral thesis, Queensland University of Technology, Brisbane, Australia.

Times Higher Education (7 February, 2008). *Barbarous scratching or universal system? The Chinese puzzle on paper.*

UKCISA (UK Council for International Students Affairs) (2010, January). *Study Methods in the UK*. Retrieved from http://www.ukcisa.org.uk/student/info_sheets/study_methods.php

Universities UK (UUK) (2009, November). *The impact of universities on UK economy*. Retrieved from http://www.universitiesuk.ac.uk/Publications/Documents/EconomicImpact4Summary.pdf. Access

Watkins, D., & Reghi, M. (1991). The Asian-learner-as a rote-learner stereotype: Myth or reality? *Educational Psychology, 11*, 21–35.

Welikala, T. (July 2008). Cultural scripts for learning: Realising the pedagogy of international higher education in the UK. *The Higher Education Academy*. Retrieved from http://www.heacademy.ac.uk/resources/detail/events/annualconference/2008/Ann_conf_

Wink, P., Gao, B., Jones, S., & Chao, F. (1997). Social values and relationship with parents among American college women of Chinese and European descent. *International Journal of Psychology, 32*, 169–179.

Winter, S. (1996). Peer tutoring and learning outcomes. In D. Watkins & J. Biggs (Eds.), *The Chinese learner: Cultural, psychological, and contextual influences* (pp. 221–242). Melbourne, Australia: Australian Council for Educational Research.

CHAPTER 28

Conceptual Bases of Problem-Based Learning

Kenneth Mølbjerg Jørgensen, Anete M.
Camille Strand, and Anja Overgaard Thomassen

Teaching strategies in higher education have been biased toward mono-logic and monomodal approaches to learning, whereby learners are pacified and their knowledge measured according to their ability to repro-duce what teachers say. Implicit in this approach is the conception of learn-ers as depositories of knowledge, and in which cognition and perception is hegemonic to other forms of knowing.

Problem-based learning (PBL) denotes a range of different educational strategies characterized by more holistic and, more recently, multimodal approaches to learning (e.g., Iedema, 2003). We view learning as identity transformation that encompasses knowing, being, doing, and relating in a complex multivoiced oneness: The focus is on practice understood as a social phenomenon that involves both individual and social dimensions that exist in mutual constitutive relationships.

There are important differences among PBL approaches. We will sketch four different approaches. Our starting point is U.S. pragmatist John Dewey, who also laid the foundation of PBL and its implications. We develop and supplement Dewey's pragmatic approach with emancipatory pedagogy

Authors' Note: The authors acknowledge valuable comments made by the editors and by Lone Krogh.

(Freire, 1996), storytelling pedagogy (e.g., Boje, 2008a; Jørgensen & Boje, 2010; Jørgensen & Strand, 2011), and intra-active pedagogy (Barad, 2007; Taguchi, 2010).

Despite differences, these four approaches share a concern in taking a holistic approach to what teaching should accomplish, namely transforming the whole person as well as transforming societal or organizational situations. PBL is one means for these achievements—it organizes learning and education around the practical matters to change the world and people. However, there are also important differences among these approaches in the ways in which they address political issues involved in education and regarding what kind of modalities (language, space, artifacts, and bodies) they integrate into the teaching and learning processes.

PBL is often regarded as an important instructional method for bridging theory and practice to make the subject matter more comprehendible to students. Although this point is important, we stress that PBL's goal is not merely instrumental in producing more effective learning. It is also focused on determining that learning produces desirable effects on organizational and societal problems.

The four different approaches to PBL sketched here are thus all characterized by being located within specific philosophies of education in which the micropractices of teaching and learning are linked to broader societal issues of democracy, ethics, and emancipation. U.S. pragmatism serves as the overall framework for our discussion on the three other approaches to PBL.

Pragmatist Pedagogy

We will concentrate our description on three important concepts in Dewey's thinking: experience, thinking, and problem orientation. *Experience* concerns the construction of meaning, which is developed in interaction with the social circumstances in which the individual is situated. For Dewey, experience is actively living and interacting (transacting) with the world in such a way that individuals experience the consequences of their actions. Experience involves action as well as the subsequent consequences of that action (Dewey, 1916).

On one hand, experience is trying (an active side), and on the other hand, it is undergoing (a passive side). Experience is thus always interaction with the social world, and it would be impossible to understand experience as disconnected from the social world. Experience is culturally embedded, which means that people are created through the relations in which they participate. Dewey argued that education is the means of continuity of life and that everyone is born immature regardless of the social group to which they belong (Dewey, 1916). People are cultural products created through continuous processes of transmission, or communication, without which society could not sustain itself.

For this reason, communication becomes central in organizing desirable communities and societies. They do not emerge by themselves. "Unless pains are taken to see that genuine and thorough transmission takes place, the most civilized group will relapse into barbarism and then into savagery" (Dewey, 1916, pp. 3–4). The need for learning and education is framed from this perspective, and the purpose of education becomes the development of reflective thinking as a tool to solve problems in society.

Thinking has to be organized around the practical matters of the world—the complex issues and problems of the world. This idea follows from Dewey's conception of experience. More specifically, because it is an active-passive process, experience is not primarily cognitive, and further, it happens through relations, which has important implications for education.

Dewey (1916) argued that in traditional school systems we have separated mind and body: "The former is then thought to be purely intellectual and cognitive; the latter to be an irrelevant and intruding physical factor" (p. 140). This notion is unfortunate because it breaks the intimate connection between activity and undergoing in experience. There are at least three consequences of this separation. First, bodily activity is seen as a disturbing element. Teaching is instead organized so that it suppresses and disciplines bodily activities and focuses instead solely on the cognitive aspects, which according to Dewey, is an abnormal and artificial situation where bodily activity is a negative activity in which people are deprived of the opportunity to play.

Second, learning becomes mechanical in reproducing what the teacher says but without understanding what it means—learning's focus is on knowing-that in the form of theoretical and abstract knowledge, but knowing-how (knowing how to apply knowing-that in practice) is completely ignored (e.g., Ryle, 1949). Third is that people learn to focus on things in themselves, without being able to see relationships and consequences among them (Dewey 1916).

For Dewey, *problem orientation* is the answer to avoid the separation of mind and body in education and learning. Education and learning have to be organized around practical problems to obtain a creative oscillation between abstract theoretical thinking and the practical matters of the world. According to Donald Schön (1983), this idea is what characterizes professional practice. He argued that knowing-that is embedded in what professionals (leaders, engineers, doctors, architects, etc.) do in practice (knowing-how). He argued with Dewey that the practical world is characterized by complexity, uncertainty, contradictions, and value conflicts.

The solution to this problem in education is not to presume that these complexities, uncertainties, and value conflicts do not exist. Rather, Dewey and Schön would argue that education and learning have to be embedded within these ambiguous, uncertain, and contradictory matters of the world. When the reflective practitioner (Schön, 1983) reflects, he or she thinks in Dewey's sense of the word. Thinking is an individual's tool for adapting to the environment, and that means thinking is a tool for solving practical problems. Thinking is valid if it is capable of solving the practical problems of the world. Thinking is about creating relationships between abstract concepts and models and practical problems.

Dewey's concept of reflective thinking is not the same kind of thinking we do every day, which he referred to as habitual thinking and which is characterized by seeing that certain ways of acting and certain consequences are connected, but we don't see how they are connected—thus, we do not understand the connection (Dewey, 1916). Reflective thinking is present in practice (i.e., reflective practice) when we can justify our thoughts and actions. Reflective thinking does not include habitual thinking. Rather, reflective thinking is more systematically explorative, and therefore, it is also strenuous and exhausting. It includes long periods of disturbances and insecurity. "Reflective thinking, in short, means judgment suspended during further inquiry; and suspense is likely to be painful" (Dewey, 1991, p.13).

Reflective thinking is unlike habitual thinking in that it is not an instrument that people naturally possess. Most people are born with the potential for reflective thinking, but it has to be nurtured and stimulated, and this is where education and learning come in. Education has to stimulate reflective thinking for helping people develop themselves and develop society. Education and learning are therefore central for the accomplishment of the highest form of society, which for Dewey was democracy.

Dewey's pragmatist pedagogy implies a holistic approach to teaching and learning in trying to overcome mind-body and individual-social dualities in education. Thus, the goal of learning is not primarily instrumentally understood in the sense of cognitive perception and ability. Instead, Dewey's concern was the development of the whole person, which involves learning to know, learning to be, learning to do, and learning how to relate with other people.

In relation to James Groccia's (Chapter 1, this volume; St. Clair & Groccia, 2009) model of teaching and learning, the learning outcomes in Dewey's pragmatist pedagogy involve holistic identity transformation of individuals and a change or a new sustainable order in the transformation of practice. Because learning involves more than just habitual thinking, it is not mechanical reproduction. Instead, learning is characterized by critical thinking in which people use and test theories directly on real-life problems. In this light, a theory is an instrument or a suggestion of how actions and consequences might be connected in regard to those problems (Dewey, 1991). The learning process is thus organized around a practical problem defined as the experience of a new bothersome and doubtful situation (Dewey, 1991).

The function of reflection in the learning process is to identify linkages between actions and consequences with the end goal of bringing about a new situation in which the difficulty and confusion is resolved (Dewey,

1991). Thus, learning involves understanding of how and why phenomena are connected the way they are and is characterized by reflective practice in which learners are able to justify their thoughts and actions.

Pragmatist Pedagogy and Problem-Based Learning

Instructional processes may be organized in a variety of ways and include a variety of teaching techniques. Teaching and learning in any curricula are organized around the practical matters of the world, and in such a way that the students learn reflective thinking. Different universities have applied the PBL model in different ways. For example, Aalborg University uses the project as its most important teaching and learning strategy: Teaching and learning are organized around problems/projects throughout its undergraduate and graduate curricula. The problems/projects include many types of teaching, including lectures, workshops, and seminars (Kolmos, Fink, & Krogh, 2004).

At Aalborg University, teachers present to groups of students a portfolio of theories and methods within any given discipline. During a problem or project work, students work in groups for an entire semester and together, argue for, select, apply, and assess specific theories and methods in regard to their appropriateness for dealing with the specific problem they have chosen for their area of inquiry. At the end of the semester, faculty evaluate students on their problem and project performance. The Aalborg model is one way of trying to promote reflective thinking in education: The teacher guides students in reflective thinking by having a dialogue with them organized around students' arguments for framing the problem and their theoretical and methodological choices, applications, and assessment(s) for addressing the problem.

This model implies that learners' identities become important starting points for the learning process. Dewey (1936) described this idea through the principle of continuity: Students' interests, intentions, and perceptions of self are the basic starting points for the design of learning processes. Thus, PBL is based on the premise of active student involvement in which they and their teachers meet in fruitful dialogues that enrich them both. This approach meshes well with Dewey's (1936) notion that a learning process involves collaboration, negotiation, and dialogue among students and teachers involved.

Because of globalization, technological developments, and multiculturalism, problems are increasingly multifaceted and contain important intercultural issues as well as differences in gender, race, religion, and so on. For that reason, PBL—in particular, the Aalborg model—seems well suited to meet future educational challenges because of its ability to integrate many different voices in the learning process.

Emancipatory Pedagogy

In many ways, emancipatory pedagogy resembles Dewey's experiential learning approach in emphasizing problem-posing education and the importance of reflection. However, in its emphasis on the societal concerns embedded in education, emancipatory pedagogy is much more explicitly critical in linking a call for revolution with reflective pedagogy. Paulo Freire (1996) spoke of education as a holistic identity transformation, whereby students and learners gain a different awareness of self and become participants in societal development rather than being the subjects of dominant discourses.

To understand Freire's perspective, it is necessary to remember that he wrote in a South American context during the 1960s and 1970s—a context characterized by oppression, and huge economic and social differences in relation to the distribution of economic resources and political power. Problem-oriented learning thus becomes fused with the peoples' right to speak and amid efforts to transform society from tyranny to democracy. As such, Freire spoke of sustainability as social and economic justice. Of what relevance is Freire's work to education in Western societies? The answer to this question is that it is sometimes useful to take things to the extreme to make certain points crystal clear. Freire's work supplements Dewey's contributions to education in emphasizing the importance of fusing democracy with the design of educational systems to reflect multiculturalism: Education should provide and nurture many different groups' right to speak.

For Freire, problem-oriented learning, praxis, and dialogue guide democratic education. His approach is described in his classic book, *Pedagogy of the Oppressed* (1996), in which he argued for a close relationship between education and societal concerns. He essentially echoed Dewey in criticizing the traditional school systems for mechanical reproduction characteristic of its learning methods.

Freire uses the term *banking* to describe the traditional school system, in which educators perceive students as depositories of knowledge and not as human beings. He argued that a fundamental narrative character constitutes the teacher-student relationship at any level in schools: The teacher narrates and students listen passively, and in the process, the contents of the narration become petrified. Education is suffering from narration sickness. Because the traditional school system stresses mechanical reproduction of knowledge, it disciplines the mind to hear only the voices of the dominant elites.

An alternative is problem-posing education, which breaks the vertical patterns characteristic of banking education and leads to authentic liberation. Thus, we have chosen to use the term *emancipatory education*, in which oppressed voices and oppressed matters enter onto center stage to overthrow the dominant elite. Freire argued that this praxis is characterized as the action and reflection of men and women to transform their worlds. Thus, for Freire, problem-posing education is a way for students to apprehend problems as being real and interrelated with other phenomena and problems within the context of their lives. As a result, students experience less alienation, face real challenges, and become committed and involved in genuine critical inquiry and transformation. It is education as the practice of freedom—not as the practice of domination.

According to Freire, people develop their powers to perceive the way they exist in the world. In this process, people are affirmed as beings in the process of becoming completed beings in an unfinished transformational reality and where education must be seen as an ongoing activity. Emancipatory pedagogy thus resembles Dewey's notion of experience as ongoing transactions with the world. Freire also stressed the importance of reflection-in-action or reflective action and emphasized that reflection and action occur simultaneously. Human activity consists of both—it is praxis. Liberation occurs through praxis, and leaders who deny praxis to the oppressed undermine their own praxis because liberation cannot proceed without the action and reflection of others.

Genuine communion and dialogue with others who are granted the right to praxis define authentic revolution. Such change can only be accomplished by the oppressed when their leaders ensure that both groups grow together: Leaders are authenticated in their praxis with the praxis of the people. Dialogue is thus essential for any true praxis. The word is not the privilege of some few persons but the right of everyone and for that reason, nobody can say a true word alone or say it for another. The importance of dialogue, the word, and the importance of granting everybody the right to speak are thus absolutely essential for transforming and humanizing society. This outcome cannot be accomplished through the banking concept of education.

Emancipatory Pedagogy and Problem-Based Learning

Emancipatory pedagogy supplements Dewey's account of PBL by emphasizing the importance of fusing democratic ideals with considerations about the design of educational systems, which reflect many different groups' right to speak and to be heard. In this respect, the notion of dialogue is stressed even further than in Dewey's original ideas of PBL. Freire, of course, has a much more outspoken political agenda in explicitly questioning the relations of power embedded in the social order compared with Dewey, who simply sought to solve world problems without questioning political structures.

The educational system becomes a tool for a redistribution of power from the dominant elite to the oppressed people. Praxis or reflective inquiry becomes the process by which citizens' thinking becomes independent of power structures embedded in the traditional educational system. The learning process is not just targeted toward solving problems—it facilitates learners becoming independent and critical citizens who transform the world into a better place characterized by social and economic equality.

The instructional process is organized around the practical matters of the world because it aids students' apprehension of problems as being related to other phenomena within the larger context of life. Dialogue is absolutely essential for effective instructional practice. The teacher's role is to stimulate praxis by supporting and affirming students as they critically inquire about the world. Teachers are "leaders," who strive to ensure that they and students grow together, and in the process, teachers become affirmed in their praxis through the praxis of their students.

Freire's approach is revolutionary in calling for an empowerment of learners through dialogues that crisscross teachers and students and crisscross education and society. Through praxis, actions are qualified with reference to a relatively fixed notion of power—that is, a fixed narrative of redistributing power from the powerful to the powerless. Freire worked with a centralized notion of power, in which power is located with a particular group of people and thus where oppressors and oppressed can be clearly identified (e.g., Hardy & Leiba-O'Sullyvan, 1998; Lukes, 1974).

Storytelling Pedagogy

Central to the idea of storytelling pedagogy is a different understanding of being and becoming and of the relations of power that shape being and becoming in a particular society. Identity transformation is addressed as the emergence of joint storytelling practices, but it is likely that these storytelling practices will always privilege some voices in society instead of others (e.g., Jørgensen & Boje, 2010). Therefore, problem solving will never dissolve inequality or injustice in society but will produce new kinds of inequalities and injustice.

The task of education and PBL are to solve the problems of the world by (a) creating multivoiced storytelling practices where stakeholder interests and intentions are represented and (b) providing the conditions for critical reflexive inquiries into how these stories affect others (Boje, 2008b). This process raises the stakes of social responsibility in society. The notion of storytelling is highly relevant for teaching and learning because stories are seen as important memory sources that help individual and collective identities. In storytelling, experiences are recounted socially to formulate lessons that serve as precedents for individual assumptions, decisions, and actions (Boje, 1991). David Sims (1999) argued that experience has little value if it is not fused with stories.

It follows that storytelling pedagogy shares Dewey's and Freire's skepticism about the ways in which we have constructed our educational systems because learners implicitly are perceived not as storytellers or homo narrans (e.g., Tally, 2001) but rather as passive depositories and consumers of instrumental and monologic knowledge. Storytelling is considered the alternative to the rationalist, scientific, and objective discourse that, according to Justine Tally (2001), has left humankind morally bankrupt.

In rationalist discourse, truth is understood monologically as impersonal propositions. In storytelling, however, truth can only be represented by conversation, and it demands by its very nature many voices and points of view. The instrument for storytelling's resistance to authoritarian discourse is the plurality of experiences that is embedded in stories as well as storytelling as it occurs in communities, organizations, and other groups, in which many different storytellers are contributing to the unfolding of collective story lines. Storytelling is what distinguishes humans from other species. Self-evident truths are demonstrated as being based simply on stories we all accept as communal (Tally, 2001). Moreover, storytelling explains group consciousness with implied shared emotions, motives, and meanings and thus is what makes a community a community.

David Boje (2008a) invented a new way of talking about storytelling by introducing concepts such as *antenarrative* and *living story*. These concepts represent a challenge to the notion of narrative that has dominated the literature on narrative and storytelling in which events are seen as following a linear logic of beginning, middle, and end. Narrative is usually backward looking and is characterized as retrospective sense making of particular events. According to Boje (2001), antenarratives are before narrative closure and are (contrary to narrative) prospective (forward-looking) bets on the future (see also Boje, 2008a).

Also present in his storytelling model is the concept of living story. Living story is what characterizes the here-and-now, and it is characterized as collective, dialogical, plural, and emergent. Kenneth Jørgensen and David Boje (2010) noted that a story is living in the sense that it is becoming and can therefore morph into narrative. It shapes our identity, whether individual, organizational, or communal, and it shapes our imagination. Story fragments are often marginalized, reduced, or forgotten in the official accounts of history, but nonetheless, much of memory and identity is shaped in conversation and has no logical beginning, middle, and end, and no linear predictable and stable connection among events.

To represent practice as narrative with a clear, beginning, middle, and end is illusory (e.g., Jørgensen & Boje, 2010). Practices are living stories that are continuously becoming, are spontaneously expressive, and take place within a multiplicity of force relations present in any situation (Jørgensen & Boje, 2009). Plurality and many different voices are thus always embedded and embodied in living storytelling and are affected by innumerable, conflicting wills and intentions. Therefore, nobody is the sole author or producer of his or her life stories (Arendt, 1998). These stories are always co-constructed in interaction with other people, technologies, and material artifacts in particular historical and geographical circumstances. To look at practices this way is to denounce that they are the products of a continuous linearity. Instead, the here-and-now moment has a local identity, which means that the future is not given nor is it headed in one particular direction. Rather, the future may unfold in many different directions (Morson, 1994).

Storytelling Pedagogy and Problem-Based Learning

Storytelling pedagogy introduces familiar elements into PBL, but also elements that are novel compared with Dewey's and Freire's notions of PBL. PBL is consistent with the image of storytelling for three different reasons. First, storytelling implies that learning has to emerge in interaction with the practical matters of the world. The learner is thus conceived as a joint storyteller who needs to adapt to the world and change it in a joint effort with other storytellers.

Second, living storytelling highlights that an important part of learning is the co-construction of meaning. Human activities are not merely instrumental but are given symbolic meaning through stories. Learning activities must therefore be linked with learners' narratives and stories through PBL because it is a way of making teaching activities meaningful to learners. This meaningfulness implies understanding, commitment, desire, affection, interest, and responsibility to transform the world.

Third, living storytelling implies co-construction of practices. Storytelling pedagogy thus implies being able to do something—to build, to act, to leave your mark on the world within its concrete historical and material conditions. In other words, the learner has to balance different stakeholder interests and value conflicts in appropriate and responsible ways and build sustainable relations among people.

These characteristics are not particularly new to PBL. They are consistent with the idea that learning is holistic identity transformation and should be concerned with practical matters of the world. Storytelling pedagogy is, however, different in its diagnosis of problems and its approach to problem solving. The dance between narrative voices and living storytelling is crucial for storytelling pedagogy (e.g., Jørgensen & Strand, 2011). Narratives are seen as relatively institutionalized and stiffened story lines that are embedded in dominant discourses, which in turn, are embedded in teachers' and learners' perceptions of self and of the world.

Problems are seen as results of complex and multivoiced living storytelling in which many different voices, intentions, and interests are intertwined and unequally distributed. Inquiry into the problem is primarily a question of deconstructing (e.g., Jones, 2003) the problem, or more specifically, mapping the politics of the problem through genealogical analysis (Jørgensen, 2007). The focus is on figuring out why the problem was framed a particular way in the first place, and then turning the process of becoming into a political process in which some voices are privileged and heard but others are marginalized.

Thus, the understanding of the problem is re-situated such that we become more aware of the different positions and the different intentions and interests instead of relying on official language for understanding the problem. In this process, an alternative memory of the past is produced that might lead to different ways of thinking about the present and the future (Jørgensen, 2007). The learning process is thus organized as a critical reflexive inquiry into the problem.

Theories, concepts, and models are seen as suggestions of how to solve problems and provide a systematic vocabulary for solving problems that can be used by the actors in the problem-solving process. In that respect, management theories, concepts, and models illuminate some phenomena and disregard others. Theories, concepts, and models have their shadows, where a shadow is defined as censored emotional and cognitive contents (Fitzgerald, Oliver, & Hoxsey, 2010).

Storytelling is a call for inclusive processes such that many different stakeholders can participate in problem diagnosis and solving. Learning to organize dialogue and to participate, collaborate, and negotiate are thus important for learners because it is through such processes that multiple and multi-futuristic stories of stakeholders can be brought into a creative interplay toward a joint future.

In the context of storytelling, critical reflexivity implies gaining an awareness of the dark effects of actions in the sense that actions always imply listening to some voices while marginalizing others. Gaining a reflexive relationship between the light and shadow means confronting narrative with what takes place in the here and now and in which narrative intentions are being pushed, pulled, negotiated, and changed in the interaction of many different voices. It also implies becoming aware of how stories interweave with other stories and still other stories whereby a sense of joint responsibility, answerability, and complicity in the relations to others are gained (Boje, 2008b).

Finally, critical reflexive practice requires personal development, in which narratives of personal identities, goals, and perceptions of how to achieve these goals are confronted systematically by partners in conversation, by historical scrutiny of one's own narratives or by confronting one's own narratives with what takes place in the here and now. Thus, a deconstruction of one's own narratives occurs, which allows for new perceptions, new ideas, and new ways of thinking about one's relations to others.

Similar to prior approaches to PBL is the active involvement of the learners in the teaching process in which the narratives and stories of learners are the important starting points in the learning process. The active involvement of students in the learning process can be accomplished through the use of many different dialogical methods and can also be furthered through joint collaboration in designing the teaching practices and learning spaces so that the curriculum really becomes a personal aspect of one's future storytelling.

Intra-Active Pedagogy
(Material Storytelling)

Intra-active pedagogy is inspired by a new material turn in social science studies (e.g., Barad, 2007; Taguchi, 2010). Whereas the move from pragmatist pedagogy toward emancipatory pedagogy and storytelling pedagogy was accompanied by a growing emphasis on language and discourse as the primary modality of learning, intra-active pedagogy is characterized by a (return) to a multimodal approach to teaching and learning (Iedema, 2003).

We have bracketed "return" because intra-active pedagogy can be seen as a post-humanist performative rewriting of Dewey in the sense that Dewey tried to overcome dualities of mind/body, individual/social, nature/culture in his essays and books. For example, Dewey did not emphasize language as a particular important modality compared with the body. In this way, intra-active pedagogy emphasizes a more democratic relationship among body/mind, language/materiality, nature/culture in understanding being in relation to the world and it can be seen as a return to one of Dewey's basic lessons. In her elaboration of intra-active pedagogy, Hillevi Taguchi (2010) referred to reconceptualized evolutionary thinking, which in many ways resembles that of Dewey, who was inspired by Darwin's evolutionary theory.

However, intra-active pedagogy is innovative in going beyond presumptions of interconnectedness and interaction inherent in the other approaches. The words *interconnection* or *interact* implicitly assume that the world consists of separate entities that interact with each other. Intra-active pedagogy is inspired by quantum physics and stresses that phenomena never exist in themselves but always must be seen in relation to each other. Karen Barad (2007) used the word *entanglement* to capture this notion, which according to her does not simply imply being intertwined with another, "but to lack an independent, self-contained existence" (p. ix).

The motor of change, learning and a story, is thus not interaction but rather what Barad (2007) termed *intra-action*, which denotes the dynamic mutual constituent forces of meaning and matter and time and space. For instance,

> Time and space, like matter and meaning, come into existence, are iteratively re-configured through each intra-action, thereby making it impossible to differentiate in any absolute sense between creation and renewal, beginning and returning, continuity and discontinuity, here and there, past and future. (p. ix)

This statement implies that sustainability does not just concern the I-other relationship, but is expanded to include the stories of nature, bodies, space, and material artifacts in a complex, entangled, and multivoiced oneness, which is why Camille Strand (2011) used the term *material storytelling* to re-situate the hegemonic relationship of language over matter. As such, intra-active pedagogy emphasizes a more balanced and complex understanding of how humans intra-act with nature, how language intra-acts with materiality, how mind intra-acts with body, and how (human) time intra-acts with space.

As beings, we are not outside the world (observing and manipulating it from a distance), or in-the-world. Rather, we are of the world (Taguchi, 2010). We live in particular historical, geographical, and material circumstances. The human body lives and breathes intra-actively as an entanglement of multiple temporalities, multiple spaces, and multiple materialities. As teachers and learners, we are made from the same substances as the rest of the world: "In other words we cannot produce knowledge and learn about the world without being totally dependent on it" (Taguchi, 2010, p. 42).

Subsequently, material storytelling focuses on the stories that emerge from within, are integral to practice, and have spatial, temporal, and material effects. Material storytelling emphasizes that storytelling is a practice of joint speaking, acting, grasping, thinking, doing, and so on that we consider result from material-discursive intra-action (Barad, 2007).

Diffraction illuminates the indefinite nature of boundaries as enactments that emerge from within. Barad (2007) understood the relationship between the natural and the cultural as a diffractive wave pattern of what she called *exteriority within*, which means that what is separated out as outside is done by means of diffractive interferences from different material, natural, linguistic, or bodily forces that combine in a mutual constituent relationship, whereby the world and its boundaries are enacted through what she called *agential cuts*. The exteriority within mechanism allows material-discursive forces to become meaningful as agential realism. Diffraction and the exteriority within this dynamic is thus what accounts for the intra-dynamic aspects in intra-action.

Material storytelling thus denotes that stories emerge as agential cuts through material-discursive intra-action. Material storytelling is different from storytelling, including living storytelling, in emphasizing storytelling's intrinsically material nature. Whereas storytelling used to be a domain of discourse, material storytelling emphasizes the materiality of meaning making. With material storytelling, a more democratic relationship is accomplished in which both materiality and discourse are considered to have agency.

Barad also elaborated on Niels Bohr's conception of apparatus in framing her agential realist account. Apparatuses are material-discursive practices. They do not merely embody human concepts and take measurements. They are far more active and produce differences that matter. Apparatuses are formative of meaning and matter; they are productive of, and part of, the phenomenon produced; and they are continuously (re)constituted as part of the ongoing intra-activity of the world, which implies that they are also open-ended practices. Finally, apparatuses are considered to be material configurations that reconfigure spatiality and temporality as well as mattering

(Barad, 2007). Apparatuses thus "enact a local cut that produces 'objects' of particular knowledge practices . . . they enact what matters and what is excluded from mattering." Matter is "not a thing, but a doing, a congealing of agency" and is "a stabilizing and destabilizing process of iterative intra-activity" (Barad, 2007, pp.147–151). Matter is intra-active and is implicated and enfolded in its iterative becoming and thus implicated in storytelling.

Intra-Active Pedagogy and Problem-Based Learning

Intra-active pedagogy can be seen as taking PBL even further because of its emphasis on organizing teaching and learning around the world's problems. What is characteristic of intra-active pedagogy is the emphasis on more multimodal approaches to teaching and learning in which other modalities are given a far more agential role compared with traditional teaching and learning, which is dominated by spoken or written words. As such, more voices are included in the learning process such as voices of animals, nature, artifacts, and bodies (Strand, 2011). Inclusiveness reveals a different understanding of memory than the one revealed in storytelling. In intra-active pedagogy, memory does not reside in linguistic expressions alone but in the apparatus of the whole situation.

What belongs to this apparatus is, for instance, apart from books, teachers' and learners' knowing and values, material artifacts, technologies, spaces and bodies, and the historicity of the situation, including traditions and conventions. Thus, learning emerges from these apparatuses of storytelling, which are embedded in the whole learning context. Intra-active pedagogy works with a more complex notion of identity and identity transformation than do emancipatory pedagogy and storytelling pedagogy, which work strictly through language. Working with apparatuses of teaching thus becomes the central point of attention when we want to produce desirable learning.

The pedagogical instruments and tools we use in our teaching matter, as does how we think about students' learning (e.g., Taguchi, 2010). The apparatus of pedagogical documentation is, for example, itself an active agent in producing stories of learning. The documentation we get is not a fixed matter with a fixed essence but a substance in process of intra-active becoming in which the meaning of pedagogical documentation becomes what it does in relation to the pedagogical practice that produced it. How the apparatus is used matters (Taguchi, 2010) and teachers, including their competencies and experiences, are themselves part of the apparatus.

Pedagogical development thus relies on continuous experiments with the totality of apparatuses of teaching, including how teachers work with their own thinking and doings as part of the apparatus. There is no privileged or best way of teaching, no privileged or best pedagogy, and no privileged or best way of doing pedagogical documentation. There is no privileged or best way of doing PBL; nor is it possible to define precisely what PBL is. When we stick to the idea of PBL as one that may produce desirable learning, we do so from our experiences and our apparatus as teachers. However, it would be the ultimate disaster for us and for PBL if we decided on one best way of doing PBL and one best way of documenting it. Such a disaster would result from misunderstanding one of the basic implications of Barad's perspective, which according to Taguchi (2010) is that learning "takes place right in the middle of things, in our very living and doing pedagogical practices" (p.61).

The very idea of PBL is that it should take place right in the middle of the organizations, communities, or societies in which learning occurs. It requires that we are capable of opening up to what happens in the here-and-now and the multiple potentials and possibilities that it affords instead of following a fixed narrative of how to organize learning events or how to respond to students. Teachers are invited to work with the students' potential for learning in any given situation, and it requires a careful and open attitude toward alternative understandings and interpretations rather than being controlled by the teachers' prejudices of the situation at hand.

Learners are entangled becomings, who have been produced by material-discursive practices, which constitute their apparatus of storytelling. The learning process becomes through the diffractive relationship between apparatuses of teaching and learners' apparatuses of storytelling. There is no best way to organize this relationship between apparatuses of teaching and learners' apparatuses of storytelling other than to note that we need (a) engaging, activating, and involving pedagogies, in which learners' stories are the ultimate goal of the learning process, and (b) the learners' efforts to become aware of and work with their own apparatuses of storytelling.

Conclusions

We have sketched four different approaches to PBL: pragmatist pedagogy, emancipatory pedagogy, storytelling pedagogy, and intra-active pedagogy, and have drawn implications of these approaches in relation to Groccia's model of teaching and learning (St. Clair & Groccia, 2009). The sequence in which these pedagogies have evolved illustrates different movements in PBL. First, the sequence illustrates a movement from learning as reflective practice (pragmatist pedagogy and emancipatory pedagogy) toward learning as reflexive practice (storytelling pedagogy) and diffraction (intra-active pedagogy). Second, there is a circular movement from multimodal pragmatist pedagogy toward relatively monomodal approaches that focus on discourse and language (emancipatory pedagogy and storytelling pedagogy) and back to a multimodal approach to teaching and learning (intra-active pedagogy). Finally, the approaches conceptualize the goals of education differently.

Whereas pragmatist pedagogy has an agenda of solving problems, emancipatory pedagogy is explicitly political in aiming to redistribute power from the powerful to the powerless through education. This goal has shifted toward a more micro-political agenda in which the distinction between powerful and powerless becomes blurred and dissolved. Critical reflexive practice and diffraction are principles that invite teachers and learners to explore the prejudices of their own language and performances to develop solutions to problems that are more sustainable than they would be otherwise.

References

Arendt, H. 1998. *The human condition.* Chicago, IL: University of Chicago Press.

Barad, K. (2007). *Meeting the universe halfway: Quantum physics and the entanglement of matter and meaning.* Durham, NC: Duke University Press.

Boje, D. M. (1991). The storytelling organization: A study of storytelling performance in an office supply firm. *Administrative Science Quarterly, 36,* 106–126.

Boje, D. M. (2001). *Narrative methods for organizational & communication research.* London, UK: Sage.

Boje, D. M. (2008a). *Storytelling organization.* London, UK: Sage.

Boje, D. M. (2008b). Contributions of critical theory ethics for business and public administration. In D. M. Boje (Ed.), *Critical theory ethics for business and public administration* (pp. 3–27). Charlotte, NC: Information Age.

Dewey, J. (1916). *Democracy and education.* New York, NY: Free Press.

Dewey, J. (1936). Creative democracy: The task before us. In J. A. Boydston (Ed.), *John Dewey: The Later Works, 1925–1953: Vol. 14. 1939–1941, Essays, reviews, and miscellaneous.* Carbondale: Southern Illinois University Press.

Dewey, J. (1991). *How we think.* New York, NY: Prometheus Books.

Fitzgerald, S. P., Oliver, C., & Hoxsey, J. C. (2010). Appreciative inquiry as a shadow process. *Journal of Management Inquiry, 19,* 220–233.

Freire, P. (1996). *Pedagogy of the oppressed.* London, UK: Penguin Books.

Hardy, C., & Leiba-O'Sullyvan, S. (1998). The power behind empowerment: Implications for research and practice. *Human Relations, 51,* 451–483.

Iedema, R. (2003). Multimodality, resemiotization: Extending the analysis of discourse as multi-semiotic practice. *Visual Communication, 2,* 29–57.

Jones, C. (2003). As if business ethics were possible, "within such limits." *Organization, 10,* 223–248.

Jørgensen, K. M. (2007). *Power without glory: A genealogy of a management decision.* Copenhagen, Denmark: Copenhagen Business School Press.

Jørgensen, K. M., & Boje, D. M. (2009). Genealogies of becoming: Antenarrative inquiry in organizations. *Tamara Journal for Critical Organization Inquiry, 8,* 32–47.

Jørgensen, K. M., & Boje, D. M. (2010). Resituating narrative and story in business ethics. *Business Ethics: A European Review, 19,* 251–262.

Jørgensen, K. M., & Strand, A. M. C. (2011). Towards a storytelling ethics for management education. In C. Wankel & A. Stachowitz-Stanusch (Eds.), *Effectively integrating ethical dimensions into management education.* Charlotte, NC: Information Age.

Kolmos, A., Fink, F., & Krogh, L. (Eds.). (2004). *The Aalborg PBL-model: Progress, diversity and challenges*. Aalborg, Denmark: Aalborg University Press.

Lukes, S. (1974). *Power: A radical view*. Basingstoke, UK: Palgrave Macmillan.

Morson, G. S. (1994). *Narrative and freedom: The shadows of time*. New Haven, CT: Yale University Press.

Ryle, G. (1949). *The concept of mind*. London, UK: Hutchinson.

Schön, D. A. (1983). *The reflective practitioner: How professionals think in action*. New York, NY: Basic Books.

Sims, D. (1999). Organizational learning as the development of stories. In M. Easterby-Smith, J. Burgoyne, & L. Araujo (Eds.), *Organizational learning and the learning organization: Developments in theory and practice* (pp. 44–58). London, UK: Sage.

St. Clair, K. L., & Groccia, J. E. (2009). Change to social justice education: Higher education strategy. In K. Skubikowski, C. Wright, & R. Graf (Eds.), *Social justice education: Inviting faculty to transform their institutions* (pp. 70–84). Sterling, VA: Stylus.

Strand, A. M. C. (2011). *Creating an oasis with a good conscience: Posing material storytelling as intra-active identity rework* (Unpublished doctoral dissertation). Department of Communication and Psychology, Aalborg University, Aalborg, Denmark.

Taguchi, H. L. (2010). *Going beyond the theory/practice divide in early childhood education: Introducing an intra-active pedagogy*. New York, NY: Routledge.

Tally, J. (2001). *The story of Jazz: Toni Morrison's dialogic imagination*. London, UK: LIT.

CHAPTER 29

Problem-Based Learning and Its Application to South African Medical Education

TED SOMMERVILLE AND VEENA SINGARAM

Problem-based learning (PBL) is a relatively recent (ca. 1970) pedagogy. It appeared with few obvious antecedents, but there was indeed theory and research to support it. Medical teachers at McMaster University in Canada are generally credited with the creation of PBL (Barrows & Tamblyn, 1980; Neufeld & Barrows, 1974), which has been called the signature pedagogy of medicine and nursing (Maistry, 2009). In Denmark, Roskilde (1972) and Aalborg (1974) universities devised project-based learning (De Graaf & Kolmos, 2007), which is more practically orientated and is associated with engineering, but with principles similar to those of PBL. Nowadays, PBL appears as either a pedagogy or a curricular organizing tool in many guises in many disciplines.

Toward a Definition of PBL

Howard Barrows and Robyn Tamblyn (1980) provided few details of PBL, although they gave the rationale for its introduction: a rapid fall-off in students' knowledge of basic science when they reached the clinical years of their medical training. By presenting students with problems couched in terms of practical clinical situations, Barrow and Tamblyn hoped to contextualize and stimulate learning. "[PBL] is the learning that results from the process of working toward the understanding or resolution of a problem. The problem is encountered *first* in the learning process!" [italics in original] (Barrows & Tamblyn, 1980, p. 1). PBL has since been claimed as a vehicle for a plethora of programs in a multitude of disciplines in an increasing variety of settings (Savin-Baden, 2000).

Various kinds of small-group work, teaching around problems, problem-solving exercises, interdisciplinary teaching, and use of trained or untrained, expert or nonexpert facilitators have all been described as "PBL." Barrows (1986), recognizing this variety, proposed a taxonomy based on two aspects of PBL: the extent of description of the problem and the extent to which the thinking process is directed by the teacher or the learner. Interestingly, he did not clearly enunciate what is one of the generally accepted characteristics of PBL—small-group discussion (Slavin, 1996), although his descriptions imply it. An earlier account (Neufeld & Barrows, 1974) described small-group learning as a component, although they devoted more space to discussing the role of the tutor (small-group facilitator) than the significance of the group process. Mark Albanese and Susan Mitchell (1993, pp. 53–54), in their review of PBL, included "patient problems as a context . . . actively involved in the discussion . . . the problem is presented first . . . Small-group tutorials and independent study" as the key elements of PBL. The Network Towards Unity for Health recorded, "Problem-Based Learning (PBL) is a method of learning in which students first encounter a problem, followed by a student-centered inquiry process. Typically, five to eight students work collaboratively in a group (tutorial), together with one or more faculty facilitators (tutors)" (Mennin & Majoor, 2001, p. 1). Maggi Savin-Baden (2000, p. 3) summarized PBL in much the same way: "The focus here is in organizing the curricular content around problem scenarios rather than subjects or disciplines. Students work in groups or teams to solve or manage these situations but they are not expected to acquire a predetermined series of 'right answers.'"

More recently, David Taylor and Barbara Miflin (2008) attempted to define the core of PBL by revisiting its roots to trace its development. In their description of PBL, they included,

> Self-directed learning . . . the problem comes first . . . problems for PBL must be those that are prevalent and important in practice . . . the sequencing of problems should allow students to build upon their acquired knowledge in a structured and logical way . . . genuinely small groups (up to 8 students) . . . good facilitation . . . perhaps generalists . . . the qualified medical practitioner . . . certain qualities in the students that were accepted into their programs, namely "self-motivation, ability to cope with ambiguity, effective interpersonal skills, and self and peer assessment skills. (pp. 753–758)

Synthesizing these conceptions, without wishing to oversimplify, but to establish a conception of PBL that will serve as background to this discussion, we envision PBL to be a pedagogy that

- foregrounds student learning (rather than faculty teaching);
- nurtures and stimulates self-directed learning;
- expects students to work in collaborative groups analyzing the problem, activating prior knowledge, processing and restructuring new knowledge while guided by a trained facilitator; and
- presents as a stimulus for learning a contextualized practice-based "problem," not necessarily to be solved, but that requires understanding of basic scientific concepts to grasp the nature of the problem.

Having chosen a working definition of PBL that we hope would be recognizable to the majority of those who espouse this pedagogy, we now trace the forerunners of PBL in medical and general education.

Antecedents in Medical Education: Push Factors

Without ignoring or decrying health care systems that have an honored history in other parts of the world, we trace the history of Western-style medicine because PBL grew out of this background. Richard Harrison Shryock (1965) described the development of medical education in Europe and its colonies as a coming together of practical apprenticeship and theoretical teaching. This process was accompanied by progression from loosely structured opportunistic teaching to structured discipline-based programs (Papa, 1999). Despite progress over many years, the record over much of the last century reveals pleas and plans for change on either side of the Atlantic (Bloom, 1988; Christakis, 1995; Goodenough, 1944), but little actual change occurred until the 1960s and 1970s (Editorial, 1971).

Some of the undesirable features of the medical curriculum during that period included overcrowding of content (Bowditch, 1900; Osler, 1913; Smith, 1989), didactic lecturing (Smith, 1989), subjects taught one at a time, in sequence (Bowditch, 1900), separation of basic science from clinical study and of medical teachers from medical practice (Editorial, 1911), and a deficiency of scientific approach and research (Flexner, 1910; Goodenough, 1944). More recently, the rapid expansion of scientific knowledge, changing social and demographic factors, and a greater understanding of the principles and practices of teaching and learning has increased pressure to change medical curricula. Although much of medical education's prior development was perhaps specific to that field, we imagine that these last three factors may have been responsible for the adoption of PBL in other fields also.

Recommendations to address these features included limiting content to core concepts (Bowditch, 1900; Smith, 1989); affiliating medical schools with universities; developing mathematics and science requirements for entrance; having laboratory science teaching preceding clinical teaching (Flexner, 1910; Regan-Smith, 1998); minimizing or abolishing lectures (McMillan, 1965; Osler, 1913), allowing students more free time for study; continuous assessment; cultivating of self-reliance and reflection (Osler, 1913); emphasizing principles rather than accumulation of facts; active partnership of students, teachers, and the general public in the determination of the curriculum; and a leaning toward the needs of the general practitioner (Daubenton, 1965; Goodenough, 1944; Taylor, 1965). Responses included delineation of a core curriculum, emphasis on basic principles, integration of subjects, teaching how to learn, and a move toward social relevance and re-humanizing the field, with a view to producing general practitioners able to find and assess information and to continue their education in any direction (Editorial, 1971; Read, 1971). Use of rural hospitals for teaching, provision for electives, and assessment of skills and attitudes as well as knowledge (Rundle, 1971), although specific to medicine, no doubt find resonance in other fields.

Against this background, teachers at McMaster University and elsewhere were drawn to a new form of teaching and learning, focusing on core material of practical importance, downplaying didactic lecturing, and guiding students into learning how to learn, using small-group discussion as the primary vehicle. Other than in the sense of moving away from overburdened curricula and a dry scientific atmosphere in which patient care was perhaps not considered foremost in importance, could the innovators have expected PBL to succeed? Was there educational theory or practice to support their ideas and draw them in a particular direction?

Developments in Educational Theory and Research: Pull Factors

As support for their innovation, Barrows and Tamblyn (1980) mentioned only discovery learning and W. H. O. Schmidt's (1965) and Ernest Hilgard, Robert Irvine, and James Whipple's (1953) studies. These two studies showed that students who were helped to understand problems took longer to work through examples, but were able to solve similar and progressively more complex problems thereafter compared with those shown what to do, who could solve only the problems they had been shown. Although no other writers were directly cited, authors such as John Dewey (Garforth, 1966), Carl Rogers (1969), Jerome Bruner (1960/1977, 2006a, 2006b), and Paulo Freire (1992) might have been quoted in support of PBL. Over a span of decades, these writers had expressed similar ideas about pedagogy, whether applied to young children, students in tertiary education, or adults with little formal educational experience.

More than a century ago, Dewey espoused an active, structured, practically based form of learning. He described education as both a psychological and a social experience (Garforth, 1966). Dewey regarded school as a community rather than merely as a site for giving out information. Encouragement of the learner's "active side" (Garforth, p. 46) was the heart of his educational methodology, and the search for knowledge arising out of practical work was a tenet of his school. Dewey's watchwords were *experience, growth, transaction*, and *inquiry*. He envisaged the learning sequence as follows:

Generating possible solutions to a problem

Intellectualization of the problem

Generation of a hypothesis

Elaboration of the supposition

Testing the hypothesis in some way

Rogers (1969) stated, "Teaching, in my estimation, is a vastly overrated function" (p. 103). His opinion was that "facilitation of change and learning . . . how to learn" was more important (p. 104). His basis for facilitating learning included sharing his puzzlement about things, being genuine with his learners, trusting them, and living with the uncertainty of discovery. Rogers himself worked largely with postgraduate students but was able to support his views with evidence from studies over a range of educational situations. At the time when PBL as a pedagogic methodology was being constructed, Rogers described the principles by which learners could be empowered and encouraged to take responsibility for their learning in an atmosphere of support and with the expectation that they could and would *learn* adequately without being *taught*.

Bruner wrote voluminously about education. In the 1960s, he depicted a "structuralist view of knowledge" (Bruner, 1960/1977, p. vii), following Jean Piaget, Noam Chomsky, and Claude Lévi-Strauss. Bruner described the importance to the learner of understanding the structure of the knowledge being acquired and proposed that "the foundations of any subject may be taught to anybody at any age in some form" (p. 12). He encouraged the development of intuitive thinking and stimulation of the desire to learn. He wrote of the need to "create intellectual skill" (pp. viii–ix). In terms of praxis, he wished to start "where the learner *is*" [emphasis in original] and follow a "spiral curriculum," revisiting topics and modes of thinking at successively higher levels, scaffolding learning to present at appropriate times what learners could discover on their own (pp. ix, xiv). Bruner (2006a) documented studies on discovery learning, a methodology that used ideas akin to those of Dewey and Piaget. Bruner's philosophy of discovery learning reads very like that of PBL:

> Our aim as teachers is to give our student as firm a grasp of a subject as we can, and to make him as autonomous and self-propelled a thinker as we can—one who will go along on his own after formal schooling has ended. (p. 58)

Freire (1992) spent many years in teaching-learning sites, learning with his "educands" (p. 36), recognizing that he had to start from where his learners were. He recognized that teachers and learners are both agents of knowing and that teaching and learning are each part of knowing. Freire understood about starting from learners' prior knowledge and encouraging active learning. He appreciated the danger of the teacher's "directivity" interfering with the learner's creative capacity and declared "The real evil is not in the expository lesson . . . [but when] . . . the educator regards himself or herself as the educands' sole educator" (Freire, 1992; p. 102).

We read in these four writers the ideas of displacing the teacher from a central position, attracting the interest of learners and helping them engage actively with their material, connecting with learners as individuals, acknowledging inequalities of power in the field of education, empowering learners to construct their own knowledge, acknowledging and building on prior learning, and equipping learners for ongoing autonomous learning. These annotations, scattered over the last century, support the theoretical and practical legitimacy of PBL as a pedagogic tool. It was an idea whose time had come.

Subsequent Support for PBL

Albanese and Mitchell (1993) ascribed the following elements to PBL: activation of prior knowledge, use of clinical problems, and elaboration of knowledge. Geoffrey Norman and Henk Schmidt (1992), using cognitive psychology, were able to corroborate that activation of prior knowledge, elaboration of new knowledge, and placing knowledge in context, as PBL strives to do, all enhance subsequent recall.

In their position paper toward unity for health Stewart Mennin and Gerard Majoor (2001) described PBL as contributing to active learning, being more satisfying for learners than passive transfer of information from teacher to learner, and leading to better retention and recall. They claimed that discussion of clinical problems in small groups encourages making connections between ideas and concepts and cooperation rather than competition among students. Mennin and Majoor asserted that PBL provides conditions for the development and practice of self-directed learning and lifelong learning in the face of the exponential expansion of knowledge.

Recently, several conclusions were drawn from a synthesis of eight previous meta-analyses comparing traditional lecture-based teaching and problem-based learning (Strobel & Barneveld, 2009). Basic medical science knowledge, when assessed in the short term by recognition of material in multiple-choice questions, appeared better served by didactic lectures. However, longer-term retention, understanding, and recall of material in response to open-ended questions appeared better served by PBL, which also resulted in improved clinical performance requiring both knowledge and skill. Johannes Strobel and Angela Barneveld (2009) noted that learners and teachers generally found more satisfaction with PBL, and stated, "Preference should be given to instructional strategies that focus on students' performance in authentic situations and their long-term knowledge retention, and not on their performance on tests aimed at short-term retention of knowledge" (p. 55). (We note that this sort of exercise, though providing a rigorous comparison with traditional pedagogy, perhaps does less justice to PBL than would documentation of its strengths in those aspects of learning not served by traditional teaching and assessment.)

Insights Into PBL Pedagogy

Two prominent writers in the field of medical education have described the intricacies of PBL. Mennin (2007) described PBL's roots in cognitive psychology and, from his interest in complexity science, claimed that self-organization can be expected—the spontaneous emergence of new structures, patterns, and properties from an environment characterized by multiple feedback loops and nonlinear dynamics (p. 307). To effect change, such a system has to be perturbed and moved away from its state of equilibrium. He noted, "Important phenomena happen at the edge of chaos: cognition, metabolism, new organizational rules, self-organization. Learning takes place in a zone of complexity" (p. 307). A degree of metacognition by all the group members is needed if the whole group—rather than a few individuals—is to succeed in its task.

David Prideaux (2007) also acknowledged the complexity of the PBL milieu, and argued for a structured approach to PBL pedagogy. He saw five major elements—end points, content, teaching and learning, assessment, and evaluation—interacting with each other, making it problematic to pursue or document change in one element in isolation. For Prideaux, PBL was salient in the drive to reform medical education, having the effect of focusing medical education on learning rather than teaching alone, and of re-focusing curriculum from content to end points and assessments.

PBL arose out of frustration with the inability of the traditional curriculum and its positivist mind-set to keep pace with developments in the fields of medicine and education. Theory and research evidence to underpin it have been gathered largely in retrospect, and at the same time, claims beyond the conceptions of the originators have arisen around it. What then of experiences of PBL in practice?

Learners' and Teachers' Experiences of PBL Pedagogy

Beneficial Aspects of Teaching With PBL

In a variety of disciplines and settings (e.g., preclinical, clinical, undergraduate, postgraduate) in which PBL has been employed, similar patterns of experience have emerged. Among students, PBL is said to be popular (Barrows & Tamblyn, 1980), enjoyable (Michel, Bischoff, & Jakobs, 2002), stimulating (Breier & Wildschut, 2006), and engendering enthusiasm (Burgun, Darmoni, Le Duff, & Weber, 2006). In terms of cognitive skills, PBL researchers claim that it stimulates inquiry and information-gathering (Becker, Viljoen, Botma, & Bester, 2003; Horne et al., 2007; Williams, 1999), self-directed learning (Horne et al., 2007; Williams, 1999), lifelong learning (Breier & Wildschut, 2006), improved learning styles (Baker, Pesut, McDaniel, & Fisher, 2007; Kivela & Kivela, 2005; Michel et al., 2002), enhanced learning skills (Horne et al., 2007; Nalesnik, Heaton, Olsen, Haffner, & Zahn, 2004), improved retention (Hsieh & Knight, 2008; Michel et al., 2002), reduced reliance on "spoon-feeding" information to students (Kivela & Kivela, 2005), and improved performance on assessments (Nalesnik et al., 2004). One report expressed that PBL required fewer staff and less time than conventional teaching (Nalesnik et al., 2004).

With regard to the way that PBL shapes students' attitudes and skills, researchers have claimed that it promotes a holistic viewpoint (Becker et al., 2003; Williams, 1999), an ability to take different views of problems, practical reasoning, an appreciation of community (Becker et al., 2003), linking theory and practice (Becker et al., 2003; Horne et al., 2007), increased relevance of the information being learned (Kiesseling, Schubert, Scheffner, & Burger, 2004), and making meaning for oneself (Kivela & Kivela, 2005). Other positive aspects of using PBL include reduced competition, increased contact with teachers (Kiesseling et al., 2004), improved interpersonal and communication skills (Horne et al., 2007), and reduced stress (Jones & Johnston, 2006).

Challenging Aspects of Teaching With PBL

Although PBL has been found to promote many positive aspects of student learning, it is not without its detractors. For example, researchers have discovered the following aspects of PBL to be problematic for some of its practitioners: time expenditure (Breier & Wildschut, 2006; Horne et al., 2007; Kivela & Kivela, 2005; Michel et al., 2002), wishes for more didactic teaching (Breier & Wildschut, 2006; Miflin, Campbell, & Price, 1999), less basic science knowledge (Williams, 1999), generally less coverage of the breadth of the field (Nalesnik et al., 2004), ambivalence about resource allocation (Horne et al., 2007), and staffing needs (Michel et al., 2002).

Among teachers, discomfort in an educational setting quite different from their own experience (Barrows & Tamblyn, 1980; Williams, 1999) and the effectiveness of PBL depending on teachers' perceptions (Williams & Beattie, 2008) also have been noted as limiters to using PBL. In a recent paper, Barrows (Hmelo-Silver & Barrows, 2006), while acting as an expert (neurology) facilitator, wrote "In PBL the facilitator is an expert learner, able to model good strategies for learning and thinking, *rather than providing expertise in specific content*" [emphasis in original] (p. 24). Whether facilitators' expertise in fact makes a difference to the learning of their groups is moot. Some studies have supported the notion that an expert facilitator's students achieve more learning (Hay & Katsikitis, 2001), but other studies have found no significant influence (Kwizera, Dambisya, & Aguirre, 2001; Park, Susarla, Cox, Da Silva, & Howell, 2007). Some authors have suggested that subject experts might affect facilitation negatively by interfering with discussion among students (Silver & Wilkerson, 1991). The Maastricht group, after surveying research on facilitators, concluded that studies on facilitators' content expertise provided "contradicting findings" (Dolmans et al., 2002, p. 179)—so the debate on facilitator background continues.

Local Experience—How We Use PBL

For 10 years, the Nelson Mandela School of Medicine has offered the first 3 years of the undergraduate medical degree in PBL format. Material is presented in 6-week "themes" that divide content according to the body's organ systems. During each theme, discipline-based content is integrated into a series of weekly "cases." These cases are written as descriptions of a patient with a problem(s) to provide a context for new knowledge. Students meet twice a week in groups of between 10 and 15 (larger than we would like), with facilitators trained in educational principles as applied to PBL group work, questioning techniques, handling difficult individuals, and so forth. Before the theme starts, the head of the theme planning group briefs the facilitators by discussing the cases and highlights salient points related to the envisaged learning outcomes of the cases. Because facilitators are generally not experts in the subject matter of the theme, we provide them with notes on each case so that they can guide their group's thinking.

As part of leadership and interpersonal skills development, students in the group rotate chair and scribe positions. They discuss PBL cases following an eight-step process adapted from Maastricht (Schmidt, 1983). At each step, the group (not the facilitator)

1. defines ill-understood terms in the description of the week's case

2. identifies issues arising from the case

3. brainstorms possible explanations for the issues

4. formulates questions to be researched to understand the issues

5. determines learning goals to be achieved relative to this week's case

6. researches information related to learning goals

7. reports back, discusses, shares, clarifies

8. reflects on group process and individual progress

The first five steps occur during the week's first meeting, Step 6 occupies most of the week in which the case is presented (we follow a hybrid model, with a number of lectures rather than pure self-directed research) and the last two steps take up the second meeting at the end of the week. In each week of each theme, the group deals with a different case using the same process. Some PBL programs stretch a problem over a longer period and may have an intermediate group meeting at which further details of the case are provided. *Project*-based learning poses a practical design problem for the group to construct, which may stretch over several weeks with multiple group meetings. As in medicine, where the case diagnosis is less important than the group's learning, the functionality of the design project's output is less important than what the students learn along the way.

Group Function in Diverse Settings

Globally, student populations are increasingly multicultural and multilingual. The majority of studies evaluating the effectiveness of PBL curricula have been conducted in academic settings where students have similar educational and linguistic backgrounds (Connolly & Seneque, 1999). We conducted several studies exploring the relationship between diversity and the collaborative small-group PBL tutorial (Singaram, van der Vleuten, Stevens, & Dolmans, 2011; Singaram, van der Vleuten, van Berkel, & Dolmans, 2010; Sommerville, 2011), and developed and validated a tutorial group effectiveness instrument (TGEI) based on Slavin's (1996) theoretical framework of collaborative learning using cognitive and motivational perspectives (Singaram et al., 2011). The TGEI provides diagnostic information about group performance and student learning.

Diversity has been described as a double-edged sword (Milliken & Martins, 1996) and a dark cloud with a silver lining (Watson, Kumar, & Michaelsen, 1993). Veena Singaram et al. (2010) noted that students who are segregated in tutorials along racial lines and other diversity factors disempowered students and reduced their productivity. However, we found that students working in heterogeneous groupings interact with students with whom they wouldn't normally intermingle learn a lot more from each other because of their differences in language and academic preparedness and are better prepared for their future profession in a multicultural society. We recommend that attention be given to creating the "right mix" for group learning in diverse student populations, and that teachers receive both facilitation and diversity training to deal with heterogeneous groups and the tensions that arise.

The PBL collaborative learning environment holds in equilibrium a number of creative tensions ideally suited to help students mediate and explore the discomfort of diversity within the safety of collegiality and teamwork. These tensions include academic under-preparedness versus academic achievement, associative friendship/collegiality versus racial/cultural divisions, group dynamics arising from personality differences versus those from diversity issues. The small-group collaborative tutorial is a forum to address biases and deepen understanding as we focus on improving learning and academic success.

Our Experiences With PBL Pedagogy

The following insights have arisen from our experience of teaching with PBL—specifically from interviews with students and faculty and analyses of their responses thematically and in terms of Basil Bernstein's (1971) eight-fold schema of classification and framing (Sommerville, 2011).

Access to Medical School

Particularly for students from disadvantaged backgrounds, physical access to higher education does not necessarily equal epistemological access (Breier & Wildschut, 2006). All of our student respondents were aware of a significant distinction between everyday knowledge and medical knowledge. Some argued that this difference should be minimized, particularly because, as students and future practitioners, they have to be able to negotiate that barrier in either direction on behalf of their patients. This barrier was only partly in terms of the language of communication. (We teach in English, but English is the first language of only 45 percent of our students.) What was more of a problem was the discourse of medicine—the specialized terminology—which was a problem for all language groups. Indeed, when we asked if matters would be improved if the language of communication were isiZulu—the vernacular in our province—the reply was resoundingly negative. IsiZulu does not yet include a large number of technical terms, and the circumlocutions to cope with this lack of vocabulary can be problematic. Exploring the language issue further, a multifactorial analysis of students' test results during 3 years of PBL revealed that, overall, language itself was not a significant influence.

Distinctions Among Disciplines

Whereas faculty members were aware of a strong discipline-based structure, students were not—probably because of the integrated nature of the PBL cases. They see, for instance, the physics, biochemistry, anatomy, and physiology of the circulatory system as naturally belonging together.

Distinctions Within Disciplines

Interestingly, opinions were reversed at this level. Faculty members saw no division among subsections of their disciplines, whereas students perceived significant distinctions. This undoubtedly also results from the curriculum structure. For example, although a physiologist is conscious of the commonalities among the function of the heart, the lungs, and the kidneys, a student encounters cardiac, respiratory, and renal physiology in separate themes. Our students were not fazed by the distinctions either way.

Control of Content, Sequencing, and Pacing

Responses were similar for all three of these elements. Faculty felt that they largely controlled what, when, and for how long they exposed students to curricular material. Students felt, with few exceptions, that the faculty ought to decide on these aspects on their behalf. This state of affairs contrasts sharply with the theory of PBL—that learners determine what they need to know, how they will arrange their learning, and the time they take to learn. We see several causes for these perceptions, and several important consequences.

Reasons for Strong Framing of Content, Sequence, and Pace

- Fourteen years after the end of apartheid, South Africa's schools still show large variability in quality of teaching, learning, and administration. (Students' high school was the greatest influence on test results in the multifactorial analysis.) Despite an attempt to introduce outcomes-based education (OBE) in schools, many of our students are still being taught in a very teacher-controlled way. Students are accustomed to being told what to do and when to do it.
- Our faculty members were all educated in the traditional teacher-centered lecture-based style. They are accustomed to the idea that faculty control the content and the process of teaching and learning.
- Medicine, like other professions, entails certain outcomes that the profession, the public, and the regulatory body demand. There is less leeway than in other fields for leaving students to decide for themselves what learning will sufficiently exercise their minds.

Consequences of Strong Framing

- The number of lectures has slowly increased over the years, probably resulting form anxiety that if faculty do not teach, students don't learn.
- Students feel that they have little leeway to explore beyond what they need to cover because there is already so much material in the cases.
- Although this shared anxiety about content coverage is common to PBL programs generally, it has the effect of reversing some of the sought-after effects of PBL. One issue that we and others in the faculty have noted is compartmentalization of knowledge—something learned in one theme is not easily recalled in another. This outcome is a symptom of content overload, which also tends to lead to surface rather than deep learning.

Control of Evaluation

Learners and teachers recognized strong control by teachers, although learners acknowledged that post-assessment feedback and faculty's willingness to debate contentious questions and answers gave them a sense of influence over assessments. Students noted that our predominant use of factual recognition multiple-choice questions was another factor encouraging them to adopt surface learning. (The deep learning strategies encouraged by the tenets of PBL call for higher cognitive levels of assessment—a challenge that our resource-constrained faculty is still grappling with.) Students were aware that their feedback at the end of each theme is taken into account when planning the theme for the next year.

Control of Staff-Student Relations

All respondents acknowledged the existence of a hierarchy between teachers and learners. Some learners took this relationship as a guarantee of the quality of the teaching—rather than the converse, which is probably another effect of the authoritarian regime to which South Africans were previously accustomed in education as in all else. The feeling was that in the small-group meetings, the atmosphere was more egalitarian, but students in the clinical phase observed some attitudes among their teachers that had decidedly negative effects on their participation and learning.

Conclusions

We have reviewed PBL as student-centered, self-directed, collaborative contextualized learning. Inculcation of generalized problem-solving skills that can be learned and transferred across disciplines and contexts continues to be elusive. Anxiety about content coverage appears to be shared by faculty and students throughout the realm of PBL. The trade-off for breadth of coverage is depth of understanding and improved retention. If the philosophy driving the curriculum as a whole is that of PBL, disciplinary experts work together to reinforce students' understanding of important areas of knowledge (which inevitably overlap several subjects). Allowing learners to work through these salient topics necessarily means that they cover these topics thoroughly and other topics to a lesser extent or not at all.

In our circumstances—a diverse student population in a developing country—we have particular constraints and challenges. However, we feel that PBL offers unique opportunities to address these challenges and that our students benefit from this pedagogy. They graduate with better understanding of the subject matter, improved retention, and the cognitive skills to find out what they do not know. The decision to implement PBL requires a significant—dare we say—paradigm shift (Kuhn, 1970). Are we interested in efficient teaching or effective learning? The two may not be mutually achievable.

We are aware that PBL requires a mind-shift by faculty and students. Faculty may be uncomfortable allowing students to learn for themselves under the eye of nonexpert facilitators. Fortunately, experience shows that students do not merely pool ignorance when they come together for the report-back meeting, but are astute enough to challenge and correct one another's misconceptions. PBL also has implications for resources and physical infrastructure—our local library facilities, computer labs, and small-group meeting venues have greatly expanded. We represent a numerically expanding program (currently 200+ students per year) in a developing country. We feel that PBL is a well-founded pedagogy that supports student learning within and after university life—but it does demand a long hard look at our own ideas of teaching and learning.

References

Albanese, M. A., & Mitchell, S. (1993). Problem-based learning: A review of the literature on its outcomes and implementation issues. *Academic Medicine, 68,* 52–81.

Baker, C., Pesut, D., McDaniel, A., & Fisher, M. (2007). Evaluating the impact of problem-based learning on learning styles of master's students in nursing administration. *Journal of Professional Nursing, 23,* 214–219.

Barrows, H. S. (1986). A taxonomy of problem-based learning methods. *Medical Education, 20,* 481–486.

Barrows, H. S., & Tamblyn, R. M. (1980). *Problem-based learning: An approach to medical education.* New York, NY: Springer.

Becker, S., Viljoen, M. J., Botma, Y., & Bester, I. J. (2003). Integration of study material in the problem-based learning method. *Curationis, 26*(1), 57–61.

Bernstein, B. (1971). On the classification and framing of educational knowledge. In B. Bernstein, (Ed.), *Class, codes and control: Vol. 1. Theoretical studies towards a sociology of language* (pp. 202–230). London, UK: Routledge & Kegan Paul.

Bloom, S. (1988). Structure and ideology in medical education: An analysis of resistance to change. *Journal of Health and Social Behaviour, 29,* 294–306.

Bowditch, H. T. (1900). The medical school of the future [address to the Congress of American Physicians and Surgeons]. *British Medical Journal, 1,* 1373–1374.

Breier, M., & Wildschut, A. (2006). *Doctors in a divided society. The profession and education of medical practitioners in South Africa.* Cape Town, South Africa: HSRC Press.

Bruner, J. S. (1977). *The process of education.* Cambridge, MA: Harvard University Press. (Original work published in 1960)

Bruner, J. S. (2006a). *In search of pedagogy* (Vol. 1). London, UK: Routledge.

Bruner, J. S. (2006b). *In search of pedagogy* (Vol. 2). London, UK: Routledge.

Burgun, A., Darmoni, S., Le Duff, F., & Weber, J. (2006). Problem-based learning in medical informatics for undergraduate medical students: An experiment in two medical schools. *International Journal of Medical Informatics, 75,* 396–402.

Christakis, N. (1995). The similarity and frequency of proposals to reform U.S. medical education: Constant concerns. *Journal of the American Medical Association, 274,* 706–711.

Connolly, C., & Seneque, M. (1999). Evaluating problem-based learning in a multilingual student population. *Medical Education, 33,* 738–744.

Daubentor, F. (1965). The challenge of the curriculum. In J. V. O. Reid & A. J. Wilmot (Eds.), *Medical education in South Africa* (pp. 316–319). Pietermaritzburg, South Africa: Natal University Press.

De Graaf, E., & Kolmos, A. (2007). History of problem-based and project-based learning. In E. De Graaf & A. Kolmos (Eds.), *Management of change: Implementation of problem-based and project-based learning in engineering* (pp. 1–8). Rotterdam, Netherlands: Sense.

Dolmans, D. H. J. M., Gijselaers, W. H., Moust, J. H. C., De Grave, W. S., Wolfhagen, I. H. A. P., & Van Der Vleuten, C. P. M. (2002). Trends in research on the tutor in problem-based learning: Conclusions and implications for educational practice and research. *Medical Teacher, 24*(2), 173–180.

Editorial. (1911). South Africa's embryo medical school. *South African Medical Record, 9,* 225–226.

Editorial. (1971). Curriculum development in the medical schools. *The Medical Journal of Australia, 1,* 1357–1359.

Flexner, A. (1910). *Medical education in the United States and Canada.* New York, NY: Carnegie Foundation for the Advancement of Teaching.

Freire, P. (1992). *Pedagogy of hope: Reliving pedagogy of the oppressed* (R. R. Barr, Trans.). New York, NY: Continuum.

Garforth, F. W. (1966). *John Dewey: Selected educational writings with an introduction and commentary.* London, UK: Heineman.

Goodencugh, W. (1944). *Report of the interdepartmental committee on medical schools.* London, UK: Her Majesty's Stationery Office.

Hay, P. J., & Katsikitis, M. (2001). The "expert" in problem-based and case-based learning: Necessary or not? *Medical Education, 35,* 22–26.

Hilgard, E. R., Irvine, R. P., & Whipple, J. E. (1953). Rote memorization, understanding, and transfer: An extension of Katona's card-trick experiments. *Journal of Experimental Psychology, 46*, 288–292.

Hmelo-Silver, C. E., & Barrows, H. S. (2006). Goals and strategies of a problem-based learning facilitator. *The Interdisciplinary Journal of Problem-Based Learning, 1*, 21–39.

Horne, M., Woodhead, K., Morgan, L., Smithies, L., Megson, D., & Lyte, G. (2007). Using enquiry in learning: From vision to reality in higher education. *Nurse Education Today, 27*, 103–112.

Hsieh, C., & Knight, L. (2008). Problem-based learning for engineering students: An evidence-based comparative study. *The Journal of Academic Librarianship, 34*, 25–30.

Jones, M. C., & Johnston, D. W. (2006). Is the introduction of a student-centred, problem-based curriculum associated with improvements in student nurse well-being and performance? An observational study of effect. *International Journal of Nursing Studies, 43*, 941–952.

Kiesseling, C., Schubert, B., Scheffner, D., & Burger, W. (2004). First-year medical students' perceptions of stress and support: A comparison between reformed and traditional track curricula. *Medical Education, 38*, 504–509.

Kivela, J., & Kivela, R. J. (2005). Student perceptions of an embedded problem-based learning instructional approach in a hospitality undergraduate programme. *Hospitality Management, 24*, 437–464.

Kuhn, T. S. (1970). *The structure of scientific revolutions* (2nd ed.). Chicago, IL: University of Chicago Press.

Kwizera, E. N., Dambisya, Y. M., & Aguirre, J. H. (2001). Does tutor subject-matter expertise influence student achievement in the problem-based learning curriculum at UNITRA Medical School? *South African Medical Journal, 91*, 514–516.

Maistry, S. M. (2009). Applying a partial problem-based learning environment to a non-major economics course: A case of cognitive dissonance. *South African Journal of Higher Education, 23*, 329–339.

McMillan, R. G. (1965). Some thoughts on the problem of method in teaching. In J. V. O. Reid & A. J. Wilmot (Eds.), *Medical education in South Africa* (pp. 235–238). Pietermaritzburg, South Africa: Natal University Press.

Mennin, S. (2007). Small-group problem-based learning as a complex adaptive system. *Teaching and Teacher Education, 23*, 303–313.

Mennin, S., & Majoor, G. (2001). Problem-based learning (Position paper). Retrieved from http://www.the-networktufh.org/publications_resources/position content.asp?id=6&t=Position+Papers#

Michel, M. C., Bischoff, A., & Jakobs, K. H. (2002). Comparison of problem- and lecture-based pharmacology teaching. *TRENDS in Pharmacological Sciences, 23*, 168–170.

Miflin, B. M., Campbell, C. B., & Price, D. A. (1999). A lesson from the introduction of a problem-based, graduate entry course: The effects of different views of self-direction. *Medical Education, 33*, 801–807.

Milliken, F. J., & Martins, L. L. (1996). Searching for common threads: Understanding the multiple effects of diversity in organizational groups. *The Academy of Management, 21*, 402–433.

Nalesnik, S. W., Heaton, J. O., Olsen, C. H., Haffner, W. H. J., & Zahn, C. M. (2004). Incorporating problem-based learning into an obstetric/gynecology clerkship: Impact on student satisfaction and grades. *American Journal of Obstetrics and Gynecology, 190,* 1375–1381.

Neufeld, V. R., & Barrows, H. S. (1974). The "McMaster philosophy": An approach to medical education. *Journal of Medical Education, 49,* 1040–1050.

Norman, G. R., & Schmidt, H. G. (1992). The psychological basis of problem-based learning: A review of the evidence. *Academic Medicine, 67,* 557–565.

Osler, W. (1913). Examinations, examiners and examinees. *The Lancet, 2,* 1047–1059.

Papa, F. J. (1999). Medical curriculum reform in North America, 1765 to the present: A cognitive science perspective. *Academic Medicine, 74,* 154–164.

Park, S. E., Susarla, S. M., Cox, C. K., Da Silva, J., & Howell, T. H. (2007). Do tutor expertise and experience influence student performance in a problem-based curriculum? *Journal of Dental Education, 71,* 819–824.

Prideaux, D. (2007). Curriculum development in medical education: From acronyms to dynamism. *Teaching and Teacher Education, 23,* 294–302.

Read, J. (1971). Dilemmas facing curriculum framers. *The Medical Journal of Australia, 1,* 1388–1391.

Regan-Smith, M. G. (1998). "Reform without change": Update, 1998. *Academic Medicine, 73,* 505–507.

Rogers, C. R. (1969). *Freedom to learn: A view of what education might become.* Columbus, OH: Merrill.

Rundle, F. F. (1971). A new medical education and training programme based on five years of undergraduate study and two years of graduate study. *The Medical Journal of Australia, 1,* 1392–1395.

Savin-Baden, M. (2000). *Problem-based learning in higher education: Untold stories.* Buckingham, UK: The Society for Research into Higher Education & Open University Press.

Schmidt, H. G. (1983). Problem-based learning: Rationale and description. *Medical Education, 17,* 11–16.

Schmidt, W. H. O. (1965). Processes of learning in relation to different kinds of materials to be learnt. In J. V. O. Ried & A. J. Wilmot (Eds.), *Medical education in South Africa* (pp. 228–32). Pietermaritzburg, South Africa: University of Natal Press.

Shryock, R. H. (1965). European backgrounds of American medical education. *Journal of the American Medical Association, 194,* 119–124.

Silver, M., & Wilkerson, L. A. (1991). Effects of tutors with subject expertise on the problem-based tutorial process. *Academic Medicine, 66,* 298–300.

Singaram, V. S., van der Vleuten, C. P. M., Stevens, F., & Dolmans, D. H. J. M. (2011). "For most of us Africans, we don't just speak": A qualitative investigation into collaborative heterogeneous PBL group learning. *Advances in Health Science Education, 16*(3), 297–310.

Singaram, V. S., van der Vleuten, C. P. M., van Berkel, H., & Dolmans, D. H. J. M. (2010). Reliability and validity of a tutorial group effectiveness instrument. *Medical Teacher, 33*(2), e133–e137.

Slavin, R. E. (1996). Research on cooperative learning and achievement: What we know, what we need to know. *Contemporary Educational Psychology, 21,* 43–69.

Smith, R. (1989). Medical education and the GMC: Controlled or stifled? *British Medical Journal, 298,* 1372–1375.

Sommerville, T. E. (2011). *People and pedagogy: People and pedagogy: Problem-based learning in the MBChB curriculum at the UKZN Medical School* (Unpublished Doctoral thesis manuscript). Durban, South Africa: University of KwaZulu-Natal.

Strobel, J., & Barneveld, A. V. (2009). When is PBL more effective? A meta-synthesis of meta-analyses comparing PBL to conventional classrooms. *The Interdisciplinary Journal of Problem-Based Learning, 3,* 44–58.

Taylor, A. B. (1965). Presidential address. In J. V. O. Reid & A. J. Wilmot (Eds.), *Medical education in South Africa* (pp. 1–4). Pietermaritzburg, South Africa: Natal University Press.

Taylor, D., & Miflin, B. (2008). Problem-based learning: Where are we now? *Medical Teacher, 30,* 742–763.

Watson, W. E., Kumar, K., & Michaelsen, L. K. (1993). Cultural diversity's impact on interaction process and performance: Comparing homogeneous and diverse task groups. *Academy of Management Journal, 36,* 590.

Williams, A. F. (1999). An antipodean evaluation of problem-based learning by clinical educators. *Nurse Education Today, 19,* 659–667.

Williams, S. M., & Beattie, H. J. (2008). Problem-based learning in the clinical setting: A systematic review. *Nurse Education Today, 28,* 146–154.

CHAPTER 30

Confucius and Buddha in the College Classroom

Relational Virtuosity in Teaching and Learning

Peter J. Giordano

How do we understand the behavior and character of good teachers? We may assert, for example, that good teachers are powerful mainframe computers who download knowledge into their students' heads with the skillful dispensing of information in lectures. Or we might suggest that superior teachers are "good company" to students, like bicycle instructors who help less experienced riders navigate ever more complex turns and twists on a mountain highway (Baxter Magolda, 2002). Good teachers are midwives, we might aver, helping students give birth to ever more complex understandings of the world (Belenky, Clinchy, Goldberger, & Tarule, 1997). We might propose, too, that good teachers are also first-rate metaphor makers. Good teachers are reflective about their craft, seeking to find metaphors that describe their approach to effective teaching. They then teach in harmony with their guiding metaphors.

Because I view teaching and learning as a fundamentally relational activity, I have been drawn to teaching metaphors that put relational dynamics at

Author's Note: I thank Dr. Peter Hershock of the East West Center (Honolulu, Hawai'i) for offering comments on a draft of this chapter.

the center of the craft of teaching (e.g., midwives and good company). Good teaching involves navigating important interpersonal and developmental issues with students (Giordano, 2010b) as they shift their focus from external sources of authority (e.g., parents) to their own interior voice of self-authorship (Baxter Magolda, 2001, 2002).

In this chapter, I will develop the idea that relational dynamics run through or cut across *all the specific skills* of good teaching. By analogy, it is well established that the relational alliance is key to the effectiveness of psychotherapy and counseling (Martin, Garske, & Davis, 2000). Ample evidence also supports the assertion that even if health care providers of all stripes have excellent technical training in their specialty, their effectiveness is diminished if they lack sensitive "bedside manner" or pay too little attention to the collaborative bond with their patients (Hall, Ferreira, Maher, Latimer, & Ferreira, 2010).

Highlighting the relational dimensions of good teaching is not new. Authors such as Mary Field Belenky, Blythe McVicker Clinchy, Nancy Rule Goldberger, and Jill Mattuck Tarule (1997); Marcia Baxter Magolda (2002); Parker Palmer (1998); and Ken Bain (2004) have all underscored the centrality of teacher-student relational dynamics. In addition, in a series of empirical studies of excellent teachers and superior teaching, William Buskist and colleagues have highlighted the importance of relational dynamics in effective pedagogy (Buskist, Sikorski, Buckley, & Saville, 2002; Epting, Zinn, Buskist, & Buskist, 2004; Keeley, Smith, & Buskist, 2006; Schaeffer, Epting, Zinn, & Buskist, 2003). Janie Wilson, Rebecca Ryan, and James Pugh, (2010) also have emphasized the significance of rapport in the teacher-student relationship, developing a scale to measure rapport and using it as a meaningful predictor of important college student outcomes.

I will augment this valuable literature by drawing ideas from two traditional Eastern systems of thought that place relational skill at the forefront of what it means to be an exemplary person and, more germane to this chapter, an exemplary teacher. By using the Confucian and Buddhist traditions, I hope to demonstrate that relational virtuosity, not merely relational competence, is something that all teachers should seek to develop. Relational virtuosity is the ability to develop, maintain, and continually improve the quality of interpersonal relationships in a particular context. In our case, the context is the college classroom. In the Groccia model of teaching and learning (St. Clair & Groccia, 2009; Chapter 1, this volume), relational virtuosity is central to the domain of instructional processes because it (relational virtuosity) is connected to virtually all instructional practices in the classroom.

Confucius in the College Classroom

Confucianism and Buddhism are typically described as religions, philosophies, or systems of political thought, but their relational psychology is most germane to this chapter. Because they each developed and flourished first in Asia, their perspectives emphasize dimensions of relational dynamics that are likely unfamiliar to most Westerners.

The Confucian tradition stretches back 2,500 years to mainland China. This same time frame corresponds roughly to the time of Pythagoras or Heraclitus in Western philosophy (Liu, 2006). The founder of Confucian thought is obviously Confucius (551–479 BCE), but others are also responsible for the development of Confucian philosophy and ethics, notably Mencius and Xunzi. The most widely known of the Confucian texts is *The Analects of Confucius* (Ames & Rosemont, 1998), a collection of Confucius's sayings written down by his pupils (Liu, 2006). The *Analects* is considered one of the "Four Books" or canonical material of Confucianism (Gardner, 2007). The other three are the *Zhongyong* (The Doctrine of the Mean), the *Da Xue* (The Great Learning), and the *Mencius*.

Familiarity with Confucian thought in the West is typically superficial, with knowledge running no deeper than opening a fortune cookie to read an aphorism starting with the stem, "Confucius say . . . " (Giordano, 2010a). Globalization and the economic and cultural rise of China, however, makes the time ripe for a keener awareness of the Confucian tradition (Ames, 2010). Unfortunately, stereotypes of Confucianism may erroneously convey that it is, by its very nature, antiquated, feudalistic, coercive, and paternalistic (Littlejohn, 2009; Rosemont & Ames, 2009). The so-called New Confucianism movement (Bell, 2008; Makeham, 2003), however, has been rendering Confucian ideas in ways that are more accessible to contemporary thinking and society. Herbert Fingarette (1972) provides a case example of how an initial impression of Confucius can mature with time:

> When I began to read Confucius, I found him to be a prosaic and parochial moralizer; his collected sayings, the *Analects*, seemed to me an archaic irrelevance. Later, and with increasing force, I found him a thinker with profound insight and with an imaginative vision of [humans] equal in its grandeur to any I know. Increasingly, I have become convinced that Confucius can be a teacher to us today—a major teacher, not one who merely gives us a slightly exotic perspective on the ideas already current. *He tells us things not being said elsewhere; things needing to be said. He has a new lesson to teach.* (p. vii, italics mine)

The Confucian idea of the relationally constructed person is most central to our discussion of teaching and learning. As an example, consider what Fingarette (1983) underscored about the construct of fatherhood. Adopting a Confucian perspective, "fatherhood" cannot be captured in a mere biological relation. The fundamental meaning of fatherhood is represented in the degree to which I *behave* in a fatherly way to my child, in how I fulfill my roles and responsibilities in living out this relationship.

Ultimately, a father is not something I am, a father is something I *do*. And over time, I attempt to be a father or, rather, *become* a father with increasing virtuosity. Therefore, Confucians would be quite comfortable with modern phrases such as "talk is cheap" or "walk the walk." My behavior is what signals the degree to which I fulfill my roles and responsibilities in the interpersonal domains of my life. Indeed, my identity is created within these interpersonal domains.

Because we are "irreducibly interpersonal" as Fingarette (1983, p. 336) observed, we can extend the fatherhood discussion into all spheres of human interaction, including the teacher-student relation. Following Fingarette's line of thinking, or rather a Confucian contour of thought, the term *teacher* has no meaning without *student* in the mix. Teachers do not exist independently of students; conversely, students do not exist autonomously of teachers. The two exist and fulfill their roles and responsibilities only in relation to one another. This nuance has a very practical and significant implication. We cannot think of teaching without invoking learning, and we cannot envision teachers without imagining students in relationship with them. Teachers and students, teaching and learning are inextricably bound together. In Confucian thought, the family is the locus where the roles and responsibilities of relational dynamics are first learned, as the Xiaojing, the Chinese Classic of Family Reverence (Rosemont & Ames, 2009) demonstrates. The family is so vital because it "is an ecology in which the interdependence of the constituent members means the prosperity in one sector redounds to the health and well being of the whole" (Rosemont & Ames, 2009, p. 23). Persons learn to behave in exemplary ways by fulfilling their roles and responsibilities first within the family and within the so-called "five relationships" in traditional Confucian thought: father-son, husband-wife, ruler-minister (subject), elder brother-younger brother, and friend-friend. But the process of relational virtuosity is endless, as we move out from the family in ever-widening concentric circles of interpersonal relationship (Tu, 1994), including the teacher-student relationship.

The fundamental insight of Confucianism therefore is that human identity is always constructed in the context of relationships, and persons evolve, mature, and become exemplary to the degree that they fulfill with integrity their various roles and responsibilities in life. As Fingarette (1983) so aptly summarized, "Where there are not at least two truly human beings, there is not even one" (p. 340). In life, our identities are shifting moment by moment, as we move into and out of our various interpersonal roles. Throughout the course of a day, I am father, husband, friend, supervisor, supervisee, benefactor, beneficiary, teacher, and student. These *relationships* constitute who I am, and in the Confucian tradition, my identity resides in between each of these relationships.

How then do these Confucian ideas translate into classroom practice and instructional processes? Undoubtedly, Confucius would be comfortable in the context of a college classroom because, at its core, Confucian thought expounds a philosophy of education (Lai, 2008). The *Analects* (Ames & Rosemont, 1998) opens with the question, "Having studied, to then repeatedly apply what you have learned—is this not a source of pleasure?" (p. 71, 1.1). Throughout the *Analects*, we also find repeated references to the "love of learning." According to Chen Lai (2008), the meaning of learning in Confucian thought can have both a narrow and broad connotation. In the narrow sense, learning may simply mean "to learn something," as in the acquisition of a skill or the development of a cognitive understanding. More broadly and, by implication more importantly, learning in the context of Confucianism also means the "cultivation of excellence in one's character." The development of this exemplary personhood is a lifelong project, never complete, always in process and always playing out in the context of careful attention to relational responsibilities. Roger Ames (2010) argued, "The theme most persistent and pervasive in shaping the Chinese philosophical tradition broadly is the project of personal cultivation" (p. 66).

Consider the current climate of higher education today, at least in the West. College students and their parents often ask such questions as, "What can I do with this degree? What are my employment opportunities after I graduate? What is the average starting salary for someone who majors in [pick the academic discipline]? How can I increase my chances of finding a job after I graduate?" These careerist concerns are legitimate, although from a Confucian perspective, they tap into only the veneer of what education should entail. The questions do not reflect the deeper, more important connotation of learning. As I have noted, education for Confucius is a lifelong process of self-cultivation, self-improvement, and of "expressing virtue in activities connected with other people" (Kupperman, 2008, p. 412).

This type of educational discourse may sound quaintly idealistic, according to some. In an age of understanding students as "customers" and viewing education as a path to the development of specific skills or particular careers, Confucius calls on us to remember what some describe as the liberal arts orientation to our work as teachers. Importantly, one does not have to teach literature or philosophy to appreciate the Confucian perspective on education as a process of personal cultivation. Accounting or marketing professors, for example, can still emphasize values of lifelong learning, character development, ethical behavior, and relational virtuosity. The specific domain of education or disciplinary territory does not matter when we understand education as more than the teaching of career related skills.

The first implication of the Confucian viewpoint, therefore, is to keep these values of personal cultivation front and center in whatever it is that we are teaching. Indeed, one of the principal contributions of Confucian thought is that the qualities of exemplary character can be taught to or, more accurately phrased, *learned by* anyone, provided the person dedicates him or herself to this self-cultivation. That is, exemplary character and consummate behavior are not products of a noble bloodline (as was thought during the time Confucius started teaching), but was and is something open to everyone

(Lai, 2008; Rainey, 2010), including both students and teachers. In addition to teaching disciplinary content, therefore, teachers should emphasize aspects of personal development including integrity, honesty, dependability, working well with others, and so on.

Adopting a Confucian perspective in the college classroom has a second important implication for our work as teachers in the college classroom. Our *identity* as a teacher is reshaped by adopting a Confucian perspective on teaching and learning. Relational virtuosity in the classroom connotes an understanding of the interdependence of teachers and students. As I argued earlier, a Confucian viewpoint locates a teacher's identity in the midst of or in between each of his or her relationships with students. Behaving skillfully in the classroom, therefore, requires paying exquisite attention both to the broad relational dynamics in the classroom and to individual relationships with each student. Such virtuosity requires great skill in that we must attend to and appropriately respond to multiple domains of teaching, including the content of instruction, the mode of instruction, the macro-relational climate (the entire class) and the micro-relational climate (individual students). Because a teacher's identity depends on how well the teacher fulfills his or her responsibilities to students, teachers must therefore exhibit relational virtuosity in understanding the uniqueness of each student. If a student comes to the teacher for help because she is not performing well on exams, the relationally skilled teacher does not offer "canned" advice on how to study more effectively. Instead, the teacher tries to understand the particular educational background, study skills, and strengths and weaknesses of this student and then offers advice that is tailored to this student's unique situation, personality, and skill set.

A final key implication of the Confucian perspective connects to the Chinese notion of change and transformation. In Chinese thought, ongoing transformation is at the heart of all things and events. The concept of "teacher," therefore, would not convey a fixed or static state of being; nor would the idea of student. It would be more accurate to think of teachers as always transforming into students and of students as continually changing into teachers. If we adopt this perspective, we can readily perceive how this dynamic dance unfolds in the classroom. When a teacher spends time reading and thinking in preparation for class (rather than pulling out the same old lecture notes), the teacher has transformed into a student during those times of preparation. When a student asks a question that the teacher cannot answer, the teacher becomes a student at the moment he or she appropriately responds by saying, "That's a great question, and I don't know the answer. But I will see if I can find information for us to discuss when we meet again." The same holds true when a student, either to the entire class or when working in a small group, offers an insight that elevates the level of discussion and understanding in the classroom. All teachers have had the experience of a student offering an insightful perspective that they never considered before. At that moment, who is the teacher and who are the students? The teacher exhibiting relational virtuosity recognizes the dynamic nature of the student-teacher relationship and welcomes the role of student as a way to model what it means to be a lifelong learner. This shift in perspective is empowering and liberating both to students and professors. For students, offering an informative example or intellectual insight, especially if acknowledged overtly by the teacher, can be a life-changing event (Giordano, 2010b). For teachers, it is liberating because it allows them to model what it means to be curious, honest, humble, and collaborative. Besides, as Joel Kupperman (2008) observed, "There is little more deadening than having a perfect-seeming teacher" (p. 406).

Buddha in the College Classroom

The Buddhist tradition is distinct from Confucianism yet shares with Confucianism exquisite attention to relational dynamics. Like Confucianism, Buddhism's origins trace back 2,500 years, although not to China but to northern India and the teachings of Siddhartha Gautama, the Buddha's given name. There is some debate about the details of the Buddha's life because the first full-length biographies about him were not written until 400 years after his death (Robinson, Johnson, & Bhikkhu, 2005). He probably lived between 563–483 BCE, born as a prince into an aristocratic family in what is today the border between Nepal and India. Siddhartha grew up living a luxurious life by the standards of his time and locality. At the age of 29, however, he left his wife and young son to pursue a variety of religious practices, with the aim of understanding the nature of suffering and its resolution. After 6 years of dedicated and diverse religious practice, Siddhartha sat in meditation facing east under the Bodhi Tree (the tree of awakening) and ultimately gained the insight he sought. Siddhartha thus became the Buddha or the awakened one (Robinson et al., 2005).

After his enlightenment, the Buddha began teaching, and his ideas spread quickly through India and within five or six centuries had become firmly established throughout all of Asia (Liu, 2006). Ultimately, Buddhism migrated to other continents including Africa, Europe, and North and South America (Hershock, 2005). In all of these migrations, Buddhism adapted to its new cultural environs. In the United States, the writings of William James, Carl Jung, and Abraham Maslow had a significant impact on how Buddhism was received, understood, and practiced (Robinson et al., 2005). Because of these writers and others, Buddhism is more familiar to Westerners than is Confucianism. Contributing to this relative familiarity are also contemporary research scholars who are scientifically investigating a variety of Buddhist ideas and practices. These researchers have studied Buddhist teachings as applied to addictive behaviors (Marlatt, 2002), drug-using persons and behaviors that increase risk of HIV infection (Avants & Margolin, 2004), anxiety-disordered conditions (Toneatto, 2002), grief reactions

(Michalon, 2001), and the general benefits of Buddhist (and other) meditative strategies (Wallace & Shapiro, 2006; Walsh & Shapiro, 2006).

The Buddhist tradition is extraordinarily complex and commonly classified into three main schools—Theravada Buddhism in Southeast Asia, Mahayana Buddhism in East Asia, and Vajrayana Buddhism in the Indo-Tibetan region (Wallace & Shapiro, 2006). To speak of Buddhism as one monolithic system is misleading because Buddhist traditions are so varied in their teachings, in the canonical literature they value, and in the practices they promulgate. Nevertheless, Buddhist ideas of interdependent origination, skillful means, and relational virtuosity are all conceptual resources we can use in our teaching craft. By understanding and acting on these resources, we may cultivate "an ever increasing sensitivity and flexibility in our responses to others" (Hershock, 1996, pp. 70–71). If relational virtuosity matters in the classroom, as I have argued, then a Buddhist perspective has much to offer.

Interdependent Origination

A central Buddhist teaching is that all things arise interdependently, and all things and events are related to all other things and events. To illustrate within the biophysical domain, consider the patella or knee-jerk reflex. If a physician's hammer strikes the patella tendon, the foot and lower leg will suddenly jerk forward. What caused the patella reflex? Was it the hammer strike? Was it the sudden stretch of the patella tendon, which the hammer strike produced? Was it the resulting signal sent from the stretched tendon to the spinal cord, which was then interpreted as notification that the lower leg was rapidly flexing? Or was it the return signal sent back to the quadriceps to compensate for the perceived flexion by extending (jerking forward) the leg? Or should we factor in the moment when this person first scheduled the appointment to see the physician? The dilemma is apparent: All these events are interrelated and interdependent. It would not make sense to identify only one of these factors as *the* cause because each event in the chain is related to and dependent on all other events. This fundamental idea, that all things and events are interdependent and interrelated, was one of the Buddha's chief insights into the nature of how our worlds are organized. Missing the inherent interdependency of all things and events is to make the same error as overlooking the fundamental relational construction of human identity as seen in the Confucian tradition.

Interdependency in the context of education argues against the sharp lines that are sometimes drawn between academic disciplines. Recognizing the interconnection and interpenetration across disciplinary boundaries suggests educational benefits of multidisciplinary teaching and learning, benefits that accrue for teachers and students as well as for college curricula (Hershock, 2010).

Paradoxically, interdependent origination cannot be fully understood without considering its connection to other conceptual ideas within the Buddhist tradition, ideas such as the changing nature of all things, the impermanence of self, the troubled relational nature of all things and events (suffering), and the idea of karma (Hershock, 2006). This conceptual matrix reflects the intricate psychology and cosmology of the Buddhist tradition and takes us far afield from the central purpose of this chapter. For interested readers who want a comprehensive consideration of these conceptual ideas and their interrelationships, consult Peter Hershock's work (1996, 2005, 2006).

Skillful Means

The Buddha is known to have adapted his teaching to fit his audience. If he was talking with a group of well-educated aristocrats he taught in one way, whereas if he was teaching an assembly of lower-caste laborers, he taught in another way. As Buddhist ideas spread from India to other parts of the world, other Buddhist teachers did the same. This adaptation of teaching style, technique, and approach is known as *upaya* (Sanskrit), which is typically translated as "skillful means," "skill in means," or "expedient device" (Jiang, 2008). Pedagogy within the Buddhist tradition, therefore, always entails highly creative, flexible, and spontaneous strategies to maximize the impact of teaching.

Relational Virtuosity

Recognizing the interdependence of all things and events and using skillful means when working with others is connected to a highly attuned sensitivity to relational dynamics in all interpersonal situations. Like the Confucian tradition that pays exquisite attention to relational roles and responsibilities, the Buddhist perspective adopts a similar virtuosic attention to relational dynamics. Hershock (1996, 2005) invoked the metaphor of an improvisational jazz performance to bring to life this quality of relational virtuosity. Improvisational jazz involves the in-the-moment creation of music as the musicians work in concert to create new and evolving musical structures. One member of the jazz group might set out a melody and others play off it, sometimes following, sometimes leading, while new variations are discovered in the act of music creation. When done well, jazz improvisation is hypnotic in the sense that one gets lost in appreciation for the unfolding developments. When done well, such improvisation also reflects extraordinary skill, not only in playing the musical instrument but in attunement to what the other musicians are doing. It may *appear* effortless, but it is not. This metaphor is compelling as we think about pedagogical improvisation and relational virtuosity in a college classroom.

Buddhist Ideas in Classroom Practice

How would a college classroom look if we kept in mind the concepts of interdependent origination, skillful means, and relational virtuosity? First and foremost, the casual observer might not notice anything unique in the behavior of the teacher. Teachers skilled in using these conceptual resources might not behave in ways that would *overtly* signal they were putting these ideas into practice. The teacher also would not necessarily adopt any particular techniques or pedagogical strategies. The implementation of these Buddhist ideas would fit with any number of teaching approaches—lecturing, collaborative group work, Socratic dialogue, problem-based learning, or teaching with technology.

Instead, one might simply observe that the class flows well, that things just seem "to work." On an attitudinal and behavioral level, teachers skilled in understanding the interdependence of all things and events would be less likely to blame students for problems in the classroom. They would also be less likely to impugn themselves. Instead, these teachers would recognize the inherent interconnections among all students as well as the interdependence of the teacher with the students. These teachers would connect previous classes and experiences with the present class. If a class went poorly last semester, how does that experience relate to what is unfolding in this class today? In a nutshell, these teachers would have keen insight into how, over time, things have come to be as they are in their classrooms. With this insight, they would be better equipped to respond spontaneously, nondefensively, and effectively to enhance the learning environment. They would be less likely to respond recklessly out of frustration or anger.

Second, teachers who put into practice these conceptual ideas would also be skilled at modifying their communication patterns or course assignments to fit with the particular class or mix of students. As teachers, we have all had the experience where an assignment that worked well in the past is just not working well now. It might be best, in this instance, to work with the class to modify the assignment so that it fits better in the present context. This flexibility is skillful means. Teachers who use skillful means also are more likely to encourage an attitude of lifelong learning in their students. Such lifelong learning is not directed necessarily toward achieving more advanced degrees or certifications, however. In the best sense, lifelong learning reflects an attitude of curiosity and enthusiasm toward intellectual pursuits, whether or not these pursuits lead to concrete recognition in the form of more academic degrees. Teachers adept at the nuances of skillful means are the ones remembered by students as inspirational. Such inspirational teachers are not necessarily eye-popping dynamos in the classroom. Rather, they are more likely to be teachers who connect with students at deep intellectual levels to inspire students to learn for years to come.

A third implication of a Buddhist perspective on teaching and learning is that, on the face of it, the interpersonal dynamics in the classroom might not be particularly remarkable. As I noted earlier, the class just seems to work, to develop effortlessly. There is not much interpersonal dysfunctional drama among students or between students and professor. Like the jazz ensemble jamming, the class works together in what appears to be effortless collaboration, spinning out new levels of understanding through pedagogical improvisation. Teachers skilled in this kind of relational virtuosity are not front and center in the class, at least not overtly, as I have already noted. In the thinking of Palmer (1998), a "great thing" (e.g., a great idea or an important concept) is in the foreground, not the teacher.

Hershock (2005) has related an instructive story from the oral tradition in Korean Chan Buddhism. Chan is a form of Chinese Buddhism that migrated to Korea and later to Japan where it became known as Zen Buddhism. The story goes something like this. One of the senior students at a Buddhist monastery questions the leadership of the Buddhist master. The student thinks the master is a bit of a slacker, just indulging in the privileges of being in charge—enjoying the food, taking leisurely strolls around the grounds, and relaxing in front of sunsets. At one point, the senior monk directly confronts the master and asks him what he does that qualifies him to be the master. Unperturbed the master replies, "Not much I guess." After a time, the master has to leave the monastery for about a month and places the senior monk in charge. The interpersonal quality of life at the monastery rapidly declines as petty arguments develop and grow. Soon, many monks are leaving despite intensified efforts by the senior student to restore order and harmony. When the master finally returns, life at the monastery is in a shambles. Cool and collected, the master looks around and says something to the effect of, "I guess I better get back to not doing much once again."

The parallels with teaching and classroom dynamics are clear. Sometimes, despite our best efforts, things just do not work well in the classroom. Certain mixes of students may be difficult for us to work alongside, for example. One event in the classroom, a moment critical to the evolution of the class, might shut down learning opportunities, both in the short and long term (Palmer, 1998). Teachers who are relationally virtuosic are better equipped to use skillful means in ways that often go unnoticed, behavior akin to the head monk "not doing much." Like the leader of a dynamic improvisational jazz group, the teacher skilled in using these Buddhist resources can set a tone or help create an environment in which the individual talents and personalities of the students coalesce to reach new heights of learning. As Duke Ellington is purported to have said, "You've got to find some way of saying it without saying it." Clearly, it would be a joy to be in that classroom as a teacher or a student.

Conclusions

The ideas I presented in this chapter speak to a general approach to teaching and learning, rather than to specific techniques that one might develop and use, although these conceptual ideas have clear implications for instructional processes. At the outset of the chapter, I asserted that teaching is a fundamentally relational activity, and I defined *relational virtuosity* as the ability to develop, maintain, and continually improve the quality of interpersonal relationships in a particular context, in this case, the college classroom. In making this claim, I do not diminish the importance of specific techniques or strategies that one might employ in teaching. A well-organized and lucid lecture delivered with enthusiasm is clearly preferable to a disorganized one conveyed in monotone. A well-structured problem-based learning exercise with a thoughtfully designed assessment component is better than a quick-and-dirty exercise that leaves students wondering what they did and why they did it. My claim is that relational dynamics are central to the success of *all* specific approaches to teaching and learning, and therefore developing relational virtuosity has significant payoffs in the classroom, both for students and for faculty.

The Confucian and Buddhist traditions offer conceptual ideas that suggest both attitudinal and behavioral strategies that a teacher might employ. Within the Confucian tradition of Chinese philosophy, the notion of the relationally constructed self has important implications for teaching and learning. In this chapter, I emphasized that (a) good teachers will underscore knowledge acquisition and personal cultivation (in the spirit of the liberal arts tradition), (b) will seek to understand the unique story of each student and respond sensitively to this individuality, and (c) will understand the dynamic nature of change and transformation, allowing teachers and students the freedom to exchange these roles when appropriate. In a classroom anchored in relational virtuosity, teachers are intermittently transformed into students and vice versa. Within the Buddhist tradition, I highlighted several conceptual ideas of interest. These ideas suggest that good teachers (a) keep a broad and curious perspective on their classroom work by understanding that their teaching is affected by interconnections among their past and current teaching experiences and groups of students (interdependent origination), (b) remain creative and flexible in the instructional processes they use in the classroom (skillful means), and (c) stay highly attuned to the macro- and micro-relational climate of the classroom (relational virtuosity). I used Hershock's (2005) metaphor of jazz improvisation to illustrate the climate of a classroom using these conceptual resources. To extend this metaphor, consider that John Coltrane, a virtuoso of jazz improvisation, *first* became a technical master of the saxophone. He could not improvise to such an exemplary degree before he had mastered the techniques of playing the instrument. Similarly, teachers typically cannot effectively improvise until they have mastered other, more basic, aspects of what it means to be a good teacher, such as developing content and creating an organized framework for the course. The paradox of the Buddhist perspective is that, much like in the story of the master of the Buddhist monastery, you may not notice what the relationally skilled teacher is doing until someone else steps in and tries to do it.

Putting into practice the conceptual ideas I outline in this chapter is not easy and requires a good deal of time and disciplined personal cultivation, an idea that both the Confucian and Buddhist traditions would endorse. The irony is that after all this work, which may help create deep learning experiences for our students (and ourselves), we may never hear a word from students about their positive experiences (Giordano, 2010b). The *Analects of Confucius* (Ames & Rosemont, 1998) may have another lesson to teach us: "To go unacknowledged by others without harboring frustration—is this not the mark of an exemplary person?" (p. 71, 1.1).

References

Ames, R. T. (2010). *Confucian role ethics: A vocabulary.* Hong Kong: Chinese University Press.

Ames, R. T., & Rosemont Jr., H. (1998). *The analects of Confucius: A philosophical translation.* New York, NY: Ballantine Books.

Avants, S. K., & Margolin, A. (2004). Development of spiritual self-schema (3-S) therapy for the treatment of addictive and HIV risk behavior: A convergence of cognitive and Buddhist psychology. *Journal of Psychotherapy Integration, 14,* 253–289.

Bain, K. (2004). *What the best college teachers do.* Cambridge, MA: Harvard University Press.

Baxter Magolda, M. B. (2001). *Making their own way: Narratives for transforming higher education to promote self-development.* Sterling, VA: Stylus.

Baxter Magolda, M. B. (2002, January–February). Helping students make their way to adulthood: Good company for the journey. *About Campus, 6*(6), 2–9.

Belenky, M. F., Clinchy, B. M., Goldberger, N. R., & Tarule, J. M. (1997). *Women's ways of knowing* (10th ed.). New York, NY: Basic Books.

Bell, D. A. (2008). *China's new Confucianism: Politics and everyday life in a changing society.* Princeton, NJ: Princeton University Press.

Buskist, W., Sikorski, J., Buckley, T., & Saville, B. K. (2002). Elements of master teaching. In S. F. Davis & W. Buskist (Eds.), *The teaching of psychology: Essays in honor of Wilbert J. McKeachie and Charles L. Brewer* (pp. 27–39). Mahwah, NJ: Lawrence Erlbaum.

Epting, L., Zinn, T., Buskist, C., & Buskist, W. (2004). Student perspectives on the distinction between ideal and typical teachers. *Teaching of Psychology, 31,* 181–183.

Fingarette, H. (1972). *Confucius: The secular as sacred.* Prospect Heights, IL: Waveland Press.

Fingarette, H. (1983). The music of humanity in the conversations of Confucius. *Journal of Chinese Philosophy, 10,* 331–356.

Gardner, D. K. (2007). *The four books: The basic teachings of the later Confucian tradition.* Indianapolis, IN: Hackett.

Giordano, P. J. (2010a). Culture and theories of personality: Western, Confucian, and Buddhist perspectives. In K. Keith (Ed.), *Cross-cultural psychology: A contemporary reader.* Malden, MA: Wiley-Blackwell.

Giordano, P. J. (2010b). Serendipity in teaching and learning: The importance of critical moments. *The Journal on Excellence in College Teaching, 21,* 5–27.

Hall, A. M., Ferreira, P. H., Maher, C. G., Latimer, J., & Ferreira, M. L. (2010). The influence of the therapist-patient relationship on treatment outcome in physical rehabilitation: A systematic review. *Physical Therapy, 90*, 1099–1110.

Hershock, P. (1996). *Liberating intimacy: Enlightenment and social virtuosity in Chan Buddhism.* Albany: SUNY Press.

Hershock, P. (2005). *Chan Buddhism.* Honolulu: University of Hawai'i Press.

Hershock, P. (2006). *Buddhism in the public sphere: Reorienting global interdependence.* New York, NY: Routledge.

Hershock, P. (2010). Higher education, globalization and the critical emergence of diversity. *Paideusis, 19*(1), 29–42.

Jiang, T. (2008). The dilemma of skillful means in Buddhist pedagogy: Desire and education in the Lotus Sutra. In R. T. Ames & P. D. Hershock (Eds.), *Educations and their purposes: A conversation among cultures* (pp. 157–173). Honolulu: University of Hawai'i Press.

Keeley, J., Smith, D., & Buskist, W. (2006). The teacher behavior checklist: Factor analysis of its utility for evaluating teaching. *Teaching of Psychology, 33*, 84–90.

Kupperman, J. L. (2008). Fact and value in the Analects: Education and logic. In R. T. Ames & P. D. Hershock (Eds.), *Educations and their purposes: A conversation among cultures* (pp. 405–419). Honolulu: University of Hawai'i Press.

Lai, C. (2008). The ideas of educating and learning in Confucian thought. In R. T. Ames & P. D. Hershock (Eds.), *Educations and their purposes: A conversation among cultures* (pp. 310–326). Honolulu: University of Hawai'i Press.

Littlejohn, R. L. (2009, March). *Hidden commensurabilities? Tu Weiming's New Confucian political theory and the Lockean civil libertarian tradition.* Paper presented at the National Conference of Asian Studies Development Program, Philadelphia, PA.

Liu, J. (2006). *An introduction to Chinese philosophy: From ancient philosophy to Chinese Buddhism.* Malden, MA: Blackwell.

Makeham, J. (2003). (Ed.). *New Confucianism: A critical examination.* New York, NY: Palgrave Macmillan.

Marlatt, G. A. (2002). Buddhist philosophy and the treatment of addictive behavior. *Cognitive and Behavioral Practice, 9*, 44–49.

Martin, D. J., Garske, J. P., & Davis, M. K. (2000). Relation of the therapeutic alliance with outcome and other variables: A meta-analytic review. *Journal of Consulting and Clinical Psychology, 68*, 438–450.

Michalon, M. (2001). "Selflessness" in the service of the ego: Contributions, limitations and dangers of Buddhist psychology for Western psychotherapy. *American Journal of Psychotherapy, 55*, 202–218.

Palmer, P. J. (1998). *The courage to teach.* San Francisco, CA: Jossey-Bass.

Rainey, L. D. (2010). *Confucius and Confucianism: The essentials.* Malden, MA: Wiley-Blackwell.

Robinson, R. H., Johnson, W. L., & Bhikkhu, T. (2005). *Buddhist religions: A historical introduction* (5th ed.). Belmont, CA: Thomson/Wadsworth.

Rosemont, Jr., H., & Ames, R. T. (2009). *The Chinese classic of family reverence: A philosophical translation of the Xiaojing.* Honolulu: University of Hawai'i Press.

Schaeffer, G., Epting, K., Zinn, T., & Buskist, W. (2003). Student and faculty perceptions of effective teaching. A successful replication. *Teaching of Psychology, 30,* 133–136.

St. Clair, K. L., & Groccia, J. E. (2009). Change to social justice education: Higher education strategy. In K. Skubikowski, C. Wright, & R. Graf (Eds.), *Social justice education: Inviting faculty to transform their institutions* (pp. 70–84). Sterling, VA: Stylus.

Toneatto, T. (2002). A metacognitive therapy for anxiety disorders: Buddhist psychology applied. *Cognitive and Behavioral Practice, 9,* 72–78.

Tu, W. (1994). Embodying the universe: A note on Confucian self-realization. In R. T. Ames, W. Dissanayake, & T. P. Kasulis (Eds.), *Self as person in Asian theory and practice* (pp. 177–186). Albany: SUNY Press.

Wallace, B. A., & Shapiro, S. L. (2006). Mental balance and well-being: Building bridges between Buddhism and Western psychology. *American Psychologist, 61,* 690–701.

Walsh, R., & Shapiro, S. L. (2006). The meeting of meditative disciplines and Western psychology: A mutually enriching dialogue. *American Psychologist, 61,* 227–239.

Wilson, J. H., Ryan, R. G., & Pugh, J. L. (2010). Professor–student rapport scale predicts student outcomes. *Teaching of Psychology, 37,* 1–6.

CHAPTER 31

Learning, Teaching, and Assessment Using Technology

GEOFFREY CRISP

E ach year the New Medium Consortium publishes the *Horizon Report*, a summary of key technology trends that are likely to affect education in the next 1 to 5 years (Johnson, Smith, Levine, & Haywood, 2010). These reports have highlighted the rapid pace of development in digital technologies and the resultant changes in expectations that have been placed on teachers and educational institutions by students and the wider community. Today, it is almost impossible to conceive of a learning environment that does not make some use of technology; the challenge for teachers, students, and institutions is to use the potential of digital technology to deliver quality learning, teaching and assessment, in addition to flexible and timely access to content.

The key themes emerging from the 2010 *Horizon Report* include the rapid uptake of technologies that promote social interactions and the seemingly insatiable demand for more flexible and distributed learning environments (Johnson et al., 2010). One of the practical consequences of the universal adoption of centralized learning management systems has been a gradual shift from a largely teacher-controlled classroom to one where students are expected to take a more active role in engaging with the curriculum. This change manifests itself in students being offered more opportunities to undertake self and peer-review, in students being active rather than passive participants in classroom sessions, and in the expectation that teachers will create more vibrant learning communities that foster participation and engagement. The image of a typical learning environment is no longer one of a physical location or even the synchronous physical presence of many students, but of a more dynamic and interactive environment where the roles and actions of teacher and student move along a continuum defined more by the learning and assessment tasks themselves, rather than formal roles.

Changing Teacher Expectations

Teachers are expected to be more flexible in providing students with a variety of learning experiences and are often required to respond in real time to students' needs as we move more to the concept of "just-in-time" teaching (Simkins & Maier, 2010). Another recent trend that will further promote the distributed nature of the learning environment is cloud-based computing, where content and software resources exist on remote servers, rather than on local computers. Cloud-based approaches allow students and teachers to interact with content, resources, and each other, from anywhere in the world. Such environments also mean that students and teachers do not have to have access to single, isolated computers as the content and software that they need to access is available from any computer with Internet access. These changes have been challenging for many teachers as they reflect on the nature of their role in the educational environment and their relationships with students. As the educational space becomes more technically demanding, the skill base for teachers expands dramatically. Although the manner by which teachers interact with students may be changing, the core role of scaffolding and facilitating learning and providing mechanisms to measure student performance remain the same.

Changing Student Roles

The act of being a student is also changing as students become more mobile and large numbers travel to other countries to complete their higher education. Quality content and learning experiences are becoming more ubiquitous, so students can remain in their local environment and still be part of an international classroom. Students do not necessarily have to physically travel to experience different learning environments; they can remain in their local community for local social interactions, yet be part of a different community for their educational interactions. This ability to remain in a local physical environment and simultaneously be part of a global classroom is likely to change the economics of education significantly in the near future (Allen & Seaman, 2010).

Effective Use of Technology ───────────

The physical devices that students and teachers use to access their educational environments will continue to become more portable and feature-rich as vendors compete to bring new devices into the market. Wireless access to cloud-based learning environments will become more common, so that the educational experience of students will be less dependent on physical access to resources. As open source content becomes more available, the main issue for teachers and students will be to determine the quality of the content they access and of the learning experience itself. Measuring the quality of teaching, learning, and assessment will become an important consequence of the increased use of a digital educational environment. Online education can provide more widespread access to content and learning, but the curriculum design that surrounds the content and the scaffolding provided by the teacher provide the quality experience for students.

To describe how technology can be used for quality learning, teaching, and assessment, we must first determine the space that defines the educational experience (Keengwe & Kidd, 2010). The online educational environment involves various interactions among students, teachers, content, and technology. These interactions can be summarized as cognitive, affective, and managerial (administrative) (Coppola, Hiltz, & Rotter, 2002). Students are required to undertake cognitive tasks such as thinking about discipline content; using information to construct a reasoned hypothesis and completing assessment tasks that demonstrate the development of skills and capabilities at an appropriate level. The affective domain is concerned with feelings, behaviors, and relationships and involves interactions between students and with their teachers. Managerial tasks involve numerous activities such as student access to information, students submitting artifacts to meet course requirements, institutions processing data related to students' performances, and institutions certifying learning outcomes and monitoring or evaluating student feedback.

Quality learning, teaching, and assessment depend on successful integration of all three of these domains; this is relevant whether the environment is online or face-to-face. Undertaking educational activities in an online environment provides both new opportunities and responsibilities for students, teachers, and institutions. Numerous guidelines have been written about how to use technology effectively in education (Fry, Ketteridge, & Marshall, 2009; Joint Information System Committee, 2004); however, the issue is not a shortage of advice, but rather the practical means to appropriately integrate advice into the workload constraints of many teachers and the limited financial resources of many higher education institutions. Online teaching inevitably demands an initial investment of teacher time, so the reward should be an enhancement in the quality of the learning environment and student outcomes. Over time, the initial increased investment in time should translate into workload efficiencies with a payback in the time commitment to construct new learning experiences for students; teachers should be able to leverage their own previous endeavors with the work of colleagues to reduce their own future workloads. The effective use of technology should include a strategic approach to designing learning activities and assessment tasks, incorporating a plan to reuse and repurpose materials and curriculum designs, as well as using sound pedagogical guidelines about how students learn (Ablin, 2008).

Some teachers question the efficacy of new online learning environments. There have been numerous studies comparing the performances of students using traditional face-to-face instruction and those using online methodologies (Lim, Kim, Chen, & Ryder, 2008; Means, Toyama, Murphy, Bakia, & Jones, 2009; Shachar & Neumann, 2010). Teachers involved in online courses have often had to demonstrate that their educational environments produce learning outcomes at least as good as those arising from traditional teaching approaches, the assumption being that assessment outcomes from traditional learning experiences should be used as benchmarks for quality education. This is an assumption that should be challenged. By using the potential of the online environment, learning activities and assessment tasks themselves are changed, so the same outcomes as traditional modes of learning would not necessarily be measured. Many standards and norms that are historically associated with learning have been constructed using traditional text-based or face-to-face learning activities and their associated assessment tasks have been determined by the limitations of this educational environment. Digital environments change this situation, so it is interesting that the same learning outcomes should be measured even though there are radically different ways of engaging and assessing students.

The Conversational Framework

Diana Laurillard is well known for her work on the Conversational Framework, a model for designing online or blended learning environments using technology (Laurillard, 2010). The framework proposes a synergistic interaction between students and teachers where learning and teaching is facilitated by conversations or dialogues between teachers and students. Although the framework can become quite complex when all the interactions between the teacher, the learner, and the learning environment are included, the framework can be summarized as activities involving learning through acquisition, inquiry, discussion, practice, collaboration, and production. Laurillard's framework symbolizes a design approach that facilitates the integration of the cognitive, affective, and managerial components described previously. The framework does not try to privilege any one epistemological approach, but draws on elements of instructivism (teacher-centered approaches based on lecture style delivery of content), constructionism, social constructivism, and collaborative engagement.

Technology makes many of the pathways in the framework practical, such as the provision of timely feedback to large numbers of students, the facilitation of peer feedback processes for students in different physical locations, and the scaffolding of learning activities where students can obtain both synchronous and asynchronous assistance through online communication tools. Technology enables students and teachers to traverse the pathways in the framework numerous times, allowing multiple practice sessions that reinforce key concepts and the development of key capabilities. Table 31.1 summarizes how technology may be used to implement the elements of the Conversational Framework.

Table 31.1 Online Activities That Can Potentially Facilitate Laurillard's Conversational Framework Elements

Conversational Framework elements—students are required to	Relevant online activities that facilitate students engaging with the elements
Access explanations and presentations of the theory, ideas, or concepts	Audio narrated presentations, accessing open educational resources
Ask questions about their understanding of the theory (by providing the opportunity for answers from the teacher or peers)	Discussion boards, virtual classrooms, blogs, Skype
Offer their own ideas and conceptual understanding (by providing comment on students from the teacher or their peers)	Blogs, wikis, peer review
Use their theoretical understanding to achieve a clear task goal by adapting their actions in the light of their understanding, or in response to comments or feedback	Scenario-based activities, role-plays, peer review, game-based learning
Repeat practice (by providing feedback on actions that enables students to improve performance)	Diagnostic and formative online quizzes with feedback
Repeat practice (by enabling students to share their trial actions with peers, for comparison and comment)	Blogs, wikis, e-portfolios, self-review, and peer review
Reflect on the experience of the goal-action-feedback cycle (by offering repeated practice at achieving the task goal)	Formative online assessment with feedback
Discuss and debate their ideas with other learners	Discussion boards, virtual classrooms, Skype
Reflect on their experience (by having to articulate or produce their ideas, reports, designs, performances for presentation to their peers)	Podcasts, blogs, wikis, e-portfolios
Reflect on their experience (by having to articulate or produce their ideas, reports, designs, performances for presentation to their teachers)	Wikis, blogs, e-portfolios

New Learning, Teaching, and Assessment Spaces

Web 2.0 is a term used to describe many of the emerging collaborative spaces now available through the Internet; the key feature of a Web 2.0 environment is not the technology itself, but the virtual space that facilitates and encourages a user-centric approach to creativity and peer review (Lee & McLoughlin, 2010). Web 2.0 services that are readily available to students and teachers include blogs (Edublogs, WordPress), wikis (Wikispaces, MediaWiki), collaborative word processing (Google Docs), aggregation tools (RSS, Bloglines, PageFlakes, iGoogle), social bookmarking (del.icio .us), shared calendars (Google Calendar), and shared content (Flickr, YouTube).

Web 2.0 services allow anyone to aggregate or create content; users can publish their insights or interpretations about an issue to a worldwide audience and receive feedback and commentary from virtual colleagues. Software applications such as blogs, social bookmarking, podcasts, and wikis allow students to be active creators, rather than just passive receivers, of content or the experiences of others. Traditional higher education delivery is often associated with the passive transmission of information or the retelling of the experiences of others. Students will often sit in face-to-face lectures copying notes and complete assessment tasks where they must wait, sometimes weeks, to receive feedback on their performance levels. This passive educational environment has the potential to breed dependency on the teacher for continual affirmation of whether the student is right or wrong, or meeting the expected standard of performance. Although teachers have a critical role in assisting students to understand the standards for a discipline and to guide learning activities, students need to be able to develop skills in self-assessment so that they can regulate their future learning activities. Students need skills to be able to self-review and to apply performance criteria to their own learning and to obtain timely feedback from a variety of sources (Boud & Falchikov, 2006; Nicol, 2009). Technology by itself does not produce self-regulated active learners, but the tools are able to facilitate activities that promote an active approach to learning, provided teachers have used the tools wisely to design activities that promote creative opportunities for students, rather than simply efficient methods to passively transmit content.

Learning environments are becoming more blended in nature as students make choices about whether to attend all traditional face-to-face sessions or to adopt a mix of asynchronous and synchronous activities. Fully online programs also require this mixed mode approach, with synchronous activities such as virtual classrooms, Skype sessions, or avatars meeting in three-dimensional (3-D) virtual worlds; these active sessions facilitate the development of communities of active learners. New types of learning and assessment spaces are becoming available to teachers and students, including online role-plays and scenario-based activities; serious games; virtual or remote laboratories and field trips as well as 3-D virtual worlds using avatars.

Role-Plays and Scenario-Based Learning

Online role-plays allow students to take on the role of a persona and to respond as that persona to a scenario constructed by the teacher (Linser, Ip, Rosser, & Leigh, 2008). Role-plays are designed as authentic learning activities where students can interact with other students (through their personas) to collaborate, collude, negotiate, or debate an issue. Both role-plays and scenario-based learning provide students with decision points and branching opportunities. Technology allows decision points to be recorded and a map of a student's decision-making capability can be used for grading purposes and for students to understand their own strengths and weaknesses in decision making. Scenario-based activities also provide branching and decision points for students, but in this case, students would normally respond as themselves rather than as personae, and the branching is more prescribed compared with a role-play. When a scenario-based activity is undertaken, students follow a limited number of set branches and usually arrive at a prescribed end point; in a role-play, each group of students can take the activity in a new direction and the end point is often different each time the role-play is run. The teacher needs to determine priorities for activity learning outcomes, whether the weighting for assessment will be on the quality of student decision making and the justifications for those decisions, or whether weighting will be on the pathway that the student has chosen to solve a problem. Scenario-based activities are usually used where there are preferred pathways for students to follow and the point of the exercise is to test whether the student could recognize the preferred pathways. Role-plays are more often used when students are required to understand different stakeholder perspectives in a complex situation where there are no prescribed pathways, simply different consequences for each action for different stakeholders.

Role-plays offer rich learning environments for students as they can receive timely feedback on their actions in the form of the responses from other personas; students can reflect on the consequences of their decision making by interpreting whether their actions have had a productive or non-productive influence on other participants in the role-play. An important characteristic of role-plays is their ability to allow students to take on a particular persona yet remain anonymous to other students thereby permitting students to act out the behavior of their persona without feeling that it is a direct reflection of their own beliefs. For role-plays that involve controversial social or political issues, it is important that students feel they can participate fully and explore all options without their own cultural or social beliefs being compromised.

There are specifically designed software tools for role-plays (http://www
.fablusi.com), but they are not essential for designing and running a role-play.
Using a combination of tools from any common learning management system
will enable teachers to conduct a role-play (Maier, Baron, & McLaughlan,
2007). Teachers can use group features to define personas, e-mail and discussion board features to allow communication between personas, quiz tools for
formative or summative tests, wiki features to capture content creation, blogs
to capture student reflections on their decision making, and assignment
upload features to capture student assignments. Examples of role-plays using
common learning management systems can be found at the Project EnRole
website (http://enrole.uow.edu.au) and for the purposely designed role-play
software at the Fablusi™ website (http://www.fablusi.com).

Assessment of an online role-play can be conducted using many common
Web 2.0 tools such as wikis, blogs, discussion forums, and e-portfolios.
Teachers designing role-plays should reflect on the capabilities that are
being developed within the role-play and ensure that the weightings for the
assessment marks appropriately mirror what is being valued. If the key
learning objective for the activity is the acquisition of content knowledge,
then a role-play is not the appropriate activity to develop and assess this
capability. If the capabilities to be developed involve decision making, analyzing the consequences of a solution from multiple social, political, or cultural
perspectives, negotiating outcomes with others, or resolving conflicts within
group situations, then a role-play is likely to be an appropriate learning and
assessment space.

Scenario-Based Learning

In scenario-based learning, the students will normally respond as themselves
and solve the problem or follow the path that they themselves would follow
in the context presented. Scenario Based Learning Interactive (SBLi) is an
example of software designed to facilitate the creation and delivery of scenarios for problem-based learning or enquiry-based learning (http://www
.sblinteractive.org). SBLi software allows teachers to incorporate multimedia
to provide a more authentic experience and quizzes so that students' declarative knowledge can also be assessed in addition to their decision-making
capabilities (Stewart, Brown, & Weatherstone, 2009). The assessment of
scenario-based learning is similar to role-plays, and should be closely aligned
with rewarding the development of valued skills and capabilities, not just
those amenable to scoring easily. Interactive Multi-Media Exercises (IMMEX)
is an example of problem-based assessment using a scenario and attempts to
track students' strategic problem-solving ability and the efficient use of
resources, as it tracks the path the student takes through a problem solving
activity (Cooper, Sandi-Urena, & Stevens, 2008). IMMEX activities model
the use of authentic assessment environments as students are provided with

resources and must decide how to use them in the most efficient manner. There is a "cost" to using the resources (students lose grades or points for redundant or irrelevant information), just as there would be in real life. Hazmat is an example of a chemistry problem using IMMEX; students must identify an unknown compound and can request physical and chemical tests that assist in identifying the substances (Cooper, Cox, Nammouz, Case, & Stevens, 2008). Students must develop strategies for efficiently identifying unknown compounds, a skill relevant to developing attributes of a professional chemist who would be required to identify an unknown compound with the least number of tests.

Serious Games

Serious games represent a recent attempt to design sophisticated digital learning and training activities based on principles of participant engagement found in digital games designed for entertainment purposes (Aldrich, 2009). Marc Prensky (2001) has promoted use of computer games in education and training, particularly games that address complex social issues; he was also an early advocate of computer games for competency-based training in business and military environments. Games cover many elements of Laurillard's Conversational Framework outlined in Table 31.1, especially repeat practice cycles and timely feedback that can be incorporated into new learning activities. Business, health, and military training programs have tended to dominate current serious game-based learning use, and these games are often designed to promote drill and practice-based activities (Pivec & Pivec, 2010). Serious games have not been widely adopted in higher education, probably because they are associated with adventure and fantasy equivalents in the entertainment industry and because most teachers do not have the skills or time to produce high-quality, visually appealing games.

The main reason computer games are now being investigated for higher education learning and assessment is the similarities between the characteristics of well-designed games and those of well-designed learning and assessment activities (Pivec & Dziabenko, 2004). Digital games are designed to be engaging and to keep participants on task. They are characterized by a high degree of interactivity, contain appealing multimedia sequences, and have clearly articulated goals, outcomes, and rewards. The game players are expected to develop specific skills as they proceed through the game, and these skills are used to proceed to higher levels within the game. Game players are provided with constant feedback in response to their actions, and they are rewarded at regular intervals to keep them motivated to play; communities of practice evolve around how to master the skills that are required to reach advanced levels in the game. Each player often takes a different path on his or her journey through the game, and players share their experiences and insights with other players. If one were asked to summarize what an effective learning and assessment environment might look like, it would be very similar to this description of the digital game environment. Teachers and institutions should look seriously at designing learning and assessment activities around these key characteristics of games. Engaging students in meaningful activities that encourage time on task would be a significant enhancement to our current approaches to teaching and assessing students. A summary comparing the design principles for games and learning is shown in Table 31.2.

Table 31.2 Design Principles for Games Compared With Learning (adapted from Pivec & Dziabenko, 2004)

Game design principles	Learning design principles	Laurillard's Conversational Framework elements
Clear vision of goals or mission	Clear learning objectives	
Player experience is paramount	Student-centered learning approach, active learning approach	Ask questions about their understanding of the theory (by providing the opportunity for answers from the teacher or peers)
Easily recognized structure and rules	Uses a logical sequence of learning and assessment activities that are aligned with learning outcomes	Offer their own ideas and conceptual understanding (by providing comment on students from the teacher or their peers)
Adapts to different skill level of player	Offers open-ended tasks, acknowledges different ways of learning	
Easy to learn, hard to master	Communicates high expectations, challenges students to higher level learning	Repeat practice (by providing feedback on actions that enables students to improve performance)
Does not interrupt the flow of play	Embeds assessment tasks in learning activities	
Provides frequent rewards, not penalties	Use authentic assessment activities, gives frequent and immediate feedback to students	Reflect on the experience of the goal-action-feedback cycle (by offering repeated practice at achieving the task goal)
Includes exploration and discovery	Uses active forms of learning, provides constructivist activities	Access explanations and presentations of the theory, ideas, or concepts
Repeat practice (by enabling students to share their trial actions with peers, for comparison and comment)		

(Continued)

Table 31.2 (Continued)

Game design principles	Learning design principles	Laurillard's Conversational Framework elements
New skills assist in progressing toward goal	Scaffolds student learning, assist students become strategic learners	Use their theoretical understanding to achieve a clear task goal by adapting their actions in the light of their understanding, or in response to comments or feedback
Intuitive interface, no need to read manual	Ready access to learning resources that can be used independently by student	
Includes the ability to save progress	Use of student portfolios to demonstrate skill development	Reflect on their experience (by having to articulate or produce their ideas, reports, designs, performances for presentation to their teachers and peers)

Virtual Worlds Using Avatars

Second Life is a well-recognized example of a 3-D online virtual world that has been adopted widely by many educational institutions (http://www .secondlife.com). Virtual 3-D worlds can be characterized as multiuser online role-plays; these environments allow participants to be represented "in world" in the form of an avatar so that they can explore the simulated world, create their own digital objects, and complete specific tasks within this world. Virtual worlds have the potential to facilitate authentic learning and assessment. The main disadvantage of these worlds, from a teacher's perspective, is that creating the 3-D virtual environment and scripting learning activities often requires professional expertise. Several commercial and open source software packages are available for constructing virtual worlds, including Second Life, Active Worlds, OpenSimulator, On-Line Interactive Virtual Environment (OLIVE), and Multiverse. The Joint Information Systems Committee (JISC) "Serious Virtual Worlds" report contains a comprehensive list of virtual world platforms used in education and training (de Freitas, 2008).

Virtual 3-D worlds provide an opportunity for students to experience presence and immersion. Presence is the feeling students have about being in a particular environment and context (either by themselves or with others), and immersion is associated with the properties of the system that give rise to the feeling of presence (Dalgarno & Lee, 2010). The fact that students construct avatars, both in physical form and in presentation format, makes 3-D virtual worlds different from many of the role-plays discussed earlier. In most 3-D virtual worlds, students will have a close affinity with their avatar; it is a representation of them in the digital environment. The virtual world itself is usually constructed to match the 3-D characteristics of the physical world so that students would expect certain physical laws to be adhered to in the virtual world, although clearly some exceptions are permitted (such as avatars being able to fly unaided). Educational activities need to make use of the specific attributes of the 3-D environment, and students should be given tasks that require navigating the 3-D environment or investigating the components of 3-D objects or terrains. Many tasks being assigned to students in 3-D virtual worlds, when mapped against learning outcomes, could be completed just as effectively in two-dimensional (2-D) digital environments. The issue for teachers is to appropriately map the learning outcomes set for the development of specific capabilities with the real attributes of a virtual 3-D environment so that the time and resources spent on the activity are appropriate. Design principles associated with experiential learning and task-based learning (Kolb & Kolb, 2005) can be used to design appropriate activities for 3-D virtual worlds. Learning activities in 3-D virtual worlds generally emphasize student performance rather than knowledge recall, so authentic assessment activities in these environments involve criteria relevant to these performances, rather than the recall or manipulation of content knowledge (de Freitas & Neumann, 2009; Richardson & Molka-Danielsen, 2009).

Objects within virtual worlds can be linked to external webpages, as well as to external wikis, blogs, or discussion boards, where students can assemble evidence of their learning (Hobbs, Brown, & Gordon, 2009). Many virtual world activities have been constructed with the assumption that students spontaneously develop capabilities simply by entering or moving around the virtual world. Virtual world tasks should be purposely designed around pedagogy that clearly demonstrates the worth of undertaking the activities. Virtual worlds may not be appropriate if students are expected to follow a linear sequence of prescribed tasks; alternative technologies could be more appropriate and less complex, such as Flash simulations or Java applets. The use of virtual worlds in higher education appears attractive to some teachers because students can exercise control over the actions of their avatar within the virtual space, in addition to receiving feedback from the system or other avatars (Kalyuga, 2007). Virtual worlds can also be a creative platform for students as they can construct their own objects or explore social, cultural, or political issues in a safe space. The assessment of student actions in virtual worlds needs to emphasize those skills that are specifically developed within this particular environment, rather than skills or capabilities that could be assessed quite readily outside of the virtual world.

Assessment tasks within virtual worlds can rely on the use of external tools such as wikis, blogs discussion forums, and e-portfolios, but it is difficult for many teachers to set "in world" assessment tasks themselves because the scripting language used to create interactive activities and feedback for students is a professional activity that takes time to master, frequently more time than most teachers would be able to allocate. Teachers need simple tools with which to design a wide variety of assessment tasks within the virtual world, similar to the quiz and survey tools available in learning management systems. An example of a quiz and survey tool that can be used within Second Life and OpenSimulator is Simulation Linked Object Oriented Dynamic Learning Environment (SLOODLE) (http://www.sloodle.org). This tool integrates common selected response items from Moodle into Second Life or OpenSimulator so that an avatar can answer questions at key points within the virtual world (Kemp, Livingstone, & Bloomfield, 2009). SLOODLE offers a variety of "in world" learning and assessment activities, including a set of tools for designing "in world" assessments. The question types are familiar to students and allow them to be tested using the quiz chair (selected response questions presented from Moodle quiz tool), the web-intercom (chat facility that can be archived in Moodle), the distributor (vending machine distributing content from Moodle), the choice tool (archiving voting in Moodle), the postcard blogger (students take screenshots of their activity "in world," annotate with text and upload to Moodle blog), and the awards system (presentation of Moodle grades "in world"). The SLOODLE system is an interesting example of linking various tools available in a learning management system with a virtual 3-D world so that students do not have to move in and out of various online environments. Integrating learning and assessment tools so that a seamless interface is presented to students will incorporate one of the key elements of good game design that maintains flow and keeps students engaged with the task.

More sophisticated approaches to using technology for assessment will be required in the future; the incorporation of evidence-centered assessment design that allows data to be collected from student activities "in world" is needed (Shute, 2011). To date, the reporting of a student's performance level and capability is often reduced to a mark or grade—a poor articulation of the student's abilities. Although e-portfolios are becoming more common as a representative sample of students' work, they do not necessarily provide a map of capabilities against defined standards because they are designed to display examples of individual objects. *Stealth assessment* has been the term introduced to describe the unobtrusive collection of data about a student's ability to complete a particular task (Shute, 2009). This concept of collecting data about the pathways chosen by the student to complete a task, and then being able to convert these data into a meaningful map of the students' capabilities, is an important step in redefining the reporting of student performance. Teachers need to examine new ways to report what strategies students have actually learned, in addition to discipline content, and so provide employers and student themselves, with a more sophisticated measure of capability development.

Virtual or Remote Laboratories and Field Trips

Virtual laboratory activities and field trips can be simulations that are entirely virtual and designed to provide students with a prescribed range of options, or the manipulation of physical objects by remote access. Both formats are educationally useful as either replacements or complements to expensive laboratory sessions or difficult to organize field trips. Students can be given access to remote laboratories or field sites where they can download data to their local computer from a remote sensor for use in learning activities or assessment tasks. Virtual activities allow students to collect and analyze authentic data, which means that the tasks can include requirements for students to reflect on the real life consequences of their responses (Michigan State University, 2008). Remote access to equipment is particularly useful for science and engineering disciplines because access to many relevant and authentic laboratory sites may be impossible because of cost or safety reasons. Access to virtual labs and field trips would be particularly beneficial to institutions in developing countries where expensive equipment for student laboratories is likely to be beyond the budgets of local universities. By allowing free remote access to appropriate laboratory equipment, institutions possessing teaching equipment could provide a valuable service to many students in developing countries. Even in developed countries, there are often inequities in access to laboratory teaching equipment and free remote access can assist in a more equitable access to a quality higher education experience.

There are continuing discussions of the efficacy of virtual or remote laboratory sessions compared with hands-on experiences in terms of student learning outcomes (Murray, Lowe, Lindsay, Lasky, & Liu, 2008). Virtual laboratory sessions can be used as formative activities to ensure that students are adequately prepared for summative hands-on laboratory sessions. This use of virtual laboratories is less controversial than the complete replacement of physical laboratory sessions. Simulations can also be used to provide students with opportunities to complete the learning cycles outlined in Laurillard's Conversational Framework and to test hypotheses by engaging in "what happens if I do this" activity. The development of simulations and experiments on virtual animals (see http://www.clabs.de) has occurred because of the heightened awareness of ethical issues associated with physical experiments on live animals.

An interesting approach to integrating the educational benefits of virtual and physical laboratories can be found in the Trilab project, which offers students a holistic laboratory experience (Abdulwahed, Nagy, & Blanchard, 2008). Trilab requires students to complete virtual, remote, and real activities, although the format could be adapted to provide options for teachers and students. Similar learning outcomes are observed from students who have completed purely remote laboratory sessions compared with students who have completed hands-on sessions (Nickerson, Corter, Esche, & Constantin, 2007).

Although some virtual and remote laboratory experiments require students to download special software to their computers, other computer-based activities require only a recent version of a standard web browser using standard plug-ins. The JISC-funded Remote Access to Academic Trials and Testing (RATATAT) project demonstrates how Web 2.0 technologies can be integrated with remote laboratory assessment tasks (http://ratatat .pbworks.com). The integration of virtual or remote laboratory sessions with the collaborative tools of the Web 2.0 environment allows teachers to facilitate group and project work. This integration could transform the nature of laboratory sessions in higher education institutions by allowing students to participate in larger, more complex experimental projects that could promote higher-level learning.

Many higher education institutions, especially those in developing countries, cannot afford a comprehensive array of expensive laboratory equipment, nor can students necessarily afford to travel to remote locations for field trip experiences. By sharing expensive equipment through remote Internet access, institutions could cooperate to reduce their costs yet still offer an extensive range of educational experiences for their students. Such sharing could involve industry partners and government laboratories, which frequently possess more sophisticated laboratory equipment than universities have.

An example of an integrated learning and assessment model for remote field trips is the 3-D-compound virtual field trip system developed by Ming-Chao Lin and Chun-Yen Chang (2009). This model uses four components: a streaming video server, the use of instant messaging, an automatic marking and feedback system, and a dedicated website for student access to resources. Student assessment tasks are linked to specific video sequences or objects in the virtual environment with multiple-choice questions providing timely feedback to students. Students are able to capture still images from the video sequence and incorporate these into their extended written responses to assessment questions. Although this type of integrated approach is still novel, it illustrates the possibilities for new virtual and remote learning and assessment spaces that offer new experiences for students and allow teachers to develop and assess higher level skills.

Conclusion

Technology offers many new possibilities to enhance the educational experience of students and the quality of teaching in higher education. However, technology itself does not ensure the quality we strive to achieve; good learning and assessment designs are required in combination with an informed use of the appropriate technology. Students should be considered active partners in this new educational environment and not just the recipients of teacher-designed experiences. For students to become self-regulated and future-focused learners, they need to develop skills that promote self-review and be able to apply performance criteria to their own learning. Teachers and technology, working together in a synergistic manner, can facilitate the development of these characteristics.

References

Abdulwahed, M., Nagy, Z. K., & R. Blanchard, R. (2008, July 14–16). *The TriLab, a novel view of laboratory education: Innovation, good practice and research in engineering education.* Presented at EE2008 Conference, Engineering Subject Centre, Loughborough, UK, P051. Retrieved April 26, 2011, from http://www.engsc.ac.uk/downloads/scholarart/ee2008/p051-abdulwahed.pdf

Ablin, J. A. (2008). Learning as problem design versus problem solving: Making the connection between cognitive neuroscience research and educational practice. *Mind, Brain and Education, 2*(2), 52–54.

Aldrich, C. (2009). *The complete guide to serious games and simulations.* San Francisco, CA: Pfeiffer.

Allen, E., & Seaman, J. (2010). *Learning on demand: Online education in the United States, 2009.* Babson Survey Research Group. Retrieved April 26, 2011, from http://sloanconsortium.org/publications/survey/pdf/learningondemand.pdf

Boud, D., & Falchikov, N. (2006). Assessment with long-term learning. *Assessment & Evaluation in Higher Education, 31*(4), 399–413.

Cooper, M. M., Cox, C. T., Jr., Nammouz, M., Case, E., & Stevens, R. (2008). An assessment of the effect of collaborative groups on students' problem-solving strategies and abilities. *Journal of Chemical Education, 85*(6), 866–872.

Cooper, M. M., Sandi-Urena, S., & Stevens, R. (2008). Reliable multimethod assessment of metacognition use in chemistry problem solving. *Chemical Education and Research Practice, 9*, 18–24

Coppola, N. W., Hiltz, S. R., & Rotter, N. (2002). Becoming a virtual professor: Pedagogical roles and ALN. *Journal of Management Information Systems, 18*(4), 169–190.

Dalgarno, B., & Lee, M. J. W. (2010). What are the learning affordances of 3-D virtual environments? *British Journal of Educational Technology, 41*(1), 10–32.

de Freitas, S. (2008). *Serious virtual worlds: A scoping study.* Retrieved April 26, 2011, from http://www.jisc.ac.uk/media/documents/publications/seriousvirtualworldsv1.pdf

de Freitas, S., & Neumann, T. (2009). The use of "exploratory learning" for supporting immersive learning in virtual environments. *Computers & Education, 52*, 343–352.

Fry, H., Ketteridge, S., & Marshall, S. (2009). *A handbook for teaching and learning in higher education: Enhancing academic practice* (3rd ed.). New York, NY: Routledge.

Hobbs, M., Brown, E., & Gordon, M. (2009). Learning and assessment with virtual worlds. In C. Spratt &P. Lajbcygier (Eds.), *E-learning technologies and evidence-based assessment approaches* (pp. 55–75). Hershey, PA: Information Science Reference.

Johnson, L., Smith, R., Levine, A., & Haywood, K. (2010). *The 2010 Horizon Report: Australia–New Zealand Edition.* Austin, TX: The New Media Consortium. Retrieved April 26, 2011, from http://www.nmc.org/pdf/2010-Horizon-Report-ANZ.pdf

Joint Information Systems Committee (JISC). (2004). *Effective practice with e-learning. A good practice guide in designing for learning.* Retrieved April 26, 2011, from http://www.jisc.ac.uk/media/documents/publications/effectivepracticee learning.pdf

Kalyuga, S. (2007). Enhancing instructional efficiency of interactive e-learning environments: A cognitive load perspective. *Educational Psychology Review, 19*(3), 387–399.

Keengwe, J., & Kidd, T. T. (2010). Towards best practices in online learning and teaching in higher education. *MERLOT Journal of Online Learning and Teaching, 6*(2), 533–541.

Kemp, J. W., Livingstone, D., & Bloomfield, P. R. (2009). SLOODLE: Connecting VLE tools with emergent teaching practice in Second Life. *British Journal of Educational Technology, 40*(3), 551–555.

Kolb, A. Y., & Kolb, D. A. (2005). Learning styles and learning spaces: Enhancing experiential learning in higher education. *Academy of Management Learning & Education, 4*(2), 193–212.

Laurillard, D. (2010). *Rethinking university teaching: A framework for the effective use of learning technologies* (3rd ed.). New York, NY: Routledge.

Lee, M. J. W., & McLoughlin, C. (Eds.). (2010). *Web 2.0-based e-learning: Applying social informatics for tertiary teaching.* Hershey, PA: IGI Global.

Lim, J., Kim, M., Chen, S. S., & Ryder, C. E. (2008). An empirical investigation of student achievement and satisfaction in different learning environments. *Journal of Instructional Psychology, 35*(2), 113–119.

Lin, M., & Chang, C. (2009). Incorporating auto-grading and feedback tools into an online 3-D Compound Virtual Field Trip system. In G. Siemens & C. Fulford (Eds.), *Proceedings of World Conference on Educational Multimedia, Hypermedia and Telecommunications* (pp. 3698–3703). Chesapeake, VA: Association for the Advancement of Computing in Education.

Linser, R., Ip, A., Rosser, E., & Leigh, E. (2008, November). On-line Games, Simulations and Role-plays as Learning Environments: Boundary and Role Characteristics. In G. Richards (Ed.), *Proceedings of World Conference on E-Learning in Corporate, Government, Healthcare, and Higher Education* (pp.1757–1765). Chesapeake, VA: Association for the Advancement of Computing in Education.

Maier, H. R., Baron, J., & McLaughlan, R. G. (2007). Using online roleplay simulations for teaching sustainability principles to engineering students. *International Journal of Engineering Education, 23*(6), 1162–1171.

Means, B., Toyama, Y., Murphy, R., Bakia, M., & Jones, K. (2009). *Evaluation of evidence-based practices in online learning: A meta-analysis and review of online learning studies.* Washington, DC: U.S. Department of Education, Office of Planning, Evaluation, and Policy Development, Policy and Program Studies Service. Retrieved April 26, 2011, from http://www2.ed.gov/rschstat/eval/tech/ evidence-based-practices/finalreport.doc

Michigan State University. (2008). *REAL: Remote Environmental Assessment Laboratory.* East Lansing: Michigan State University. Retrieved April 27, 2011, from http://www.real.msu.edu

Murray, S. J., Lowe, D. B., Lindsay, E., Lasky, V., & Liu, D. (2008). *Experiences with a hybrid architecture for remote laboratories.* In D. Budny (Ed.), *FiE 2008: The 38th Annual Frontiers in Education Conference* (pp. 15–19). Piscataway, NJ: IEEE.

Nickerson, J. V., Corter, J. E., Esche, S. K., & Constantin, C. (2007). A model for evaluating the effectiveness of remote engineering laboratories and simulations in education. *Computers and Education, 49*(3), 708–725.

Nicol, D. J. (2009). Assessment for learner self-regulation: Enhancing achievement in the first year using learning technologies. *Assessment & Evaluation in Higher Education, 34*(3), 335–352.

Pivec, M., & Dziabenko, O. (2004). Game-based learning in universities and lifelong learning: "UniGame: Social skills and knowledge training" game concept. *Journal of Universal Computer Science, 10*(1), 14–26.

Pivec, P., & Pivec, M. (2010). Collaborative online roleplay for adult learners. In P. Zemliansky & P. Wilcox (Ed.), *Design and implementation: Theoretical and practical perspectives* (pp. 393–408). Hershey, PA: Information Science Reference, IGI Global.

Prensky, M. (2001). *Digital games-based learning.* New York, NY: McGraw-Hill.

Richardson, D., & Molka-Danielsen, J. (2009). Assessing student performance. In J. Molka-Danielsen & M. Deutschmann (Ed.), *Learning and teaching in the virtual world of Second Life* (pp. 52–60). Trondheim, Norway: Tapir Academic Press.

Shachar, M., & Neumann, Y. (2010). Twenty years of research on the academic performance differences: Traditional and distance learning: Summative meta-analysis and trend examination. *MERLOT Journal of Online Learning and Teaching, 6*(2), 318–334.

Shute, V. J. (2009). Simply assessment. *International Journal of Learning and Media, 1*(2), 1–11.

Shute, V. J. (2011). Stealth assessment in computer-based games to support learning. In S. Tobias & J. D. Fletcher (Eds.), *Computer games and instruction* (pp. 503–524). Charlotte, NC: Information Age.

Simkins, S. P., & Maier, M. H. (Eds.). (2010). *Just-in-time teaching: Across the disciplines, across the academy.* Sterling, VA: Stylus.

Stewart, T. M., Brown, M. E., & Weatherstone, A. (2009). Interactive scenario design: The value of flowcharts and schemas in developing scenario-based lessons for online and flexible learning contexts. *Journal of Distance Learning, 13*(1), 71–90.

Author Index _____

508

Subject Index _____

⑤SAGE research methods online

The essential tool for researchers . . .

. . . from the world's leading research methods publisher

Discover SRMO Lists— methods readings suggested by other SRMO users

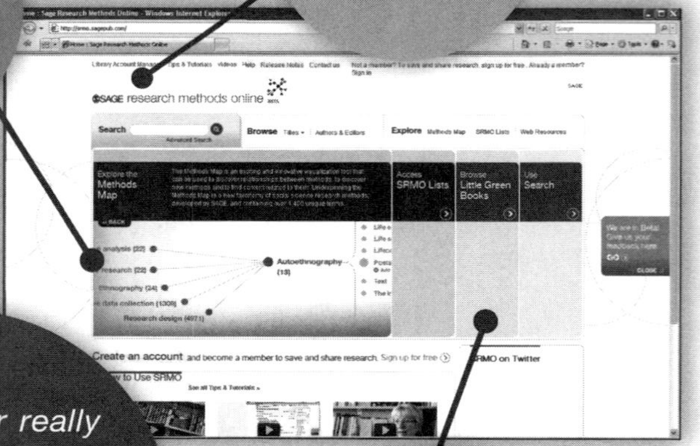

"I have never really seen anything like this product before, and I think it is really valuable."

John Creswell, University of Nebraska–Lincoln

Find exactly what you are looking for, from basic explanations to advanced discussion

Explore the Methods Map to discover links between methods

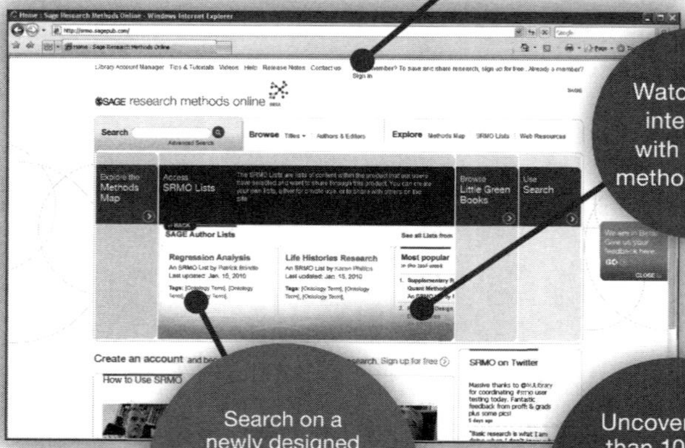

Watch video interviews with leading methodologists

Search on a newly designed taxonomy with more than 1,400 qualitative, quantitative, and mixed methods terms

Uncover more than 100,000 pages of book, journal, and reference content to support your learning

find out more at
www.srmo.sagepub.com